Extraordinary acclaim for

Dr G Sundaram's
PLIGHT OF HONESTY

"The author's candour makes his autobiography different from many other officers' memoirs".

—*The Hindu.*

"Engaging narrative, encompassing a variety of areas".

—*The Hindu Business Line.*

"....shows that side of public life that a citizen does not get to see."

—*Consumer Voice.*

"....talks about his days as negotiator for the Bofors deal".

—*gfiles* (leading journal on governance.)

...."Emandar, Moolyavan aur Nishtavan Logo ki Dhurghati ki kahani kahthi hai".

—*Prabhat Khabar* (leading Hindi daily).

"Candid confessions jiggle across the book".

—*Organiser.*

"Book questions Bofor's truth".

—*The Statesman.*

"....publicly very relevant and necessary memoirs.

—*News Today* (leading eveninger of Chennai).

Plight *of* Honesty

The Untold Bureaucracy

Some of our Learned Authors

General S Padmanabhan; General VP Malik; Admiral Vishnu Bhagwat; Dr. A. Sivathanu Pillai, DRDO; Dr. R.K. Tiwari, Scientist; Parvez Dewan, IAS; PS Bhatnagar, IAS; N Vittal, IAS; PK Agrawal, IAS; Sudhir S Baloeria, IAS; NS Sisodia, IAS; J.K. Bagchi, IAS; Maloy Krishna Dhar, IPS; BR Lall, IPS; PC Dogra, IPS; DC Pathak, IPS; Dr. S Subramanian, IPS; R.K. Ohri, IPS; SR Arun, IPS; Birbal Nath, IPS; VK Agarwal, IRS; Virendra Gupta, IFS; Lt. Gen. SK Sinha; Lt. Gen. Raj Kadyan; Lt. Gen. HB Kala; Lt. Gen. Arjun Ray; Lt. Gen. CK Kapur; Lt. Gen. NS Narahari; Lt. Gen. Chandra Shekhar; Lt. Gen. ML Chibber; Lt. Gen. Ashok Joshi; Maj. Gen. Nilendra Kumar; Maj. Gen. Vinod Saighal; Maj. Gen. VK Singh; Maj. Gen. Samay Ram; Maj. Gen. Dipankar Banerjee; Maj. Gen. Y Behl; Air Cmde RV Kumar; Air Marshal SR Deshpande; Air Vice Marshal AK Tiwary; Air Vice Marshal Samir K Sen; Air Cmde (Dr.) CN Ghosh; Air Cmde NB Singh; Air Cmde RV Phadke; Arvind Gupta, IFS; Ambassador Kishan S Rana, IFS; Cmde Ranjit B Rai; Cdr. Alok Bansal; VK Singal, IRS; Sudha Raman; Carlos Ramirez-Faria; Brig Yash Mohan, VSM; Brig. Kim Yadav; Brig. DK Khullar; Brig. Trigunesh Mukherjee; Brig. (Dr.) HK Kar; Brig. MS Patial; Brig. Parmodh Sarin; Brig. RP Singh; Brig. Jaspal Singh; Col. PK Gautam; Col. MN Gulati; Col. MS Jaswal; Col. Anil Shorey; Col. Anil Bhatt; Anuj Dhar, Journalist; Sapna Gupta; Prakash Nanda, Journalist; Ranjit Kumar; Vijay Naik, Journalist and many more.

Plight
of
Honesty

The Untold Bureaucracy

Dr G. Sundaram, IAS (Retd)
Former Secretary to the Government of India

2nd Edition

Manas Publications
New Delhi-110002 (INDIA)

Manas Publications
(Publishers, Distributors, Importers & Exporters)
4402/5A, Main Ansari Road, (Opp HDFC Bank)
Darya Ganj, New Delhi - 110 002 (INDIA)
Ph.: 23260783, 23265523:, 23842660 (R)
Fax: 011-23272766
E-mail: manaspublications@vsnl.com

2nd Edition 2010

ISBN 978-81-7049-327-3
Rs. **495/-**

Typeset at
Manas Publications

Printed in India at
R.K. Offset Process, Delhi
and Published by Mrs Suman Lata for
Manas Publications, 4402/5A, Main Ansari Road,
(Opp. HDFC Bank), Darya Ganj,
New Delhi - 110 002 (INDIA)

To

my parents,

and

my wife

whose constant compassion

for the poor is more than even mine

Preface to Second Edition

As anticipated, the book evoked different reactions. General readers reacted differently from civil servants; even among the civil servants, the senior ones of the old vintage reacted differently from the junior ones. Dyed-in conservatives of 'sweeping things under the carpet' culture did not approve of the transparency of the book. One of them, although there is nothing about him in the book, went to the extent of preventing a man who was ecstatic about the book from talking about it in a Book Club or writing a review in a special fortnightly in Chennai! But many others of the old vintage felt that the book called a spade not a spade, but a shovel! Most of them read it in one sitting. One of them told me that he read it twice to know some of the nuances of the various incidents or policies.

After all, what is the purpose of a book? It should read well. Secondly, if possible, it should give a message. Many general readers appreciated the truth, boldness, frankness and the courage of conviction—I am again reminded of the Mahatma and "the Profiles in Courage" of Kennedy.

For a book of this kind, I am happy that it has seen a second edition, reminding me of the exchange between Churchill and Shaw! It has received eight reviews in a year from important newspapers and journals--although the 'jute press' as R.K. Karanjia used to call totally ignored it, not surprisingly–since it was "received" (a word for "release" by President or PM) by Dr APJ Abdul Kalam in September, 2008.

Contents

Prologue

Only when I started writing this autobiography or memoir, I realised how difficult it was to be truthful. Throughout my life, I have been inspired by Mahatma Gandhi and his *The Story of My Experiments with Truth*. He had stated that "I know no diplomacy save that of Truth". The portrait of Mahatma Gandhi adorned my room throughout my career and still does in my home.

Jawaharlal Nehru wrote: "... Gandhi was always there as a symbol of uncompromising truth to pull us up and shame us into truth. What is truth? I do not know for certain, and perhaps our truths are relative and absolute truth is beyond us. Different persons may and do take different views of truth, and each individual is powerfully influenced by his own background, training and impulses. So also Gandhi. But truth is at least for an individual what he himself feels and knows to be true. According to this definition, I do not know of any person who holds the truth as Gandhi does. That is a dangerous quality in a politician, for he speaks out his mind and even lets the public see its changing phases."

Moreover, the public has a right to know. They are not well conversant with the happenings, the methods and machinations in government. They blame the politicians all the time which the politicians deserve. At the same time, they may not know about the civil service politicians (second rung of politicians!) who are in fact more dangerous than the professional politicians and who, of late, have sacrificed merit for other considerations; only brute political force or backing works with them, and no more fine sensibilities like an honest and straightforward appeal work.

It is the endeavour of this book to tell the truth; only two or three instances have been suppressed because, they if told, might be totally twisted by the wicked world, which would affect my private interest, though in a small way, or more than mine that of others to whom I owe a duty of silence.

Rajaji chose not to write his autobiography. R.L. Stevenson felt that biographies and autobiographies were not good forms of literature. But I have read many of them, the last one being Nelson Mandela's *Long Walk to Freedom.* Mine does not belong to any of these categories. Although I have avoided self-praise, it is perhaps unavoidable in places. So I have indicated the policy issues in italics so that readers need not waste time reading my personal details unless they want to know. But Chapter 14 on 'Bofors' or 'Tehelka' or 'Corruption' and Chapter 20 on 'Bureaucracy' and also the Postscript may be read in full. I would also request readers to avoid piecemeal reading because no individual or organisation is criticised everywhere. Good and bad aspects are stated so that a true picture is available without any hurt to individuals or denigration of institutions.

Often I thought that in what way this account of mine would be of interest to the general public. But I have felt that it is always advisable for persons associated with public affairs to leave an account so that it might be of use however little it might be to some one who wants to know about public affairs and how these are conducted with what effect, even if it is just a footnote to history. There is a lot of duplicity in politicians and bureaucrats in the world. That is the reason why, the bad politicians (there are many good politicians too, as there are many good civil servants) are able to dupe the public. But for a detailed diary of Ananda Ranga Pillai, one would not have known the corruption of Dupleix, his wife and others. We would have known only their empire-building abilities. This does not mean that all of them were bad; there were many among the rulers who were honest and good.

This is also my perception of men and matters. It may be right, wrong or indifferent. So readers could come to their own conclusions. As Voltaire said: "I disagree absolutely with what you say, but I will defend to my death your right to say it".

I have written or dictated this entire work myself from memory although there are supporting documents or diaries wherever necessary or available. Secretarial assistance has been efficiently provided by S. Manimozhi to start with in his spare time and later by Ramkumar.

Dr G. Sundaram

* * *

1

Kilpattu, my birth place

It is a small village of 2,000 people in the semi-arid part of the old North Arcot District in Tamil Nadu, which included some parts of the present Andhra Pradesh long years ago, and recently divided further into North Arcot Ambedkar District with the historic Vellore as the headquarters and Tiruvannamalai-Sambuvarayar District with the equally historic Tiruvannamalai as the headquarters. One has to confess that, till the district was renamed Sambuvarayar, one had not heard of the name except for a scholarly few.

No other country lives so much in the past as we do, as is evident from the garlanding of statues or celebration of birth or death anniversaries almost every week with the President (happily President Kalam had given up this practice) or the Prime Minister with their retinue and a whole lot of dignitaries in attendance wasting time and money. There is no need to celebrate anyone's birth or condole death except that of the Father of the Nation and at the most Panditji, the Father of modern India. This does not mean disrespect to a whole lot of leaders, national or regional, who contributed to freedom or development of the country. It is only to save time and use it for useful purposes in a country where time has no value and where people spend days on some holiday or the other or in the simple habit of lazing around. Laziness should be only for a person who cannot employ himself or herself forced by economic circumstances of a country.

Added to this is our anxiety to change the names of streets, districts and universities. Some universities bear the name of the almost unlettered. We pretend that the names obliterated have been erased from history. True to our hypocrisy, we keep the names of the other invaders, but not those of the white invaders. In this respect, a region of India which had changed for the better long ago was Gujarat by abolishing old names for the districts. (Following caste riots against names of districts and transport corporations after caste leaders, the entire practice has been happily given up in Tamil Nadu).

People of Kilpattu always looked to the skies for rains. Frequent droughts played havoc with their lives. However, rains used to lash every year during the season and I remember as children we tucked ourselves inside the house or on the pial in those days of no electricity. The lightning before the thunder enabled us see each other covered in warm cotton blankets because it was never that cold. Occasional fever or cold was treated by grandma's home remedy, which was generally effective and, if fever persisted, the doctor with a Licenciate in Medicine with robust common-sense was called in. My cultivated taste for Campari always reminded me of the 'mixture' he gave in those days of no antibiotics. He improved his knowledge of medicine and practice by getting to know the names of the modern medicines prescribed by the doctors in the famous Christian Medical College Hospital in nearby Vellore.

Rains filled tanks around the village, which enhanced the beauty of the landscape when filled fully and the wells, too, which were our swimming pools. One is straightaway pushed into water as a method of teaching swimming. The dalliance of the water-snakes, although a deterrent to a person like me, was inconsequential for others, for they knew that these snakes were harmless. These tanks and wells provided water to the fields the year round and the farmers had to put in a lot of hard work to raise the crops as compared to their counterparts in the Cauvery delta, though the delta is starving for water now.

1

Kilpattu, my birth place

It is a small village of 2,000 people in the semi-arid part of the old North Arcot District in Tamil Nadu, which included some parts of the present Andhra Pradesh long years ago, and recently divided further into North Arcot Ambedkar District with the historic Vellore as the headquarters and Tiruvannamalai-Sambuvarayar District with the equally historic Tiruvannamalai as the headquarters. One has to confess that, till the district was renamed Sambuvarayar, one had not heard of the name except for a scholarly few.

No other country lives so much in the past as we do, as is evident from the garlanding of statues or celebration of birth or death anniversaries almost every week with the President (happily President Kalam had given up this practice) or the Prime Minister with their retinue and a whole lot of dignitaries in attendance wasting time and money. There is no need to celebrate anyone's birth or condole death except that of the Father of the Nation and at the most Panditji, the Father of modern India. This does not mean disrespect to a whole lot of leaders, national or regional, who contributed to freedom or development of the country. It is only to save time and use it for useful purposes in a country where time has no value and where people spend days on some holiday or the other or in the simple habit of lazing

Ours is a semi-agricultural family in the sense that my grandfather was working for the old Madras and South Maratha (MSM) Railway, a private company. He was awarded a medal for meritorious work. That was the reason why we could find some old railway artefacts in our house. He was posted in Madras with frequent trips out to disburse salary and safe-keep of cash in those days of no cheques or banks. He did not wait for his retirement or pension and, in fact, missed only a few years before his retirement was due because tale-carriers from the village informed him that his brothers were planning to deprive him of his share of the huge property since he had no children. So he decided to fold up from Madras and get back to the village to claim his share, which he did. A battle royal ensued with litigation in different courts and walls were constructed blocking the common passage connecting the four houses. The family had lands all around the village and the fields were sub-divided and fragmented so that each brother could have a bit in every corner of the village, and much long after I was to read about the sub-division and fragmentation of agricultural lands in rural India in the works on rural economics for my Honours Degree. To quote a funny or ridiculous instance, one of the two wheels of a big cart and another wheel of a small cart were shared among brothers so that the carts were not useful to any one of them!

The other brothers felt that all this was a vain venture on the part of my obstinate grandfather because the property had to revert to them on his death or he would be constrained to adopt one of their sons as his heir. But grandfather decided to stump them by adopting my father when he was only six months old from his wife's side. My father was my foster grandmother's brother's son. This disappointment made the brothers adopt a more aggressive and belligerent posture. A battle royal was on.

Years rolled by, but time did not heal the rupture. My father could not complete his education because of the belligerence of the brothers and one had to go ten miles to have high school education. Since the income from the farms was declining and my grandfather himself was constrained to sell away some lands, my father wanted to supplement his income by taking up any job. The immediate avenue was the second world war. His brother was in the far-away Batavia, in the South East Asian theatre of war. He wanted to join the army. He also thought that it would provide him an opportunity to see some far-off places and countries. I was a young lad then and would not be of much help to look after. So, my grandfather felt that his foster-son should remain by his side. My father dropped the idea.

Rural indebtedness was a scourge of the rural society those days. It was to swallow us gradually as it did many others, particularly in an arid area like ours. Much later, for my honours degree I was to read a scintillating Rural Credit Survey by the Reserve Bank of India. This survey was done under the chairmanship of the redoubtable A.D. Gorwala, ICS More than a report, it was a piece of literature. I quote: "When local cooperation gets into the charge of the village moneylender, and more especially the landlord-cum-moneylender, he becomes the society, the depositor and the borrower, all of them together or each in turn, with the ease with which one Godhead becomes Brahma, Vishnu and Shiva – Creator, Preserver and Destroyer – in the more picturesque expressions of Hindu philosophy, or with the elusiveness with which matter and energy exchange roles in the more recent refinements of nuclear physics". **A famous suggestion of this Committee was "Cooperation has failed, but cooperation must succeed."**

I could not resist quoting *mutatis mutandis* from this literary piece in my report in 1993 on export credit. This Committee was appointed under my chairmanship by S. Venkitaramanan, the then RBI Governor, a highly rated and brilliant civil servant, although somewhat controversial, or made controversial by the press later.

My father was not allowed to visit any other house. He was able to go outside the village only when permitted by my grandfather. My grandfather himself was also not in the habit of visiting anyone. But he commanded some sort of respect and any relation who came to the village invariably visited him. He was not on talking terms with his brothers. When one of his brothers died, he did not even come out of the house to see the body—a normal custom in our country. As death is a great leveler, one is expected to pay the last respects even if one has avoided occasions like marriage on account of some enmity. But he refused to budge so much so that when he himself was in his death-bed, his other brother came to see him with a lot of trepidation because he feared that he would be booted out even in such a situation. Normality among the families was restored long after the demise of my grandfather and, in fact, perhaps for psychological and other reasons, my father started visiting his cousins with a vengeance.

I am the first and only son of my father, K. N. Gopalan. Other five are sisters, including a twin-sisters who are alive. One of the sisters passed away at the age of 30. Another two boys died very early in life. My mother was from Kulitalai on the banks of Cauvery. It is a beautiful place on the banks of 'Akanda' (broad) Cauvery with picturesque scenery. It was always a pleasure visiting this place on holiday—a contrast to the semi-arid Kilpattu—bathing in Cauvery early in the morning, witnessing those doing 'Suryanamaskar'(worshipping Sun God) standing in knee-deep water for the benefit of their physical, mental and spiritual health. I was too young to admire the women bathing in the canals of Cauvery while the train meandered through beautiful scenery on both sides from Trichy to Kulitalai. I see it still in dreams woven from earliest memories. Now, the Cauvery has almost become dry; there is not much water. Urbanization along its flow has taken its toll.

I studied in a small school situated in a nearby village, Vadamadimangalam, run by a single teacher. In fact, Vadamadimangalam and Kilpattu are twin villages with lush paddy fields in between. No examinations were held in this school. As soon as one finished a single book meant for a standard, one was promoted to the next class and so on. These books related mainly to Tamil literature and as a result general knowledge was zero. When I appeared for a small test for entry into the Polur school, I did not know who Gautama Buddha was or which was the capital of India. A boy who studied with me in the village school became my good friend. Later he rose to the position of Parliamentary Secretary to the M.G.R. Ministry—more about him later.

The teacher used to come to my grandfather every month on the new-moon day (*amavasya*)—perhaps he chose this day to remember it or for whatever reason—and collected six annas as monthly fee. He reported to my grandfather about my progress in the school although he was getting daily or weekly signatures on a notebook about my homework. At that juncture, an incident happened. My grandfather started teaching me English. With a little knowledge of English, I could copy his signature in English on the notebook as a mark of work done at home. The teacher did not know English at all. During one of his visits, he said that he was satisfied with the work of the boy on the basis of my grandfather's signatures. My grandfather was surprised and he called for the notebook. He was shocked to see his signatures forged. But he did not beat me for my first act of innocent forgery and truancy. He only told me that it was wrong to copy any other person's signature. But when I went to the school later in the day, the teacher did not spare the rod. Although he had not even heard of the Bible, he instinctively believed in the Biblical dictum of sparing the rod and spoiling the child. He made me stand—there were no benches in the school—and gave a few beatings on my hand so that I learnt that one should not copy another's signature. The teacher was also in the habit of boxing the ears of the children with one of his long nails so much so my ear remained often wounded with a nail mark.

After walking a mile and a half to the railway station in half slumber, I had to take a train at 6 a.m. for the Polur school and return home at 10 p.m. My father invariably, or a servant, used to escort me from the station to the house both in the morning and in the evening, with rain on occasions, wading through the slush because there was no road those days between Vadamadimangalam and Kilpattu. The family stayed at Polur for a short while. On some days, if the guard of the train was a nice fellow, I used to get into an early evening goods-train from Polur. The goods-train never stopped at Madimangalam because there were no goods to discharge. But, a kindly guard applied the brake and literally dropped me from the train. It was a boon to reach home early on a few days. On one such evening, I slept off and did not get down at Madimangalam. My father was naturally anxious and got in touch with the next station over the railway phone, thanks to the station master. My teacher who was also on the train assured my father that he would keep me at his residence for the night. The next morning, I went straight to the school at

Polur by the morning train and my father met me at Madimangalam station with an eight anna piece for my mid-day meal.

At the Polur school, the head-master was Natesa Aiyar who used to come to the school to pluck flowers at about 6.30 a.m., for his daily Pooja (worship) and he used to see me and the other boys. So to avoid this torture of early rising and late coming to home, my father decided to transfer me to Madras. While at Polur, I had done fairly well in the school. I also felt that my friend M.S. Parthasarathy was the best student, coached by his father-teacher. His English was impeccable and he did his college with me in Madras. He did not sit for the IAS unlike almost all of us although he would have made it with brilliant colours. He joined the Reserve Bank of India, married a beautiful girl, and was later with the Asian Development Bank in Manila. He took his old father also to Manila. (I saw in the newspapers a few years ago that he died at the ripe age of 90. I contributed a small amount still later for a fund in his memory)

The notable events, while at Polur, were the Indian Independence in 1947 and the assassination of Mahatma Gandhi in 1948. There was a lot of excitement all around. My father felt that my grandfather should have been alive to see the Indian Independence for, the latter unlike my father, was not a nationalist and felt that the British would never give independence to India. He also felt that the idea of landing a man on the moon was moonshine - my grandfather who represented the common run of thinking those days felt that this would be an impossible task for the mankind to achieve like the belief of the earth being flat.

You start having doubts about the man-woman relationship, which were the precursors of adolescence and sex deeply embedded in every human being, which comes to surface as one grows up. Such thoughts started sprouting as the rudiment of a leaf on an autumn tree on the verge of spring or some plant sprouting in a field. It was always by association with some more naughty boys who pretended to know a bit more. I felt that a baby was born just by the marriage of a man and a woman, whereas they felt that there was something more to it, which kindled my curiosity although it was not pursued further.

My father decided to move me to Madras. His elder brother, who was working in a textile firm, goaded him to do so. He was also toying with the idea of taking up a job or starting a small business like running one or two autorickshaws to supplement his dwindling agricultural income. He gave up the idea later out of sheer diffidence and also for astrological reasons. More on astrology later. He could not also secure a good job and his brother's promises were in vain. Meanwhile, I was admitted into the famous Madras Christian College High School whose famous headmaster for forty years, Kuruvilla Jacob, interviewed me. I wonder even now how he agreed to admit me looking at my village background and my father's.

In fact, the Scots Mission's General Assembly's school of 1837 became Madras Christian College School. This was headed by John Anderson who was keen on strong education. He also founded a Muslim Girls School in Triplicane, Saint Colombus in Chengleput and Anderson School in Kancheepuram. But his pioneering General Assembly School was started in 1835 with 56 students which became the Scotland Mission School in 1837 and later as the Madras Christian College High School. College classes began in 1866-'67.

This school was located on the premises of the Ophthalmic Hospital, Egmore, and later was moved to Armenian Street. There was a further move to Errabalu Chetty Street and again it moved to Linghi Chetty Street in 1846. The institution was christened the Madras Christian College in 1876-'77. The college moved to a sylvan 360 acre campus of the Selaiyur forest in Tambaram in 1936-37. The college still nestles in this rich fauna and flora where I had the privilege of working as a lecturer in Economics in 1959-'60. The school still remained on Linghi Chetty Street before it moved to Chetpet in 1949 or so. The old handsome buildings of the school have now been pulled down on Linghi Chetty Street. The premises of the school that remains in George Town today is Anderson Church with its unique steeple. It was also convenient for me because my father's real father in life (as narrated earlier my father was given in adoption to Kilpattu) was working for the Andhra Scientific Company in a beautiful building opposite where I could have my lunch. He used to stay there too because he had divorced his wife who was actually my father's mother through a court of law – a rare thing those days—and, as a result, his eldest son with whom I was staying, was not on talking terms with him. They did not meet for years and my father was the only connecting link with another brother in between who had gone to the South East Asian theatre during the second world war. This grandfather was also kind to me. He used to take me to different places of interest in Madras. The next room to his was that of the famous Pilot Pen Company. Although they were Christians, they used to consult my grandfather on astrology. In fact, he had correctly cast my horoscope years ago spending a couple of days, which years later, took only a couple of minutes on a computer. I marvelled at his labour and correct predictions. He made me contribute a princely sum of Rs 5/- to the Madras Christian College High School building fund. I was happy to see my name in print in the school magazine indicating this donation along with numerous other contributors. When I mentioned this to a friend years later as puerile juvenile satisfaction, he said my small contribution was also important because had I decided to take back my Rs 5/- by removing a few bricks from a crucial part of the building, it might have collapsed!

It was under Dr William Miller who came out in 1862 as the school's principal, that the institution began to grow and it was he who made it a college. He also founded the country's first alumni association here in 1891. His statue across the road in front of the college and the school and the High Court on the other side was a reminder of his contribution to education in Madras. In fact, it was popularly known as Miller's School and College.

The first Indian professor in this college was Prof J.B. Raju, professor of philosophy in 1916. The first Indian headmaster of the school Dr Kuruvilla Jacob, was appointed in 1931. However, it took a long time for the college to appoint an Indian as principal. Dr Chandran Devanesan, who was my affectionate colleague with a Ph. D., from Harvard, became the principal in 1963 and he was also kind enough to take me round the college a few years later.

I did well in the school. I obtained certificates of Honour in some subjects. I had no difficulty in sailing through the curriculum of this important school. Although I wanted to pursue my studies further, I was not happy in my father's brother's place. My aunt practically used me as an errand boy. I never went to the provisions stores in the nearby village except to dispose of old papers and to have some eatables with that money in the nearby hotel. Otherwise, our household chores were mainly performed by servants. I also had to cover a long distance from their residence in Park Town to the school in George Town. On the way, there were many good hotels and magazine shops. I used to buy children's magazines like the famous 'Kalkandu' of Tamilvanan, hide them from the prying eyes of my uncle's son. Somehow I developed an urge to become a writer or a journalist. I did make one or two attempts which were not published. While buying these magazines from pavements, the 'kokokam shastra' magazines with nude women on cover attracted my attention. There was some latent curiosity which was not pursued, however!

I was struck by typhoid almost the day I joined the Madras Christian College High School. I went back to my village for a month, suffered from fever for the standard twenty-one days in those days of no chloromycin and came back. The excellent eats of the Modern Café on Thambu Chetty Street, the Ramakrishna Lunch Home on the China Bazaar (now the N.S.C. Bose Road) and the Arya Bhavan in Park Town were welcome to the extra hungry stomach after the severe fever and starvation. My visits to the hotels had to continue later in Vellore, too. My daily allowance from my father was two annas, which was just enough for a cup of coffee. At times, I used to accumulate this amount for three or four days so that I could have a regular sweet, savoury or 'dosa' and coffee.

My father made suitable amends in kind and money - he was rather punctilious about such matters - to his brother for having kept me for one year. As soon as I finished the examination and passed, I was moved to Vellore.

My grandmother was a great influence on me more than my mother. She used to wait till late in the nights for my return from Polur, feed me, put me to sleep and wake me up again at 5 a.m. to catch the train at 6.10 a.m. She did that when I moved to Vellore, too. One can find a psychological reason for this: she did not have a child of her own because my father came to her in adoption when he was six months old and refused to go back to his parents later. His fondness for his foster parents was much more than for his own, as the old Tamil saying on the subject emphasized. My grandmother passed away on 1st January, 1955 and I still dedicate my annual diaries to her on the first of every year.

The house faced the paddy fields at Kilpattu with the lake at a distance. Beyond the lake is the mountain of Tirumalai (not to confuse with the famous Tirumala of Andhra Pradesh) with a Jain temple and caves with beautiful paintings.The chemists from the Department of Archaeology who came to restore and conserve these ancient paintings became our life-long friends - one in the DGTD in Delhi, one who remained in the Department of Archaeology throughout and another one became a well known professor of archaeology at the M.S. University, Baroda. A visit by our friends from the nearby towns for a couple of days on holiday was not complete without a visit to this Jain temple. On a festival occasion, I saw for the first time a District Collector in my life, an Englishman in khaki shorts and a sola-hat. He warmly waved at the crowd.

Our garden abounded in different types of fruit-bearing trees—mango, lemon, guava, bublimas (citrus), pomegranate, country badam and a host of others like plantains, drumstick, coconut, jasmine, parijath, crotons and manoranjitham. Parijath and manoranjitham provided a nice fragrance in the evenings and it was difficult to locate the flower, which merged with the leaves because of the same colour and one had to locate the manoranjitham flower by going towards the smell. My grandfather was fond of gardening and I followed him by drawing water from the well to water these plants. We used to play hide and seek in the midst of these plants and on occasions organized community lunch for the children. **I am sad to find that the economy of the village has changed and these trees have disappeared by the indiscriminate planting of 'babul' trees for firewood. It is no longer possible to see the lake from the house, which to my dismay I discovered during my visits to the village in later years. We have destroyed the environment everywhere, whether it is in a village, town, city or a mountain.**

My father's real mother visited us occasionally. She was a loquacious lady separated from her husband. She and her sister lived in a village near Vellore with a lot of rich agricultural lands. Her village is green on the banks of Palar, a river without water (even Cauvery has become a river without water now, thanks to Karnataka). But the sub-soil water made the soil fertile, which yielded good sugarcane. Her sister's husband came to live with her unlike the normal practice of the girl going to the husband's place. These two ladies were very proud of their father who was a 'Dubash' in Madras – a person who in British days could speak the native tongue as well as English. These 'Dubashes' worked for the East India Company interpreting for the Englishmen or with other English commercial houses. They were well paid. They were living in a palatial house on Nattu Pillaiyar Koil Street—a sought after address by these people. Her father's house still remains in a dilapidated condition on the same street. He also used to go in a horses-drawn coach to the office – an office of status. His name was Sundaram born on the star 'Moolam'. Moolam, as the saying goes, true or not, is good for the boys who are born to rule and not for the girls. When my real grandmother came to see me when I was born, she advised my father to name me after her father since my star was also the same.

2

To School

I have felt that I should devote a separate chapter to Vellore though it overlaps Kilpattu.

Although Vellore has a reputation of a town with certain wonders like 'a river without water', it is a beautiful town on the banks of the river, Palar. Thanks to the then Government of Karnataka known as Mysore State, Palar was rendered waterless by construction of a check-dam upstream. Andhra Pradesh proposes to make it worse by another dam at Kuppam, the birth-place of a Chief Minister. Thus Tamil Nadu is constrained to fight all the three States around in the absence of nationalistion of rivers. Be this as it may, the town has spread beyond Baghayam where the Christian Medical College hostel is situated at the foot of a beautiful hillock and also the famous Central Jail of Vellore, which housed many leaders during the Independence struggle and since Independence too, the latest being the Kanchi Shankaracharya. Otteri which nestles in the Jhawadi hills and the blue hills provide a backdrop from a distance to the town. A very recent addition in this area is a Golden Temple by the recent Narayanee Peedam which attracts huge crowds like the Golden Temple at Amritsar. Another small hill with the remains of an ancient fort rises almost in the middle of the town adding beauty, though it also adds to the heat in summer and cold in winter by the South Indian standards. The town also has an ancient fort right in the middle of the town with a moat around. The temple of Jalakhandeswara inside the fort abounds in beautiful sculpture, which the British were supposed to have planned to dismantle and assemble again in England. The French plundered many sculptures from Gingee and other places and took them away to Pondicherry of France. Some of these beautiful pieces could be seen even today in Pondicherry. A similar plan to dismantle the 'mandapam' at the Vellore temple was fortunately given up because the ship meant to carry the dismantled 'mandapam' sank on its way from England to Madras.

Apart from 'the river without water', the next wonder of Vellore was 'a temple without God'. For some reason or because of pillage by the Moghuls, there was no 'God' in the temple within the fort at Vellore. The citizens could not satiate their spiritual longings by starting worship in the temple because it was in the care of the Department of Archaeology; a bureaucratic department, as usual, would not permit anything new or a positive step. So the citizens, with the tacit connivance of the then Collector of North Arcot, staged a strange coup by installing an idol in the temple one fine morning and started the worship.

Once the worship is started, the legal provision in such cases is very interpretational that the government or the department of archaeology could not remove the idol. They could have only prevented it, but obviously failed in doing so because of the surprise element. The Government of India wanted to take action against the officials of the department of archaeology for not having discharged their duties and also against the Collector. But good sense prevailed and the matter was allowed to rest there so much so worship was resumed in the temple. Incidentally, the Collector Gangappa resigned from the Indian Administrative Service and stood for election thinking that he would be able to cash in on the crest of popularity generated for him by this action. Although he managed to secure sizeable votes for a stranger and novice in politics, he did not win the election—a reminder and a warning to many of his colleagues who make similar attempts.

Strange are the ways of the government indeed that a Tamil film by my good friend, K. Balachandar, depicts how the villagers in a village starve for water and their repeated representations to government for starting a small water supply scheme fall on deaf ears. Ultimately, out of sheer disgust, they take the initiative of diverting a water-way which will quench their thirst, but the benevolent government prevent them from action because under the land revenue regulations no one has the right to divert any water-way.

I told the film director that I almost had a similar experience. When my villagers were experiencing continuous drought for a few years and there was no water, I requested one of my colleagues who was the head of the Water Supply Board in Madras to sink a bore-well in the village. He was good enough to order it immediately in order to comply with my request. But his orders could not be implemented for about a year because the district administration was obliged to go according to their own priority in these matters. After repeated efforts, the bore-well was sunk and it was the only well supplying water to the entire village while all other wells had gone completely dry because of continuous failure of monsoon for a few years.

The fort at Vellore also housed important offices like the Collectorate, the Sessions Court and the oldest police training college of the country. Since the police training college was situated in Vellore, the citizens were used to seeing a lot of police officers roaming around town. People might not fear the police these days because of the complicated political connections but it was not so in those days. However, since so many policemen were seen all over, another uncharitable attribute was attached to Vellore as a place with 'police without power'.

A similar uncharitable attribute is 'college without knowledge' – perhaps these words are spun more for rhyme than for real meaning. Vellore was the home of the famous Christian Medical College and Hospital started by Dr Ida Scuddar more than 100 years ago. People feel even now that it is a privilege to study in this medical college. The hospital is now surrounded by the dusty town, no doubt, but it still attracts patients from all over the country influenced by its reputation and patient-care. The hospital also believes in equity by charging the rich more and the poor less, if not free for the poorest. The Christian missionary zeal is still reflected in the services of this institution.

Similarly, the Voorhees College and the Voorhees High School have been there for more than 100 years. The Voorhees College was for a long time an institution teaching only up to the intermediate level. Famous people like Dr Radhakrishnan, Dr Adiseshiah and O. Pulla Reddy, ICS, passed through Voorhees College as students. Of course, Dr Radhakrishnan studied in an equally good Sri Venkateswara School of the famous Tirumala Tirupati Devasthanam, popularly known as the Mahant School at Vellore, before going to the Voorhees College. There were also other good schools like Don Bosco and Auxilium. The Voorhees College celebrated its Centenary in 2004 actually after 106 years. It transpired the alumni included President Dr S. Radhakrishnan, Dr Malcolm Adiseshiah, acting Director General, UNESCO (his father was the first Indian principal), O. Pulla Reddy, I.C.S., P. Ramachandran, the former Governor, Dr S. Chandrasekhar the well-known population expert and Minister, V.L. Ethiraj, Barrister, S. Ratnam, former finance secretary to the Government of India, R. Velu, IAS (Rtd.) and Union Minister, A.M. Raja, a well-known playback singer, Dr Vedagiri Shanmughasundaram, well-known economist, G. Viswanathan, former Minister and founder of the famous Vellore Institute of Technology an incredibly beautiful campus with students from many countries, M.A. Jayavelu, former M.L.A., and Parliamentary Secretary to Chief Minister M.G.R., humble self and many others who distinguished themselves. Living now on Dr Radhakrishnan Road close to his house, I always joke that Voorhees is from Dr Radhakrishnan down to Dr Sundaram. Such a place with such a galaxy of people cannot be without knowledge with quite some wisdom thrown in!

The Auxilium College for women is located across the river in the New Vellore towards Katpadi railway junction. The Katpadi junction is on the main route between Madras and Bangalore. A branch goes to Tirupati and Renigunta on one side and another branch connects Villupuram on which Madimangalam is located, which was my daily beat as a student.

The sugarcane and paddy fields, and also coconut groves, connect Sathuvachari across the river at the foot of the hills. The Collectorate has been moved from the historic building in the Fort to a modern characterless building named after some present-day leader. Perhaps this is the beginning of new history. My parents now live here.

So Palar flows only when there are heavy rains, particularly on the west of Tamil Nadu, and in Karnataka. Otherwise, it is still 'a river without water'. But it is certainly with polluted water from the tanneries for which North Arcot is famous in the country since the East India Company days. The EI (East India) tanned leather is famous all over the world although its export is now restricted in favour of the value-added finished leather or leather goods. (The clock has again been put back by allowing export of EI leathers under the WTO dispensation!). I was to serve the Leather Export Promotion Council and initiate this policy of value–added exports much later. The Police Training College has been moved from Vellore to Madras and thereby perhaps the policemen are no longer powerless in Vellore. The temple also has a 'God' as stated above and there is no temple without 'God' any longer. The colleges have never been devoid of knowledge, and there is also a college for Arabic in Vellore – a fact not known to many.

There was no problem in getting admission to the III Form at the Voorhees High School because I was coming from the famous Madras Christian College High School. Besides, it was a sister Protestant institution. My father did not want me to go to the nearby new Board High School at Kalambur. He felt that standards would not be high in these schools. He also somehow preferred Christian institutions. I had no difficulty in coping with studies despite my travel everyday from the village to the town by train. A walk of a mile and a half to the station to catch the train at 7.30 a.m., reach Vellore at 9.15 a.m., well in time for the school at 10.00 a.m., In the evening, the travel was between 5.15 p.m., and 7.30 p.m., till I reached home. My father or a servant invariably came to the station in the evenings to fetch me back home. My companion was my cousin Ramu (K.R. Ramamoorthy) who was studying in the Board School at Kalambur. I feel even now that this was a rigorous schedule for a youngster and so much so I missed the games in the school and the college, but physically compensated by the fairly long walk to the station both in the morning and in the evening.

I followed my father's advice not to get into or get down from the train in motion as most boys tend to do out of sheer thrill. I scrupulously followed his advice and earned the name of a good or ideal student from the railway staff and some permanent passengers. As also advised by him, I always travelled in the last compartment which was also clean and comfortable. Some of the station masters of those days are friends even now and I recently met the grand-daughter and wife of the famous film producer of Madras, late GV (G. Venkateswaran). Her two grandfathers, VRS and VRV—V.R. Subramania Iyer and V.R. Viswanatha Iyer—of Polur always admired my discipline and comport. They too travelled always in the last compartment or bogie.

We were quite a few in number and were known as 'train students'. We prepared for the examinations in the beautiful Children's Park by the side of the fort at Vellore, sitting at times on the trees. There was no sense of caste or creed or religious feelings amongst us. I must also give credit to my father who was always catholic in his outlook and allowed me to go to the school in the Harijan colony in those days of strict segregation. So much so, on occasions when I had to stay at Vellore, I slept in the school or the college or with a classmate in the Harijan hostel near the Children's Park. I obtained prizes in Bible contests in the college and the school. A beautiful picture of Chirst, with a lamb in hand, with the words, "Not to be ministered unto, but to minister", adorned our home for a long time. There was no attempt at proselytisation those days and I hardly knew any one who changed his faith by conversion.

The emphasis was on English or Tamil literature, both in the college and the school. We borrowed books from the library particularly to enrich our skills at the language. The books of Nadodi in Tamil and A.S.P. Iyer's (A.P. Venkateswaran's father who was in the ICS) *An Indian in Western Europe* and *The Stories of Tenali Rama* are still green in my memory. Mahatma Gandhi's *The Story of My Experiments with Truth* left an indelible impression on my young mind. I used to buy by VP Post from Madras books like Louis Fischer's *The Life of Mahatma Gandhi*, Maxim Gorky's *Mother*, *Great Essays*, etc. for reading during the long vacations. I came out with flying colours in the examinations throughout including the SSLC. I never failed as feared by the headmaster at Polur at the time of my admission. C.A. Samuel was the headmaster of the Voorhees High School for a long time. James D. Isaac for discipline,

Titus and Alexander for Science, Mathews and V. Subramania Iyer for Mathematics and K.V. Subramania Iyer for Social Studies, which included Geography and History with multiple-choice questions where I stood first always were some of the well known teachers of the school.

But the stint of two years in the Voorhees College in 1953-55 is a memorable period in my life. Our financial problems by then became immense, and my sister having got married with considerable expenditure as is common for a south Indian Brahmin household, my father was already steeply in the proverbial rural debt. "The Indian farmer is born in debt, lives in debt and bequeaths debt" (Rural Credit Survey of the Reserve Bank of India). He felt that I should stop with the SSLC. But my high marks and a college in Vellore itself induced him to agree to my application to do the then two-year intermediate course.

When I had to apply for the college, I was interested in doing liberal arts. My heart was not in science somehow. There were only three combinations available those days: (1) Physics, Chemistry and Mathematics; (2) Physics, Chemistry and Biology; (3) Indian History, Modern History and Logic. I had filled up the form for the so-called third group. But, a day prior to the date of submission of applications, a family friend from a neighbouring village arrived and enquired about my preference. It is a marvel that there are some seemingly uneducated, but highly intelligent people in our villages. He was one such person who always read *The Hindu*, and could talk on many matters with authority. He felt that my choice of logic and history was totally wrong. He talked to me for two hours and convinced that I should do at least the combination of Physics, Chemistry and Biology, if not the first group itself with my high mathematics marks. Despite my excellent performance in mathematics, I always felt that I was weak in mathematics and did not have the confidence to do it. It was also too late to get a new application form after this brain-washing. Since the form had to be submitted the next day, I simply added the second group as the first choice and made the history group as my second one.

We had to give these applications only to our headmaster since it was a sister institution. The red-brick structure of the school and college with a lot of trees in the compound was separated only by a small gate. To use Goldsmithian expression, it was only a migration from "the blue bed to the brown". Admissions were decided purely on merit and performance those days. I got my admission into the second group in no time although I could have very well got the first too. My trepidation for mathematics was still lingering in me because 40% were allocated for problems in physics, which required knowledge of mathematics. I depended upon the balance 60% where I always scored around 50%. I was also worried about dissecting cockroaches and earthworms. The final examination in Intermediate was removal of the cockroach's brain to a glass and insertion of a coloured paper to show your skill. Whenever I see a cockroach even now, I immediately remember how this creature used to test my skills!

It was a remarkable and enjoyable period of two years. The curriculum was excellent. The very first day, Dr B.G. Swamidoss came up with a library catalogue and recommended books starting from Panditji's *Glimpses of World History*, the entire range of Dickens, Hardy, Walter Scott, etc. He and the American Rev Blaise Levai taught Shakespeare with great facility and Lockhart's biography of Walter Scott; in fact the former excelling the latter. Perhaps while Swamidoss spoke English, Levai spoke American. The handsome Narendran, whose obituary I read in the papers, taught S.T. Coleridge's *Rhyme of the Ancient Mariner*. I still have these books.

My childhood friend and classmate from the village, Jayavelu always wondered why Fridjof Nansen should write on his journey through Greenland and the worry of the ancient mariner about the albatross should trouble us. After studying with me in the village school, we lost touch because he went to the Board school at Kalambur for his high school. He did well in the SSLC and secured admission to the second group in the Voorhees College on merit and secured a Government of India scholarship for students belonging to the backward communities. He could not have afforded higher education otherwise.

He was a jolly companion in the second group. He believed in enjoying life. He had never read Oliver Goldsmith's magnum opus, *The Vicar of Wakefield*. Scholars like the late silver-tounged orator, Rt. Hon. Srinivasa Sastri, I believe, used to read this book every year twice or thrice to improve their English. One was interested in playing the 'sedulous ape' as R.L. Stevenson tried to improve his own style. I still feel that style is somewhat inborn and effort could improve it only to a certain extent. I have known first class English Honours students with gold medal from the Madras University whose English is just ordinary. Raja, the leather technologist, and some others I knew could write beautiful English. I consider one of my brothers-in-law, the Oxford educated, S. Krishnamurti, as a good pen-man. Botany student and Ambassador in Brussels, P.K. Dave was another good pen-man in English.

On the eve of the Intermediate final examination, Jayavelu wanted me to tell him the story of the *Vicar of Wakefield* and the possible important questions. Since I had no time myself, I told him that I could do this for an hour on the way to the hotel from my room to have our dinner, which took twenty minutes, during the dinner for another twenty minutes and on the return walk for another twenty minutes. He absorbed the whole thing, wrote the examination and passed it, too! He was always lucky in examinations.

Jayavelu naturally got only a third class in the Intermediate. He filled up all possible combinations on the application form –about eighteen or so –and secured admission to the geography course in the Presidency College, Madras. He was a good companion in Madras and I visited the Victoria hostel many a time. The boys used to troop in the evenings to the then famous Queen Mary's college on the world-famous Marina beach. Not only Marina has declined since, but also the Queen Mary's. Colleges like the Stella Maris have taken its place both in education and feminine fashions. Jayavelu went up later to do Law and became an advocate at Vellore. Law was not a specialization those days. Getting admission into Law was easy and every one got it just for the asking. So, the then Principal, the ever-humorous A.S.P. Iyer, ICS, said on the first day while welcoming the students, "Ladies and gentlemen, you are here today because you could not be elsewhere".

I was still going to Vellore from Kilpattu by train everyday and we were known as 'train students'. The time on the train was used either for study or for reading books recommended by Swamidoss. I preferred boarding the train at Vellore Town because it used to be practically empty. Whenever the door of the last compartment was locked, I used to open it with a key of mine inherited from my grandfather who was in the railways. The key is still with me. The train with a steam engine stopped at the stations and meandered through the beautiful Kannamangalam forest and the pass. I am still in touch with some of the 'train students'. Balaraman became a Member of Parliament and I met him years later in Delhi. He was also a member of the Consultative Committee of the Ministry of Commerce.

I did extremely well in the studies. Whenever the train was late in the mornings, Principal Jesuratnam asked me "Oh! Your train was late today" or "Oh! Your train was on time today". He also taught us physics. But my strong point was chemistry and I often stood first apart from getting a rank in English or biology, but never in physics. Once the train was late by half-an-hour for the chemistry exam and I finished it with a first rank. The laboratory work was very interesting. I should also mention Profs Hariharan who taught us physics, Hastings who taught us biology and Raja Pillai who was a professor of Tamil.

There were quite a number of girls, particularly in the second group. The girls always remained in their waiting room with windows covered by a metallic screen so that boys could not see through. (I was surprised to see this still caged room in 2004 when I was invited to the centenary celebrations of the college!). Instructions were issued on the very first day that the girls should stand outside and enter the class only after the entry of the lecturer and the lecturer should see that they left first before he or she left the classroom. The girls sat at the entrance or at the back of the class depending upon the location of the door. I was so shy, particularly coming from a non-coeducational school, that I never spoke to a girl on any occasion in the college; this was true of most others except a bold few. The bold few attracted canards by such acts in a conservative college and town. People were busy all the time spinning stories in a hush-hush manner connecting a boy and a girl. There was perhaps a lot of repressed sexuality for want of a free atmosphere.

I emerged with flying colours with a first class in the second group, which was supposed to be difficult. Only four out of sixty-four students got a first in the biology group which was relatively common in the first group. No one got a first in the liberal arts group. Unlike these days, first classes were a few and far between even in history, economics, politics and English B.A., or M.A., or Hons of the Madras University. For some odd reason, no first class was ever awarded in the B.Com. course of the University of Madras. A good second class in these subjects was considered very good.

With a first class in hand, the question arose again what to do next. B.Sc., or B.Sc (Hons) Chemistry was a sought after course. I could have walked into the medical course of the CMC, Vellore, but my father's financial position did not permit it. In fact, he wanted me to stop here. But some inner urge made me clamour for further pursuing my studies. My father's real father advised him to allow me to go to Madras for further studies. He told him not to bother about further indebtedness or erosion of property. I was keen on doing my Honours leading to M.A. Perhaps astrology also prevailed with my grandfather and another astrologer, reading my horoscope, said that in any case I was destined to study for another three years and would become a gazetted officer like a Collector or IGP because of the 'Gajakesari Yoga'. This was too much for a villager like my father who was a village-munsiff, a position he took up in a nearby village to compete with his rival cousin who was the village-munsiff of my village. He was not content with the appellation of 'landlord' or 'mirasdar' written by people on his post-cards or letters. He wanted a governmental position. He later became the unanimously elected village Panchayat president, met the Ministers who visited the area and played a notable part in the elections. I learnt a bit of electoral politics on these occasions. He has remained a staunch Congressman or sympathiser throughout despite his foster-father's sympathy for the British. I was also toying with the idea of going to the National Defence College, which would have meant study for another three years and a gazetted position as predicted in the stars! More on astrology or some metaphysical explanations of life later.

I applied to all the three leading colleges in Madras – Loyola, Christian and Vivekananda. I was very keen on Christian. Pat came the replies giving me admission in the Economics Honours course of Loyola and Vivekananda. Christian also replied granting me admission in B.Sc., Chemistry or Zoology Honours. Their policy, I was told , was not to give admission into Economics to students of biology. But the replies came swiftly, something unthinkable these days – city colleges responding favourably to a lad sitting in a village. ***One has to run from pillar to post for an admission these days that also with recommendations. India has become a country of 'sifarish' or recommendation for each and every thing. Even to get an appointment from an officer, who is a public servant, one needs recommendation – a sorry state of affairs indeed. In many a developing country, one needs a local partner to start an industry or trade. Similarly, one needs 'a word to be put in' for everything now in our country even at the highest levels in Delhi.***

I again toyed with the idea of doing English literature for my Honours or a subject like Psychology. But my friend in the village advised me again not to waste my first class in the Intermediate and insisted that I should do at least Economics so that it might lead me to the IAS. Students were clear those days and perhaps are so even now. The moment I told my classmates that I was applying for Economics Honours, they felt that I must be setting my eyes on the IAS. However, unlike medicine where one was assured of a good position, IAS was a gamble because of the tough competition. My friend, even in those days, always felt that it was wasting precious time studying history or English, which could be studied at home. But I always felt that these subjects were delectable and provided one with finer senses of perception and satisfaction. Nevertheless, one could derive such satisfaction even by reading these books otherwise. But my close friend, Jayavelu, felt that I should have gone to the Psychology Honours of the Presidency College because there were three beautiful girls from some prominent families of Madras and they were known as 'the big three of the Presidency'. Inter-collegiate classes in psychology were being held in the far-off Tambaram MCC and the three used to take the lone boy in the class in their car. My friend used to tell me that I missed this enviable opportunity by not applying for Psychology – I could have been the cynosure of all eyes.

The Honours course of the University of Madras was an excellent one which was misunderstood in the other parts of the country. It was a three-year course for the bright ones to get an M.A. degree in three years. The post-graduate students of the normal M.A., sat with the second and third year Honours students. The curriculum and the examinations were the same with the same question papers, the only difference being that the normal M.A. students were graduates and the Honours students were undergraduates. Moreover, while one could appear four times in the examination for an M.A., degree, one could appear only once for the Honours. So it was clearly meant for the very bright ones with stringent admission requirements unlike for the normal B.A., or the B.Sc.

I secured admission in the free hostel at Guindy by the Manali trust because of our financial position and I spent two years there. M.S. Parthasarathy of Polur also came in here. He was working for B.Com (Hons). During the third year, I moved to the nice Loyola hostel, which boasted of six messes – one with morning meal known popularly as 'Brahmin mess' because the Brahmins are supposed to be in the habit of having lunch in the morning, a mess with afternoon meal, a Malayali mess, an Andhra mess, a so-called cosmopolitan mess and a European mess meant mainly for the Fathers from abroad. The food was excellent for fortyfive rupees per month. There were more than a thousand rooms, all for single occupancy. The Catholic Church on the campus was a tourist attraction. A new railway station was opened for the campus. Sports and athletics were given equal importance and Loyola produced well known players like Tennis Krishnan who was my senior by one year. It was a pleasure seeing players on the numerous tennis courts – a game which I could not afford financially and even otherwise I was not a sports enthusiast on account of my missing the games during my earlier years because of the train journey every day.

The curriculum was rather rigorous with the well-stocked library open till 10 p.m. Librarian Michael was interested in his job and he mentioned the names of books, authors, whether it was readily available for lending and other details – a quality which even the sales girls in book shops do not possess these days – although he was in the habit of cracking same poor jokes again and again. To give an instance, whenever we wanted Crowther's *Money*, he would look into his pocket and say that there was nothing.

On top of the library was the Bertram Hall – the biggest hall in the city then. Apart from being used as an examination hall, it saw many an entertainment programme, and in my days many a leader in their particular fields, addressing the students, and also people like Jesse Owens and Ranjan in my days. It was also converted into a movie-hall every Friday night for a nice English film after an excellent special dinner, where boys roared invariably with the MGM lion. Fathers always futher censored the films the previous night by their private viewing. The joke was the salacious and sexy scenes were only for the Fathers. Once the irresistible A.S.P. Iyer, ICS, was invited, who punned on the word, 'nun' and 'none' by saying 'Fathers marry none (nun), but bring forth orphans'. After this humorous remark, Loyola stopped inviting him for ever! Rajaji was a regular visitor every year.

One should appear before the Vice-Principal and obtain a late-slip, if one was late for any class. Entry is not permitted otherwise and absence would attract a fine of Re.1/- or reprimand the next day. All students are given a number at the time of admission which will be their identity throughout. Students have to sit in the order of the number so much so the same person would sit by one's side for years. If a black dot appears against one's number on the notice board, one has to appear before the Vice-Principal for an act of commission or omission. One of my friends followed an ingenious method of 'cutting' Fr Basenach's – a German Father who studied in the London School of Economics, a strict disciplinarian and an institution by himself, students held him in high esteem – class. He would deliberately appear late before the Vice-Principal, take a 'late-slip' and disappear in the hostel for an hour. He would sneak just after the class was over and place his 'late-slip' in the attendance register, which used to go to the Vice-Principal's office every hour and by looking at the slip, they would mark him present as though he had attended the class!

Those were good three years for me, though I missed the co-educational atmosphere of the Voorhees and regretted for not having gone to the more than hundred-year old Christian. Loyola was comparatively a young college and its distinguished alumni included many persons of eminence like former President R. Venkataraman. In fact, R.V. left the college for the National College,

Trichy, without completing his graduation because the college objected to his nationalist activities as a student. When he became a Minister, the college was naturally proud of him and eventually the President of India with whom I had the privilege of working.

The boys and girls of the Christian were known as the 'gentlemen and ladies' of Christian, the 'princes' and 'princesses' of Presidency, the 'rowdies' of Pachaiappa's but the 'slaves' of Loyola because of the rigour of discipline and the rule to be in the hostel room before 8.30 p.m. The Father would go round and if a room was locked, he would put a lock of his own so that you could not enter without meeting him. Of course, some enterprising inmates like me on occasions kept the light on and locked from inside by climbing on the door. You could open the same way through the ventilator by climbing. We wanted to change at least the appellation by calling ourselves 'the lords of Loyola'. The question of 'ladies' did not arise as there was none. (The college is now co-educational). It was true that even station-masters or ticket examiners let off the Loyolites when there were lapses so much so the nearby Pachaiappites used to utter a falsehood as Loyolites whenever they were caught. Pachaiappas is also an old college which produced many leaders particularly of the DMK including the late C.N. Annadurai. He spoke in English with the same facility and alliterations as in Tamil despite a heavy accent. I used to go to Pachaiappas to listen to him. He always said that while Loyola admitted only horses and sent them out only as horses, Pachaiappas admitted donkeys and sent them out as horses!

Although the flamboyant Prof V. Ganapathi felt that I should have got a first class, I got a high second class. First class was rare and some years there was no one getting a first. During our year, three got unusually first from our class and one or two from St. Joseph's of Trichy. So it was a matter of regret for me while V. Krishnamurthy got a first who became my colleague later in Gujarat and Radhakrishnan entered the I.D.A.S., Fernandes Varkey George made it only to the IPS during the first attempt and the I.D.A.S., during the second and resigned later. Sripal, though considered a top class student whose notes some of us borrowed, was never lucky at examinations and got only a high second. Years later in 1992, I met Sebastian Zachariah in the ESCAP Conference at Beijing who was a Director in the UNDP, New York. My companion on the left in the class for three years, Frederick Moses, a rare Protestant boy in the Catholic Loyola, was my colleague and good friend in the IAS who died a few years ago. My companion on the right, Sadasiva Reddy became a flourishing lawyer in Hyderabad with whom I was always in touch. I used to go to his house in Lakshmipuram in Madras quite often and also used to listen to the lectures by eminent persons arranged by the Lakshmipuram Young Men Association whose members were all above 70!.

Sadasiva Reddy is in the habit of collecting old books like Crowther's *Money*, Sabine's *Political Philosophy*, etc. as I do. He tried to get Fr. Royappa's notes on political philosophy and Constitutions which we studied, but in vain. I preserve mine even today and read it occasionally. Those were comprehensive notes culled from great works on political philosophy and also the world Constitutions. Fr. Royappa did not want us to confine ourselves only to his notes, but frightened us in such a way about the examinations that we were forced to delve deep into the originals also. These notes were popular in the other colleges too, although these were given strictly to the boys in Loyola. Two boys from the Pachaiappas used to borrow these notes from me. One of the boys Mohanarangam accosted me years later at an airport. He was an AIADMK M.P., from Alandur, Madras – a lean boy who had become very fat and I could not naturally recognise him. He became a confidant of MGR and got interviews for MGR at very short notice from Mrs. Gandhi. In fact, he could practically walk into Mrs. Gandhi's room because while Mrs. Gandhi was sure of being disqualified from the predominant Janata Parliament when she was an M.P. and was to be disqualified for the emergency, she did not want that to be a unanimous verdict and wanted at least a lone voice in her favour. Mohanarangam obliged her under orders from MGR of course and thereby won her confidence. I was told that she removed her costly watch and presented it to Mohanarangam when he came out of the room after casting his dissenting vote in her favour. The other constant companion of his, Rahmathullah Khan became a commercial tax officer in Karnataka. Mohanarangam died a few years later. I had read Fr. Royappa's notes after my retirement just to feel whether they were up to the mark and our fascination was not just juvenile – indeed these notes were comprehensive and erudite.

Prof Ganapathi was noted for his handsome features, good dress, flamboyant style of delivering lectures and flowery language. He particularly used to wax eloquent on Keynes and post-Keynesian dynamics of Kurihara, etc. He wrote a book on trade cycles and one on 'general economics'; the chapter on Keynes was very illuminating and comprehensive. I wanted to possess these books after many years. The book on economics was out of print and was not available anywhere. But the Loyola library was good enough to spare one of the two copies they had because the book was no longer in demand years later from students. The librarian Father charged me, of course, rupees eight for the book! The alumni celebrated Prof Ganapathi's seventy fifth year or so years later. He himself did not appear for the IAS unlike his contemporary G. Ramachandran, later Finance Secretary, Tamil Nadu and Government of India. Ganapathi was supposed to have missed his university first because it was supposed to have been given to Dr A. Ramaswamy Mudaliar's daughter who was in Honours in the Presidency college that year. T.V.A. Seshan, later of the *The Hindu* (not to confuse with his equally brilliant cousin, P.A. Seshan) was absolutely brilliant for his mastery of the subject, content and good English prose, but was a soporific lecturer. Rajendran and a few others only took pride in having taught IAS or IFS luminaries like A. Madhavan, Hirji, Coelho and Khaleeli. **Lecturer C. Rangarajan of the commerce department rose to become Governor of the Reserve Bank of India and Governor of Andhra Pradesh. He also became the chairman of the Finance Commission and Economic Adviser to PM Dr Manmohan Singh. This is the bane of our system of not looking beyond one's nose. I have no quarrel with the knowledge or competence of Dr C. Rangarajan whom I know well. But Dr Manmohan Singh or any other PM should cast the net wide all over the world and bring in new people. There is no dearth of them. Similarly for the Planning Commission or the Ministry of Finance, we could think of only a Montek Singh or Rakesh Mohan. We should be able to see beyond Kirit Parikhs and Deepak Parekhs- as an economic newspaper wrote that these two were connected with several**

bodies that they spent more time in the air! Late Prof Samar Sen's son Abhijit Sen is a member of the Planning Commission and his brother is an adviser. Our governments – be it Congress, BJP or UF – are not free from this in-breeding.

Loyola always used to compete with St. Stephen's of Delhi in making the largest contribution to the IAS and other Central Services. Every year, there used to be a gallery of IAS or IFS or IPS successes, which was an inspiration to the successive generations of students. Madras University hardly contributes to the Services now so much so even the character of Tamil Nadu Cadre has changed with many officers from other parts of the country. I believe that Loyola has also lost its lustre now and rests on old laurels. The Father Principals have become pedestrian by not donning the cossacks and two of them did not even reply to my letters – what a contrast to the principals of MCC and Voorhees.

I always packed my baggage in such a way in Loyola that I would leave for Kilpattu by the next available bus immediately after the examinations. I spent time during holidays in the village by studying the various classics and meeting Jayavelu and other friends in the evenings. N. Krishnaswamy, a teacher and a staunch DMK man even today (since died) was a constant companion. We used to walk up to the railway station invariably every evening talking about all sorts of topics under the sun, mainly politics. One of the station-masters was a great student of Theosophy and he used to talk about Madame Blavatsky, Annie Besant, etc. Looking back, some of them, despite their station in life, were really knowledgeable on many matters and were also well read.

I was called for an interview to the post of a lecturer at the Avinashalingam College even before my results. This was my first interview. Although nothing came out of it, I took this opportunity to see the beautiful lush Ooty and stayed with an army friend from my village at Wellington. Ooty was much more beautiful those days. Over the years, there was a gradual onslaught on vegetation and it lost much of its charm. It is now good or attractive only in parts. Incidentally, my district contributed a lot of people to the Indian army including one of the famous Chiefs of Staff, Gen. K. Sundarji with whom I worked closely in the Ministry of Defence.

As soon as I returned to my village, my results were out and I was quite happy.

Job-hunting took me to Bombay and I was quite excited to be there for three months with some of my close relatives. They were very good although our relationship was disrupted later. A certain amount of jealousy persists among close relatives and they do not go all out to help. They stop at a point and would not like you to get something really good, and that has been my experience throughout my life. My father cannot think beyond a clerkship, naturally for a man of his background, and he wanted me to return to Madras to join the Accountant General's office. My relatives in Bombay, too, did not want me to get a good position in the Bank of India for which I got a call. As soon as I reached the village, I was struck with typhoid for the second time. I was in the bed for twenty-one days. I thought the AG's office job would go and I would be happy about it. But they gave me extra joining time and I joined a month later. My heart was not in the work there and I wanted to get out. I was awarded a scholarship to do M. Phil., by the University of Madras. But they stipulated that I should not appear for the IAS or the IPS and so I was forced to decline. I was staying in a little room in Triplicane, thanks to the good offices of an Iyengar contemporary, R. Parthasarathy from the Vivekananda College. The highly orthodox Iyengars would not think of giving a room to a bachelor boy with all Iyengar girls around and that, too, an Aiyar. The land-lady, otherwise a kind person, used to shut the windows of the kitchen whenever I passed by. She used to speak kindly and highly of me to her neighbours although I was an 'outcaste' for her. Those orthodox Iyengars would not even think of going to a Shaivite temple and omitted the word 'si' in 'Arisi' (in Tamil for rice) because 'si' may refer to Lord Siva!

My existence was hand–to-mouth and I was without money even to have a cup of coffee on some days since I had to send money to my father every month. He was steeply in debt and was finding it difficult to make both ends meet. He led a very honest life and paid for it heavily. He never accepted money or anything in kind for the numerous services like writing a registration deed, filing it, registering it, taking people to lawyers, government officials and so on. Our house was a free guest house for a host of officials visiting anywhere in the vicinity for years. There was no hotel and officials had to be fed with good food, preferably cooked in a Brahmin home. So all and sundry were diverted to our place even at odd hours and he fed them without grudging. Even now he is a person who will pay more than what is demanded or vacate a house before the land-lord actually demands so much so he has become a man on the run. Creditors converged on him at a particular point of time because there was virtually a run on him encouraged by some jealous elements in the village and he easily and quickly capitulated particularly during these days when creditors used to capitulate before debtors. He sold valuable lands in a hurry and that too to the proverbial village money-lender as graphically described in the RBI's Rural Credit Survey. His first cousin and rival, with whom he was not even on talking terms during his foster-father's days, became a wily friend, lent him money and used this opportunity to grab our house too. I was too young and innocent to intervene. He sought the help of my maternal grandfather at Vaiganallore, Kulitalai, only after having lost everything. It was all too late by then to rescue him.

One evening, he came to Madras and expressed his desire to move the family to Madras. I lost my temper with him for the first time for his haste and irresponsibility. Jayavelu was also present. Nothing could be done and tears rolled down his cheeks. Had he pulled on a year more, everything would have been intact because I got into the IPS in 1960 and my position and power even without any exertion on my part would have saved him in the village. He became an epitome of 'haste makes waste' and he is that even today in spite of his scrupulous honesty and Gandhian principles. (He is no more now) He had pangs of conscience at times for some of the numerous promissory notes he recklessly wrote for a higher amount to start with and added interest to principal while renewing. I too wanted that this amount be made good in course of time. But people advised against it because more than the creditors' due was already paid off. He landed in Madras with my mother and four younger sisters to live on a salary of Rs.150/- Since we could not live in the city with a high rent or in a hovel alternatively, we decided to go to Old Pallavaram, a village near Madras, where a relative's house was available for twenty rupees a month. It was really comfortable to live there.

The cruel thing was that even before my family left, my father's cousin's son and my play-mate chose to electrify our house with utter disregard for our feelings. The long chapter with Kilpattu was over for my father except for occasional visits there, for, after all, he went there on adoption although he became full part and parcel of it.

A visit to the village was incomplete for any one without a visit to our house though my grandfather never visited any one, not even a wedding or funeral except on only one occasion – funeral of his close friend and relation, a retired deputy collector, Nageswaran. After my grandfather's demise, perhaps as a psychological urge to free from repressed boyhood and also for the need to move in society to get his children accepted or married, my father started visiting people and socialising with vengeance. But the cruel relations and friends or, at least, a large part of them stopped visiting us during our days of poverty till I was selected for the IPS. I was to have a similar experience later in the capital of India, Delhi, when I got an innocuous and not-so-important a posting. However, I remembered Goldsmith's words, "Family misfortunes. The loss of fortune only serves to increase the pride of the worthy". I also recalled the Biblical saying that "blessed are the poor in spirit; for theirs is the kingdom of heaven", true or not!

***

3

Studies and Aspirations

I was trying all the time for a better position. I called on Prof. Namboodripad, Head of the Department of Economics, in the A.M. Jain college and enquired whether the position of a tutor or lecturer was available. He told me that if I had come a fortnight earlier, perhaps it would have been possible and at that moment there was no vacancy. From there, I proceeded straight to the sylvan surroundings of the Madras Christian College and met Prof John Healy, an Englishman, who was the head of the Department of Economics, in his beautiful bungalow in the midst of a forest. He was cordial in spite of my gate-crashing without an appointment. To my similar enquiry, he stated that they were having a tutor on the staff, Balakrishnan, who of course was not interested in becoming a lecturer perhaps out of sheer diffidence to face the students. My relations with him were extremely cordial later and he rose to a senior position in the Reserve Bank of India. Perhaps he was also worried about the students because a lecturer who rose to be the DGP of Tamil Nadu later had a lot of trouble with the students. Prof Healy also told me that they had promised one of their old students the post of lecturer in Economics, but the person concerned sought a few more days to make up his mind because he was already holding a government position in the

Census Department of the Government of India. So, Prof Healy retained my address and promised to get in touch with me in case the other person declined the offer. I reminded Prof Healy after about ten days and pat came a reply stating that I could come and join immediately. I resigned my AG's office job and felt relieved. Kind K. Balachandar, my immediate boss (who became a famous film Director later and was still a good friend – he used to stage dramas in the AG's office) enquired whether I was doing some thing in haste because the AG's office provided about six attempts those days to sit for the I.A.A.S., I told him in confidence that I had secured a position in the Madras Christian College and was taking a risk in the sense that it would not be a permanent position, but my heart was not in the AG's office.

I went to the college one fine morning and I was introduced by Prof Healy to the principal, Rev. J.R. Macphail and other lecturers in the staff room straightaway as a new lecturer in Economics. Some of my colleagues like Rajarathnam and Chiranjivi Nirmal were completely taken aback because Prof Healy was also telling them till the other day to find a new lecturer and how the Englishman suddenly found himself a person having the briefest address as "G. Sundaram, Old Pallavaram P.O., near Madras". I had to explain that the village consisted of hardly two streets and it was not difficult for the postman to know each and every one there (it is now a town).

Prof J.R. Macphail enquired in his own way whether I needed an appointment letter "to show my friends", as he put it nicely and diplomatically, for the practice was to issue a formal letter of appointment only after the approval of the Syndicate of the college, which was however only a formality. I told him not to bother about the letter, which could wait for the Syndicate's approval. At no stage they demanded to see my certificates. They took my word for having passed out from the Loyola college with a high second class. I found a similar practice years later in the University of Brussels. Unlike our practice of collecting the certificates or mark-sheets for record and at times these things even being forged by people, the students there do not bother to collect the degrees or mark-sheets at all. No convocations are held in the University of Brussels except once in a blue-moon to confer a degree of Honoris

Causa on some dignitary or the other. I have seen myself degrees lying in the drawers in the registrar's office uncollected. When my M.Phil., (Licence Special) results were announced orally as was their custom, everyone disappeared except me and another boy from a Latin American country. We wanted a certificate, that too, in English, for having qualified for the degree, which they gave.

The Madras Christian College was an institution of fine traditions. There was no attendance register to sign for the lecturers, nor was there any compulsion to remain in the college whenever there was no class to handle. For instance, during the first quarter, they gave me only a few classes to handle perhaps to test me out and I had no class at all on a working day every week. I did not have to be present in the college on those days.

The relationship between the teacher and the taught was close and it was fostered. Even day-lecturers like me were attached to a hostel known as 'Hall' and I was attached to the St. Thomas'. The teacher was expected to take care of the needs of the students, both academic and personal. There were mostly single rooms for the students. The three different Halls around the college, St. Thomas, Selaiyur and Bishop Heber used to compete with each other in upkeep, sports and entertainment. Hostel Days were great attraction to the students and the parents alike.

My work had increased during the second and third terms, including responsibility to handle tutorial classes for B.A. Hons., and E.A. Srinivasan, a student in M.A., became the Head of the Department of Economics some years later. Sarala joined the IAS and married another IAS officer, Gopalan. Luckily I hit off well with the students in the first month or two and that was very important. If one failed to hit it off well in the first few days, one would have problems throughout. This depended not only upon one's ability to lecture well and the academic content but also on the approach and ability to get along with the students, particularly the troublesome ones outside the college hours. One met them often on the train because the college was situated away from the city and a large number of them frequented the station to go to the city. Rapport at these times strengthened the bond and it helped.

The ladies hostel was tucked away in the far-off Guindy near the Race Course, so much so the girls had to travel up and down every day. This was intended perhaps to keep them away from the boys. One of the former principals was supposed to have remarked that if the girls hostel were to be on the campus, there was need for a maternity ward too! The hostel was sensibly moved to the campus during the time of Dr Chandran Devanesan and there was no need for a maternity ward!

Dr S. Chandrasekhar, the well known population expert who became a Minister in the Central government later, was a frequent visitor to the college. In fact, he was the head of the Department of Economics for some time. He was a scintillating speaker who could hold the audience for hours with his jokes about the population policy and the manner of his delivery despite some repetitions. His diction was excellent. He was a popular speaker even in the IAS Academy. He was also an examiner in economics by the U.P.S.C. for the IAS examinations. He explained how the system was foolproof and what was expected in the IAS exam was not scholarship or capacity to remember things, but an ability to analyse and state things to the point. To give an example, when the question was on Gandhian economics, while it is pardonable to write about Mahatma Gandhi's life also in a university examination, it is not accepted in the IAS examination. That was the reason why, some brilliant students who wrote 50 or 60 pages in three hours in answer to five questions in the Madras University economics examination with high marks failed to make the grade in the IAS examination. Of course, perhaps apocryphal, Dr Chandrasekhar actually asked a bright student to prepare draft question papers in general economics for him meant for the IAS examination and he perhaps made only minimal changes because he was more of a demographer than an economist.

I had made up my mind to remain in the Madras Christian College and pursue an academic career if I failed to make it to the IPS or the IAS. I was under-aged to appear for the IAS examination in 1959. Since age stipulation was one year less for the IPS I decided to try and came out successful. This also gave a boost to me in the college. Those days, the people who made it for the IAS/IPS or the Central Services were fairly well known immediately after the announcement of results in the Madras society because a lot of importance was attached to the civil service. There was always an 'IAS Gallery' in the Loyola College every year. As a result of this, a lot of persons from Tamil Nadu occupied high positions not only in the Central Government but also in other States. This trend has been reversed over years and the reverse is true now about which I do not want to pass an opinion.

When the academic year ended, one was paid for the whole period of summer vacation in advance and one was told about the classes to handle during the next academic year so that he or she could prepare during the summer vacation. I was also paid similarly and told that I should be able to handle even post-graduate classes during the following year.

Meanwhile, I decided to accept the offer of IPS and travel to Mussoorie and Mount Abu. That was the first year the IPS probationers were asked to report for a foundational course in Mussoorie with the IAS. So, contrary to expectations of joining only in October, I had to leave the college in May itself. It was summer recess and no one was available although I had given an indication to this effect both to Prof Healy and Rev. J.R. Macphail. After reaching Mussoorie in May, 1960, I had sent a letter to Rev. J.R. Macphail and enquired whether I should return 15 days salary because I was also getting a salary from the government. He wrote back immediately stating that I could be rich by that Rs.100/- or so and there was no need to return it. *"I do think it is a pity that you were not able to stay on as teacher, but I hope that in your new career you will be useful and happy", he also wrote.*

Thus ended the teaching career although the urge continued in different forms later. I visited the college thereafter whenever possible. Dr Chandran Devanesan, the first Indian Principal was kind enough to show me round the college. He became the Vice-Chancellor of the North Eastern University in Shillong later. When I went to the college some years later as Election Commission's observer to oversee counting which was going on on the campus, I did not see much of a difference in the surroundings except that there was a controversy between the environmentalists and the college because there was a proposal to clear the forest in some parts on the vast campus.

During those days, the visit of C.D. Deshmukh as chairman of the University Grants Commission was a memorable one. The college became an autonomous university and there was also some wrangle between the college and the government of Tamil Nadu.

The Alumni Association in Delhi was active. Although I was not an alumnus, they practically treated me as one and as a friend. Recently, I was pleased to hear from a colleague, Secretary Mohandas Moses, that on reading my name in the newspapers that I had been posted as Secretary to the Government of India, an old colleague in the college, George Jacob, enquired from him whether I was the same person who was "an outstanding lecturer" in the college with him in 1959. This is a type of satisfaction one derives, I suppose, in one's life.

4

Success

Orders were received for the IPS probationers too, for the first time, to report in Mussoorie in May, 1960 to have the Foundational Course with the IAS and other Central Services. Those selected for the IPS were proceeding hitherto straight to Mount Abu in Rajasthan in the month of October for specialised police training. The foundational course was introduced to promote inter-services camaraderie. Although it did achieve the purpose of a lasting friendship among the members of the various Services till the end of their career, it also introduced a certain amount of complexes and a mentality of subordination among the members of the other Central Services particularly the IPS because the IAS dominated the show in Mussoorie. This was also aggravated, as noted by me in the register of comments and remarks by the probationers at the time of parting, for want of a unified civil service with common scales of pay. In fact, I had also advocated this idea later in an article for the journal of the Indian Institute of Public Administration – immediately after the publication of the report of the Committee on Administrative Reforms under the chairmanship of Morarji Desai. Different hierarchical structures do produce a feeling of subordination although it may perhaps be inevitable.

Incidentally, Pakistan made an experiment by abolishing all services. The service-labels were done away with. The services were re-christened as the District Administration Group, Customs Group, Police Group, etc. Even today, the preferences of the people is for the District Administration Group and secondly for the Police or the Customs Group. In other words, the categorizations remain and consequently the exercise has turned out to be only a change in name. Though the examinations have been made a unified one instead of the three different examinations in a combined examination earlier, the distinction persists because those who obtain high ranks prefer the IAS. The preferences for other services vary from time to time and the IFS seems to have lost its attraction at the moment because of its problems of living abroad since the services mostly attract people belonging to the middle class families and from a society still based on a joint family system and certain moorings. **However, I would attribute it more to the ignorance of the service conditions and certain privileges of the IFS among the candidates, and the IFS also still preserves it as a closely guarded secret for the fear that the privileges may be eroded by government action. In this regard, a book written by one Raman, an IFS-B officer, a few years ago, was revealing.**

There was a lot of activity and rush because of the short notice for stitching one or two suits, getting warm sweaters and so on. The people of Madras do not have to wear a sweater even during the so-called winter of Madras. All this had to be done within a period of five days or so and there was naturally a great rush. Meanwhile, some elderly relatives who were living away from Madras had to be taken leave of, particularly my paternal grandfather who was living in a village not connected by any motorable road for a radius of four miles or so. It was good I met this well-wisher because he passed away when I was in Mussoorie. His astrological forecasts were nearly accurate. He predicted that I would get into the IAS also, should I attempt it. After all this hurry-burry, it was all set and the first journey towards the north had begun.

On the train, there were other fellow probationers like Sripal who was also a companion for three years in the Loyola College and so also Rajmohan, and new companions like Ramalingam and P.B. Rajagopalan. This friendship was to last for a long time, particularly among the first three, who were eternal fellow-travellers for the next two years. P.B. Rajagopalan was the best informed among the lot and he felt that he should try for the IAS. The others did not feel like doing so because no one was selected so far from the IPS to the IAS or other Services and also thought perhaps the distinction between the two Services was only small. **But it was learnt later in the Academy itself that the distinction was quite substantial in the sense that the IAS District Magistrates wrote even the Confidential Rolls of the Superintendents of Police indicating clear subordination and so also was the Police Act. This has become a bone of contention in the administration over years and some times the CR writing by the DMs has been done away with. However, the overall control of the District Magistrate and Collector over the police still remains and the Home Secretary controls the State Police. Over a period of time, by chronic wrangles and demands from the police and also, because of their proximity to the politicians for obvious reasons, the system has taken a beating and in some States even the police officers are appointed as Home Secretaries. While no police officer was appointed a Governor those days, it had become a common practice now despite the colour of a police state in practice. Thus the distinction has become blurred over a period of time though the preference still remains for the IAS because of the variety of experience it provides. While, on the one hand, the police officers claimed that they had the same kind of education and passed a similar examination and consequently could occupy any position open to the IAS officers, they claimed conveniently later that they were "experts". In any case, the definition of an expert in India is that an "expert is one who is not in the IAS". This generalist tag is also changing over the years by allowing the entry of doctors, engineers, accountants, and IIT graduates into the IAS, which is a step in the right direction. Although many feel that technical people are wasted by allowing them to enter the civil services, it is a step in the right direction because an avenue should not be denied to these highly educated persons, and, moreover, the IAS becomes a technical pool**

instead ot being a generalist service with only students of literature, politics or history. A small number of engineers or doctors entering the service does not deprive the country of technical talent. On the contrary, these persons occupying positions of authority do help the country. For instance, a cost-accountant Collector is able to apply his knowledge of cost consciousness even to programmes like IRDP, municipal administration, etc. A particular municipality, since the Administrator is not trained in cost consciousness, has deposited crores of rupees in a current account with a bank. The cost-accountant Collector advised the Adminstrator to deploy the funds in such a way as to earn good income so that he could usefully spend it on municipal services.

IAS officers may not be intellectual giants. But their exposure to various jobs equips them well both physically and mentally. The intellectual challenge of each job makes them learn all the time in the service. This may not be true of the other Services, particularly the IPS. I have observed that the intellectual ability or the ability even to grasp simple things decline in the IPS officers as they progress in service. Perhaps this is an unavoidable phenomenon on account of the monotony of the same work unless somebody tries very hard like, Sripal, to keep one's intellect sharpened all the time. This may be true of many IAS officers too, but the damage is not to the same degree. Perhaps this is the reason why, there is failure of intelligence in many important government matters and situations. I would like to cite the instance of the assassination of Rajiv Gandhi – it is a sad commentary on our Intelligence that they were not able to detect a plot, which was made over a period of a few months and the assassins, though strangers in a new place, masqueraded as journalists and ordinary persons, also carrying out rehearsals of assassination, what they called 'dry runs'.

This kind of a feeling of difference between the IAS and other Services was also aggravated, though in a small and humorous way, by the Director of the National Academy of Administration, the late Dr A.N. Jha, a great scholar and a remarkable civil servant of the U.P. cadre, known for his wit and humour. He used to sit on the Selection Board of the UPSC for the IAS and other services.

He was fond of narrating an instance: a candidate was asked why he had not applied for the IPS. He replied that it was for the reason that he was 'rather intellectually inclined' and Dr Jha told the Board that he should be given a few extra marks for that intelligent answer. He also used to advise the IPS probationers in particular to appear for the IAS. He felt that it would be better for the central service probationers to remain in the central service discarding even the IAS in order to be free from the clutches of petty politicians in the districts (politicians were not that bad in those days in State headquarters and at the Centre).

With all these thoughts, we reached Delhi and stayed in the Madras Hotel in Connaught Place for a princely sum of Rs. 6/- per day those days. Sripal and I were always adventurous as compared with the docile Rajmohan and Ramalingam. Our enquiries indicated that there was a bus service from Delhi to Mussoorie. So to make sure we enquired from the Railways whether the refund for the part of ticket from Delhi to Dehradun was possible and after ensuring that, we made the reservation by bus the next morning to Mussoorie. After tying up all this, we returned the train tickets and also saw a film, "The Nun's Story" featuring Audrey Hepburn.

The next morning on the way to Mussoorie, K.S. Bains, son of a high ranking police officer in the Punjab, joined us. The young Bains had given up his class I engineering service (he was an engineer) to join the IPS, which commanded greater respect than even the IAS in the Punjab. However, he joined the IAS in the subsequent year and ended his career as the chairman of the Punjab and Sind Bank. In the course of his career, he got a 'Padma Shri' for his outstanding work in the Asiad in New Delhi though he did not become a Secretary to the Government of India. This was because of the panel system of selection for promotion on which I will elaborate later.

The bus was not a very comfortable one unlike the buses of the modern day. The bus passed through fairly beautiful scenery of Uttar Pradesh and also through the dusty towns. In some towns, it was a sad sight to see Tamils begging. Perhaps they made it a side-occupation. This is similar to one's first experience of seeing Indian or Pakistani women cleaning the toilets in the Heathrow airport in London.

The bus reached the fairly beautiful town of Dehradun, which nestled in a valley. 'Dun' itself means 'valley'. Contrary to our expectation, it was hot in Dehradun. The ascent to Mussoorie was fairly steep and we reached there late in the evening to be greeted by a hailstorm. We reached the Academy in the midst of lashing rain. The Academy was housed in an old hotel, "Charleville'. Of course, one felt that being greeted by rain was supposed to be auspicious.

The rooms were not cosy and one had to wear a suit or at least a sweater to protect oneself from the cold weather. The place was full of boys – mostly young boys and a few girls – and this association was to continue for another three decades or more. One did not realise at that time that there would be many ups and downs and the association would take different shapes and facets from time to time–an ideal or innocent one as that of a child to that of a cantankerous one, with a lot of back-stabbing in the run-up to plum offices particularly in the evening of one's career just before retirement.

We were greeted by the Director the next morning with his usual humour and panache. It was a stay of five months for the IPS and the Services other than the IAS. There were many lectures on topics like etiquette to high philosophy to atomic energy. A variety of lecturers came and lectured on a broad spectrum of subjects – some of them interesting and some others boring. This was in addition to the permanent lectures on law, history, economics, politics, etc. The officers were expected to wield the broad brush in their careers instead of getting into a narrow hole and they were trained here for that purpose. Swami Ranganathanandha came and delivered three lectures on the motto of the academy: "Yoga Karmasu Kaushalam". Dr Chandrasekhar talked on the importance of population control. There were also many cultural programmes and an opportunity was provided to the probationers to show their hidden talents. Deputy Director, R.K. Trivedi, lectured on service etiquette, behaviour in the district, relations with fellow officers of the police, the judiciary, the engineering, and the social calls to be made after reaching the district etc. There was also an Assistant Collector's manual of the old Bombay province, which served as a guide to the youngsters.

I understand now that computers have mainly replaced the old curriculum, which is not bad in itself in the modern world. But one should not forget, as Queen Elizabeth said, "Mastery of technology may blind us to the more fundamental needs of people – electronics cannot create comradeship; computers cannot generate compassion; satellites cannot transmit tolerance".

Even in the highly materialistic United States, 'ethics' has been introduced as a new subject in the management institutions and in big corporate training programmes. This is with a view to improving the moral fibre of the executives and consequently the society. There are norms laid down for acceptance of gifts, hospitality, etc. even in the corporate world. One would recall the moral instruction classes one had to attend, not only in the schools, but also in the colleges. This part seems to be missing in the Academy today and as a result the probationers come out with mercenary ideas or totally devoid of idealism. Social etiquette has also become a thing of the past.

During our stay in Mussoorie, Gopi Krishna Handoo, a tall and handsome Kashmiri with a flock of fine silvery gray hair who was the Commandant of the Police Training College, Mt. Abu, visited and addressed the probationers. In his talk, he stated that even now he did not know the exact scale of his pay or the total emoluments. He was more interested in being a proud member of the old Indian Police than in other mundane matters. Similarly, I read in the memoir of an equally outstanding police officer of the old IP, E.L. Stracey that he did not know for quite a few years after joining the service that medical reimbursement was available for the medical expenditure on the officer and his dependents. Whereas the modern-day probationer makes it a point to know the privileges first and constructs a house within a few years of service as though he is retiring soon. Of course, this worldly-wise approach is in marked contrast to the old world approach of service first and self later, even to the extent of not owning a house till the day of retirement, as it really happened in a few cases including mine.

I was a non-entity in Mussoorie. The Mess Committee was dominated by Dr Ramaswamy Mani from Harvard whose ascending career in the United Nations later was cut short by a small slip-up and his life was cut short by cruel cancer. He opted for Bihar and so was the topper, Jagannathan Murali from Cambridge who later joined the World Bank. Many other Tamil Brahmins opted for States other than Tamil Nadu fearing the virulent anti-Brahminism in Tamil Nadu. These fears were unfounded or perhaps they were partly true. (In any case, there was a recrudescence of anti-Brahmin venom and vituperation recently after l'affaire Kanchi Shankaracharya). I was allotted to the Andhra Pradesh in the IPS and regretted for not having been allotted to Tamil Nadu. I had many non-Brahmin friends since my boyhood and so had no fears on this score. But it is true that anti-Brahminism has been carried to the extremes in Tamil Nadu more than it is necessary and disproportionate to the supposed injustice done to the non-Brahmins in the past. But Tamil Nadu is a paradoxical state in the sense the common people are not swayed by such emotional appeals at least as far as the top leader is concerned. Otherwise, a non-Tamil MGR could not have ruled the State for over a decade and so was Jayalalithaa for an equally long time. Besides, chief ministers of this highly literate State were not even graduates or did not even cross the school – Omandur Reddiar, Kumaraswamy Raja (Intermediate), Kamaraj, MGR, Karunanidhi and Jayalalithaa. In politics, charisma matters, particularly in Tamil Nadu. But this is not true in my State of IAS allotment, Gujarat. Although not a highly literate State then like Tamil Nadu, stalwarts and scholars were the CMs who were noted for erudition, though not for glamour – Dr Jeevaraj Mehta, a medical doctor, Dr Balwantrai Mehta of the Panchayati Raj fame, Hitendra Desai, Madhavsinh Solanki, a scholar and voracious reader, bird-watcher, interested in Urdu poetry and Babubhai Jasbhai Patel who could keep statistics at his finger-tips and who wrote articles on the Budget of the Government of India, which even many civil servants might not be able to do. Even Chimanbhai Patel was clever in his own way and was a graduate. Amarsinh Choudhary was an engineer and the first tribal to become a chief minister in India, leaving aside the North East. And so was

Chhabildas Mehta and Shankarsinh Waghela. Keshubhai Patel was the only one who did not know English that well but clever. Corporate Chiefs feel that Narendra Modi was one of them for his ability to project Gujarat and its impressive economic growth.

I would not go anywhere near the girls. I took the curriculum seriously. No adolescent pranks. We were suddenly asked to spend about Rs.700/- on police uniform which came as a bolt from the blue. For many of us from the middle classes, it was too harsh. Moreover, we were told that G.K. Handoo was in the habit of making the probationers spend all their money on the mess in Mt. Abu. We were worried about this aspect and luckily Commandant Bannerji came on the scene and changed all this.

Five months were over and we moved on to Mt. Abu with a feeling of sadness for not having got into the IAS who were the real rulers. P.B. Rajagopalan, Bains, Reddy and Kuppu Rao took the IAS examination and got in too—after perhaps some long years IPS probationers were selected to the IAS. They had to spend a few months in Mt. Abu before they went back to Mussoorie for the IAS training. Sripal and I felt all the more sad for not having appeared for the IAS. We felt that our stars were sealed in the IPS because the month-long, tough IPS final examination coincided with the IAS examination. For people like us from the middle class, a bird in hand was worth two in the bush.

Sripal, Ramalingam, Rajmohan and I travelled together to Madras and then on to Mt. Abu via Bombay and Ahmedabad, Mehsana and Palanpur after the joining time. Little did I realise at that time or during our sight-seeing visits to Baroda and Ahmedabad that I would have to spend a few years in that region in the IAS. In fact, my IAS career was to start, of all places, in Palanpur! We were travelling companions always later – one looking after reservations, one logistics, another after miscellaneous expenditure, etc.

On the day I landed in Mt. Abu in Novemeber, 1960, I straight landed in the hospital with paratyphoid. I listened to G.K.Handoo's welcome speech because he was on orders of transfer to Bombay to master-mind the 'Goa operations'. He was so good at man-

management that he came to the hospital to see me though he was leaving Mt. Abu, spoke a few words in Tamil (although a Kashmiri, he was born in Mangalore or Udipi and studied in the Madras Christian College) and instructed the medical officer to look after me well. He was tall, handsome, very good at riding and high-jumps in full uniform and was an institution in Mt. Abu. He was also the personal security officer to Panditji – more a glamourous post those days unlike in the present day. Incidentally, in spite of his high connections, he was sent only as an adviser to the Lt. Governor of Goa because the then policy was not to appoint police officers as Governors in order not to give the impression of a police State. Even defence officers were appointed only sparingly. But now, particularly under the BJP dispensation, too many police officers were appointed Governors even for important states like Tamil Nadu. Also, in this regard, from my own experience in the Defence Ministry, it is advisable to appoint Generals like Krishna Rao or Sinha to States like J&K and the North East because the army officers generally detest police officers at the helm – they feel that they are pseudo-civilians. If at all the defence officers respect civil officers, it is only the IAS. Cabinet Secretary also ranks above the Chiefs in the Order of Protocol.

The officiating Commandant, E.L. Stracey, was an embodiment of correct behaviour and a man of very high integrity. He was also a strict disciplinarian with a lot of humanism. As his well written memoir would indicate, he was not treated well in Tamil Nadu and true to the name of his bungalow in Mt. Abu, "Wilderness" (I called him once the man from 'the wilderness' and he took it sportingly); he was in wilderness in Mt. Abu for seven years or so. He returned to Madras to face the virulent anti-Hindi agitation, and MGR, taking note of his integrity, made him the IGP and later the first DGP of Madras. There was some bickering in the Madras Police about him but I feel that those were because of his strict maintenance of discipline.

Stracey was a good pen-man as is evident from his memoir. His English was also grammatical. On a few occasions, he was good enough to correct some of my articles before sending them to the press. Looking back, he never misunderstood my requests for draft correction. Most of us held him in great reverence.

After a year or two, I was walking on the Edward Elliots Road in Madras. An imported, beautiful limousine stopped by my side and Stracey stepped out of the car to greet a junior officer in the IAS from some other cadre walking on the road. He invited me to the Police Medal Parade that evening. This gesture of his greatly touched me and such small acts of good manner remain green in one's memory. Even junior officers do not talk to you these days if you are not useful to them. He used to teach us that demi-official letters should be addressed only by name even by an Assistant Superintendent of Police to the IG and not as 'Sir'. There was no need to 'Sir' a superior in the club or in the mess – Mr 'so and so' will be more appropriate and it would be the correct form of address.

The last examination was over on October 4th morning and twelve of us left for Delhi the same evening to appear for the IAS examination. Sripal, Rajmohan and I stayed at the Madras Hotel in Connaught Place and appeared for the three compulsory and three lower papers. We left for Madras directly. Sripal was to stay on in Madras because he was allotted to that cadre and I was to go to Ananthapur Police Training College in Andhra Pradesh. Rajmohan proceeded to UP (he later changed his cadre to Madras).

Adventurous as we were, Sripal and I thought of an idea of requesting the UPSC to allow us to take the higher two papers in Madras three weeks later. We did not want to travel again to Delhi. The UPSC was very accommodative to the candidates those days and they readily agreed. We took the examination in higher papers for the IAS in Madras.

The period of my stay in Mt. Abu from November 1960 to October 1961 was also important for me in another respect. During a visit to Madras in 1961, I was asked by my father and father-in-law to be, Dr Venkateswaran, to see my future wife in the traditional fashion. It was the only visit I did for the purpose and I decided to marry her.

We were woken up in the cold early morning of Mt. Abu at five by the 'reveille' of the bugle. We were naturally reluctant to get up and the bearer literally shook us up with a cup of tea. A quick wash, shave and we got into a smart uniform – we were ready to march at 5.30 sharp. One of us became the squad leader by turn and we were marched to the parade ground, two or three furlongs away, in front of the college. I had difficulty in keeping up the step with others because I was absent for about a month on account of paratyphoid and I was scolded on occasions for this lapse. In fact, I was given special training for a few days by the kindly Menon, an elderly instructor. Some of us who were weak in drill were pulled out for some time and formed into 'an awkward squad' to make us have a sense of shame so that we would do better and get out of the awkward squad and also avoid getting into it again!

This reminded me of my days in the Voorhees College, Vellore. On the first day, among the two hundred and odd boys and girls, a few of us including Jayavelu did not stand up for any game. I was poor at sports because of my daily train journey from home to the school and the college. But I was more fit physically and mentally than the city boys because of my long walks to the station both in the morning and in the evening and also because of swimming. About ten of us who did not stand up for any game were sent to a playground away from the college for playing base-ball. Since the physical training instructor hardly visited this far-off ground, we practically did not play even this game.

I felt that there was an undue emphasis on brawn rather than on brains in the Central Police Training College so much so that I called it in the college magazine as the Constant Physical Torture Centre! To my surprise, this article was selected and reproduced in the Golden Jubilee special issue of the National Police Academy in 1999. They did not know that I had 'deserted' the police. When I was in the hospital down with paratyphoid, there was another boy from Bihar suffering from rheumatism which aggravated in the cold climate of Mt. Abu. He held the same view about physical training in the police training college. But Stracey rightly felt that although we would not have to do it ourselves once we left the college as police 'bada-saabs' as he used to pronounce in his Anglo-Indian accent, we should be fit physically and correct the jawans and other subordinates on parade. I realised this later in Ananthapur and Guntur. It was a mystery how Sahaya got into the IPS at all with his rheumatism as another short boy also from Bihar. It transpired later that both of them were highly connected in Bihar. But, true to his non-performance on the parade ground, Sahaya turned out to be a highly successful police officer in Bihar and I used to read about him in the newspapers – he was always mentioned in dispatches, so to say. (He also became Governor of Chattisgarh, in 2001! This paragraph was written before he became a Governor).

What I learnt there - the sixth table of PT – I do even today for a few minutes in the morning. After PT, one had to change within a few minutes into another uniform – every thing was done with clock-work precision – and go on parade with a rifle resting on the shoulder. Marching, formations, presentation of arms, etc. were done. Apart from Stracey who was often there on the parade ground, English Tommy, Davenport was invariably present. His daughter, Elizabeth, was an ace javelin thrower. Spadigm, Menon, Nambiar, Joseph – all from the highly specialised Malabar Special Police – a force mainly meant to quell rebellions – were the drill instructors. They would not allow even the eye-balls to move while at attention and Spadigm would shout from a distance. (I was reminded of this years later when a President of India was always in the habit of looking around when the National Anthem was played. No one seems to have corrected him). They were also using expressions perhaps taken from some books, like "no molly-coddling here", "no butter fingers here", "you there, don't move or shuffle", etc. It was a perfect parade and training. Spadigm – a Malayalee – was harsh with good intentions, but some probationers complained to the Commandant. Stracey explained these situations and good intentions to probationers during dinner-nights.

Stracey trained the probationers in proper etiquette at social gatherings, to the ladies while calling and also he conducted almost a mess-drill as to how to hold the spoon, eat without making noise, eating bread in bits and small pieces and so on. Probationers used to avoid sitting near him at dinners to be free from his prying eyes. But he would catch them and make them sit near him and learn the dinner-drill. The neck should always be covered by a tie or scarf even at informal dinners every night. He taught us to say only 'Yes, thanks' or 'No, thanks', 'coffee or tea' to Mrs. Stracey whenever we called on them.

After the parade, there was a short break to have a bath and breakfast. Since the time was too short, while one had breakfast, the other room-mate had a bath. Classes started sharp at ten in the morning. One had to be in the class exactly five minutes earlier and Stracey's click of opening the door could be heard exactly at ten. When one of the probationers was in the class-room earlier than five minutes, Stracey told him off for lacking confidence in oneself and hence the presence earlier – good logic! The classes went on till 1 p.m., with a short tea break of fifteen minutes. Probationers eagerly rushed out for letters from parents or loved ones. On one such breaks, Sripal rushed and told me that he had seen the Government of India Gazette and the IAS exams were to start on October 6th that year. The usual date of September 18th for many years was dispensed. He asked me whether it gave me a clue and it did. I told him that this change of date might change our destiny too because we could have a try at the IAS after finishing our IPS final examination. We consulted the kind Tekchandani, the administrative officer from the Central Secretariat – all of them were generally good because Abu was a small place and we used to meet the families too on holidays by making social calls. He told us that he would prepare a time-table finishing the IPS final exam on October 4th so that we could leave for Delhi the same night to appear for the IAS exam on 6th morning. He said that the Home Ministry would not bother about these minor details and approve the time-table suggested by him.

Sripal, Rajmohan and I applied only for the IAS and Stracey had no objection to forward our applications. But when a few others applied for the Central Services, he was livid with anger because it was tantamount to looking down upon the IPS, an all-India Service. So Sripal, Rajmohan and I called on him at his residence and requested him not to penalise us for the fault of others. But government regulations did not allow Stracey any discretion and he had to forward all the applications to the UPSC.

One had to change into shirts and blazers in the afternoon for driving classes or games. Riding was also done generally in the evenings including scrubbing of horses and cleaning the stables. Hurdle-jumping on the horse-back was a difficult physical exercise. Again one had to change into a uniform or formal dinner dress depending upon the nature of dinner nights. The mess was overlooking the beautiful Nakki lake and the reflection of lights added beauty to the dinner nights as though candles were lit in the lake. Rowing was also taught or done in the Nakki. Incidentally, one had to spend a sizeable amount on the uniform. The government grant for the purpose was small. I had to borrow money for the purpose. When I got into the IAS, these uniform became useless. But an IPS Probationer, Dave bought the uniform from me for Rs.500/-. He told our common friend and Minister, Yashwant Sinha, in a party years later that my uniform was lucky for him because he did not have to buy a second set – he got into the RAW. He became a Governor on retirement and I could not!

It was both a rigorous physical and mental training for about a year with many subjects on law, crime, criminology and so on, and the final examination itself took a month. I came out with flying colours with a high all-India final rank, above Sripal, Rajmohan and Ramalingam. Despite the general impression of being weak on the parade ground, I stood second in revolver-shooting. I missed the cup for shooting because of an unintentional affectionate kick by Davenport. In rifle-shooting competition, all my four shots hit the bull's eye. Before the final shot went, Davenport who was observing me from behind thought it was over and gave me an affectionate kick. My lying-in position changed and the final shot went slightly off the mark and I lost the cup.

For the final passing-out parade drills, I opted for the horse-squad to avoid the rigour and also because of the fact that I was preparing for the IAS, though it was considered somewhat infra-dig to sit on a horse in a parade. But I felt that it was mostly left to the horse and I could go on it with ease rather than marching with a rifle and a stiff back, all the time worrying about the steps.

Another highlight of the our stay was that for the Republic Day in New Delhi in 1961, Queen Elizabeth was the chief guest and it so happened that I was placed in front of the President's Box to control the numerous photographers and as a result my photographs appeared in many journals and film-documentaries. After the parade, a lot of rural folk rushed to touch the seat where the Queen sat!

* * *

5

Stint in the Indian Police Service

After finishing the IPS final examination, twelve of us left for Delhi the same evening. The day after was the examination in compulsory papers. The three compulsory and the three lower papers were over in less than a week. The examinations were held in different centres, in some colleges and schools.

This was followed by a brief so-called joining time in Madras. I reached Ananthapur in Andhra Pradesh. Ananthapur is a small town in a semi-arid area known as Royalaseema. The other districts of Royalaseema are Cuddapah, Kurnool, and Bellary. Bellary is now in Karnataka. Kurnool was the capital of Andhra when it was carved out of the Madras State after Potti Sriramulu's death and before it was expanded as Andhra Pradesh.

The weather is generally dry in Ananthapur. The State Police Training College was located there. The mess was located in a rented building with poor furnishings and a cook who could not cook properly. The food was generally brought from the hotel and the Andhra food was full of chillies. There were two or three probationers in the mess directly recruited to the State Police Service.

V. Srinivasan was the Principal of the Police Training College. He was a religious and pious person. I was told by his deputy that it was customary to call on the principal for the first time in full ceremonial dress, which I failed to do because I was not aware of this practice. But he was not offended. The other members of the staff were generally very friendly. The fellow probationers of the State Police Service and other cadres in the police training college were generally deferential to the IPS probationer because he or she (there was no lady IPS so far. Indu Passy was the first one to be selected in 1962. But she preferred the Railways. Since she was my batch-mate, I used to tease her that she missed all the glory to Kiran Bedi!) would become a Superintendent of Police within three or four years by making a big leap as compared with them.

Early morning drills were important and one should be able to command the constables on training by one's own conduct and also by the ability to perform the same tasks oneself. This reminded me of the training given by Stracey in Mount Abu.

I had learnt car driving very well in Mount Abu. So I tried my hand at motor-cycle driving. But the bike tumbled one day and I stumbled and held it by sheer force before switching it off. But for the timely switching off, it would have been a serious accident. So kindly Srinivasan advised me to give up motor-bike riding because I would have no occasion to do so in the service.

Joe Saldhana was the superintendent of police who wanted me to conduct the district police meet. I had trepidations because I hardly knew anything about sports. However, I had a manual which I had carefully studied and under his overall guidance I could make it a highly successful event which made me known all over the district.

During this period, the IG of Police made a brief visit to the college. There was a lot of fanfare during these visits. The IG or even the DIG used to be conducted by motorbike policemen from the border of the district and they would be seen off again at the border as was done for the VVIPs. Nambiar was almost a demi-god in Andhra Pradesh. He belonged to the old IP. I was told that he was a great devotee of the Shankaracharya of Shringeri and had issued orders to the police stations that the Shankaracharya should be given all facilities wherever and whenever he entered any part of Andhra Pradesh. Nambiar, because of the efflux of the British officers after the Indian independence, became an IG with 15 years of service or so. He was there for a long time. Perhaps this unbridled power made him or some members of his family commit acts of indiscretion which landed Nambiar in jail.

Similarly, a DIG used to be given a high profile treatment whenever he came to Guntur when I was there. He never stayed in the government circuit house. He always preferred to stay in posh guest houses with swimming pools belonging to the rich tobacco merchants of Guntur district. On one such visit, the superintendent of police inspected the guest house fifteen minutes before the arrival of the DIG with his family. He saw that the town-inspector had brought a portable transistor and not the usual radio. The transistor used to cost about 500 rupees those days, which was quite a sum, more than one's pay. He scolded the inspector and ordered him to take away the transistor and put a huge radio because he feared the DIG's wife would walk away with the transistor at the time of leaving the guest house in the pretext of listening to some music and he would not be able to stop it in any way! This DIG was also jailed later for corruption.

After a month's stay in Ananthapur, I moved to Guntur. Kind Srinivasan advised me to be careful about the high profile superintendent of police in Guntur, T. Ponnaiya. Srinivasan had also known that I had appeared for the IAS and was expecting the results. He advised me to get out of the police at the earliest opportunity, for some persons like Ponnaiya might advise me to stick on or I myself might be carried away by the pomp of the police in Andhra Pradesh.

But the Ponnaiyas were actually very kind to me. He was considered a very efficient police officer in spite of some of his idiosyncrasies. He was always close to the powers-that–be and felt that he was superior to his colleagues in his work. Once he was called to the neighbouring district for law and order maintenance when Panditji came there to address a meeting. He took me along with him. He advised me to carry a baton always so that it would be useful on such occasions although it was not a part of the uniform. He felt that he was specially called because the local police chief was not up to the task. He used to give open expression to such feelings, which earned him perhaps some enemies in the Service. He also had a running battle with the IAS so much so an IAS Collector-cum-District Magistrate issued a bailable warrant against him when he avoided meeting the District Magistrate. Of course, because of his clout with the IG of Police Nambiar and the latter's proximity to the politicians, the Collector was transferred immediately by a telegram from the district and Ponnaiya felt one-up over the IAS.

So I felt that he would have some animosity against me for my attempt to get into the IAS. On the contrary, he used to discuss with me the pros and cons of the IAS and the IPS and invariably came to the conclusion that the IAS was far better than the IPS and I should leave the IPS, if successful. He always felt that it was no use carrying on a battle as he did against the IAS who were the real rulers. He felt that though he had won a few battles, they would wait for an opportunity to strike him ultimately. Of course, there were some rumours about his integrity which I had to believe because those were coming from my own colleagues. But these were not very serious by the present-day standards of corruption. In any case, after a few years, he was suspended for corruption and perhaps exonerated later. He also died after some time.

I was sent to Guntur because the district had the largest crime rate in the entire Andhra Pradesh. I was attached to an inspector for about a month. Surprisingly during this period, not even a theft took place, although even murders were common in that district. After the early morning parades again, time was spent in the police stations. I was living all alone in a rented house. Food used to come from a hotel. Ponnaiya advised me to be very careful about Andhra food lest I would be laid up with dysentery. T. Padmanabhan was the Assistant Collector on training who was noted for his Victorian English. Ponnaiya used to be quite deferential to him by taking him in his car wherever he went and allowing him to enter his office without prior appointment or waiting outside. He started giving me these privileges only after my IAS results were announced and I was successful.

We always played tennis in the evening with Ponnaiya. The town police sub-inspector was one of the main players. I was attached to his police station. He was always very well-dressed and used to come on a motorbike. He was a sign of prosperity. He never wrote the case-diaries himself. He had employed a retired police writer by paying Rs.150 or so per month, which was a sizeable amount those days. As a probationer, one is generally close to these people and could learn a lot of things including the seamy side of life provided one does not assume the airs of an IPS officer. If one does so, one will not be able to learn things *sub rosa.* So I asked him one day why he was not writing these diaries himself and how he could afford to employ a personal clerk. He was frank. He told me that he himself was from a fairly rich family and was not particularly after money. In fact, he had not taken money from any one. But the town police station was important for the rich merchants particularly of the tobacco trade that they paid him three or four thousand rupees per month either in cash or in kind without asking for. If he had been active in this regard as some others who were there, he could have easily earned ten thousand rupees or so. Case-diaries were routine documents and he gave only the points to the clerk to build on and make it presentable.

The railway station was the only good place where there was a restaurant and a good book shop. There was also an American library though in town. There were many cinema theatres and prostitutes used to come and sit by one's side if one was alone during the night shows. They also used to hang around hotels and the PWD guest house. The town of Tenali in the same district was quite notorious in this regard. Ponnaiya advised me in the beginning itself to be careful in this regard, for one should not try to paint the town red as some probationers did in the past. His theory was that if one had to do, one should take off to a big city and indulge in so that there was no notoriety in the work place. He also told me that whenever I went to any village on camp or for investigation, I should never stay in any private house although the police inspectors would advise one to do so. He advised me that I should be prepared to sleep in a temple or even under a tree, but not in any one's house under any circumstances. One of the Assistant Superintendents of Police went to a village to investigate a murder case. In Guntur district, villages had beautiful and comfortable houses belonging to rich tobacco farmers. The inspector of police advised this ASP to stay in one of those houses, which this officer unwittingly did. The next day hundreds of telegrams were sent to the IG of Police and the Chief Minister stating that the lady of that house was involved in this murder and the ASP compromised himself by sleeping with her. So much so this hapless poor officer was immediately placed under suspension. It took long years for him to get over the stigma and problem although he rose up in the hierarchy eventually and retired with honour.

Although he was a senior to the SP, he happened to work in the same district as an ASP on account of this punishment. I was also attached to him for training. This was one or two years after his punishment. I found him to be an extremely honest person. Whenever even fruits or coffee were kept for him in a circuit house before his arrival, he either paid or asked these to be removed immediately. Only for the cinema shows he did not pay. Cinema was the only entertainment in the district. So I asked him why he was not paying for the shows when he was paying for everything else. He told me that the theatre owner would unnecessarily create a scene for nothing if you tried to pay. **Moreover, he was of the view that in this sea of corruption, other people should have at least some thing to say against you because it would be extremely difficult for a puritan to exist and to avoid a graver charge being thrust upon you.** Of course, perhaps his mind was a bit coloured because of his personal experience. Ponnaiya always used to joke that for all the hardship this ASP had undergone on account of this charge, if he had at least slept with the lady of the house, he could have had some secret satisfaction!

I was moved to another area of great crime, Bapatla on the Andhra coast. It is a small beautiful town on the main line between Vijayawada and Madras. There was also a criminal settlement nearby, Stuartpuram. The criminals from Stuartpuram did not spare some of the trains running on this main line. I was in charge of the police station for a month. Surprisingly in this high crime area, no crime occurred. Ponnaiya was really aghast and felt that I was missing on my training. I used to tell him jocularly that my preventive work was so good that no crime occurred. I used to tell the sub-inspector to book some cases instead under the Motor

Vehicles Act. On one occasion, at about 4 o' clock in the evening, he asked me how many months of conviction I wanted for a person. It was a strange question to me because I thought that this was a matter entirely in the hands of the magistrates. But the sub-inspector told me that these magistrates were generally uncared for people unlike the other executive officers and they could not mingle freely with the public and ask for some small favours because of their position. So they could only depend upon the police for small favours like a wife wanting a car on some occasions or to get a ticket for the cinema and so on. So he took care of these things and consequently could convince the magistrate about the period of conviction according to my wishes. But I told him to leave this to the magistrate. These small favours are nothing when compared to the rampant corruption of a high magnitude, which has now gripped even the judiciary.

There were beautiful guest houses on the coast at Chirala. The sea, unspoilt by man, presents a beautiful picture and is also unpolluted for sea-bathing. The district is rich because of the Virginia tobacco cultivation. Tobacco is also an important item of export for the country. The Tobacco Board is located in Guntur, which was in my charge later when I was in the Ministry of Commerce. The soil was somewhat black in colour. The farmers generally indulged in luxury and the wives generally spent time in pleasurable pursuits in nearby towns. Somehow many of the film actresses in Madras those days hailed from the coastal districts of Andhra Pradesh, particularly from this belt.

The people of these districts had a nasty habit of using the road-sides and rail-sides for their ablutions. One should not look on either side in the morning when the train passed through these districts. In the evenings after sun set, one used to see hoards of village women going on the roads with a small brass vessel. A new Assistant Superintendent of Police during his first days in the district asked the accompanying inspector whether there was any festival or 'mela' in the village. The inspector thought that the ASP was trying to poke fun at him. He learnt later that the people which he thought were in a 'mela' were actualy moving around to answer the call of nature.

R. Rajamani was the Sub Collector in Ongole. He used to visit Bapatla frequently. He lived in a beautiful old bungalow in Ongole with a huge banyan tree. It is now the Collector's residence because the district has been bifurcated. He had a good cook and the Rajamanis were always hospitable. We used to have lunch or dinner together and go to films. They were good companions.

Meanwhile, I was called for the interview in Delhi by the UPSC. I had requested the UPSC to call me a bit late because of the general elections that year. So I was the last person interviewed by the UPSC. On my way to Delhi, I was browsing through Galbraith's *New Capital State* which was a popular book then. I was also reading a book by Sardar K.M. Panikar because he was on the Board and was also in the habit of asking the candidates whether they had read his books. There had been practically no crime, so crime investigation did not take much of my time. I had been busy with the elections and some other routine work. Therefore I did not get much time for preparing for the interview. The time on the train was the best time to do this.

I was busy preparing for the interview in the AC chair-car. Generally I do not like to be disturbed by co-passengers on a train or on the aircraft. But a youngster who was pacing up and down accosted me and straightaway enquired whether I was going for the IAS interview. He wanted to impress me and every one else in the compartment that he was going for that, as I also discovered later in the service that he was in the habit of trying to impress people about his importance. I simply shrugged him off by telling that I was going for some other purpose. But, to my amusement, he came on the same afternoon for the interview just before me. While I was the last person interviewed, he was the last but one or two. Even at that time, he boasted that he was actually from Manjeri although his initials indicated 'Madras' and his family had known K.P.S. Menon who was on the Board. He claimed that K.P.S. Menon even came out and patted him for his good performance. I had no such claims! (These characteristics somehow persist throughout one's life. He used to boast that but for his posting to Washington, he would have become the Cabinet Secretary although the entire batch of 1961 and also many others including me in 1962 were above him. Knowledgeable people used to laugh at him behind his back). When I went in, the only familiar face was that of Dr. A.N. Jha who was our Director in Mussoorie. They asked some interesting questions like why a superintendent of police should not become a district magistrate and again revert as superintendent of police, the need for a separate IAS and IPS, etc. As expected, there was a question on Galbraith's new book. Sardar Panikar spared me of his usual egoistic questions. Dr. A.N. Jha asked me in the beginning itself, since I was the last person being interviewed, whether I had read Greek mythology where Hercules was the last person to meet the giant Cyclops who was gobbling up everyone who encountered him. He asked me whether I was aware that Cyclops told Hercules that he would gobble him up too! Although I could not readily answer the question, I recalled having read somewhere and more than that having seen a film where Hercules killed Cyclops. So, before leaving the interview, I told them that as the last person and as Hercules I should perhaps survive after killing Cyclops. Apparently this answer at the end impressed them.

The results were to be announced the same evening or the next day. So I was hoping at least to hear about it on the All India Radio on my way back because they used to play the All India Radio and particularly the news in the air-conditioned coaches. But there was no news and I reached Bapatla the next day. The Rajamanis arrived and the radio gave the first ten names while we were having dinner in the guest house. So I eagerly went to the railway station at about 2.00 in the morning to get the newspaper from the train coming from Madras. As soon as I opened the paper, I could see my name straightaway somewhere in the middle. I heaved a sigh of relief and had an urge to meet the Rajamanis immediately. But, on second thoughts, I did not want to disturb them and went to my room in the club and slept. They came over to the club early in the morning when they saw the results in the paper and woke me up. I was the only one from IPS who had completed the two years of police training. There was a reference to this in the interview. All the money that the government spent on my training was a waste.' And so on. I thought I was finished. But it was to be otherwise as destined. M. Gopalakrishna, a Deputy Collector in the same district also got into the IAS along with me.

He was allotted to Assam, but managed a transfer to Andhra Pradesh after a few years. He never worked in Delhi, but came there later as an Additional Secretary. He was a good colleague throughout.

On my return, I went on leave to Madras for about a month. I was expecting orders any time. The highest mark was on April 23, 1962: I married Lakshmi. After getting his Ph. D., from England, her father was workiong in Burma when the war broke out. When the Japanese invaded Burma, after evacuating his wife and children by the last ship out of Burma, he started for India on foot through the jungles of Burma and Manipur. He did not reach India for a few months and was given up as dead. In fact, many, who came with him, died on the way.

The Burma Indians were a happy and prosperous lot those days. They knew one another. My father-in-law was very well known. When a Burmese Prime Minister and some other ministers came to Madras after the war, they called on him. His house in Rangoon had escaped the Japanese bombs while the houses on both sides were destroyed. This was a miracle. This was also what had to happen to the *Last Supper,* Leonardo da Vinci's famous painting, which escaped undamaged when bombs fell on the church where it was painted whereas everything around was ruined. All such properties whose holders had fled were grabbed by the local Burmese. But friends in Burma guarded it against predators and wrote to him. He went back to Burma and could sell his property.

The Government of India employed him for a short while in the erstwhile Supply Department and DGTD and he retired to Madras from there. He constructed a house and named it "Burma House" in memory of his good days in Burma. He moved the family who were in Trivandrum to Madras in 1954. He had only five daughters and my wife was the fourth one. She wrote a 'middle' on 'Burma House' which is reproduced below:

"**A magnificent obsession**": Burma House – that's the name of our house in Madras built years ago when we shifted from our home town of Trivandrum in Kerala to live in Madras. My father had very pleasant memories of his career, life and stay in Burma, a place he left when the Second World War broke out. When he constructed this house he named it Burma House.

"As children having been brought up in Kerala, my sisters and I had this great fascination for the sea and as a child I have spent hours on the seashores of the Trivandrum Beach and Cape Comorin.

"So, Burma House was built very near the Marina Beach in Madras and our family spent our evenings on the Marina shores, playing, discussing, etc. My father, who had been a professor in Rangoon University and a versatile genius, enlightened us on subjects as varied as chemistry and English literature. I can say I learnt more listening to my father on the shores of the Marina with the waves lashing than I picked up in the stuffy classrooms!!

"Burma House had its moments of glory when a grandson achieved the distinction of becoming a successful cardiac surgeon and last year another grandson bagged the President's Gold Medal as the outstanding student of IIT, Madras. Many of its members are well settled and doing professionally very well—as distinguished bureaucrats, technocrats, doctors, environmentalists and teachers. It also witnessed the joys and sorrows of life—the joy like a wedding in the family or a birth of a child, the sorrow when some one dear departed.

"On my parents' death, the house seemed to react like a human being at the loss of two precious lives. There it was lonely, desolate and so vulnerable in the midst of its grandeur. The question was how well to maintain it and protect it. With a slight remodeling and renovation, Burma House could still be maintained. Minimum alterations were done as everyone was agreed on one point—the house, a magnificent one, shall not lose its character.

"Throughout the months when the contractor's men were busy breaking, building, plastering, varnishing and painting, all of us were on tenterhooks, physically and mentally worried, exhausted by the shifting of valuables and the strain of supervision. The operation made a dent in our bank balance.

"Today the renovated house stands in all its glory. It is the only bond to unite us—sisters placed in different places and diverse circumstances.

"As we assemble there on our holidays, there is so much of warmth and cheer. Every nook and corner of the house reminds us of our parents—the chair my father sat on to read his morning newspaper, sipping a tumbler of steaming hot filter coffee, the verandah my mother used to sit down to string the Pavazhamalli flowers from our garden. The house is no more just a construction of bricks, stones and cement. It has become almost human like with feelings and concern for its members.

"As for me, though physically I am now hundreds of miles away, penning my thoughts as a 'middle', mentally I am there in the shelter and security of a home built by my dear father who lovingly named it 'Burma House'." ("Hindustan Times", June 9th, 1992)" Later in 2004, my wife brought out a book on "BH" commomerating its 50 years.

His first cousin was S. Venkateswaran, ICS, a former Chief Secretary to the Government of Tamil Nadu. In fact, it was my father-in-law who had sent him to England for doing the ICS. My father-in-law was very attached to him so much so he too went to England to be with him while the former did the ICS. My father-in-law's sister's husband was one Dr. S. Venkateswaran, a scientist who worked with Sir C.V. Raman and later to become the Controller General of Trade Marks & Patents in the Government of India. Common people used to refer to them as "big three 'V_s'" (Venkateswarans) – a Professor, a Collector (he was referred to as Collector even when he was Chief Secretary!) and a Scientist. When the marriage proposal came, we hesitated to have an alliance with such a family; we agreed for we found them to be compassionate and cultured. My father-in-law told my father that his father too had started only in a village as an ordinary person and generations improve themselves in status and wealth. I find this great quality of compassion for the poor and absolute freedom from class consciousness in my wife even today even more than what I have; she feels revulsion even today when she has to go to a five-star hotel and eat in luxury while so many poor struggle even for a morsel of food. Her father always helped the poor and needy and many remembered him even today for his helping hand for their upliftment in life. **She also feels that there will be a revolution in this country. But I tell her that with deep religious beliefs,**

there would be no revolution. That was the reason why, Karl Marx felt that 'religion was the opium of the people'.

My father-in-law was a person of phenomenal memory to the extent that sometime it was a burden on his mind. He could always recall events with dates. He wrote in his fine hand, apart from chemical equations, the history of the co-operative movement in India, which he studied for his daughter's examinations, with great accuracy, which I cannot do after studying for my examinations for three years or so. Even S. Venkateswaran, ICS, did not possess that kind of memory. My wife has inherited this memory to a certain extent so much so she always stood first in the French examinations where grammar and spelling were nothing but memory power. The French Professor in the Alliance Francaise at Pondicherry always complimented her for that.

So our wedding was a big event in Madras with many politicians like R. Venkataraman, Kamaraj, TTK and Bakthavathsalam, many civil servants and star-neighbours and friends like Lalitha and Padmini attending it. IGP Shetty's daughter Beena was my wife's classmate. I met her years later in Coonoor in an UPASI Convention since her husband was the Managing Director of the Consolidated Coffee Works – now Tata Coffee. My entire village Madimangalam-Kilpattu turned up for the wedding by a special bus. After our marriage, there was time only to make a visit to the shrine at Tirupati. On return immediately, we started for Guntur.

We went straight to Guntur to meet Ponnaiya. Since he was not there, I went to Bapatla with my wife. There was a dinner on the terrace under moonlight by the Rajamanis. While we were having dinner, a motorbike police messenger came from Guntur carrying my orders from Delhi. The next morning I met the Ponniayas who were camping at Vadrevu and he relieved me in anticipation of the orders from the IG of Police. Meanwhile, two murders occurred in the area, but Ponniaya told me to forget about them and leave for Madras. He later wrote to me in Mussoorie that, in fact, my relief camé the same afternoon by wireless from Hyderabad and he made it appear as though he relieved me after receipt of the orders.

There was a tearful farewell at the station to me and my wife from the sub-inspector who had taken the trouble of coming to

Madras to attend our wedding and also from my two orderly - constables. I was moved to see tears rolling down the cheeks of these policemen. I consoled myself thinking that I would meet them again in my new capacity as an IAS officer in Andhra Pradesh. But it was never to be. I had neither gone to Andhra Pradesh, nor was destined to meet them anywhere again. That is human destiny. I had read that Krishna never returned to Gokulam, nor did he meet the Gopis later including his beloved Radha.

6

Indian Administrative Service

The summer special from Madras took a long time to reach Delhi, for the special trains to cope with the summer rush or as they call 'summer exodus' did not get priority over the normal trains and hence the delayed running. Since it reached late some time in the afternoon, my brother-in-law and his friend could not meet me at the station as planned. I went to the Madras Hotel at Connaught Place as usual. I could not locate the name of my relatives in the telephone directory and hence gave up the attempt of meeting them. I went to the station the same evening to catch the train to Dehradun. My relative and his friend were there and they felt a bit disappointed for not having had me at their home. They were apologetic that they could not receive me because of the late arrival of the train and I had to apologise to them for not being able to locate their address. I missed the reception and dinner to a new groom ('Pudhu Mappillai'). In any case, it was all bonhomie and they saw me off to Dehradun.

On this trip, no one was with me and I was reminded of the earlier first trip when Sripal, Ramalingam and Rajmohan were with me. Dehradun was hot in summer in spite of being at the foothills of Mussoorie. It was a relief to reach Mussoorie after about an hour or so by bus on the hair-pin road. There was neither excitement nor anxiety because I had been there at 'Charleville'. It was two or three days after the Academy had opened for the session. The weather was fine and salubrious. The Director always felt that the Academy should be in a hill-station so that the young officers had an opportunity of staying in a hill-station for fairly a long time, which they might not have later. Moreover, it is free from the hustle and bustle of the city and also free from other distractions. The main distraction, I was told, when the Academy was in Metcalfe House, Delhi, was from the bride-groom hunting fathers who were mostly senior civil servants in Delhi. However, a place like Delhi had its own benefits and it was a pity that Mrs. Gandhi decided to turn the campus to the present JNU which was actually constructed for the Academy.

After settling down, I called on the Director, Dr A.N. Jha, ICS, who was known to me because of my earlier stint at Mussoorie. He told me that the government had already spent a lot of money on my police training for two years and I would be on training for another two or two and a half years. In fact, it was a long, long training for me! So he told me that I should also do some work and asked me to take the physical training class for the probationers staying in somewhat far-off buildings. By this time, the probationers could not be accommodated in 'Charleville' and they had to be scattered to other locations. This did disturb the camaraderie to a certain extent, which was the purpose of this training. In fact, it became worse in the subsequent years and the probationers of different services had to be called at different times defeating the very purpose because of the sheer increase in numbers.

I used to get up early in the morning to go to a nearby building on a bicycle to take a PT class. This was no doubt an interesting exercise. I used to come back, rush through my bath and breakfast to be present in the class on time. Many others were not worried about the classes. They used to take their own time to come in and some of them used to enjoy the rare warm sunshine on the lawns. On one such occasion, Director Jha came and saw a few boys not attending the class. He never took it amiss and enquired about their health in his own inimitable way and whether there was any health reason for not attending the class! He did not believe in compulsion in these matters. In fact, he rightly felt that it was a well earned freedom for about a year and there would not be many such occasions in one's career. He too used to be in a relaxed mood always. On an occasion, a probationer had the temerity to ask him the real job of the Director. He did not take the question amiss at all. He said that he had put a similar question to the captain of the ship while sailing to England for his ICS because he saw the captain not doing anything in particular and socialising all the time. The captain of the ship answered him that 'the captain works only when the ship starts sinking'. Dr Jha said that he would give the same answer!

He was a tall, fat man with a cherubic face. My association continued with him for a long time. Mrs Jha was a simple lady who used to sit on the floor and cook. They had paternal interest in the probationers. I met him in his office after a few years when he was Secretary of the I&B Ministry. Mrs Gandhi was the Minister – her first position in Government during Shastri's time. Jha was relaxed and I enquired how he could do that with a Minister like Mrs Gandhi. He told me that he kept her informed orally of important happenings and delegated administrative matters to his joint secretaries who kept him posted orally in turn. This was quite in contrast to the functioning of the present-day Secretaries.

On another occasion, he was attending a meeting of all Chief Ministers and State Ministers of Agriculture in his capacity as Lt. Governor of Delhi. After the inaugural session, Mrs Gandhi left and Dr Jha also left the meeting. I was there from Pondicherry with my Chief Minister. I followed Dr Jha talking to him. For some odd reason, Mrs Gandhi came back and enquired of Jha in the corridor when they crossed each other as to why he was leaving. He told her that he had been listening to whatever was said at the meeting for the past twenty years and so was leaving!

Badr-ud-din Tyabji, ICS, visited the Academy and delivered an interesting talk on 'officialese' and how to avoid it. He pointed out two mistakes from the notice board of the Academy itself: one notice read: "Probationers are requested to come in their formal dresses"; another notice read for another formal dinner:

"No dress is required". When Mr Justice Dhawan came, the president of the Mess Committee introduced him as Justice Dhawan. Jha corrected him to say 'Mr Justice Dhawan' (A common mistake these days which even the judges do not know). Dr Jha also narrated an instance when he was Chief Secretary of U.P. The then Chief Minister G.P. Pant was a stickler for drafting and he was not happy about a particular word in a draft letter to Delhi put up by Jha. After discussing this word for quite some time, he approved the draft stating that after all who was going to bother so much in Delhi about the content itself, let alone a word!

Dr Jha was ably assisted by R.K. Trivedi who later became Secretary, Personnel, Chief Election Commissioner and Governor of Gujarat. (The newspapers used to cite this for a long time to come as a bad example of a former Chief Election Commissioner becoming a Governor). He taught the probationers correct manners, etiquette, certain dos and don'ts in one's career and a host of other things useful. He was succeeded by Brig. M.K. Sheriff and M.A.S. Rajan. Brig. Sheriff, a Sandhurst trained retired military officer, had special affection for me because he hailed from my native town, Vellore. His brother was in the Madras IAS and a sister of his was married to B.G. Swamidoss, my professor of English in Voorhees College. Mrs Sheriff was a charming Punjabi Hindu and our association continued for a long time. Brig. Sheriff played a notable role in containing the Delhi riots immediately after Independence and was mentioned by V.P. Menon in his monumental book on the transfer of power.

We had Profs Bhattacharya and Ramaswamy teaching Economics. They could not stand each other. Bhattacharya was a puny man without much humour. Ramaswamy was burly and he was full of jokes. In a subsequent year, a probationer sent a telegram to the Academy during the Bharat Darshan stating that 'Prof Ramaswamy was dead', in order to play a practical joke. The efficient administrative officer Narayanan informed every one including Mrs Ramaswamy of this sad news. When the Bharat Darshan party was visiting a place, the officer receiving them informed Prof Ramaswamy that there was a sad news to the effect that a professor of economics from the Academy was dead. Ramaswamy, in his usual hurry to crack a joke, interjected to say that it must be Prof Bhattacharya who should have 'kicked the bucket'. But the officer concerned informed him that it was not Bhattacharya but one Ramaswamy, without knowing the identity of the person. Ramaswamy immediately said that 'it could not be because he was standing before him in flesh and blood'! The Academy was by then like a military institution, with numbers to each probationer, sitting in that order in class rooms and the Director listening to the lectures in his room through a microphone device and so on – thanks to the martinet Director Pimputkar, ICS.

Since the probationers were still coming in to join the Academy, the inaugural session by the director was kept after a few days. During the session, there was natural exhibition of scholarship from Director Jha and also his usual quips and jokes. For instance, a colleague of mine had the name, 'Rajajee' but his initials were 'Mysore Sriraman'. So the director, while calling him out, stated that 'this Rajajee was from Mysore'.

Within a few days, we were packed off to Jammu & Kashmir for the army attachment. Since I had seen the border posts on high-reaches during my earlier attachment while in the IPS, I wanted to avoid travelling all the way to Rajouri or some other place in an army truck. So I opted for Jammu. But I realised later that it was a terrible mistake because Jammu was like a cauldron in summer and we had to remain in a tent. This was too much to bear, so much so, during the free afternoons my colleague from Bangalore, Muddappa and I used to spend long hours in the only air-conditioned theatre seeing the same film just to escape the intolerable heat. Jammu was an ordinary town with a river or canal flowing through a big park. The water was crystal clear and fresh. The people of Jammu, men and women alike strangely not so well clad as is the wont in our country, flocked to the park in the evenings and had a dip in the river or canal to escape the heat.

It was a welcome comeback to Mussoorie after the army attachment, which was useful, and we could appreciate the hardships of the soldiers. The mess elections were on and I was generally not interested in the elections. But friend Gopalakrishna roped me in at the last minute and there were real two parallel lists of contestants. I was in the second position of Mess Secretary, which was a crucial post next only to the President of the Mess Committee. There was hectic canvassing on both sides and I realised the spirit of electioneering. We gave our list to a number of probationers and somehow the probationers felt that we would do better than the other snobbish group mainly from the St. Stephen's of Delhi. At the time of voting, the candidates of our list by and large did extremely well and although one person on our list had actually withdrawn in the last minute, he too got a number of votes because most probationers blindly voted for this list. It was a bit of groupism, no doubt, because it indicated the president of the mess committee belonging to a particular group and the secretary belonging to another group. Of course, this did not affect the functioning of the committee in any way.

It is generally the responsibility of the president and secretary to receive the VIP visitors and take care of them. The president always welcomes the visitor and the vote of thanks is proposed by the secretary. The mess work also kept me busy for the whole day apart from the PT coaching and other classes. Since I was also interested in equitation, I did it in the evenings. All this kept me busy for the whole day.

Like the group of four in Mount Abu with Sripal, Ramalingam and Rajmohan, it was again a group of four here with the other Sundaram, Narayanan and Moses. Frederick Moses sat by my side in Loyola for three years and he was a rare Protestant in the Catholic Loyola. The other Sundaram, like me, got in after two years of training in Income Tax. He too did not appear for the examination in 1960. In fact, we were the only two who had completed two years of training and were in the Academy again.

The same name created a lot of confusion which continued even today. While the people in the north expected us to know the difference between one Mehta and the other or between one Mathur or the other, they confused the South Indian names freely. For them, Sundaram, Subramaniam and Srinivasan are the same and they freely misuse them, let alone mispronouncing them. They also generally do not understand the peculiar system of writing the village name first, the father's name second and then one's own name as in Tamil Nadu and Kerala. In my opinion, this is the most rational way of identifying a person. The surname is really the caste name which is dropped now-a-days in Tamil Nadu. These are still used in other parts of the country. The other Sundaram was known as Sankaranarayana Gomathi Sundaram. He thought that people were further confusing him for a girl because of the middle name. So he started writing S.G. Sundaram which added to the confusion further. Even today,some of my colleagues erroneously call me 'Gopalan' which is actually my father's name or 'Gomathi' mistaking for the other Sundaram's name. We were good friends and took these mistaken impressions in our normal stride. When I got a Doctorate, he was congratulated by some. Whenever my articles appeared in the newspapers, he was congratulated by some others. But he used to tell me that he never corrected these people, but coolly accepted their compliments. In fact, the confusion started in 1960 itself when we went for the medical examination along with a few others. The clerk in the Madras General Hospital changed the forms and was about to dispatch the less stringent norms of the other Sundaram for me. This would have meant another medical examination for me because I was for the IPS and my namesake was for the Income Tax Service. Luckily, the mistake was detected in time and proper forms were sent. So the confusion was from day one!

After some years, one of our colleagues wanted some favour in the Commerce Ministry and he contacted me. In fact, he was under the impression that I was the other Sundaram. From his talk on the phone, I knew well that he had taken me for the other person. So, to have some fun, I enquired from him whether he remembered the other Sundaram and told him also that the other Sundaram remembered him well. I also gave some instances of his visit to the USA to do some studies, etc., He simply stated that he remembered the other Sundaram which was actually me and called me the 'equestrian Sundaram' because of the medal I secured in the Academy for best equitation. It was Director Jha's medal for the best rider. Luckily, he did not abuse me for some reason or the other and I put down the phone after telling him to come on a particular day. When he entered my room, he felt sheepish for having mistaken me for the other Sundaram. In any case, his job was done.

S.G. Sundaram was a chartered accountant after doing his B.Com (Hons)., from the Pachaiappa's College. He got a gold medal and was a bright person. In fact, we were close friends along with R. Narayanan and Frederick Moses. Sundaram made a name in Kerala by being the chairman of the Rubber Board, Cardamom Board and also held charge at some time or the other of all organisations of the Ministry of Commerce in Cochin like the Marine Products Export Development Authority, Coir Board, Cashew Board, etc. He was also working for sometime with the Industrial Development Corporation, on deputation to the Government of Kerala. In fact, he would have been absorbed there but for the cadre transfer rules and also resistance from the Kerala IAS cadre. He returned to his parent cadre, Haryana, and got a UN posting in Gautemala after a few years. Unfortunately, he died when his motor car was involved in an accident in Gautemala. When the news of his death appeared in the newspapers, some people mistook it for me and made kind enquiries. A few months after this incident, a cousin of mine rang me up in Ahmedabad where I was posted and enquired whether there was any thing wrong with my health and whether I was in the hospital. I told him that I was hale and hearty and enquired the reason for his sudden enquiry. He told me that a relation of mine had told him that something had happened to me obviously mistaking me for the other Sundaram. This cousin told me that he got the telephone number from my mother-in-law in Madras and was making this indirect enquiry because of his concern for me. I requested him to inform my mother-in-law immediately that there was nothing wrong with me lest she should be worried. Frederick Moses also passed away a few years ago after playing tennis for long hours. Perhaps his system could not stand this strenuous exercise after the age of fifty. He spent a few years in the United States on posting and on leave and, in fact, had planned to go there and settle down. So only Narayanan is left in this close-knit group and is happily settled in Kerala.

We four used to take a long walk to Kulri in the evenings, rain or thunder, every day and occupied the same table in the Kwality restaurant over-looking the Mall. M. Venkatachalam and B.C. Balasubramaniam also used to join us. This was a 'religious' trip every evening so much so people used to enquire about us whenever we were absent at our table in the restaurant on some rare days. Some friendships also blossomed with some local girls. As far as I was concerned, this long walk was an additional exercise besides my PT classes and riding every day. But it was all great fun and good for one's health. One's mind also remained fresh.

At the end of the term, we had to take the mid-term examinations and the probationers belonging to the other Services left the Academy. The usual Bharat Darshan for the IAS during the winter months was cancelled that year because of the Chinese aggression. The probationers allotted to Gujarat and Andhra Pradesh and of course Assam were sent to Assam and the North East. We spent a useful one month at Guwahati visiting Shillong and the nearby areas. There was a lot of excitement and sorrow immediately after the India-China war. Gopalakrishna who was then allotted to Assam cadre was with me and he was aghast to see the practice of the Assam administration and his prospect of being there. After some years, he managed to get a transfer to his native Andhra Pradesh. E.S. Parthasarathy was the popular Assistant Commissioner at Guwahati. He took great care of us. He was killed after a few years by a bomb planted in his office in the thick of an agitation when he was Deputy Commissioner. I read about this in the London *Times* when I was posted in Brussels in 1979-81 and felt very sad about it.

Some of us were also lucky enough to go to Bomdila and beyond near the Sela Pass. It was an exciting journey through thick tropical forest for almost a day to Bomdila. It was within a few days immediately after Chinese aggression and the guest house was bereft of mattresses which were taken away by the Chinese. We had seen the numbers of the Indian prisoners written in chalk on the walls. Beyond Bomdila near the Sela Pass, there was a huge pit, full of bodies of dead Indian soldiers.

It was a good experience to visit the villages of the Moplas and have their hospitality. K.V.R. Chari and his charming wife were there for a number of years. They gave us South Indian dishes that cold morning before prayers by the monks in the Buddhist monastery.

Back to Mussoorie and the preparations almost started for the final examinations and departure. The examination was not a serious affair because there were only four papers. There was also an examination in riding. I stood first in the riding examination and got two marks more than my rival Yugandhar who was also competing for the Director's medal. This news, two days prior to the riding competition, somewhat unnerved him. Although the competition was to be held only among the top six, six more were also added by demand and the contest was held on a particular day. There was no Director by then because Jha had already been transferred to Delhi. M.A.S. Rajan and Brig. Sheriff were in command. Luckily, the horse also behaved properly for me and I was adjudged the best rider and I was lifted from the ground by my friends. They also extracted a small party from me which cost me Rs.109/-, a hefty amount those days. In fact, I regretted that expenditure for quite some time. Since Yugandhar belonged to the other group, he felt bad and this kind of a divide, despite the absence of any apparent ill-feeling, remained till the end of our service. In any case, he scored over me by becoming a secretary in the PMO when my name was also considered in 1995 during Rao's time, because of his Andhra connection. One or two probationers failed in the riding examination and they had to make trips to Mussoorie in the subsequent years, but they were passed in the third attempt in spite of their continued bad performance because the government could not afford to spend on their joy rides to Mussoorie every year from their places of posting.

I was a virtual non-entity during my first stay in Mussoorie. Since I was experienced, I could make better use of my second stay and make it useful and enjoyable as well. During the second stint, I was well known among all the probationers because of my Mess Secretaryship and I always used to say I was making a mess of the mess! The dinner nights were generally enjoyable. Dinner nights were followed by some entertainment or the other mostly from the probationers. I was in charge of the table plan. PMC and I used to sit on either side of the chief guest. We generally sat a good looking lady probationer in front. Some boys used my good offices to sit by the side of some particular lady probationers; some others complained against me for not placing a good-looking lady-probationer by their side.

It was by then spring in Mussoorie, but it could not be enjoyed because of the preparations for the examinations and the eventual departure. Since I had to attend the wedding of a cousin of mine in Madras, I decided to fly back. It was considered very costly those days because a flight would cost Rs.210/-. I reached Madras in time for the wedding and before my departure for Gujarat. As happened for Guntur and Bapatla, I was never to visit Mussoorie again except once when I was secretary to the Government of India after long years. After some years, there was a fire in the Academy which consumed the library and its books and also a board which carried the names of the best riders. Perhaps this board was not replaced because by then riding was made optional. In fact, the government very nearly abolished it. But Mrs. Gandhi as Prime Minister intervened and rightly retained it as an option.

The results came later when I was in Palanpur in Gujarat and I was happy to find that I had done well. My rank in the final list had considerably improved, by twenty places or so. Although I had not attached any importance to this, I realised years later that this placing was also important because one got one's promotion as additional secretary or secretary earlier, for the movement up was slow at this level. There could be a gap of even one year between the first and the last officer in getting promotion.

I was also told years later that M.A.S. Rajan had recorded in the first CR on me that, according to Dr. Jha, I would be one of the outstanding officers in the service. In some CRs, I saw the Directors remarked very adversely on some probationers even stating that so and so would not make a good officer, etc. and I felt that it was very uncharitable to pass such remarks in the first year of one's service since it would be difficult to foresee one's performance at that length of time.

My happiness of the year, 1962, was also marred by my allotment to Gujarat. There were not many vacancies in the southern states that year. The State Reorganisation Commission's formula of 50% of the vacancies to be allotted to outsiders and our batch being 1/3 reserved categories (only SC and ST those days) to be allotted to their home states as far as possible resulted in many of us having to go far away from home. My own family problems and the prospect of stay far away from Madras made me feel sad. Andhra Pradesh, where I was allotted to in the IPS, was prepared to have me back. But the Central Government was stubborn and refused to consider our requests for cadre transfers. A boy from Delhi allotted to Andhra Pradesh, facing family problems, was prepared to have a mutual change to Gujarat. But the Home Secretary L.P. Singh was stubborn.

Allotment to a particular State cadre is a bad but perhaps unavoidable feature of the All India Services. In fact, the very term, All India Services, becomes a misnomer because of the State allotment. Moreover, people are getting into these Services from the middle class and the lower middle class families. The family moors and responsibilities are an important part of the Indian society. So, a posting to a far off state for life in a sub-continent like India creates personal problems. Transfers to different places once in three years or four years may not pose such problems. Of course, the other side of the hedge is always greener and the people in the Central Services who face such transfers feel that allotment to a single state would be convenient because you do not have the problems of frequent shifts. However, all things considered, the people who are allotted to far-off states like Jammu & Kashmir and the North Eastern states all the time try to get deputations to Delhi or to their home states. At the same time, in the All India Services, a certain amount of knowledge of the local conditions and the people including language is necessary. Perhaps a compromise could be allotment on a Zonal basis or compulsory transfers to other states, not necessarily to Delhi, at least twice or thrice in one's career will not only preserve the all-India character but also take care of the personal problems of the officers. The Department of Personnel should consider these matters seriously and evolve a system instead of taking a negative view and finding excuses for not doing a thing all the time. But the department finds a solution or changes the rules when it suits them. A powerful ICS Home Secretary, L.P. Singh, who was totally opposed to inter-cadre transfers for needy persons like me, changed the policy and made it possible only for the ladies when his daughter got into the IAS. Another Home Secretary got his daughter's cadre changed from Tamil Nadu or Tripura to the Punjab or Haryana. This is Indian hypocrisy.

* * *

7

Starting off

I started with a heavy heart for Gujarat and most of us were in a similar frame of mind. When the train passed through Baroda and arrived in Ahmedabad, I thought that I never knew two years earlier when I took photographs of these places that I would land there almost for my life time.

Eight of us were allotted to Gujarat and we synchronised our arrival at Ahmedabad station. There was some one to receive us and we were taken through the gray and dusty streets of Ahmedabad to government rest house at the New Mental Hospital. The name itself was quite shocking and we realised later that the entire Gujarat administration was in some hospital or the other because there was no proper accommodation immediately after the formation of Gujarat in 1960. As a result, many government departments were housed in some hospital or the other, like that of the Inspector General of Police in the Old Mental Hospital, the Collector in the Civil Hospital and the State Administrative Training School in the Old Nurses Quarters making us wonder whether the adjective qualified the nurses or the quarters. The Secretariat itself was housed in the Polytechnic building. So we were in a state of sorrow and also anger for having arrived there. We deposited our luggage in the rooms on the top floor and our luggage was naturally heavy.

When we came down for breakfast, a tall and handsome man entered the dining hall to welcome us. He introduced himself as A.S. Gill, Deputy Secretary, General Administration Department. In fact, he had apologised for not having come to the station to receive us. He enquired whether we came to Gujarat by choice or by accident. We had no answer. We realised later that all those who were allotted to Gujarat on the bifurcation of the old Bombay State were not a happy lot. The ladies particularly missed the glitter of Bombay. He wanted us to shift to the Circuit House in Shahibaugh because our accommodation had been arranged there and, as usual, some one had brought us here by mistake. Although we were a bit reluctant to bring down all our heavy luggage again, we had to obey his orders. But we discovered that the Circuit House at Shahibaugh was a beautiful one, in more agreeable surroundings with a lot of trees, true to the name of the area, and also it was a historic building because Mahatma Gandhi was tried by the British in that building. Opposite was the Moghul Emperor Shahjahan's Palace, which was at this time the Governor's residence. Poet Rabindranath Tagore had stayed for about a year in this building and wrote his famous novel, "Hungry Stones" when his uncle was a Sessions Judge in Ahmedabad. One of our senior colleagues had also occupied this beautiful building earlier in his capacity as Collector of Ahmedabad in the erstwhile Bombay. This building, on the banks of Sabarmati, is now converted into a museum after shifting the 'Raj Bhavan' to the new capital, Gandhinagar, in 1978.

Shahibaugh also had other beautiful residential buildings. All big industrialists lived here and there were also other Government bungalows. In fact, I was to live in one of these bungalows some years later. The private residential buildings are not seen from the road because the occupants have the good sense of covering the compound with a lot of trees. Sarabhai's 'Retreat' is also located in this area. U.S. Ambassador Galbraith also used to stay with one of the industrialists here, residing in a beautiful bungalow in a big compound with all types of trees. But the area is highly polluted by the thermal station of an otherwise efficient Ahmedabad Electric Company on the other side of Sabarmati. Although the Raj Bhavan also received a lot of dust from the thermal station across, the various Governors had preferred to stay there rather than in the rural Gandhinagar and also for the usual psychological reasons of staying in a historic building. Staying in a historic building gives one sense of power or being a ruler in succession.

Gandhinagar was thought of as the capital immediately after the bifurcation of Gujarat from Bombay on the recommendations of the States Re-organisation Commission. But it took a long time for the government of Gujarat to conceive a plan and execute. Many Chief Ministers themselves were rather reluctant to move out of Ahmedabad. In fact, when I was posted in Mehsana as Assistant Collector in 1966, I saw broad roads being laid since Gandhinagar was to fall partly in the district of Mehsana. However, it took another fifteen years for the capital to take shape and start in a small fashion. Although the distance of 20 km was not so long by the city standards, from the Governor down to an ordinary employee were reluctant to move there till the time Morarji Desai became the Prime Minister of India under the Janata Party rule. He was keen that every one including the Governor should stay in Gandhinagar.

When Sharda Mukherjee was appointed Governor in 1977 or 1978, she came with the expectation of staying in the Shahjahan palace in Ahmedabad. Moreover, she had certain close family connections with Gujarat and all the more she thought it would be convenient to stay there. Normally, the interregnum after the departure of a Governor and the arrival of a new Governor is only a few hours or at the most one day. In this case, when Governor Viswanathan left, there was a gap of two days. During this short period, the Government of Gujarat staged a veritable coup by engaging about 200 or so trucks and shifted the entire 'Raj Bhavan' to Gandhinagar. The Shahjahan palace was made almost empty. So when Sharda Mukherjee arrived at Ahmedabad airport – situated between Ahmedabad and Gandhinagar – and her cavalcade started moving towards rural Gandhinagar, she enquired where they were heading to. She was also aware of the topography of the place. When some one told her that she was being taken to the 'Raj Bhavan', she wondered why it was not to the Shahjahan Palace in Ahmedabad. She was told that they had already shifted the 'Raj Bhavan' to Gandhinagar. She became very angry and her tantrums could not help because it was already a fait accompli. However, in order to mollify her feelings, the Government of Gujarat converted one of the bungalows in Shahibaugh as 'Raj Bhavan Annexe' so that she could meet the petitioners and friends and be accessible to the common public of Ahmedabad.

Ahmedabad of those days when we landed in 1963 was a real provincial town. It was highly polluted by the hundred and odd textile mills. There was not even a single English book shop. English journals were also practically not available. There was only one restaurant of some standard, named 'Kwality'. There was only one three-star hotel being run by a local Parsi. So we cursed our destiny for having landed in such a place. But Gujarat is one State in the country, which completely changed over years for the better. When I went back in the seventies, I saw many boards asking people to learn English; when I went back again in the eighties, there was an Alliance Française and Max Muller Bhavan. **Gujarat has also become a leading state in industrialisation. After travelling all over the world, I have come to the conclusion that the Gujaratis are straightforward and are good people. So, if I were given a chance again, I would certainly opt for Gujarat.**

But the fifteen-day stay and the transition from Mussoorie to the district was smoothened by the enterprising deputy secretary of the general administration department, A.S. Gill. During this period, we were expected to call on all Ministers and Secretaries to the Government. Gill had told all secretaries to throw us a lunch or dinner at their places so that we could see the cross-section and in the bargain some secretaries could also possibly locate bridegrooms for their daughters. When the IG of Police, the formidable Nagarwala, complained to Gill that the IAS probationers were not calling on the IG of Police, Gill told him that he would direct them to do so provided they were entertained to a dinner. Nagarwala was considered a very powerful man and he had no time even to meet us although he spoke to me over the phone purely by chance. He was suspended after some time for having been involved in some scandal.

I was appointed or elected informally the leader of this group because they perhaps felt that the senior most K.G. Ramanathan was never punctual. Besides, as also in Mt. Abu, I was always made the group leader. Others never even bothered about the names of the officers or the ministers on whom they were calling. They simply followed me or were herded by me from one room into the other. This kind of a practice results some times in certain comical situations by somebody dropping a brick or committing a faux pas. On a similar occasion in Maharashtra, one probationer asked a secretary, when the secretary was talking about his good old days as a successful Collector in Pune, whether he was there 'after or before Mr Yardi'. The secretary replied that he was Yardi himself for the discomfiture of the probationer because he was not even aware that he was in Mr Yardi's room. But, on the whole, this was a good practice and a good exposure to the State.

I knew we were calling on Mankodi, Secretary (Panchayats). But I was also taken aback and wondered whether I was in a minister's room because Mankodi was in a kurta and pyjama and looked like a politician. He was very genial. Others as usual did not bother where they were. Sensing our puzzlement, he stated that he was from Saurashtra and the senior politicians of Saurashtra became ministers and the junior politicians were inducted in to the IAS! That was the explanation for the sartorial preference of Mankodi. He also entertained us to tea at his residence as stipulated by Gill. Mankodi was of the view that a stint as District Development Officer made the junior IAS officer 'seasoned'. He was right.

Dr Jeevaraj Mehta was the Chief Minister of Gujarat at this time with a Tamil IAS officer, R.V. Chandramouli, well conversant in Gujarati, as his private secretary. Gujarat had successively good and knowledgeable chief ministers.

These ministers here were speaking about Gandhian ways, which was somewhat annoying to the young probationers. For instance, they did not have air-conditioners for their rooms, but perhaps were spending more money on a number of fans running and watering the 'Khus-Khus' (a kind of grass for cooling) all the time. To us, it appeared to be pesudo-Gandhism. We were also annoyed by their invariable question whether we knew Gujarati. One or two of them did not even know what an All-India Service was. Madhavsinh Solanki was the Deputy Minister for Revenue and he struck us as a highly intelligent man even at that time.

We were also entertained at the Gymkhana by the IAS Association. We landed at the wrong Ms. Parekh's place for evening tea and as usual one or two of us already started settling down in the sofa when the lady appeared. She looked different and she told me that although she was also one Ms. Parekh, we should be looking perhaps for her neighbour, Ms. Parekh, a deputy secretary to the government – a comely person. We were highly scandalised when we had difficulty in locating the residence of the Chief Secretary. While the residence of the chief secretary must be a well known place in other states, even a person walking in front of the house did not know about it. Even the institution of chief secretary was unheard of perhaps because it was a new capital. More than this, after the dinner, there was not even a driver for the chief secretary to drive us down to the Circuit House. The chief secretary, who himself was an ICS, drove the car. So some of us were really convinced that we had landed in the wrong State.

The two weeks of calls, dinners, entertainment and also hopes and frustrations came to a close. We started dispersing in different directions. The people posted to Baroda and Surat were happy because every one said that these places were extremely good. They all gave a meaningful smile when they heard about my posting to Palanpur in Banaskantha district. I was the first probationer to be sent there. I had had a glimpse of this town on the way to Mt. Abu when I was in the IPS. In fact, it was the last main station in Gujarat on the way to Mt. Abu and Delhi. Mt Abu was a part of this district in the erstwhile Bombay. Even that small attraction of a hill station had gone when Mt. Abu was allotted to Rajasthan during the States Reorganisation. As one of the Secretaries remarked during our stay in Ahmedabad, Gujarat was 'singularly devoid of natural beauty in any form'.

A jeep was waiting for me and it took me straight to the Collector's residence for lunch. J.V. Vyas was the Collector and was considered a competent person. That was the reason why the government allotted me to that district for training. Of course, he was colourful in his own way and was suspended from service after some years for corruption. His wife was a simple and kind lady. After the lunch and some preliminaries with the Collector, I was lodged in the Rest House, which was the only good place to stay and also to eat in Palanpur. There was no other hotel at all. I started my house-hunting within a few days because I wanted my wife to join me as early as possible. There were a number of good buildings at Palanpur belonging to diamond merchants staying in Bombay and Belgium. But none of them was prepared to rent out the house and kept it locked for their occasional visits to celebrate some religious chores or the other. I happened to meet a rich man, however, staying there for most of the year, for renting some accommodation from him. He was known as the 'Towerwala Sheth' whose one daughter was in Belgium, another one in New York and the third one in Tokyo. He was naturally not prepared to rent out any accommodation. I met his daughter in Belgium some years later when I was posted there and recalled this meeting with her father. My house-hunting experience was described by my wife in an article in *Pondy Observer* of Pondicherry and also in the erstwhile Madras *Mail*: *Pondy Observer* 2nd October 1967 "House Hunting-An Experience" by Lakshmi Sundaram.

"It is a great consolation to many of us to know that no less a person than the Prime Minister is in search of a residence for herself. Of course, she wants a house to suit her requirements.

"The Problem: After a year of 'theoretical indoctrination', my husband was posted to a State for field-training. It was the headquarters of a big district. It was formerly a princely state with all the regal pomp and splendour of a Nawab. We had landed at the place with full of hopes, my heart brimming with joy, ready to move into one of the mansions of the former Nawab Saheb. I was also afraid that I would go mad, gazing at the 'hungry stones' like Tagore's hero. The Nawab has become poor and is no longer in a position to maintain his old mansions.

"But I was disappointed. I was told that it would be quite a job to get decent accommodation in the town. The rich landlords of the place do not let out their houses, specially to the Government servants who always quote the rent-rules to their advantage. They prefer to lock up their houses during their absence.

"We had to occupy a suite in the Government Rest House where accommodation was available according to priority and seniority. We could establish ourselves there for quite some time in spite of the constant danger of our ever-mobile V.I.Ps barging in with their entourage and throwing us out of our temporary shelter.

"With a foothold in the Rest House, we had started looking for a house. We never had a more interesting experience in life.

"We were shown a house which had everything but water. Water had to be brought from a distance of at least a furlong. We had to reject the offer. The house at a desolate corner of the town was well furnished with all facilities, but I objected, for it has a bad reputation of being 'haunted'. My husband liked the house and he thought that I was more haunting than any of these invisible visitors.

"After a month's running about, we could find a place. The land-lord was a leading businessman who was also very proud of his only daughter living in Paris. He had to get her consent for allotting a portion of the house. The landlord came out with a printed sheet. My husband signed the agreement, in his anxiety to have a roof over our head without even reading the conditions.

"It was late in the evening when we moved into our new abode. Of course, we had to get it furnished ourselves. We discovered to our dismay that there was not even a single bulb. When my husband turned to our landlord, he replied that it was one of the conditions of the agreement that we should get our owns bulbs!"

Ultimately with great difficulty I got a small house in a vast compound but without a proper terrace. Almost the whole building was covered with a zinc sheet which was a playground for monkeys all the day.

However, the company at Palanpur was congenial. There were the Georges working in the Burma Shell whose car was available to us all the time to go round. The civil surgeon, Dr Shah, was one of the only two doctors in the entire district who lived very close to my house. He treated every patient complaining of fever for typhoid! My wife was also treated that way once and true to his nickname he very nearly killed Subramaniam who was an Assistant Superintendent of Police. But Dr Shah's wife was very kind and did not mind my daily visits to their place in the evenings.

There was also a small club in an old princely type of building where people played tennis and cards. There was an American couple who were actually protestant priests whose house was used as a church for the few Christians including the Georges. But the house itself was a mini-US. They occasionally entertained us to sumptuous dinner and on one such dinner night unfortunately the news of the assassination of President Kennedy came.

There were also frequent picnics to Balaram where there was a small rivulet and a beautiful palace of the Nawab, which was all the time locked. (It is now a beautiful hotel). The picnics also included visits to Ambaji, a fairly picturesque place on the way to Mt. Abu where a famous Hindu temple was situated. The trips were always in jeeps because there were practically no cars those days and the visit to Ambaji was through Danta, a fairly picturesque and green part of the Banaskantha district. The maharajah of Danta was a keen cricketer and his palace was situated almost on a mountain. One had to wade through many passages before meeting this somewhat dull person. His brother, Madhusudan, was a more active person who dabbled in local politics and became the president of the Taluk Panchayat. Perhaps he also became the President of the District Panchyat later. Ambaji had also a famous Jain temple – Kumbharia. I wrote an article on the "Temples of Kumbharia" in *The Hindu* on October 10th , 1965:

"Gujarat is famous for its exquisite Jain temples. These temples are generally grouped together on high places and they have an air of aloofness and seclusion. The temples at Kumbharia too nestle among the hills with scenery around, at an altitude of 1,500 feet.

"Kumbharia is seventeen miles from Abu Road Railway Station on Delhi-Ahmedabad metre-gauge. The temples are approachable by a motorable road. Many pilgrims visit the Hindu shrine at Ambaji, two miles from Kumbharia, and they never fail to visit this enchanting place.

"The marble carvings in the temples are masterpieces of the sculptor's art and are a feast for the eyes, not only for the casual holiday-maker but also for the ardent pilgrim, especially of the Jain faith. The temples present an attractive appearance even from outside.

"Kumbharia is the name of the village, though there are no houses now. When Akbar invaded Mewar, a chieftain known as Kumbha took shelter here and the place was named 'Kumbharia.'

"Many historians have mentioned these temples in their books, though minute historical details are lacking. The temples of Neminath and Mahavir were built by the same Vimal Shah, in the eleventh century, who built one of the famous Dilwara temples and many other temples in this part of the country. He had spent crores of rupees in building these temples. The tablets in the temples give the years and names of the persons who installed the idols. Vimal Shah built these temples before the more famous Dilwara temples. This is the reason why the architecture of Dilwara is slightly superior though it is of the same pattern.

"The temple of Parshwanath was built by Maharaja Kumarpal. The names of the builders of the Shantinath and the Shambawanath temples are not known. The temple of Shantinath might have also been built during the same period as the temple of Neminath or a little later. The temple of Shambawanath, with a prosaic appearance and devoid of the architectural grandeur of others, belongs to a later period.

"These temples also fell a prey to the ravaging forces of Alla-ud-din Khilji. Some of the structures were reconstructed in the later centuries.

"The aesthetic instincts in man are kindled by the richness of sculpture in four temples, out of this group of five. The imposing towers invite the visitor as he approaches. The towers appear black, weather-beaten over centuries and the carvings are hidden by moss.

"All the sanctums contain imposing statutes of the Jain Thirthankers. One sees the richness and magnificence of marble sculpture. The most attractive feature is the central dome in Mahavir's temple with its richness of pendants and carvings. This compares well with the central dome of the Dilwara of Abu which we see often in pictures. The visitor loses himself at the intricate carvings on each inch of this dome. The central dome in Neminath's temple is conspicuous by the absence of sculpture. It is plain, but attractively painted. The painted designs appear fresh even to-day.

"The most attractive features apart from the central domes are the fourteen ceiling panels in the temple of Mahavir. They are intricately carved and speak volumes for the sculptor's art. These enchanting bands depict the various scenes from Jain mythology.

"These temples are of the same pattern except the temple of Shambawanath. The shrines are surrounded by beautiful mandaps with pillars of spotless marble. There is no structural difference between the Hindu and Jain temples except for the provision of space for the various Thirthankers in the latter. The inner temple are surrounded by quadrangle with columns of cells. The various Jineswaras are presented in these columns of cells. Many cells are also empty".

When Moosa Raza became the Collector for a short time, we started playing tennis at his residence. It had a beautiful tennis court. There was also a swimming pool in the compound though it had gotten into disuse. This was the residence of the English Resident, somewhat far away from the town during the pre-Independence days in the kingdom of Palanpur. The Indian number two used to live in a bungalow somewhat far away from this residence and the Indian's residence was known as the 'Kala Bungalow'!

The training for over a year included the usual attachments to the Dy. Collector's Office, S.P's office including police stations, Panchayat Office, District Health Office, Magisterial work and so on. During attachment to a police station, I saw in the diary a **member of women dying of stove-burns. As recorded else where, one could really learn about things *sub rosa* if one did not assume airs. The sub-inspector confided in me that these were mostly suicides or murders of young women faked as accidents about which the police could not do anything for want of evidence. In any case, I brought this to the notice of the SP and the Collector and they were aware of it. The only attraction of** this district in the whole state was that all Assistant / Dy. Collectors of the three sub-divisions were provided with jeeps for tours because it was considered a difficult district for travel and without many buses. There were not many roads.

Collector Vyas believed in giving a shock treatment to the new probationers. When he was the Collector of the neighbouring district of Mehsana, he took an IAS probationer on tours to remote and dry villages bordering the Runn of Kutch. This probationer, who was from the London School of Economics and from Bombay and had not seen a village in his life, seeing the life of an Assistant Collector and the Collector, decided to resign. He felt that all this was not worth the trouble. However, he regretted his action later in life because he could not do all that well in the private sector. Being a rare Gujarati with such seniority in the IAS in Gujarat, had he remained he would have done extremely well. There are only a few directly recruited Gujaratis in the Service because the commercial-minded Gujaratis always feel that they could hire a Collector for about Rs.1000 or so! So, Collector Vyas perhaps decided to give me a similar treatment and took me all the way to Varahi, a God-forsaken place then bordering the Runn of Kutch.

Collector Vyas was a night-bird even otherwise. We left at 11.30 p.m., for Santalpur and reached early in the morning – about a hundred miles away from Palanpur. This was also because of a stipulation that the Collectors should make seven night halts with total ten days of touring in a month. If one leaves the previous night, one night is counted! Even in the eighties, a chief secretary imposed such a rule on the heads of departments, which I defied because it was not at all necessary for the Commissioner of Sales Tax who should, on the contrary, be available in the headquarters on most days. Another rule made by the bureaucracy was a sizeable travelling allowance per kilometer for senior officers if they drove their own car. This was not a bad rule. But three or four officers including one or two Finance Secretaries used to go from one corner of Gujarat to the other almost throughout the week, work or no work, to earn a sizeable TA packet per month. Madhavsinh Solanki tried to curtail this by stipulating that all officers in the Secretariat should remain in the HQ on Tuesdays and also by keeping meetings on Thursdays. Despite this, week-end trips went on. Chief Secretary Chandramouli once remarked while these officers were constantly on the road disposing of files, some others had open air-tickets all the time in their pockets and spent all their time in the air.

When we reached there in the afternoon, there was a sand storm from the desert which converted the day into almost night.

Although I cursed my fate, unlike Shah, I did not decide to resign. I was made of sterner stuff. However, I thought of resignation several times later to the anxiety of my parents, parents-in-law and friends. I felt that life was not worth living. There was turmoil behind my calm and handsome visage although I did not show it. Looking back, it was good or the will of Providence that I did not do such a foolish act.

However, I went on trying for a change of cadre to one of the states in the south. My trips to Madras were always via Delhi for this purpose. On one such visit, some one told me that I must try for a deputation to Andhra Pradesh where I was well known already. This was possible since a similar kind of deputation was agreed to in a case where the candidate concerned was influential. A kindly relative, V.V. Nathen, took me to the Deputy Home Minister, L.N. Mishra because he had known him and worked as the Collector of the district where from he was hailing. The Deputy Minister agreed to this deputation and the secretary was convinced by Dr. A.N. Jha. But Mr. L.N. Mishra was over-ruled by Joint Secretary P.K. Davé and the former could do nothing about it. But times changed and the same L.N. Mishra was my Minister when I came to the Ministry of Commerce eight years later. At that time, he had risen so much in political stature that even a Secretary dared not show any such recalcitrance to any of his decisions. If he had done so as the Joint Secretary in the Home Ministry had the temerity to do, he would have literally kicked him out and locked his room. In fact, it really happened to some officers in the Commerce Ministry and the State Trading Corporation – they were transferred one fine morning because they opposed him on some thing or the other and the rooms were locked and there was no one in the Government including the Prime Minister to question Mishra. Incidentally, P.K. Davé was my ambassador in Brussels years later and time had changed a lot for him and the civil service. I never told him how he came in my way! I wrote in my diary in June 1963 in Ahmedabad: "I am reminded of my Guntur days with no money – literally shed tears at my condition and my family"

So I resigned myself to my fate and stayed on in Palanpur. My wife joined me a few months later and the stay was enjoyable. Of course, some relatives were aghast when they visited us there because there was no running water, nor a proper bath room. There was no bread available in the town and the Gujaratis always stated 'they had no bread and butter mentality'! One had to go to the railway station to get some loaves of bread from the pantry car of the Delhi – Ahmedabad Express.

Since we had no Bharat Darshan during our training in Mussoorie on account of the Chinese aggression, we were called for a Bharat Darshan along with the subsequent batch. It was a great welcome relief for a month, which took me to different places in India. I was again made the leader of the group and I had to take care of the needs of the group and the programme. It was no doubt very enjoyable. During this Bharat Darshan, Sarala who was my student in the Madras Christian College who got into the IAS in the subsequent batch, and her batch-mate Krishnakumar and two others, visited us in Palanpur and saw my house without a terrace. Krishnakumar became a Minister in the Central Government later having resigned from the Service.

I was about to be posted to a sub division on completion of my training. I very nearly completed my training and was expecting my orders, which were expected for Radhanpur in the same district because the post was vacant. Suddenly, orders came from the Government asking me to officiate as District Development Officer for about twenty days when Jayaraman was to be on leave. **This post is equivalent to that of a Collector. In fact, there was a lot of hooplah about the Panchayati Raj and Balwantrai Mehta and others wanted the colonial institution of the Collector to wither away. So Maharashtra and Gujarat created a parallel institution with a non-official district panchayat president as the chairman and an IAS officer, some times even senior to the Collector, working as secretary to the district panchayat**. In many districts, Collectors were even asked to vacate their offices and go to smaller buildings because they were in charge of only law and order and assessment of revenue and not even collection of revenue. Most of the revenue officials and all departmental heads like PWD, Health, Agriculture, etc. were transferred to the District Panchayat. In all districts, the Collectors refused to obey this dictat to vacate their offices except in Palanpur where the Collector found it convenient to shift the office from the Nawab's old palace to his residence because there was a railway level-crossing in between which was closed most of the time for the passing trains. The Collector thereby avoided this nuisance and started functioning from his residence. I officiated as DDO for about twenty days.

By sheer coincidence, when Jayaraman returned from leave, my Collector Capt. Bhambri, an ex-army man from the transport department with somewhat a dubious reputation, proceeded on leave for one month and I was asked to officiate as Collector. This was indeed a great surprise to every one as to how a probationer who had not even seen a subdivision was asked to work as Collector straightaway. In any case, the period of one month passed off peacefully in spite of a visit by the Chief Minister. **Perhaps this was something unique in the entire country where an IAS officer started off as a Collector straightaway**! After about twenty years, when I visited Palanpur, I did not find my name on the board in the Collector's room. Normally they are in the habit of inscribing the name if one officiates as Collector even for one or two days. It was an unintentional omission, which was rectified by the then young Collector at my request with documentary proof, of course, and thereby I earned a small place in history along with V. Shankar, ICS, who became Principal Secretary to the Prime Minister and B.G. Deshmukh, IAS, who occupied a similar position after having been the Cabinet Secretary. Once, when Madhavsinh Solanki as chief minister was on a visit, a young IAS officer hailing from the south requested him for a transfer to a comfortable district like Baroda or Surat or Kaira. Solanki happened to see this board and remarked to the young officer that 'this was a unique district which produced a cabinet secretary, two principal secretaries to PM, three chief secretaries, adviser to the governor in Moosa Raza and secretaries to the Government of India like Dr Sundaram. So you should be here and get yourself well-trained. Draw inspiration from this board!'.

Palanpur, which I visited in 1986, was altogether a different town. The place, where no bread was available for want of a bakery when I was there earlier had transformed itself into a place of buzzing activity thanks to the diamond trade. **The place was full of constructions although in the usual Indian haphazard fashion. We generally have no aesthetic sense and we spoil**

things in course of time. In other words, things only deteriorate with the passage of time unlike in the west where beauty is added from time to time. We do not believe that a thing of beauty is a joy for ever. For instance, wherever I had parked my well-kept beautiful cars, passers-by made an indelible scratch on them. This is our mentality. People in Palanpur told me that I could name anything under the sun – a VCR, TV, any French perfume, Scotch whisky and what have you, it was available there. In a district where there were only two doctors including the civil surgeon, there were now about 100 doctors of almost all specialities. This kind of prosperity is true of many towns in Gujarat.

The compound where I stayed was no longer visible from the road because there were far too many shops in front. But I was surprised to see the building, where I had stayed still in existence. It was a greater surprise to my niece who was accompanying me as to how we stayed there without a proper roof.

I landed in Radhanpur on 1st January, 1965. This is a sub division bordering the Runn of Kutch.: My article in *The Indian Express* in 1965:

"Except perhaps for students of geology and geography, few people know much about the Runn of Kutch. It is one of the most interesting regions in India from many points of view.

"It covers a considerable part of the district of Kutch in Gujarat. It is considered a great strategic barrier between India and Pakistan and the border in this sector was considered peaceful till it flared the same year.

"The Runn is a peculiar geographical formation. It is both a desert and an arm of the sea.

"A close observation of the map will reveal that it is shown in a slightly different shade of sea-blue.

"According to history, it was a navigable lake in Alexander's time and a shallow lagoon in the third century A.D. It is believed to be the bed of an arm of the sea raised above its original level by a natural convulsion of the earth.

"The other view is that a bund was formed in the west during an earthquake and the eastern portion became shallow and consequently occupied by a lake or lagoon.

"Geologically, it is of recent formation. The larger Runn of Kutch extends about 150 miles east to west and about 80 miles south to north. It has an estimated area of 7,000 square miles. The eastern or smaller Rann occupies an area of about 2,000 square miles and a narrow channel connects it with the larger Runn.

"The road and the railway lines to Kandla from Palanpur (on Delhi-Ahmedabad line) pass through this strip. This region is assuming great importance because of the free-trade zone and the Kandla port.

"This part of the country is prone to earthquakes even now though the volcanoes under the surface of the earth are not active. There was a violent earthquake in 1819. This is the main reason for the treeless, barren and rocky appearance of the country· bordering the Runn.

"The islands in the Runn are known as *beds*' These regions contain geologically an extremely varied succession of strata. It is supposed to be a series of sediment, the series containing sand-stone, white clay, alum and salt petre.

"Other minerals are also believed to be available here. Iron and coal mining was started some time ago but subsequently given up, as it was not a profitable proposition. It is also believed that this region is rich in oil.

"The Runn in inundated between June and October. The passage across is almost impossible and it is dangerous to venture to cross the region during this period.

"The ground appears even on the surface of the water but it is a morass in which anything will sink.

"One will sink deeper and deeper if one tries to wriggle out vertically; it means slow and painful death. The inundation is by salt water, water driven by strong winds from the sea and also of rain water.

"It is an interesting place to visit during the winter months. Birds, antelope and wild asses are seen. The wild asses appear in herds and they are a feast for the eye. Migratory birds are also seen in plenty.

"The Runn is intolerable in summer. The salt water, as it dries, leaves a hard flat surface covered with stone, shingle and salt. It is a very interesting experience to drive a vehicle for miles at the maximum speed possible without any obstruction.

"As the heat increases in the summer, the ground is baked by the sun. The salt shines with dazzling whiteness and the distance appears uncertain. It would be almost impossible to trace one's route back if one got lost in the Runn.

"No vegetation is seen anywhere except some raised beds which appear like oases. There is an air of desolate loneliness except for the presence of some stray birds.

"The villages in this region are buffeted by winds in the summer months. Clouds of sand and dust, blown about by hurricanes, are a daily occurrence. The neem, pipal and babul trees are seen in the villages. The Forest Department has taken up the task of afforestation to arrest the spread of the dreadful Runn.

"The average rainfall in this region is about twelve inches and scarcity conditions prevail almost every year. This region is beyond the range of the southwest monsoon. It is among the places in India which receive the lowest rainfall.

Apart from being a strategic barrier, the Runn of Kutch is a dismal, but interesting region".

Unlike Palanpur, Radhanpur had not changed even a bit even in 1986 when I visited again. The addition was only a good government guest house. During my early days, people had to stay in the Nawab's guest house. (Radhanpur has now a good hotel!)

The Nawab of Radhanpur was an old man with two begums. If he had had lunch with one begum, he would have dinner with the other. The two begums did not meet at all except on formal occasions. Each one had her own personal staff with the Nawab as the only common factor. Only the family doctor had access to these begums. Once my wife accompanied the doctor and met these begums out of sheer curiosity who were living in a world of their own. It was also helpful to accompany a doctor because he could also act as an interpreter. In fact, one of the begums was not even aware that Winston Churchill was dead and gone. The Nawab used to take them every year to a particular hotel in Bombay on the Marine Drive. He would be in a suite in the middle with the two begums on either side in different suites. They would also travel separately with their entourage. The son-in-law of one of the begums had a fixed time every week to call on each begum.

The Nawab was very fond of playing cards, which he did with the local gentry far into the night. He had a peculiar protocol – whenever a Minister visited Radhanpur, he would receive him and see him off at his guest house where the Ministers had naturally to stay. Whenever the Collector of the district visited, he would receive him and see him off at the gate of the palace. Whenever I visited him, he would get up and shake hands. When others visited or called on him, he never used to get up.

It was reported that the Nawab of Radhanpur, along with his cousin the Nawab of Junagadh, wanted to accede to Pakistan. But he was prevailed upon to accede to the Indian union by his brother-in-law, the Nawab of Palanpur. As quid pro quo, the Government of India bought his place at Palanpur for about Rs.18 lakhs or so which was a huge amount those days. The Nawab of Palanpur was also nominated to the Parliament and made Honorary ADC to the President. Unlike the Nawab of Radhanpur, this one was a very informal person and visited the Collector. The Collector and other officers were expected to call on former rulers and also address them as 'Your Highness'. The Nawab of Palanpur had retained a small guest house for himself and entertained us whenever he came from Bombay. He was successful in many business ventures in Bombay.

The so-called bungalow of the Assistant Collector at Radhanpur was located in the midst of the dirty town. One could see the desert there from this building. It was our good fortune that a disciple of Gandhiji and resembled him a bit, Ravi Shankar Maharaj, visited us at our residence. The office was located in a compound where donkeys were standing almost for the whole day. However, it was a sensitive town because of its proximity to the border with Pakistan. There was no place to go in the evenings except to a small cinema theatre or to the railway station.

The Assistant Collector was expected to tour for 20 days with 15 night halts. Since a jeep was given to the Assistant Collector, there was no need for one to travel by train or by bus. The landscape of the villages bordering the Runn of Kutch was really interesting. The people of this area, as in the neighbouring Rajasthan, were really leading a difficult existence because they had to cover four or five miles to get drinking water. I was advised not to drink water at all because of the likelihood of getting the disease known as 'guinea worm'. I had some knowledge of this disease because my own village in Tamil Nadu was infested with this disease. Only in our house we did not get this disease because we were drinking from a protected well. All those who drank water from the village tank got this dreadful water-borne disease. With this experience, I advised the Department of Health to clean up the wells in the area.

My special assignment during this period, apart from maintenance of law and order and disposal of magisterial cases, was allotment of lands to the landless poor. This I did by extensive touring with an efficient Thasildar and Sheristadar. This way some thousands of acres were allotted to the landless poor in a short time. I recorded on 24th April, '65: "**Last day of this marathon touring, but I do not know our orders will be implemented – the local Congress MLA is not in favour in spite of their professed ideologies of democratic socialism and Harijan welfare. He does not want implementation because a few influential people lose their excess land, though many landless persons are benefited**".

Here I must record that most of the top officials in the State administration functioned in a mechanical manner. They were 'signing-machines' without applying their mind. Why I say this is that while I disposed of so much of land and satisfied so many landless villagers, there was a letter from the Government of Gujarat when I was in Belgium in 1970 asking why I had not allotted land to some particular person while I allotted land to some chap below him in the list. Of course, I dashed off an angry reply stating that this should be looked at in the totality of the work I did and I could not even recall this case after so many years. Of course, they kept quiet and closed the matter. To my dismay, I found most of the officers including

the chief secretary, barring a few honourable exceptions, functioned in this fashion even in 1987. Some section officer or a minion in the secretariat wants to needle a collector or the head of a department and puts up a file to the secretary or the chief secretary with a draft of caution or warning. The secretary or the chief secretary, instead of applying his mind, simply signs it and thereby gives a handle to these minions in the secretariat to harass the field officers. Once when I questioned an additional chief secretary about this, he told me that most people simply signed the note for the first time and took it somewhat seriously only when it came again for the second time! Perhaps this kind of a situation of giving importance to trivialities was fortunately not in vogue in the Government of India.

We visited Deesa, a small commercial town, on the way to Radhanpur from Palanpur. Surprisingly it was reported that Deesa had an airport in the pre-independence days with flights from Karachi to Bombay touching Deesa. The air strip was still there.

There was a small section of the army in Deesa and the Second Lieutenant found it difficult to kill time. So he used to visit us in Palanpur. He also visited us after so many years in 1990 in New Delhi remembering us and taking the trouble to find our whereabouts. But, by February 1965, there was a lot of activity because of the problem with Pakistan and, if I remember right, a Brigade moved into Deesa. Many army officers started meeting me in Radhanpur wanting something or the other.

We had planned to go to Madras on leave for the summer. So we left in the first week of May, 1965. I wrote to the Government to recall me in case there was a war with Pakistan. I was pleased to see in Madras a reference to my article on Kutch in Rajaji's "Swarajya".

I went via Delhi because I was still pursuing my request for a transfer. After spending a few days in Delhi, we reached Madras. There was a sudden surprise because the Government of Gujarat transferred all of us to the newly formed Panchayats. I was transferred from Radhanpur to Mehsana District Panchayat. So I was in a sub-division only for four months and so were my batchmates. The Government wanted to change the emphasis from law and order to development administration.

I was not happy about my posting to Mehsana. So I wrote a letter to A.S. Gill, Revenue Secretary, stating that this practice of keeping the assistant collectors in the same revenue division was wrong. They should also be changed from a bad to good place and vice versa.

Because of this transfer, my wife stayed behind in Madras. I was returning via Delhi. In New Delhi, Mrs. Jayaraman somehow contacted me and told me that T.K. Jayaraman was already transferred from Palanpur to Ahmedabad and they were eagerly expecting me in Palanpur to officiate as DDO. It was again a surprise and I went there to officiate as DDO for about twenty days. In the mean time, I packed my luggage at Radhanpur.

A drilling machine was to be shifted from Radhanpur to Tharad, a place bordering the Barmer district of Rajasthan, where there was no water. I recorded in my diary: "They do not take bath or wash their clothes because of acute scarcity of water". On account of local politics, the District Panchayat President did not want to shift it. But I forced it and the well at Tharad yielded very good water. He went there for a formal inauguration and was good enough to say that the well was dug at my good intentioned protestations and he would name it 'Sundaram well'.

This reminds me of a similar situation in my native village, Kilpattu, years later. All wells went dry because of continuous drought for years. I persuaded my friend and batch-mate who was the MD of the Tamil Nadu Water Supply and Drainage Board to sanction a bore-well. But this was opposed because it was not on the Collector's list. However, it was sanctioned despite bureaucratic objections and it was the only well giving water to the entire village for a long time till it rained. This reminded me of my friend K. Balachandar's picture "Thanneer Thanneer" where the villagers on their own turned a rivulet to have water for the village after their repeated pleadings for water supply fell on deaf ears of the officialdom. They were proceeded against under the revenue law for changing the course of rivulet without due permission.

A conference of Collectors and DDOs was on and I had to attend it in this capacity. On the way to Ahmedabad, I saw the conditions in Mehsana. The DDO, one Parmar, a nice gentleman with a string of degrees following his name was keen on having me there. He belonged to the old Baroda State Service. The old Baroda State had the good practice of sending their Deputy Collector recruits to the London School of Economics. Baroda was a very progressive State and had also taken care of people belonging to the backward sections of the community. Dr. B.R. Ambedkar was also a product of the Baroda State. My DDO Parmar also belonged to the Scheduled Caste and he had done his BA (Hons) and LLB in India. He got his DPA from the London School of Economics. He also got his fellowship of the Royal Economic Society from London.

Mehsana Collectorate was located in a beautiful old building of the Baroda State. The officers' colony was a congenial place nearby and full of trees. Parmar had reserved a nice bungalow for me in this area. Although the government of Gujarat was prepared to change my posting following my letter to Gill, I changed my mind and preferred to go to Mehsana. The stay in Mehsana was enjoyable because of a club nearby where we played tennis and bridge in the evenings. By some coincidence, the Collector was alone there, his family staying in Bombay and so was the SP. "The SP's wife", I wrote in my diary on 4th Nov., 65: "was a pseudo-sophisticated lady from Bombay, condemned arranged marriages. and advocated pre-marital affairs and finally love". I used to be ready in the evenings to go to the club while Joseph and Namboodhri, IPS Probationers slept. She pulled them out one evening, advised them to be like me, told me to take her car out of the narrow garage, which she could not do and drove us to the station for dinner, which was the only place in Mehsana to have dinner or lunch. (Again, Gujarat has experienced a sea-change now for the better. There is a five-star deluxe resort and many water-parks now in Mehsana). The Sessions Judge was a bachelor and I used to take lifts from him during some week-ends to go to Ahmedabad. Even otherwise, my trips to Ahmedabad were frequent because I had some problem of some pain in the chest. The doctors with high-sounding degrees from London and other places in Ahmedabad were really useless. They could never diagnose what it was. The pain disappeared the moment I left Mehsana because it was nothing but a problem on account of the hard water of Mehsana. The electro-cardiogram in Vellore also indicated that there was nothing wrong with my heart.

There was no compulsion of tours in the Panchayat job. Although I took some interest in the development projects and had to travel in the district mainly to conduct some enquiries, the job was not taxing as that of a Sub-divisional Officer. I finished reading all the six volumes of Winston Churchill's book on the Second World War.

During one of the visits to Palanpur, Chief Minister Balwantrai Mehta, who was the father of the Panchayat Raj, took some fancy for me. **He spent a lot of time talking to me and wanted me to suggest a similar set-up at the state and the national level. I had sent him a note of possible indirect election from the district to the state level and the national level. In other words, the national level parliament would be a National Panchayat. During the Collectors and DDOs conference in Ahmedabad, I met him again. He told his wife at a dinner, 'true to his name, he is handsome'. Unfortunately, a few months later, the plane in which he was travelling was shot down over Kutch during the Indo-Pak war and he died.**

The senior politicians also felt in course of time that the District Panchayat Presidents were becoming too big for their boots. The local satraps were behaving like the chief ministers of the districts so much so the state-level ministers and the government found it rather difficult to control or manage matters in the districts. As a result of this, the institution of Collector, which was supposed to wither away, became important again and the government really started depending upon the Collectors once again. They also gave up the practice of posting the senior officers as DDOs and thereby avoided the usual conflict with the junior who was a Collector and number-one-man in the district. The district panchayats were slowly and quietly downgraded.

My wife was not in Mehsana with me for most of the time because she had the traumatic experience of her father passing away in Madras. So she could not return to Mehsana at all. I had to take my food in the only place, which was the restaurant at the railway station. There was no other hotel worth the name in Mehsana. Again I found that Mehsana had vastly changed in 1985, but the official colony with a lot of trees had deteriorated miserably. I would not like to stay there at all again.

I should record here about the Rabaris of Gujarat. A Rabari was our servant at our home and we used to admire his dress and his wife's. A Rabari is best described in the words of one Ms Winifred Bose, a foreigner who wrote from Ahmedabad in *The Indian Express* in 1963: "Milkmaids of Gujarat" – "Some times when I see youngsters drooling over pictures of film stars, foreign and native, I feel like taking them by the scruff of the neck and propelling them to the countryside of Gujarat, to see what is Indian beauty displayed at its best. The round, high-breasted fullness of a female creature, tapering to a handspun waist, swells and curves voluptuously to hips immortalised in Indian sculpture, captured centuries ago in stone, today alive in the flesh of the milkmaids of Gujarat.

"I refreshed my memory anew this year, lingering by the road-side to watch a bevy of Krishna's Gopis laughingly swinging their way to celebrate the birthday of their Lord. What a phantasmagoria of colour they presented in their vivid costumes, predominantly red, but gaudily slashed with every hue of the rainbow. No wonder Krishna found them as irresistible as Ahmedabadis find them today.

"Yes, it is so. A few years ago, the milkmaids who poured daily into the city of Ahmedabad, leaving their men folk behind, were temporarily forbidden for a spell to come to the city. Made for love-making, could they be blamed if the city youth succumbed to their rustic charms, and pursued them as avidly as did the navy-blue god of yore? Could they be scolded, when their eyes sparked off only laughter, if some of them fell a prey to the lure of romance, these eternal symbols of love and of love-play?

"Their tall, handsome males, turbans of cycle men atop proud heads, ears winged with gold, are men indeed, begetters of striking masculine boys and beauteous maidens. Jealously, they withdrew their tantalising wenches from the wicked temptations of the city.

But the merry maids who are the milk-life of the city, the love-life for the village, could not be subdued for long.

"Often have I paused on some remote bullock track to admire a passing string of girls, single, double and treble tiers of glinting brass and copper vessels balanced on their queenly heads. They move from village to village, mile after mile, in a curious trotting gait, perhaps for speed, perchance for balance, but executing a swirl of skirt, and a sway of hips to tempt a saint of a man and men are not saints. Cultivated or natural, no model school could turn out figures as twitchingly alluring as these, pirouetting along the paths like multitinted columbines.

"On a country road in the dusk of evening, the milkmaids, still tripping, went their homeward way with empty milk pots to their native places. A passing car reflects its headlights in a myriad tiny mirrors embroidered thickly in bold vari-coloured threads on the full hipster skirts of the maids. Light flashes from their mirrored head veils, and scintillates off, their firm, star-studded bosoms, sprinkled with inlaid pieces of glass. With an occasional cow-bell tinkle, glass meets glass, as the voluminous folds of cloth swirl force and waft around the ballet-dancing forms of grace.

"There are moments when I wonder if Krishna's Gopis are immortal. Do they hide their aging womenfolk, or do they never age? Tall, erect, proud like queens, each one a Rani, their figures never run to fat. Fun-loving black eyes may dim, but faces with bone structures like an artist's dream, seldom age. The beauty of the bone outlives the shrinking of the flesh.

"The milkmaids are back in Ahmedabad. They have been back for a year or two. I hope they will not retreat again. Every day I look out for them for they pass, hoping for a cheery chat by the roadside. Such interludes are never dull, for the milkmaids are rarely glum. Quickly they respond to a friendly smile with a flash of teeth against the dusky beauty of a face, or a skin as golden as a peach. Their beauty is disturbing.

"I can only imagine the effect upon a man. A trim ankle turns on the road, sunshine sparks off a diamond glitter in a purple red, a brilliant blue, or floral skirt. A hand is raised, long and slim fingered to steady brimming bowls of milk; heads turn. The milkmaids are a common sight on the streets of Ahmedabad, but they never cease to fascinate with their grace and beauty, which has become a legend in Gujarat."

It was time for my promotion. I was told that the chief secretary proposed my name for collectorship of Rajkot. But the chief minister Hitendra Desai turned it down because he felt I was too young to be a collector, that too in a district like Rajkot. If Balwantrai Mehta had been there, he would have readily agreed. But he was also in the habit of cancelling the orders whenever the local leaders protested against certain postings so much so when some one was going to a district to take over as collector, the traffic police constable stopped him on the way and told him that the orders were cancelled. Some one else was pulled out of a train, when he boarded it to go to the place of his new posting. Hitendra Desai, on the contrary, checked about the person from the local leaders and consulted the leaders in the new place about acceptability before posting a person. So I came to know about my possible promotion from the Mehsana District Panchayat President who was otherwise a good person and also told me that he had given a good chit to the higher-ups in Ahmedabad about me and I could expect a good posting. This he told me on his own without my asking. He was right and I was posted to Junagadh as District Development Officer.

Junagadh is fairly a beautiful town at the foot of a big hill, atop with Jain temples. The Jain temples are beautiful structures of the 12th and 13th century with rich architecture in the western part of India, the prince among them being the famous Dilwara at Mt. Abu. The cluster of 863 temples on top of the hill of Palitana in the Bavanagar district are also equally attractive. The temples at Ambaji in Banaskantha known as Kumbharia temples and the ones at Ranakpur in Rajasthan are also rich in intricate architectural beauty. Junagadh also has an Ashokan edict on a rock.

The district is famous for the Gir forest and the lions, which are seen in the world only in Africa and in the Gir forest. It is believed that Gir must have been a part of Africa some million of years ago because the lions as also the people living in Gir closely resembling the Africans. A visit to Gir is a must for all those visiting Junagadh.

The famous Porbandar, the birth place of Gandhiji with his house, is also a part of Junagadh district. Porbandar has also assumed some notoriety in the recent past for its smuggling and mafia dons. The Hindi picture, "Godmother" with Shabana Azmi in the lead is supposed to be a true story of the first woman-don (The first woman dacoit was Phulan Devi who, through Mulayam Singh Yadav's populism, was elected to the Lok Sabha and rubbed shoulders with Sonia Gandhi and Atal Behari Vajpayee in the Lok Sabha chamber.) The palace of the Hindu king at Porbandar on the beach is an imposing structure.

The famous Somnath temple is also a part of Junagadh district. The coastal town of Veraval from where a vertical line could be drawn to Antartica without any habitation in between is the seat of the Somnath temple and also a place where Lord Krishna fell dead to a hunter's arrow.

The district is easily the best in the dry, desert-like Saurashtra. The paddy and sugarcane fields make the district very green. The 'Kesar' mangoes of Junagadh are also famous. I wrote in my diary on 26th March 1966: "Junagadh is like South India with a lot of trees. I love trees and nature's beauty anywhere". In fact, I wrote a number of letters to *The Hindu* requesting the police not to cut those huge trees to widen the roads in Madras. They did not listen. Those were not the days of environmental preservation. Years later, Mrs Gandhi saved the trees in Delhi when they widened the roads for the Asiad. There are different varieties of grapes from Mongrol, a small Muslim State whose Nawab ran away to Pakistan with the Nawab of Junagadh. Being a coastal district, it has many places of tourist attraction. Starting right from Porbandar, Mongrol, Chorwad, Veraval and Una, the coast is dotted with beautiful buildings. Some of them are now converted into hotels. For instance, the building at Chorwad right on the beach is a hotel although with poor upkeep. The state ministers and officials generally rush to Junagadh during summer to escape the heat of Ahmedabad or Gandhinagar.

I took over as DDO in Junagadh in February, in 1966. My gas problem at Mahesana disappeared the moment I landed in Junagadh, thanks to the good water there. To start with, I stayed in the beautiful Manoranjan guest house. The Nawab of Junagadh was fond of buildings and dogs. Thanks to him, there were many beautiful buildings in Junagadh. The kennel of the Nawab became the Government of India Institute of Community Development! The Agricultural University was housed in another building of the Nawab. The Nawab used to perform marriages of his dogs. I saw one or two cemeteries of his dogs too. I was told that when he flew off to Pakistan in a plane, he made it a point to carry all his dogs with him but left behind one or two begums!

Among these buildings, the best official building was that of the Dewan, known as the 'Administration House'. It was in a huge compound with quarters for the servants, 'dhobi' and the barber. It was planned in such a way that from the portico one could enter the drawing room on the right and the dining hall on the left and personal rooms with attached bathrooms, having imported bath tubs and fittings. The guest suites with attached bathrooms were on the right, adjoining the drawing room. Apart from the staircase, there was also a lift in the building installed for a Dewan who was not well. The kitchen was on the back and well planned in such a way that the bearers could come to the dining hall straight without disturbing the inmates or guests of the house. The inmates generally lived on the top floor with a balcony, a study and many bed rooms. The whole house is furnished with Persian carpets and beautiful furniture. There were very fine mirrors from Belgium. Refrigerator was a luxury those days. There was one on the ground floor and another one on the top floor. Shah Nawaz Bhutto, the grandfather of Benazir Bhutto, was the last Dewan. An old Goanese cook and other servants used to talk about the young Zulfikar Ali Bhutto, who became the Prime Minister of Pakistan.

After the integration of Junagadh, the collector moved into this house. A small good building in the same compound was given to the Resident Deputy Collector. After the introduction of the Panchayati Raj, the DDO was also housed in the main building because the collectors were finding it difficult to occupy the whole building. So the collectors occupied the top floor and the ground floor was given to the DDO. The collectors generally allowed no interregnum, when they were transferred, for the fear of the PWD taking away the furniture and carpets. This could not be ensured for the DDOs and there was a small spell after my predecessor's transfer and my taking over. As a result, the PWD removed many of the furniture and carpets to the residence of the Executive Engineer and I could retrieve only some of them with great difficulty. One of the refrigerators was moved to the Manoranjan guest house. In fact, the Executive Engineer lived in a beautiful building well furnished with these carpets and furniture. Even now the crockery and cutlery at the Manoranjan guest house and also at Rajkot Circuit House belonged to the period of the Nawab of Jungadh. **I found to my dismay, as usual, not only this compound but also the entire area spoiled by haphazard construction of flats. The beauty of the place was simply ruined as is our wont.**

The District Panchayat Presidents were supposed to trouble the DDOs a lot and there were many stories about this. Luckily for me, the District Panchayat President was the Prince of Porbandar, Shri Udyabhansinhji who lived in Bombay. He came to Junagadh for two or three days every month. Since he was also the President of the Land Development Bank, he used to spend a lot of time in Ahmedabad, Delhi and in other places. In fact, the joke was that he spent more time in the air than on the ground. He could easily reach Junagadh from Bombay because the district had two airports. So I had full freedom in my work and was considered the most powerful DDO in the state. Of course, this was not to the liking of some of the non-officials of the panchayat including the Vice-President who was a troublesome man. He used to tell people that he would get rid of me ere long. I had an occasion to call on the Maharaja of Porbandar who had married an English woman. I was told that three or four successive generations including Udyabhansinhji had no issues. As a result, Udyabhansinhji himself was an adopted prince.

The Finance Minister Maldhevji Odedra belonged to the district and he came almost every month. The understanding was that either the collector or I should accompany him on tours, which was to every nook and corner of the district. He was a kind person from Porbandar, belonging to the Mehr community, who were also considered somewhat fierce. Murders were common among them. The Godmother' referred to earlier belonged to this community. But I found them in the villages on the coast with slight Arabic features perhaps because of the connections with Arabia on the other side of the sea. Their skin, particularly that of women, had a slight bluish tinge, which made me wonder whether they were the descendants of Lord Krishna. Lord Krishna's kingdom was the nearby Dwarka, which was now an established historical fact and he picked one of his spouses, Rukmini from Mahuva in Bhavanagar district and died at a place near Veraval. Perhaps Mehrs and Ahers were the descendants. But surprisingly Odedra was defeated in the Elections in 1967 as it also happened to the Congress in Tamil Nadu and in other places.

My office, and the office of the collector, were housed in a huge and labyrinthine palace of the Nawab abounding in pigeons. The administrative work involved was somewhat heavy because all development departments were under the Panchayat, as also the thousands of teachers and hundreds of medical and para-medical personnel. I wrote on 6th April, 66: "I like such busy life, which keeps one active and alert!" The Collector of a district earlier exercised only coordinating supervision over the technical heads of the departments and direct supervision only over the revenue and the police departments. Whereas in the Panchayati Raj system, the control of the DDO over the departmental heads was direct and it involved close supervision. **Development works had to be taken care of and the president and I were particularly interested in check-dams in different parts of the district to contain and conserve the rain water. This is similar to the tank system established by the early kings of Tamil Nadu.**

There was no compulsory night halts for the DDOs. So, on some days, I used to go by my jeep all the way to Una which was 110 miles away and return in the evening. Similarly, Porbandar in the district was about 60 miles away.

By this time, I was reconciled to my stay in Gujarat. In fact, I had given up my attempts to get a transfer to the south. I was also considered for the post of secretary to the Governor. But Chief Minister Hitendra Desai ruled it out by saying that the post was not meant for active young officers and posted a retiring officer instead. Some time in the month of September, 1966, I was asked to go for a training for two months in the Indian Institute of Public Administration in New Delhi. This was naturally a welcome change.

The kindly relative who was still in Delhi told me that I should list out the possible postings in the south so that he could try again for a change. But I was no longer interested in these attempts partly because I was disgusted and also secondly for the fact that **those days representations to Government were not looked upon with favour. So I thought I would not make a representation again. But the situation has changed over years and now even officers of the level of Cabinet Secretary make representations to the government for something or the other. Court cases by civil servants have also become so common that nobody takes them seriously. Those days an officer going to the court was always looked down upon and became a marked man. This was also because of the fact that justice was generally done without asking for it.**

I was successfully completing my training in the middle of December, 1966. On the last day of training, my relative V.V. Nathen made it a point to contact me. Since I was not there, he left an urgent message for me. When I contacted him, he told me that there was a post of a Collector being created in Pondicherry and I should apply for it since the Chief Secretary U. Vaidyanathan was from the same Bihar cadre as Nathen and was known to him. In fact, he wanted me to go and meet the chief secretary who happened to be in Delhi. This was a welcome development no doubt and before taking the train to Junagadh, I met all the people concerned who told me to send a representation through the government of Gujarat. In fact, I had met chief secretary U. Vaidyanathan even a year earlier in a friend's place in Delhi and it did not even occur to me that one from some cadre could go to Pondicherry on deputation. That is how destiny works, I suppose.

On the way back to Junagadh, I gave a representation to the chief secretary at Ahmedabad who this time was not inclined to forward it. But, after a month, he proceeded on leave and the officiating chief secretary was inclined to forward it with a favourable recommendation. An under secretary who was really ruling the General Administration Department was also inclined to help me. Meanwhile, the chief secretary of Pondicherry wrote me that the vacancy was to go to an under secretary from Maharashtra who was working in the Home Ministry in Delhi and I should wait for the second vacancy if at all it would arise. So I was disheartened, again. I wrote in my diary on 4th March, 67: "Failure, frustration and pessimism have become a part of my life". But he wrote me a letter himself after about a fortnight stating that the Maharashtra officer would not be able to take this post because the government of Maharashtra wanted him back and would not agree to another deputation. This helped me and my orders for Pondicherry came in the last week of March, 1967. When Udayabhansinhji arrived from Bombay, some one told him at the airport after reading the newspapers that I was transferred to Pondicherry. The Vice-President who was at loggerheads with me claimed that he not only got me transferred out of Junagadh, but out of Gujarat itself! We were seen off at the railway station by Sessions Judge Bhatia and also Collector R. Balakrishnan apart from the other officials and friends. The Bhatias, the Balakrishnanas, my wife and other ladies were good friends. Living in the same house with the Balakrishnans created better intimacy.

This was perhaps the first instance which made me feel that "there is an inscrutable destiny which shapes our ends". I had given up all attempts for a transfer to the south. I was never deeply religious. Although I prayed before deities in temples including Tirupati, I always had a lurking doubt whether this was all true. Although the village astrologer was categorical that I would become a gazetted officer like a Collector, I did not attach much importance to it. Although my father-in-law was a London-returned professor of chemistry, he strongly believed in astrology. When I was unhappy about my posting to Gujarat, he always assured me that things would change for the better after 1966 and they did. I will narrate later some more such instances not based on rationality.

* * *

8

Winning Laurels at Pondicherry

It was on April 9th, 1967 that I landed in Pondicherry. I was advised to take over on that very day. It was a Sunday but that happened to be an auspicious day. For the same reason, a new Ministry under Chief Minister M.O.H. Farook was also sworn in that morning. I discovered later despite long French influence and having a large number of Christians, Pondicherry was also highly superstitious. Christians were still divided on their original caste lines. I happened to call a meeting on Tuesday at 3.00 p.m., It was an important meeting to put Pondicherry on the international map by participating in an international exhibition to be held in Madras. But nobody turned up. People started trickling in after 4.30 p.m., Most of them told me that they chose not to come between 3.00 and 4.30 p.m., because it was 'Rahukalam' and particularly the first meeting for a good cause should not be held at such an inauspicious time.

Hindu-Muslim conflict is peculiar to North India, may be for historical reasons and the invasions. The South was comparatively peaceful and if at all there were some religious troubles, they were confined to the north of Tamil Nadu. Whereas in the South, particularly in Karaikal, which is a part of Pondicherry and the surrounding area, the people are really secular in the sense that the Hindus visit the Darga at Nagore and the Muslims visit the famous and only temple for Saneeswara in Karaikal. The Hindus also worship at the famous church at Velankanni. The Christians too tonsure the head of children in fulfilment of a vow as the Hindus do at Tirupati, Tirutani and in other shrines. **That way, Pondicherry-Karaikal region is so secular that others should emulate!**

On the eve of my departure from Junagadh, there was news to the effect that the Venkatasubba Reddiar Ministry in Pondicherry was about to fall. It went out of office in the first week of April, 1967 when I was having my joining time in Madras. I was in touch with chief secretary, U. Vaidyanathan, and informed him that I would reach Pondicherry by bus on the afternoon of 9th April and take over immediately. From my experience later in Pondicherry, I felt that he could have very well sent a car to fetch me from Madras or asked some one coming to Madras to pick me up because too many officials and persons were travelling up and down between the two places out of sheer necessity and official work. Perhaps he did not do this because some one had already floated a rumour that I was related to him which was not a fact. In fact, even his sub-sect was different from mine! Such type of rumour mongering is very common in our country and is being indulged in even by knowledgeable people and high officials. In fact, such rumours were to haunt me throughout my career. **May be because ours is a 'sifarish' culture, which has become worse in course of time. Perhaps the competition is also very stiff that a stage has come where no one can get any thing done in this country without knowing some one in an office, including the private sector, or by some recommendation or by sheer corruption. Of course, the wheel is almost turning a full circle now because there is so much of recommendation and favour-seeking that nothing can be done without recourse to this; the politicians and the civil servants do this as well in such a rampant fashion. For instance, the ministers issue sanctions either for house allotment or for telephone connections that the list itself is so long that it has lost its meaning or sanctity. In olden days,**

things were done mostly in the normal course and the ministers did a favour only on rare occasions so that it had some value. Now it has no value at all because the ministers have become executives and many of them perform practically these clerical functions instead of concentrating upon policy making. I am glad that the courts are coming down heavily on these practices.

Travel to Pondicherry takes about three hours by road from Madras. It is generally through pleasant places. When the lake is full at Chengalpattu, it presents a beautiful pictures with small hillocks as the back-drop. I have always felt that this lake is as beautiful as a lake in Switzerland. The bus crosses the waterless Palar after Chengalpattu and stops at a place where all buses stop so that the passengers and the crew could have coffee or tea. Even a sumptuous meal is possible. After this stop, the bus is on a fairly good road wherefrom one could go to the bird sanctuary at Vedanthangal or to a nearby hillock with a small and beautiful temple on top. The journey is also through Madhurandakam, which is famous for its temple. Beyond Madhurandakam, the journey is via Tindivanam from where the road branches off to Pondicherry from the main Madras-Trichy highway and this is one of the routes. The scene immediately changes and it gives the picture of a coastal area with a lot of casuarina trees. This road in Tamil Nadu, although connecting the capital of another state, is a narrow one and is not well kept. It remained so for many years because of the negligence of the government of Tamil Nadu.

The other road is via Marakkanam. It is more beautiful because the road for a long stretch is right on the beach and one could have a good view of the sea. Years later, a five star hotel had come up in this area right on the beach. The Central University of Pondicherry years later was also located on this road facing the sea. So also was the not-yet-full-blown Auroville.

The foundation for Auroville was laid during our time on Feb 28th, 1968, by President V.V. Giri. In the words of the Mother: "Auroville belongs to nobody in particular. Auroville belongs to humanity as a whole". The inauguration was done with a lot of fanfare with soil from about 150 and odd countries. But after the demise of the Mother, the project did not take its full shape as per schedule because of the internal squabbles in Sri Aurobindo Ashram.

Beyond this area, the road passes through Kalapet, a picturesque area of Pondicherry, with numerous coconut palms and thick vegetation. Later it was also the constituency of M.O.H. Farook. So it was a very pleasant journey, unlike the road journeys in the desert-like north Gujarat and Saurashtra. A comparable scenery could be the landscape in south Gujarat particularly in Kaira with canals and green vegetation. Somehow I have always appreciated scenic beauty and a lot of vegetation and not desert-like places although I find that these things do not disturb the mental equilibrium of many persons and even people from Kerala being quite happy in Rajasthan or Gujarat.

While on the way to Pondicherry, I saw the photo of M.O.H. Farook, the Chief Minister to be of Pondicherry, in *The Hindu*. The face appeared somewhat familiar although I could not really place him. But when I called on him for the first time, I realised that he was my contemporary in Loyola College. He also could recognise me instantly. He was the youngest Chief Minister ever in the country and earlier he was a Speaker of the assembly --the youngest Speaker of any Legislative Assembly in India. Perhaps it is also a record in the world.

I was duly received by Under Secretary C.D. Dayal at the bus station in Pondicherry. I was told later that he was one of the aspirants, wrongly though on account of his seniority, for the post of Development Secretary, which I was to occupy. Although his misplaced aspirations were not fulfilled, he turned out to be a kind and good friend with whose family I am still in touch. Some years later, he had died, prematurely.

He took me to the government guest house, which was located in a private building. Although it was comfortable, it was quite a contrast to the circuit houses or rest houses of my days in Gujarat. The circuit houses and rest houses in Gujarat are well furnished with beautiful furniture, crockery and cutlery. Even a small rest house in a village in Gujarat had a kitchen attached. Whereas a government rest house or circuit house in the south including Tamil Nadu did not have a kitchen and they got even a cup of coffee from the nearby hotel. So the food had to be brought in a tiffin-carrier from a hotel although it was not a new experience for me to eat from a plantain leaf. In fact, I welcomed it. Since my predecessor, a Sardarji from the North, was leaving on transfer, there were a number of farewells in the typical South Indian fashion. It was a welcome change from Gujarat and I could also meet the cross-section of Pondicherry straightaway in these parties.

Next door, there was a bar although I had never used it. The owner of the bar was a dark looking African-like man whose daughter also looked typically African. I was told later that there were quite a few such 'creols' in Pondicherry because of the French connection. I reproduce below my article – 'A New Comer in Pondicherry '- published in the *Pondy Observer*: August 7th, 1967. "AUGUST 15th – the most important day in our national life; more so in Pondicherry because it is also Sri Aurobindo's birthday. The Government Tourist Home is being inaugurated during this week, this year – the International Tourist Year. The importance of the Tourist Home could be more well understood only by one who stayed in the former Inspection Bungalow, once declared a jail to accommodate the Jagathguru in the sixties!

"The Public Relations Officer requested me for an article for the special supplement being issued on the day of inauguration. He wanted the article to be in a lighter vein, for he had seen only my recent jaunts in journalism. To start with, I had contributed only serious, factual articles on high-brow subjects like anthropology and archaeology. I wanted to write something humorous, if not, childish and flippant, for a change. So. I was wondering whether this article also should be of the same category. I hope that no organisation or individual will feel offended by this unadulterated nonsense (unlike the local toddy).

"Pondicherry is well known all over the country. It is well known in the North (includes east and west India) because of Sri Aurobindo and the Ashram. It was a strange coincidence that Pondicherry was hitting the headlines in the press and on the A.I.R. when the Government of India issued orders posting me to Pondicherry in the last week of March, 1967. A Tamil film 'Madras to Pondicherry' was also running in Madras. Some of my friends joked that my posting itself portended trouble for Pondicherry. Some others were envious and felt that I was a wrong choice for Pondicherry – Pondicherry caters to spiritual as well as spirituous cravings of men and women and I am not interested in either. I became the envy mainly of those who sought the so-called paradise of the inebriates!

"Pondicherry also conjures up some visions in the minds of those who are far away from it. They feel that it is a little Paris in India. The pent-up emotions of the people in the neighbouring areas find a vent in this 'pleasure island'. Week-end excursions to Pondicherry are very common.

"When my posting to Pondicherry was announced, the eyebrows of the orthodox in the family went up. They wanted me to be careful here, to confine myself to my house after dusk, to seek refuge in the Ashram and not to frequent the beach in the evenings. So I was full of ideas and apprehensions before landing up here.

"It was again a coincidence (not by design; I assure you) that I took charge of office on the same day the present Ministry took office. The reason was that it was an auspicious day!

"Immediately after assuming office, I was eager to explore the place and know the spots. I went to the beach, saw the beautiful coast edging the town. The beach was beautiful. Contrary to my great expectations, I could not see even a single sea-bather let alone bikini-clad nymphs. The Public Relations Officer was quite sore that his plans to beautify the beach with bathing facilities, fresh-water cubicles, multi-coloured umbrellas and what not were not agreed to. He had plans, I believe, to convert Pondicherry into another Nice or Miami. I enquired about the people who were likely to use the beach. He told me that he did not anticipate any difficulty, for a norm had already been struck here. The people of India do object to the bikini because it is the barest minimum. Even the people in England object to the modern-mini because it exposes the bikini underneath. A via media (or golden mean) is the shorts – half-quarter pants, if I may say – which serve the purpose without any risk of exposure. So, no one should have objection to the provision of bathing facilities on the beach. This will indeed be a great tourist attraction.

"I believe that the Public Relations Officer thought of another attraction, rather a useful information to a complete stranger to

Pondicherry, the addition of the words, "wet area begins" on the welcome-signs at Gorimedu and the Cuddalore Road. Sage counsel prevailed and the words were omitted. I told him that the purpose was fulfilled by the numerous boards with the inscription, "Here is the toddy shop"!

"When I met my sceptical relatives in Madras again, I told them that the bonnet of my car was still in shape and it had not been damaged by any tottering drunkard. No one who has visited Pondicherry will say that the government square or the beach is another New Harlem, which should not be frequented after dusk. On the contrary, we see a concourse of respectable citizens breathing fresh air from the sea on the beach till late in the night. I was also surprised to know from the Police Chief that grave crimes were practically nil in Pondicherry. Liquor and crime are supposed to go together according to common belief – perhaps this is another popular misconception.

"I, for one, like the attire of the policemen in Pondicherry. The colourful French cap adds grace to them – it is far better than the ugly head-dress of the policemen in other parts of the country. It reminds one of de Gaulle in his uniform.

"Pondicherry is a beautiful town. Perhaps it is one of the most well-planned towns in the country. The plan (reproduced in the leaflet of the Information Department) and an aerial view will confirm it. It is surrounded by a palm-fringed beach, beautiful, tall coconut palms, paddy fields and the backwaters. You see the touch of Kerala on the way to Cuddalore. A trip to Villianur will convince one about its soil fertility. The Ousteri lake could be a delightful picnic spot.

"But the town is not free from the vagaries of man – the vandalism, the destructive nature in man have wrought havoc on the face of the town. The irregularly arranged shops, the roads within the town and the drainage are an eye-sore. I for one will be glad if a committee is appointed to look into the question of beautification of the town – a real active committee of the citizens and not one which will go into voluntary liquidation like some of our co-operative societies.

"It is a quiet town with a veil over her. It will be open only to those who seek and knock. Even the houses look drab from outside with high doors and windows. One has to go into a house to see its beauty. One should not mind the liquor shops, which provide relief to those who need relief and who come all the way covering long distances. The liquor is also supposed to provide inspiration to some of the literary cranks who have produced great masterpieces. I would like to give the homely example of Alexander Dumas and Jean Jacques Rousseau. Spiritual inspiration and beauty are concealed inside the Sri Aurobindo Ashram. It is open to those who seek. On the cultural and educational side, the Alliance Française, Sasi Kala Manram, French College and the Institutes provide vast scope to those who are thirsting for knowledge. Pondicherry is no less important as a place of historical interest and pilgrimage. There is a famous temple at Villianur.

"I feel it is perhaps the best town from the point of view that it contains people from all parts of the country and also a few foreigners. It is a place which provides a cosmopolitan life with a composite culture in the deep South. You can see a cross-section in the "Cercle", which is another place of attraction with a bar, tennis courts and other facilities for recreation. It is the only place in India where one can acquire a good knowledge of the sweet (but illogical, as indeed most other languages are) French language. One has a good opportunity to converse in French, which is widely spoken. (Of course, most of the French knowing persons fumble in pronouncing and speaking English though it is no less true that the English-knowing lot fare much worse when essaying French!) I hope there will not be any Gaullian controversy of English versus French here. It is a place where English and French co-exist.

"Lastly, a word of caution to the tourists. You are neither going to land up in hell, nor are you going to be shot up to high heavens by your visit here. But, you are bound to knock off some one or get knocked off at one of the many perpendicular, blind-corners within the town, if you are careless in driving."

Pondy Observer's M.P. John was an institution in Pondicherry. He was a Malayalee settled there. He had been bringing out his weekly, *Pondy Observer* – later changed the name as *New Times Observer* although I told him that it was losing its distinct Pondicherry touch – for more than thirty years or so. He was sending this to me regularly even in 1998 and perhaps to all the people who had were posted in Pondicherry earlier. It never stopped even when he was almost dying in a hospital. Fortunately he survived and brought out the journal even when he had some personal bereavements.

It was never a scandal sheet as most such local papers turn out to be. For that matter, even the so-called national dailies and journals have become scandal sheets now. The leading newspapers in Delhi are obsessed with gossip about the ministers or top officials, very often totally wrong, and so are the journals. Even the business journals are mostly personality oriented with photographs of some industrialist or the other on every page. As a result, the correspondents tend to take favours from these industrialists for publishing a column on them with a photograph. The newspapers and journals in the South, barring some honourable exceptions like *The Hindu* (slightly changing now) are obsessed with gossip about film stars.

If one has read a journal in India, there is no need to read the other one because it turns out the same story or gossip a few days later in a different language. There is practically nothing new. There is not even a single journal of the type of the *The Economist* of London in our country today. Perhaps *India Today* is somewhat good with less gossip. But *India Today* also goes off the rail carrying some incredible articles at times.

Luckily and happily, M.P. John did not belong to this category. He may not be even making money out of his Weekly. In fact, it presented a poor appearance and he depended upon a few advertisements to keep it going. But whatever articles it carried, they were of some value. He was not flippant like the modern journalists. (It is totally changed now in 2002 with change of management. He was too old to edit himself)

It was an ambition of mine to become a journalist once. So I started contributing articles and many of them appeared in different journals and newspapers. Later my wife followed. But, after some years, I decided that one should not take to journalism as a profession. The old-world values of correct journalism have disappeared except in a few newspapers and journals like *The Hindu*. Even *The Hindu* has slightly swayed from this path because of its young correspondents or editors.

Lot of young girls and boys have taken to journalism, particularly in Delhi. As Mani Shankar Aiyar put it to me once, perhaps many of them have failed to make it to the IAS or any other Service and consequently they tend to snipe at the civil service all the time. Most of them do not even verify the facts before churning out their stories. There is hardly any investigation in their so-called investigative journalism, which has become a byword after the Watergate in the USA. These young journalists move around all the time without knowing the conditions in the countryside in modern Levi jeans or ethnic 'kurtas'. There is no dearth of lunches, cocktails or dinners for them. As President Zail Singh remarked once, you can make any journalist write any story by giving a bottle of scotch whisky. Many people also use them to get some publicity. "Publicity is a frailty, compounded with naivete, even of noble minds", wrote Mr. Justice V.R. Krishna Aiyer. They meet these journalists, invite them and pamper them so that some stories could be written about them and some stories planted about the adversaries so much so that these journalists have become a set of new exploiters in society.

The well-known journalist-author, Shobhaa Dé herself wrote: (I am not an admirer of Ms Dé, but I have read her memoirs. I was struck how her father was keen on returning a loan of rupees hundred or so, as I was keen to do the same to the Madras Christian College). "But newcomers or veterans, I've learnt the hard way that journalists are not nice people to know. Fascinating, fun, stimulating, gossipy, yes. But also devious, malicious, vindictive and petty. Most journalists are conceited, despicable jerks with dandruff and pyorrhea to boot. Conduct your own survey and tell me if I'm wrong. Most lead fairly wretched personal lives (they make perfectly insufferable spouses). Most lack a healthy sense of humour—the only time they laugh is at someone else. Most walk around with intellectual hernia, weighed down by the world's problems. I prefer to stay away.... Remain on the fringes".

In a TV interview which I happened to see , Ms Dé was equally forthright about the corrupt practices of journalists nowadays

The expression 'bureaucrat' itself is a pejorative. However, it has come into common use. Our journalist friend in the North call them also 'Babus' to which I strongly object. I call them 'Kauaas' –

meaning 'crows' or 'Kakkai Koottam' in Tamil. A letter of mine to this effect was published by *The Hindu* itself. So **there are journalists and journalists as bureaucrats and bureaucrats. As a government or society, which cannot do without a bureaucracy, democracy cannot do without journalists.**

'Unfortunately even some senior civil servants have fallen prey to this kind of an approach. It may be necessary to have the friendship of the Fourth Estate to project correctly the image or the views of the government. But it has to be done within limits, keeping the anonymity of the civil service in view. But even civil servants occupying exalted posts have sought cheap publicity for their official duties, which they are in any case expected to perform, and also for getting certain posts on which they have an eye. They have tried to get these posts by appointing themselves in newspapers and these correspondents have also thought of getting certain benefits by projecting these persons and their objectives. But, by and large, they have turned out to be miserable failures and some of these appointments remained only in newspapers. I call them 'the newspaper heroes'. M.P. John did not belong to this category of journalists, but to the old guard.

I also remember when there was a raging controversy on the question of restriction of export of semi-processed leathers in Madras, the chairman of the Leather Export Promotion Council requested *the Hindu* to write an editorial, but they checked the facts from me. I gave them the correct perspective and the need to restrict the export of semi-processed leathers. They did not write the editorial, which would have become the view of the newspaper in a way reflecting the public opinion. Since they refused to write an editorial as requested by the chairman of the Leather Export Promotion Council, they published an article written on his behalf reflecting his views on the subject. Whereas some other newspapers rushed with editorials as demanded by him and also contradicted these editorials after a month or two, **depending upon public memory being short. All this does not mean that I am against the Fourth Estate. In fact, the press and the media are the guardians of democracy and the path of rectitude. It is not fair to generalize. Many of them are sincere to the cause. They themselves have realised that many of their young**

colleagues have let them down as happened in the civil service and in the society at large as well. As Jawaharlal Nehru said once that 'it is better to have a bad press than to have no press'.

When I was introduced to some other officials with names like François de Condappa, I was amused. Ramu was spelt in French as Ramou and Palaniswamy as Pajanissamy and Jayaraman as Djayaraman, etc. This was quite an amusement in the beginning but I got used to it later. In fact, many representations were still received in French. French was the official language according to the Treaty of Accession and the Acts and Rules were also translated and printed in French. The street names are still in French in Pondicherry. I saw some files on which the then Chief Minister, Goubert, wrote 'approvè' for approval. Even the servant at home said 'hopital' for hospital, 'cuisine' for kitchen and so on albeit with a heavy Tamil accent. When I went to Karaikal for holding a magisterial inquiry into a police firing as District Magistrate, the witnesses were freely mixing French words while deposing in Tamil as we mix English words while speaking in Tamil. A sample sentence is "I walked on the trottoir (pavement) and reached the carrefour (junction) and heard the loud noise of firing".

Since Pondicherry was the place to learn French, my wife and I immediately joined the Alliance Française. Many colleagues felt that all new comers to Pondicherry were very enthusiastic about joining the Alliance but left within a month or two because it was a difficult language. Of course, they always give the excuse of pressure of official work for leaving. It was true that in Pondicherry Alliance, they would not even utter a word in English or Tamil while teaching French. I realised that this was the correct way of learning a language. Once you start learning a language through another language, the substance is lost and the other language always dominates the learner. This is how Sanskrit or French is taught through English in other schools and colleges in our country. Moreover, one has to survive the first three or four months in learning French so that it becomes smooth later. Many people find it difficult during this break-in period and give up. Luckily this did not happen to us and we stayed on learning the language for nearly three years. We were the first officials in Pondicherry to learn the language fully. Perhaps this example was followed only later and the attempt was not given up as done by the officials earlier. The teachers were also accommodative in the sense they did not mind our frequent absence because of my tours. They were not much worried about attendance as long as one was diligent and willing to learn. The Director of the Alliance, a French man, was not a good teacher at all. His wife was staying for some time in Pondicherry who taught us for some time. She was not bad at teaching. But in the first year we were taught by a lady from Pondicherry, Rose Felix, who had also studied in France, with excellent diction, pronunciation and also strong in grammar. In fact, it was she who laid this strong foundation. We are still in touch with her. My wife always stood first because she was good at grammar. French grammar requires a lot of memory too. The Director used to tell her, 'Madame, Vous avez beaucoup de memoire'. I always managed to pass, not that they were considerate to me in the examinations.

Jawaharlal Nehru called Pondicherry 'a window on France'. It was true with its French culture. We lived in a historic building which was more than a hundred and fifty years old. I read about the building in the famous Anand Ranga Pillai's diaries because the government press was located here. We lived on top of the press which was still housed here. Our flat was spacious, with six big rooms with high ceilings. There was an impressive verandah and a terrace to walk. The roof was almost crumbling because the huge old Burma teaks were giving way at the edges. I invited the wife of the chief engineer, CPWD, one day and switched on the fan. The fan started splashing water all around since water had collected inside the fan through the loose ceiling. She told her husband to re-do the ceiling which was done in an agreeable fashion so that we could climb on a ladder to have a bird's-eye view of Pondicherry. Once our young niece had gone up the ladder to hide herself there, but she could not come down and thereby caused us some anxious moments. This house was on rue de l'Eveché, a difficult name to pronounce, meaning Bishop's street. Perhaps a bishop lived in our house in the distant past. But recorded history showed that it was more than a hundred and fifty year old house with the government press on the ground floor.

We had a hectic social life there because of the warm, fun-loving and entertaining people. The French crowd of the Consulate was also friendly. There were frequent parties in the houses and also in the club known as Cercle de Pondichery, located in a nice corner of the park opposite 'the Raj Niwas' near the beach. I was the president of the Cercle de Pondichery for a year and I improved the interior further by engaging an architect from the Ashram.

Since Pondicherry was a Union Territory, the officials and the ministers had to make frequent trips to Delhi, almost every month. Since half the government was in my charge, I had to be out often, driving down to Madras after the French class and dinner, flying to Delhi from Madras and back and motoring down often in the night after dinner–perhaps one cannot do such nocturnal trips these days for security reasons. During the three year period I had covered more than twelve thousand miles - half the circumference of the globe. Driver Jagadisan was tireless and he came and saw us years later at our residence in Chennai. Since we were in the South and nearer home – in a triangle of Pondicherry - Madras-Vellore – many friends and relatives visited us. I felt rather unhappy for a moment when I was reading the literature on Pondicherry, in the first few days after my arrival there, that the entire territory was hardly 180 sq. miles whiles Junagadh district was about 4500 sq. miles and one of the taluks was a hundred mile way from Junagadh. I wondered for a moment whether I made a mistake by opting to come to Pondicherry. But the people, the French culture, the alien touch and the Tamil dramas and cultural programmes, frequent trips to Madras and Delhi and the thrill of working directly under the Lt. Governor made me feel happy. Moreover, this small territory had a sub-continental jurisdiction in the sense that Karaikal was about sixty miles down on the coast – one had to go through the famous Tanjavur district of Tamil Nadu – Mahe on the West coast of Kerala with a beautiful building for the Administrator and Yenam in the east on the coast surrounded by Andhra Pradesh. Chandranagor near Calcutta luckily merged with India immediately after the transfer of power by the French in 1954. Travel to these places was a veritable excursion.

During our period, Pondicherry was sanctioned the All India Radio. The station was opened with a music concert in the 'Marie'

– Mayor's office or 'Hotel de Ville' – not to be confused with the English hotel – a beautiful building right on the beach where the Legislative Assembly also used to meet. The first director was an active person who brought in leading artists like M.S., Lalgudi, etc., every month to perform. There was a story after his departure that he took money from a lot of people to feature them on the AIR those days and did not pay even the great artists whom he made to perform. Whether these stories by his less active colleagues were true or not, he was good at conception and execution of ideas in a new station. The then Minister for Information and Broadcasting, Nandini Satpathi, was an ardent devotee of the Ashram and she was in Pondicherry every month. With all that contact, he managed a trip to France to study the French Radio. On his return, he was promptly posted in Rajkot. But Pondicherry should remember this active man which generally the people of Pondy do always.

My wife and I are fondly remembered there even now. She for her writings (mostly middles in *The Indian Express*, *The Mail*, and *The Pondy Observer*) and broadcasts over the AIR. Without our asking, chief secretary Anjani Dayanand made her a member of the State Social Welfare Board. In fact, these boards were not politicised those days. So a few socialites, but dedicated to the cause, were on them. They were mostly the wives of officers or professors or some scholarly persons from the Ashram who functioned with dedication. They added stature to the office and not the other way round.

The narration above should not mean that it was all fun and no work, as also wrongly construed by people outside Pondicherry. Whether it is a small state or big one, the entire paraphernalia of a Lt. Governor who is the Administrator, a Ministry, a Legislature with all Committees including the Public Accounts Committee, etc. were there to keep one fully occupied. I wrote in my diary on Sunday, July 23rd, 1967: "Busy with files throughout the day. Somehow, I cannot keep quite when files are there. They weigh on my mind. I wonder how some officers sleep over files for days and months." (This practice of disposing of files in time continued throughout my life and such recordings became common in my diaries. I was in the office till 00.30

a.m., to clear the files even on the eve of my departure for Brussels from Pondicherry.) I should mention here my tireless personal assistant J. Ambroise (Ambrose in English) who did not hesitate to put in long hours of work. I am still in touch with him.

It is a microcosm where so many things happened. More than this, in a small place like this, the scope for development work was immense and many new ideas could be implemented without much hindrance. The Central grant-in-aid was available to take care of the budget deficit. When some one asked the late C.N. Annadurai, chief minister of Tamil Nadu, whether he was interested in the accession of Pondicherry with Tamil Nadu, he wisely replied that he was not at all interested in that merger because a few crores of rupees were flowing into the territory from the Centre every year, which was virtually a part of Tamil Nadu. As a result of this heavy pumping in of money, the doctor-patient ratio, the bed, the student-teacher ratio, the per capita income were very high in Pondy. To put it in modern lingo, the per capita income and the human development index were far above the neighbouring states. The people of Pondicherry also would not prefer such a merger because they could approach a government easily on the spot. The Treaty of Transfer of Power also stipulates that the peoples' wish should be ascertained before such a merger, if at all. But it is advisable to keep it as a distinct entity because I believe that it is still distinct, different from Tamil Nadu in spite of a lot of Tamilisation over a period of time and the people of Pondy feel more at home in Paris than even in Madras. It is also a distinct, cosmopolitan town with people from different parts of the country in the Sri Aurobindo Ashram and the Jawaharlal Institute of Post-Graduate Medicine and Research.

Sri Aurobindo Ashram is somewhat a controversial place in Pondicherry, although for no reason. The ministers themselves, including the chief minister Farook, admitted to me that Pondicherry without the Ashram would have no importance. The Ashram should not be misconstrued as a single, fenced place where people stayed and meditated. It is spread all over Pondy where people live in different buildings and lead a normal

family life. It is entirely left to the individual to adopt a particular mode of life – a family with children, a life of celibacy, a vegetarian or non-vegetarian food, given to alcohol or not although these are not permitted on the main premises. The main motto is 'perfection in whatever one does' and as a result many industrialists have set up fine industries there, giving a part of the income to the Ashram and a few others doing whatever they could do for the Ashram in a perfect manner – like teaching, photography, painting, etc., Some have given their entire wealth to the Ashram and all their day-to-day needs are taken care of by the Ashram. This was all done, by or in the name of the Mother – a French lady who decided to stay on in Pondicherry with Sri Aurobindo. I had met her several times because as District Magistrate I had to escort many a VIP. She always gave a benign smile although she hardly spoke to any one, perhaps because of her old age and also because she spoke only French. She used to give a flower to every one, each one had a special meaning like peace, prosperity, calmness, etc. There was a guide book to this. At least on one or two occasions I knew of, she seemed to have given the appropriate flower according to the mental condition of the devotee. Mrs. Gandhi made a visit and spoke to her in French.

However, there was certain amount of antagonism between the Ashramites and the local people. Ashram was considered a north-Indian pocket in an essentially Dravidian town. Pondicherry is also somewhat noted for its anti-brahmin feelings – an influence of the neighbouring Tamil Nadu. But my wife and I were very popular there because we mixed freely with every one there. Even the former chief minister, freedom fighter and Mayor, Edouard Goubert (pronounced as Edward Guber), was a known and outspoken anti-brahmin. The Pondy Cinema Theatres Association invited him to preside over a farewell function for me and my wife when we left Pondy, in 1970. It was a touching function. Mr. Goubert specially came to this function and declared that of all officials posted in Pondy, he liked only two brahmins – one me and another one who was there a few years earlier – because of our catholic outlook. He was considered very formidable that no one could shake him politically – a myth blown off later by the astute and crafty Farook who managed to be the chief minister for a number of years in spite of changing parties. Goubert retired to Bangalore. Mrs. Goubert was our good acquaintance and we used to visit her some times.

On account of the antagonism between the local people and the Ashram, it was foolishly attacked during the virulent anti-Hindi agitation in 1965. It was an emotive issue and the whole of Tamil Nadu was exercised about it. In fact, it sounded the death-knell of Congress power in Tamil Nadu because the people of Tamil Nadu felt that the Congress leaders including Kamaraj let them down badly in this regard. Congress has yet to regain its lost ground in Tamil Nadu. So, the Aurobindo Ashram, which was considered a pocket of North India in an otherwise placid Pondicherry had to face the wrath of the people. The Ashram always had a powerful lobby in Delhi and naturally there was a furore. The Government of India appointed a Committee under joint secretary, Union Territories, A.D. Pandey and Balakrishna Shetty IP, a former IG of Police of Madras. The committee found that there was no proper District Magistrate (Executive) for the Union Territory. The chief secretary himself was notified as district magistrate under the Criminal Procedure Code, which was not only an odd situation, but he was also away on leave during the agitation. The powers of the Collector were curiously being exercised by the Administrators of Karaikal, Mahe and Yenam who were actually of the rank of Deputy Collector. There was no Collector at all for Pondicherry. Since the chief secretary who was also the district magistrate was away on leave and the lacuna was discovered during the peak of the agitation, the judicial district magistrate was requested to perform the duties of maintenance of law and order which he naturally and rightly refused. So, the Pondicherry Administration had to issue post-haste a notification under the Criminal Procedure Code empowering the Development Secretary as District Magistrate. So the Pandey Committee recommended creation of a post of a full-fledged Collector and District Magistrate for Pondicherry. I was appointed to this post and thereby I became the first full-fledged Collector and District Magistrate of Pondicherry. Since it was felt that the

Collector could also undertake other development functions, I was also Development Secretary to Government.

When I landed there, I was only Development Secretary for a few days. There were several departments under the control of Development Secretary. A notification under the Criminal Procedure Code was issued empowering me as District Magistrate for the entire Union Territory. Somehow it was called District Magistrate (Independent) in order to distinguish it from the judicial District Magistrate. Perhaps a more appropriate designation would have been District Magistrate (Executive). The Departments of Health, Education and Welfare were taken away from me and given to a new secretary, J. Anjani Dayanand, from the Tamil Nadu cadre, who later became chief secretary. **She was an ardent Ashramite and the Lt. Governor had certain hesitation before taking her on deputation. But eventually he agreed. Incidentally, there is no such hesitation these days. A business- tycoon's son or son-in-law is appointed to the most sensitive post of Revenue Secretary or Finance Secretary to the Government of India or even in the PMO!**

The powers of the Collector were vested in different Administrators. The powers had to be withdrawn and vested in me by a notification. At that time only did I realise the enormous powers being exercised by a Collector. There were about 200 and odd Acts mentioned specifically in annexure to the Notification indicating the powers of the Collector. In other words, wherever the institution of the Collector was mentioned in these Acts, the Collector had some powers to exercise. Apart from the well-known Arms Act, Cinematograph Act and the Indian Railways Act, etc. the Collector had some role to play under the other Acts. It also included the Indian Lunacy Act, Forest Act, Wildlife Act, Postal Act, etc. The Collector could stop a train moving out of a station by issuing an order to the railway authorities in a law and order situation or prevent a plane from taking off and, in fact, one of my colleagues had to do this in Bihar. The Collector and District Magistrate could also prevent a telegram or letter being dispatched under certain circumstances. The last one was done by one of my colleagues in Haryana during the Emergency and he had to pay a price for

it later. Thus, these powers were all vested in a single functionary – perhaps the most powerful official in the entire world. But these powers are expected to be exercised carefully, without even consulting the chief minister or government. The District Magistrate-cum-Collector should exercise his judicial mind. The public have become naturally highly critical when a Collector went on signing orders under the 'Gundas' (notorious criminals) Act at the behest of the government. When the Venkatasubba Reddiar Ministry was tottering, they wanted to give a twist to it as often politicians do on such occasions. Reddiar and Kangeyan, a respected and competent minister who was good at Tamil, French and English and who thought well of me even after I left Pondicherry – called me and asked me to impose Section 144 Cr.P.C., in the Ashram area, which I refused point blank. The same night, the Reddiar ministry fell. Because of our heavy schedule, we always used to go to the late night cinema show. I was called out by the Lt. Governor – I always used to tell my whereabouts to my servant at home in those days of no mobile phone – from the show and the papers were rushed to Delhi for imposition of President's rule.

Reddiar was a noble man. His son also became chief minister years later. His son-in-law was one Bhaskaran. He applied for a post in the department of agriculture. People knew that I would go purely by merit and told my minister, Subbiah, a highly respected Communist, that I would select or equally rule out Bhaskaran not just because he was Reddiar's son-in-law. Bhaskaran did well in the interview and I gave him the job. Subbiah did not interfere with my decision because he was always fair.

I should also mention here Farook's political rival in Congress, P. Shanmugham, a fine person. He was no match to Farook in political manoeuvres and as a result could not become chief minister for long years although he was an M.P., I was glad that he became chief minister at last in 2000 or so.

In the short-lived Venkatasubba Reddiar ministry, one Nagarajan was the minister. He was a humble person who managed to become an MLA. P. Shanmugham was staying with him and the rumour was that he was disposing of the files and Nagarajan was just signing! At that time, there was a royal barber! I call him a royal-barber because he was making the Lt. Governor and other big-wigs in Pondy including me presentable. He always used such occasions to influence us on some matter or the other. I was reminded of Cheiro's observation in his book on palmistry that one would be an influential royal-barber if one barber had the line of Apollo or sun on his palm and it would not mean that the barber would become the king. This barber's nephew was a peon in the co-operative department and was alleged to have been involved in a murder case and was jailed for three years. The royal-barber's contention was that he was really innocent and was wrongly framed; so he should be re-instated in service. Since he was prodding the Lt. Governor almost every fortnight when he was trimming and decorating him, the Lt. Governor told me to look into it again, although the request had been rejected a few times earlier. I too, in my youthful enthusiasm felt that why should not I give new life to a man and a prisoner should not remain a prisoner throughout his life; this would be an experiment in prisoner-reform; but this should not be quoted as a precedent.

I wrote a note to this effect and marked it to Nagarajan, the minister for co-operation, and the LG for approval. But Shanmugham came in the way and made Nagarajan over-rule me after explaining the position to me. Shanmugham knew where the influence was coming from and more than that he was a stickler for rules and norms; he rightly felt this case might open a Pandora's box. After a year or so, Farook was the chief minister again. When I entered his chamber, I saw a man sitting outside his room whom I could not readily recognize. Farook told me that it was my once minister .Nagarajan who was seeking a peon's post because he had nothing to live on. But Farook rightly felt that it was not proper to give a peon's post to an ex-minister and gave him the post of a librarian. (**What a contrast to the present day MLAs or MPs, let alone Ministers!)**

Apart from being a Collector and District Magistrate, I had a whole range of departments like Agriculture, Animal Husbandry, Cooperation, Industry, Civil Supplies and so on. Almost nearly half of the Government was with me. This provided ample opportunities not only to discharge regulatory functions like arms licensing and cinema licensing, but also to perform a wide range of development functions.

The institution of Collector and District Magistrate was unknown to Pondicherry at that time. In fact, I was better known as Development Secretary. This resulted once in a funny situation. Pondicherry was noted for interesting cultural programmes. Many cine artists and theatre personalities from Madras used to come and perform there. They came there not only to spread culture, but also to have spirituous inspiration since Tamil Nadu was 'dry' then with 'prohibition'. So when the famous film star, Padmini, who was our neighbour in Madras came there, she naturally wanted to meet us and enquired for my whereabouts as Collector and District Magistrate. The attendant and the manager in the government guest house told her that there was no such person. She was somewhat aghast because the Collector and District magistrate was not known in that place. But the manager immediately caught on and clarified that I was also the Development Secretary and I was known by that designation only. So I had to sort of publicise the post in Pondicherry.

The revenue administration was totally different because the French system was still in vogue. The Indian revenue laws were yet to be extended. The Revenue Department was known as the Contributions Department and the head was known as the CCD (Chef de Service Contribution). So the concept was completely different in the sense that the people contributed revenue although 'Contribution' in French also meant 'tax' and it was not collected as was in British India. I was asked by the Lt. Governor within a few months after my arrival about some loss of revenue to the exchequer because some revenue officials failed to collect land revenue. During a long drawn inquiry, it transpired that the officials of the Revenue Department had no concept of collection of revenue at all and they were not trained for the purpose. So they collected whatever 'contribution' came in, but allowed the assessment to lapse after a period of three years. So I recommended to the Lt. Governor practically to exonerate them with a simple warning because of the prevailing legal situation.

Similarly, the office of Registration was known as 'Hypothecation'. The French registration, survey and settlement laws were still in force. There was also some local resistance to change these laws. The Lt. Governor was rather eager and he was almost having a running battle in the Assembly. The Leader of the Opposition, E. Goubert, always used to state that why we were so anxious to introduce these new laws which were actually the alien laws of the English and not the Indian laws. Of course, no one was aware in Pondicherry that the Indian Civil Service itself was an Indian concept copied later in England. There is no institution of Collector in England and it is more akin to the Prefect in France. The civil service examinations were also introduced in England after they were conceptualised in India for the Indian administration.

Consequently, the Lt. Governor had placed the responsibility upon me to replace all the French revenue laws. I had to contact frequently the Government of Tamil Nadu and draw hundreds of personnel for introducing these laws in the Legislature with the obligatory translations in French, Tamil, Telugu and Malayalam and implement on the ground. These contacts with the Government of Tamil Nadu and had naturally to be at the highest level. So whenever I met my batchmates in Tamil Nadu, I used to tell them jocularly that I was there to meet my counterparts who were Secretaries to Government and not the small fries. It was due to the dedication of the officials drawn from Tamil Nadu and also the cooperation of the local officials particularly Subbaraya Pillai, who as the CCD and eventually promoted to the IAS, that a smooth implementation of replacement of the French revenue laws was done within a short period of time. Apart from the establishment of a normal revenue system with Tahsildars, Village Munsifs and Karnams, many other allied departments like Registration, Weights and Measures and Survey and Settlement were established.

The Department of Agriculture also had its own expansion programmes with many officers, agricultural engineers, and scientists drawn from the neighbouring Tamil Nadu. There was a conference of the Agriculture Secretaries of the Southern States in Pondicherry. **Secretary, Agriculture of the Government of India, an ICS man was, impressed with my work that without my asking** recommended me for a FAO post in Rome. Of course, this did not come through as usual. But by a strange coincidence my posting to Brussels some years later was also from the Ministry of Agriculture.

The department of cooperation as usual had its own scandals. The president of the Cooperative Marketing Society, D. Ramachandran, used to take me to lay some foundation stone or the other and to open some building during the President's rule in Pondicherry. He became a chief minister a few years later.

My predecessor Vaidyanathan had planned a dairy for Pondicherry. I had made arrangements to execute it during my tenure. I had brought in the National Dairy Development Board as consultants to execute the project. Pondicherry administration was also procedure-ridden in a way that any transfer of money to another government organisation would require the approval of the Home Ministry of the Government of India which was long drawn because they had to consult the ministries concerned in Delhi. In order to cut short this delay, I transferred the money to the local Cooperative Milk Marketing Society, which, in turn, placed the money at the disposal of the NDDB. So the dairy became possible although it was actually executed during my successor's time. I had left Pondicherry after completing all the formalities like the land allotment and laying the foundation. We also planned to introduce distribution of milk in sachets, which was a novel concept unheard of in India then; it was to be done by a French Company through the NDDB. In these tasks, under secretary Pajanissamy (Palaniswamy in English or Tamil) was of great assistance to me. He is still in touch with me. His French is also very good.

The Act and Rules regarding the land reforms were introduced rather late because they were stalled by the local agricultural gentry who were powerful. As in other parts of India, by the time the Act and the Rules were passed and notified, it remained only an exercise on paper, lands having been brought already within the Land Ceiling Act limits.

Pondicherry did not have many industries except for one or two languishing industrial estates and five composite textile

mills. One of them in Mahe ran into trouble; I was one of the members of the investigating team appointed by the Ministry of Commerce to suggest a solution. Chief Minister Farook and I used to try hard for attracting new industries to Pondicherry. Whenever we went to Delhi, we talked to the French Ambassador without much result. We requested the Ministry of Defence to establish an ordnance factory which was not agreed to. When we saw some reports about a Free Port, we wrote to the Government of India to establish it there. At our request the Development Commissioner, Small Scale Industries and the National Small Industries Corporation, conducted an industries intensive campaign, which attracted hundreds of applications. We started another industrial estate in Pondicherry and another one in Karaikal.

The Finance Secretary, one of my batchmates, particularly made it a point to oppose all my proposals. He was close to the chief secretary and tried to snatch the post of Collector and District Magistrate from me. But, since the Chief Minister Farook was close to me, he did not agree to his request. In fact, he did not know much about these manoevres of the bureaucracy and the importance of the posts during his first tenure as chief minister. So once he asked me why others were asking only for my post of Collector and District Magistrate. I explained it to him. The chief secretary also made a move through the Home Ministry during the President's rule again to take away the post from me and hand it over to my batchmate. The chief secretary told the Lt. Governor that I would be an ideal secretary to him. But the Lt. Governor also felt that I could also continue as Collector and District Magistrate while being his secretary. **This was an unexpected development and the chief secretary resiled from the proposal by some other manoeuvres. This was the first time I had a taste of bureaucratic manoeuvres by colleagues which of course became a common feature later in one's career, particularly in Delhi. So I had to get the finance secretary overruled by the Lt. Governor on the question of sanction of a five-year sales tax holiday for new industries. This gave some boost to the industrialisation of Pondicherry.**

There was a very old distillery from French government days producing only arrack, which was sold in auctions. There was some idea to scrap this old distillery and have a new one. But the proposal to have a new one, particularly during the Gandhi Centenary Year, would not go through with the Government of India. So I called it modernisation of the old distillery and obtained approval of the Planning Commission of the Government of India. In fact, it was a new distillery and since there was no expertise to build a new one in Pondicherry, I was looking for an expert. During a chance conversation with a relative of mine in Delhi who was working as Finance Director of the Engineers India Limited, I got an idea that the Engineers India Limited could do this job. So I got the necessary approvals for entrusting this job on turnkey basis through the 100% Government owned Engineers India Limited. **In fact, even the present Engineers India Ltd., may not be aware that this was the first Government project of M/s. Engineers India Ltd., a Government of India undertaking and the then Chairman Rao and Technical Director M.S. Pathak were enthusiastic about it.** After finalisation of arrangements including the financial aspects, I asked Pathak, who became chairman by then, to come down to Pondicherry to sign the agreement lest it be torpedoed out of sheer jealousy after my departure from Pondicherry. **His father was the Vice President of India who had also come to Pondicherry a few months earlier to open a super-market named by me as 'Amudhasurabhi'; naturally the younger Pathak stayed with the Lt. Governor B.D. Jatti. He was happy to sign the agreement.** The finance secretary who was my batchmate tried to raise some unnecessary points after my departure but the Chief Minister and the Lt. Governor overruled him. But he himself somewhat fell out later with his mentor, the chief secretary and had to face the problem of having to pay a sizable amount for his rented official accommodation. Chief Minister Farook was always kind to the officials and he had the knack of taking work out of the bureaucracy. So he came to the rescue of this officer by giving the file to him. He asked him to record a note as though it was done by Farook himself. Thus he baled out my colleague out of this necessity of having to pay a few hundred rupees extra.

Farook was a handsome, nice person who had drawn sword with the bureaucracy during his tenure as Speaker and thereby got into the clutches of a wily Lt. Governor. He once told me that after learning this lesson, he became friendly with the bureaucracy and tried to take the best out of them. He was successful in this game and remained the chief minister of the territory for a long time. He belonged to a rich Muslim family in Karaikal with overseas business connections. He was completely secular in approach and visited the temples at Karaikal, Rameswaram, Tirupati and so on. He was also a good astrologer and I used to consult him now and then. His brother was even more well conversant in astrology and it was almost an obsession with him. Whenever he had spare time, he used to call astrologers and discuss with them; not a day passed without looking at the stars. Farook became a Union Minister of State some years later when I was also in Delhi as Additional Secretary in the Ministry of Commerce. (He always had an eye on the ambassadorship to Saudi Arabia – Holy land for Muslims – right from his Pondy days as chief minister. Although he was very good at political manoeuvres, he used to feel tired at times at this constant politicking. He used to ask me whether he could try for Saudi Arabia. I told him that would be political hara-kiri for a young politician like him. But he achieved it in 2005 when his political career was almost over.)

During his tenure as Chief Minister, he wanted to put down firmly the liquor lobby, which was meddling in local politics. Lt. Governor S.L. Silam from Bombay was a wiry, slim and tall man sporting a moustache with somewhat a comical appearance. He was earlier the Speaker of the Bombay Legislative Assembly. He was wily in his approach and played one politician against the other in Pondicherry so that he could remain on top. He was also keen on finishing the machinations of the liquor lobby.

The Pondicherry Assembly consisted of only 30 members and it was always a delicate balance between the Congress having 16 or 17 seats, and the other parties the remaining seats particularly the Communists. One or two independents always played havoc by crossing the floor, either for a liquor licence or for money. The Assembly used to be held generally once in six months according to the statute and would adjourn immediately. Some MLAs were kidnapped on the eve of the sessions and kept in the neighbouring Madras with the

connivance of the local government and local police and brought in only on the morning of the Session so that they did not cross the floor. So the liquor auctions according to the old French system in what was known as 'Cahier des charges' had to be changed. This was changed by the Lt. Governor in spite of the opposition from the local ruling party. At that time, Farook was not the Chief Minister. Whenever there was a difference of opinion between the local government and the Lt. Governor, the matter had to be referred to the Home Ministry of the Government of India. So on one such occasion, the Lt. Governor overruled the local cabinet on the basis of a note he told me to record and the matter was referred to the Home Ministry in Delhi. As Secretary to Government, I was functioning directly under the Lt. Governor and did not have to go through the Chief Secretary. This was the system for a long time. So I was apprehensive that I had come down south on a posting after having taken all the trouble but I should not be axed by the politicians in this kind of a wrangle. However, luckily for me, they were also well disposed towards me and also went out of office within a short time. Silam was fully in charge and his policy was upheld by the Central Government.

However, the liquor lobby challenged the Administration in the courts of law. Incidentally, the local judicial system was both on the French and the Indian pattern. The Indian pattern was slowly being introduced. The Chief of the Judiciary known in French as Chef de Service Judiciare used to call himself the Chief Justice. But the Pondicherry cases used to go to an ICS Judge in the Madras High Court who knew French well. He promptly pulled up the Chief of the Judiciary in Pondicherry who was only a Sessions Judge in Tamil Nadu for wrongly translating his designation as Chief Justice. The Madras High Court issued orders that he should call himself 'the Chief of the Judiciary' by the correct translation from French to English. So when the liquor case was handled within the Pondicherry administration, the Law Secretary was somewhat a wobbly person by nature and his actions were not free from local influence. He recorded a note almost opposing the policy laid down by us on the file. But the Lt. Governor wanted me to give

him a draft note overruling the Law Secretary. Lt. Governor Silam never dictated a note. He always wanted draft notes from the Secretaries and copied them personally in red ink and signed them so that it looked as though it was his own note on the file. When the case came up in the High Court of Madras, challenged by a number of liquor merchants from Pondicherry, he told me to be present in the High Court personally myself so that the government pleader would also present the case properly. When the government pleader was arguing the case, by some mistake and forgetfulness he gave the file itself to the judge. The judge stopped the proceedings for about five minutes and read the entire note portion. My heart sank because, I thought as a judge and legal person, he would agree with the law secretary's opinion and we would lose the case. In my heart I was cursing the government pleader for this stupid mistake of his. But, to my utter surprise, the judge came down heavily upon the liquor merchants and dismissed their petitions straightaway. He also paid a compliment to the Lt. Governor for having taken the trouble of writing a note in his own long hand! That was the first occasion I learnt that at times writing a note on tricky issues in long hand indicated application of one's mind and created a good impression. I saw some years later Ambassador Davé adopting a similar practice in Brussels on a tricky though small issue, which would have attracted Audit's attention. But the Auditor did not object because Ambassador Davé had applied his mind and took the trouble of recording a note in his own long hand! Dictated notes some times may give an impression that some other person recorded it or the party wanting a favour recorded it and the higher officer simply signed. Whereas a note in long hand indicates a conscious decision. In this regard, Farook was not noted for good English although he was a graduate from the Loyola College and whenever a note came from him in good English, Lt Governor Silam thought it was written by his personal secretary Somasundaram. Chief Secretary Anjani Dayanand and I were left red-faced once when Farook as chief minister wanted us to take a visiting lady-dignitary, who was the head of a government, in an open car (no security problems those days) because "she was after all a public woman", he said.

Although the liquor policy was kept at bay for some years, it got itself revived later. The distillery was an accomplished affair, which I was happy to see on a visit to Pondicherry. They were also producing good rum, which was marketed in different parts of India. It was my intention to export it. But the powerful liquor lobby from Karnataka with a notional base in Pondicherry for tax purposes, which was to play a major role in the Karnataka administration later, bought over the politicians in Pondicherry and stopped production of rum lest it would pose competition to this firm's production in Karnataka. So the distillery was selling only arrack and industrial alcohol although it was functioning well.

While at Pondicherry, I always wondered why Mr. Silam was writing in red ink, but I discovered later that in the old Bombay and the present Maharashtra and Gujarat, the chief ministers used red ink, the ministers green ink and others blue ink by a government order so that it could be distinguished.

Wily Lt. Governor Silam did not want to part with lands for Auroville easily. Unlike Karaikal, Pondicherry is not a compact or contiguous territory. There are many enclaves of Tamil Nadu interspersed with those of Pondicherry. Even some houses are partly in Pondicherry and partly in Tamil Nadu so that in olden days fugitives from law took easy shelter in Pondicherry. Silam alerted the Government of Tamil Nadu about the need to take care of the roadways, canals and water channels flowing from the Tamil Nadu territory to Pondicherry while leasing land for Auroville. However, Government of Tamil Nadu did not take a long time to lease lands for the project. Silam dragged the matter and an Auroville Committee was formed with him as the head and me as the member-secretary. I took a firm view that the Pondicherry administration should provide lands on a 99 year lease basis, which the committee approved. But, after the meeting, Silam told me that he thought that I would take a bureaucratic negative view on the subject so that he could intervene and take credit and I did not provide him that opportunity. Of course, he liked me and my work and he made these remarks in good humour and not in anger.

Silam was succeeded by B.D. Jatti, a short but sharp person. He was always fond of telling that he was more of an administrator than a politician. **He rose from the position of a village panchayat president in his native village Jamkandi to the position of acting President of India at a crucial moment of Indian history when he had to exercise enormous power and take certain crucial decisions.** He was deeply religious with 'viboodhi' (ash) on his forehead. He refused to use the kitchen in the 'Raj Niwas' used by non-vegetarian Silam. He was also a pious and religious person. He was reputed to be an honest politician. When I happened to call on Rajaji once in Madras with my brother-in-law, S. Krishnamurti, who was secretary to Rajaji earlier, Rajaji spoke highly of B.D. Jatti. When I was posted in New Delhi some years later, he was the Vice-President and I did not want to disturb a person in such a high position. Some common friends however told me that he had enquired about me. So I called on him. Whenever I wanted to meet him later, he always received me during his evening walks even if he had no time otherwise.

But a posting in Pondicherry might pose a problem at times. Although one does a lot of work there, the other persons may have an impression that it is only a cushy posting without much work. This problem was compounded by the Lt. Governor writing the CRs of the officers. In the Union Territory set up, the Lt. Governor who is the Administrator under the Act is all powerful and consequently the Chief Minister and his team always suffer from a complex. Lt. Governor Silam was in the habit of writing only one or two sentences in the CR, which was not enough for the Government of India. At a particular point of time, Lt. Governor Jatti told chief secretary Anjani Dayanand not to hand over a particular file to the chief minister Farook. Farook was annoyed and left for Delhi and got the powers to write the CRs of the chief secretary. In that process, the secretaries came under the control of the chief secretary who started writing the CRs. Years later, this to a certain extent was to affect my promotion in the government of India under the 'panel system'. More on this later.

* * *

9

New Horizons in Brussels

The Administrative Reforms Commission submitted its report in 1968 and suggested certain structural changes and specialisation in the civil services. Following this, I also pleaded for a unified civil service in the IIPA journal of the Pondicherry branch which I was editing at that time. Although nothing much came out of the Report, because of some thoughtful minutes of dissent in the report in order to preserve the unity of the country through the All India Services, it impelled many IAS officers to specialise in some area or the other. This was also combined with an urge to go abroad and study in a good university. So many officers applied for scholarships through the Scholarships Division of the Ministry of Education of the Government of India, the British Council, the U.S. Educational Foundation, etc.

I had also applied for a scholarship to go to the East-West Centre in Hawaii. After an interview and group discussion, I was placed first on the list of selectees. But the East-West Centre did not give admission because they erroneously thought that the B.A. (Hons.,) course of the University of Madras was equivalent only to a B.A., Prof. D.N. Rao of the U.S. Educational Foundation, Madras, who was also earlier in the Academy in Mussoorie, clarified this point stating that the Honours carried greater weight than the M.A., course. But it took almost a year for the clarification to be accepted.

Meanwhile, I thought that it might be more useful to specialise in the EEC matters by getting a scholarship to go to Belgium, since many IAS officers had already gone to the East-West and other US Universities. Moreover, knowledge of French was essential to go to Belgium which I had acquired in Pondicherry. Accordingly, I applied for a fellowship through the Ministry of Education to go to the University of Brussels. It was sanctioned after the usual interview.

I was to reach Brussels in the month of September, 1969. I was reluctant to leave Pondicherry and was in two minds. But chief minister Farook persuaded me to take up this fellowship because it might be useful in the long run. At the same time, he wanted me to stay on and also promised a change of cadre. But I deeply weighed the pros and cons between localising or internationalising myself. The Minister-Counsellor in the Belgian Embassy in Delhi, Noppen granted an extension till January, 1970 to make up my mind and proceed to Brussels. Noppen's daughter, Christina became Ambassador of Belgium in New Delhi when I was Additional Secretary in the Ministry of Commerce. In fact, she had studied in Delhi and also had a stint earlier as Second or First Secretary in Delhi.

So I left Pondicherry in January, 1970 although it was a difficult decision. The Government of Gujarat as usual granted only leave due and not even study leave. This policy was later changed by that government at my instance when I returned, although the benefit was not given to me. But others were benefitted. Taking this benefit, Dr. T.K. Jayaraman had gone to the East-West for the second time, this time on study leave.

I stayed with a relative of mine in Bombay for a couple of days before taking off for Brussels in January, 1970. After crossing the immigration, my relative left the airport. There was some confusion on account of a hockey team travelling by the Air-India flight, each one having heavy personal luggage. So they wanted us to go out again and weigh our personal baggage also. I had some books with me and my personal baggage was heavy. I had to jettison them and request my relative to collect them the next day. Luckily, the thoughtful agent of the SBI in Pondicherry had given me a cheque book and I paid the Air-India by cheque for some excess baggage. However, it was an unpleasant experience with the Air-India during my first travel abroad.

The plane stopped in Beirut. We could go only to the duty-free shopping centre. Beirut of those days was a lively place, which I had visited later. French was the main language although English was also understood. It was the main banking centre in the Middle East. Currencies from all over the world, including the Indian rupees were freely accepted and changed by the numerous money changers. It was also a place for the Muslims of the Middle-East to free themselves from orthodoxy and freak out. The casino was world famous. But after a few years, this beautiful place was spoiled and destroyed.

I had to get off the Air-India plane at Geneva. When they announced that the temperature was zero, my blood almost froze. It was a wrong part of the year in January to undertake a trip to Europe by a first-time traveller. However, the airport was beautifully situated in the midst of mountains. The sky was overcast but the planes had no difficulty in landing and taking off. It was a clean airport with clean bathrooms and toilets.

The flight to Brussels took about an hour. On arrival I was received by an official of the Ministry of Education. The taxi driver was also with the official and he was so well dressed that I mistook him for another official of the Ministry of Education. The official concerned took me by that taxi to the Ministry of Education which was not very far off and paid me the scholarship for the first month. She had already reserved my accommodation in a small hotel nearby where the proprietrix was an English woman. Students from India and other English-speaking countries were lodged in that small hotel for the first few days because of the need for interacting in English. When I enquired from her for a bathroom to have a bath which was important for we Indians after a long journey, she told me, to my horror, that there was no bathroom in that hotel. Later I learnt that there were many such small hotels in Europe and England without a bathroom or a shower.

Since this hotel was giving only breakfast, she showed me a restaurant where people understood English. Although I could speak French, perhaps there was some difficulty of accent in the first few days. I discovered that this restaurant was situated on the famous Rond Point Schuman with the famous 'Berlaymont' building of the EEC on the other side. So I could have a first look at this building and the institution on this cold and gray afternoon, which was to play many an important role in my life.

I contacted V. Krishnaswamy, who was an IAS officer from the Tamil Nadu cadre, in charge of the local office of the Cashew Export Promotion Council. T.V. Antony of the same cadre was in this post earlier. Krishnaswamy told me to come to cocktails at his residence the same evening so that I could meet the cross section of the Indian community in Brussels. I took a taxi although, it was quite a bit on my small pocket of a student, and reached his spacious apartment on Avenue Louise. His apartment was just in front of the Olympic Airways. Avenue Louise is a famous thoroughfare in Brussels which one has to pass through to go to different places with the tram lines running in between. The Olympic Airways is still situated in the same place, and whenever I went there which was on numerous occasions over years later, I always remembered Krishnaswamy and his apartment and that cold evening. With the passage of years and increase in traffic, Avenue Louise lost its importance as a residential area and people started moving out to the suburbs. However, some old families like that of Prof. Hatry still live there in their ancestral homes.

It was a farewell party to Ambassador T. Swaminathan who was leaving for India the next day to take over as secretary, Industries. In fact, he was known to my in-laws. Malcolm Subhan, who wrote for *The Economic Times* was also there. He was also working in the South East Asian Centre of the University of Brussels. Mr. & Mrs. Mukherjee of the Tea Board were also there who were an institution in Brussels. Mukherjee was supposed to be a class-mate of Swaminathan and had close links with him. As a result, he was not paying much attention to the other officers of the Embassy and they were quite sore about it. There were the usual bickering between the Embassy and the Government of India offices outside. Even Krishnaswamy had his own problems, particularly with

Ambassador Swaminathan. It was a fashion for many of them to talk about the EEC in intimate terms because it was like the United Nations Organisation in New York. In fact, the EEC officials were getting about 15% over and above the UN scales of pay. So all this was naturally something strange to a newcomer like me. At the end of the cocktails, Mr. & Mrs. Krishnaswamy gave me South Indian food and requested his accounts officer Jagannath to get me back to my hotel. Jagannath took me to his small apartment on the way, although it was late in the night and he personally walked with me to my hotel. Jagannath joined later the Air-India in Brussels and settled there comfortably. He even bought a house and I attended the 'Grahapravesam' (house-warming) with my wife during our second stint in Brussels. Another person in the Air-India I met was Jagdish Manickam who had gone to Belgium earlier as an ace player of hockey from India and also as a coach. The Air-India had a direct service to Brussels from Bombay at that time and the flight used to carry Indian vegetables for the Embassy and the other Indians also used to get it by turn. Jagdish was good enough to put me also on the list although I was only a student. Mrs. Jagdish was from Bangalore and both of them were extremely hospitable. They had two charming daughters. Our association continues even now. Jagdish is the longest living Indian in Belgium. He will complete half a century there next year!

I went to the University the next day and reported to Prof. Guy Spitaels, a labour economist in the tall Sociology building on Avenue Jeanne, which housed many departments. Malcolm Subhan's South East Asia Centre was also located in this building. Spitaels became the Deputy Prime Minister of Belgium later and I met him when I was posted in the Embassy there. Spitaels told me that the department would decide about my exact work and I should meet one Prof. (Mrs) Duprez. She was rather a peculiar lady although she was all right otherwise. She had visited Bombay once and felt that the poverty and slums around the Santa Cruz airport were rather appalling. Although she knew English fairly well, some time the usage was funny in the sense that instead of using the word 'appalling or striking', she used the word 'impressive' for the French 'impressionner' while talking about the slums.

She straightway ruled out a Ph.D. for me although the fellowship was for a Ph. D., because it would take about four years. The Department of Economics also had a bad experience with an Indian student and the Indian Embassy at that time. This I came to know later. A student from Bihar went there to do a Ph.D., and he already had a prepared thesis with him. After staying for about a year, he started applying pressure through the Ambassador for a Ph.D. which the Ambassador, in all his kindness particularly for those from Bihar, did. The Embassy wrote a letter to the Head of the Department impressing upon them the need to give a Ph.D., at short notice. The academic world there was very particular about the academic autonomy and they were naturally appalled by this letter. In fact, it was all left to the individual professors to teach the student without any interference. In other words, the professor was all-in-all. So this student from Bihar had to be turned out. What was more appalling was that he managed to get admission in the University of Ghent in Belgium by taking the help of the local Honorary Consul General of India who was a Belgian. So, since I was a government servant, they wanted to be on guard from the beginning. She also felt that it would be more useful for me to do an M. Phil., (Licence Special) for a year on the EEC which had all features including macro-economics, foreign trade, politics, EEC law, etc., It was a composite course in the Institute of European Studies involving all important departments including the Institute of Applied Economic Research. She told me that this course would take only one year. I could also perhaps usefully do a 'stage' (training) at the EEC, which would be useful from my career point of view. By then I was also worried about the weather conditions in Belgium and settled for her suggestion.

After settling these matters, I looked for an Indian student. One was Narasimhan working for Ph. D., in the Department of Botany. He readily took me to his land-lady who had a good apartment of two rooms in a house overlooking a lake. Although the rent she was demanding was somewhat high, I requested her to settle it for me straightaway because of the comfort and also the beautiful view overlooking the lake and a church on the other side. This building is on one side of the small lake on Avenue du Generale de Gaulle with swans and winter birds. In that house too, there was no proper bathroom, but Narasimhan had done up one for him and his wife although it was a complicated contraption, he made the land-lady buy. So I could not have my bath there too for the second day. I met another student, James from Kerala working for a Ph. D., in Botany in another institute. He suggested that I could move into one of the rooms in his house near the University for a few days before my apartment would be ready. His apartment had a good shower attached and it was a great relief to have a bath there and move out of the hotel.

The next day I did the customary reporting to the Embassy and met some diplomats who later became life-long friends. Shashank was particularly good whom I had already met at Krishnaswamy's cocktails. Since his wife Kalpana was away in India, he took me home for dinner and also showed me a bit of Brussels by night. Ranjit Sethi, another Second Secretary, who spoke flawless French and Chinese became an Ambassador to France years later. Association with the Shashanks continued and it turned out to be a close friendship between our two families. As the Georges sustained our spirits in Palanpur, the Shashanks sustained us during our difficult days as a student on a shoe-string budget in Brussels. However, we did not take any monetary help from them.

After a few days, I moved into the apartment on Avenue du Generale de Gaulle. The land-lady Cambier Libbrecht was exceedingly good and she particularly liked the Indians because they were quiet as compared with the African students. In fact, when my wife joined, she was exceedingly helpful to her by doing the shopping, taking the clothes to the laundry, cleaning, etc., which a normal Belgian would not do particularly for an Indian or for a black person. She absolutely had no bias for colour. She was simply surprised to see a tall and healthy vegetarian and told many of her friends in the same street about this miracle man. Our association became very close and I invariably visited her whenever I went to Brussels later. On one or two occasions, I even stayed at her place. Her husband, who lived practically in a village died later. Since she was not prepared to live in a village, she was managing this house for a rich man who owned many houses in Brussels. We had never seen this rich man because he never bothered to visit and see the house as people or landlords do here. Whatever she wanted to do in the house, she could do and he paid for it. She never went to a church. She told us that she was through two world wars and if a man could perpetrate so much of atrocity on fellow human beings, there was no God. She was never happy to see a German in her house when a friend of mine came.

The winter was rather long drawn in Europe that year. It was quite depressing for a person from a warm and sunny country not to see the sun at all for months together and also the bleak leafless trees standing everywhere. Whenever I felt depressed, my landlady used to assure me that there would be a sudden splurge of leaves and the trees would be full of leaves within a few months. The entire scene would get itself transformed. She also used to tell me jocularly that I could even have a bath in the lake opposite in summer although it was not done or permitted. True to her word, the entire scene changed in the month of May. The trees had so much of leaves sprouting and there was lush green vegetation. It looked as though a green carpet was laid in front of our house and the church presented picture-card beauty. The winter birds, which came from the Polar regions to escape the biting cold there disappeared from the lake in summer. They went back. People used to spend time under the sun by sitting on the banks of the lake and fishing.

The University was not very far. The Institute of European Studies was situated on Avenue Franklin Roosevelt. Many streets and Avenues in Brussels carry the names of world war heroes and leaders. The Free University of Brussels was founded as a religion-free University with free or liberal thinking unlike the ancient Catholic University at Louvain. The University of Louvain was also known as the Cambridge of the Continent.

The classes in the University were quite instructive. Many classes used to start at 8 o'clock in the morning and some late in the evenings, because many professors worked elsewhere too particularly in the EEC or in Government. For instance, Paul Hatry, the professor of Foreign Trade, was working for the Federation of Petroleum Companies in Belgium. He was their chief negotiator. At the same time, he was a Senator of the Liberal Party and became the Finance Minister of Belgium when I was posted there. The president of the university – similar to Vice-Chancellor- Henri Simonet who taught us public finance was also the Foreign Minister of Belgium and the Mayor of Anderlecht, a part of Brussels. Similarly some other professors were Ambassadors.

The faculty of the Institute of European Studies had also an impressive array. It included the Father of European Union, Paul Henri Spaak and Jean Rey who was the then President of the European Economic Commission.

The Drew University of the United States used to draw students from different universities in the U.S.A., and conducted a six month course in English on European affairs in the Institute of European Studies. So whenever I had difficulty in following a particular lecture in French, I used to listen to the same lecture in English sitting in the Drew University class. In this regard, there was perfect freedom for the students.

There was also a system of 'free students' (eleves libres) in the University where students like me could attend whatever course I liked. If I passed the examination, I would be given a certificate to the effect of having passed in those subjects. If one had not passed, the certificate would simply say that one just attended those courses. But I wanted to take a degree because of the emphasis upon degrees in our country whatever be the worth of those degrees. The complete course included about twenty four papers. The examinations were mostly oral although it was left to the professors to have a written examination or a combination of both. One had to write a thesis also for the degree. My thesis was on 'the Indo-EEC trade' on which there was also an oral examination with three professors, Paul Hatry, Duprez and another nice lady Poelmans Kirschen who also worked in the Belgian Foreign Office as a Director. Her husband was the chief professor who wrote a book in English, 'Economic Policy in our Times' giving the theoretical aspects of economic policy too.

My wife joined me three months later. She was there for about twelve months by leaving three months early, and I was there for eighteen months. It was a shoe-string budget. Luckily for her, the Belgian Radio Station was just opposite our house. There was an English woman who was kind to her and made her broadcast every week over the external services of the Belgian Radio beamed towards Africa, the U.S.A., and Latin America. This kept us going and we could also visit quite a few places in Europe.

My wife had gained some experience of broadcasting in Pondicherry and she was actually carrying a certificate to that effect from the Station Director of All India Radio, Pondicherry. The Director of Belgian Radio did not want to see the certificate. They simply told her to read a passage in the studio, which the Director was listening to in his room on another floor without her knowledge. He could easily make out that she was not broadcasting for the first time or mike-shy.

The examinations were held in the month of July and luckily I made the grade in all the subjects except one which was macro-economics. It was highly mathematical. Since it was only one subject where my marks were a bit low, they decided to award the degree to me. They were satisfied with my thesis and placed a copy in the central library which is there even today. As soon as the jury announced the award of degree to a few students, the Belgian students immediately disappeared from the place. They were not in the habit of collecting the certificate or even the degree. No convocations are held in the University of Brussels except for conferment of Honoris Causa on some distinguished dignitary or the other once in a few years. But to satisfy people back home, only a student from Latin America and I stayed behind and requested for a certificate. The Institute gave it in English to me. The degree was sent a few months later signed by numerous professors and also the Rector of the University. The Belgian students were not keen on collecting the degrees because their word was taken for truth and it was also a verifiable fact, which could be done directly with the university as the director in the Belgian Radio had tested my wife for her skills in broadcasting without looking into any certificate.

The academic work in the university was between September 1970 and July 1971. Meanwhile, between April and September, 1970, I did a 'stage' (training) in the Foreign Trade Division of the EEC. There was no Ambassador in the Embassy of India because Ambassador B.R. Patel was posted after a few months from the time of departure of Ambassador Swaminathan. The interregnum was filled by Chargé d'Affaires, Kesavan, a Mysore Aiyangar related to H.V.R. Iengar, married to a German lady. After retirement he settled in Hamburg. He was kind enough to give a letter to the EEC recommending my training. So I became the first Indian trainee although, before acceptance of my candidature, I was asked to meet a high official who was not all that friendly with India. This was done by Klaus Ewig and von O'svath just to have some fun at my expense. But I was admitted to the course starting on April 1st, 1970. In fact, they were happy to have an Indian.

The trainees were also given a room in the 'Berlaymont'. They were attached to different advisers who, of course, hardly found time to guide them. Although de Soye was my formal adviser, my advisers in effect were Klaus Ewig and von O'svath with whom I am still in touch. There were many seminars, lectures and papers to be written. The trainees were taken for a week to Berlin to show its special status and also to the European Court of Justice in Luxembourg and the European Parliament in Strasbourg. However, it was all left to the trainee to imbibe whatever he or she wanted. A German adviser remarked once about a German trainee with us that he had not seen any other man who had done so little in so long a time! However, later he could join a big company.

To many Europeans, knowledge about the Indians is sketchy. Unlike Englishmen, they do not know much about us. So when I talked about the Second World War, Hitler, etc., this German trainee was really surprised at my knowledge, although it was something very common in India. So he and his friend took me and my wife to some parts of Germany to show their great country. National pride, capacity for hard work and punctuality are the qualities, which one could learn from them.

During this period, I also came across the very first book on Indo-EEC trade written by Prof. R.S. Nigam of the Delhi School of Economics. Another book was written by Dr. (Mrs) Dharma Kumar of the same school. These books were available in the EEC library. On my return to India, this helped me have an abiding relationship with Prof. R.S. Nigam who became my Ph.D. guide in the Delhi School of Economics. From the time I was posted with the Leather

Export Promotion Council in Madras till I completed my tenure as Director in the Ministry of Commerce in 1976, I was in touch with him. He also registered me for a Ph.D. On completion of my tenure with the Ministry, I wrote a thesis with the help of material available with me. In fact, it was a feverish activity for about sixteen hours a day continuously for nearly three months. In fact, the then Commerce Secretary, Bose-Mullick, told me once that from his experience of writing a book on the game of Bridge, which he played well and also an authority, it would be very difficult to write a book, give references, make corrections, etc., - the clerical work takes half the time. He was right; the thesis became rather bulky. Two of the examiners commented upon the bulk. But while publishing it as a book, I removed two chapters giving descriptions of the organisations of the EEC. But a reviewer caught on and remarked that this aspect was lacking in the book! After an oral examination and defence of the thesis, the University of Delhi awarded the degree in the beginning of 1977. I just missed the convocation in spite of the rush and I could take the degree only next year from the Chancellor of the university, B.D. Jatti who had been my Lt. Governor in Pondicherry and Vice-President of India at this time. He was happy to see me taking the degree. Morarji Desai was also on the dais as PM giving away the degrees. I saw B.D. Jatti telling him something about me because I had never met Morarji although he was from Gujarat.

In all this, one tends to feel that an inscrutable destiny shapes one's ends. I could not go to the East-West University in Hawaii. Circumstances compelled me to go to Brussels which was also something unique from my point of view. The then Ambassador B.R. Patel, an ICS man, was also from the Gujarat cadre and he felt that I should go into the Ministry of Commerce on my return, which I did. My job also took me to Europe almost every year and I visited Brussels on my own during my visits to Europe. I could thereby continue my association with my landlady and other friends there. During one such visit, when I rang my landlady, there was no response. My sixth sense told me that there was something amiss. When I contacted her relative and my friend, Gui Meert, he informed me of the demise of my landlady and her funeral that very evening. It was the will of Providence perhaps that I should attend her funeral and place the gift I usually carried for her on her coffin in the cemetery. The bells of the church opposite my apartment sounded sad for me that day where I was purely by chance. The same study and stay in Brussels took me there again on a posting in the Embassy without my asking or working for the post as most civil servants do. Although I could not deal with the EEC during my first stint in the Ministry of Commerce, I dealt with the subject during my second stint as Additional Secretary and it also so happened that I had to negotiate the third enlarged Agreement with the EEC, the first one by K.B. Lall and the second one by P.K. Davé. So, in all this, there seems to be an invisible thread running through.

10

Back in India

I was in two minds whether to leave Pondicherry or not. My wife did not want to leave at all. Ultimately, we left with a heavy heart. Another important factor also weighed with me for such a departure; I hardly had any money to get my four sisters married. A deputation or study leave would have helped me accumulate some money, but that was shattered by the Government of Gujarat. However, my earned leave and half-pay leave enabled me save some money and I got the twins married. My father had nothing.

Moreover, all sorts of peculiar problems crop up for a middle or lower middle class person going abroad. My first sister's husband and his family thought that I had left India for good and started ill-treating my sister. There was near separation and in my absence, my father had to approach some influential relatives to bring about a patch up. This pressing problem and my sisters' marriage made me again seek a posting to the south. Luckily, Pondicherry was not counted as a deputation and my own earned leave, half-pay leave and extraordinary leave for a few months sanctioned by the Gujarat Government – in fact, a problem created by the chief secretary, Pondicherry at the last moment before my departure – came in handy and it was treated as reversion to the state.

Ambassador B.R. Patel's recommendation for Commerce and my training in Brussels helped. I was posted in the Leather Export Promotion Council in Madras under the Ministry of Commerce in October, 1971.

I met T. Abdul Wahid, Vice-Chairman of the Leather Export Promotion Council, Madras, in the absence of the Chairman Nagappa Chettiar, on October 12th, 1971 to inform that I would like to take over the next day. He told me that there would not be any problem as far as he was concerned. He would also try and convince the Committee of Administration of the Council at a special meeting before allowing me to take over because the appointment had to be endorsed by the Committee of Administration and there had been problems in the past. The Export Promotion Councils are non-profit making companies under the Indian Companies Act. So there is a Committee of Administration instead of a Board of Directors. Although the Government could issue certain orders including appointment of certain officials at their request, the Committee has to endorse it formally. In some Councils, the Committee members tried to be difficult and they even went to the court of law to stall certain appointments. In order to get over difficulties of this kind, the Government of India introduced a clause in the Articles of Association of all Councils to the effect that the Government directives would be binding upon them because they were, in fact, Government companies taking grant-in-aid from the Government.

Luckily for me, there was no such problem and I could take over on October 13th, 1971. There are two Export Promotion Councils for leather – one dealing with raw hides and skins, which, of course, were banned for exports in the sixties and consequently the Council was left with the export of semi-processed hides and skins. The semi-processed hides and skins from Madras were of the famous EI tanned variety. The name was acquired because of the East India Company and a particular tanning process introduced by the Company those days. It was also a historical accident that the EI tanneries were located mostly in Tamil Nadu, that too in a particular district known as North Arcot District. The second largest cluster for semi-processed hides and skins, but of a different variety known as chrome tanning variety, were located in Calcutta. Although there were tanneries in Kanpur, Agra and Bombay, these centres were known more for leather goods and footwear. Since it was felt that the semi-processed tanners would not pay sufficient attention to value-added leather goods like leather garments and footwear, a separate Export Promotion Council was set up at Kanpur by the Government of India for these items. This Council was also functioning in tandem with the Madras Council.

The Leather Export Promotion Council at Madras was a small office of about fifteen persons including the peons. But the office was one of intense activity in the field of exports and the semi-processed leathers occupied the third or fourth position in the export structure of the country. The office was situated in one of the important leather trading complexes in the world known as Periamet. The leather people, wherever they had their offices in the city, would come there in the mornings to have a feel of the ever-changing leather markets and to meet their foreign customers. Both their 'mandis' and offices were located in the narrow lanes between the Poonamallee High Road and the Vepery High Road and the Sydenhams Road bordering on the one side in front of the old and historic Madras Corporation Building. The place is a hive of activity. As one goes along the Sydenhams Road and Vepery High Road by bus or by car, one could smell leather – a trade predominantly in the hands of Muslims but, curiously, the Brahmins of Madras and also a few Chettiars occupied a pride of place, some of them exporting more than the Muslims. A. Nagappa Chettiar was one among the pioneers who also accounted for the largest exports in some years so much so the Government of India awarded him a 'Padma Shri'. He was not even a matriculate and could speak only haltingly in English, but he had an alert mind and could comment upon any commercial or economic situation, say, the impact of devaluation, like an economic wizard. He made me realise that one's alertness or sharpness had nothing to do with one's education or acquisition of a degree – some **one may be educated, but not intelligent. More than that, he brought in a scientific infusion into the trade by involving the Central Leather Research Institute, Madras, of course, with the active**

assistance of Dr. Nayudamma, the then Director. Those two men set an example to other scientists and scientific institutions, not to function from an ivory tower or in a closed cocoon, but by close interaction with the trade and industry. Perhaps it was the only scientific research institute at that time to have an economics wing and could transfer technology to the industry and trade.

Above all, Nagappa Chettiar changed the colonial pattern of the leather trade. The EI tanned hides and skins used to go to England, get sorted out and exported to West European countries, at times after finishing there. It was thought that only an Englishman could ensure quality and honesty. Chettiar broke this myth and established direct contact with the importers in Western Europe. He was a pioneer in this regard and other exporters followed him.

It was the only Council which wanted an IAS officer as Secretary now known as Executive Director. My predecessor, T.S.R. Subramanian from U.P. cadre, had made a big name in the Council and also later in the Service. (This draft was made by me three years ago. He has since become the Cabinet Secretary – the highest position in the civil service). Although he was the senior most in the 1961 batch with all qualifications, some of his batch-mates tried to pip him at the post. As stated by me earlier, some tried to become heroes through newspapers. In spite of the unseemly and unnecessary controversy created, Prime Minister Deve Gowda made him the Cabinet Secretary. V.N. Narayanan, Editor, wrote much later in *The Hindustan Times*: "Bureaucrats on TV are like contestants in a beauty parade. Careful preparation and training precede beauteous exposure. And the mandarins do not depend on special training for occasional exposure. They appear before select committees, give evidence and explain policies to MPs, media and the public at large. Reticence will vanish once they get accepted as TV personalities with a presence on the small screen. I have a strong feeling that Delhi's Lt., Governor, Tejendra Khanna, owes his present post to the mass media exposure during his days as Commerce Secretary. That and other things, perhaps."

But I must also add that Tejendra Khanna and I worked together twice in Commerce. He was a pleasant, competent and helpful person. In fact, when this controversy between the relatively unknown T.S.R. Subramanian versus Tejendra Khanna was going on, I happened to have a word with their batch-mate, K.A. Nambiar, Defence Secretary and Chief Secretary, Tamil Nadu. He told me categorically that he would give only four to six marks out of ten for competence to TSR, but easily nine to Tejendra.

Chettiar wanted an IAS officer in order to ensure good administration free from petty politics. This also enabled him to function smoothly as chairman while also attending to his own affairs. He never claimed any TA or DA from the Council for his numerous trips either within the country or outside.

We used to participate in quite a few fairs abroad and he was present in the important ones. The Paris Semaine du Cuir was the most important of them all, held every year in the first week of September. It was a big affair and one floor was exclusively devoted to footwear. While taking a look around, I was surprised to see a board, 'Madras'. I was wondering who this man was from Madras without my knowledge. But when I entered, I was told by the proprietor that it was a well known chain of shoe-stores in Italy. Since I did not disclose my identity, he took me for a Latin American. When I asked him why he had chosen the name, 'Madras', he told me that it was a place in India known all over the world for good quality leather and hence he chose the name. He also told me that he had never visited Madras, but was buying the Madras leathers from agents in London and Paris. Then I disclosed my identity and gave my card. I told him that he could very well buy these good leathers from Madras directly instead of through middlemen who would be charging a higher price. He said that he would visit Madras in response to my invitation and was also anxious to see the place after which he had named his important shoe-chain.

True to his word, he came to Madras within a few months. I arranged for his visit to leather centres like Ranipet, Vaniyambadi and Ambur. He was so impressed by the quality of leather and also the abundance that he felt that we could straightaway have at least twenty shoe factories. He wanted to enter into a collaboration with Hafizur Rahman of the South East Tanning Company, which I facilitated when I moved to the

Ministry of Commerce. It was practically the first shoe factory in India with foreign collaboration. It is functioning even today albeit under different management, producing shoes for Florsheim.

Nagappa Chettiar, and also a few others got into financial trouble because the leather trade was generally based on a slender capital base. If one tried to do too much with the slender capital base, it would function well with profits as long as the rotation was good, but even a small trouble would throw the rotation out of gear and one would fall flat. This happened to a number of persons including the knowledgeable and vigilant Chettiar because others including some political bigwigs encouraged him to do more and more of exports, though out of good intentions.

The small office had to be streamlined though the people were good and efficient perhaps because it was a business organisation. The organisation was also free from the usual governmental files and procedures and at the same time it needed improvement because many aspects had to be changed. First of all, the building itself, although an ancient one, did not have rudimentary facilities including a good toilet. Secondly, it did not have a good library. Thirdly, the monthly journal was looking like an unattractive government bulletin. Luckily, telex was there next to my room and I could even converse over the telex with the foreign buyers with the help of an efficient typist.

The library was properly arranged and the additions to the library were published in the monthly journal. A close link was established with the Economics Wing of the Central Leather Research Institute. A man from Ms Hindustan Thompson Associates was invited to redesign and print the monthly journal in an attractive form, with my editorial. Although these were important features, the tradition-bound semi-tanned exporters felt that all this was an unnecessary luxury although Chettiar and the subsequent Chairman, Wahid did not feel so. There was also yet another person from Gujarat, Ahmad Ali Parpia, who was settled in Madras for generations with a modern office of his own and a modern mind. He encouraged me in these ventures and used to send some of his letters on the telex machines from his office only a few metres away – a rare practice those days. Some members also felt that the monthly editorials were somewhat strident and consequently an editorial board was formed to check on my writings. Although the Council gave me a loan for purchase of a car most willingly, it did not permit a staff car. They were also reluctant to move into a modern building away from the Marble Hall of the Vepery High Road. On these two counts, I could not convince them. But looking back it was a good idea not to have a staff car which, according to the right thinking Chettiar, would be misused by the non-official members and also by all sorts of officials coming from Delhi. So it was a wise move not to have a car with a driver with all problems but to pay taxi charges to each and every one in the Council for movement on official work.

However, this traditional approach also acted as a damper against modernisation. Regarding tanneries, I wrote in my diary on January 12th, 1972: "I was deeply moved to see the labourers working in the traditional tanneries. They must be really God-cursed to work in such surroundings. It is really a pity. Tanners should modernise the tanneries and remove such appalling conditions". Those days the International Leather Fair in Madras was international only in name. I repeatedly wrote in the journal to invite at least the South East Asian neighbours so that it would become international. I am happy to know that it is now a big affair with people coming from different parts of the world. The fair always had a fashion parade. During January, 1972, immediately after my taking over, the chief guest was the then Deputy Minister of Commerce, A.C. George. He had started as a trade union leader while working in the Fertilizers and Chemicals of Travancore (FACT) at Cochin. The factory sent him to Harvard perhaps to brain-wash him. He obtained an MBA from Harvard and did become a bourgeois. On his return, he took to active politics after resigning his job. He succeeded in becoming a Deputy Minister at the Centre in the Commerce Ministry. Somehow he came close to Mrs. Gandhi but did not make it obvious or exploit it. He was considered a knowledgeable minister. In the fashion parade, he enquired from me whether those beautiful garments were being produced in Madras. I told him that they were produced only for the fashion parade because there were many problems in producing them on a large scale. He directed me to give a note on his return from Cochin en route to Delhi. I gave him the following note which I had to give informally because the accent was on finished leather, leather goods and footwear while I was in charge of a Council which was for promotion of export of semi-processed hides and skins. This was the starting point of Leather Policy in 1972. "A Note on Increasing the Export of Finished Leather: The Leather Export Promotion Council, Madras is concerned with the export of semi-tanned EI hides and skins. The export per annum is of the order of Rs.50 crores out of the total leather export of about Rs.100 crores from the country.

The export of raw hides and skins is virtually banned except for the goat skins, which are being allowed on a quota basis. This is also likely to be stopped by 1973-'74.

A new product of semi-tanned category, viz. wet blue chrome tanned leather was a new development in the sixties along with vegetable tanned hides and skins.

The policy of the Government is to encourage the export of finished leather and leather manufactures by transformation of the semi-tanned hides and skins and it is expected that the export of leather in finished form will be augmented considerably in the years to come.

The American manufacturers have started looking for finished leather rather than for the semi-finished categories because of the mounting wages in this somewhat labour-intensive industry and also the very nature of the tanning process. This trend is likely to prevail in other advanced countries of Western Europe and Japan and most of them will even be prepared to shift their tanneries and tanning factories to developing countries with good raw material potential.

In this context, our country should not lose the opportunity and the industry should try to hasten the process of switch over from the semi-tanned leather to finished forms.

B. But the process of switch over is rather slow in the case of EI tanned leather because of the fact that this category has a fairly steady market abroad. Production of finished leather and leather manufactures involves much labour like getting the necessary licences from the Ministry of Industrial Development for a large-scale unit, getting quality raw material and development of better marketing techniques and know-how to push finished leather and leather manufactures in the foreign markets. Besides, the traditional nature of the EI tanning industry and the established quality of this leather ensure an adequate margin of profit although the margin would be higher in the case of finished leather.

In order to encourage the production of finished leather and leather manufactures, a certain amount of restrictions, physical and fiscal, on the EI tanned and chrome tanned semi-finished leather and very liberal incentives for finished leather and leather goods industry, are necessary.

Time and again, people in the industry complain about inordinate delay in obtaining the licences from the concerned authorities. The units, which now produce and export semi-tanned leather, will also apply for industrial licence in due course to manufacture finished leather. Diversification plans of the industrial units to this effect should be agreed to without delay by the Ministry of Industrial Development.

It is suggested that some essential machinery could be brought under the Open General Licence by the Government of India. If this is not feasible, the State Directorate of Industries could be instructed to issue essentiality certificates in consultation with the Export Promotion Councils dispensing with the present cumbersome procedure of taking the assistance of the Assistant Directorates of Industries which are located in the districts. This will considerably reduce the delay.

The Ministry of Foreign Trade could make separate allocations for import of machinery other than what is allowed under the REP provisions without reference to the DGTD. The DGTD, after taking into consideration the present policy of import substitution in consequence of the cut in foreign aid and the capacity available in the country, could make a list of foreign machines available to the Chief Controller of Imports and Exports and the Ministry of Foreign Trade for issue of licences".

He gave the note promptly to the Commerce Secretary, H. Lal, ICS, and impressed upon him the need to exploit this promising sector for exports. Commerce Secretary convened a meeting and emphasized the need to restrict the export of semi-processed hides and skins as the raw hides and skins were excluded for exports in the sixties. This meeting naturally sent shock-waves in the leather circles all over the country particularly in Madras. There was immediately a furore and delegations started rushing to Delhi. They wanted to find out what prompted the government to do this so suddenly. Somehow they came to know that some note was given by me to the minister. Naturally I had to hide my note and pretend some innocence. Perhaps it was in a sense wrong on my part to have given a note suggesting restriction of the export of a commodity, which I was charged to promote. But I felt that as an IAS officer it was my moral duty to look at the larger and broader interest of the country. This was the moral justification for this act. In fact, this kind of a conflict occurs in the career of almost every IAS officer. They fight for a particular cause when they are in one Ministry. For instance, while in Commerce, we may argue for exports and against some measures of the Ministry of Finance. But when some one moves from Commerce to Finance, he does just the opposite because he is in the Finance Ministry. Similarly, one fights for a particular measure of the Central Government and tries to impose it on the State Governments. But when one goes back to the State Government, one does just the opposite. According to me, this is a wrong approach particularly for an IAS officer. He is there for the correct interest and should fight for a correct cause wherever he is. His immediate or sectoral interest should not come in the way and that should be his conviction. In other words, his conviction should not change according to the place unless the facts presented to him warrant so. So, on this basis, I think what I did was correct.

However, I was apprehensive of one point that the government was always good at giving the stick immediately but not the carrot as suggested in my note. In any case, there was so much of controversy on this question that the government decided to appoint a Committee under Dr Sitharamiah of the DGTD. The Committee went into the pros and cons of the subject of my note and recommended gradual restriction of the export of semi-processed leathers for smooth switch-over and also several incentives including abolition of industrial licensing. Meanwhile, I had published a small book on the new and tangled 'GSP (Generalised System of Preferences) and the Leather Trade'. This book was also incorporated in the report of the Sitharamiah Committee which turned out to be a land-mark document in the history of the leather industry. **(Some years later, I was surprised to see this booklet also along with my Ph.D thesis in the Harvard, East-West and UN libraries).**

Following this report, there was a lot of activity and I was called almost every fortnight to the Commerce Ministry in New Delhi to work out a system of restriction of semi-processed leathers on the basis of a quota system. This was primarily done by a Director by name Rajpal. We did consult many persons including those in the DGTD and the STC. My counterpart in the Kanpur Council was not involved. He was a good person, but could not produce results. He was a technical man although the industry felt his knowledge was outdated. For all practical purposes, I wrote all the notes and Rajpal signed with some corrections here and there, but, I must say, after full application of his mind and discussion. He was an efficient Secretariat officer. He was essentially in the Ministry of Defence and came over to Commerce where he spent a few years. He and one more Director were the only two Directors in the Ministry of Commerce who had not gone abroad at all while all others hankered after foreign trips and some joined the Ministry only for that. Ultimately, Rajpal made a single trip to Bangkok before his retirement. He was naturally proud that he gave shape and direction to India's leather policy before his retirement, with all my assistance.

There was quantitative restriction on the export of semi-processed hides and skins, which should decline every year and peter out over a period of time. There was always controversy about the basic and the reference years for quota. Although the cottage and small tanners were promised common facility centres, they felt that the entire policy was not called for. There was a divide between the North and the South in the sense that the leather goods producers in the North welcomed these restrictions. Abdul Wahid and other big exporters with their modern outlook welcomed this policy. Although Chettiar did not have much to gain, he too welcomed it because it was in the country's interest. In fact, it was his idea which I recorded in my note and gave practical shape with the help of the Government. So some of these actions had naturally become controversial. There was a court case against the continuance of Wahid as Chairman. The Committee of Administration was also influenced to ask for my transfer and to appoint only a Council official in my place. Somehow this resolution was carried through and I was expecting a shift. My anxiety was that I should not be sent back to Gujarat because it would have amounted to some sort of punishment for good work done. Luckily for me, the Commerce Ministry was unusually wise, thanks particularly to A.C. George who had known the problem I was facing, I was accommodated in the Ministry for the rest of my tenure of two and a half years and also placed in charge of leather perhaps to the chagrin of the tanners in Madras. However, our relations remained cordial not only because I did not nurture any ill-will against them but also because of the good nature of these people. **They were to thank me later after a few years for this new direction in policy which was ultimately for their benefit, in spite of the initial turbulence. There was a sea-change in the composition of leather exports of India from semi-processed to finished leathers, leather garments and full footwear over a period of fifteen years. Many foreign collaborations had also come up. In other words, it was an area where the Government's policy direction took the right course and paid rich dividends. All this was on the basis of a two page note. That was one of the reasons why a Government post at policy-making level was considered important and a decision affected or benefited a large number of people. (Years later in 2004, I was surprised to see T.S.R. Subramanian claiming entire credit for the leather policy in his autobiography. When I was asked to introduce the book in the Madras Book Club in his presence, I told him**

on his face that he was nowhere there and was back in his cadre, in UP. When the policy was initiated by me and A.C. George and I faced the full brunt of the wrath of the semi-processed lobby, he was not there. He had nothing to say. He never thought that I would be there to speak on his memoir. JFK had said that 'success has many claimants and failure is an orphan'!)

I feel that this experience was rewarding although even a business-oriented Minister like P. Chidamabaram felt that the Councils should not have officers on deputation. I told him, when he was my minister in the Commerce Ministry years later, that this experience was useful because a government official learnt time was money or precious and he became time-and- target oriented which many government officials woefully lacked otherwise. For instance, government policy changes were known to the exporters in Madras from their liaison officers in no time, whereas I got to know after a few days from the Commerce Ministry in the normal course. I could never set right this situation. Similarly, Parpia moved the entire world when many exporters defaulted on their contracts in a bullish market and the Commercial Attachés of the various embassies descended on the Commerce Ministry within two days. All this was done by him on telex or telephone. In fact, it was the same view expressed later by the Prime Minister Indira Gandhi that the Commerce Ministry and other economic ministries should function in this fashion without delaying policy decisions for years. So I consider my stint in the Council as a rewarding experience of my career.

Delegations are common for many ministries, particularly for Commerce, and I was invariably the leader of such delegations. There were many amusing incidents or experiences during such visits.

When I went from the Leather Council all by myself, I was accommodated in the then famous 'Sun-N-Sand' in Juhu. A film function was on and I could see the whole lot of stars from Helen to Hema Malini and Dharmendra at close quarters.

My experience with the Air-India the next morning was narrated in the following article which was published by me in the then widely-read Indian "PUNCH" viz. *Shankar's Weekly*: January 12th , 1975:

"The CIPs : It is human nature to feel thrilled at being treated as an important person. The VIP treatment meted out to some of our people, say the ministers, diplomats and visiting dignitaries had aroused in me a longing to be treated as a VIP some day.

I am a great one for travelling. Often I go abroad and on one such trip I went to the 'check-in-counter' and presented my ticket and ordinary passport. The chic receptionist at the counter filled in my embarkation card and after checking in my luggage ushered me into a VIP room I was dreaming of. To make it good, she ordered coffee for me and said that she would see me through the customs and emigration at the right time.

When she left, I started wondering about the special treatment meted out to me. Was it a part of the airline's PR work or was it to make amends for some bad reports of neglect of the passengers? After some time, the receptionist came and took me through the Emigration and Customs and she told me to go through the security check. It was not only just this alone. You could have knocked me down with a feather - a posh imported car was waiting at the tarmac to take me to the plane and I was the first to be taken inside.

I was the first one to ascend the steps of the jumbo jet named "Emperor Vikramaditya" – 'a palace in the sky'. I really felt like a live Maharajah.

When the jet took off, it looked as though a big building had sprouted wings and gone up.

I was feted and pampered on the best in the wine list.

On reaching the destination, I was warmly received. I just looked around for the other VIPs. There was none.

I became curious and glanced at a disembarkation paper of the air-company. It was written in bold letters against my name- CIP. What is this CIP? When I reached the hotel, I asked for a dictionary and looked into it. There was no mention of CIP at all. I could not contain myself. I rang up the air-company and asked for the meaning without disclosing my identity. They said,

"Commercially Important Person", and that explained the special treatment. So I was a CIP, though not a VIP!"

Narayan Bhatt had become the top most exporter of leather garments in the country with numerous awards (I believe he has since declined and practically disappeared – that is the vagary of business). He was a part of my three member delegation to the then Soviet Union and a few other East European countries in 1975 and it was his first official visit abroad for selling garments.

We had a very useful talk with the Foreign Trade Office of the erstwhile Soviet Union with the assistance of the well-known G.K. Arora who was our Minister there and also V.N. Singh of the STC who was a son-in-law of Lal Bahadur Shastri. Our official itinerary included the then Leningrad (now St. Petersburg, as in the distant past). Since even cities required visas, I had a visa for Leningrad. But Narayan Bhatt and Aslam of my delegation did not have visas because they could not read Russian and thought they had one. In any case, the Foreign Office was kind enough to arrange visas for them at short notice. In fact, they had gone out of the way to get these visas because in the then Soviet Union nobody was to be given a visa without hotel accommodation, particularly in the Intourist hotels and all hotels were full in Leningrad on that day. But we told them that we were very keen on visiting Leningrad and would spend the night in the airport itself. They reluctantly agreed. When we went to the airport to take the last flight at about 10 p.m., we were told that it was delayed by about four hours and we felt happy because our problem of accommodation was automatically solved. We spent the first half of the night in the Moscow airport itself in the company of our friends from the Embassy and the STC.

Finally our plane landed in Leningrad at 4 a.m.,and to our utter surprise, in bright sun light. We realised that Leningrad was very near the Artic Circle and, in fact, in summer they did not have to switch on the street lights for about two months because of the twenty-four hour Artic sun. The girl at the counter enquired about our accommodation. Narayan Bhatt gave her a small leather wallet; such small gifts like leather articles, cigarettes or whisky worked wonders in the then Soviet Union. She allowed us to leave the airport to go to the Intourist hotel.

When we reached the hotel, the girl at the counter wondered how we could come there without proper reservation. She refused to allow us to go inside the hotel. In fact, she was angry with the girl at the airport and banged her over the telephone for having sent us there. Narayan Bhatt again tried his tricks and told her that we were from a friendly country like India. She told us not to enter the hotel till about 6 a.m., After that, she allowed us in for a wash in the bathrooms attached to the lobby and allowed us to go up only to have breakfast.

When we were having breakfast, a man from one of the southern republics of the erstwhile Soviet Union accosted us and talked about India and Raj Kapoor. In spite of our friendly remonstrations, he told the hotel to give us breakfast at his cost!

After the free breakfast, we came down and cajoled the girl again. She spoke to some one and arranged our accommodation for the day in another hotel. It was all terrible bureaucracy and we had to take the reservation slips from the Intourist office. Luckily, it was only next door. We reached the hotel and did our official business in the forenoon.

We had already reserved our accommodation in a tourist bus to visit the famous St. Peter's gardens near Leningrad. Meanwhile, we saw the famous Hermitage Museum. When we boarded the bus, we realised that we were the only three passengers. But they did not cancel the trip. At a museum en route, we could make out from their talk that they were making fun of our girl-guide stating that we were the only three black chaps for her that day. In any case, the driver and the girl-guide were very polite and we reached the garden. To be very frank, we were disappointed with the garden and it was nothing compared with the Brindhavans near Mysore. We were also told that it was a habit with Peter the Great to drench the guests from surprise-fountains in the garden. The girl also wanted us to get drenched as it happened to many a visitor. But we were very careful in stepping on anything and wanted to find out the exact trick. When some one stepped on a particular area, a fountain or water dropped on his head drenching him completely. We wondered whether the fountain was working on some pressure when you stepped on the area. But we actually discovered that a man was sitting at a distance and was operating a switch under his foot. In other words, it was not a tremendous contraption.

Similarly, some one was asked to enter a cubicle or hut. The moment he entered, there was a gush of water on all sides around him and if he tried to get out, he would be drenched! Again our alert eyes discovered that a man was operating this, hiding at a distance in a bush. So our girl-guide was totally disappointed by our alertness. Perhaps she did not expect the black chaps to be so alert or brainy. So, to her great dismay, we refused not only to get ourselves drenched but also discovered the trick. It was also a great disappointment to the driver of the bus.

11

In the Capital

The Vice- Chairman of the Leather Export Promotion Council, C.K. Duraivelan, a mild mannered and a steady individual in business without taking much risk, was travelling with me to Delhi for a meeting. In the leather trade, people operate on a small capital base. If one tries to speculate and reach high with a small capital base, like a magician balances many balls in the air, one is likely to fall badly should something go wrong. Some leading figures in Madras did it and paid for dearly. Duraivelan was not of that type. But he was also worried about my exit from the Council because of the controversy. But he knew the rule that unless the Central Government issued orders withdrawing my services, the Council would not be able to do anything. But situations of this kind always created a certain amount of uncertainly for both the parties.

When we reached the hotel, I immediately contacted Director Rajpal as usual. There was a pleasant surprise for me. He told me that only that evening a telegram was sent to Madras transferring me to the Ministry as Deputy Secretary. He also told me that I should join immediately as desired by the Commerce Secretary, Y.T. Shah. No doubt, I felt happy about this tiding.

After the meeting, we went back to Madras and I packed up quickly. I came to Delhi on April 14th , 1974 and reported to the

Ministry of Commerce. It was a very hot summer that year. I stayed with one of my relatives as usual. But hostel accommodation was allotted to me on Curzon Road within fifteen days. It was in a centrally located area, built for the UNCTAD conference. Although the accommodation was small with only two rooms, it was more than enough for two persons. It was not far from the office and I could go home for lunch. It was also good from the security point of view because one could lock the flat even for months together. The flats in other buildings would attract thieves even if they were locked for a few days.

There was no problem for me in settling down in the ministry because I was already familiar with the surroundings and the people. Normally they take some time to allot a room or work. But, there was an Additional Secretary, R. Tirumalai, who was on top of the IAS because he stood first in the first batch of 1948 and he gave me some work straightaway. He wanted me to process the report on SCOPE-AIR – Standing Committee for Promotion of Exports by Air – an interesting acronym. So I had to get down to work almost on the first day and I became *the first Member Secretary of SCOPE-AIR.* The then Director, Transport, T.K.Sarangan, who prepared the report was at loggerheads with Tirumalai. They could not get along with each other. Sarangan was from the Directorate of Shipping where he had spent some years and became an expert and consultant to the UN. This was his first Secretariat posting and naturally was perhaps a bit excited about it. He used to tour around the country and also abroad on UN work. During these tours, he made it a point to meet the press. Somehow Tirumalai did not like all this. Under Sarangan, there was an efficient but somewhat mischievous Section Officer who also added fuel to the fire. In any case, Sarangan had to go back to the Directorate of Shipping although the public opinion was in his favour. One of my colleagues had put it humorously that it was a fight between a 'fair' Aiyangar (Sarangan) and 'dark' Aiyangar (Tirumalai) (Some say that there was some such ethnic conflict in the past among the followers of Sri Ramanujacharya)

Tirumalai was no doubt an efficient and kind officer. But his style of functioning was such that he annoyed many persons including the minister. He used to call me at least about a dozen times to his room every day. He wanted the notes to be revised endlessly and as a result there was delay in some matters and the minister was quite annoyed about it.

My task became really difficult because I was reporting to Tirumalai directly for two-thirds of my work and to V.C. Pande for one-third of my work. V.C. Pande was a difficult person in his own way. Though he was kind at heart, he was often moody and brusk in his manners. He could not get along well with Tirumalai. He also had the impression that I was very friendly with Tirumalai. Pande was also somewhat against the South Indians. He openly stated, although in good fun, that he was not able to function well because of one 'Southy' above him and another 'Southy' below him. He also went hammer and tongs against the south Indian leather industry. He was for the Agra footwear industry supported by the footwear and leather goods lobby and also by the Executive Director in the STC, Seth, who came over from the Batas, the husband of Mrs. Leila Seth who became a judge of the Delhi High Court later and the father of the present famous novelist, Vikram Seth. This crowd always felt that I was always supporting the Madras lobby although I was the initiator of the policy against semi-processed leathers. Of course, all of them were my good friends otherwise.

As a result, things were difficult for me although the other Joint Secretaries, Commerce Secretary Y.T. Shah, Secretary, Foreign Trade, Dr P.C. Alexander and Bose-Mullick thought well of me. But I fell between these two stools and on one occasion I asked both of them to relieve me from one of the charges so that I could function only under one person. But they did not do so and asked me to carry on.

Pan-chewing Pande was also an astrologer. Several officers in Udyog Bhavan used to consult him about their future. This was common particularly at lunch time. Dr Arjun Sengupta and S.M. Ghosh were permanent fixtures there. But I was the only one who had not consulted him and perhaps that also annoyed him a bit. Perhaps he thought that I did not have sufficient faith in his astrological capabilities. But I told him once that not that I did not believe in astrology but I did not want him to look into my horoscope because he would know my weak points and it was not good for me working under him! He found this explanation rather funny as it was intended to be.

Pande prepared a paper on leather policy. He never attended to routine matters of administration. He left all these matters to us. He was always interested in preparing papers as they did in the World Bank and other UN organisations. He also prepared a paper on leather industry, which went before the Cabinet. Mrs. Gandhi felt, on the advice of G. Ramachandran from the Tamil Nadu Cadre who was then in her office, that the suggestions were quite explosive and would annoy the tanners in Madras. The paper was rejected. Pande did not come to remain present in the ante-room during the Cabinet meeting as was the practice. Since it was late in the evening, he had sent me. After the meeting, Ramachandran was almost furious because he thought I had prepared that paper and coming from the Leather Export Promotion Council, Madras, I should have known the ground realities. I had to tell him indirectly that I was not responsible for the paper although I did not let down Pande. On coming back, I felt that all this was too much and some Parliamentary Committee might find fault with the quota policy itself, which was assiduously evolved and implemented. So I consulted Rajpal and wrote a critic of Pande's paper. I circulated it only to Rajpal and Pande. I requested Pande not to take it amiss and it was being done with all good intentions to keep the record straight. But I must say to his credit that he had not mistaken me.

He also never bothered about the Parliamentary Committees and their procedures. The rule was that the Secretary himself should appear. I had already appeared before the Chairman of the Petitions Committee and explained that there was no Joint Secretary for the subject and both the Additional Secretary and Secretary were out of station. So, for the second time, the Commerce Secretary told V.C. Pande to appear before the chairman for this subject. The chairman was also from U.P. So they exchanged pleasantries in Hindi to start with. But, when Pande told him that this matter was lying in some other section of the ministry and delay had occurred, the chairman told him that this was not a correct explanation and he was concerned only with the ministry and not with this or that section. After a brief discussion, he enquired from Pande as to how soon he would be able to send a report on the subject. Pande, without knowing the procedure, told him that he would send the reply the same evening. The next question of the chairman was that how long Pande was working in the Government of India. He stated that he was here for more than a year during this second spell of his. The chairman was more annoyed and fired him stating that he did not even know this simple procedure; he had to get the approval of the minister for sending any report or reply on any subject to the Parliament and it had to be made in many copies including Hindi translation. All this Pande was ignorant of and the chairman gave a fortnight to complete the procedure. I was quite amused and felt that it served Pande right.

Pande also did not appear before the Public Accounts Committee. The Public Accounts Committee had a long session of a day and a half to discuss the leather policy. They had gone round the country and had collected a lot of information from the different lobbies. Prof. Hiren Mukherjee was the Chairman. Tirumalai and I and also the then Commerce Secretary Bose-Mullick appeared before the Committee. It was easy for me to explain things because I was closely associated with the evolution of the policy and also worked in the field. *The Illustrated Weekly of India* was carrying a series of articles on different industries. I had written an article on the leather industry when I was in the Leather Export Promotion Council. By a strange coincidence, the article appeared after about a year when I was in the ministry and that too two days before the hearing by the Public Accounts Committee. Prof. Hiren Mukherjee brought the article to the meeting and stated that one Mr Sundaram had written an article on the leather industry and he did not know whether he was an expert or not. The Commerce Secretary immediately told him that I was sitting there in his presence. They had a number of questions to ask on the observations in the article, but on the whole things went off very well.

Tirumalai was a very meticulous person in his preparations although he wanted us to collect a mass of unnecessary details. There was a holiday preceding the meeting. He called me to his house at 9 a.m., and started preparing for the meeting. He also gave me lunch. Perhaps he was afraid that should I go out for lunch I would not come back for quite some time. He went on and on till 8.30 p.m. Since my wife was out of station, I had to go to dinner at her niece's place. But he wanted some further exercise to be done on the export figures. This exercise would not be possible but for the assistance of the officer concerned in the STC. Luckily, the officer concerned, Mrs. Roy, was a 55 year old lady and I could request her to come to my apartment at about 10.30 p.m., She was kind enough to do so. She was also the president of the STC staff union. She was the daughter of B.R.Sen, ICS, former Director General of the FAO. She told me once that her father ranked higher in the UN Protocol than C.V. Narasimhan because he was the Head of a Department while C.V. Narasimhan was not and he was only a Chef de Cabinet in charge of the Secretary-General's office. After getting the figures from her, luckily I had a calculator which was a rare thing those days. I could work on it till 2 o'clock in the morning.

Another important achievement was the creation of the Hindustan Diamond Corporation. There was an old, somewhat cranky person by name S.G. Zaveri in the diamond trade. He wanted to have a collaboration with an Israeli company. His request was handled before my arrival and the collaboration was almost approved. He must have refused to oblige the then Commerce Minister, the formidable L.N. Mishra, who very rarely wrote a note on the file, but in this case wrote three or four lines in his own hand stating that in such an important collaboration the public sector undertaking like the MMTC should be associated. Much to Zaveri's chagrin, the proposal fell through. It was being revived in another form, the Hindustan Diamond Corporation. Zaveri left no stone unturned to sabotage it.

The Ministry of External Affairs was dead-set against this proposal, because of the Israeli angle coupled with the South African angle. The South African company, De Beers, controls even now about 70% of the raw diamond trade in the world (It is declined to 60% in 2004). India was one of the main clients particularly for the 'smalls'. The representatives of the Diamond Trading Company of London used to have meetings regularly in

the Ministry of Commerce presided over by the Joint Secretary. Their local representative was one retired Maj. Gen. Virendra Singh. He was a very rich man who owned the Modern School in Delhi. His brother-in-law Kishore Prem Chand was another collaborator and the MMTC was the third partner. But the proposal was turned down several times by the Ministry of External Affairs from the Israeli and the South African angle. Commerce Ministry could not convince them at all.

Luckily for Maj. Gen. Virendra Singh, Y.B. Chavan became the Minister of External Affairs and the General had known him. The Secretary was also Vishnu Ahuja who was known to him closely. So they had suggested a way-out for this important collaboration by giving a solution. Instead of having a collaboration directly with the Diamond Trading Company of London (De Beers), it would be the Bank of Bermuda – an organisation on paper in order to avoid the South African and Israeli angle. This turned out to be a good solution and the paper was revised accordingly and the proposal was approved. My tenure came to an end in October, 1976.

Maj. Gen. Virendra Singh was very happy and told me that I did not ask him anything at all including an admission in his school as many civil servants did for their children. I told him that I would keep that offer in mind and use it on some other occasion when it was needed for some one else because I had no children. In fact, I used it for a relative and a friend later. He readily obliged me although some years had gone by. The Hindustan Diamond Corporation was an important landmark and it contributed a great deal later to the growth of the Indian diamond industry.

After my reversion to Gujarat, I used to come to Udyog Bhavan frequently because I was the Additional Industries Commissioner in Gujarat. I had to attend the Industrial Licensing Committee and also the Free Trade Zones Committee representing the Government of Gujarat. Immediately after my reversion during one such visit, I encountered Pande in the corridor and he called me to his room. He told me that he just then had consulted Dr Alexander about my posting as chairman and managing director of the newly created Hindustan Diamond Corporation because Gen. Virendra Singh and also the then Finance Minister H.M. Patel from Gujarat

(although he had not known me at all) enquired whether I could be posted since I would be the most suitable person. But Dr Alexander ruled it out because I had just then gone back to Gujarat and it would be difficult to get me back so soon. Moreover, Pande was also interested in one Sharma who became the chairman and managing director. Although Gen. Virendra Singh and the Diamond Trading Corporation were not happy with him in the beginning as told to me by Gen. Virendra Singh in Frankfurt airport, he continued as CMD for a long time and made it a great success. He had to go some years later though Gen. Virendra Singh and the Diamond Trading Corporation wanted to retain him. By then, I was back in the Commerce Ministry after fourteen years as Additional Secretary. He was succeeded by a competent officer from the MMTC. The Corporation contributed a lot to the development of the diamond industry in India particularly in Gujarat, Bombay and Surat.

Since I had made a name in the Leather Export Promotion Council and was also considered for the Hindustan Diamond Corporation, the Gem and Jewellery Export Promotion Council were after me to become their Executive Director. They offered many perquisites like free house, car, etc. in Bombay. But I was not much interested in the offer. At one point of time, the then chairman, Mahendra Mehta wrote a letter to the Ministry of Commerce asking for my appointment. The Ministry of Commerce told me that they would be able to put it through if I was interested. But I declined the offer. **Perhaps had I accepted it, I would have been decorated with an award for the rapid strides the diamond industry and exports made since.**

Although it was only a short period of two and a half years in the Ministry of Commerce, it was a rewarding one. I was pleasantly surprised to receive a letter one day from the Government of Gujarat stating that I was promoted as Director in the State and I could claim the pay under the one-below rule. But when the question of promotion as Director came up, some elements in the Commerce Ministry as usual put hurdles. Four of us had to become Directors and there were vacancies to accommodate us. We wanted the ministry to write a letter to the Department of Personnel, but the ministry did not do it as usual. There was a

Joint Secretary in charge of administration who was two years senior even to the Commerce Secretary. He could not get his promotion because of some charges against him. He was always taking orders from N.K. Singh, Special Assistant to the Commerce Minister because he was there at his mercy. But, when both of them went abroad once, A.N. Varma who was then a Joint Secretary shot off this letter to the Department of Personnel asking for my promotion. (The same Varma totally turned against me years later when he was Principal Secretary to the Prime Minister). I thought it would not come through and in the meanwhile I had gone abroad. When I returned on June 15th, 1976, there was a pleasant news from my personal secretary stating that the letter had come for my promotion. So I took charge the same afternoon which gave me another four months of tenure in the Ministry of Commerce.

Meanwhile, Tirumalai, although number one in the IAS, was not accommodated in the ministry or in any other important ministry. He went as Secretary, Supply – fairly an unimportant position. Both Pande and he wrote two different CRs on me. Pande perhaps thought that I would avoid a report by him. This is common in the Government of India. When they worked under two or three officers, they would channelise the form to an officer who was likely to give an outstanding report. So I told the Vigilance Section to send him also a form to avoid this misunderstanding. The Director, Vigilance, told me that two reports were written and Commerce Secretary decided to send only Tirumalai's report. But both the reports were well written, almost on the same lines. In fact, Pande's report was even much better than Tirumalai's because the latter was always very conservative in his approach.

Looking back, it was really a formidable team at that time in the Commerce Ministry. Quite a few of them – A.N. Varma, S.P. Shukla, P.K. Kaul, A.S. Gill, Prem Kumar and Tejendra Khanna became Commerce Secretaries later. Although he was not Commerce Secretary, V.C. Pande became Cabinet Secretary. Dr Arjun Sengupta occupied important positions in his own way including Ambassadorship to Brussels. Mani Narayanaswamy became Secretary, Textiles and resigned from the service to join the private sector. Had he remained, with all his competence and bonhomie, he would have even become Cabinet Secretary. Tejendra Khanna,who became Commerce Secretary later, was also a Deputy Secretary there with us. **I too would have become Special Secretary or Commerce Secretary as expected by many, but it was scuttled as a subsequent chapter would explain.** Anwarul Hoda, the Deputy Director General, World Trade Organisation, was also a Deputy Secretary. He spent long years in the Ministry of Commerce almost without break dealing with the same subject. I was told that this single specialisation came in his way at the time of his empanelment for Secretaryship, but he was cleared for the obvious reasons while his batch-mate, Samar Singh was turned down for the same reason of single specialisation. Hoda became Special Secretary for a few days before proceeding to the WTO. Samar filed a case in the Central Administrative Tribunal and won although he lost in the Supreme Court when the Government went on appeal.

Another important area of controversial policy-making was in respect of the Free Trade Zones and Export Processing Zones. There was a demand from the Government of West Bengal for starting a Free Trade Zone in the vacant Salt Lake area near the Calcutta airport. R. Tirumalai led a team which included me and found a suitable site. But the proposal was opposed by the Ministry of Finance and the Planning Commission. P.N. Haksar was the Deputy Chairman of the Planning Commission assisted by Prof. S. Chakravarti. T.L. Shankar, IAS, was the person in charge of the Programme Evaluation Division. They were left-oriented economists who did not believe in free trade. Prof. D.P. Chattopadhyaya, the then Commerce Minister accompanied by the economic adviser, Dr Arjun Sengupta and I, had a discussion with them in the Planning Commission. But, they were opposed to the idea. The Ministry of Finance also opposed the idea for a different reason – Pranab Mukherjee who was in the Finance Ministry did not want Prof. Chattopadhyaya to get any credit for starting this zone in Calcutta.

Meanwhile, the Indian Institute of Foreign Trade prepared a report, which was processed by me. S. Rajgopal, who became Cabinet Secretary later, was the Development Commissioner of the Santacruz Electronics Export Processing Zone. He gave his own ideas for inclusion in the paper including the concept of a 100% export oriented unit. N. Vittal was in charge of the Kandla Free Trade Zone and he was striving hard to revive it with his usual enthusiasm. The Kandla Free Trade Zone was always quoted by every one as a bad example for not starting more zones in the country. Incidentally, during the period of Vittal, the export from Kandla went up from rupee one crore to rupees five crore and he claimed a lot of credit as he did always like a 'school boy'. He had not grown over this syndrome even when he became Central Vigilance Commissioner in 1998. He was succeeded by my batch-mate, Niranjan Singh. Many exporters complained that he was not very active and it was also very difficult for any one to appear as active as Vittal. But during his tenure, the zone became a hive of activity because of the exports to the then Soviet Union and the Rupee Trade Area and the exports touched Rs. 150 crore or so.

When this paper on FTZs and EPZs was under active consideration in the Ministry, *Blitz* of Bombay wrote an article stating that this was an attempt to get the multinationals by the back door. With this article, the Government developed cold feet and the entire concept died a natural death including the proposed Salt Lake Area Free Trade Zone. But years after, the concept took shape again and a number of zones was developed in different parts of the country. By then the economic policy and philosophy had totally changed.

Similarly, I processed a paper for the Government on the Delhi Dry Port. This was in 1974. Many people had told me that they had dealt with this concept during the last decade or so. When the paper went to the Cabinet with a recommendation for establishing it at Tughlaqabad, Mrs. Gandhi on the morning of the Cabinet meeting wanted to know about the presence of any possible archaeological monument in the area. I had to contact the Director General of Archaeology and gave a reply at short notice. There were many claimants for the dry-port including Tughlaqabad, Palwal, Meerut and so on. So the paper was referred to the Planning Commission for further study on the locations. When I became Additional Secretary in the Ministry of Urban Development in 1990, I found the issue still hanging fire for want of clearance from that ministry from the Delhi urban agglomeration point of view. I played my small role again and it was cleared by the Committee of Secretaries with great difficulty. Finally, it took off as a container terminal at Tughlaqabad nearly 30 years after the concept was born and this was cleared by me as Additional Secretary, Commerce.

Another aborted case and a missed opportunity was the question of establishment of a Free Port on the Andaman and Nicobar Islands. The then Trade Development Authority (now wrongly merged with the Trade Fair Authority of India and known as the India Trade Promotion Organisation) made a comprehensive study of the islands and recommended establishment of a Free Port on the southern most island of Great Nicobar. This was a comprehensive study covering all types of legislation to be amended for the purpose, investment, climatic conditions and so on.

This would have been an ideal location because it was located on one of the busiest international shipping routes and ship repair yards could have been easily started there. I processed this report and prepared a paper for the Committee of Secretaries. I got the clearance of all the Ministries including the Intelligence Bureau because many foreigners would visit the area and also the Ministry of Defence. Navy also cleared the proposal. The Ministry of External Affairs also found it an ideal proposal because some possible claims in the area on these islands could be warded off. There was no Ministry of Environment those days to object to a proposal of this kind on the Andaman & Nicobar Islands. The investment was of the order of Rs. 1800 crore spread over 18 years. It included all types of infrastructure including an airport, ship yard, etc., But the Committee of Secretaries killed the idea in the first meeting itself. Curiously, the Committee of Secretaries included Dr Manmohan Singh who also opposed the proposal. I wrote in my diary on August 16th, 1975: " I accompanied Commerce Secretary to the Committee of Economic Secretaries . Discussion was on Free Port/ Export Processing Zones. I was not much impressed by the performance of these stalwarts". Dr Singh was a Left-oriented economist then who changed to the Right

in the Narasimha Rao government as Finance Minister with great ease as also reported in the press then and this was also the reason for his continuous success in career.

The idea was actually mooted by a Foreign Service officer, Siddharthachari. He was our Commissioner in Hong Kong in the early sixties and had a vision to suggest that a Free Port on this Island would be a good substitute for Hong Kong, which would revert to the Chinese in 1997. As it happened to many new ideas, it was also rejected forthwith by the Ministry of Commerce. But, Mohammed Yunus as Special Secretary revived the idea and got the report made by the Trade Development Authority. When I went back to Gujarat in 1977, I again wanted to have a look at this bulky, but comprehensive and useful report of two volumes. When I contacted Dr V.R. Panchmukhi, who was with the Trade Development Authority then, he told me that all copies were destroyed because they were marked 'secret'! That was how the Free Port died. Although Dr Subramanian Swamy tried to revive it with a report by the Raunaq Singh committee, it was yet to have a resurrection because of some inherent problems. Meanwhile, Great Nicobar had become a defence base and they would not allow it there. Moreover, the Ministry of Environment has become a reality and they would not allow any such activity on Andaman & Nicobar Islands because the tropical forests would be destroyed. (The recent Tsunami of 2004 brought back these thoughts to me how situations changed in human life. Perhaps it was good we did not establish a Hong Kong on Great Nicobar).

An account of the Commerce Ministry would be incomplete without mentioning about N.K. Singh who was Special Assistant to the Commerce Ministers L.N. Mishra, Prof D.P. Chattopadhyaya and later Pranab Mukherjee. At that time, the Special Assistants of different Ministers who were actually junior officers had formed an informal caucus and they went about as super-Secretaries and super–Ministers. Most of them, particularly N.K. Singh, wielded enormous powers and also made this clear to others. He was well disposed towards me and got me an extension by issuing a letter to Gujarat Chief Minister from L.N. Mishra although the latter just signed it. This was also because of a relative of mine who was in the same Ministry and was much closer to him. However, when I returned from Brussels, I was to come into the Ministry. But they diverted me to Madras in the Leather Export Promotion Council and I did not mind it in a way. But, when I wanted to come into the Ministry later, he resisted it, but could not completely stall it because of A.C. George. Because of this high profile, Mrs. Gandhi herself abolished the posts of Special Assistants except in the case of R.K. Dhawan and downgraded others as Private Secretaries. N.K. Singh was also packed off to Japan by Pranab Mukherjee on the orders of Mrs. Gandhi. N.K. Singh had his own problems years later and no one was prepared to take him back to the Government of India in 1990 except for Commerce Secretary S.P. Shukla of the Bihar cadre who himself was brought to Commerce from Industry earlier as Joint Secretary by N.K. Singh. V.C. Pande, as Cabinet Secretary, ruled out Commerce for N.K. Singh. But he landed in the Home Ministry. Being a competent officer and with the knack of getting on well with the powers-that-be, he landed in the Economic Affairs. I was a witness to all this because I was attending the selection committee meetings of the cabinet secretary every week in my capacity as additional secretary in charge of administration of the ministry of urban development.

In 1990, I fell off my chair in the Ministry of Urban Development when N.K. Singh entered my room. It was like Mahomet going to the mountain. He wanted to retain his late mother's bungalow till he was posted back in Delhi. I helped him. Of course, years later, he also came in my way and got the post of Expenditure Secretary to the Government of India when Dr Manmohan Singh considered or recommended me. Our paths crossed again in 1998. On a recommendation from the Gujarat Chief Minister, I was considered for the post of a Secretary in the PMO since there was no Cabinet Secretary or Secretary to the PM from the Gujarat Cadre since Independence. N.K. Singh naturally stole a march over me.

Another notable mention of this period was my close working with V.P. Singh. He had just started his Ministerial life as Deputy Minister for Commerce. He was mostly dealing with my subjects including leather and I had to brief him on many occasions. He was extremely polite and pleasant to work with. In fact, I did not know his close relationship with V.C. Pande although the latter was my Joint Secretary. Singh told me on many occasions that he wanted to do many things, but did not know how to go about in government. Sharma was his private secretary – a pleasant and warm officer who remained with V. P. Singh throughout even when he was the PM. V.P. Singh, Bose-Mullick and I had a long trip to Kandla. Since the plane was detained at Jamnagar for the so-called technical reasons, we had to undertake a long journey by road to Kandla. We exchanged a lot of anecdotes, particularly Bose-Mullick entertaining us on the way to while away the tedium of the journey.

I had met V.P. Singh later once or twice in the airports. He enquired about my postings. However, he could not take me into Economic Affairs or Commerce. When my file went to him in 1990 for my appointment as Additional Secretary in the Ministry of Commerce, Sharma told me that V.P. Singh as PM enquired whether I was the same Sundaram who worked with them earlier. He spoke to me once at a Rashtrapati Bhawan reception after laying down office as Prime Minister. He was the only Prime Minister whom I had known personally well. (Now, of course, Dr Manmohan Singh too).

His wife's sister's husband and my batch-mate, B.K. Singh lived in the same building on Shahjahan Road. BK, after having been an additional secretary, became a member of the Central Administrative Tribunal. He suddenly died of heart failure one morning. His wife and Mrs. V.P. Singh were away in Jaipur. I met V.P. Singh again here at the funeral. He remembered me well. Since I had difficulty with the Rao Government in getting a proper posting, I requested him later over phone (he spoke to me over phone when I wanted an appointment) to put in a word to the then Prime Minister Deve Gowda. He told me that it would be misconstrued as interference, but would certainly tell the Prime Minister or any one that I would be a very good officer or suggest my name, should the Prime Minister or any one enquire for good officers for some positions, as they did though rarely.

I also met him in 1997, presented a copy of my new book, "India and the EU" which he appreciated. Because of his Commerce back ground, he felt that it was an important book.

I requested for his intervention with Gujral for a post-retirement position, for such positions were given only to a chosen few, not necessarily on merit, but for other considerations. He did not intervene although promised to help. Perhaps he was too sick by then or was deeply immersed in caste politics which was actually his undoing although he was otherwise an honest and efficient Prime Minister.

12

Dr. V. Kurien: Right Recognition

When I was in Brussels in 1970, I came across two books on the Indo-EEC Trade in the EEC library. The first book was written by Dr R.S. Nigam of the Delhi School of Economics and the second one was by Dr (Mrs) Dharma Kumar, a South Indian married to former Petroleum Secretary Loveraj Kumar. I had interacted with Loveraj when he was in the Planning Commission on the Dry Port location. On my return to India, I got in touch with Dr Nigam so that I could work for a Ph.D., But he told me that residentship in Delhi was necessary. So when I was transferred to Delhi in 1974, I immediately got myself registered for my Ph.D., with Government permission. There was no need to attend any class. In fact, I had gathered a lot of material and had only to consult Dr Nigam now and then.

When I was almost finishing my tenure with the Ministry of Commerce in 1976, Dr Nigam directed me that I should submit my thesis immediately, in any case, before the end of December, 1976. I had no other option but to write the thesis at a feverish speed. I was always in the habit of taking long leave only when I had to move from one place to the other at the end of a tenure.

So I had already taken four months leave. Commerce Secretary Bose-Mullick also told me that writing a book was not easy particularly a thesis because it also involved, apart from repeated proof-reading which was boring, a lot of clerical work like foot-notes, tallying with the reference, page number, etc. A number of my personal assistants both in Delhi and in Madras cooperated with me, particularly Ambroise came from Pondicherry, stayed in my wife's house in Madras for a fortnight and assisted me. I had mentioned all of them by name in my thesis when it was published. Those days facilities like photo-copying were also not available in many places. Some exporter- friends like Parpia very kindly offered to do this for me on payment of course despite the fact that he wanted me out of the Leather Export Promotion Council because of my initiation of the new leather policy. I did not have any rancour. I also got the voluminous thesis bound in leather. In any case, it was a feverish activity for about sixteen hours a day. The thesis was completed by the third week of December, 1976. I had planned to take the train one fine morning to reach Delhi to submit the thesis. But it had rained heavily the previous day and the roads in Madras city got water-logged in no time. I thought of reaching the station by taxi, but it was providential no taxi was available. Had I got into a taxi with a box full of six volumes of my thesis, the whole thing would have been spoiled with water because even the buses had to wade through a lot of water which was up to the height of the whole tyre. In any case, the trains were also cancelled. So, after two days, I flew to Delhi and submitted the thesis on the last due date of the month. I really heaved a sigh of relief.

Evaluation of the thesis was an elaborate exercise. Once the thesis was submitted to the university, the professor had no control over it. The Vice-Chancellor would select three professors one of whom would be from a foreign university from a panel of names submitted by the professor. Of course, some informal understanding worked depending upon the relationship and standing of the professor with the Vice- Chancellor. Prof. R.S. Nigam felt that there would always be some criticism or attribution of motives in the case of an IAS officer. So he took care to appoint very eminent people as examiners. This was a closely guarded secret till the date of viva voce examination because on that day one of the examiners would come and interview the candidate in the presence of a number of invitees. This viva voce examination is announced on the board and any one can be present. While in Delhi the invitees have no right to put questions, not even the professor concerned but only the external examiner, in Brussels anybody can put a question. The Delhi system is better because the examinee would not be able to give some ready-made questions to his friends before the examination.

Although Prof. Nigam took a lot of interest in expediting the reports from all the three examiners, it just missed the convocation. In Brussels, results are announced then and there and certificates are given on the spot. Whereas here it has to be formally confirmed by the Syndicate of the University. This meeting was to be held later after that year's Convocation.

Meanwhile, the University Syndicate took a decision to impose a two year leave rule for all candidates for the Ph. D., including the lecturers in colleges. In other words, every one had to take leave for two years compulsorily for working for a Ph. D. When my result was considered for formal approval by the Syndicate, I was told that some one had raised this point. But the Vice-Chancellor and the Syndicate took a rational stand stating that in my case the examination was already over and the result was also out and it would not be fair to apply the rule at this stage. Moreover, it would not serve any purpose. So they declared the result formally and I was given a provisional certificate. I had to take my Ph. D. only in the Convocation next year from the hands of the then Prime Minister Morarji Desai and the then Chancellor of the University, Vice-President, B.D. Jatti, with whom I had worked. He was obviously pleased to see me receiving the degree and told the Prime Minister also that I belonged to the Gujarat Cadre. Although I belonged to the Gujarat Cadre, I had no occasion to meet Desai at all.

Meanwhile, the Government of Gujarat had posted me as Joint Commissioner of Industries. Unlike in the Government of India, the Government of Gujarat as far as possible kept in view the qualifications and experience of a person before posting him or her to a post. I was posted joint commissioner of Industries because of my industries and trade background. I

was preparing to report there in the middle of February, 1977. I was going there after a decade and so had my own apprehensions. But, a day before my actual departure, Dixit, a competent officer from the Revenue Department working on deputation in the office of the commissioner of industries rang me up to say that I was to hold additional charge of the post of Additional Commissioner because the then Additional Commissioner M.P. Parikh was transferred. This was a pleasant surprise to me because the post of additional commissioner carried heavier responsibilities and was more interesting than the post of joint commissioner. I held charge of these two posts for nearly four months. I was confirmed additional commissioner of industries. My place as joint commissioner was taken by an affable promoted IAS officer from the sales tax department, C.N. Shah, who remained my friend for long years to come. The Shahs took American citizenship after retirement because some of their children were settled there. I was on the Boards of many companies. I had to attend Industrial Licensing Committee and other meetings every month in Delhi. It involved frequent touring to Bombay, Delhi and also within the State. I was Member Secretary of a coordinating body of the Commissioner of Industries known as Industrial Extension (INDEXT) covering all industries corporations like the Gujarat Industrial Investment Corporation, Gujarat State Finance Corporation, Gujarat State Industrial Development Corporation, Gujarat Export Corporation, etc.,

Gujarat has made rapid progress in industrialization after its formation in 1960 mainly because of the inherent capabilities of the people for commerce and industry. Even an average Gujarati like a clerk or a peon in a government office will have some other business to fall back upon and will be familiar with matters like shares and stocks. They are also pragmatic and straightforward in their approach and in their dealings. They do not want to waste either their time or your time in unnecessary, meaningless and hypocritical courtesies as people in the north of India do. (This was written in 1993. The same point was made by B.K. Nehru who was Governor of Gujarat in his autobiography published in 1997)

Apart from these characteristics of the people, the Government of Gujarat also created a corps of officials in the IAS to manage the Department of Industry and the numerous corporations under its control. Unlike in the Government of India, a corporation job was always sought after because of the nature of the work and also the perquisites. Of course, this also had taken a beating over a period of time because many other officers in the IAS itself felt that this core group became a cadre within a cadre. So they wanted this to be thrown open to others too. **In any case, may be because of the atmosphere, the officials were capable of taking quick decisions for the development of the state. In fact, the officials went out of the way to pursue licences, etc., for the state from the Central Government. This was something unthinkable in other states. In fact, it would have attracted disciplinary proceedings elsewhere. In almost all the other states, there is always an antagonism between the bureaucracy and the industry. The bureaucracy had always put obstacles against the industry and it was for the industry to get over by all means whereas Gujarat was the only state in India where the government and the industry functioned together as partners for a common cause as in Japan. (Incidentally, this has also changed in other states to the extent that the bureaucrats, businessmen and politicians have become partners in corruption).**

Gujarat was the first state in the country to attract investment from the NRIs. The Gujaratis are still the largest Indian community abroad. Almost every household, even the ordinary people, had a son or daughter abroad. A team had gone out under the chairmanship of the then Finance Secretary, M.G. Shah. In my entire career, he was the only Finance man whom I found always positive in his approach. After visiting some European countries and the USA and meeting the NRIs, he suggested that there should be a separate office to attract and assist the NRIs to establish industries in Gujarat. He had recommended in his report that the Additional Commissioner of Industries, whoever it was, should be in charge of this office and the entire operation should be under the overall supervision of the Commissioner of Industries. So the office by the name, Industrial

Extension Bureau, was created in early 1978. It was a modern, almost paperless office, with telex and necessary requirements. The office had even an attractive receptionist. It was christened iNDEXTb and I was the first chairman. The idea was that a foreign NRI should first of all find the atmosphere business-like and congenial, free from stacks of dusty files as in the office of the Commissioner of Industries. Once an NRI had come to the office, all his requirements like industrial licence, the numerous permissions and also essential requirements like school admission for children, gas connection and telephone connection should be taken care of. There was an energetic chief by name Jai Narain Vyas who was the chief of the office directly reporting to me. He demanded from time to time for a hike in his salary because he was in great demand from the private sector, too. M.G. Shah used to grant his request on the spot. But the officer did a lot of good work as per my guidance and direction. It was a good team of youngsters. He became an authority on these matters and later wrote two or three books on the subject. He resigned later to become a BJP MLA and Minister. He has now his own Consultancy firm. (He did become a Minister again, I suppose).

I was also acting as the Managing Director of the Gujarat Mineral Development Corporation for some time. We used to have many meetings of the iNDEXTb in Bombay and other cities of India to attract investment to Gujarat. During an important visit to Calcutta by the team, a flap occurred and somehow many entrepreneurs were not informed about the visit. This was discovered at about 10 o' clock the previous evening after our arrival. N. Vittal was the leader of the team as the Commissioner of Industries. The entire visit would have been a flop, but we had an enterprising agent in Shilpi Advertisers. They had even produced films for attracting entrepreneurs. This company was a part of the Sarabhai Group and they used to do an excellent professional job for us. In fact, even the logo of the Industrial Extension Bureau – iNDEXTb – was one of their suggestions selected by us. Seeing our predicament, this agency man met his contact in *The Statesman*. He persuaded them to carry an advertisement on the front page – about a quarter of a page – the next morning. It required a lot of persuasion to shift

the news from the first page and print the advertisement about the visit of the Gujarat team. Of course, the newspaper had to be paid for it. But it was a timely move, which made our visit meaningful and attracted a huge number of entrepreneurs.

Several policy initiatives were taken. In one of the meetings, I made a suggestion to the then Secretary, Industries, S.J. Coelho that a time had come for us to have a District Industries Officer in each district as the District Agricultural Officer, District Health Officer and so on. He made a note of it and gave a better dimension to it by calling it a District Industries Centre when he moved over to the Government of India as Joint Secretary in the Ministry of Industrial Development. This concept was accepted all over the country and District Industries Centres were started in all states with the financial assistance from the central government. When the government changed after a couple of years, this concept was not scrapped. If Coelho had continued in Delhi, he would have certainly become Secretary, Industries and possibly even Cabinet Secretary with all his competence. But, unfortunately, he returned to Gujarat to head the Gujarat Narmada Fertilizers Company, but resigned mostly because of the machinations of some of his jealous colleagues. One of them was all along in Agriculture and had an eye on Industry. He managed to come into Industry with Coelho's exit. But he too played a very important role in the industrialization of Gujarat and in the affairs of the state for a long time. I also had to prepare a comprehensive five-year plan document for the industrialization of Gujarat at the instance of S.M. Ghosh, Secretary (Industries), Gujarat who was on reversion then to the State Cadre. Apart from all this and frequent tours, file work was also very heavy-bundles and bundles- as recorded by me on many days in my diary. I was also made in charge of Administration by Commissioner N. Vittal.

When one looks at some of these exits of brilliant officers like Mani Narayanaswamy and Coelho from the IAS, one really feels sorry for the great loss to the government. They also do not seem to be happy in the private sector for obvious reasons. About fifty IAS officers all over the country left the IAS for the private sector at that time. All of them were brilliant and competent men. Perhaps that was the reason why, they could leave! But they have not done all that well in the private sector for the inherent constraints of the private sector in India. Whenever there is a voluntary retirement scheme in the public sector or in government, it always happens that the better or the best ones leave and the worst ones remain.

It was also a phase in one's life, I suppose. Looking at all this philosophically, it was a period when I was offered many jobs without my seeking them – starting from the CMD of the Hindustan Diamond Corporation, the Bharath Leather Corporation by Dr Seetharamiah himself, the Executive Director of the Gem and Jewellery Export Promotion Council, Joint Commissioner of Industries converted into the Additional Commissioner and numerous other Directorships and first chairmanship of the iNDEXTb and so on. This was crowned by an offer to go to Brussels. But there were also times when one did not get any thing at all even if one tried hard as it was to happen after my retirement.

In November 1977, hardly after completing a year in Gujarat, a friend of mine, U. Vaidyanathan, Joint Secretary and Financial Adviser in the Ministry of Agriculture who was also my chief secretary in Pondicherry, came to stay with us on his way to Anand to attend a Board meeting of the National Dairy Development Board and the Indian Dairy Corporation. Normally one did not bother to travel all the way to Anand from Delhi to attend a meeting. But this time he had a compulsion to do so and he stayed with me. On his way back also, the next day after attending the meeting, he stayed in our house. At that time, I overheard him talking to my wife about when we would go to Brussels. I thought he was enquiring about our earlier stay in Brussels. But he told me that at Anand Dr. Kurien was making an enquiry for posting an officer in Brussels from the Ministry of Agriculture to handle their affairs for 'Operation Flood – II'. He did not want an IFS officer because they were not aware of the ground realities in India. He wanted an IAS officer or one from any other Service and wanted a name from the Board members. Nobody had any name to suggest. But,

U. Vaidyanathan remembered that I studied in Brussels and was also with the EEC. So he immediately mentioned my name to Dr. Kurien.

I am deeply indebted to Dr. V. Kurien. Needless to say that he is a remarkable person. But for him, I would not have got a posting abroad. Our relationship has been good always and also with that remarkable lady, Dr Amrita Patel, daughter of H.M. Patel, ICS, former Finance Minister. H.M. Patel started as an Assistant Collector and ended as Finance Secretary. He again started as President of the Vallabh Vidhyanagar Panchayat and ended as Finance Minister! My close relations with Dr. Kurien continued when I became Secretary, Civil Supplies and also partly when I was in Commerce as Additional Secretary. **I always saw that many an award came to him without his seeking or manoeuvring as it happened often but the Nobel Peace Prize should have also come to him. (This might have sounded a bit far-fetched at that time but, now, if the Peace Prize could be awarded to Dr. Muhammad Yunus of Bangladesh for rural micro-finance, it could as well have been given to Dr. Kurien for the White Revolution in India and for making India the largest producer of milk in world) Incidentally, there are many awards in this country including 'Padma' awards and 'Kalaimamani' awards in Tamil Nadu, to cite a few. As Inder Malhotra wrote in "The Hindu", these awards were more 'extracted' than 'given'. In some cases like Dr Chenna Reddi Award for good governance, it does credit neither to the name, nor to the recipient. But, for Dr Kurien, Dr M.S. Swaminathan and Mrs. M.S. Subbalakshmi, awards came without seeking. There are also numerous other awards of doubtful credibility. Mr. P.K. Davé, my Ambassador in Brussels who was Adviser to the Governor in Tamil Nadu told me that there was fearful lobbying for 'Kalaimamani' awards in Tami Nadu. As a result, deserving persons also do not get these awards in time. To quote an instance, a Tamil comedienne Manorama got a 'Padma Shri' after a long stint in films and after getting into the Guinness Book of Records.**

Both of us were somewhat reluctant to go back to Brussels. In fact, my wife was not inclined at all. But Vaidyanathan felt I should accept because it was always difficult to get a posting abroad and, should Dr Kurien select me, it would go through without any difficulty. So it was quite a temptation at least as far as I was concerned. I called on Dr Kurien within a few days and had a chat with him. He gave me an indication then and there that he would be inclined to consider me seriously.

After a few days in January 1978, the secretary to the chief minister, Chandubhai Patel, told me that there was a letter from Dr Kurien addressed to the chief minister, Babubhai Jasbhai Patel, a highly competent but Gandhian-like simple-looking chief minister, asking for my services for a posting in Brussels. Chandubhai also told me that Dr Kurien had written in his letter that I was 'tailor-made' for the post and since it was a request from Dr Kurien, it would not be refused by the chief minister. After about ten days, it was a pleasant surprise to hear from R. Balakrishnan, secretary in the General Administration Department, that they had already replied to Dr Kurien stating that should Government of India make a request to the Government of Gujarat for my services, they would have no objection to spare me. I naturally felt very happy. But when I told this news to my wife, she was very unhappy and started crying. In any case, I decided to ignore her feelings because only I decided in all such matters.

Dr Kurien took up the matter immediately with the Ministry of Agriculture of the Government of India. He not only took it up, but also told some of my friends in Gujarat in the airport one fine morning, the news spread like wild fire. Many colleagues of mine were really unhappy. Perhaps they tried their best to scuttle it. The Government of India also raised some objections. But, Dr Kurien told them point-blank that he did not believe in fake panels as they did in the Government of India, but would be prepared to consider a candidate as good as me, if there was one. There was none with the experience of studying in Brussels, training with the EEC and knowing French well. The Government of India had no other go but to clear my case. Perhaps it was one of a few cases of foreign posting decided purely on merit and not on other extraneous considerations. Dr Kurien used to tell people even later that many in the Government of India wondered for a long time whether he had known me personally or was related to him in some way because all such postings were decided on the basis of these considerations. Later too, I had hardly come across a person being posted abroad purely on the basis of suitability without the backing of a minister or secretary for extraneous reasons.

In any case, it dragged on. I insisted that I should go only with diplomatic status. I had known that otherwise one would not be able to function effectively in an office abroad particularly in dealing with organisation like the EEC. If one had no diplomatic status, one would not even be able to enter the portals of the EEC and one had to deal through a Second or First Secretary in the Embassy. Dr Kurien realised it and got me the diplomatic status although the Ministry of External Affairs was dragging their feet.

Meanwhile, I was placed in charge of a UNDP Conference to be held at Anand. This meeting was to take place in the first week of December, 1978. Although my orders were received in October 1978 itself and Dr Kurien wanted me to leave immediately, the chief secretary to the Government of Gujarat, H.K.L. Capoor wanted me to complete the Conference and go because perhaps he was hoping against hope that my posting would be cancelled for some reason or the other. He held the post of Establishment Officer as joint secretary in the Government of India. He became the chief secretary to the Government of Gujarat and held the post for seven long years. He got an extension for six months which was challenged by one of the IAS officers in the High Court on the ground that the extension was not in order because more competent officers were available to take his place and Capoor was also not that competent and that he was rejected by the Government of India for secretaryship. The CRs had to be produced in the court and it was quite amusing for a junior batch-mate of mine to read the Confidential Reports of the chief secretary and handle the case along with the Advocate General. Meanwhile, six months had gone and the government decided not to give him further extension. The IAS officer concerned had also resigned from the IAS meanwhile and became a lawyer and pressed for a decision on merits. But, the High Court dismissed the case stating that there was no cause for further action. People joked that Capoor was the chief secretary for seven years which was made seven and a-half years by the government as the seven and a-half year cycle of 'Sani' in one's horoscope or 'Sadesathi'! Of course, he did not harm me in any way.

He was a strict person who used to tick off even his wife not to interfere in official matters. In other words, it was difficult even for his wife to influence his decisions. So it was perhaps fitting that he was appointed chairman of the UPSC two or three years later although the appointment came as a great surprise to many.

The UNDP Conference was a great success. For the first time in the country, a wireless simultaneous translation system was installed. One could listen to the proceedings of the conference while moving from place to place. The delegates for the conference arrived by a special plane from Delhi. When they were transported to Anand in about ten luxury buses from Ahmedabad, there were crowds on both sides of the road and I realised it was not difficult in India to collect crowds for anything. But the conference delegates from abroad thought the crowds were there to greet them! They enjoyed their stay in rural Anand, but on the ultra-modern campus of the National Dairy Development Board. Since there was Prohibition in Gujarat, Government of India's permission was sought to give alcoholic drinks to the foreign delegates attending the conference. Since Morarji was the Prime Minister, George Fernandes as industries minister, though convinced himself, could not permit the Government of Gujarat. But the orders of the Government of Gujarat had a stipulation that foreigners could be given a special dispensation. So Babubhai, Chief Minister, cleared in spite of Morarji and the foreign delegates had their drinks!

The officers of the Government of India kindly offered to transport me and my wife and the huge baggage to Bombay by the special plane when they left on December 2nd, 1978 from Ahmedabad. But I had to tie up some loose ends. I handed over charge and left the same night by train for Bombay and farther on to Madras. One had to change from the Bombay Central station to Victoria Terminus. This was a cumbersome process. But some relatives and the regional office of the Gujarat Industries Commissioner in Bombay helped me.

After reaching Madras, I had to finish some orientation training with the Tamil Nadu Dairy Development Federation and the new dairy coming up in Erode. This helped me compare the conditions in Gujarat and Tamil Nadu in the dairy sector. I was also ready for take-off to Brussels.

One of the remarkable persons I met during this period was Mrs. Shashikala Kakodkar, the former Chief Minister of Goa. She was on a four day visit to Gujarat. The Government of Gujarat, for some reason, rolled out the red carpet for her and asked me to be the officer-in-waiting. I travelled with her for four days. I found her to be a very balanced person who did not talk more or less and her behaviour was just correct although her husband appeared to be a bit eccentric or, as they say in French, 'un peu gaga'. I was told that her father, Bandodkar, as the first Chief Minister of Goa never took any pay, nor travelled anywhere at government expense. This reminded me of Nagappa Chettiar of the Leather Export Promotion Council who never used Council's money even when he travelled on official work. The Maharajah of Bhavanagar too as the first Governor of Madras did not take any pay. It is very difficult to find such public persons these days.

This period was a high watermark of my career with many important job offers and finally a posting to Brussels purely on merit, thanks to Dr Kurien and hence this chapter under the name of this remarkable man.

* * *

13

A Second Stint Abroad

It was a cold, grey winter afternoon in the middle of December, 1978. I landed in Brussels and was received by the Embassy staff. I did not feel bad about the grey sky or cold weather as I did during my first arrival in Brussels because I was mentally prepared for it. Moreover, by now it was a familiar place with annual visits since I left in 1971.

I was taken to the Hotel Palace, a familiar hotel because every one who came from India to Brussels on official work stayed there and I too was lodged there. It was an old regal type of hotel located in Place Rogier in the heart of the city opposite Hotel Sheraton and the famous Martini Centre. I had to stay there for nearly three months because my post was a new one and everything had to be done afresh including office room and house accommodation. In such a situation, one had to rough it out and work a great deal. But I had no difficulty whatsoever because I was familiar with the place and I could explore on my own.

I reported to the Embassy on December 18th , 1978 situated in a building on Avenue Moliere which I had frequented several times earlier. Since Ambassador Davé was away on tour, I was told by one of the Counsellors holding charge, to occupy a room on the second floor in the old building. Ambassador Davé and other Counsellors were sitting in a hired building two buildings away. I did not make this an issue because such things happened whenever new posts were created. But, when Ambassador Davé returned from tour, he told them to give me a fairly spacious room on the first floor. This room was facing a garden. In fact, years ago, the Ambassador himself used to sit in this building and that room was now being occupied by the secretariat of the Embassy. But, on the whole, they were all friendly and Mrs. Navarekha Sharma, the Head of the Chancery, took a lot of interest in searching for an accommodation for me and acquiring other things like crockery, cutlery, etc., which were essential not only for the house, but also for discharging representational duties.

When one goes into an Embassy, one is often invited to some party or the other. It so happens that at times people are out on transfer and there is a chain of farewell parties. There could be a chain of welcome parties too. In other words, entertainment is a part of diplomatic life and one should be mentally prepared for it. A totally new person who does not belong to the Foreign Service may find it a bit difficult to cope with. Even within the Foreign Service, many Foreign Service wives find it difficult and boring because they have to entertain all and sundry all the time throughout one's career although they are paid for it by the government in the form of representational grant.

I had no difficulty whatsoever in establishing contacts in the European Economic Commission because it was a familiar place for me. In fact, when Dr Kurien wanted something urgently, the Director concerned was not inclined to grant it. But I directly approached the Director General who was also a close friend of Dr Kurien. When he instructed the Director to do it, he naturally wondered how I could operate at that high level so soon after my arrival. But some one put him wise by telling him that I had been a trainee in the Commission and was familiar with the set-up.

Apart from settling down at work, I was also looking for a suitable apartment. Although many apartments were available, they lacked something or the other. I had to do these wanderings in spite of the inclement weather of December. Whenever the weather was still with the sky overcast for a day or two, it was a sure sign that it would snow. On one such evening, we went for a dinner at a colleague's place. The road was absolutely clear at about 8 p.m., But, when we came out at about 11 p.m., there was about six inches of snow all over the place. It was also Crristmas eve. My friend's car at some stretches started going back in snow because most people there had no special tyres for snow as they had in Scandinavian countries. So he requested me to stay with him at his place for the night, which was nearby, instead of driving me all the way to my hotel which was at a long distance. So I stayed with him at his residence with which too I was familiar because of my earlier visits to one of his predecessors.

The place was full of snow the next morning also and hardly any traffic was moving. In any case, since I was in that area, I contacted a land-lady's agent on phone. I thought he would not show me the apartment that day because it was Christmas Sunday and the weather was also very bad. But, to my surprise, he was willing to show me the apartment. For the Belgians, the holidays were sacrosanct, but they would sacrifice it if it was a question of business. He told me the same thing and wanted me to come within an hour to see the apartment. I did not want to trouble my colleague because it was risky to drive. So I took a tram, although the distance was only about two kilometres. But even the tram took about half-an-hour because they had to remove the snow on the track. I reached the place with great difficulty.

I was rather surprised because when I reached the building I realised that I had seen it under construction during my first stay. It was a nice modern building just in front of the tall Sociology building of the University of Brussels where I reported first as a student in 1970. The University area itself was a good residential area. It was also not far from the Etang d'Ixelles (artificial lake in the commune of Ixelles within the city of Brussels. Once I asked a lady whether she was from Brussels or, as they say there, a Bruxellois; she corrected me to say that she was an Ixellois!) and the apartment where I stayed first. The Bois de la Combre (forest) was just across the road so that one could go for a walk in the evenings. More than all this, apart from being modern with new wall paper, fittings, etc., all the three bed rooms had attached bath rooms which was not the general case in Belgium. They always economised on bath rooms and toilets. Even big apartments with three or four bed rooms had only one bath room and two toilets, one mainly for the use of the visitors. Whereas this apartment was very well planned with this luxury and also a separate room for the servant on the ground floor with a shower attached which indeed was a greater luxury in Belgium. The apartment was also not that expensive, much below my ceiling stipulated by the Ministry of External Affairs. So I straightaway agreed to take it.

Hotel Palace was convenient because it was located in the heart of the city and there was a self-service just opposite in the famous 'City-2' shopping complex. I have always preferred the self-service while eating out because it is easier to pick up whatever you want particularly for a vegetarian like me. After seeing me for two to three months eating only rice, vegetables, yoghurt, etc., which were side-dishes for them, the girl at the counter asked me one day how I managed to survive on this type of food. This was similar to my land-lady's surprise during my first stay as to how a vegetarian could be so tall and hefty!

Meanwhile, an officer who was familiar with the arrangements for shipping came from the Indian Dairy Corporation, Baroda, and took me to London, Dublin, Paris, Hamburg and Frankfurt for familiarization. These visits were useful for acquainting oneself with the people who mattered for one's job. I must mention here that on these visits and during other visits, I never liked the question at the Immigration in London, although polite, about the purpose of the visit and the number of days of stay in spite of the fact that I was travelling on a diplomatic passport. My friend was telling me that we would not encounter any such problem in Dublin. But the Immigration at Dublin too had put such silly questions and they would not budge at my protests.

At Dublin, Ambassador N.N.Jha had a small office with a Second Secretary Jagannathan to assist him. The Ambassador had hardly any work. So he was always happy whenever somebody visited Dublin on official work. He was kind enough to place the Embassy car at the visitor's disposal and arranged to take the person around. I was reminded of my visit to New Zealand where the High Commissioner complained as soon as I entered his room that it was a place meant for unwanted people

like him. I suggested later to the Government of India, when they appointed a committee to go into the question of economy in the diplomatic service, to do away with Embassies in such places which could be looked after by a big Embassy from the neighbouring country like England or Australia. But the committee, as usual, suggested an increase perhaps as a measure of cadre management of the IFS rather than economy. Parkinson's Law is universal in its application.

It was customary for some one to hold a New Year Eve Party inviting others, particularly from the Embassy. That year, it was left to Rahman of the Tea Board, which was located in the Martini Centre. So it was not a problem for me just to walk across and meet the other members of the Indian community despite the biting cold. But Ambassador Davé could not come because he was snow-bound in his small but good bungalow in a posh area on a huge plot which stretched from one road to the other. He had tennis courts on the compound. The government of India did well to buy this property years ago.

Perhaps it was the smallest office I had in my entire career although the work was day-to-day and involved a lot of touring. There was only one file to deal with. There was a PA attached to me whom I used to send out quite often on tours because he was naturally interested in seeing places. He also developed an expertise in shipping matters by supervision of loading, handling bills, etc., But the entire operation was streamlined within a few months so much so the Ambassador felt to my great disadvantage that there was no need for a person of my rank to handle the job any longer. I was told later that he had recorded in my CRs that I had worked with such efficiency and organised things so well that my post became superfluous. At the same time, I believe he contradicted himself by asking for a substitute. May be what he meant was a lower level person although he was wrong because the job involved high level contacts not only at the member-states level but also in the Commission; in fact, he appreciated my very high level contacts including at the Minister level in Brussels, which the other officers in the Embassy did not have. This remark also perhaps came in the way of my extension two years later. Normally the post would have been for a period of three years. But when Dr Kurien made it for two years, I felt it was good because in case I did not like it I would be able to get away. Otherwise, an extension for another year would be in the normal course.

However, the job involved apart from field operations in regard to shipping of commodities, constant interaction with the Commission and the Member Governments to tie up and operate the allocation of the aid commodities for Operation Flood – II which was a massive project. Although my function was mainly aid coordination, I submitted notes to Ambassador Davé from time to time on EEC matters and at that time on the current topic of EEC-ACP Relationship. He appreciated some of these notes much to the annoyance of the members of the Foreign Service. In fact, he wanted to give me a part of this job on a regular basis, but could not do so because of the opposition from the members of the Foreign Service who dominated this Economic Mission, too. But I kept him informed of many other matters. He appreciated this because many IFS officers did not bother about many local matters, may be because of the language difficulty. One such information provided by me was how Belgium recorded automatically all overseas calls and a similar practice was prevelant in the EE Commission. This was to guard against the then Palestinian terrorist attacks although it was against privacy laws which could be relaxed for national security reasons.

At that time, there were some bright and friendly officers from the Foreign Service. In fact, the set which came in one year after my arrival along with Ms. Arundhati Ghose was more friendly than the previous one. Arundhati made efforts to move me from the other building to the main building where the Ambassador also sat. The interaction was better. The other Counsellor, S.K. Shunglu, became a long-time friend. So were Nalin Surie and Poonam. There is always some antagonism in the Embassies between the Foreign Service and the officers belonging to other Services. But, Brussels being an Economic Mission had the tradition of having always a non-IFS Ambassador with a number two from the Foreign Service as a matter of convention. On a few occasions, Foreign Service Ambassadors were also posted and it was the convention to have the number two from the IAS. In spite of all this, the Foreign

Service officers by their long stints in small Embassies had lost the capacity to wield the broad brush and consequently their horizon always became narrow and small so much so there were petty bickerings even amongst them too. What would have been a matter of ordinary importance to be handled by a middle level officer for the IAS would be a big thing for the IFS. The visit of a minister or a delegation was a big event and they would plan months in advance. They would concentrate on petty details like who should be excluded from which party, how not to treat a fellow Indian living there and so on. This kind of pettiness was also carried to the Foreign Office in New Delhi. But it was all insular right up to the Foreign Office for a long time and things did not come out. The IFS always felt that the IAS were the whipping boys for the politicians and they were in a position to please them on the contrary by extending all types of hospitality during their visits abroad.

Even in the Foreign Office in New Delhi, the Prime Ministers have always been in the habit of dealing with the Foreign Secretary directly. Moreover, unless a Minister was an expert in diplomacy for a long time like Swaran Singh or Narasimha Rao, it was difficult to function. In any case, the Foreign Ministers had to go strictly by the advice of the Foreign Service bureaucracy lest some diplomatic faux pas should be committed. In other words, barring a few ministers who were well versed in foreign affairs, others found it difficult to deal with the Foreign Service bureaucracy. But the A.P. Venkateswaran affair exposed the entire Foreign Service to the outside world and the Foreign Service too came under political pressure. Although they have a good system of rotation for postings like Super A stations, A stations, B stations, C stations, etc., many officers have put the system to disuse or abuse by seeking political favours. A system of coterie administration also came to light immediately after the retirement of J.N. Dixit, a highly competent diplomat and Foreign Secretary. So the Foreign Office is no longer beyond the public glare.

One Mr Raman, an IFS officer also wrote a couple of books highly critical of the Foreign Service. The intention of the author was to improve the service and to free it from even minor corruption like misuse of representational grant, excessive office expenditure, etc., because they were located far away from the headquarters. I was told that the entire Foreign Service did not take kindly to these books of Raman. Interestingly, the book carried a foreword by a highly acclaimed Foreign Service officer of old vintage, Badr-ud-din Tyabji.

During this period, the India Trade Centre was also started with the assistance of the EEC. A number of non-IFS experts came into the Trade Centre. They could not be given diplomatic status because of the nature of their function. Although this resulted in a bit of tension between the Embassy and the Trade Centre, the Trade Centre by and large worked well and served its purpose. It continued to function under the budget of the Commerce Ministry. I had dealt with it later when I was Additional Secretary in the Ministry of Commerce.

It is not known to many people outside Government that the Ministry of Commerce controls nearly seventy commercial posts in different Missions abroad. But most of these posts barring perhaps three or four are monopolised by the IFS. So a wrangle has been going on for a number of years about the non-IFS commercially trained officers manning these posts. In spite of the recommendations of many committees including one under Dr P.C. Alexander to this effect, the IFS has not given up its hold on these posts. On the whole, a major restructuring of the IFS is necessary and it is possible to cut down many Missions abroad. But this cannot be achieved unless there is political will at the level of the Prime Minister – even a Prime Minister should be of a type like Margaret Thatcher. (It is reported that the present Foreign Secretary Shiv Shankar Menon is trying to increase the strength of the IFS and the Missions abroad)

Brussels was one of the big Missions with about a hundred officials including the Trade Centre. These hundred families constituted the main nucleus of Indians in Belgium. There are about a hundred families in Antwerp in the diamond trade. Apart from these two hundred families, there are about fifty families of Indians scattered all over Belgium. Since Brussels was a small city where one could go from one house to the other in about fifteen minutes by car, it gave a feeling of cohesion in spite of the prevalence of the small-town mentality otherwise. The Antwerp Indians in the diamond trade lived by themselves in great luxury. However, they were very much an Indian community transplanted from Gujarat and Bombay because they followed all traditions and observed religious festivals like Deepawali although these festivities were held in the luxurious Europa Hotel in Antwerp. They could also get all Indian vegetables by the then direct Sabena flights from Bombay. In fact, I had seen Zaveri in the Brussels airport carrying only a small bag on his shoulder. He did not have to carry anything else at all because for him a trip between Antwerp and Bombay was like going from Bombay to Poone.

The snowfall of Christmas eve continued now and then and snow was lying all over the place. Since Christmas holidays were sacrosanct for the Belgians, no Municipal employee was there to remove the snow and as a result there was many an accident. The Government of Belgium also did not have the requisite equipment to remove the snow because the heavy snowfall was rather unusual. The newspapers also wrote that it would have been an ideal time for the erstwhile Warsaw Pact countries to invade Belgium because no one was available.

One of the highlights of our stay, as far as we were concerned, was the visit of Dr Kurien. He also brought a copy of the film, 'Manthan' which was shown to a large audience after a reception. Later I sold the film to the Belgian Television. Malcolm Subhan had shown it several times to the Belgian trainees going to Africa in order to give them an idea about the problems they might encounter in developing countries. So the film must have had about hundred and odd shows during my period. Ambassador Davé also made the visit of Dr Kurien highly successful.

During my stay, my former professor of Public Finance, Prof. Henry Simonet was the Foreign Minister. He was also the Mayor of the Anderlecht commune within the city of Brussels. He was also the President – equivalent to our Vice-Chancellor – of the University of Brussels. Later on, he got into trouble on account

of some minor financial dealings with some foreign country in Latin America and had to resign. He could not recover himself from that and faded away from public life. In fact, when he was out of office, he spoke to me once to arrange for an interview with Mrs. Gandhi during a private visit of his to New Delhi. Perhaps he thought he could retrieve his position by meeting a few world leaders of the stature of Mrs. Gandhi. I had to keep Ambassador Davé informed in any case and the latter was not perhaps helpful in his report to Delhi and as a result the interview did not come through.

No politician had gone to jail (now some of them have gone at least for a short while) or lost his political career ever in our country so far for any act of commission or omission despite the numerous inquiry commissions and cases in courts of law. If at all, it was only a temporary loss of face which was accepted at ease by the common public. (This was drafted three years ago. The situation has changed somewhat now, thanks to the Judiciary). Whereas in western countries, some politicians might have been corrupt. But, whenever they are caught, there is no other alternative but to subject oneself to the rule of law. No one could escape punishment, legal or political. For instance, one of the prime ministers of Belgium was indicted for some wrong-doing in a business deal. Despite his best efforts, he was fined heavily and given a suspended sentence instead of actual imprisonment taking into consideration his services for the country. That was the end of him. Such dispensation of justice is yet to be practised here.

Guy Spitaels was the first person whom I met in the University in 1970 because he was attending to the affairs of the department of economics and any new entrant had to see him. During my tenure in the Embassy, he was the Deputy Prime Minister of Belgium and received me warmly on two occasions. But I was really close to Prof Paul Hatry who taught me Foreign Trade. He was also the chief negotiator of the petroleum companies in Belgium. He was also a member of the Liberal Party of Belgium and became the Finance Minister during our stay there. When I invited him to my residence for a dinner, he readily accepted and came waiving the protocol. It was very

unusual for a minister to participate in a dinner at the residence of a Counsellor. Ambassador Davé felt that among the officers in the Embassy I had the best contacts. The top bureaucrats of the EEC did not believe much in protocol because they were mainly technocrats and consequently used to receive even a Counsellor in their office and also on some occasions attended a dinner or cocktails at the residence. During a dinner, one such person who attended was David Williamson, Additional Director General of Agriculture and also Von Verchauer, another Additional Director General. Both were A-1 i.e., equivalent to Director General in the EEC hierarchy. Williamson later went back to England to be the Permanent Secretary of a Department and came back a few years later as Secretary-General of the EE Commission to succeed the legendary Emille Nöel, who held the post for a long time ever since the inception of the EEC and retired.

The post of Ambassador to the EEC is a difficult one unlike the other Ambassadorial assignments to some other countries. Apart from dealing with Belgium and Luxembourg which is not difficult, the Ambassador has to understand the complicated organisation of the EU: Council of Ministers, Committee of Permanent Representatives, Commission, European Parliament, Court of Auditors which is like our Comptroller and Auditor General, European Court of Justice and also many lobbying groups and should be able to establish proper rapport with all of them. Dr K.B. Lall was highly successful and was even known to ordinary people even during his first tenure. He also unusually had a second tenure with a break in between as Secretary to the Government of India. The late T. Swaminathan also did well by sheer intellectual ability and connections in the GATT. Incidentally, for a long time, Ambassador to the EEC was also India's Permanent Representative to the GATT and the UNCTAD in Geneva. This was done away with later as the Geneva work involved a large number of days in negotiations and also the Permanent Representative to the UN Organisations in Geneva – I think it was A.P. Venkateswaran – claimed that he would also cover the UNCTAD as it was a part of the UN system unlike the GATT. Many other Ambassadors were neither trained, nor intellectually equipped or hard working to fill this post. They could not make a mark for obvious reasons. Although Ambassador Davé did well by and large, he could not be considered a tremendous success because he carried with him the Indian bureaucratic hierarchy and aloofness. He became rather sensitive whenever a Director General did not accept his invitation to dinner. This was not out of any discourtesy on their part. There are about two hundred and odd Missions to the EEC in Brussels and if a Director General attends a dinner in a Mission every day, he would take more than a year to cover all of them. They did give importance to a country like India although they unnecessarily clubbed Pakistan and other countries like Sri Lanka and Bangladesh with us. The trade agreements were also copied every time with small changes. Moreover, before the entry of Britain, their exposure to India was also small. They thought it was like an undeveloped African country. For instance, the Chief of the Court of Auditors, a French, came to India to audit the accounts of the Operation Flood – I. He was simply surprised to see the type of accounts maintained and the handling of commodities in India. When he returned, he gave a glowing report. A Scottish officer, Lorimer Mackenzie, who accompanied him during the visit told me that the gentleman was simply carried away by the knowledge of the Indians because his earlier exposure was only to Africa!

In fact, during our first stay, in spite of the shoe-string budget, we visited a number of places in Europe. During the second stay, the official work itself took me to a number of countries and we could do that by our own car although I did not tour as much as I was expected to. I sent my Personal Assistant instead. But a personal memorable trip was to North Cape in Norway – the top most point of civilisation in the world. My wife wrote an interesting article in *The Illustrated Weekly of India* with some photographs taken by me.

But the stay was not without tears. As it happens some times in life, things go wrong in succession. Since I got this post with selection by Dr V. Kurien, the officialdom got cross with me and did not place my name on panel for Joint Secretaryship. In fact, my name was on the list as confirmed by Joint Secretary, the late N.Rajagopal, a highly rated officer selected by Dr V. Kurien to deal with Operation Flood –II as he did in my case. It was removed along with few other names because the then Cabinet Secretary, N.K. Mukherjee, felt that the list was long. But the committee blundered so much that the then Cabinet Secretary Krishnaswami Rao Sahib – a very upright and highly regarded officer, one who was brought to the centre by the Janata Government, but was retained by Mrs Indira Gandhi as her Principal Secretary when she came back to power and also made him later the Cabinet Secretary superseding many officers – introduced the system of consulting the state governments too and thereby included many good officers – one of them was M.S. Rajajee from Andhra Pradesh – on the panel. In any case, this caused me mental anguish at least temporarily although our names were also included again in consultation with the state government.

I also exposed myself to the cold weather in winter so much so my health deteriorated. Although I was functional, I had to take treatment. My servant too fell sick and he had to leave the place with his wife. So we had to manage without a servant for more than a year – this was particularly difficult for official entertainment. Never in my life was I involved in a serious road accident. The sturdy London taxi dashed against a steel barricade on the motorway from the London Heathrow airport to the city and made a complete turn – it did not capsize because it was the heavy London taxi. I thought I would be finished by the oncoming cars on this highway. But, luckily, there was not even a single car and I escaped with minor bruises. Similarly, once in my early life, a man tried to pick my purse but failed. But my purse was pick-pocketed at a London tube-station. The police behaved in the same way as in India in spite of the fact that I was a diplomat. My complaint elicited a routine reply from the Metropolitan Police after a few months.

I had listed about thirteen such bad incidents or experiences over a period of one year and I got a bit disgusted. I requested Dr Kurien to relieve me after the tenure of two years. It was nearly three years before a substitute arrived. In fact, these persons were lucky in the sense that these technical officers from the NDDB got straightaway the diplomatic rank of Counsellor without having to undergo the hardships I had to. Ambassador Davé and I left

Brussels almost at the same time. We arrived in Delhi on August 15th ,1981 and I did a bit of searching for my next posting.

Dr Kurien wrote of me: "I am happy the visit of the Director General of EEC, Klaus Meyer, went off very well. I was happy to hear him speak very highly about your work in Brussels.

I am indeed sorry that it may not be possible for IDC to continue you with us. I had not fully realised till now how the IAS is just as bad as other Government services in fighting for posts and in the jealousy they display towards their colleagues. I suppose this is an Indian trait and we will have to learn to live with it."

More than all this, my youngest sister was keen on getting married. My father was far from a good counsel to her. She got married without us a month before our arrival back, of course, with the funds provided by me as I did in the case of my other three sisters, too. In any case, we were happy about her marriage. After a few days stay with my brother-in-law, C. Venkataraman in New Delhi, we arrived in Madras on the evening of August 20th, 1981. There was no one to receive us strangely. We reached "Burma House". There were no lights because of power failure. It was inauspicious. But power came with in a few minutes. We felt happy that every one was hale, healthy and hearty. But, within a few minutes, my father came with my brother-in-law Ramachandran to announce that my newly-wed sister died that evening. They admitted her into a government hospital thinking that she could be revived. In fact, she died in the taxi on the way to the hospital. Since it was late in the night, the hospital would not give her body away. I had to spend the whole night in the hospital, take that out in the morning and attend the funeral the next day. Sripal was the Commissioner of Police whom I woke up at 1 a.m., and as usual he was helpful. The Brussels posting started with tears as soon as the proposal was initiated and ended in tears.

* * *

14

Bofors or Tehelka or Corruption

It is not for nothing that India is one of the most corrupt countries in the world; it is also not a country for the common man.

The word, 'Bofors' became a synonym for corruption. I should add at the outset whether there is any truth at all in this controversy or alleged corrupt deal. This doubt has arisen because the way in which the various governments including that of V.P. Singh and the BJP have dealt with this matter. Only Gowda did get some papers from Switzerland. So, while 'Bofors' is still a presumption, 'Tehelka' has become a reality of corruption because of the visuals. The DMK had kept cut-outs of the 'Bofors' gun at every nook and corner during a Parliament election in which I was an Election Observer and the DMK did not get even a single seat.

Many people may not know that the spade work for the 'Bofors' negotiations was done by me and, in fact, I held the first meeting of the negotiating committee after getting government approval under the chairmanship of the then Defence Secretary S.M. Ghosh. By that time, my tenure in the Ministry of Defence was over and there was a thinking whether a short extension of three to four months should be given to me exclusively to attend to and finish these negotiations. But Cabinet Secretary Krishnaswamy Rao Sahib rightly felt that these negotiations would not be over so soon and there was no point in retaining me. Moreover, the then Defence Secretary, S.M. Ghosh, also suddenly died. His successor, S.K. Bhatnagar, did not believe in doing things fast which was also supported by the then Secretary, Defence Production, M.C. Sarin. There are always two views on such matters. Defence Secretary P.K. Kaul finished the 'Mirage' negotiations in about five months and there was no scandal. If something is dragged on, particularly on a matter like this, several people jump into the fray and create confusion. Of course, some auditor may find fault if things are done fast in government – it may be construed as unseemly hurry or haste to do certain things. So it cuts both ways. One of the deputy secretaries working with me who had long experience in Defence, P. Ray, always used to tell me that whoever was going to handle a big purchase like this would be the centre of a first-rate controversy. Subsequent events proved him right. Defence Secretary, T.K. Banerjee, who succeeded me as Joint Secretary, always used to joke that I should have started these negotiations at an auspicious time! I hasten to add that the negotiations (only one meeting) for the 155mm guns with the French gun as the first preference were scrapped and the entire controversy arose because 'Bofors' was preferred.

It was on 1.1.1982 that I joined the Ministry of Defence. In fact, I was not inclined to go to that Ministry. Many people at all levels do not want to be in the Ministry of Defence or Home. Contrary to the general belief, these are considered, according to a classification done by the Government of India itself, unpopular Ministries. Commerce and Economic Affairs are the most sought after followed by Petroleum, Industry, Petro-chemicals, (now Power), Agriculture, etc., In all these, the main attraction is the opportunity to travel abroad although many want job satisfaction too. Of all the Ministries I worked for like Commerce, Environment, Urban Development, Civil Supplies, Defence, Cabinet Secretariat and Tourism, Commerce Ministry provided the best satisfaction and one had to read and learn a lot there although I found job satisfaction everywhere except in the Cabinet Secretariat.

Since I was going to be in charge of Administration, I found to my surprise that my name board was already there at the time of my joining on the morning of 1.1.82. My predecessor was one Narayanan who was only a Matriculate and joined the Ministry of Defence as a 'boy' those days at the age of 15 or so. He remained in Defence throughout. He was a highly competent person with good ability to draft. In fact, some of the officers belonging to the Central Secretariat Service are really good at secretarial work. They could analyse things well and present the pros and cons in such a way to enable the superiors to take a quick decision. I could recall C.P. Kapoor in the Ministry of Defence and M.C. Jayaraman in the Ministry of Commerce. P.C. Jayaraman was another one in the Ministry of Commerce earlier. These two were far superior even to some of the IAS officers.

When I returned from Brussels, I was looking for a posting for the rest of my tenure. It was a pleasant surprise to learn from one of my colleagues in Gujarat that the Government of Gujarat had already agreed to my further deputation to Delhi when a reference was made by the Government of India on telex. In fact, such reference was unnecessary because I had not completed five years. However, the Government of India is in the habit of making such references to the parent cadres with the hope that they would decline. Later Patankar, who was principal secretary to the Chief Minister, told me that when the telex came from the Government of India, he straightaway replied without even consulting any one. He also told me that I could have stayed on in Brussels and he would have cleared things for me if there was any difficulty. Incidentally, Patankar who became Chief Secretary to the Government of Gujarat is from a royal family and so also his wife and both of them are very suave. It should be recorded here that Mr & Mrs H.K. Khan were also very friendly and suave and they belonged to the same batch although Khan joined a year later. S.J. Coelho also belonged to the same 1956 batch. One of our Chief Secretaries used to call them 'Mummoorthys' (the Trinity) of the 1956 batch in Gujarat. The 1956 batch also had people like A.N. Varma, Naresh Chandra, M. Varadarajan and S.K. Misra. Each one was unique in his own way, good or bad. Some batches have the so-called stalwarts who have become either famous or notorious. The 1962 batch, although started well with a lot of people getting into the panels by hook or by crook, earned a bad name because it was the only batch the panel of which was bandied about in the press. As a result, many felt perhaps rightly that it was not at all a good batch. However, 1962 batch of mine surpassed all others again by hook or by crook, by having a Comptroller and Auditor General, two in the PMO, one in the IMF, one in the UNIDO, one in the World Trade Organisation, and one as the head of an Inter-Governmental Institute in the former Yugoslavia after having been Secretaries to the Government of India, let alone many others who became Secretaries to the Government of India and Chief Secretaries to the State Governments. But the batch missed the important slot of Cabinet Secretary, thanks to the machinations of the previous cabinet secretary in getting repeated extensions. His extension was also challenged in the court of law. Similarly, repeated extensions and politicisation of the post knocked off the entire 1960 batch although a high-ranking and competent officer was available. This does not speak well of the bureaucracy and also the PM's office.

There were not many vacancies at that time of the year in the Government of India. There was a vacancy in the Ministry of Surface Transport and I was selected both by the then minister and the then secretary. Meanwhile, I happened to call on the Defence Secretary P.K. Kaul with whom I had worked earlier in Commerce and he wanted me to come over to Defence. When I told him that I had already tied up something in the Surface Transport, he simply told me not to bother about it. In fact, this caused some embarrassment to me with Yashwant Sinha, the then joint secretary in Surface Transport who became Finance Minister later. Of course, K.S. Bains was to leave the Surface Transport Ministry for the Asiad. But he was in two minds. Moreover, Mrs. Gandhi herself was the Defence Minister and once my name was cleared by her, there was no need to go to the Appointments Committee of the Cabinet again – or it was just a formality. Since I was also in a hurry to get a posting, this helped. I was also in a hurry to get accommodation in Delhi because my car and luggage were lying with P.N. Writer, the DGP of Gujarat. In this regard, my personal assistant C.V. Kurian was of great help and this association still continues. Some part of the luggage was also kept by my colleague, C.N. Shah and another friend Chib during my stay in Brussels and I had to relieve them of this burden.

I was in charge of Administration for three months. During this period, I could find my feet and learn about this complicated Ministry with numerous organisations. Every newcomer was asked to read a book written by one Venkateswaran who spent all his career in the Ministry of Defence and retired as joint secretary to join the Bharatiya Vidya Bhavan. His book was indeed useful and it gave a good account of the transition from the British when the Commander-in-Chief was a member of the Viceroy's Executive Council which was like the present day Cabinet. In the post-Independence days, the supremacy of the civilian power over the armed services in a democracy was well established. The President of India became the Supreme Commander. Many people remember H.M. Patel as Finance Secretary. But he was actually Defence Secretary for a long time and all this smooth transition took place during his period. There is a demand even now from the three Chiefs of Staff for a Joint Chief System. But it is not being agreed to because India is a democracy and the armed forces have to be kept in their place.

Very often a question arises as to why unsavoury developments as in Pakistan or Bangladesh have not taken place in India. This is for two reasons: One is that luckily like the civil services in India (may no longer be so), the Armed Forces are highly professional and they do not want to dabble in politics. Secondly, India is a highly individualistic, complex and vast country so much so that even for the armed forces it would be difficult to control for a long time particularly when the hostile neighbours have to be contained. In other words, the armed forces cannot afford to have an internal rebellion while having to guard the long borders. Even a charismatic leader like Mrs. Gandhi found it difficult to control things during the so-called Emergency. However, I would like to sound a note of caution here. The young IAS officers are rightly rebelling against their corrupt seniors. (This is also changing now for the worse and they seem to be losing their idealism). Judiciary is trying hard to contain and cleanse the rot. (Corruption is also creeping into the Judiciary). If the politicians try to perpetuate corruption or if institutions are demolished and if people witness constant wrangles in the legislatures, there is every possibility of our democracy being in danger. Rebellions are not started by Generals but by Colonels like the young IAS Turks of the UP who questioned their corrupt seniors. Besides, we in the country, including the Press, have started badgering the democratic institutions like the Parliament, administration, etc. Once these institutions are weakened, there would be no alternative to military rule. Or, even the country might disintegrate. Of course, this is not a solution because the military governments in Pakistan and also in Bangladesh have not covered themselves with glory. In fact, these two countries rank far below India in the Transparency International's corruption index. So democratic institutions have not only be protected, but should also be kept free of corruption.

Many people in this country were also under the erroneous impression that a man in uniform was free from corruption. I had seen even knowledgeable MPs giving expression to this impression in the Parliament during debates on Defence grants or subjects. 'Tehelka' completely demolished this feeling.

After one Rao from Madhya Pradesh left the Ministry of Defence at the end of his tenure, I was made the Joint Secretary (Ordnance). This should not be confused with the Joint Secretary in charge of ordnance factories in the Department of Defence Production. This was a unique post because it gave complete exposure to all branches of the Army and also the Departments of Defence Production and Defence Research and Development. The job required high level coordination. Since Joint Secretary (Ordnance) is in charge of all purchases for the army, both from within and abroad, he has to play an important role. Since many purchases of important equipment were languishing by sheer negligence of some of my predecessors, I was asked to hasten and I was brought in specially for that purpose with my Commerce background. Many civilian colleagues used to avoid these purchases or delayed them out of sheer fear of getting into some trouble or the other later. But I always felt that there was always a reputation and if one was not hanky-panky one did not have to bother. So I started the process with a lot of gusto. Although I had done my customary call, this brought me to the notice of the then Chief of

Army Staff, General Krishna Rao. He was quite appreciative of my work and used to invite me to his house even for some social dinners. Years later when I met him in a group of officials in Jammu & Kashmir in my capacity as Secretary, Civil Supplies, and he was the Governor, K.R. Venugopal, Secretary, PMO, happened to make an off-the-cuff remark by saying that there was some delay in making grains available by the Ministry of Civil Supplies to J&K. But, Governor, Gen. (Retd) K.V. Krishna Rao remarked that he knew me well and when I had acquired the much-needed equipment for the army within a short time, it would not be difficult for me to get the grains. On a later occasion also, when my Minister, Buta Singh, was to travel in the Governor's helicopter to Amarnath to have a 'darshan' of the famous ice-Lingam, Governor Rao instructed his private secretary to make it a point to put me also on the same helicopter so that I too could have the 'darshan'. This he did without my asking.

So naturally I had to be in close touch with the General Staff particularly the Deputy Chief of Army Staff who was in charge of all procurement in the army. Maj. Gen. N.N. Khanna was actually the person working under the Deputy Chief, Lt. Gen. K. Sundarji. I was always under the impression that he was a 'mechanised' Sardarji. But, on an occasion, he suddenly broke into Tamil to my utter surprise and I gathered that he hailed from North Arcot District of Tamil Nadu which incidentally used to send the maximum number of soldiers to the army. He was one of a few Generals who always kept themselves abreast of the various developments particularly in armament. In the defence service, unlike in the civil service, one cannot stay on in the headquarters for a very long time. One has to do the obligatory field posting if one wishes to go up the ladder. So even a Deputy or Vice-Chief does a Command before becoming the Chief. These frequent postings outside the headquarters make one lose touch with the fast, ever changing technology, particularly in armament. Unless one takes great care to get the journals and read them up even if one is in a far-off place like Ladakh or Sela Pass, one cannot be up-to date.

Incidentally, this fast changing technology is also a gimmick by the Western arms manufacturers to exploit the countries who buy these arms. They will sell a missile for a few crores of rupees. They will make some small change the very next year and charge a higher price saying that it would be more effective. This kind of a game goes on and on; they also keep telling Pakistan that India has acquired this or that weapon and vice versa. In other words, this is a big commercial proposition for them. Of course, the Generals are also fond of importing things perhaps because of our general belief in things foreign. India was the only country in the free world then outside the then Communist countries, which had a big armament industry with about thirty ordnance factories (now forty), ship building yards and aerospace manufacturers. However, it could not be helped that many items of warfare had to be imported and the Ministry had to be in a state of alert all the time for obvious reasons. For instance, the development and manufacture of an indigenous tank took a very long time crossing many target dates. So the army had to rely upon huge imports. In this task, I had to give the right of first refusal to the ordnance factories. In other words, it had to be ascertained whether they were in a position to produce an item before taking an import-decision. Once an import-decision was taken, technology transfer for indigenous production in the ordnance factories had to be negotiated and it had to be a part of the purchase programme. In this, research was also involved and in many cases the defence research and development laboratories were in a position to produce some of the items. Of course, very often they were in the habit of claiming that they would be able to produce any and every item under the sun. So the Joint Secretary (Ordnance) under the over all control of the Defence Secretary had to coordinate all these matters and take important decisions. The department of Supply in the Department of Defence Production in charge of indigenisation had also to be consulted. All this meant a lot of wrangle among these organisations and attendance at these meetings taken by Defence Secretary and Secretary, Defence Production to arrive at a decision, time schedule for purchase, time schedule for transfer of technology, time schedule for indigenisation in ordnance factories and so on. So I found this extremely interesting with a lot of job satisfaction.

At times, the defence personnel would not tie-up some matters like repairs and refurbishing of even items like tanks. This had to be tied up at the time of purchase itself so that we did not lose the negotiating advantage and cost reduction. Similarly, there was no control over spare parts or proper assessment at the time of purchase. So the sellers, whatever they had lost during the negotiations, would gain at the time of selling the spare parts years later by charging higher prices. I had plugged this practice by wanting the EME (Electrical and Mechanical Engineers) to make a proper assessment at the time of purchase itself so that the value could be fixed. In fact, this was also quoted in the report of the Joint Parliamentary Committee on 'Bofors'. Similarly, subsequent medium or long term repair and maintenance could also be tied up at the time of purchase itself. Since this had not been the practice in the past, the country lost a lot of money.

The army was on the look out for a good field gun. They had ruled out the Russian 152 mm guns. Incidentally, the Russians always had a peculiar calibration like 152 mm and not 150 or 155 mm because of their philosophy that in a war should the guns fall in the hands of an enemy, he should not be able to use them. The Russians were also generally following the general strategic practice as other super powers also did that they would give any number of main weapons like tanks, guns, etc., but not sufficient ammunition and spares so that the receiving country would always be on leash and in the event of a war would have to beg them unless the receiving country had a good industry like India and smart enough to produce the ammunitions and spares within a short time. Of course, we were not that smart. The erstwhile Soviet Union was also helping the satellite countries like Bulgaria, Czechoslovakia and Poland by asking the receiving countries to get ammunitions and spares from them against free foreign exchange. (There was also a Rupee Payment regime in operation then with the East European countries). But some ammunition manufacturers in Western countries like Germany were smart enough to produce ammunition for the Russian peculiar calibration guns and sell them.

So when the question of short-listing of field guns arose, the choice fell on the French gun. The French manufacturer also had an advantage because he was also producing the Self Propelled version. The second choice was the 'Bofors' gun. But it was not second quality-wise. Quality-wise it was equal to the French gun and was in no way inferior. The poor third was a trilateral cooperation version with joint manufacturing in the U.K., Germany and Italy. At this juncture, an Austrian firm also jumped into the fray. But Lt. Gen. Sundarji felt that this was a poor gun, but wanted to keep the firm on the list in order to generate competition for this big purchase. He called me and the Additional Financial Adviser Swaminathan one day to his room and confided that he would not say 'no' to the Austrian gun in order to have a good deal with the first two lest they would exploit us. But Finance should not insist upon the purchase of the Austrian gun at the time of negotiations because it was definitely of poor quality and consequently the price was low. Normally Finance insists upon accepting the lowest offer and he did not want this to happen. So he took us into confidence. At the same time, he told us that he would not like to put this on record because it would immediately leak to the Austrian party. Such leaks from the Services HQ were not uncommon as 'Tehelka' also proved later. After a few months, Lt. Gen. Sundarji was moved away to a Command and Lt. Gen. H. Kaul came on the scene. The Director of Weapons and Equipment also changed and Gen. Mayadas was appointed. When I informed Lt. Gen. Kaul of Sundarji's views about the Austrian gun, he wanted a record as it always happened in government and in that respect, as I have already recorded elsewhere, the professionals are more bureaucratic than the bureaucrats themselves. But he wrote a letter to Lt. Gen. Sundarji to have it in writing and the latter confirmed it. So as already reported by the JPC and as it appeared in many newspapers and journals in the welter of the 'Bofors' controversy, the Swedish and French guns were on a par. It also happens often in government that the shadow becomes a reality. A powerful minister from Kashmir was backing the Austrian company and their Indian agent was also a retired Kashmiri General's son-in-law. So there was a lot of pressure to accept the Austrian version which was also supported by Lt. Gen. Mayadas. It could be recalled that Lt. Gen. Mayadas gave many interviews and wrote a few articles during the 'Bofors' controversy projecting himself. Perhaps somebody put the government wise at that time and the noise of Lt. Gen. Mayadas died down. But he wrote a book on the subject and I was surprised to learn from it that a technical evaluation was ordered again even after a round of financial negotiations for the Swedish or French guns.

It was recorded in the JPC that Lt. Gen. Sundarji gave a recommendation in favour of the 'Bofors' gun on the basis of some 'shoot and scoot' theory. I felt that perhaps the politicians and the Secretariat played a trick upon him or he acquiesced himself for a favour done by Rajiv Gandhi – there was a rumour that Lt. Gen. H. Kaul may supersede him with the help of the Kashmiri lobby although this lobby became less powerful during Rajiv Gandhi's time. As a professional, he should have stated both the French and 'Bofors' guns would be acceptable equally to the Army depending upon the commercial advantage instead of giving an opinion in favour of a gun of the two equally acceptable guns but placing the second one above as inter se seniority and inviting criticism upon himself. The rest is history.

I must also add that Rajiv Gandhi became unnecessarily nervous when the controversy broke out, nor was he guided properly even by civil service luminaries in his office like Gopi Arora. It was a fact that the Swedish PM Olof Palme was lobbying hard for this gun. He even flew down to Copenhagen to meet Mrs. Gandhi when she was on her way to some international conference in the UK or the USA and spoke to her about the gun, as a letter from C. Garekhan, IFS, of the PMO (We thought that he was a Muslim from UP but he turned out to be a Nagar Brahmin from Gujarat. So he started expanding his initial and started writing Chinmay Garekhan) and later our PR to the UN, indicated. We had bought 'Mirages' from France, 'Jaguar' from the UK and 'HDW' from Germany and so this item from Sweden to please all Europeans, we could have explained. The trilaterally produced 155mm gun, as indicated above, was not good enough. This crucial explanation was missing from Rajiv's Government and he was not guided properly.

Even if the Government of India had decided to buy the French gun, there would have been a similar controversy because the Indian agents of 'Bofors' would not have kept quiet. In all big purchases, the agents try to create a controversy if they are losing out. These agents, very often retired Defence Service officers, are fronts of big industrialists. I was told that even 'Bofors' agent was a front-man for a well-known industrialist although I would not be able to confirm it. In fact, for some odd reason, the 'Bofors' agent never met me. For one or two other items of purchase, the 'Bofors' men from Sweden negotiated directly and they could not get the contracts because, as I told them, their items were good quality-wise but not competitive cost-wise on account of the high cost Swedish economy. But I was aware of some of the other leading industrialists dabbling in arms sales for obvious reasons. They generally operate only through front-men. When one or two of them operated directly, they burnt their fingers very badly.

Up to a point of time, the Ministry of Defence was recognizing these agents and providing a commission for them in the contract itself. Some how this system was given up and at the same time agents were being entertained right from the Defence Minister downwards. They had their access to the Ministry and also to the Services headquarters. In this dispensation, at times two agents were claiming to be representing the same company and it was a problem to check the facts. So I suggested to the Ministry of Defence that we could restore the old system with proper registration so that there was transparency and we would know 'who was who'. Per contra, if we did not want to have agents, there should be a legislation banning people or agents from dabbling in defence matters or purchases. This suggestion was not acted upon and the nebulous situation continued resulting in controversies of this kind.

At the same time, the agents are also in a way useful because some of them have given very valuable information to the Ministry and the Defence Services. For instance, when a proprietary item was being negotiated from a single producer in the world, an agent unconnected with this purchase but knowledgeable informed me that the manufacturer was trying to charge an exorbitantly high price for which there was no justification and should I drive a hard bargain, he would sell it at a lower price. This tip was useful. Of course, it was quite possible that this person could have tried to be an agent by pretending to be a friend of some person or the other in authority and perhaps that was not agreed to by the manufacturer. Actually in this case, it was a government manufacturer who was using only his Military Attaché in the deal.

But he could not get the useful information and the course of negotiations for want of an Indian agent! That was the reason why, barring the erstwhile Soviet Union, the other East European communist countries too had Indian agents. I do not know the prevailing system. But it would be worthwhile to examine my suggestion for transparency within the Ministry or a total ban by legislation. CVC Vittal was asked to look into the matter and he had suggested the first course as suggested by me. But this only legalises a bad system. A better course would have been total ban of agents, Indian or foreign, by legislation. (It is now reported recently that Sri Lanka has done this).

There were several other purchases. The work-load pertaining to the Indian purchases for the Canteen Stores Department was not heavy. On the very first day, when a file came for purchase of some items costing about Rs.100 crore, I was paying a lot of attention to that file reading it in great detail. I used to tell my colleagues jocularly that while I signed such agreements while walking down the corridors, my colleagues invited the TV even for signing an agreement of three crore or so of some aid from some European country. In fact, during my stay of two years and three months, I signed agreements worth about Rs. 2,300 crore. When Mrs. Gandhi visited the United States once, the Russians got a bit frightened and suddenly wanted me to visit Russia to negotiate and decide upon some major purchases. I never thought that they would call me so soon and I was not ready. But I had to leave at short notice on government orders. Defence Secretary P.K. Kaul could get the requisite clearance of the Cabinet within sixty hours flat from the time of drafting.

The Russian General was very well informed about India. Any small news item appearing even in a language paper in India regarding defence would be put up to him every week. Since he was doing this job, as it was their custom to specialise on a particular country, he knew every thing about us. But on our side even the defence personnel were not knowledgeable because as I have already stated, they have to do field jobs and they are not kept in the headquarters for more than three years at a stretch. Since a foreign trip was involved, they would not call the person who had actually inspected the equipment earlier. The new person would again ask them to show the equipment. They would always say that they had shown the equipment two or three times. But they had known our system and also the consequent ignorance on our part which was useful to them. Although I told the army headquarters to call the same person who had seen the equipment earlier, they did not do it because of the trip. Of course, the civil side of the Defence Ministry at least at that time was rather harsh on the top army officers who had spent long times on mountains and on the borders and naturally wanted to make a few trips abroad while they were in the headquarters. The officers of the Ministries of Defence and Finance could have been more charitable. On one or two occasions, I had to fight with the Finance Secretary for getting such trips approved. In fact, on one such occasion he asked me (P.K. Kaul moved by then to Finance) what was my personal interest in the matter. Unfortunately, in our country, people think that a quid pro quo is always involved, and it is forgotten that we fight on the basis of merits of a case. I told him that I had no personal interest at all and I felt that the officers should have a chance to go out at least in the evening of their career while the civilian officers had made umpteen number of trips throughout their career.

I conducted the negotiations successfully with the assistance of the Generals and the Financial Adviser Swaminathan for about a week. It was the biggest ever contract signed with the Soviet Union. After that, the biggest deal has been by the then Defence Secretary T.K. Bannerjee in 1996 as reported in the press. Ambassador Vishnu Ahuja, Defence Secretary Kaul including the Minister appreciated my work. P.K. Kaul jocularly said that I was made an honorary member of the USSR Communist Politburo. Similarly a contract was concluded by me with the USA for the first time after 1965, but it had also to be called off much to our regret and that of the US Ambassador here.

In the subsequent year, I was ready for negotiations with the Russians. But they never came forward and in fact were dilly-dallying the matter because there was no such urgency and the urgency arose the previous year because of Mrs. Gandhi's trip to the United States and the Russian feared that India might enter into some major deal with the USA. So in brief it was very high level international politics which one could experience in the Ministry of Defence.

Lt. Gen. H. Kaul spoke to me about the importance of Siachen and sent a note for sending a team out for purchase of some snow equipment for about Rs.50 lakhs for the first time. These equipment had to be bought on the spot. It was also an important purchase because Pakistan had already encroached into this area and farther encroachment had to be stalled. But at that time nobody in the Ministry had heard of Siachen and since it was a small purchase, it was felt there was no need to go for it immediately and also there was no need for a joint secretary to go along with Lt. Gen. Hoon in charge of Jammu & Kashmir area. The financial adviser opposed it and Defence Minster R. Venkataraman was inclined to agree with him. Defence Secretary S.M. Ghosh was also not much in favour. But I almost fought with the Secretary and Minister and impressed upon them the importance of the mission. But they agreed to send only my Under Secretary Gautam Sen who was also a finance man to handle these small but crucial purchases on-the-spot. In any case, the Lt. General and the under secretary went and made successful purchases of these much needed items. In fact, the Pakistani Intelligence was informed about this by some one and one or two companies in Europe, although promised to sell the equipment, went back on it when the team visited them the next day. As a result of this purchase and mounting of that operation which subsequently appeared in newspapers in an innocuous fashion and our army wrested a few hundred meters of the area, the Defence Minister claimed credit. Of course, there is no harm because every thing is done in the name of the Minister in a democracy and a civil servant is supposed to keep silent except perhaps while writing his or her memoirs!

There were reports in newspapers in 2004 that troops would be withdrawn at least in parts from the Siachen heights. Since I felt that this would be a wrong move, I wrote a letter to the Defence Minister Pranab Mukherjee explaining all this and the efforts put in, with a copy to PM Dr Manmohan Singh. PM asked the late J.N. Dixit to reply to me thanking me for this input and assuring me that this crucial aspect would be kept in view during negotiations. Of course, Lt. Gen. (Rtd) Hoon, like the Minister, claimed all the credit to himself in his book. He did not even mention Gautam Sen's name. The controversy still continues. Army is not in favour of withdrawal. I wrote again to the present Defence Minister, A.K. Antony, a fine person, with whom I had the privilege of working. It is also a good move to send tourists from our side too as Pakistan did long ago.

As far as I was concerned, it was a good stint with good experience of high level coordination, high level politics and transfer of technology in a particular field. I was also happy that I could be of assistance to the armed forces although they also tended to exploit here and there with constant demands for increase in salaries and numerous perquisites, most of all free rations. Free rations were available only for the Jawans in the forward areas at a particular point of time. Then it was made available up to the rank of Brigadier in the forward areas. Later it was extended to the level of Brigadier and equivalent ranks throughout the country. Later it was raised to the level of Generals and equivalent wherever they were posted. This resulted in some resentment among the Jawans. The joke was that should the soldiers and Generals consume that much of calories every day, they would only become obese and not battle-fit. I am told that many of them sell a part of these rations in the market. It is unfortunate that we Indians are always up to such tactics wherever we are.

One should read Anthony Sampson's book, "Arms Bazaar" to know about the nature of the industry and the widespread corruption because of big money. People like Adnan Kassoghi thrived on these deals. Several scams like 'Bofors' have taken place in the country and generally the politicians got away with it till recently. It is good that the judiciary has woken up and started bringing every one corrupt to book. During the Narasimha Rao government, corruption was raised to the level of an art and I myself became a victim of this system and I could not get a proper position in an economic ministry. In fact, things came to such a pass as in many state governments that honest officers were considered fools. I reproduce below Inder Malhotra's article on 'The Exponential Increase in Corruption' in *The Hindu* dated December 13th, 1995: "Parliament's paralysis over the "Telecom Affair" will be overcome or bypassed one way or another. But there is no getting away from the fact that it has once again pushed to the fore the phenomenon of corruption as an integral and expanding part of India's life. Until the Lok Sabha election at least it just will not go away.

Time was, not very long ago, when the Capital's smart set, dazzled by the glitter of globalisation and virtually consumed by consumerism, had begun to declare smugly that corruption had "ceased to be an issue" in this country. How wrong they were was demonstrated first by the slow-motion and wholly involuntary exit of those tainted by the securities megascam and the stinking sugar scandal, and then by the applause the Supreme Court is receiving for exposing the loot and wrong-doing in almost every nook and cranny of governance.

There must be something sick about a society in which the apex court, and not the top political leadership, has to put its foot down on such lucrative pastimes as the out-of-turn allotment of government housing or petrol pumps on the one hand and the masterly display of the "gift of the grab" in the award of contracts worth hundreds or even thousands of crore on the other. The figures being bandied about in connection with the telecom transactions are so mind-boggling that even if a fraction of what is being alleged is established on inquiry, this affair could truly turn out to be the mother of all scandals.

What has accentuated the public outrage against flagrant and still growing graft and bribery is that South Korea has imprisoned and indicted two former presidents for having built up private slush funds while in this country the tolerance for corruption is limitless and unashamed. Indeed, the suspects and the guilty are often coddled, to say nothing of being shielded.

For instance, when a diligent Customs officer levied a penalty on the Minister for Textiles, Kamal Nath, trying to bring in luxury goods without paying duty, it was the official who was summarily transferred. Nothing happened to the errant Minister. And so it goes on down the line.

The CBI raided the Customs at the Indira Gandhi International Airport, confiscated some "ill-gotten" cash and made an arrest. Immediately, the entire Customs staff went on a strike. A subsequent raid on the Income-Tax Office led to exactly the same result. In other words, to make money "on the side" has become a birth-right with which no interference is to be tolerated.

At the higher echelons the governing principle seems to be that it is perfectly legitimate to amass truckloads of black money under cover of collecting funds for the "party".

To be sure, corruption in India is not a new or recent phenomenon. Kautilya had catalogued, 25 centuries ago, 40 different ways in which the king's minions were likely to cheat him of the revenue. In the 18th century, Clive could boast of "a lakh and a lass" each day. Warren Hastings, responding to the impeachment proceedings against him in the British House of Commons, had the temerity to declare "Given my opportunities, I am astounded at my moderation".

In Hyderabad, even today, the bribes regularly paid to officials are called "maamool" (routine), a phrase that goes back to the Mughal days. In modern and metropolitan Bombay, the same payments are called "hafta" or weekly. In the rest of the country, the phrase is "tea money" or "chai paani ke wastay".

The point, however, is that the exponential increase in corruption , not just in areas where its cutting edge touches the common people, but in the higher reaches where millions and billions change hands, has acquired the quality of tyranny in Stalin's Russia or Hitler's Germany. Unless this tidal wave is stemmed, it is bound to sweep away the whole system".

The Hindu also wrote in an editorial on December 20th, 1996, when Narasimha Rao resigned as leader of the Congress Parliamentary Party: "In a sense, the Rao era had come to symbolise corruption at high places eroding the credibility of not only the party but also of the democratic polity as a whole".

When I joined service in 1960 and even for long years later, corruption, particularly in the IAS, was unheard of. Officers were hesitant to accept even small gifts or dinner invitations. Whenever an IAS officer was caught for corruption, even lay public invariably checked whether he was a direct recruit or a promoted officer. So people had not lost faith in the IAS. But things have changed totally today. Corruption starts at the very top coupled with casteism, nepotism and favouritism. The politician-bureaucrat-businessman nexus has become too close. For a moment I am not stating that a bureaucrat should shun businessmen. I belong particularly to a cadre – Gujarat – where there is a close and healthy relationship between the industrialists and the bureaucracy as in Japan and this has made quick industrial development of Gujarat possible. But, in such a relationship, one has to be careful not to cross the 'Lakshman Rekha'. If this is relaxed even by a few officers, there is scope for corruption as it has happened in a few cases of IAS officers in Gujarat and also in the bureaucracy in Japan. Industrialists or businessmen also know who-is-who. But the situation has totally changed for the worse and we hear complaints even against IAS officers every day. The less said about the other civil services, the better.

Even now many Ministers would always like to have a corrupt or a wheeler-dealer as Secretary. An honest man has become insipid for them. In this regard, I know three highly rated former ministers to the extent of being treated statesmen and not politicians from Tamil Nadu who occupied high positions were not free from the tinge of corruption although they presented an honest face to the public. They functioned through reliable agents. Only perhaps A.K. Antony was totally free from even a shade of a shadow of doubt in this respect. But he too, as he himself told me and naturally so in such a milieu, could not control corruption by others. When I did not believe the talk about the prevailing corruption, I was told authentically by a person that one of my batch-mates himself demanded Rs. 25 lakhs stating that it had to be given to the higher-ups. When this person wanted my advice, I told him to lay a trap through the CBI. But he told me later that he was a small industrialist who would not like to antagonize the bureaucracy or the politicians and settled the matter to start with for Rs. 10 lakhs. We do not know how many such Rs. 25 Lakhs this batch-mate of mine demanded and got and where all that money had gone.

Some wives of officers do business; some produce TV programmes and thereby derive an advantage of their husband's position; some give dance performance even when they are old and grab government accommodation for ever from the artists' quota. Plot-grabbing is a favourite pastime with IAS officers. No one seems to question all this these days as they used to do in the past. Perhaps the government also feels that the income has to be supplemented by the wife's earning these days. Some have got lucrative employment in the banks for their children while they are in the Finance Ministry. Whether the government turns a blind-eye or not, it is a question of personal ethics.

S.S. Gill, former secretary, Information and Broadcasting, wrote an article stating how the norms had changed over years that dinners and gifts had become acceptable. A Tamil Nadu officer told me once that corruption should be measured by a device like the Richter Scale! 0-1 on Richter Scale relates to acceptance of things like calendars during the new year; 2 would relate to acceptance of small gifts of practically no value; 3 would relate to acceptance of things like watches, pens, etc.; 4 would relate to acceptance of air-tickets, diamond necklaces, grabbing of plots, different types of nepotism etc.; 5 on Richter Scale of corruption relates to acceptance of hard cash, opening of accounts in India and abroad, flats, etc. and turbulence is caused.

Although one or two Cabinet Secretaries talked about integrity, they themselves accepted welcome or farewell dinners on assumption of office from some industrialists or traders in five star hotels, also inviting other officers in large numbers, thereby sending a clear wrong signal to the bureaucracy. The CVC himself was present in such dinners! This was sad indeed. Like a judge, at least after becoming CVC, he should have kept himself aloof with much less social contacts. Some Cabinet Secretaries have kept these lunches or dinners only to a few officers, as such social contacts cannot totally be avoided. If it is a large gathering, it gives a lot of scope to the industrialist or a middleman to have a larger field of influence, which is very common in Delhi. Names are always dropped and they barge into houses, let alone offices, even without appointment. I know a particular trader who was doing this frequently dropping the names like A.N. Varma, Montek Singh Ahluwalia et al so that his job was done or intimidated the officer. Another middleman told me that so-and-so officer would not be able to become a Cabinet Secretary and he really ensured it.

A Prime Minister and Cabinet Secretary invited the Chief Secretaries to evolve a code of ethics for the civil service and talked about the politician-bureaucrat-criminal nexus. Exactly on the previous day, they had given extension in service to a bureaucrat of dubious reputation while denying it to me. When I questioned the Principal Secretary to PM after a month or so, he was honest enough to admit that it should not have been given. This principal secretary was an honest and straightforward man. His predecessor would have justified it on the basis of importance of a post as though I had declined important posts.

"Today, there is an extremely thin line distinguishing bureaucrats from politicians (Darshan Balwally in *The Hindustan TImes* dated December 13th, 1996)." This is also evident from the number of IAS and IPS officers being jailed for corruption.

A leading editor, Prabhu Chawla, wrote in *The Financial Express* on January 6th, 1998 under the caption, "Retire only the Upright": "The rule of not giving extensions to superannuated officers applies only to (upright) N.K. Singh (of the CBI) and the likes of him. Such upright officers are never good enough to serve the ends of any government caucus ——— the silent end of his term, unsung and unextended, is a tribute to the culture of favouritism perfected under———".

So one has to be true to oneself in such an atmosphere. Possible temptations by family members in such a general atmosphere of corruption and irregularities have to be avoided. Of course, such a person can only satisfy himself or herself by reading A. Pope: "The honest man is the noblest work of God".

Dwelling further on corruption, my senior colleague and also a good friend from the Gujarat cadre, N. Vittal, (this was my moral dilemma whether to comment upon or not, but I allowed public interest to prevail over private friendship and also because this account would be incomplete without such a reference because he was CVC) made a lot of noise about corruption, but did little to eradicate or even lessen it. During his tenure, the Transparency International's corruption index for India has become worse. To apply the Tamil Nadu cadre officer's application of Richter Scale of corruption, Vittal was worried only from 5 and above. He seems to have turned a blind eye or deaf ear up to 4 on the scale.

Even his frequent tours, as M.N. Buch, a highly rated former IAS officer wrote in *The Pioneer,* were not expected of a CVC because he was expected to concentrate on the voluminous file work and also there was no need to educate the people of India about corruption. May be because of his frequent absence, some one wrote in *The Economic Times* that he had to pay a bribe of Rs. 5000 to a section officer in the CVC's office to see a file – corruption under the very nose of the CVC!

Grabbing government plots is a form of corruption indulged in by many and since it is done by many, it escapes attention and is also sanctified. Constructing a house on the plot by taking a loan from the bank which may or may not be returned and leasing out the house to a public sector at a high rent is another form of corruption. He had rented out his house in Gandhinagar to a state government PSU who had made many modification or changes. When Coomi Kapoor wrote about this in *The Indian Express*, he explained it away by stating that these were temporary structures which would be taken away when the PSU vacated the house. On the contrary, he should have advertised the availability of the house in newspapers, even fixing a minimum expected rent, and rented it out to an individual and not a PSU. This was high integrity of a CVC who was making so much of noise and putting names (I appreciated this to start with) in a hasty manner on a website without even checking them. He should have checked and rechecked the names because it vitally affected other officers. There were also some details lacking and many commented upon him adversely although the not-so- knowledgeable middle class made him a hero. PSUs are in the habit of renting houses or flats of senior officers to please them even at a high rate and no private occupant would come forward to carry out improvements even temporary.

CVC Vittal could have simplifed the Vigilance Manuals and the procedures for departmental inquiries so that corruption cases could have been dealt with expeditiously instead of writing letters to High Court Judges to expedite these cases. Nor did he catch any big fish for corruption. When the house of an officer of the standing of the General Manager, Southern Railway in Chennai was raided under public glare with a lot of media publicity by the CBI, I told Vittal that he should bring the General Manager to book quickly if the case was true or should take action against the

CBI officer for humiliating the GM if the case was not true. Vittal gave some vague advice to the CBI officers in such cases before conducting raids. The case dragged on as usual and the officer also retired. Of course, Vittal would blame the government for not giving sanctions in time. Although I do not agree with him on this point and agree with his successor, P. Shankar, for such a prior government sanction, the matter is before the Supreme Court for a decision. (The Supreme Court has since given a judgment).

Former Cabinet Secretary T.N. Seshan was also questioned about his acceptance of a costly ring from the notorious Chandraswamy and the latter's deposition in this regard before the Jain Commission, his Desabaktha Trust and getting accommodation for it from the notorious Delhi don Romesh Sharma as reported by *India Today* and also *The Asian Age* and also his flight in a Reliance plane and under-payment (?) were subjects of discussion. As A.J. Phillip wrote in *The Indian Express*: February 9th , 2002: Cabinet Secretary Prabhat Kumar was caught while many others were not. Kiran Bedi was reported to have grabbed a medical seat for her daughter which was meant for the Mizos. What is the yardstick for corruption in India? Particularly for the officials. Where is the rule book on ethics for civil servants thrown away by no less persons than the CVC and Cabinet Secretaries? There is no such thing as 'conflict of interest' for these persons.

In respect of an ICS officer, "the History of Services" which gave their details – place of birth, date of birth, educational qualifications, etc., — also indicated that he owned lands in Tanjavur – the idea was that he should not be posted to that district. Even when I joined Service in 1962, an IPS batch-mate of mine was asked to give up his property in Tamil Nadu or should go to some other Cadre because he was fairly rich. But all this seems to have been thrown to the winds now.

Political corruption is always justified in this country. When a minister was making money, a friend of mine asked him, "why don't you be a gentleman?". He replied , "Look, the people whom I represent are not gentlemen!" Huge money flows even in Municipal and Panchayat elections, let alone Assembly and Parliament elections. Civil servants try to justify their corruption by saying that political corruption is the root-cause. Consequently, the dealings of the government in sensitive economic ministries are suspect. Things have come to such a pass that even in budgets, people suspect some big companies or NRIs or some other influential sections are being favoured and the schemes for the common man are only an eye–wash. This is also possible because sons, daughters or relations of the ministers or civil servants work for these companies either within the country or abroad. When the value-system has taken a terrible knock, such suspicions of big corruption, apart from small corruption, cannot be ruled out.

I think and hope that the people distinguish between official and political corruption. Officials have no business to be corrupt with their fixed income for a good part of their life and pension till their death and even beyond as family pension. As far as political corruption is concerned, perhaps the people feel that they are helpless. The politicians and political parties have started collecting money through the officials also. They have thrown their ideologies to the winds. Since parties change sides so often and get themselves aligned with diametrically opposite ideologues, the people are taken for granted and political parties feel that they can easily fool them. Common man in this country cannot get his ration-card, ration, kerosene, patta-transfer or what have you without 'sifarish' or plain bribe to an official or politician. Political parties feel these days that they are carrying conviction to the people about their changing sides of policies. But this is a mistaken impression.

While the Congress took nearly four decades to become corrupt yet nurtured honesty and honest officials for a long time, the BJP hardly took four years to become corrupt and did not encourage honesty, merit or honest officials. Of course, Modi's Gujarat is an exception.

Very often it is stated by political parties and politicians that people's verdict or people's court is more important than ordinary courts of law –this is the logic they apply. But we cannot say that this means corruption has become a non-issue in the country. Just because a corrupt government gets reelected, it does not mean corruption has disappeared. If you still insist that it has become a non–issue, I can only say that is not for nothing India is one of the most corrupt countries in the world!

You cannot dub the electorate illiterate barring states like UP and Bihar because if it is so, they will not be changing the governments as they do. Having lived in a village for long years, I am aware that the people know what is what and what they want. But they are helpless at least for five years. They have also started feeling unfortunately whether it is Rama or Ravana – Congress or BJP – DMK or ADMK – corruption cannot be escaped in politics and why we cannot also have a share in this milieu. I saw a voter telling this on camera during an election in the North-East and it equally holds good in many states.

The selections to the IAS, IPS, IFS, etc. are still purely on merit, I believe. The recruitment and interview systems are such by several boards that there is practically no scope for manipulation. This also appears to be so because the sons or daughters of some of my colleagues could not get into the IAS! They could go only into the less glamorous central services. But the same thing cannot be said of the other recruitments or promotions by the UPSC. This is because of the proverbial dangling of the post of Governor or a Rajya Sabha nomination before the chair of the UPSC. At least in one case I was aware of, the UPSC had given a lot of importance to letters from the MPs particularly from Andhra Pradesh during Rao's time and telephone calls from the PMO. Unfortunately, the government changed and the wait for a gubernatorial post was in vain. Also in this regard, a member of the UPSC was dismissed for corruption. Another from the Punjab was about to become a member of the UPSC with political influence. But he was suspended for some acts of corruption when he was a chairman of the State Public Service Commission. Luckily, the country was saved of his services!

P.C. Hota, my batch-mate and former chairman, UPSC, started heading a committee on administrative reforms and thereby retained the government house and other perquisites. He was also going round the country with a team under him to gather evidence for improving or reforming the civil services. Former CVC and my friend, N. Vittal, took up a job with the government of Andhra Pradesh trying to reform the AP administration. In fact, this issue of Constitutional functionaries like the Chief Election Commissioners and Election Commissioners, Comptroller and Auditor General, Chairman and Members of the UPSC, Judges and CVC (only statutory though) accepting gubernatorial post or Rajya Sabha nominations came to the fore when the former Chief Election Commissioner, M. S. Gill, accepted nomination to the Rajya Sabha. This practice was adversely commented upon by intellectuals and newspapers. I wrote to the government that this practice could be stopped only by a Constitutional amendment. However, these functionaries cannot be prevented from standing for elections, but they should be permitted only as Independents. Unless this is done, people will have no faith in these functionaries.

When P.C. Hota was appointed member of the UPSC, he was secretary, Department of Personnel. He got his orders two or three days before his retirement and the orders contained two or three more names. He handed over charge and practically ran from North Block to the UPSC to take over so that he would have the seniority to become the chairman over the other two or three. In personal matters, civil servants show great fore-sight! But IAS officers are borne on State Cadres and the State Government had to issue an order after getting due Vigilance clearances stating that the Government or the President was pleased to allow so-and- so to retire. There are some cases where the officers are suspended even on the last day of service without being allowed to retire. I am not suggesting that P.C. Hota needed such a clearance. I also do not know whether he got all this done on the same day by his State Cadre on fax. However, this kind of a technical flaw was not expected of a person to hold an important Constitutional office dealing with service matters and rules. For argument's sake, if any thing had been discovered, the State Government would not have been able to do anything because of this fait accompli and Constitutional immunity and the procedures thereof.

Leaving aside the tortuous topic of corruption, when I was in the Defence Ministry, some jawans or even officers used to get recommendation letters from MPs for transfers to places of their choice. The Services headquarters invariably used to write that these personnel violated conduct rules by approaching the MPs. K.P. Singh Deo, who was a Deputy Minister and who himself was in the Territorial Army, took strong exception to this as people's representatives MPs had every right to write and it should not be construed that the defence personnel had approached them. He had submitted the file to Defence Minister R. Venkataraman who not only agreed with him but also recorded that any exception to MPs' letters could even be construed as a breach of privilege of an MP. (Incidentally, Deputy Ministers figure far below the Chiefs in the order of precedence and this created a piquant situation in the ministry where these are followed in letter and spirit even in ordinary meetings, let alone ceremonial occasions. In fact, a Chief even refused to call on him. So an order was issued post-haste by the Cabinet Secretariat stating that only in the Defence Ministry, the Deputy Ministers would rank above the Chiefs.)

I wrote the following letter to the Generals and others while leaving the Defence Ministry on June 30th , 1984: "This is just to say ' au revoir' and thank you and your colleagues, on the eve of my transfer to Gujarat on completion of my extended tenure in the Government of India (with the Embassy of India, Brussels and the Ministry of Defence), for your kind co-operation during my stay here. Although I am somewhat a conscientious objector to arms, particularly the 'arms bazaar', my tenure in the Defence Ministry has been an eventful one, and a unique experience which one does not get in a State Government. Arms and arms race are perhaps necessary evils for any human society, but let it be for preservation of peace".

* * *

15

Back in the Home State

After a successful stint in the Ministry of Defence, I arrived on one fine morning in October, 1984 in Ahmedabad and drove down to the beautiful circuit house (no longer so) in Gandhinagar. Although it was October, the weather was hot and naturally Gujaratis were in the habit of drinking a lot of water throughout the day. As soon as one enters an office room or a house, a glass of water is invariably offered. In fact, it is considered highly impolite if one is not offered water. Perhaps this has also some thing to do with their innate sense of economy in life.

I was warned that I would get a house at Gandhinagar either immediately or it might take even six months. The latter part of it turned out to be true and it took exactly six months to get a nice bungalow in the green city of Gandhinagar, not far from the Secretariat. Meanwhile, I had to spend all the time in the circuit house taking my food also there. Whenever the circuit house was full, I moved to room number 13 because others were not prepared to occupy it. Similarly, one would find only a vacant plot on number 13 in the row of bungalows for ministers – this is superstition.

The posting also took a long time. The secretary to the Chief Minister was somewhat hostile because of my posting abroad followed by a posting in Delhi. Chief Secretary Sivaraj, who was interested in me, could not carry conviction to the Chief Minister Solanki who in turn was advised by the Industries Secretary Sivagnanam. Sivagnanam did not see eye to eye with Sivaraj. In all this conflict, about twenty days elapsed. Chief Minister wanted me to go as a member of the Electricity Board which I felt was for a junior super- time scale officer. Sivaraj wanted me to become Home Secretary. He was promptly over-ruled by the secretary to the Chief Minister. After all this confusion, H.K. Khan, a debonair bureaucrat of Gujarat, called me and asked me to take over as chairman of the Gujarat Pollution Control Board. They felt that an officer with experience in industry would be able to take a balanced view in such matters because establishing industries was important for Gujarat. He also assured me at the same time that I would be shifted to a good post in the industries department within a month or two although this promise was never fulfilled. Meanwhile, I found the Pollution Control Board job, although not considered important by many, an interesting one. It was a new field which infused some sort of enthusiasm and missionary zeal in one. So I did not try for any change and settled down in the job. Meanwhile, when I called on Chief Minister Solanki, he offered me the post of Secretary, Agriculture, which was generally a very important position in any state. Moreover, Solanki was a strategist in any matter. He must have felt that I should owe him a good post and thereby he could control the Minister of Agriculture, Mahant Vijayadasji who was not in his camp. Incidentally, Mahant Vijayadasji used to wait on me when I was District Development Officer in Junagadh years ago and even planted a news item in a paper that I was not giving interviews properly because he had to wait for a while on an occasion before meeting me. Chief Minister Solanki must have also felt that Secretary, Agriculture, could be in the hands of a man known to Dr Kurien. But I declined this offer because I was not interested in Agriculture. I told him that I would prefer a position in the department of industry or else would continue in the Pollution Control Board. He must have felt that I was obsessed with industry and left the matter at that though I always believed in specialization in the Service.

The Bhopal gas tragedy took place on December 4th, 1984. I had already planned to go to Delhi to load my luggage for

Gujarat. But the briefing by the Member Secretary of the Pollution Control Board was faulty and the newspapers carried on the front page that I left for Delhi to discuss the fall-out of the Bhopal gas tragedy with the Central Government. So there were frantic phone calls from the Chief Secretary asking me to return. But I informed him that my purpose was entirely different and the news item was totally wrong. So he permitted me to stay on as per my plan for sending my personal luggage to Gujarat. In any case, this accident was a storm in the tea cup. But it enhanced the importance of the Pollution Control Board and Chief Minister Solanki, clever man he was, issued a note written in his own hand to all departments, particularly to the department of industry to carry out a survey of all industries in Gujarat so as to avert any accident of this kind in any of the numerous chemical units in Gujarat. The Government of India also directed the State Pollution Control Boards to gear up to face any untoward incident of this kind. Bhopal gas tragedy was the worst tragedy of its kind in history and I had to deal with it later in the Government of India. The victims did not get their due compensation for years on end, thanks to the inefficiency of the Government of Madhya Pradesh and the long-drawn procedures of the courts.

The Solanki Government got into a lot of trouble because of the reservation issue. He propounded the famous KHAM – Kshatria, Harijan, Muslim and Adivasi – theory and came to power in the elections with a massive majority. Unlike in other parts of the country where the forward communities constituted only a small percentage and consequently cannot fight the KHAMs, the Patels constituted about 49% of the population in Gujarat. They thought they would be totally finished if Solanki continued in power for a full term of five years which was likely with his massive majority. So they thought of an agitation of the kind of the earlier Nav Nirman Movement of Gujarat, launched against the then Chief Minister Chimanbhai Patel (this was Chimanbhai Patel's first tenure as Chief Minister). **This was a student movement started against a corrupt government which was removed purely by public agitation (for the first time in the country) in spite of a majority in the Legislature. Similarly, this time, the people decided to**

oust Solanki come what may. The agitation assumed massive proportions all over Gujarat. Solanki tried hard to control it but miserably failed. But he tried to escape removal from chief ministership by giving a communal colour to it. He informed the Central Government that it was a communal agitation. Chief Secretary Sivagnanam also fell in line and sent similar reports to the Centre. At a particular point of time, Home Secretary C.G. Somiah visited Gujarat and he was also told that it was a communal agitation. But it went on and on for about four months without the agitation abating. Army was also called out in many places and they could not do any thing because the Gujarati women folk came out in huge numbers in the streets. In Gujarat, the womenfolk are always in the forefront including the daily household life. To use a slang, they wear trousers and not the men! Naturally the army could not kill the women and incur the wrath of the people. But Governor B.K. Nehru was reported to have informed the Centre of the real reason for the agitation. In other words, they got the correct picture from the Governor and not from the Chief Minister or the Chief Secretary. Naturally Chief Secretary particularly came in for adverse notice.

The Congress at the Centre and the Rajiv Gandhi Government decided to change Chief Minster Solanki. V.P. Singh, who was at that time a Minister in the Rajiv Gandhi government, was dispatched to Gandhinagar to change the leadership and install Prabodh Rawal or Natwarlal Shah as chief minister, but Solanki wanted to have his own crony Amarsinh Choudhary, an Adivasi as chief minister so that he could control from behind. He insisted upon this and Rajiv Gandhi was constrained to agree, as also recommended by V.P. Singh. Amarsinh Choudhary, who had worked as an engineer in the State PWD and an Adivasi from Surat, became the first Adivasi Chief Minister of an Indian state. He was a competent man who completed his tenure. But he was asked by the Centre not to follow the Solanki line and within a short time he was at loggerheads with Solanki. Such things are very common in politics. As Kennedy said there is no friend or foe in politics, but they are only colleagues. Chief Secretary Sivagnanam was also removed. Solanki was otherwise a well-read and competent man although the wily Delhi politics swallowed him later.

In this context, people outside Gujarat wonder how the vegetarian, generally peace-loving and religious Gujaratis could turn violent on occasions. The communal riots in the aftermath of Godhra massacre of Kar Sevaks (including Hindu women and children) in a train compartment in 2002 have raised the question again about the Gujaratis. The Gujaratis are extremely good and straightforward people - there is nothing devious about them as it is with the people in the North or in the South of India. But there is a mulish obstinacy in their psyche which is also their courage of conviction. Mahatma Gandhi was an example of this streak in one's character. If they are convinced what they are doing is right, they will pursue it to the very end come what may. So the 2002 communal riots were a mass upsurge as the anti-Hindi riots of Tamil Nadu although different versions appeared and as a result real truth became the casualty.

I continued in the Pollution Control Board. The work was interesting because it was the other side of industry. There was also a lot of activity after the Bhopal gas tragedy. The Central Ministry of Environment was impressed by my work so much so they included me in a delegation to West Germany. During this period, we visited a number of forests which had been affected by acid rain. We also visited the automobile factories of Mercedes, Volkswagen and BMW. It was a very educative visit. **Pollution control in the thermal power stations in West Germany was particularly remarkable and one could not find even a spec of coal dust. On the other hand, this was a great problem in and around the thermal stations in India. I had brought quite some literature with me from Germany. I sent the literature to all Electricity Boards in the country, but they never bothered as usual. In fact, Gandhinagar itself, a new city, was spoiled by locating the thermal power stations there. So I am glad that now the courts have started enforcing these laws strictly.**

During this visit, I also called on the famous Petra Kelly in Bonn. I wrote an article in *The Economic Times* in 1985: "The Irrepressible Petra Kelly": " I was a member of a delegation to the Federal Republic of Germany at their invitation to study 'Environmental Protection and Industrial Development'. It was a normal practice to invite commercial, economic and cultural delegations from India to the FRG.

But it was felt by the Government of the FRG, particularly after the Bhopal accident, that a delegation concerning environmental protection should be invited.

The delegation had a useful discussion with some members of the Bundestag at a reception hosted by an official of the Indian Embassy. But the delegation was sorely disappointed because the Green Party leader, a staunch feminist and a Gandhian, Ms. Petra (pronounced Peetra) Karin Kelly failed to turn up although the invitation was accepted on her behalf. Another Green, Gen. Bastian also failed to turn up. An official of the Foreign Office remarked that this was common with the Greens because they were non-conformists.

However, we did not want to give up the attempt of meeting Ms. Kelly about whom we had heard a lot. Besides, my Ph. D. guide and professor at the Delhi School of Economics also told me to make it a point to meet her because they had studied together; I had also another common factor with her; she had been also a trainee like me in the European Economic Commission in Brussels. So I tried to speak to her over the phone for an appointment. But I could not get her private telephone number at all.

I learnt later from her secretary that this was removed from the telephone directory for security reasons. However, a Foreign Office official told me that she was living in one of the apartments next to the hotel where I was staying in Bonn. So I made a personal attempt to contact her there. But there was no indication at all.

A German journalist-photographer passing by enquired about my search and when I informed him, he was also rather surprised to know that her number was not in the telephone directory. But he was good enough to take me in his car without my asking to the office of the Die Grunen (The Greens) in Bonn, though it was late in the evening. But she was not there though a few Greens were quite active in the office. They told us that she only occasionally turned up there, but could not tell me her whereabouts. All of them looked young.

At the request of my colleagues again, I made a telephone call the next morning to Kelly's secretary in her office. I left all the details about our delegation and she said that she would certainly leave a note for Ms. Kelly and contact me back. Ms. Kelly was bound to come to the office and see the note.

There was a call the next morning asking me to come to Kelly's office at 11 a.m., My colleagues had to deny themselves the pleasure of meeting Ms. Kelly because they had committed themselves to certain prior engagements and I was to join them in the afternoon.

I did not want to be late for this appointment which was difficult to get. So I was in Ms. Kelly's office near the Bundestag exactly on dot at 11 a.m. But Ms. Kelly was not there. Her secretary, a charming and vocal Ms. C. Queller, was helpful and she got me a cup of coffee. She checked on telephone with the Parliament, too. When I enquired whether Ms. Kelly had forgotten the appointment, she stated that it would not be the case because Ms. Kelly's memory was good. She also told me that I had a wrong idea that the Germans were punctual! But I really found them always punctual including their trains and buses. And half-an-hour delay or even more was not something uncommon for Kelly and she would have been dragged by somebody for some other important work, she added. At about 11.45, Ms. Kelly herself rang up and told Ms. Queller that she was held up in the Parliament because some voting was on and I could go for a short while and come back. But I did not want to miss Kelly in any case. Her room was full of books and documents piled up everywhere. Two or three pictures of Mahatma Gandhi, a picture of Martin Luther King and an appeal from eleven former Generals of the NATO against deployment of missiles in Europe adorned the wall.

As people had told me, she also looked charming and attractive in some of the photographs there. I also enquired from Ms. Queller as to how to address Ms. Kelly-Mrs. or Miss. She told me that in Germany even unmarried woman would prefer to be addressed Mrs. rather than Miss because the latter indicated that she was at a loose end. I told her that it was just the opposite in India or in France!

While waiting, I read a few pages of her book in English. It was full of appeal for environmental protection, maintenance of peace, abolition of nuclear weapons, emphasis upon Gandhian values of non-violence and peaceful struggle and feminist views like freedom for a married woman to have relations outside marriage since it was something accepted for men, etc. She had also studied in the United States.

In fact, she had already kept a packet of literature ready for me and my professor in Delhi. It was 12.30 p.m. But she did not turn up at all. At about 1.00 p.m., there was a telephone call stating that she would come within 5 to 10 minutes. But she actually arrived only at 1.30, but told me that she would be with me within two minutes. But she disappeared, perhaps to meet her colleagues like Gen. Bastian who had also peeped into the room meanwhile. She finally turned up at 1.45 p.m. I felt that it was just like meeting a film star in India, or perhaps it was easier to meet Grace Kelly. I was also wondering whether it was just a habit or her non-conformism or she wanted to keep an MCP wait. I thought of telling this to Ms. Kelly, but restrained myself lest she should misunderstand. In any case, I was determined to see her. She profusely apologised for the delay because of the Parliament session.

She fondly enquired about my professor in Delhi and enquired about the delegation, whose member I was. She also told me that she could not come to the embassy reception because the invitation reached her only that morning and there were certain prior commitments. She felt that we should also have met the Greenpeace organisation in Bonn. She said that she would arrange a meeting for us at Hannover or Berlin, which she did.

Incidentally, Greenpeace organisation is not a political organisation. They are in touch with not only the Greens, but also with any other political parties, individual or organisation, dealing with environmental matters. Their main concern is protection of the environment, the whales and anti-nuclear measures. It is an international organisation with a million contributors, which also refuses to have any Governmental assistance.

Since the time was short, I started putting specific questions to her. One of the questions related to pollution control measures in West Germany. According to her, these measures were not at all satisfactory. For instance, if a person committed theft, it was a crime and the person was promptly locked up. But it was not a crime to pollute the atmosphere or the water. In fact, two thirds of Germany was highly polluted. Although the laws provided for penal provisions, they were not being implemented properly and no one had been sent to jail or paid a fine so far for polluting the environment.

She was of the view that the Government was very tolerant of pollution. They did not take effective steps at all. For instance, some chemical and paper factories were polluting the water in Hamburg. When the Greenpeace volunteers went and closed the pipes carrying the effluent, they were chased out.

She also talked about the effect of acid rain on trees in Europe. She advised us to visit some of the forests and see for ourselves. The delegation, in fact, visited some forests and found to their horror that many of the trees were dying and there was no cure to prevent air pollution. She also felt that the high incidence of cancer was due to the faulty treatment of the environment.

I raised the specific question as to how to remove poverty in developing countries without going in for development including industrialisation, since poverty was the main pollutant in the developing countries. To this, Ms. Kelly stated that agricultural development would be more desirable for developing countries than industrial development. She stated that particularly the chemical industries should be avoided. She also said that she would talk about Bhopal, what happened there, and how the multinationals misguided and exploited the developing countries by keeping the peoples of these countries in dark about what they produced. She felt that Bhopal was a standing example of such dangers to the entire world and, of course, proved later by Chernobyl, Rhine pollution from Switzerland, etc.

I specifically referred to development-oriented industries like fertilizers. A green revolution would not have been possible in India without these industries. She was of the view that even in respect of fertilizers, the developing countries should not go in for chemical fertilizers. They should concentrate upon organic fertilizers, which were much more desirable for preserving the quality of the soil, whereas chemical fertilizers damaged the soil permanently.

Of course, she agreed that progress would be somewhat slow this way, but it would be preferable to the damage to human beings, the environment and human health from pesticides and chemical fertilizers.

She enquired about the role of voluntary organisations in India and wanted to have a list of them. I explained how the Government itself encouraged voluntary organisations in India. In fact, voluntary organisations had a great role to play in environmental preservation and pollution control rather than governmental organisations which had their own limitations. Even financial assistance was being provided by the government to voluntary organisations. Incidentally, voluntary organisations or associations have no right to sue the government in Germany for violation of pollution control laws or norms.

Only individuals have such rights. This is political question which perhaps the government in power is not willing to give to voluntary bodies. I asked her about nuclear plants. She stated that in spite of the resistance by the Greens and the public in West Germany, the government was going ahead and the Greens might have to think of some other course of action. She suggested that the developing countries like India should not go in for nuclear plants at all because of the possible dangers involved. They should concentrate on other sources of energy.

It was more than half an hour and she had to rush to another appointment. She said she would come to India to see the conditions here and also to see her adopted Tibetan child growing up at Dharmashala. She also told me that she was in touch with our former Ambassador to the FRG, R.D. Sathe, living now in Pune.

I requested her for a copy of her book. But she said that the book was a mutilated version of the German original and she had sued the publishers. But she lost the case.

So she gave me only the original German version. When I requested her for a photograph for possible publication, she jocularly remarked that she was not interested in publicity and consequently did not keep her photograph all the time. During this discussion, I found her to be a very sincere and forthright person.

I found many admirers of Kelly. They felt that though the ideas were laudable, the solutions offered by the Greens were not practical. Some felt that the Greens were losing ground. Some officials merely shrugged off the Greens. However, it was gathered from one and all, including business associations and chambers of commerce, that environment was the prime subject today in West Germany and would remain so, next only to the preservation of peace including social security.

This has been amply vindicated in the recent elections in the FRG. Ms. Kelly not only returned to the Bundestag, but her party secured 42 seats with 8.3% of the votes as against 27 seats with 5.6% of the votes in 1983. This is considerable".

(I met her a few years later in New Delhi in the company of my professor, Dr R. S. Nigam. Unfortunately, for reasons not known, she and Gen. Bastian committed suicide some years later cutting short her promising career and also an international role).

The work in the Pollution Control Board naturally involved treading on the toes of powerful industrialists. There were pressures from time to time from the department of industry to clear polluting units. However, the work was carried out on an even keel with adequate safeguards. We did not want to be eco- fundamentalists. But a particular industrialist came from Haryana to locate a unit for manufacturing Polycarbonate, a substance used in the place of steel for cars and a replacement for steel sheets. But the process of manufacture involved phosgene – the killer gas of Bhopal for which chlorine was the raw material. In fact, only two units were producing phosgene in the country apart from the Bhopal unit and these were located in Gujarat. After the Bhopal gas tragedy, these units stopped producing phosgene. Since the Gujarat Alkalies and Chemicals were producing chlorine, the Haryana industrialist wanted to locate his unit near Baroda or in south Gujarat. I very strongly objected to this and asked him to go to a place where there was no habitation within a radius of 10 km. I had evolved a system of distance-criterion for various types of dangerous industries so that the minimum distance of no-habitation was assured. In fact, this criterion was adopted later by the Government of India.

It would have been possible for this industrialist to locate such a place in North Gujarat or Saurashtra. But he was not inclined to go to those places. He started applying a lot of pressure through Industries Secretary H.K. Khan and the Chief Minister himself. Chief Minister Amarsinh Choudhary himself spoke to me. But I was not prepared to sacrifice the interests of the people of Gujarat. As a result, one fine evening, I was transferred as Commissioner of Sales Tax. I felt very unhappy about it – although years later I felt that it was a transfer in the right direction.

I requested Chief Secretary Chandramouli to reconsider this decision. But he felt that the Pollution Control Board was a small unknown organisation of about 250 officials whereas the Sales Tax Department was a huge organisation with about 5,000 officials accounting for almost the entire budget of the Government. He felt that the transfer was in my own interest. However, I rushed to Delhi and informed his batch-mate, T.N. Seshan, Secretary, Environment & Forests, who also thought well of my work. He wanted me to stay on as Chairman of the Gujarat Pollution Control Board. But Chandramouli did not agree because the Chief Minister also wanted me out of it for obvious reasons. In fact, this incident and the perception about the pollution control and the environment was brought to the notice of Prime Minister Rajiv Gandhi by the environmentalist Anil Agarwal when he was asked to educate the MPs on pollution control and the environmental problems. In fact, the idea of educating the MPs was borrowed from me because, for the first time in the country, I had held an educating seminar for the MLAs in Gujarat. In any case, as a result of this transfer, I took over as Commissioner of Sales Tax on January 1st, 1986 in Ahmedabad.

Gujarat government had a silly rule that those who were posted in Ahmedabad should move residence from Gandhinagar and not vice versa. In other words, if one is transferred from Ahmedabad to Gandhinagar, one need not move residence. It was my view that option should be given to the officer concerned. This rule was silly because it was quite possible that somebody might be transferred two or three times in a year and every time that person cannot move residence. At that time, Chief Minister Amarsinh Choudhary readily gave me this dispensation in order to assuage my feelings. So we stayed on in Gandhinagar. This rule was also changed later with the facility of using government car on payment. Of course, I had to use my own car. But there was not much of a problem because the Finance Minister or the Finance Secretary used to call me and other officials of the Sales Tax department almost every day because it was the only important source of revenue and there were many discussions.

Sales Tax law is a complicated one. Although the file work was not very heavy because of very clear delegation of powers down the line and decentralisation, one had to know the nuances of the law. One had to be alert because of the powerful staff unions having access to the Chief Minister and the Finance Minister. However, in the teeth of opposition from the unions, computerisation was introduced in the department and I wrote a detailed article in *The Economic Times* for the benefit of other states on August 24th, 1988. Only one other state, Karnataka, had resorted to full scale computerisation at that time. Needless to state that computer was a convenient tool in the modern world, particularly in tax management and in an organisation like the Sales Tax Department.

"Sales Tax is important because it accounts for 60 to 70 per cent of the tax revenue of the state governments. This is true of Gujarat also. Besides, the department has about 128 offices spread all over the state with a staff of about 5,000. There are nearly 3 lakh registered dealers and this number expands every year by about 8 per cent. Thus, this organisation accounts for a revenue of over Rs. 1,000 crores per year.

The Sales Tax laws of almost all States have become complicated over a period of time. For instance, in Gujarat, the rate varies from half per cent to 45 per cent comprising nine structures.

Apart from this, the Sales Tax Act and Rules with a host of exemptions have resulted in numerous forms being prescribed from time to time. The law has the unique feature of 'set-off' i.e., giving back the tax collected in respect of raw materials used for manufacturing commodities or the dealers being allowed to claim the 'set-off' themselves in their returns. In many cases, the dealer has to give just a form instead of paying the tax. He has to get these forms typed or printed himself. In Gujarat about 3 crores of such forms are being issued every year which are supposed to be at least sample crosschecked by the authorities.

Often, certain details are lacking in these forms or tax returns. The dealer is expected to show his turnover with details of commodities he has traded in, but, he indicates only the total turnover and not commodity-wise. So, besides the difficulty of keeping track of these forms, it is difficult to collect data of turnover pertaining to each and every commodity.

Also, under the law, the assessment has to be completed within a period of two years, but with the increasing number of registrations and without corresponding increase in the staff, assessments are kept pending for years which amounts to loss of revenue to the state.

The state governments increases or decreases rates on different items every year in the budget. But, it is not possible to know their exact impact because of the spread and the lack of data.

Similarly, there is no scientific system of keeping track of the problems of the large number of employees like pay, allowances, date of retirement, etc.

In order to obviate these difficulties, it was decided to have computer-aid for the department. Though punchcard operators were appointed a few years ago and the main computer of the government was being used, data collection and analysis was a few years behind".

This was the situation in 1986 and it had not since changed much. I explained the various difficulties of the old style computerisation in my article. Perhaps seeing the examples of Gujarat and Karnataka, other states also resorted to computerisation of their sales tax department for their benefit.

Since I had spare time, I could also learn operating the computers. Since 'iNDEXTb' undertook the computerisation of the department, they also taught me for a month or two. In this regard, as a part of IAS compulsory training every year introduced by P. Chidambaram, I did computer courses in the well known

CMC, New Delhi. One Srinivasan from the Orissa IAS Cadre also came to lecture on the computerisation of the land records which he had already done in a few states. He was on the verge of his retirement from the IAS. He gave us an interesting story to drive home the point that it was not difficult to learn operating the computer although many grown-up persons thought it would be difficult. His son and his friends made fun of him that he was not a modern man because he did not know anything about computer. So he took a bet with them stating that he would learn the computer well within a period of six months. In turn, he gave them a book on the political philosophy of Plato which both of them had to study during this period and take a test at the end of six months. After the period of six months, Srinivasan came out with flying colours in operating computers. Both his son and his friend miserably failed in the test on Plato's political philosophy. This anecdote gave us enough confidence.

Since Sales Tax was a complicated legislation and there was immense scope for its simplification, I wrote ten papers on the various aspects in consultation with some Deputy Commissioners and Assistant Commissioners who were real stalwarts in the law and the rules. These papers were submitted to the Finance Department of the Government of Gujarat. But they gathered dust as usual because as usual, the Government was not receptive to any suggestion. I would like to observe here that the Indian society is conservative by nature. This is both its strength and weakness. It is a strength because there are no convulsions in the form of revolutions. At the same time, it is a weakness because it is difficult to introduce changes. It is a stagnant society or a cesspool.

Similarly, the IAS officers are good at maintaining the status quo and implementing certain regulatory laws, but they are not good at innovating. Most of them are neither time-bound, nor target-bound. In fact, the various economic liberalisation measures were possible during the Narasimha Rao Government because of Dr Manmohan Singh as Finance Minister and his Finance Secretary, M.S. Ahluwalia who was an economist. The budget took entirely a different philosophy, shape and turn because of them. Although some budgets prepared by S. Venkitaramanan, V.P. Singh and R. Venkataraman were really good with some new features, there was not a major departure or path-breaking because of the conservative attitude of the civil servants and their unwillingness to experiment.

I wrote a couple of articles also on the simplification of Sales Tax laws in *The Economic Times.* Some industrialists thought that those were written by a sales tax expert and one or two of them without knowing that I was a civil servant wrote me through the newspaper that I should become their tax consultant!

At the same time, I also wrote a couple of articles in *The Economic Times* on the need for introduction of Value Added Tax in the country on the EEC pattern. So I was the first one to advocate introduction of VAT in this country. The idea was picked up later by Dr Manmohan Singh and Dr Raja Chelliah and they also knew that I advocated it first. When I lectured on the need for introduction of VAT in the National Institute of Public Finance and Policy in New Delhi, my own colleague Sales Tax Commissioners from other States, who were IAS officers, opposed it stating that it was not practicable. But the States fell in line later with economic liberalisation although it was to gain currency slowly. Finance Secretary Gurumurthi introduced it in a way in Tamil Nadu in 1996. There was still opposition from many quarters.

The period of two years and three months as Commissioner of Sales Tax was quite rewarding before my shift again to Delhi in March, 1988. During this period, the near stagnant sales tax collected with a growth rate around 12% every year for some years shot up beyond 20% crossing the Rs.1000 crores mark for the first time. The Government of Gujarat commended me as follows:

"M.S. Dayal *D.O.No.GST/1087/2339/TH 88-1537*
Addl. Chief Secretary

Government of Gujarat,
Finance Department,
Sachivalaya, Gandhinagar – 382010.
Phone 4059/6704.
Dated July 14, 1988

Dear Dr Sundaram,

During the year 1987-88 the receipts from Sales Tax reached its new heights by crossing Rs.1000 crores for the first time in the history of Gujarat State. I convey the appreciation of government for the efforts put in by you.

With regards,

Yours sincerely,
Sd/-
(M.S. Dayal)

Dr G. Sundaram,
Joint Secretary to the Govt., of India,
Ministry of Environment,
New Delhi."

Octroi is an obnoxious tax. So we introduced a Bill in the Assembly for adopting Entry Tax in its place. We plugged all the loopholes of the Sales Tax system in this levy. The industrialists and traders felt that they would not be able to evade as they did with Octroi and opposed the Entry Tax Bill so much so that the Government was constrained to withdraw it from the Assembly. Maharashtra also studied the proposed system of Entry Tax of Gujarat under Finance Secretary M.D. Godbole because Octroi constituted a huge revenue for the Bombay Municipal Corporation and the other Municipalities in Maharashtra.

I was happy VAT became a reality in 2005. I wrote the following letter to Prime Minister Dr Manmohan Singh with a copy to Finance Minister P. Chidambaram. P. Chidambaram was good enough to reply.

Respected Sir,

Greetings.

You might recall (I had informed you when I was in the GOI) that it was I who suggested introduction of VAT in this country (my articles in "The Economic Times" dated 4.6.'86 and 15.11.'86) when I was Commissioner of Sales Tax, Gujarat. I did this in the light of my studies in Brussels (M. Phil.) and also as a measure of sales tax reform. In fact, I delivered two or three lectures too in the National Institute of Public Finance and Policy (Dr A. Bagchi should recall). Of course, my own colleagues felt that this would be difficult to implement! So, the Hon. FM's observation today that this would be the most important tax reform since Independence was right indeed.

I am justifiably glad today although it has taken a long long time to fructify as it always happens in our country. Congratulations to you, our FM, your Government and the State governments.

with warm regards, as ever,

Yours sincerely,

(G. SUNDARAM)

To

Dr Manmohan Singh,
Hon. Prime Minister,
New Delhi

Dy. No. 51 /FMP/FM/05
FINANCE MINISTER
INDIA
NEW DELHI – 110001
January 24, 2005

Dear Dr Sundaram,

Thank you very much for your letter dated January 17, 2005. It is interesting to learn that you had suggested introduction of

VAT as long back as in 1986 when you were Commissioner of Sales Tax, Gujarat.

Thank you again for your congratulatory remarks.

With regards,

Yours sincerely,
(P. Chidambaram)

Dr G. Sundaram
Former Secretary to the
Government of India
"Burma House"
33/18, 9th Street
Dr Radhakrishnan Road
Chennai-600 004

* * *

16

Panel and Promotions or Postings

It is always a hassle to get a good posting in the Government of India unless one has tremendous influence at the level of the Cabinet Secretary or preferably in the PMO. Otherwise, one should have high political influence of significance. If one does not have both, one should be extremely lucky. May be I fall in the third category except on an occasion when I had an access to the then Cabinet Secretary. So when my name was sent to the Government of India for a posting again, the then Establishment Officer who had his own ideas and idiosyncrasies as well although he was a very good person and a devout Catholic and my contemporary in the college, would not send my name to any economic ministry. His idea was that I had done economic ministries sufficiently and I should go to one of the non-economic ministries. I told him that I had no objection at all to go back to Defence. Since it was not a sought after Ministry, he sponsored my name. But the then Defence Secretary, S.K. Bhatnagar, although I had worked with him, did not want me there. In life, we feel sorry some times when we do not get certain things. But it turns out to be for our own good later. This Defence Secretary got into a lot of controversy later and became the centre of a political storm. So it was good that he did not take me for his own reasons. Later on, too, I was not picked up for the post of Secretary, Petrochemcials, although my name was on top of the panel. It so turned out that the minister and his son were arrested for their alleged involvement in some scandals. Earlier in my life too, when I could not get a post in the Reserve Bank of India, Bombay, I felt unhappy. But I was happy that I became a Lecturer instead in the Madras Christian College.

It so happened that the Secretary, Revenue, in the Ministry of Finance picked up my name for a post in that Ministry. If it had been a post of Joint Secretary, I would have very happily accepted it. But there was no such vacancy at all. So when I probed into the matter, it turned out that it was for the post of the head of the Economic Intelligence Bureau. I was not at all happy about this selection. When I met the Secretary, Revenue, I pleaded with him, but he was not prepared to leave me off the hook. The post per se would not have been bad. He perhaps wanted me because of my sales-tax background and wanted one from the IAS with a broad vision to build up an organisation. One could have really built up an important organisation collecting economic intelligence about the various industries, industrialists, traders, their good and bad activities, etc. In other words, it could have been a counterpart of the political Intelligence Bureau on the economic side. But it always happens in Government that it would be extremely difficult to do some thing new or build up an organisation unless you have total freedom. In this case, I would have had to work under the Customs people who would have been naturally hostile to me. They would not have liked the presence of an outsider there. They would have put all types of obstacles so that one's efforts would not fructify at all. Luckily for me, an IPS officer from the PM's office was also interested in this post. But he had not made up his mind and he wanted to keep this in reserve for him. He kept this post as a fall-back position in case he had incurred the wrath of the then PM for some lapse or the other and had to leave the PMO. So he managed to hold up the proposal along with my dossier for about six months or so. In fact, the file was not traceable at all. The same Establishment Officer, who was my friend, had even thought of calling for duplicate copies of my dossier from the Government of Gujarat so that I could be considered for some other post. Meanwhile, the file was luckily found and in that process the post also had gone and I heaved a sigh of relief although I had lost six months.

I was later sponsored to the Ministry of Environment and Forests because of my earlier stint as chairman of the Gujarat Pollution Control Board. I was readily accepted by T.N. Seshan even without my dossier because he had known my active work in the Gujarat Pollution Control Board and the consequent sudden and abrupt transfer. He was at that time well disposed towards me. It was a different story that he had totally turned against me later for no reason. I had not even talked ill of him, but our colleagues are so clever in cutting a good relationship. That was how I landed in the Ministry of Environment. Incidentally, the definite article is always a casualty in Government. While Environment takes the article 'the' everywhere particularly in the U.K., it is dropped here. Although I was selected for a forest vacancy, Seshan on his own gave me pollution control, hazardous substances management, etc., I found the atmosphere quite congenial and the work was also interesting. T.N. Seshan was luckily transferred within a few months.

The purpose of the book is also to expose how phony the Indians are. Perhaps we are the worst hypocrites in the world. This is true of this so-called middle class hero who has written a book on the degeneration of India. The newspapers and journals had built him up more than what he actually deserved. In fact, I would not have even devoted this space to him; but the public have to be informed since many of them may not be still aware. I would only invite attention to an article written on Seshan by B.G. Deshmukh, a former Cabinet Secretary and Secretary to PM, in *The Indian Express* reproduced later in his book. (Incidentally, of all recent books by civil servants, the three books by B.G. Deshmukh including his autobiography were the best in forthrightness and truth; he never hesitated to mention names). R. Venkataraman, the former President of India, also had made some telling remarks on Seshan in his book.

Some civil servants have used the media to glorify themselves and the gullible people believe them. All that appears in the newspapers is not true. I know quite a few instances where utter falsehood is written in newspapers and people generally tend to believe what they see in print. As some media persons themselves admitted and as also indicated in an interesting TV programme 'Newswatch', many media reports were not correct.

T.N. Seshan was on his first visit to Madras after publishing his controversial book with some unsavoury remarks about the late C.N. Annadurai. I also happened to be on official visit and had arrived in Madras the previous night. The plane actually landed late in Madras at about 1.00 a.m., The State Government Protocol took me straight to Taj Coromandel in Nungambakkam. I enquired from the Protocol Officer why he was not taking me to the State Guest House as usual. He told me there was some problem in the state guest house and also added that T.N. Seshan was also expected by the morning flight from Delhi and he would also be staying in the same hotel in a suite next to mine. I became more insistent that I should go to the state guest house and did not want to face any problem in the hotel. But the Protocol Officer insisted that I stayed there and assured me there would not be any problem and there was adequate police 'bandobust' for Seshan.

T.N. Seshan arrived at the airport next morning and he was not allowed to enter the city for the whole day by a huge crowd. He was confined to the airport till about 5.00 p.m., He summoned the Chief Secretary and the DG of Police. There was high drama in the airport.

Meanwhile, I had gone out on my work and was returning to the hotel in the afternoon. But the policeman at a distance advised me not to take that road. But I told him that I was staying in the hotel and I had to go there. But he advised me that a huge crowd was sitting outside the hotel and I should put the glass down lest they would attack my government car mistaking that Seshan was inside. I did so and managed to enter the hotel with some difficulty.

Seshan arrived there at about 5.30 p.m., brought by the Chief Secretary Haribaskar and the DGP Sripal. Perhaps his vanity was satisfied. Incidentally, both of us had to attend the same wedding of a friend and there was a lot of 'bandobust' no doubt for Seshan. I am sure he must have liked it immensely as he did always.

But, in all this I noticed that even the drivers of the vehicles did not have a bad word for Seshan. I thought they would bad-mouth him because of his remarks about Annadurai. In any case, the drama was over for the day and the agitation was apparently called off. By coincidence, the newspapers carried on the front page on the same day a trenchant criticism of T.N. Seshan and his antics by the former Cabinet Secretary, B.G. Deshmukh, already referred to above.

The next day both of us were returning to Delhi by the same plane in the evening. I did not see even a single person holding a black flag or demonstration against him either in front of the hotel or en route to the airport. It was all peaceful. This was a clear indication that the previous day's demonstration was an organized one and there was no spontaneous feeling among the people. Over a period of time, I suppose people perhaps tend to forget even legends like Mahatma Gandhi or Annadurai who was considered the Gandhi of Tamil Nadu.

When Seshan entered the VIP room in the airport, I stood up. He told me to sit down. A few press persons came and interviewed him. He was very angry with *The Hindu* for some wrong reporting according to him and asked *The Hindu* correspondent to clear out yelling at him: "you are from a gutter press known as *The Hindu* on Mount Road!" Needless to state I was amused to see him again which was on many occasions in full foul temper.

His predecessor, Peri Sastri was a quiet and efficient Chief Election Commissioner. He never tom-tomed about himself from roof-tops. He also followed the right policy of sending election observers who knew the language of the State but did not belong to that Cadre. Knowing the local language gives a lot of clue to what is happening around. Whereas Seshan sent out observers most of whom did not know the local lingo and as a result they had to depend upon the translation of the untrustworthy local officials.

During the period of Peri Sastri, I was sent to Tamil Nadu. Although the DMK Government kept a cut-out of the 'Bofors' gun at every nook and corner, the Congress – AIADMK combine won all the seats. The present MP and a Minister, T.R. Balu, a confidant of Karunanidhi was an observer from the party side for this election. He was totally crest-fallen when all results were out except the South Madras parliamentary constituency. The result was a foregone conclusion in this constituency too with the Congress film-star Vijayanthimala Bali standing there. This was one of the biggest constituencies in the country where the counting took nearly thirty hours. The former Foreign Secretary, A.P. Venkateswaran was also a candidate. Being a Foreign Service man, the whole counting process appeared a scene of madness to him. But I assured him that there was some method in the madness. He fared fairly well for a total stranger to politics. Vijayanthimala Bali hardly turned up except for a brief TV shooting in the evening.

The counting was going on and I was tired by about 11.30 p.m., I thought I would go home and sleep because everything was going on well. But a thought occurred to me on the way – since DMK lost every-where, there might be some problem here and as a matter of precaution I telephoned the Chief Electoral Officer of the State, D.K. Oza, an amiable and efficient person. He advised me – which was a good advice - not to take any chance and to go back to the counting centre. So I went back. Again at about 2.00 a.m., both the State Observer and I felt that everything there was fine and we could go home and come back by about 7 a.m., after a bath. When we were coming out, T.R. Balu accosted us and said there were some unaccounted votes which was a serious matter and I should come back with him. So I had no other alternative but to go to that segment of counting and stopped the counting because there were about twenty votes which were not accounted. T.R. Balu made a lot of noise about it. But I told the counting officer to bring the counterfoils. Meanwhile, Balu was very vehemently objecting to the entire counting. But I told him that counting would go on and if he wanted he could lodge a complaint. He immediately started writing down on a piece of paper. After about half-an-hour or so with difficulty, the counter-foils were produced and the numbers tallied. But the Polling Officer failed to record these numbers and hence appeared as excess unaccounted votes. Balu had no other alternative but to feel satisfied. In any case, I reported this matter to the Chief Election

Commissioner in my report lest there would be an election petition. There was a very serious consideration for a petition questioning the election of Vijayantimala Bali on this score. But she won by a huge margin and wiser counsel prevailed and the idea of election petition was given up by the losing candidates. But she was totally unaware of this incident till I told her years later in Delhi when I came to know her.

However, we must give the devil its due. Seshan really put the politicians in their place and the fear of the Election Commission in them. Elections became peaceful and less expensive and there was real universal appreciation for the man from the common people which he really deserved. Unlike most other civil servants who were generally ineffective, he was capable of delivering the goods, law or no law, rules or no rules. After seeing him, even the supine judiciary woke up and started asserting itself much to the appreciation of the common public. The executive could no longer run roughshod over these institutions. However, when he stood for election for the highest office of the land, many people rightly wrote although he was the best Chief Election Commissioner, he was eminently unsuited to hold this high office. He had a crushing defeat. But he still had caught the attention of the common man that when once I was passing in front of his house in a taxi, the driver remarked that a man like Seshan should be the PM or President of this country. I had also known K.R. Narayanan a little because he was a colleague of a brother-in-law of mine in the Foreign Service who died a few years ago. The country could not have found a better person than this scholar, diplomat and an amiable person with humility, let alone his humble beginnings – from 'the log-cabin to Rashtrapathi Bhavan'. My wife was more happy because of her greater compassion for the poor and admiration for the people who came up the hard way (though some of his actions were considered somewhat controversial later and he did slide a bit). (Very recently too, I was going to the Election Commission to meet my Cadre-mate and CEC Gopalaswami. The gossipy taxi-driver recalled Seshan and his initials too).

K.P. Geethakrishnan became the Secretary, Environment and Forests. It was an unusual posting for him because he had spent

all his life in Finance before this. He says even now that he has enjoyed the posting, may be because he is a keen bird-watcher of the winged variety. Although he and Additional Secretary Dr A.C. Ray, IAS., gave me an outstanding chit as told by them to me, I got angry with Geethkrishnan once and walked out of his room. I wrote in my diary: "He does not read the files; if he reads, he does not understand; if he understands, he does not remember". This was more out of anger. He was a good and clever person. When I met him in Washington years later he told his private secretary, "I was Sundaram's Secretary and he had not forgiven me for that!"

Mahesh Prasad became the Secretary, Environment and Forests later. Although he was a bit controversial, I found him to be a knowledgeable person with rich finance and industry experience. He was also in the Ministry of Commerce and as our Minister (Economic) in London. He was well disposed toward me. We had initiated even during Geethakrishnan's time steps to control automobile pollution in the country. A lot of work was also done on hazardous substances management following the Bhopal tragedy. The Environment Protection Act, a path-breaking legislation which was passed during Seshan's tenure, was implemented fairly effectively. This could be done because of the close interest taken in matters pertaining to the environment by Rajiv Gandhi following the footsteps of his mother. The Prime Ministers later did not take so much interest and, in our country, even a single programme does not take off without an interest being shown by no less a person than the Prime Minister. This is indeed a sorry state of affairs. When so many things could be done by so many officials and politicians, they either lack the initiative or obstructions are put in their way that they find it difficult to achieve their objectives. It is a constant fight with the other Ministries particularly Finance. The system is such that all the time obstacles are put in the way even against good common goals and one succeeds if one is capable of crossing these hurdles. It often happens that one loses interest in this chronic battle or one falls by the way side. That is the reason why many proposals in the Government of India take a long time to fructify and it purely depends upon the high-level political will. I know many projects and ideas had taken even ten years just to be accepted. So, even in the case of automobile pollution, it took such a long time so much so what was started in 1988 started fructifying in a small way only in 1996, that too with Supreme Court intervention. Many people expressed some silly reservation or the other in the media against lead-free petrol or catalytic converter.

To give another instance of this kind where PM's intervention became necessary even in a small matter was in the case of the New Delhi Railway Station which was in a total mess. There was hardly any parking space on the Ajmeri-gate side. It was a scene of utter chaos. But no Railway official or the Railway Minister paid attention to this problem. A foreign visitor or journalist wrote a scathing article about the conditions there in one of the newspapers. This was seen by Prime Minister Narasimha Rao and he referred it to me when I was Secretary, Public Grievances, in the Cabinet Secretariat. I took a couple of meetings which was followed up by my successor and also by the PMO. Thanks to the intervention of the PM, the whole scene incredibly and completely changed at the New Delhi station within three or four months. There is huge parking space, more over-bridges have been constructed, platforms have been cleaned up and undesirable elements have been driven away. A simple thing of this kind could have been achieved by the General Manager or the Railway Board itself. Either the idea did not occur to them or they faced problems of finance and other constraints. But it could be achieved only at the intervention of the Prime Minister. Although one blames the PMO very often, in our system many decisions have to be taken by the PM himself or the PMO has to intervene. This is more true of very powerful Prime Ministers like Mrs. Gandhi and Rajiv Gandhi than others.

When I was in the Ministry of Environment, it was still not a much sought-after Ministry. People even thought that one was 'sidelined' to use the bureaucratic parlance, if one was posted in the Ministry of Environment. But it became a sought-after Ministry later mainly because of the trips abroad and the possibility for getting a UN posting. So, when I became a Secretary and the post of Secretary, Environment, fell vacant people thought I would be the natural choice because of my earlier stint there and the work in the field as chairman of the Gujarat Pollution Control Board. Of course, I personally did not have my heart there and left it without speaking to anybody and thinking that should it happen in the normal course I would go there. But things do not happen in the normal course in the Government of India. There is no place for merit or background. The post was given to some one who manoeuvred for it and would clear cases of industries easily and, of course, I was not unhappy. But I felt that the system did not work. It worked contrary to logic and what others naturally thought.

Even at the time of my promotion as additional secretary, I recorded in my diary on January 20th, 1990: " I learnt yesterday that my case had moved to the Prime Minister for appointment in Urban Development. What a slow move and what a department? It all has become a struggle. My exposure in the Government of India – Home (Pondicherry), Agriculture, Industry, Commerce, Defence, now science departments like the Environment and Bio-technology, except Finance so far. But what is the use in this bureaucratic jungle of no values" which is Government of India.

During my stay in the Ministry of Environment as Joint Secretary, I had signed, on behalf of the Government of India, the International Convention on Transboundary Movement of Hazardous Wastes, popularly known as Baslé Convention because the Convention was signed there. The minister could not attend this meeting and so I was authorised to sign it. This is an important Convention even now because there are attempts by developed countries to dump hazardous wastes quietly in developing countries. The requisite rules were also framed by me in time following this Convention. Perhaps the implementation is still not satisfactory.

During this period, Z.R. Ansari was the Minister for Environment and Forests. Contrary to the popular belief and general impression created by his personal appearance, he was a knowledgeable person about the matters pertaining to the environment and pollution control and was committed to the

cause. This was perhaps possible because he had spent a few years in the Ministry and mastered the subject adequately. He was also a good person as a human being. Unfortunately his political career ended when he was allegedly misbehaved when a lady visited his office and his life also ended thereafter.

He was followed by Mrs. Maneka Gandhi who, of course, was totally committed to the Environment. She wanted to do many things and brought in a band of knowledgeable people on her personal staff. There was naturally a lot of activity in the ministry. She started with a misunderstanding with the Secretary for some trivial reason and called in T.N. Seshan who was the then Cabinet Secretary to brief her on the subject which Seshan did most willingly. I had hit it off well with her although many others found her difficult. It was time by then for my promotion as Additional Secretary. When I was shifted to the Ministry of Urban Development, she thought I was going on my own. But it was not so. Actually T.N. Seshan wanted his protégé Madhava Sharma to stay on in that Ministry so that he could get himself informed of the happenings in the Ministry. Besides, he perhaps felt that with my knowledge of French, Ph.D., and international exposure, I would be a potential rival to Madhava Sharma in getting any UN post. So he sent my name to the Ministry of Urban Development and I had to accept it because it was a question of my promotion.

In fact, three of my colleagues knowing Seshan's good disposition towards me, prejudiced him so that he as Cabinet Secretary would not clear me for promotion. Two of them ganged up and one of them was the adviser in these matters. This so called adviser told my colleague from Gujarat that he might be the casualty because our batch-mate, K.G. Ramanathan, would have no difficulty on the basis of his record and I would be the second one to go through easily on the same basis. Since empanelment was also a question of restricting numbers, the adviser told my colleague that he would be left out as a consequence unless he managed to eliminate me. So they hatched a plot. They not only prejudiced Seshan but also another member who was related to one of them. This kind of a thing happens at higher levels. It is a job to keep one's job if it happens to be a good one! This member of the Board became a member of the UPSC later (for the first time, a Home Secretary was shunted out as member, UPSC, which in those days was only of the rank of additional secretary) and he had to please me to retain his bungalow when I was in the Ministry of Urban Development. He lost no time in congratulating me on my promotion. Taking this opportunity, I enquired from him as to how the paneling was being done for promotions. He explained by stating, perhaps he was referring to me, that in a particular case all members including the Cabinet Secretary felt that a particular officer was considered 'outstanding' and he had specialised in Commerce. But he argued that the officer did not have diversified experience and he did not do anything even in Pondicherry. This was quite contrary to the truth. But the Lt. Governor who wrote the CRs wrote only two lines on every one. In any case, he was briefed on these lines by my own colleagues and he convinced the other members to my detriment. But I got a wind of it and made a comprehensive appeal in time. My Minister also spoke to PM Rajiv Gandhi and the latter remembered my work in Gujarat as chairman of the Pollution Control Board, and my seminar to the MLAs to educate them on Environment and his replication of the same for the MPs. Since my general reputation was good as a good officer, I was included in the list straightaway thanks also to the good offices of R. Vasudevan who was then additional secretary in the PMO. There is a saying in Tamil "Than vinai thannai chudum". To give a Biblical translation, this means "As you sow, so you reap". All these three colleagues of mine perhaps indulged in the same tactics for promotion as Secretary when our turn came two years later and exposed themselves in that process and were left out of the panel. They could not make it even later despite their best efforts. However, after repeated efforts, one of them – the adviser – made it only as Special Secretary, but in the mean time, he died.

As in the case of postings, empanelment is also a dicey proposition in the Government of India. It is more of an exercise in elimination than in selection of officers for top posts. Many good officers including some who became Cabinet Secretaries or CAG or Executive Directors of ADB or IMF later had come to grief because of the system. One of my batch-mates who had

had an outstanding record throughout his career, whatever his other faults might be, lost his Secretaryship because of a single remark in his CR when he was Additional Secretary. The CRs are not written properly in some State Cadres like Gujarat and, as a result, the casualty rate is very high. Even a Harvard Ph.D., had failed to make the grade for the post of Joint Secretary or Additional Secretary, thanks to this system. In other words, the Joint Secretary or Additional Secretary is put on such a high pedestal in the Government of India that even a Harvard Ph.D., without any other fault and full of good qualities could not reach it. The system also breeds other traits like not giving fearless advice even at the level of Additional Secretary because of the chronic worry about the CRs. Even IAS officers have started requesting their superiors for 'outstanding' CRs because of this system. This request for outstanding CRs was a common trait prevailing only in the Central Secretariat Service and as a result every one in the CSS was found outstanding according to the CRs. The system has also made many people go round lobbying and seeking favours from politicians. Of course, the State Governments go to the other extreme of promoting all and sundry without leaving out any one. A balance has to be struck between these two extremes. If not, as the Government of India took a stand in Jaitly's case and as upheld by the Supreme Court, it is left to the Government to choose a person of their choice as Secretary irrespective of the various considerations. If this is so, there is no need to have a system of empanelment at all with all its attendant bad features and heart-aches to those who have no pull. In fact, one of my batch-mates started crying at mid-night much to the consternation of his wife and children because his name was not on the panel! The CRs also do not always reflect the quality of a person. The exact personality may not come out. I always advocated that there should be a self-assessment column so that you have an opportunity to state whatever you have done even though it is not read often because it is self-commendatory or adulatory. After a long time, this suggestion was accepted so that a situation where a lot was done by me at Pondicherry, but the Lt. Governor wrote only two sentences without realising the

implications, could be avoided. Again luck plays a part. Some people get 'outstanding' entries although they are not really 'outstanding'. In any case, CRs written by different people over a period of fifteen or twenty years, read together do bring out the person. But, a person may fall by the wayside because of prejudices of selection committees or by comparison with other CRs. I wrote in my diary as early as on December 20th, 1975 when I was a Deputy Secretary: "a lot of work – that is all – credit for work depends upon your destiny rather than upon performance". On the whole, it is advisable to give up the panel system in preference to selection for each post i.e., by considering a few persons in the zone by a select committee, say four persons to be considered for one post. No one is black-balled and there would be no lobbying before or after. The person left out would wait, may be in vain, or use his clout and get in as it happens always in a few cases. But the system does not lose credibility as it happens now.

Ours was a very unique batch. Out of about 90 and odd officers, about 80 and odd were on the Joint Secretaries panel. To start with, the number of persons included in the Joint Secretaries panel was very low. But a good officer from Andhra Pradesh who became Chief Secretary of that State later was not on the panel. This made the then Cabinet Secretary who was also from Andhra Pradesh to lose faith in the system. He gave a ruling that the State Government should also be consulted in the process of empanelment. As a result of this wise ruling, the numbers increased. I was told this system was given up a couple of years later. For empanelment as Additional Secretaries too, the number was less to start with. But the Governments changed twice and many people jumped into the wagon with the help of the new Governments and as victims of the earlier Governments so much so that 42 officers were on the Additional Secretaries panel. Out of this, only two did not come to Delhi. Even some of those who had never worked in Delhi came as Additional Secretaries. So, when the question of empanelment of Secretaries came up, a lot had naturally to be left out and this naturally resulted in bickering. One or two even resorted to the unusual step of planting stories in the newspapers. They thought they would be able to gain something by resorting to the press. This is a new trend where people try to gain something by resorting to newspapers although such tactics do not help often. In fact, on the contrary, they lose out often. But, on the whole, the question of selection in the Government of India even for top positions like Cabinet Secretary has become questionable over a period of time. This reached its depth during the period of Narasimha Rao. Following the destruction of the Babri Masjid, a Muslim who was never a Secretary or even Additional Secretary of a Department was appointed as Cabinet Secretary much to the surprise of the entire bureaucracy. Some of the Cabinet Secretaries were not even on Additional Secretaries panel. Having appointed him, the PM should not have spoken about his possible ouster without extension from the ramparts of the Red Fort of all places, that too on a solemn occasion like the Independence Day. Similarly, while some posts of Secretaries were kept vacant for months, some like that of Foreign Secretary Salman Haider were announced four months in advance because some elections were coming up. All these old gimmicks of the Congress party did not pay off in the elections and Narasimha Rao lost power.

As far as I was concerned, luckily I had no problem for empanelment as Secretary. S. Rajgopal, the then Cabinet Secretary, was kind enough to tell me himself that I was through. He told the Chief Secretary to the Government of Gujarat too. Principal Secretary to PM, A.N. Varma, too told me indirectly. But I could not tell this outside and some of my colleagues thought that I was not in and included my name in the non-select list in the newspaper. My well wishers and friends all over the country felt unhappy and I had to reassure them quietly that it was a wrong report. They also confused my name, 'Gopalan Sundaram' with 'Gopalakrishna' (Gopal) and wrote that he was in. It came as a rude shock to him when he discovered later that he was not in. In fact, they did a disservice to both of us. If he had known earlier that he was not in, he would have taken some corrective action, coming from Andhra Pradesh. In fact, on the day this wrong list was published, Secretary Geethakrishnan asked Cabinet Secretary Rajgopal whether he could start congratulating persons who were on the list. I happened to be there at that time; we were attending the same meeting in the Cabinet Secretariat. Rajgopal replied stating that he could do so provided he was prepared to take it back in some cases! When I was promoted, to cover up their discomfiture, the same fellows planted an item stating that I got in with the influence of the then President R. Venkataraman who was related to me ("Sunday"). Strangely enough, some people really thought that I was related to him! I had the privilege of working with him when he was Defence Minister and I think he thought well of me. Though I requested him on some occasions to help me to get some posts, he never did anything for me. For that matter, he did not help his own secretaries, Murari and Prem Kumar – they did not get anything in Government after their retirement. In any case, in a judgment by the **Central Administrative Tribunal in a case filed and won by my batch-mate, Samar Singh, the entire minutes of the empanelment meeting taken by the Cabinet Secretary on December 22nd , 1992 were reproduced and thereby came into public domain and my name was very much there. "The Committee after screening the CR dossiers of all officers and keeping in view their record and experience including the conceptual and leadership abilities, achievements and potential for general management positions, recommended the following officers of 1962 batch of IAS for inclusion in the panel for holding the post of Secretary or equivalent posts outside the Secretariat at the Centre:**

Sl. No.	Name	Cadre
(A)	FOR HOLDING THE POSTS OF SECRETARY	
	S/Shri	
1.	P.C. Hota	(OR)
2.	M.P. Modi	(OR)
3.	B.N. Yugandhar	(AP)
4.	A. Hoda	(BH)
5.	K.R. Venugopal	(AP)
6.	G. Sundaram	(GJ)
7.	R. Naryanan	(KL)

8.	M.R. Sivaraman	(MP)
9.	V.K. Shunglu	(MP)
10.	C.K. Modi	(MH)
11.	N.R. Krishnan	(MP)
12.	A.C. Sen	(PB)
13.	R.K. Ahooja	(UT)
14.	R.V. Pillai	(A&M)
15.	Arun Sinha	(GJ)
16.	R.V. Gupta	(MP)
17.	Mata Prasad	(UP)
18.	P. Abraham	(MH)
19.	R. Nayak	(OR)

(B) FOR HOLDING NON-SECRETARIAT POSTS

S/Shri

1.	D.K. Afzalpurkar	(MH)
2.	Man Mohan Singh	(PB)
3.	S.P. Upasani	(MH)
4.	R.K. Sinha	(BH)
5.	Yogesh Chandra	(UP)
6.	S.K. Basu	(OR)
7.	C.D. Tripathi	(A&M)

3. The Committee noted that there was only one lady officer, namely, Smt. M.V. Garde (Sl. No. 17). She was not considered suitable for empanelment to hold Secretary/ equivalent posts.

4. The Committee further noted that there were 12 SC officers (Sl Nos. 67, 69-73 and 75-80). Of these, one officer (Sl. No. 74) is due to retire on 31.12.1992. Of the remaining, 3 officers at Sl. Nos 69, 71 and 75 were considered suitable for empanelment.

5. The Committee also noted that there was no ST officer in the batch.

The Cabinet Secretary sought approval of the panel of the Appointments Committee of the Cabinet and finally after shifting S/Shri D.K. Afzalpurkar, R.K. Sinha, Yogesh Chandra and C.D. Tripathi to the list of officers empanelled for holding the post of Secretary to the Government of India, The list was finally approved."

This also had set at rest the false propaganda by one or two batch-mates of mine. Incidentally, Samar Singh was a pleasant and competent officer. I was told that he was left out of the panel because he did not have diversified experience. That is, he had handled almost throughout his career only Forest and Wild Life. Whereas this reason was not applied in the case of Anwarul Hoda who had dealt with for long years only the Trade Policy in the Ministry of Commerce for obvious reasons. Poor Samar, although won the case in the Central Administrative Tribunal, lost it in the Supreme Court.

Although this is all fun in a way, people tend to believe the newspapers and it does affect one. A certain amount of dirt sticks on you for no fault of yours because it is difficult to wash off the entire dirt immediately. I wanted to file a case against the newspaper and the correspondent on the basis of this judgment, but desisted from doing so because I neither had the patience, nor the wherewithal to be a court-bird. I only issued a letter to the same magazine, *Sunday* denying that I was related to R. Venkataraman, but the journal refused to believe it though it published my letter. May be because of this denial, I was not treated that well later because Delhi goes by one's connections!

B.K. Nehru felt that the word, 'bureaucrat' was a pejorative and the proper word should be civil servant. (Nowadays they are not even bureaucrats, but only 'bureaucats'). In any case, this word has come into currency. But the Indian newspapers have gone a step ahead and started referring to the civil servants as 'babus', 'babudom' and so on. Of course, as a subsequent chapter would show, I do not hold any brief for the Indian bureaucracy. It is trained to be obstructive rather than facilitating. However, it is not advisable to badger institutions

like the civil bureaucracy because the Fourth Estate would be nowhere in a dictatorship or under military rule. Besides, would they like if we call them 'kowaas' (in Sanskrit meaning crows) because they rush from place to place, particularly when food and drinks are made available? However, the 'babus' deserve it because decisions are taken these days either by a clerk which the officer is afraid to over-rule or by the minister. Clerks' decisions are generally negative or unhelpful and ministers' are corruption-prone. The bureaucrats have also become so docile and refrain from giving advice to the ministers – this is also failure to do one's duty. In fact, a corruption-free strong minister capable of taking quick decisions is an asset to the society.

The journalists in Delhi are obsessed with ministers and civil servants. Their counterparts in Chennai are obsessed with cinema stars to the extent of quoting them even in respectable journals.

However, it should be said to the credit of both the print and visual media that, but for them, some powerful politicians would have hijacked this country, the whole or a part of it.

* * *

17

Ministry of Urban Development (MUD)

Whatever be the merits or demerits, the IAS provides a variety of experience and one learns something or the other in every post one holds. For instance, I have learnt in the Ministry of Civil Supplies, which is in charge of the Directorate of Vanaspati, Vegetable Oils and Fats, that **it is not advisable to take Vanaspati because all sorts of oils are mixed and at times even re-refined rancid oil is used. It is always advisable to take conventional oils like groundnut oil, mustard oil, gingelly oil, or any other edible oil including palmolein in its natural form. Similarly, although I was in the Ministry of Urban Development only for about four months, I learnt quite a lot about human nature.**

Although Maneka Gandhi thought I was leaving the Ministry of Environment to the Ministry of Urban Development on my own volition, it was not so. Maneka Gandhi also in her characteristic pungently jocular style asked me why I was keen on going to Murasoli 'Moron'! (Maran was the Minister for Urban Development at that time and people in the North often mispronounced his name). She used to consult me occasionally later too through her confidant and my Ph.D. class-mate, Dr Sri Ram Khanna. Dr Khanna is now active in the Consumer Movement as well through his organisation, 'Voice' in Delhi. Maneka also gives support to consumer affairs. In fact, she rightly felt that it was an important Ministry and wanted to tag it on to the Environment although it was not agreed to. She is also Prime Minister material with all her intelligence provided she controls her temper.

In any case, I landed in the Ministry of Urban Development. Secretary Sivaramakrishnan had made his task easier by having an Additional Secretary for the tricky and difficult Delhi affairs and by creating another post of Additional Secretary for allotment of houses. He kept with himself the creamy Urban Development part which meant trips abroad and consultancy from international organisations like the World Bank. Of course, I must say to his credit that he was an expert in urban affairs and did not want to waste his time on Delhi matters and house allotment. Finally, he went to the World Bank for the second time.

When I called on him on the first day, he also told me that the Ministry had the dubious distinction of being in charge of the 'samadhis' in Delhi. I always wondered whenever I saw the Director, CPWD, on TV why he was going round the 'samadhis' with other dignitaries as a ritual many times every year. I realised now that this Ministry was looking after these 'samadhis' and the CPWD was with this ministry. So when Sivaramakrishnan told me that I would be in charge of this work also, my heart sank. But I could not do anything about it. So, when the death anniversary of Pt. Jawaharlal Nehru fell the following May, I dressed myself totally in black for the occasion. But no one including Rajiv Gandhi turned up in black and all of them were in pure white. So people could easily spot me several times on the TV that evening going around the 'samadhi' of Pt. Nehru along with the dignitaries. They must have also wondered the same way as I did!

There was also another Sundaram, also from Vellore, who was an expert in Urban Development. He was from the Maharashtra Cadre. He was a Joint Secretary in the Ministry at that time. **In fact, when his posting was considered for Urban Development as Joint Secretary, my name was sent because of the service card of the Department of Personnel and it was discovered in time, much to my relief, that they did not want**

me but the other Sundaram. This happened because the Department of Personnel had no separate major classification for Environment and my stint with the Gujarat Pollution Control Board was shown under the categorization of Urban Development. Although I told even earlier the officials of the Department of Personnel that this was a misleading and wrong classification, they, with their usual mind-set and no-change attitude, did not correct it. It could be corrected and a major classification of Environment could be introduced only when I myself was posted in the Cabinet Secretariat as Secretary and the officer in charge of the computers of the Cabinet Secretariat and the Department of Personnel was the same person. In fact, I could correct many such other aberrations in the list.

The other Sundaram told me on the day of my posting that I would be henceforth a very well known person in Delhi in different circles. I did not believe it. But it turned out to be true later. All sorts of people like Yamini Krishnamurthy, Shovana Narain, judges and ministers started telephoning me and meeting me because all of them occupied some government house or the other. In fact, the visitors flow was so constant that one could not do any work in the room. So one of my predecessors had even an arrangement of locking the room from his table by an electronic device.

All officials posted to Delhi, after taking care of their posting, had naturally to fix their accommodation. So they trooped in straightaway to the Ministry of Urban Development and the Directorate of Estates. Although the system was followed strictly according to the rules during this period particularly with the cooperation of the Minister Murasoli Maran, many people tried to jump the queue. Some police officers used to post their inspectors in the building to chase the papers. Without any exaggeration, some ex-MPs occupying bungalows used to come and sit in the corridor outside my room or the room of the Minister much to our embarrassment praying to allow them to continue in their bungalow. A lady officer who held the highest position in the country and also served as a Governor for some time with a fiery reputation so much so she was known as 'hunterwali' actually came and wept before the Minister for continuing in her bungalow in Delhi. So did another fashionable lady minister who was out of office at that time. Murasoli Maran avoided seeing them later because they would break down with tears flowing down their cheeks.

Many people would not know that some politics was also infused into this. Some fence-sitters of the Congress party were allowed by the then Prime Minister to continue in their bungalows. Such a 'not-to-be-disturbed list' was with the Minister for Urban Development. It was an informal list though. Some of these political bigwigs, whenever a notice was sent to them by the Estate Office in the routine course, would straightaway ring up no less a person than the Prime Minister who in turn would ring up the Cabinet Secretary and he would ring me up. Since these contacts had to be frequent, Cabinet Secretary V.C. Pande told the Home Ministry to install a RAX (Restricted Automatic Exchange phone for high officials and ministers) phone in my office and also in my residence. But the Home Ministry did not install a RAX in my residence and I was not unhappy about it.

The normal charge was that the top officials had grabbed a number of bungalows. But when I appeared before the Cabinet Committee on Accommodation and gave them the statistics that only two or three top IAS officials were occupying Type VIII bungalows particularly because they came under 'the earmarked category' and the parliamentarians had much more than their usual quota of bungalows, it came as a revelation to the members of the Committee and they tactically did not pursue the matter. Some Ministers had a room in places like VP House and Western Court for the guests in addition to their bungalows.

Some of them got bungalows allotted free of charge in the name of some political party or association. Some had converted them into memorials so that they could stay there for ever. In any case, a bungalow in Delhi was allotted to an Indian judge of the International Court of Justice in the Hague. When he died, his wife continued to occupy it under some pretext or the other. She could be vacated with great difficulty because the other Indian judge appointed to the same post in the Hague wanted the same bungalow in Delhi. He used to call me now and then for vacating the lady. **When he came to know of my background and specialisation, he had some sympathy that I was being wasted** by the Government in this post for house allotment. He could appreciate my specialisation because his son himself studied in Brussels and almost had a similar background.

Before the lady could be vacated, the government had already acceded to the demand of the judge that his present bungalow should also be free in lieu of the bungalow to be vacated. When the bungalow was ultimately vacated and before he could move in, the CPWD demanded a few thousand rupees as garden maintenance charge. This was a peculiar CPWD formula under which the garden maintenance charges per month ran into a few thousand rupees. The judge's contention was that the garden was also given free to his predecessor in the International Court of Justice and consequently this garden should also be treated on a par. But the CPWD stated that as far as the garden in the other bungalow was concerned it was not exactly free, but the maintenance was given to that judge who was spending from his pocket and the garden was in excellent shape. So this kind of a parallel cannot be drawn and the judge concerned should shell out a few thousand rupees for its maintenance. But the judge hit the ceiling as anticipated by me and rang up the Cabinet Secretary straightaway who in turn sent a rocket to me and the CPWD. But the CPWD had some formula or the other in their pocket all the time to suit different types of individuals or situations and quickly produced one where the charge was considerably reduced to a few hundred rupees! The judge was satisfied. One could multiply such instances.

Several thousand rupees were waived by the Cabinet Committee on Accommodation. A few years later, some one filed a public interest litigation against this kind of arbitrary waiver of public money. When the Defence Ministry came up with a proposal to waive about Rs. 50,000 or so due from former Defence Secretary S.K. Bhatnagar, the Deputy Prime Minister Devi Lal remarked that the then Prime Minister V.P. Singh who was also the Defence Minister must have signed this file also without reading it along with a few other hundred files. His contention was that the Ministers had no time to read and apply their mind to the files and it was all the work of the bureaucrats. So this case was shot down by the Committee. But, 'no' was never taken as a final answer in the Government of India, and the issue was brought up in the subsequent meeting and passed for waiver when the Deputy Prime Minister was not present. He would not have followed up this case. This kind of waiver of public money was stopped by the Supreme Court a few years later.

Not only some top-ranking officials and politicians but also some lower-level functionaries like clerks, drivers and teachers are involved in this huge racket of Delhi. Journalists are no exception. The press pool is an expanding one all the time because of press blackmail. Artists are no exception. One or two civil service wives have grabbed houses for ever in the name of running dancing schools. The Estate Office very often did not have an account of who occupied which house. I was told that some people had not paid the rent at all for months or years together. Many of them had sublet their houses. Although action was taken in some cases, it was not systematic. Many of them had practically appropriated the Government houses for themselves because their children got into government service and the house was transferred as fresh allotment. Some had let out the garages and made money.

I must also record a rare instance of honesty in this matter. When Dr Manmohan Singh was posted in the South-South Secretariat, Geneva, he owed about eight or nine thousand rupees for some natural over-stay. In his absence, Mrs Singh was brought to me by her friend, Dr (Mrs) Barthakur of the Planning Commission. I told her that even the minister had no powers of waiver, which could be done only by the Cabinet Committee on Accommodation. Although the Planning Commission where he was should take a note to the Cabinet Committee, I told her that we would do so as a special case, if she so desired. "If it has to go to a Committee, Dr Saab (Dr Manmohan Singh) would not like it", she said and issued a cheque on the spot - she was carrying a cheque book. I really appreciated her honesty.

The Ministers before and after Maran did not follow the system at all. The discretionary quota of allotment by the

Minister was only 20%. 80% was meant for the normal queue. Maran was remembered for a long time in the Ministry for his scrupulous adherence to this rule. But the other Ministers started operating on the entire 100% and in the true Delhi feudal style allotting houses whenever people approached them. As a result of this practice, there used to be long queues outside the Minister's office, and once when I was surprised to see such a queue, I was told that the Minister concerned was allotting houses like a billing-clerk taking the applications himself. Things came to such a pass at one stage that there were serious allegations of corruption in house allotment. Even senior officers were asked to pay huge amounts by the officials of the Estate Office or the PAs of the Ministers and some of them had to resort to the corrupt practice of asking some business house or the other to pay the money on their behalf.

File work was heavy in the Ministry. I wrote in my diary on April 21st, 1990: "sat till 00.30 hours midnight and disposed of about 500 files".

In any case, this was a huge racket where I could see how the government houses were appropriated or treated as their own much to the draining of the public exchequer. I wrote in my diary on March 10th , 1990: "I am more convinced that this is a dishonest country and Indians are hypocrites". I wanted to introduce a system of computerisation where allotments would be done as was done for some medical college admissions where everything was left to the computer. One should give a few choices and it would be left to the computer to make the choice as per the parameters. But, before I could do it, I was transferred and I felt relieved to be free from this mad-house although it was an experience in itself. (This was drafted five years ago. Subsequent events including the Supreme Court verdicts proved what I said above).

Another issue which was hanging fire in this Ministry and which is still dragging on is the question of installation of a statue of Gandhiji at the India Gate. Although I was not dealing with the subject, I saw a number of files on the subject with learned and not-so- learned notes. The original proposal was to install a statue of Gandhiji in the standing posture in the place where a British

King's statue, I believe, stood. This was under a beautiful canopy in front of the India Gate. The statue would be looking at the Rashtrapathi Bhavan along Raj Path which, incidentally according to me, is one of the most beautiful sights in the world; I have not seen elsewhere such a wide panorama overlooking from the Raisinha Hill with beautiful buildings on both sides. In fact, the French call this Champs Elysée de l'Inde. In my opinion, this is even a shade better without those artificially glittering lights of Champs Elysée of Paris. But some elements particularly close to the ruling family did not want a memorial for Gandhiji in such a prominent place in the capital. So they started a bogey that a statue of Gandhiji should not be under an imperial canopy. Some suggested removal of the canopy and installation of the statue. But the same group – the self-styled guardians of culture and the urban arts of Delhi – opposed it stating that removal of the canopy would spoil the entire ensemble of art around the India Gate. So the debate went on and on. I thought the BJP would revive it and place the statue. But they are not admirers of Gandhiji. Delhi was not that friendly to Gandhiji; that was why, he also chose to be away from Delhi even on the Independence day of 1947. Some suggested a statue in a sitting meditative posture on the India Gate lawns near the Museum, which also did not take off. **Even now, in my opinion, it is neither late nor inappropriate to install a statue of Gandhiji under the canopy in India Gate – this would be a great tribute to the Father of the Nation.**

While on Gandhiji's statue, I must narrate a comical incident. While on a visit to Moscow, a well-known Russian architect showed a statue of Gandhiji in a sitting posture to Mrs Indira Gandhi. We do not know whether she really liked it or not with her high aesthetic sense in such matters. In any case, she felt that Gujarat's capital, Gandhinagar, would be the appropriate place to install it. Since it came from Mrs Gandhi, the Congress government of Gujarat went back on their earlier order of a statue in standing form to be installed in front of the Secretariat and accepted this one. The Russians flew the statue by a special plane and placed it in front of the Secretariat to be formally unveiled on the following October 2nd . Unfortunately, the statue was not covered properly; photographs appeared in the press and immediately many

Gujaratis – prominent and ordinary alike – were up in arms. They did not like the statue at all. They felt it looked as though Gandhiji was sitting in a bathroom. The protest was so vehement that the government of Gujarat covered this statue and the proposal to unveil it was given up. A few months passed by before the following October 2nd and the statue was still there yet to be removed, but fully covered. But *The Indian Express* reproduced a news item on October 4th from a prominent Moscow newspaper stating that this statue made by a well-known Russian architect was unveiled on October 2nd, with the Russian Ambassador and other dignitaries present! Obviously, they were not aware of the fate of this statue . I believe it is now in a museum in Delhi. The government of Gujarat restored the original order for a statue in a standing posture. These are the stories of the statues.

18

Close to Top

As I have already written, postings depend upon luck or chance. In the context of my long experience in Commerce and Industry, I went on requesting successive Commerce Secretaries like Prem Kumar and A.N. Varma, with whom I had worked earlier, to take me as Joint Secretary. In fact, when the post of Director General, Indian Institute of Foreign Trade fell vacant, the then Governor of Gujarat, R.K. Trivedi himself without asking me rang up Prem Kumar and told him that I would be the most suitable person for that post. But Prem Kumar had straightaway told him that it was already lined up for Dr S. Saxena of the Maharashtra cadre. So somehow it did not click and also thanks to the Establishment Officer Lynn I had to work in the Ministry of Environment.

When my orders of promotion came as Additional Secretary, it stated that I was appointed to the Ministry of Industrial Development. I felt that there was something wrong with this order because I was reliably told that I would go to the Ministry of Urban Development. But my Secretary, Mahesh Prasad, was so sure because he was the first one to get the orders and it clearly stated that it was for Industrial Development. In fact, he goaded me to go to the Industrial Development to take over. But I refrained from doing so lest I should cut a sorry figure. So when I checked up with the Establishment Officer Lynn, the storm in the tea cup was over and he stated, although a meticulous person that he was, that it was a mistake in the order and a corrigendum was being issued. Perhaps this kind of a mix-up had occurred for the first time in the Government of India. Mahesh Prasad was also a bit disappointed because he was all the time advocating that I should go to Industry which was the other side of Environment or Environment was the other side of Industry.

So when I landed in the Ministry of Urban Development, I lost all hopes of getting into Commerce Ministry because it would be very difficult at the Additional Secretary level and there would not practically be any vacancy. In any case, I had registered my request again with Commerce Secretary, S.P. Shukla, with whom also I had worked earlier in the Ministry of Commerce. One indirect benefit of the useless job of house allotment was that all sorts of people came to know about you and your background. In fact, many of them felt that I was being wasted on this job. I had also luckily known the then Finance Secretary, Dr Bimal Jalan, who was Economic Adviser to the Ministry of Industry in Udyog Bhavan when I was Deputy Secretary/ Director in the Ministry of Commerce.

When I was pursuing this matter in spite of its inherent difficulty, Commerce Secretary, S.P. Shukla, rang me up one day to say that a vacancy of Additional Secretary had occurred and I would fit in well, although two formidable colleagues of mine were also being considered, because Minister Arun Nehru had stipulated that the Additional Secretary should be able to start functioning from day one instead of learning on the job, for it would take at least six months to know the intricacies of. Commerce. So I fitted in and was posted there in no time. So this was purely by Providence. My earlier experience also counted. But in the BJP dispensation, there is no such stipulation of earlier experience for posts at the level of Additional Secretary or Secretary – two persons became Commerce Secretaries who never worked in Commerce; an officer became Finance Secretary without any earlier experience so much so he is reported to have asked: what is the difference between 'direct' and 'indirect'

tax! A revenue secretary who had never worked in Finance was also the son-in-law of a business tycoon; an officer became our Executive Director on the World Bank who did not know what was IBRD. This was BJP's selection, to cite a few instances.

I had no difficulty in functioning there right from the beginning because I was well conversant with the subjects. As usual, there was a variety of subjects starting from plantations to STC, MMTC and Transport which was rechristened as Infrastructure Division. The idea of a holding company, Bharat Business International Limited (BBIL) for the STC, the MMTC and the PEC was also being actively floated although I myself felt that such a Leviathan would not work. In any case, the then Government and S.V.S. Raghavan were very enthusiastic about it. But it became the first casualty as soon as a new government was formed and the Minister was Dr Subramanian Swamy. In any case, the work was so diverse that one had to spend a lot of time in reading up things. Although people felt that there was always a rush for the Ministry of Commerce because of international travels, the travels were by then cut sharply by the Commerce Secretary and naturally it was not the main part of the work. Although travel was always interesting for many, the work part of it and the need to learn new things was more interesting for every one.. I do not think that in any other Ministry except perhaps in Finance or to a certain extent in Industry, the officers even at the Deputy Secretary level could learn so much.

I saw some of my own earlier notes particularly of the Leather Division, Gems and Jewellery, specially the creation of the Hindustan Diamond Corporation and the Transport Division. For instance, I was the first Member Secretary of the SCOPE_AIR (Standing Committee for Promotion of Exports by Air) as Deputy Secretary and I had to chair the SCOPE_AIR and SCOPE_SHIPPING meetings again. On one fine morning, I read in the newspaper thatl I was appointed Director on the Board of the Air-India representing the Commerce Ministry. That was a surprise. I had no knowledge at all that my name was proposed. This continued for more than two years. When the Board was reconstituted later with a lot of non-officials dropping the representative of the Commerce Ministry, I wanted the then

Commerce Secretary, A.V. Ganesan, who was also Secretary, Civil Aviation earlier, to take up the matter. He was somewhat reluctant to do so. However, when the matter was taken up, it was not agreed to: perhaps he did not press for it. Sovan Kanungo, although was in Commerce earlier as Special Secretary, did not agree. People in civil service often become jealous of their colleagues.

Minister Arun Nehru himself was a difficult person, particularly with his private sector background. His private sector background perhaps helped him in taking quick decisions. But he could also deal with some one in the same fashion if one failed to come up to his expectations. When he was succeeded by Dr Subramanian Swamy, another person of a difficult reputation and also a maverick politician, there was naturally a lot of apprehension in the Ministry. He also removed the Commerce Secretary, Special Secretary and the Chairman, BBIL, in no time. But he made a very significant statement to the officers on the very first day which I felt that everyone should note in administration. He said that officers were free to give their opinion on file, but they should be 'straightforward' in their dealings without trying to draw circles around the Minister and, if they tried to do so, he would become a difficult person to deal with. I always felt that the word, 'straightforward' was missing in the dictionary of many bureaucrats and they always tried to adopt some devious method or the other. So this was a clear and loud message from him. Of course, my heart also sank when I came to know that he was a very close friend of T.N. Seshan. They fell out very badly later after a few years.

A trip to Afghanistan took me along with Dr Swamy on December 31st, 1990. We broke the New Year there. In fact, the airport was snow-bound with the temperature down to minus 14 Degree C. Our plane had to take off late, but they cleared the airport for us and we landed there. I had been to Kabul even earlier. It was not much of a place. The poverty of the people and the housing were striking. But, on an earlier occasion, I was leading a delegation and we were accommodated in the Intercontinental Hotel on the outskirts of the town. We were the only five persons occupying the hotel of about 400 rooms or so. But they were keeping the hotel spick and span and were also running the kitchen. Some occasional marriage receptions were taking place in the hotel. We could hear rocket sounds which were being fired on the town by the rebels hiding in the mountains. When one or two of us had to stay behind, they were scared to remain alone in the hotel and moved into a less posh hotel in the town. But, when I went with Dr Swamy, we were accommodated in the State guest house. We could meet President Najibullah who even came down to receive Dr Swamy and saw him off. President Najibullah, among other things, noted that he had known that Dr Swamy had attended even the funeral of Pakistan President Gen. Zia, but Dr Swamy was "a flexible" man. Dr Swamy had taken also two press correspondents in the delegation. One of them jocularly asked how he had left out Afghanistan for such a long time from his numerous visits all over the world. **Dr Swamy stated that this was because of his pronounced pro-Pakistan stance vis-à-vis Russian dominated Afghanistan. This trip also provided proximity and understanding between me and Dr Swamy. He came to know of my qualifications and earlier stint in the Ministry of Commerce. He is no doubt an intellectual stalwart. It was not for nothing he was a Professor at Harvard for a long time.**

During my earlier visit to Afghanistan, an important task given to me was that I should be able to get the consent of that Government for prospecting copper in that country. It is not a very well known fact that Afghanistan is one of the richest countries in copper deposits and it was one of the most important reasons for invasion of this country by the erstwhile USSR. To my great surprise, the Afghans at the official level readily agreed that India could come and prospect copper because they were already familiar with many Indians who worked in their coal mines as engineers before the Russian invasion. While they would have no objection, their only problem was that some of these copper deposits and mines were located in areas which were being controlled by the rebels. But they had gone on record agreeing to this suggestion. This was welcomed by my superiors when I came back to Delhi. But, when it was elevated to higher levels in that Government, they actually started evading the issue. When Dr Swamy also

broached this subject with President Najibullah, he simply stated that he would have no objection but the documents were in Russian and they would take some time to translate and provide them. But the proposal never materialised, we were told by our Ambassador, because of the Soviet pressure. Soviet control was quite strong even then. (Later too in retirement, I reminded the GOI for including it in Indo-Afghan talks).

Dr Swamy was succeeded by another difficult person, P. Chidambaram. He had known me earlier in a cursory way although he sought my suggestions in his first meeting with officers on the very first day. When I talked to him later he had also known that I had already worked earlier in the Ministry. The problem with these important or sought-after Ministries is that there is always pressure from some quarters or the other to remove a Secretary or an Additional Secretary on the plea that the post was obtained in a devious fashion or it was a favour conferred by a different government. So the Ministers, particularly the intelligent ones, naturally tried to look into the details and once they knew that it was well-deserved or because of one's background, they did not yield to unnecessary pressures. So he must have looked into the details as it was also his habit always. I found that he was one of the brightest and one the most competent Ministers I ever worked with including persons like R. Venkataraman who was very intelligent and meticulous in his dealings. But Chidambaram surpassed many of them because he functioned more like a super–Secretary. In England, it was said of Edward Heath and one or two other Prime Ministers that they could have easily functioned as permanent Secretaries because of their competence, thoroughness and ability to plan things. As it had been said in the case of Edward Heath, Chidambaram was also a Permanent Secretary manqué. But, as a politician, he was a problem for the party. His brusque and arrogant style with a rich family lineage and Harvard education did not endear him to many. Since he was not all that well-disposed toward the IAS particularly when he was Minister, Personnel, the IAS officers floated a story rightly or wrongly, that he could not make it to the IAS and hence the intense animosity. He sobered down a great deal later particularly after his bad defeat in Sivaganga. A Minister should not function like a Secretary. He should be able to combine the qualities of both as R. Venkataraman did. As a good lawyer too, he had no convictions since generally lawyers could argue both sides of the same case. Although he was a Minister for Personnel himself for five long years, he told me once that a particular officer was not fit to be Cabinet Secretary because he was only Secretary, Personnel! In fact, this officer had an outstanding record and with his experience as Secretary, Personnel, was eminently suitable to be the Cabinet Secretary. But Chidambaram was justifying the appointment of a particular officer as a Cabinet Secretary who was not even on Additional Secretaries Panel as was known to Chidambaram himself. But I still consider him a highly intelligent Minister. Of course, many persons have questioned me about his competence as Finance Minister because he was not a student of economics or public finance. As he himself stated that he was not an economist, but an economic administrator *par excellence,* in my opinion. I should also add that in his championing of economic reforms, he should remember this is also a sort of neo-colonialism by the West and we have to be careful about it while willy-nilly have to embrace it. Both Ganesan and I were surprised that Chidambaram did not know what was LIBOR (London Inter-Bank Offered Rate) when he became Commerce Minister. **But he picked up fast and wrote the Export Import Policy of that year practically himself. He should also not forget that India has a large number of poor still. To quote an instance of English arrogance and 'white-man's burden' still, I enquired from *The Economist* of London why they were not indicating LIBOR in their weekly issues. They were yet to reply in spite of reminders. Globalisation has become a convenient bandwagon for the white westerners. So we should not become Davos-slaves of the World Economic Forum or even the World Bank or the IMF. The philosophy or the policies of these organisations are being questioned by their own right thinking people like Joseph Stiglitz.**

Shukla was succeeded by M.S. Ahluwalia and by A.V. Ganesan. They were all good in their own way. But the position of an additional secretary was a bit nebulous in many ministries. The additional secretaries were powerful only in a few ministries.

Otherwise the joint secretaries were the nodal officers and often submitted files to the secretary or the minister directly. This would be more so in case the additional secretary was not knowledgeable. Many additional secretaries by their very short tenures in a ministry only for one or two years because it is a short period (this is no longer so because promotions have become slow) before elevation as secretary or rejection in empanelment would not be very knowledgeable. Since I had no such problem and could call for files, it could not happen to me in a big way although one or two joint secretaries did try to by-pass me. To add to this, Ahluwalia also brought in a new scheme of distribution of work under which he made me and my colleague, the late V.S. Venkataraman, powerless. Perhaps he thought that we were the fifth wheel to the coach. But we did protest in our own way and V.S. Venkataraman was given the charge of Japan and ESCAP. I also used this opportunity to get the charge of the EEC which was my specialization. I allowed the joint secretary, West Europe, to deal with bilateral matters and have his trips to West Europe, but retained all matters pertaining to the EEC with me. Ahluwalia was good enough to agree to this suggestion.

It always happens in our government that one's specialisation is hardly used. Perhaps the government is afraid of knowledge or specialisation. When an officer was sent abroad for training in dairy development, he was promptly posted in mining after his return. Such examples could be multiplied and somehow unfortunately this happened all the time. So, although I had specialised in the EEC matters, I was not given this coveted charge even during my deputy secretaryship because some other influential officer managed to have it. I was conveniently dubbed as 'the leather expert' because many others were not interested in that subject at that time. Again, I was not given the charge of the EEC when I joined the Commerce Ministry as additional secretary and I did not want to make it an issue because it was directly in the charge of the Commerce Secretary. But I did not let go this opportunity and got the charge of it. By sheer coincidence, it provided me an opportunity because our ambassador in Brussels was suggesting negotiations of a new agreement with the EEC. Lot of discussions took place and

although Ambassador Sengupta's initiative was not welcomed in some quarters purely because of personal animosity against him, the idea somewhat took shape. It provided me an opportunity to negotiate the third improved agreement with the EEC. The first one was only a Commercial Cooperation Agreement which was done by Ambassador Dr K.B. Lall in 1976. The second one was done by Ambassador P.K. Davé in 1981 and it was an upgraded Economic Agreement . The third one was the upgraded Partnership Agreement which was fully negotiated by me with the guidance of Dr Sengupta and initialled by me in December, 1992. In fact, my colleagues in the Ministry of Commerce and also in the Ministry of External Affairs thought that it would not easily go through. But the EEC officials were also somewhat kind because of my earlier association with them and it was completed in record time. When something is completed in record time, people generally are not inclined to believe it in our system.

Although the draft was fully cleared by the Ministry of External Affairs, particularly pertaining to the human rights clause – the full text was faxed twice to the additional secretary in the ministry of external affairs, P.M.S. Mallik, who was sitting then in Dhaka and several telephone calls were made for clarifications - the then Principal Secretary to PM, A.N. Varma, tried to find fault with it purely because he did not like Dr Sengupta and did not want the credit to go to him. But A.V. Ganesan stood by me fully and did not go back on his earlier commitments. Commerce Secretary Ganesan recorded on the Agreement negotiated and initialled by me with the EU: "In content and coverage, the Agreement is among the best between the EEC and developing countries". Whereas the Additional Secretary from the Ministry of External Affairs tried to wriggle out of it and disown his clearance, he did not succeed because his juniors were fully associated in Brussels and they were aware of the clearance given by him at the first instance. In any case, the final signature by the Commerce Minister dragged on providing a lot of anxiety to the EEC in Brussels and the Ambassadors of the member-countries in Delhi. But, the Principal Secretary to PM allowed that to be signed by Commerce Minister Pranab Mukherjee in Brussels in December, 1993 only after

Ambassador Sengupta returned to India. He had gone to that extent. Neither Ambassador Sengupta nor could I be present at the time of the signing of this important Agreement. Public interest suffers because of private feuds. I must also mention here that there are some charmed circles even among the economists in the Government of India. For instance, Dr Bimal Jalan is perceived to be close to V.P. Singh and the BJP. Dr Rangarajan and Montek are in Dr Manmohan Singh's charmed circle. Dr A. Sengupta is outside this and hence could not become the Deputy Chairman of the Planning Commission. Since he joined the Congress party earlier and because of his West Bengal connections, he could manage an innocuous post with Cabinet rank.

Colleague V.S. Venkataraman passed away in the meanwhile contracting cancer and I had to deal with his subjects too. That made me more occupied with a trip to Beijing as the leader of the Indian official delegation to the ESCAP session. I had seen this great city earlier when I was there for bilateral talks with Dr Swamy. In fact, I had signed the Trade Agreement with China. This was done after a long time. Their Vice- Minister who was equivalent to a Secretary was not present. In fact, only a Director negotiated with us and finalised the document. But Ambassador C.V. Ranganathan who was also from a neighbouring village as mine and whose grandfather was the late Sir C.P. was strict about the matters of protocol with the Chinese. Since the Vice-Minister was not available, he did not want the Commerce Secretary Montek to sign the document. Similarly, he was also equally firm that I should not sign the document with a Director on the Chinese side. He was of the view that the Chinese were very strict in these matters of protocol and would always try to establish some unsavoury precedents for the future by subtly down-grading the other party. Since he was firm, a Deputy Minister who was equivalent to an Additional Secretary came in and signed the document. Dr Swamy was always fond of Press and TV. In fact, he wanted to take a TV crew from New Delhi, but that was ruled out by the Prime Minister Chandra Shekhar and a French TV in Beijing was asked to cover the signing ceremony on behalf of the Doordarshan. But the French girl made a mistake in handling the designations and she had telecast my signing with the Chinese Deputy Minister rather than Dr Swamy signing with his counterpart. I am sure Dr Swamy must have felt unhappy about this mix-up!

Ambassador C.V. Ranganathan was also very particular that we should meet the Mayor of Shanghai, Zhu Rongji "who would one day become an important person in China". He met us for a short while. But he really became one of the top leaders, within two or three years in Beijing, particularly in charge of economic reforms in China. He had also become the Prime Minister of China. When I saw his appointment in newspapers, I was reminded of what Ambassador Ranganathan told us. I also reminded Ambassador Ranganathan about this when he was in retirement in Delhi. But Dr Swamy did not succeed in his attempts to meet Deng Xiaoping, the top leader of China. But the Chinese appreciated Dr Swamy because this was his fourteenth visit to China, his two books on China and his capacity to speak and understand Chinese.

When I was in China for the ESCAP session, I attended the Prime Minister's banquet. Prime Minister Li Peng was going round before the dinner and since he had been in India about six months earlier, he evinced a lot of interest and spoke to me for about five minutes which was a surprise to others. I could also meet the disabled son of Deng Xiaoping in the same dinner who requested that India should support the resolution on the disabled in the ESCAP session. I told him that we would do this without any hesitation whatsoever. He was supposed to have been tossed out of his apartment during the Cultural Revolution and became crippled.

When the hostilities between Kuwait and Iraq ceased, the Government of India wanted the Ministry of Commerce to step in and coordinate the organisations in the rebuilding of Kuwait. It was thought that it would provide a lot of opportunity for India to play a role in project exports. I was made in charge of this operation and I had to coordinate with a number of ministries like the External Affairs, Power, Telecommunications, Urban Development and so on. Although we tried very hard and sent out delegations to different parts of the world, the success was not tremendous, but to start with we could achieve project exports of $50 million or so which was not considered a mean achievement. Of course, $21 million or so were accounted for by the Telecom Consultancy Corporation and its dynamic chairman and managing director, Aggarwal. He had good contacts earlier in Kuwait. The various delegations, particularly to the UK and the USA, tried to become at least sub-contractors of big companies in those countries, which would have been substantial, but they could not succeed much. Although I could have easily gone to the United States along with the delegation because I had never visited the United States, I did not want to thrust myself and wanted that to be purely a business delegation.

But, Dr Swamy was asked by Prime Minister Chandra Shekhar to go to Kuwait immediately to assuage some of their ill feelings against India following a faux pas committed by the former Minister for External Affairs, I.K. Gujral. Since there were no flights from Dubai to Kuwait immediately after the cessation of hostilities, Dr Swamy wanted to take a special plane. But this created some criticism in the Indian press although it was unfounded. But the delegation was given only a small Avro **plane by which we flew from Delhi to Jamnagar and stayed there overnight and flew to Dubai the next morning. It was a long, but comfortable flight. One should be prepared to spend time on such a flight. We could reach Kuwait from Dubai because this plane was available with us. The plane was actually passing through dense smoke emanating from some five hundred and odd oil wells which were set fire to by the Iraqis while withdrawing from that country. We could actually see the wealth of the world being burnt out and going up in smoke in this unfortunate fashion. It took some months for them to contain this fire. There was also dense black smoke hanging over the city of Kuwait. We could see Kuwait immediately after the devastation. Dr Swamy was received even at the highest level and he presented our case well. But it was still doubtful whether their feelings were assuaged with the deep damage done by Gujral. It took a long time for normalcy to return in relations between the two countries.**

One of my distant relatives who was posted in the State Bank of India in Kuwait had come to India on a holiday with his family, the war broke out during this period and they could not return. He thought his whole house was either burnt or ransacked because he was living in a posh locality. I offered to see his house if time permitted. So when I went there, there was hardly any one in that huge building except a tenant and a watchman. The tenant who was my relative's neighbour told me that almost the entire building was ransacked and things were stolen. He did not allow the marauders to enter his floor and he could succeed in doing so. In that process, he saved the apartment of my relative which was exactly in the same shape as he left even without a pin having been moved! His car was also saved in the garage while many other cars were stolen or damaged.

Among the personal contributions made by me in Commerce, other notable one was to initiate a warehousing-cum-exhibition centre at Rotterdam. EDI – Electronic Data Interchange—was also introduced for the first time in the country with the help of an able colleague for a long time, B.L. Malhotra. He stayed on as a consultant for a year or so after his retirement to pursue this project. U.K. Sen of the Customs also assisted us. RBI Governor Venkitaramanan appointed me as the chairman of a Committee on Export Credit. This report was received well. Some of the recommendations were straightaway accepted in the Budget by Dr Manmohan Singh that year and I was pleased to hear this in his Budget speech. Venkitaramanan used to refer to this report even years later in his articles on export credit. India's first anti-dumping case was also decided by me after the usual hearing. The Commerce Ministry created an Authority for this later. In fact, I had written an article on the subject in the IIFT Journal in 1974. This was based on my discussions with the EEC official concerned in Brussels.

As the earlier one, this too was an interesting stint in the Ministry of Commerce and Cabinet Secretary S. Rajgopal was pleased with my work in the Ministry of Commerce. He had also known my work earlier as Deputy Secretary in the same Ministry because he was then the Development Commissioner, Santacruz Electronics Export Processing Zone and I was dealing with some aspects of the policy pertaining to Free Trade Zones. My term was to come to a close on May 31st, 1993 under the rounding-off rule. If the rule had remained so, I would have become a Secretary meanwhile and there would not have been any interruption. But, one of our batch-mates, when he was Establishment Officer got this rule changed to the date of expiry of the tenure without rounding-off in December or May and as a result many of us had to hand over charge. In fact, he did this to get rid of many of us at one stroke! By a strange coincidence, my colleague Anwarul Hoda's repeatedly extended term was also expiring on the same day as mine i.e., March 10th, 1993. This was only a quirk of destiny since Cabinet Secretary wanted to get rid of Anwarul Hoda on that day because he was over-staying. So he had to be vehement in my case too and I also had to leave the Ministry of Commerce on the same day. Had it not been for this strange coincidence of dates, perhaps he might have agreed for my continuation for another two or three months. So this period was over.

Commerce Secretary Ganesan wanted me and Hoda to continue to come to office informally. This was actually to help Hoda to continue till his posting to the WTO came through. Ganesan, otherwise a stickler for rules, must have done this at the instance of A.N. Varma who was interested in Hoda because of their Bihar connection and also for obvious reasons. But I did not attend the office after handing over. As a result of this manoeuvre, I was denied a farewell. Hoda continued informally till he became a Special Secretary for a couple of days before he left for the WTO. His grouse was that he could not become Commerce Secretary. He is now compensated with a membership of the Planning Commission.

The Establishment Officer who was my batch-mate and who did all this failed to make the grade and he had to remain an Additional Secretary for another two years although the same rule on tenure was not applied in his case! These are the strange ways of the Government of India and the only rule strictly followed is that 'show me the person and I shall show you the rule'!

* * *

19

Secretary to the Government of India

As I have already written elsewhere, empanelment and postings are dicey affairs in the Government of India. The confidential reports themselves are not written often objectively because of a false sense of generosity prevailing in the Government of India and also in many other northern States. By calling everybody 'outstanding', one does not do justice to a really 'outstanding' person. This was proved in a few cases where officers went to the CAT including a batch-mate of mine.

Be this as it may, luckily I had no difficulty in my empanelment as Secretary to the Government of India as I have explained elsewhere. But the problem started at the time of posting largely because of the circumstances. Cabinet Secretary Rajgopal was well disposed toward me and wanted to give me a good post. In fact, the post of Secretary (Revenue) fell vacant at that time and I could have fitted in with my Commerce background. But Finance Minister Manmohan Singh wanted to have M.R. Sivaraman. Rajgopal was kind enough to ring me up and tell me that although M.R. Sivaraman was below me, he was being cleared in those circumstances and I should not become "nervous". I accepted this position. (If a person below you in the order of merit is appointed, it could also mean supersession. Hence, he assured me and Yogesh Chandra. When our other colleague, Gopalakrishna, did not get such a call, he really became "nervous").

Meanwhile, my tenure was over and also the two month leave period. So I got automatically reverted to the Government of Gujarat as in the case of many of my batch-mates. Although there would not have been any problem from the Gujarat side, no one knew and some times problems could have been created by our own colleagues there. So I requested Rajgopal to expedite my posting and he could offer me only the chairmanship of Food Corporation of India or a post in the Cabinet Secretariat. Since the post in the Cabinet Secretariat was not one of consequence, (in fact, the posts in the Cabinet Secretariat other than that of the Cabinet Secretary are of not-much-consequence), many friends advised me to take up the chairmanship of the FCI. I did not want to do so because the FCI was an organization with numerous problems, which could not be solved by any one for obvious reasons. Besides, I was told there was a lot of corruption in the organisation. It would have also created some doubt about my empanelment and rank in the context of the false news items which had already appeared. So I decided to take up the Cabinet Secretariat job. The charm of the post was lost by half since it was located away from the Rashtrapati Bhavan. The main cabinet secretariat is located in the Rashtrapati Bhavan. I discovered that there was not even a Joint Secretary and only a few staff up to the level of Under Secretary and Director in the name of a computer and officer-oriented system. Actually one could not function in an effective manner at least for redressal of public grievances for want of sufficient staff. In the beginning it was a post created for a railway service officer who wanted to become a Secretary to the Government of India. (He was a brother of the Foreign Secretary, M.K. Rasgotra, but a fine and competent officer. I processed his case to come into Defence when I was Joint Secretary there. There was only one CR of his instead of a panel. Being a stickler, Defence Minister R. Venkataraman queried why only a single name for the post! Defence Secretary P.K. Kaul explained it away. But Rasgatora's performance was outstanding). He was not sure whether he would be empanelled. So he persuaded P. Chidambaram, the then Minister of Personnel, to create a post of Director with the pay and rank of a Secretary to the Government of India for the reason of paying close attention to public grievances from departments like Railways, Urban Development including the DDA, the Posts, Telecommuication, Civil Aviation and Banking and Insurance. After the post was created ostensibly to deal with the large number of complaints against these Departments, the officer concerned suddenly discovered that the designation of Director was not good for him because he was mistaken for an ordinary Director in any other Ministry. So the designation was changed to Secretary. Cabinet Secretary Deshmukh rightly objected to this change of designation because the officer concerned was not even empanelled. But it was already agreed to by the Minister of Personnel, P. Chidambaram. Since it was a fait accompli and Chidambaram gave the ruling that the Secretary should circulate all the files to the Government through the Cabinet Secretary. In this case, the Government was the Prime Minister and there was hardly any file to be circulated to that level! Of course, the job provided a lot of clout with these Departments and they could take care of personal requirements like telephone, railway ticket, air ticket, etc., for the officers in this outfit.

Minister Margaret Alva also objected to this dispensation because she was also heading a Department of Administrative Reforms and Public Grievances which was also located in the same building with an Additional Secretary at the helm. Besides, there is a huge petition section of the Prime Minister's office. So these three offices for redressing public grievances created only confusion and the people had to go from one place to the other. But Prime Minister Narasimha Rao did not accept her suggestion of merger of her department with this office or vice versa because this was created by Rajiv Gandhi. I also suggested abolition of the post. It was accepted much later after I had left and the post was combined with that of Secretary (Coordination) in the Cabinet Secretariat.

During this period, Prime Minister Narasimha Rao referred to me Vice-President Al Gore's document on "Reinventing Government". I analysed it and submitted a report to him. I asked his Private Secretary Ramu Damodaran whether the PM

himself or he had referred the document to me of all persons. He assured me that Rao himself did it. This report, if implemented, would have been useful in cutting down posts or even departments. I suggested that an active minister (I was keeping P. Chidambaram in mind) and an active secretary in the PMO should monitor its implementation. But it never saw the light of day although Ramu Damodaran told me that PM appreciated my quick work. Some months later, when I enquired from A.N. Varma about the fate of this report, he told me not to bother.

Meanwhile, Saifullah became the Cabinet Secretary. His appointment was a great surprise to the entire bureaucracy. When it was announced on the TV, many people thought it was wrong news. Saifullah was never a Secretary to the Government of India in any department. But, S. Varadan of the Karnataka cadre had told me much earlier that Saifullah was a dynamic person however and he had a novel way of functioning. Meanwhile, my name was considered for the post of Special Secretary in the Ministry of Commerce and it was nearly cleared. But A.N. Varma who was Principal Secretary to PM did not want a rival to his protégé Tejendra Khanna in the same Ministry. Saifullah asked me whether I would like to go to Bombay as Chairman of the Export Credit and Guarantee Corporation under the Ministry of Commerce. I declined the offer because there was no point in accepting a lower position although it was of the same rank and pay. May be it was also a ruse to divert me to Bombay away from Delhi. Such tactics are often practised by civil servants in positions like Cabinet Secretary or Principal Secretary to PM in order to favour their own friends. In fact, the politicians could learn a thing or two from the civil servants. Civil servants have become civil serpents. Some of them are scoundrels to whom it is impossible to carry conviction. You can carry conviction to Stone Henge, but not to these blockheads - only brute political force works with them. Pardon my metaphysical explanation, many of them have lost their grown-up children, believe me or not, as retribution perhaps, if at all there is a God. But these fellows do not learn and they are always after power. A Cabinet Secretary held cocktails at his residence within one or two months after the sudden death of his only daughter.

Ramu Damodaran told me that the Gujarat Chief Minister Chimanbhai Patel desired my services back for an important assignment. But, within fifteen minutes, the same CM rang up to say that the matter need not be pursued. On another occasion, an influential person approached me to enquire whether I would be interested in becoming Chief Secretary to the Government of Gujarat. He was an emissary of the Chief Minister Keshubhai Patel. But, I told that I belonged to the 1962 batch and there were many others above me in 1961 batch and also N. Vittal in 1960 batch. He told me that they were aware of this fact. In fact, he was carrying photocopies of the IAS-Gujarat-Civil List! I specially asked him about Vittal who was keen on going back to become CS. He told me that Vittal was certainly ruled out because the Chief Minister stated that there would be a doubt in the mind of the public as to who was running the State because of the knack of Vittal's publicity to himself and assiduous self-promotion. **But my friendship and regard for him and his family continue to be good.** Then, I enquired about S.K. Shelat who was not only No.1 in the 1961 batch of Gujarat, but was also a competent and rare Gujarati in the civil service. He told me that he too was not acceptable because of his rude and abrasive nature. Subsequent event of Shelat not getting even a single extension as Chief Secretary when extensions were normal proved that this contention was true. Of course, he was continuously re-employed later even by Narendra Modi. This was perhaps because Waghela did not give him an extension though re-employed him in the Gujarat Industrial Investment Corporation. (Incidentally, Shelat and Padmanabhiah were the only two officers, I know of, continuously re-employed for years together without a break even for a day since retirement. N.K. Singh was also one such officer, but his continuous stint since retirement came to a close about a couple of years ago). Others, about seven in the 1961 batch, had either less than a year of service or they did not really matter.

The offer was tempting. I thought it over for a day. I told this emissary that I would not be interested in the offer because I would straightaway become a persona non-grata in the entire cadre and it would be difficult for me to function. Besides, it would also be totally unethical for me to supersede so many for no fault of theirs. S.K. Shelat, being a local man, would be a constant threat. Moreover, I would not like to get myself dubbed as a man of that Chief Minister. Of course, the emissary who was not a politician told me that the party had such a thumping majority, there would be no such danger. A news item about my possible posting also had appeared in *The Times of India* although I had firmly declined the offer. As anticipated by me or luckily for me, the Chief Minister and his Government went out of office within a few months. But when the same party came to office at the Centre, some of my batch-mates who otherwise ignored me, rang me up because they thought that I might get an important position. Once again, politicians can learn a thing or two from the civil servants. The politicians have succeeded a great deal in beating down these creatures but still many of them exist and manoeuvre in such a way to harm their helpless or hapless colleagues.

When he made this offer I took the opportunity to tell Saifullah that when his predecessor was inclined to give me a good post, the post of Secretary, Public Grievances in the Cabinet Secretariat, fell vacant as my luck would have it. Similarly, when Saifullah was inclined to transfer me to a better post, the post of Secretary, Civil Supplies, Consumer Affairs and Public Distribution was falling vacant. I told him not to place me there. But he did precisely the same thing within fifteen days.

I was told that Prime Minister, Narasimha Rao, paid a lot of attention to Civil Supplies and the Public Distribution System. Meanwhile, my batch-mate K.R. Venugopal of Andhra Pradesh cadre, who was really committed to the poor and an expert in Civil Supplies and Public Distribution System with an authoritative book on the subject to his credit, was away on leave from the PMO because he had some differences of opinion with the Principal Secretary A.N. Varma. Although Venugopal never told me, the rumour was that he was persuaded by the Prime Minister to come back either to his office or to the Ministry of Civil Supplies. Venugopal came back to the PMO and I landed in the Ministry of Civil Supplies.

The Ministry of Civil Supplies, Consumer Affairs and Public Distribution was important in its own way. A.K. Antony was the Minister who was a man of great rectitude and personal honesty. I have great regard for him. The activities of the Ministry touched the daily lives of the people all over the country. It was the responsibility of the State Governments to implement the PDS. However, the Central Ministry was also responsible because of allocation of foodgrains from the Ministry of Food and the Food Corporation of India. Sugar and kerosene were also PDS commodities. There was bumper production of sugar that year and it was my view that the government could delicense the whole operation including the sugar industry. But I could not voice this opinion as Secretary, Civil Supplies and PDS. The Ministry was also responsible for monitoring the movement of prices of essential commodities and taking corrective action wherever necessary. The ministry was servicing the Special Action Committee on Monitoring of Prices under the Cabinet Secretary and also the Cabinet Committee on Prices under the chairmanship of the Finance Minister. Consumer Affairs was also an important area and India had done well within a short time by having a legislation, thanks to Rajiv Gandhi, and a nation-wide set up of courts to decide consumer related cases. It was also an area which was subject to international exposure. In fact, during this period, at my initiative, the Ministry became an affiliate member of the Consumers International, an apex organisation of NGOs in the field. This organisation gave only affiliate membership to governments because, while benefiting from government experience, it did not want to be influenced by any government in any way. So the governments were not given the voting rights.

The Indian Airlines was in the habit of increasing the fare almost every year. The business class trip to Madras one way used to cost nearly Rs. 10,000/- which even the business men could not afford. The private airlines had not become competitive in this country (at that time). In fact, their record was dismal. They conveniently followed the Indian Airlines and jacked up the fares. At a point of time, I, as Secretary, Consumer Affairs, filed a complaint with the Monopolies and Restrictive

Trade Practices Commission against this concerted practice. They did an investigation. But I did not know the outcome and the practice went on. Of course, the convenient excuse was that the price of Aviation Turbine Fuel was high in this country. It was high because of the Central and State tax element apart from the cross-subsidy on kerosene and LPG. A way had to be found to bring the price down so that the air fares were reasonable and also feeder airlines could function as in many other countries in the interest of tourism. But our civil aviation policy was faulty. (This was recorded in 1996; things have changed now for the better by competition among the airlines)

We are also unconsciously working against national integration. Some years ago the people in the North were not even aware that there were four states in the South with four different languages. But, thanks to the leave-travel-concession and the mobility of the people, they are now aware of the difference and thereby national integration has been promoted. By jacking up the air fares and the railway fares every year, we are unconsciously acting against the unity of the country by preventing the movement of ordinary people. Incidentally, our newspapers are also promoting disintegration in a way by having different editions. What appears on the front page in Madras edition of a newspaper does not appear on the same page in some other edition or it may not appear at all. Practically, it is a separate newspaper of that region or area or even a district. These are some of the seeds of possible disintegration. The erstwhile Soviet Union with her largest airlines in the world, 'Aeroflot' had air fares almost equal to the railway fares if not less so that people could move easily from one Republic to the other in the vast country. When this was changed by liberalisation, many parts of the Soviet Union fell apart. Of course, this was one of the reasons.

Nepal has about 43 airports and they use small planes successfully for promotion of tourism. Mongolia has 21 airports with only 16 having proper runway. In other places, the planes land on hard ground. In fact, in Ulanbattor itself, my plane taxied before taking off on a 'kutcha' ground with a lot of pebbles. It was an aircraft of 50 to 60 seat capacity. In Alaska,

I saw hundreds of planes being parked near a lake. These are called sea or float-planes which take off from lakes and land on lakes. In our country, whenever we think of an air-strip, we prepare a grandiose plan running into crores of rupees which is naturally shot down by the Finance Ministry for want of funds. The Director General of Civil Aviation quotes his old rule-book whereas things have changed a lot in the modern world. We have not even used the 100 and odd air-strips constructed by the British during the Second World War in different parts of the country which are in the charge of the state governments, let alone improving the regular airports which are with the Airports Authority of India. (When I was Secretary, Tourism, I had recorded this in 1996. This seems to be changing for the better and in the right direction now).

Edible oil operation was another important work of the Ministry of Civil Supplies. I had already dealt with it when I was in the Ministry of Commerce. In fact, I used to attend many of these meetings under the Cabinet Secretary as a representative of the Ministry of Commerce. The Ministry of Civil Supplies itself was a part of the Ministry of Commerce as the Department of Internal Trade till 1976. So it was not that difficult for me to function here.

Moreover, Civil Supplies was also free from tension during this period because we were not facing any problem of scarcity anywhere of any commodity. In fact, it was a problem of plenty of rice and wheat. So there was not much pressure from the state governments making one's life miserable as it often happens in this Ministry. Only the sugar scandal broke out because of the then Food Minister Kalpanath Rai and an enquiry commission was appointed. Although my Minister and I came out unscathed, Minister Antony had to resign suddenly because of a mistake committed by the PMO in an answer to an Unstarred Question in the Parliament. Whether that mistake was deliberate or otherwise, I do not know till today. The reports were also collected back by the PMO. I feel that there was also something political. Rao perhaps felt that Antony was coming close to the Rajiv group under Mrs. Sonia Gandhi. In any case, Antony was a great stickler for rectitude and he resigned

immediately. His stock went up immediately in the country. It happens often that in such enquiries where many interests play, the innocent becomes guilty and the really guilty ones get away with the booty. This was true in this case too.

I must record here that any import decision results in a scam in our country. It is no doubt true that at times decisions are delayed and the country is put to a loss as happened in the case of sugar. But, at times, the newspapers also create an unnecessary controversy in the name of transparency. Import decisions cannot be taken and tenders cannot be opened in public because the moment the news leaks out, the foreign exporters put up the price. They already have their agents here. They get confirmation through the newspapers here. Some correspondents in their anxiety to file news were always after such news. I was told that some were employed by these agents themselves. Two commercial organisations like the STC and the MMTC bid and get two different prices. But the newspapers look for a black cat in a dark room when it is not there and try to introduce one inside. Of course, in our corruption-ridden society, presence of cats or bandicoots cannot be ruled out. However, one cannot take off one's clothes in the public in the name of transparency. I should also record here that when I was in the Civil Supplies, I came across a few young, intelligent lady correspondents – Rachna Burman, Nivedita Prabhu and Hema Ramakrishnan – who were far superior to their men-peers, although troubled me often for news, kept the facts and figures at their finger-tips.

The issue of decontrol of sugar was also examined by the Cabinet Secretariat. It was the view of every one including Finance Secretary M.S. Ahluwalia and Commerce Secretary Tejendra Khanna that licensing of sugar mills should be done away with and sugar should be removed from PDS as an item. Although I was also of the same view, I could not accept it as Secretary, Civil Supplies and PDS. So I had to record a note of dissent much to the annoyance of the Cabinet Secretary Surendra Singh and others. But I explained to them that the juncture was inopportune to implement the suggestion. Implementation of such a suggestion at that juncture could also be suspect. I gave a copy of my note of dissent to K.R. Venugopal also to keep the PM in the picture.

When I saw a news item that the imported sugar was being re-exported by taking advantage of a loop-hole in the Export-Import Regulations, I got it plugged immediately, prevented re-exports and thereby too incurred the wrath of the powers-that-be. The vested interests went to the High Court, but lost the case because we fought the case well.

I requested both Venugopal and Varma to shift me to an economic ministry though Civil Supplies was also an economic ministry in a way with an Economic Adviser in the ministry. However, the civil servants' perception was that it was not that important. Both of them promised to have it done after the elections, which were due in some of the states.

As soon as I took over, I got a comprehensive policy paper prepared on the PDS. Antony was not inclined to place it before the Cabinet lest it should create a controversy. But I persuaded him to place it so that this Ministry had done its duty for targeting of the PDS according to the recommendations of a Committee of Ministers headed by the then Tamil Nadu Minister for Food and Civil Supplies, G. Viswanathan. Incidentally, G. Viswanathan was my junior in college in Vellore and was a good and competent person. He made one mistake of changing the parties often. He gained some publicity at the all-India level because of this report. I also prevailed upon Antony that he should know the various implications figure-wise of the various recommendations of this Group of Ministers. He reluctantly agreed to place the note before the Cabinet, but marked it only for information and not for a decision. That itself was somewhat an odd practice because Cabinet was always approached for a decision. However, when the other ministers read the paper which also suggested pegging of procurement at a particular level, the other ministers, particularly Balram Jakhar, who was supposedly representing the agriculturists' lobby, vehemently opposed it. They said that this was a very sensitive paper and it would provoke a lot of public reaction before the state elections which were almost a year away. They unanimously felt that the entire matter should be considered by another group of ministers and finally by the National Development Council which consisted of all the chief ministers.

This was one way of evading the issue and putting it in the cold storage. So the paper went into a limbo. The group of ministers under Pranab Mukherjee had a few meetings spread over some months and finally wanted further papers to be prepared on the subject of PDS and targeting. Although targeting only the comparatively poorer sections was already in vogue in states like Gujarat, Haryana and Rajasthan, they were afraid of broaching the subject to the other states. Several papers were written on the PDS and RPDS. But no one was prepared to tackle the problem right from the first stage of procurement, Minimum Support Price (MSP), Central Issue Price (CIP), etc., down to the other end of distribution only to the selected sections. RPDS was adopted as some sort of a geographical targeting where poor were concentrated which was the brainchild of actually Venugopal and not Narasimha Rao.

Meanwhile, Cabinet Secretary was changed and Surendra Singh came on the scene. I renewed my request to him and he assured me that I would be changed to an economic ministry. Meanwhile, many ministries were bifurcated. Food, Industry, Urban Development and Civil Supplies were also divided into two Departments and Rural Development even into three. All Secretaries of these Ministries opposed the move in a meeting taken by Cabinet Secretary because they knew that it would create a lot of confusion. Even Yugandhar, Secretary (rural development) who always toed the line of his boss opposed this proposal. But two officers in the PMO from the 1966 batch and a few influential ones in the 1964 batch who wanted their promotions during the period of Narasimha Rao itself since he was a bit shaky in office at that time, made this suggestion so **that more posts of Secretaries could be created and there would be an upward mobility for them. So this idea was sold to Prime Minister in the name of social development and concentration on these aspects. I even now wonder how the highly intelligent Rao accepted this. But, in reality, the bifurcation resulted in** confusion, turf-battles between two Secretaries and ineffectiveness on account of artificial division of staff. I was made in charge of Consumer Affairs and Public Distribution System. But I could not do much particularly in respect of Consumer Affairs because there was no one to assist me. The only Director also proceeded on leave for some reason or the other. Meanwhile, Ministers were also appointed to be in charge of these Departments. Venod Sharma became MOS for Consumer Affairs & Public Distribution System and he wanted to do quite a lot. But we could not provide him full satisfaction for the same reason. Every year, the Indian International Trade Fair is inaugurated on November 14th. A theme is given every year for the fair. That **year, I persuaded Mahesh Prasad who was my secretary and presently chairman of the Indian Trade Promotion Organisation to accept 'Consumer Satisfaction' as the theme. I had also invited Ralph Nader from the USA. But I was so dispirited by this thoughtless bifurcation that I gave up all this. (Incidentally, Delhi never changes. To promote an officer in the PMO, about 20 officers of the same 1974 batch have been promoted *in situ* by upgrading the posts in one go recently).**

Differences between K.R. Venugopal and others in the PMO came to a head and Venugopal decided to leave for good. He wanted to concentrate upon rural development in Rajasthan and in Andhra Pradesh. While going, he suggested my name as a replacement because it was a question of dealing with rural development, civil supplies and other welfare departments from the PMO. He thought I would be the right choice because the other candidate was my batch-mate and his relative, B.N. Yugandhar, also from Andhra Pradesh who was about to retire in a few months. There was also a feeling and criticism in the press that many Andhra officers were preferred for important positions and frequent extensions in service and the PM might post me for a change. But it was not to be. A.N. Varma and Ratan Watal, PS to PM scuttled it. Venugopal was always naïve in these matters. If he had wanted to help me, he could have obtained the orders of the PM, installed me and gone. As soon as he left, the post went to Yugandhar. Before leaving, he also confided in a few of us that two or three scoundrels (he did not mean Narasimha Rao) were virtually running this country. This honest man left in disgust. Some of the IAS colleagues also who had knowledge of this proposal (to appoint me as secretary in the PMO) did not give a clue to me. That is IAS camaraderie!

Cabinet Secretary, Surendra Singh, went on promising that I would be shifted to an important ministry. This turned out to be only an empty promise. Although he suggested my name for important postings like Department of Personnel, Chemicals and Petrochemicals as I understood, these were also scuttled. In fact, Prime Minister Narasimha Rao left everything practically to Surendra Singh and Varma and they played havoc. Or, the PM was cleverly silent so that these people, knowing his "requirements", as Ratan Watal used to put it often, appointed their own people or the people who would do things unhesitatingly at their behest in important economic ministries. Finance Minister Manmohan Singh also wanted to take me as Secretary (Expenditure). He had seen my work at close quarters in the Cabinet Committee on Prices. He used to tell me that he had high regard for me and would unhesitatingly have me in the Ministry of Finance. But this suggestion of his faced stiff opposition both from Surendra Singh and Varma because they wanted to favour N.K. Singh, though junior to me. Perhaps it was for the first time that the Finance Minister, as my luck would have it, failed in his attempt to get some one of his choice. According to my information, he was having his way till then with the PM.

Meanwhile, I also established indirect access to PM and sent him some notes. In fact, I wanted to meet him myself and present my case. But the caucus around him would not allow me to meet him. He also hardly had any direct rapport with the officers. Most Secretaries did not even know whether he had even known their name or the department. This was in contrast to Rajiv Gandhi, Chandra Shekhar or Deve Gowda who knew most of the Secretaries well and had direct contact with them.

Many are not aware that in the powerful sanctum (PMO), there is also a sanctum sanctorum: the office of PS to PM. The PS could get the Principal Secretary or the Cabinet Secretary over-ruled by PM. PS also discreetly favours the Principal Secretary or the Cabinet Secretary depending upon who is likely to get a foreign posting and he could tag himself on to him! For instance, Ratan Watal, went along with Surendra Singh as PS to the Executive Director to the World Bank. Ramu Damodaran, IFS, was the only one who got a post in the UN on his own and

he was called by Rao to serve him for a short period as PS. Deve Gowda's PS Jain managed a posting to the Tea Board in London. His claim to the post was that he was drinking tea every day! Shakti Sinha, PS to PM Vajpayee was also related to him and his successor as well managed a post abroad. So this has become a regular pattern.

The post of Indian Ambassador to Belgium and Luxembourg and to the EEC located in Brussels went mostly to ICS or IAS officers because it was an Economic Mission. Only two or three IFS officers were posted there so far on account of their special expertise in economic matters. Since I had studied in Brussels, I was posted earlier there as Counsellor, thanks to Dr Kurien and also negotiated later the third upgraded Agreement of Partnership and Cooperation with the EEC. The Ministry of External Affairs thought that I would be the most appropriate candidate outside the IFS. Many officers like former Cabinet Secretary Rajgopal and M.S. Gill were also claiming the post because they were retiring from service. Of course, one should have the proper background because it was a difficult post with many organisations like the Commission, Council of Ministers, the Parliament and the Court of Auditors. An ICS officer and an IAS officer who were posted earlier with not much of an economic background were not successful. Though the Ministry of External Affairs, particularly Foreign Secretary J.N. Dixit backed my candidature if a non-IFS officer was to be taken, Prime Minister Rao chose as usual an IFS officer hailing from Andhra Pradesh who was also the son-in-law of a former President, V.V. Giri. Of course, the officer was a competent person with adequate background in economics and commerce. He was also my batch-mate. But it appeared as though he was favoured with this post because of his pedigree. He went there and for some reason or the other got tired after eighteen months or so. He also wanted to be a Secretary to the Government of India and possibly Foreign Secretary overtaking others with the help of the Andhra lobby. So, with the help of the same connections, he got a post created for himself in the MEA and naturally got himself posted and returned without completing his tenure in an important economic Mission. Perhaps he felt a bit guilty in his heart of hearts that he had scuttled my chance and so he recommended my name again to the Minister for External Affairs. Since I was not allowed by the caucus to meet the Prime Minister directly, I indirectly conveyed my interest to him. I had also sent a copy of my book (published Ph.D. thesis), "Commercial Policy of the EEC and the Association Agreements". I do not know whether it had actually reached him or not. Some of the IAS at the top level were also following the policy that if they were not getting some thing, the other IAS man should not also get it. So naturally the post again went to a batch-mate of mine in the IFS who incidentally happened to be a Bengali and the Minister for External Affairs was Pranab Mukherjee.

The so-called plum postings, although important from the country's point of view, are decided not on the basis of merit in the Government of India, but on the basis of other considerations particularly pedigree or contacts. That was the reason why, when Dr. Kurien selected me purely on the basis of my merit, the Government of India was not prepared to believe it. It was only with him, my C.V, my book and my background worked. With all others, it turned out to be a minus factor as my batch-mate, Prem Budhwar warned me not to take a Ph.D., long ago, because it immediately developed some sort of jealousy and they tried to put me down. It is advisable to be an ordinary graduate, get into the IAS., do not specialise and plod up by sycophancy. But I must say that the public opinion or the opinion of the general people who knew me, my background and my work, particularly in the Ministries of Commerce and the Environment, were in my favour. They always sympathised with me particularly the way in which the Narasimha Rao Government treated me. But they were helpless because they were not the powers that-be. One of my senior colleagues and former Finance and Commerce Secretary, S.P. Shukla used to tell me that this Government's treatment was a plus point to me because I did not oblige them the way they wanted.

Whereas the Narasimha Rao Government was particularly notorious for bad appointments starting from Cabinet Secretary. Mrs. Indira Gandhi and Rajiv Gandhi placed a lot of emphasis on merit also. She might have said something about corruption as a universal phenomenon, but she made it a point to encourage efficient and honest officers also. The two good examples were Dr. P.C. Alexander and Rao Sahib, let alone many others like G. Ramachandran, V. Ramachandran, B.N. Tandon and so on. **The officers hailing from Andhra Pradesh or belonging to the Andhra Pradesh cadre of the IAS and the IPS including technical and legal service officers from that State had a field day with repeated extensions or re-employment during Rao's period. The usually inactive Rao who kept even posts of Secretaries vacant for months on end announced the posting of Salman Haider as Foreign Secretary two or three months in advance because he thought he would be able to get the Muslim votes in the state elections. But his anticipations failed. My batch-mate and friend occupying a lower position than me in inter se seniority, V.K. Shunglu, was appointed the Comptroller and Auditor General of India to the utter surprise of every one. This was considered some sort of a coup. The swearing in ceremony was also rushed through the same evening fearing some adverse comments in the press the next morning. As feared, the press rightly commented upon this appointment adversely. Surendra Singh and Varma were mainly responsible for these misdeeds and Rao simply acquiesced in these machinations because it suited him.**

Comptroller and Auditor General of India is a very high Constitutional position. It is even a shade higher than that of the Election Commissioner because in the Constitution there is a separate chapter on the Comptroller and Auditor General with that heading, whereas the Election Commissioner is mentioned under the chapter on elections. The Comptroller and Auditor General can also attend Parliament without voting rights. Consumer Activist, H.D. Shourie, very rightly filed a petition in the Supreme Court stating that the selection for this post should be done very carefully. He was also of the view that it would be more appropriate for the new Government to choose the incumbent because the Comptroller and Auditor General could be looking into the acts of commission and omission of the previous Government. In fact, when Somiah was appointed as Comptroller and Auditor General by the V.P. Singh Government, it was felt that the timing was somewhat inappropriate. This time the post could have been kept vacant for a few months, but Narasimha Rao was told it should not be kept vacant because it was a Constitutional post. This is not correct. Posts of Supreme Court and High Court judges which are also Constitutional posts are kept vacant for months. So an IA&AS officer, even a retired one, could have been the most appropriate choice. In this connection, Inder Malhotra's article in *The Hindu* is reproduced here:

"Manipulating bureaucracy becomes fine art? Suborning of civil servants by their political masters is nothing new in New Delhi (about the State Capitals the less said the better). The pernicious practice began during the Indira Gandhi years when "commitment" became a convenient cover for shunting off "inconvenient" officers scrupulously intent on doing their duty and to promote and pamper those whose pliability excelled their ability.

"Things degenerated during the Emergency. But, far from being stemmed, the rot has been allowed to worsen, deliberately and steadily. In fact, it seems that the successive governments have competed with each other in the fine art of manipulating the services.

"In all fairness, it must be added that the bureaucrats, as a class, are not free from blame for this sorry state of affairs. For every minister anxious to bend the officials to his dubious will, there are at least three civil servants willing to bend over backwards to do his behest.

"Even by these standards, however, the appointment of Mr. V.K. Shunglu a relatively junior IAS officer from the Madhya Pradesh cadre, as the new Comptroller and Auditor-General is something of a shock, and an extremely depressing one.

"The Comptroller and Auditor-General (CAG) is a constitutional office of the highest importance. Its incumbent ranks above the Cabinet Secretary who is the headmaster of the civil service. As it happens, Mr. Shunglu is three years junior to the present Cabinet Secretary, Mr. Surendra Singh, and more than two years junior to at least eight Union Secretaries.

"What makes his selection for the prestigious and the prized post even more intriguing – to put it no more strongly than that – is that his name did not figure at all in the panel prepared by the Cabinet Secretary and endorsed by the Finance Minister,

Dr. Manmohan Singh, as minister in charge. The Secretaries included in the panel are not only all senior to the "dark horse" chosen but each of them has some distinction or the other to his credit.

"Mr. N.R. Ranganathan is Member-Secretary of the Planning Commission, Mr. M. Zutshi, the Secretary for Fertilisers was this country's Negotiator during the Uruguay Round of world trade talks. Mr. K.A. Nambiar has been Defence Secretary for four years, and Mr. T.S.R. Subramanian, the Textile Secretary, was Chief Secretary of U.P. He had to leave that post because Ms. Mayawati, then Chief Minister of the most populous State, could not countenance a Brahmin Chief Secretary!

"To make matters even murkier, the office of CAG was left vacant for five days after the retirement of Mr. G.C. Somiah, in clear violation of both the letter and the spirit of the Constitution. It was during this vacuum that Mr. Shunglu's name was drawn from a hat, so to speak, and mysteriously "approved". From all accounts, it seems that the Cabinet Secretariat was not taken into confidence while carrying out this politico-administrative coup. The whole operation took place apparently in the Prime Minister's Office (PMO).

"This raises the question whether the PMO today has not become more imperious than in the days of the lady who used to be called the Empress of India.

"The message that has gone to the civil service is that powers that be bother neither about seniority, nor distinction or even propriety. The resentment among top civil servants is palpable and pervasive. But who cares?

"Officers of the Indian Audit & Accounts Service have a grievance of their own. By long tradition the post of CAG belongs to them. But they have been deprived of it since the late seventies.

Meanwhile, at the Press Club they are saying that from now onwards "CAG has become a mere COG"."

But Delhi never changes. A relatively junior secretary, V.N. Kaul, was appointed CA & AG as successor to Shunglu by PM Vajpayee for obvious reasons.

Similarly, Gopalakrishna Gandhi's appointment as High Commissioner to South Africa was hailed in the press because he happened to be the grandson of Mahatma Gandhi and Rajaji as well. Of course, nobody questions his intellectual equipment or competence, but the posting should not be justified on the basis of pedigree. As an IFS gossip columnist wrote, this IAS officer was earlier posted in Kandy in Sri Lanka. He later became Joint Secretary to President Venkataraman. This got him a posting to London in the Nehru Centre. Although the Centre was located far outside the High Commission, he enjoyed a high diplomatic rank which was normally not done. From there, he was posted to South Africa on the basis of this qualification of pedigree. Mahatma Gandhi and Rajaji were the only two leaders who did not take care of their progeny. I was told by my brother-in-law who was Secretary to Rajaji that once Rajaji's son, C.R. Narasimhan, was about to get into the official car. Rajaji told him that the official car was meant for the Governor and not for his son. That was the sense of honesty of Rajaji. Similarly, Mahatma Gandhi did not favour in anyway his sons or grand-children. So if Gandhi had been alive, he would not have relished the appointment of Gopalakrishna Gandhi as High Commissioner because he was his grandson. So this was one of the last questionable appointments of the Narasimha Rao Government.

Again, Delhi never changes! Gopal Gandhi was in South Africa only for a short while. He became Secretary to President Narayanan. I was told that Narayanan was not that happy with the correct advice of Gandhi and he was sent away as High Commissioner to Sri Lanka – the justification was his earlier stint in Kandy. But he managed to get himself appointed as our High Commissioner to London through the R. Venkataraman and Vajpayee network. But the IFS lobby including the powerful Brajesh Mishra. Principal Secretary to PM Vajpayee, was up in arms and Gandhi was diverted to the not-so-important for the IFS and cold Oslo (Incidentally, Foreign Service is always clever in dealing with these non-IFS appointments. Former Generals and even some Secretaries were happy with ambassadorial appointments to New Zealand, Ireland, Oslo, Bucharet, even Copenhagen, etc. Only after reaching there, they realised that these were not important

Missions or IFS was not that interested in them. Once I saw General Bewoor, who commanded the fourth largest army in the world, had only a second secretary under him and sharing a PA in Copenhagen!)

Most of our Missions look like a piece of the secretariat in Delhi – cut and placed abroad. In some places, the CPWD has constructed the building so much so even from outside it has the typical CPWD or secretariat look. Inside these buildings, newspapers are strewn, rooms are unkempt and bath-rooms are smelly so that one does not miss Delhi. Only the visitors' area and the officers' rooms are kept clean with a lot of effort to please the foreigners who visit. Our High Commission in London is no exception and at one time it had about 600 employees – many locally recruited on the basis of our 'sifarish' culture and many posted from India on the same basis by the various ministries so that the visiting dignitaries or officials from India who often go to London are taken care of in their shopping and sight-seeing. In this regard, the IFS is in a better position to please people by taking such care of the visitors from home than the IAS or the IPS.

While his batch-mates are languishing as secretaries to government and many of them having fallen by the way side in the empanelment system, Gopal Gandhi has become the Governor of an important State like West Bengal. Fortune smiled on him as it does always on such people. Even if Mrs. Sonia Gandhi wanted to reward some one from the Gandhi-Rajaji family, she could have appointed Gopal's brother Rajmohan Gandhi who was active in public affairs. Incidentally, L.V. Saptharishi (I do not hold any brief for him) told me that he tried to get his cadre changed from West Bengal to Tamil Nadu because his mother wanted to see him as the Collector of Thanjavur. When he approached Rajaji through Kalki Krishnamurthy, Rajaji told him orally or wrote to him stating that he would be better-off in West Bengal than in Tamil Nadu. But Rajaji wrote a letter to the Home Minister for his grandson Gopal and got his cadre changed from Maharashtra to Tamil Nadu. When I contested this stating that Rajaji would not have done such a thing, Saptharishi told me that he saw this letter himself in a Home Ministry file! Perhaps even sticklers at times do this. For instance, when I was in the Ministry of Urban Development, the

Director of Estates told me that President Venkataraman had written a letter to allot a house to a well-known dancer who now lives in Chennai. I told the Director that it could not be and perhaps his secretary had written on his behalf. But there was a letter from the President himself!

I even wondered whether they were not transferring me to a good economic Ministry because I refused to oblige the PMO in their request for a repeat of the notorious palmolein deal for which a case was already pending in the Kerala High Court against K. Karunakaran and the company concerned, and also I refused to pay a few crores of rupees to an Andhra company for some earlier deal in which a case was pending. Both Antony and Buta Singh were under pressure from the Prime Minister to appoint an arbitrator to settle the payment against legal advice from the Ministry of Law. But I explained the position to the officer concerned in the PMO and to a relative of Narasimha Rao as well who was reasonable. In fact, I thought Law Secretary Dr. Rao would readily agree to this because he was close to Narasimha Rao and got an extension in service. But he did not.

Home Secretary Padmanabhaiah sought my help for appointment of one of his friends as a member of the Consumer Forum. So I thought I would take his help in getting a shift to a better Ministry. He told me that the Prime Minister should feel that I would be "useful" to him as Ratan Watal said that the Prime Minister knew his "requirements". In any case, without his intervention, Cabinet Secretary Surendra Singh and A.N. Varma decided to shift me to Surface Transport. I had a lot of experience because I had dealt with shipping matters from the Ministry of Commerce both as Deputy Secretary and as Additional Secretary and also visited many ports while posted in Brussels for facilitating shipment of 'Operation Flood' commodities. But again they changed it to Tourism in the last moment.

I learnt later that I was placed in Tourism because I would be retiring on October 31st, 1996 and Cabinet Secretary's protégé and D.G. (Tourism) and ex-officio Additional Secretary Ashok Pahwa would be ready to take over in his favourite department. He was also placed on Secretary panel. If my predecessor, Sundar had remained there, this would not have been possible because he would retire only in 1997. Bureaucrats may not plan for country's problems so much in advance, but plan their future in this meticulous fashion. They even write the CRs in such a way that some rivals are thrown out of the way. But, at times, these plans misfire. Minister for Tourism Srikanth Jena from Orissa wanted to get me an extension to start with. But, an Oriya officer came on the scene and I was dropped like a hot potato although the same Deve Gowda government gave extension until further orders to Padmanabhaiah, Home Secretary, on the same day. D.G. (Tourism), although promoted, was shunted off to an innocuous rural development organisation because by then T.S.R. Subramanian was in position as Cabinet Secretary.

I did not protest because I did not want to spoil my chances of re-employment. I was in need of a job because I had not built a house anywhere on account of my financial problems as explained elsewhere. Otherwise I would have to go to my wife's house in Madras. So I did mention this to both T.R. Satishchandran and Meenakshi Sundaram in the PMO. They were honest and straightforward and did not misguide others. If A.N. Varma had been there, he would have justified it saying that Home Secretary was a very important person while Tourism Secretary was not. I would have told him that it was not my fault that I did not take up important posts; he saw to it that I was not offered one. But T.R. Satishchandran frankly told me that it was not right on the part of the government to have made an exception in the case of Padmanabhaiah. In fact, he stated that such exceptions, apart from creating heart-burning in others, spoil the administration. Unfortunately no newspaper wrote about this invidious distinction although many of them wrote against the extension to Padmanabhaiah.

It has to be recorded here that, however, T.R. Satishchandran pontified to me that a caretaker Government should not move files for appointment when I requested him the very next day after Deve Gowda stepped down as P.M. to move my file for appointment as a member of the UPSC. He also told me that he himself never wanted an extension or a post after retirement. I believed him. But, a few months later, I was disillusioned by the hypocrisy of this civil servant because he accepted the position of

Governor of Goa from the caretaker government of Gujral and was rightly kicked out when the BJP came to power. In fact, I wondered whether he got the idea of Governorship from me. Gowda indicated to a friend who pleaded my case that I would not be considered for the UPSC, Election Commission, etc. because these Delhi posts were reserved for the favoured few for 'services rendered', and I would be considered for Pondicherry as Lt. Governor. Satischandran told me that when he checked, the incumbent Dr (Mrs.) Bajpai had not completed her term. I had indicated Goa also because it was vacant although I knew very well that I would not get it. But Satishchandran perhaps got an idea from my note as it happened often! Of course, in the case of Lyngdoh, Deve Gowda said that he was killing three birds in one stroke – Lyngdoh was from the North East, a tribal and a Christian. He was my predecessor in Tourism and was a highly honest person. He proved himself in the Election Commission.

But I found Tourism to be an important area of economic development particularly in India. Public perception and civil service perception are different. As they feel that Civil Supplies is not that important, they may also feel that Tourism is not that important. But, in reality, Civil Supplies and PDS and also Consumer Affairs are so vital for the common man. Tourism, of course, has also the trappings of high profile like Commerce. It has great glamour with eighteen offices abroad and many bilateral agreements with different countries. Sundar was transferred within a few months after taking over as Secretary, Tourism, while Varma always told me that I should be in a post at least for a year. When I was posted to Tourism, I always used to joke that the beautiful department was for beautiful people i.e., Sundar to Sundaram. **Jokes apart, it is the biggest industry in the world. It is the third biggest foreign exchange earner after garments and gems and jewellery for India. In fact, in gems and jewellery, the import content is almost 55% whereas in the case of tourism there is practically no import content. We have hardly exploited the tourism potential of this country. Whenever an entrepreneur thinks of doing something, he thinks only in terms of an industry, whereas hotel business has very high potential. The employment potential of tourism is also very high, far higher than the** investment-employment ratio for agriculture and industry. It also provides employment for women and ordinary people in villages. The World Tourism Organisation, an UN organisation, feels that tourism is also for poverty alleviation because of the employment potential. When I was in the Leather Export Promotion Council, the people at large particularly industrialists were ignorant about the potential of the leather industry. I initiated a new direction for the industry. Similarly, the scope for initiating a similar move was high for tourism.

I got a strategy paper made. Since I made the mistake of making my paper on PDS as a Cabinet note, it could not see the light of day. So I made this paper transparent and gave it wide circulation in the press and among state governments and opinion makers. It was well received in spite of the obduracy of the Finance Ministry.

But Minister Jena did not argue the paper at all. He gave only a sheepish smile when it came up in the Cabinet. I recorded in my diary on October 30th, 1996: "Our items on strategy for tourism in India came up before the Cabinet. Jena did not say anything at all except for a sheepish grin. P. Chidambaram pretended not to see me. Ibrahim threw the paper down. It was over in two minutes. In any case, it is country's loss. I have done my duty". But the minutes recorded and circulated to all concerned including the press later, thanks to Cabinet Secretary T.S.R. Subramanian who realised the importance of tourism, that "the Government noted the importance of tourism as an instrument for economic development and employment generation. The Government desired that the Department of Tourism take up the various proposals contained in the note with the concerned Departments, the Planning Commission and State Governments for being suitably reflected in their Plans." This meeting took place on the evening of October 30th, 1996. Only on the morning of October 31st, 1996, Minister Jena told me that I was not getting an extension. I had to meet a Japanese delegation for tourism also in the Federation of Chambers of Commerce and Industry that day. As happened to me often in my career, I was on call of duty till the last day or moment. But I retired as a happy man because the paper

prepared by me got favourable minutes from the Cabinet Secretariat in spite of the short-shrift in the meeting.

I had suggested the creation of a Board of Tourism Industry and Trade from my experience with the Board of Trade of the Commerce Ministry. In the Secretariat, all ideas may not be your own. Even a bright Section Officer would have thrown up a good idea. The strategy paper was a collective effort particularly with the assistance of Dr Ravindran and Mrs. Chudan T Misra (IAS: Gujarat Cadre). But this idea of Board was entirely mine and my own. When it was accepted by Jena later and implemented, he did not have the courtesy even to make me a member. He had included Dr Nitish Sengupta who was a D.G., Tourism once upon a time.

Little did they realise that tourism had a high potential in India for employment and it was already the third biggest foreign-exchange earner. By spending Rs.200 or 300 crore in the form of incentives per annum (many incentives are already there - only a few have to be supplemented as detailed in my paper), the country could earn another Rs.10,000 crore to Rs.20,000 crore per year. The Finance Ministry did not understand this ordinary arithmetic. The World Bank - IMF and the Harvard fellows were simply repeating the 'mantra' of 'no incentives and market forces' while many other developing countries were exploiting tourism to their benefit. In fact, my strategy paper was mainly private-sector driven. These fellows did not even mention 'tourism' in the annual Economic Survey of the Government of India. Only when I protested, they included a word or two in the subsequent year.

P. Chidambaram is also in the habit of going at a tangent. He had high regard for me, as many people knew, and this was reciprocal. But, down the line, perhaps because of tale-carriers or because of my bad-luck, he became cold toward me. The GOI tourist office in Geneva was in the process of being closed at the instance of the Ministry of Finance as a measure of economy. But the lady-officer in charge, who was the daughter of an ICS man who was dead, rushed to Delhi and met N.K. Singh and P. Chidambaran whom she had met during their annual Davos trips, requested them to continue this ofice. They wanted me to oblige her, but I could not. This was also a reason perhaps. He told my Minister that the Department of Tourism should be shut and tourism could be promoted by the private sector. In fact, we did not have restrictions as such. His department had many restrictions on tourism promotion in the Income Tax and the Customs regulations. I felt that this was a preposterous suggestion, particularly for a developing country.

Another pet theme of mine in Tourism was promotion of small airlines with small aircraft and revival of the numerous airports with the state governments. India could have a network of airports with small carriers to ferry tourists without fatigue. After years, I am glad that this is being fulfilled by the Deccan Air and other small airlines.

I have already stated elsewhere that one cannot help but blow one's own trumpet in one's memoirs or autobiography: I was the first Assistant Collector on training or 'Supernumerary' as they call in Maharashtra and Gujarat to go to Palanpur. This term was mistaken at times as 'Super' Assistant Collector or Collector. So we used to say jocularly that it could also mean 'superfluous'! Once my colleague Moosa Raza arrived in a place by bus when he was Supernumerary Assistant Collector. People there wondered how this 'Super' Assistant Collector or Collector was travelling by bus. Incidentally, Moosa Raza has devoted one full chapter to me and my wife by name in his somewhat an autobiographical novel, while he camouflaged the other names. My second first was that I was the first one to get into the IAS after completing two years of training in the IPS. I was also the first one to officiate as Collector for a month immediately after finishing my training as Assistant Collector before even taking charge of a Sub-division. I was the first Collector and District Magistrate of Pondicherry. I was the first one to conduct an Industries Intensive Campaign for a single industry – leather. I was the first Chairman of the 'iNDEXTb' in Gujarat. I was the first Counsellor for the NDDB to be posted in the Embassy of India, Brussels. The first antidumping case (PVC) in India was decided by me. I was the first to suggest introduction of VAT in the country. I was the first one to publish air-pollution levels daily in newspapers in Ahmedabad along with the weather report. I was also the first one to conduct a seminar for the legislators on environment and pollution control in the country; first to introduce distance-criterion for locating industries; first to conduct an advertisement campaign in newspapers, journals and hoardings against pollution - this has become so common now, but at that time the government of Gujarat almost called for my explanation for such wasteful expenditure! I invited the Greenpeace International in 1985 to establish their headquarters in Gandhinagar in India; they said that they would consider later. I was also the first to suggest introduction of Electronic Data Interchange (EDI) for trade in the country.

I was the first Member Secretary of SCOPE-AIR. I was a Director on the Air India Board from the Commerce Ministry for the first time and restored the Centaur symbol with the same letter-design from the ugly one introduced by Rajan Jaitly. I also went on record that Air India should have freedom without Government clearance to sell or purchase planes because the present system had spoiled the airlines and the planes were aged. When I questioned in the Board why the Air India should not change planes as the Singapore Airlines does once in five years, for after all Singapore learnt the tricks of the trade from the Air India to start with, the then Chairman told me that government clearance itself took five years here.

Although the idea of Citizens' Charter and Public Enterprises Regulatory Commission were not mine, I was the first to initiate them in the Government of India. For the first time, a citizens' charter was evolved for the hospitals with the Healthy Ministry. The Ministry was totally opposed to start with; it later wanted this to be left to them to evolve. We refused and the Ministry of Consumer Affairs brought this out. The idea was given an impetus later by Cabinet Secretary T.S.R. Subramanian and other Ministries were forced to fall in line.

Similarly, I mooted the implementation of a Public Utilities Regulatory Commission as a single entity so that utilities like electricity boards, water-supply organisations, ports and telecommunication did not put up rates without consulting the consumers as they did. I wanted a single organisation which was a new idea and Cabinet Secretary Surendra Singh referred it to a committee of secretaries under my chairmanship. All ministries opposed the idea tooth and nail except power and telecommunication who wanted to form their own organisations. Much later, the Telecom Regulatory Authority and the Electricity Regulatory Commissions became a reality and the idea was accepted for other Ministries too. Now it looks as though Parkinson's law would prevail and there would be a number of such regulatory authorities even for Information and Broadcasting and Civil Aviation to re-employ ex-judges and civil servants.

Similarly, the idea of a Pepper Exchange was mooted in Cochin as the first commodity future exchange. Meanwhile, Prof Kabra gave a report although he himself was opposed to forward trading in many commodities except two – it was a curious report where the chairman himself was recording notes of dissent! In any case, I wanted to activate the sleepy Forward Markets Commission under the Ministry of Consumer Affairs and give a push to the Pepper Exchange. I studied the subject by visiting the Chicago Board of Trade and also discussing with one of their directors, Nobel Laureate Dr Merten Miller. The Manual of the Board of Trade was also obtained. A note for the Cabinet was prepared, but the government did not want to take a risk because of some on-coming elections. I now find that the Forward Markets Commission and the commodity exchanges are active. As is my wont, I also wrote a couple of letters to the then chairman of the FMC as to how to go about it.

Dr. A.M. Swaminathan was an outstanding officer of the Tamil Nadu IAS cadre noted for efficiency although promoted from the State Civil Service and was also a good friend of mine for a long time. He told me once that he was following my career and remembered some of my 'firsts'. I told him that being the first, one is very often the guinea-pig and others who follow enjoy the fruits of one's labour. Others also claim success because 'success has many claimants' as John F. Kennedy said, 'but failure is an orphan'.

The World Tourism Organisation is a Madrid-based Inter-Governmental Organisation of the U.N. (now a UN Agency) whose Secretary-General resigned in May, 1996 or so, a year before his term was over. One Harsh Varma, an officer from the Department of Tourism of the Government of India who absorbed himself in the World Tourism Organisation at a middle or just above middle-level alerted me about this vacancy since I had made fairly a good impact in the WTO meetings with my knowledge of tourism and French. So, as advised by Varma, I got a proposal initiated nominating me for the post. The proposal was approved by CM Ibrahim, the then Minister for Tourism and later by Jena too. It was also approved by Prime Minister Deve Gowda. If my nomination had been filed at that time as advised by Varma, I had a good chance of winning the election. But Foreign Secretary Salman Haider opposed it tooth and nail. He also had a personal score to settle with me. I was the leader of the Indian official delegation to the ESCAP session in Beijing. Since the PR to ESCAP could not come from Bangkok for some reason, Haider wanted to be the leader since he was our Ambassador in Beijing. But he knew nothing about ESCAP. So I spoke to Commerce Secretary Ganesan who upheld my contention and spoke to Foreign Secretary Dixit. It would have made some sense if at least the PR had come though in that case too the nodal Ministry was supreme with a senior officer. But the IFS is in the habit of creating such problems even to other Secretaries. Though Haider did not attend even a single session, he managed to include his name over mine in the final official documents. This was done with the help of his IFS colleagues and one of whom was my Under Secretary. Salman Haider did this also so that he would automatically get invited to a trip to Shanghai with his wife and perhaps they would have excluded me for want of room in the aircraft. So I appealed to his good sense as a colleague by telling him that, as our Ambassador to China, he would have many opportunities to visit Shanghai in style, but poor me might not be able to come to China again and he should not spoil my opportunity. Although good sense prevailed, I think all this rankled in his mind and he wreaked his vengeance by spoiling my sponsorship to the WTO Secretary-Generalship and Ambassadorship to Brussels. But I blamed only my destiny although, as a normal human being, I felt like hitting such cantankerous fellows in the Services. But I felt that one should not take law into one's hands under any circumstances. But, curiously, almost all my enemies came to some grief or the other ultimately. As the old saying goes, 'King kills immediately, but the mills of God grind slowly, but they grind for ever'. Haider got himself appointed as our High Commissioner to the UK during the interim government of Gujral. He was rightly kicked out when the government changed.

External Affairs Minister Gujral was not willing to over-rule Haider although he was apparently convinced about my credibility. The excuse given was that India was fighting an election for the Security Council and so could not lobby for another election i.e., to the post of Secretary-General of the WTO. But, as was well known, India got a good drubbing with only three votes – for the Security Council seat one from Bhutan, one our own and one from Libya – not that Col. Gaddhafi loved us but he would go against whatever the US did at that time, apart from getting isolated in respect of the CTBT. So time was lost and the acting Secretary-General who was a French and who was actually waiting to know about my candidature jumped into the fray after knowing through Varma himself that my proposed candidature ran into trouble. Thus the mandarins of the MEA misguided the Government wherever India had no chance (Security Council) and missed an opportunity for the country where it was possible (WTO).

I requested Deve Gowda again and he instructed in my presence the Cabinet Secretary T.S.R. Subramanian and Satishchandran. But it invited only a frown from Subramanian on August 15th, 1996, both in the morning at the flag-hoisting and in the evening at Rashtrapati Bhavan reception. Both my wife and I wondered why he was hostile although I knew the reason and I had not told my wife about all this. Although Subramanian told me later that he did try with Salman Haider and Gujral and they were not willing to re-consider, particularly on an assessment from our PR to the UN Prakash Shah. He was apparently happy and was all sugar and honey to me on this occasion, the frown having faded! But he also told me that the MEA expressed inability to sponsor my candidature because of the Security Council election, but not questioned my suitability.

The same Prakash Shah and his deputy told me in New York that India was sure to win the Security Council election at least in the second round. Satishchandran could not do much because he belonged to the 1952 vintage and did not know the new bureaucratic class and their machinations in Delhi. In fact, after my retirement and departure, there was a move to sponsor S.K. Misra. But the UPSC-bar would have operated because he was a member of the UPSC. So Satishchandran did not pursue the matter though I told him that if a Prime Minister like Mrs. Gandhi or Rajiv Gandhi or even Chandra Shekhar had approved my case as Deve Gowda had done, the MEA would not have dared to oppose or re-submit for reconsideration. They would have meekly sponsored me. But Satishchandran swallowed all this. This is the problem with some Prime Ministers digging out old fossils for these posts like Principal Secretary which require alertness, dynamism, efficiency and political sagacity too. A.N. Varma was not at all lacking in this regard because he was not a fossil, and in a way he kept Rao in office and also himself for full five years, of course, without he being caught in any scam or scandal. Fossils are good, but only for research. (Satishchandran was awarded 'Padma Bhushan' in 2005, for what I do not know. Of all civil servants who got Padma awards that year, only S.R. Sankaran deserved it because of his dedication to rural development and the poor throughout his career with conviction. He rightly declined the award).

There is no accountability at all in our administration, particularly in the MEA. Prime Minister Deve Gowda did not take any action at all against the Minister or the mandarins for the debacle in the election to the Security Council. Foreign Secretary Shashank also told me years later that the Government of India was misguided by these people.

I was in many Departments at the wrong time. As explained elsewhere, I had to popularize the institution of Collector in Pondicherry. I was in the Pollution Control, the Department of the Environment, Consumer Affairs and Tourism at the wrong time in the sense during the formative years of struggle. When the Departments became popular, others jumped in and enjoyed the fruits as also happened in Brussels.

I must also confess, although I did not lobby with politicians for posts all along, I had to resort to it unfortunately after becoming a Secretary. As mentioned elsewhere, I went up to senior civil servants with my problems and they solved them by and large. One or two of my Ministers like A.C. George were impressed with my work and they helped me. No outside political help was sought. But, when I was on leave before my first posting as Secretary, many friends advised me to lobby and newspapers were also full of such reports about my colleagues. This was like the MMTC's best candidate lobbied because others lobbied and he did not want his case to go by default. When I was Secretary, Tourism, a panel came for a post in Tourism. A candidate did research as they always do in Delhi and made R. Vasudevan speak to me. But the other candidate lobbied with the Minister and succeeded. This is a vicious circle. The top civil servants are also responsible for this state of affairs. Since they no longer help the youngsters or junior colleagues and prefer to go by the inclinations of the political bosses, the youngsters lack confidence in the seniors and resort to outside help. This happened in my case when the top civil servants refused to recognise my educational equipment, experience and background when the whole world thought that I would land a good Economic Ministry. So I had to resort to outside help though it did not work.

Many officers became victims of corruption, communal system or other prejudices even in their early or middle career. Luckily, this did not happen to me except at the level of Secretary. The system became so corrupt that even some Secretaries demand bribes and it kept me out of a good Economic Ministry. Even Dr Manmohan Singh could not help me.

Although time had run short before my retirement, I thought the Gowda Ministry would help me. V.P. Singh was prepared to speak to the PM about my credentials, as he told me, if he was asked. Chandra Shekhar actually spoke. He was PM when I was Additional Secretary (Commerce). Incidentally, he was a natural leader with a lot of simplicity about him. A leader is not jealous of educated persons. He encouraged Dr Swamy, Mohan Guruswamy of Harvard, Yashwant Sinha and others. Whatever his political habits might be as a politician, he expected certain norms and honesty from a civil servant. He was also not afraid of pulling up any one. Dr V. Kurien, R. Venkatraman and B.D. Jatti would have vouched for my credentials. Not that I was their man – I worked with them and they thought well of my work. But the attitude of Maran – although he was well-disposed and even stated that he would get me re-employment – totally changed. Chidambaram and Maran never lifted their fingers while many thought that they would help me. In fact, a leading journalist of *The Sunday* magazine advised me to approach these big-wigs. Although the PM (Gowda) himself promised me an extension, he coolly forgot it at the crucial moment as was his wont. I was told that these people had become highly casteist within Hinduism though they blamed the BJP all the time. A Tamil film, "In a Single Village" has a dialogue, "Even if people want to forget castes, the Government or the politicians do not allow them to forget".

I wrote in my diary a few years ago (13.8.71): "People are complaining about discrimination not only against Brahmins but also against Harijans (in favour of Backward classes) by the present Government of Madras". These Mandalites or OBCs do not like the Harijans or Dalits (as they are called now) equally. While Rajiv Gandhi tried to take India into the 21st century (in fact, he was responsible for large scale computerisation in India), V.P. Singh took her back to the 19th century. When I made this statement, my batch-mate, a good friend and also a Harijan (I prefer this word to Dalit) M. Venkatachalam, IAS (Rtd.) used to tell me that in Madras the Harijans and the Brahmins were the neglected ones. (Mayawati seems to have come round to this view). The beneficiaries were the caste-Hindus. Murasoli Maran once wrote on a file that we should give preference to backward classes of the society. So Secretary Sivaramakrishnan and I collected a few CRs of Harijan officers. Maran not only did not select any one of them, but also remarked that a sensitive post like the Director of Estates should not be given to a Harijan and it would be difficult to remove the person. He also added that the Karunanidhi Government had a lot of trouble from the then Harijan Chief Secretary, Padmanabhan although Karunanidhi himself appointed Harijans as Chief Secretries and DGPs. Similarly, when I strongly recommended Harijan Sivakami, IAS, Regional Director, Tourism, Government of India,

Madras for a Tokyo-post of the Ministry with all her qualifications and suitability and practically no competition, Minister Jena did not select her for months.

Long ago, curiously my father used to hang a portrait of E.V. Ramaswamy Naicker in our home for a short period. When EVR left the Congress and turned virulently anti-Brahmin, he removed the portrait. But, looking back, EVR was an honest man of conviction. He not only condemned the Brahmins, but also the superstitions, temples and even broke a few idols of Gods. But the present-day non-Brahmins, by and large, are highly superstitious, temple-going and idol worshippers. They want Brahmin-priests for marriages, funerals and such functions and even put 'Pillaiyar Suzhi' (Ganesh's mark) on letters and invitations, but do not want Brahmins for college admissions and jobs. But Hinduism survives because of them and not because of people like me.

I was interested only in the IPS or the IAS. I did not even apply for the other Services. My wife's household had ICS, Indian Foreign Service, IA & AS, IAS, IOFS, etc. It was a civil service family. But no one has gone into the civil service now. Similarly, many civil servants' children have gone to the USA to be a part of the global village. *The Hindustan Times* carried in 1996 a series of articles on the state of civil service in different states. The lesson or conclusion was that it had become "the Indian Administrative Sewer" or "the Indian Police Sewer" because of the prevailing corruption, which no bright person should enter. However, bright persons including highly technically qualified people enter these services. So it is imperative to rectify the present state of affairs. Should we not clean up the sewer?

* * *

20

Bureaucracy: Some Thoughts

As Dr Madhav Godbole, former Home Secretary, has written in his book, "Unfinished Innings" there is unfortunately a lot of politics in the civil service itself. The poor politician is blamed often. But he could always learnt a thing or two from many of the civil servants. Or, the old camaraderie or the old-school-tie spirit has gone contrary to the popular impression that the civil servants are very friendly amongst themselves. In fact, there is a lot of skull-duggery. Some of these people also plan things in such a way even three or four years in advance so that the potential rivals are eliminated as it happens in politics so that their favourites could occupy important positions. Some of them even go to the extent of writing something in a CR which is neither adverse to be communicated, nor good enough for promotion. This has happened to me because a non-IAS secretary with whom I worked thought that, with my Ph.D., and rich trade background, I would be a claimant to some posts like Commerce Secretary or Finance and he decided perhaps to eliminate me while requesting me to take care of his own IAS brother who was working with me. Similarly, a former Cabinet Secretary too went on promising some assignment or the other after my retirement, but did nothing. I realised later that he saw a potential rival in me for some posts which he was also eyeing after his retirement, and wished my disappearance from the scene. This happened particularly to a number of south Indian additional secretaries in Commerce starting from C.S. Ramachandran, ICS, Muralidharan and myself, to name a few. Only A.V. Ganesan, although pushed out to Civil Aviation, managed to come back as Commerce Secretary.

Apart from many schemers and exploiters belonging to the IAS and other Services, there is a new set of people who belong to this category. These are the IMF and World Bank boys. Some of them failed to make the grade for the IAS. But they enter the civil service laterally at the level of Secretary because they happened to be a minor functionary in the high-profile, American-backed IMF or World Bank in Washington. They play havoc with the system. If one has a look at the career-graph of an IAS or IFS or any other Service officer, there would be ups and downs. Whereas in these cases, it is always an upward curve irrespective of the change in the colour of the Government. These persons are like winter birds. Whenever the climate gets hot for them, they fly away to the cool climes of Washington to their own houses and other comforts just to come back when the climate improves again here. They occupy only top positions in economic ministries and important ambassadorial jobs to retire as Finance Minister at the age of 58 or around 60 without having undergone the various troubles a politician had to undergo. (I hasten to add, lest it should be misunderstood, that Dr Manmohan Singh did not belong to this category. He joined as Economic Adviser–slightly less than Joint Secretary – in the Ministry of Commerce and worked his way up. So was Dr Arjun Sengupta.)

These IMF and World Bank persons get tax-free pension from those organisations besides the pension from the Government of India. They could always suggest taxation measures against the poor pensioners here. In fact, these fellows should be asked to declare their assets both within India and abroad before their appointment or re-appointment in the Government of India which should be made public. Some of these persons including some IAS go to the several institutes in Delhi. One such institute is ICRIER

– International Centre for Economic Relations – mainly created for Dr K.B. Lall with financial assistance from the Department of Economic Affairs. So mainly the persons from the DEA, during interregnums of unemployment park themselves there. It is located on the India International Centre campus on a small floor. It is not a deemed university or anything of academic kind or excellence. But even an ordinary graduate including the ones in the IAS call themselves 'Professor' – a designation or honorific more than even a 'Doctor'. One has to toil hard to become a professor in a university. But I was surprised to see one of my batch-mates calling himself a professor. In fact, he tried to knock off a Doctorate from a university, but they refused to register because he had no M.Phil or even perhaps an M.A. Who knows he will get a honorary doctorate soon, if not already managed it. Anything is possible in Delhi and anything goes.

In our society and system, time is not money, nor is it a resource which has to be managed. However, of late, some state governments like Gujarat conduct a single-day training programme for the officials on time management. In the absence of such a training for the officials of the Government of India, people including senior bureaucrats waste a lot of time. Very often meetings start late and they extend longer than it is necessary. If a top bureaucrat or minister is not able to manage his or her time, the time of all others down the line is also wasted. This also results in avoidable delay in disposal of files.

A lot also depends upon the attitudes of the people and those who come in contact with the government. It happens often that people drop in without notice or appointment. This disrupts work and encroaches on the time available for performing other tasks. "I could walk into so and so's room" is a common practice in our country, particularly on the part of the private sector lobbyists. They may impress their bosses by this practice, but this results only in problems, though this practice could be resorted to on rare occasions when it cannot be helped. But, in our country, this is more a rule than an exception.

Also in our society, we use the telephone or communication through letter much less. There is also a mistrust that a telephonic talk or even a letter will not be acted upon. Consequently, there is always emphasis upon personally seeing a person not only in government but also in the private sector for getting a thing done. This practice, apart from wasting other resources like fuel, results in wastage of the non-renewable resource known as time. Perhaps the other party who has to accede to a request also feels that a personal call by an applicant is important to establish one's authority or for explaining matters or requests. Also in our society, invitations to weddings are expected to be delivered in person at least to close relatives and friends. Unless this culture changes, it is difficult to change the output of the bureaucrats of both the public and private sectors or for that matter any other busy person.

Meetings replace a lot of time taken for moving files or correspondence provided a goal is set for the meeting in order to resolve issues. If the meetings are used only to talk shop or to postpone decisions, they become meaningless. But if the meetings are well structured with goals set, they could be very useful indeed.

Bureaucratic inefficiency has also spread of late to the private sector. The private sector is no longer efficient as it used to be in the past. Perhaps this is a general malaise of falling standards of education and the attitudes of the society in general. There are no replies to letters addressed to many a private sector organisation these days. A general attitude of nonchalance prevails everywhere. In fact, the governmental bureaucracy shines by contrast these days!

File or paper management is also an art. When one's table is clean, very often we go away with an impression that the person concerned has no work or is not fully occupied. A clean table is not attributed to efficiency. One of my colleagues who was a Collector used to carry about two hundred files always – every day to the office, spread them on the table, pack them and take them home in the evening and also when he went on tours. This was to create an impression that he was always over-burdened with far too many files. This practice prevails even in international organisations When I was in an international organisation, some people used to say that the table should be "decorated" with a lot of paper so that any one coming including the boss would get an impression that he or she was over-worked. Even during one of my recent visits, I saw one of my such friends sitting in the midst of papers and computer sheets as some people sit in the midst of piles of files in our country. I am not aware of the practice in the private sector. But it appears that even the private sector executives believe in handling far too many papers in spite of computerisation. I have read that even in the United States the volume of paper used has gone up even after large scale computerisation because far too many print-outs are taken.

This is also a country of 'sifarish' (recommendation). Even to get an appointment, people do research and find out a friend of an officer and make him speak to the officer concerned. Of course, looking at this from the other side, some bureaucrats are not available at all to people even over phone and hence this approach. This is not desirable and people should be able to transact business over the phone. The 'recommendation culture' for anything and everything should also stop because it vitiates the entire system.

All this makes us feel that there is no escape from Parkinson's law as far as the bureaucracy is concerned whether it is the public or the private sector. However, no country or organisation can do without bureaucrats. Bureaucracy generally lacks the power of positive thinking in our country. It is very difficult for a common man to get things done by the bureaucracy and the private sector bureaucracy is also emulating this. In many offices, decisions are neither taken, nor papers disposed of one way or the other. Everything has to be followed up. May be the long years of colonial rule has made it a negative organisation where obstacles or objections have to be raised to each and every proposal and the hurdles have to be crossed. Even in private sector organisations, negative aspects of a proposal are instinctively thought of first. The technical bureaucracy cannot even cut the red-tape. Although this attitude is changing slowly, there is need to develop an attitude of positivism and dynamism. This attitudinal change should come about not only among the higher echelons, but more particularly at the lower and middle levels. Training becomes important here.

It is my view that there is too much of security in the Civil Services. While a politician should not be allowed to trammel upon the Civil Services or run rough shod over them, the civil servants' security to the point of not discharging the duty should be diluted, if necessary by amending Article 311 of the Constitution. I gave this view to the Pay Commission so that they could negotiate with the employees' unions before giving pay hikes in order to ensure that good money is not put after bad money. But they did not do it and as a result governments became bankrupt.

Unfortunately, bureaucracy including the IAS are not time or target-oriented. Perhaps this is due to a lacuna in their training. For that matter, time is not a resource in our country. The Section Officer or the Under Secretary or the Deputy Secretary, as in olden days, should keep a check-list of matters to be followed up according to their urgency and put them up periodically to his or her superiors. Such practices are no longer in vogue and these functionaries in the hierarchy have almost become useless. As a result, the Joint Secretaries have become nodal officers and they also need repeated reminders from Secretaries to follow up or put up things, which very often they do not do not only in important matters but also in replying to the citizens. That is why, very often citizens complain that there is not even an acknowledgement to their letters. I recorded in my diary on September 22nd, 71: "In our administration, people care more for procedures than for the substance – more for the shadow. No wonder, common man is simply exasperated at the government. I do not know when things will change. It depends upon individuals." Again I wrote on August 16th, 91: "I pity the plight of common man. I even feel that we administrators have failed this country." I would like to emphasise that handling correspondence itself is an art, which should be taught to bureaucrats, both in government and private sector. High level officials or executives do not seem to scan the incoming letters at all. Since they are away from the office most of the time, they seem to leave it to their PAs or Executive Assistants who mark them to the officials concerned with the subject, but remain unreplied. I always used to read the letters coming to me. Whenever I was on tour, my PAs were instructed to keep photocopies of important letters and a list of people called on phone and send it to the airport itself so that I could see on my return straightaway. Any top official or M.D. well conversant with the subject could dictate a reply straightaway. Some Ministers like P. Chidambaram do this and create a tremendous good impression. The office is also kept alert and they cannot dilute a high-level decision. Important calls could be returned. Since this is an art which is not practised by many, there are always complaints that letters or complaints even to higher-ups remain unreplied to. This is a common complaint in India, both against the government and the private sector.

The Ministries of Law and Finance are notorious for their delays because of the tremendous pressure from different departments for advice in the case of the former, and in the case of the latter an expenditure delayed even for a day is a saving to government! So, although the different functionaries in different ministries are expected to function fast to decide on an issue, constant chasing of things at the highest level of secretaries has to be done to the detriment of policy formulation and advice, which they are expected to do. The Economic Administrative Reforms Commission under the late L.K. Jha clearly stated in a paper that a Secretary or an Additional Secretary should not become an operational man. He should concentrate upon policy formulation and advice to ministers.

The best satisfaction, apart from projects put up, was when people told me that they were benefited by an official act of mine when I myself had naturally forgotten it. On one or two occasions, when I was sitting in an airport, some strangers walked up to me and told me that their project had come up well or their exports had gone up by some clearance or licence given by me. I felt extremely happy. This happened also in case of the Swminarayan temple in London – the biggest Hindu temple outside India. Although I was from the Gujarat cadre, I did not know this organisation at all. But, when I was additional secretary in the commerce ministry, the chief secretary to the government of Gujarat rang me up to clear their project for the Kandla Free Trade Zone quickly – they brought raw marble from Italy, Bulgaria, etc. added value after chiseling them and exported to London for this temple.

With regard to Khairnar, Kiran Bedi and Alphons, times have changed fast and consequently there is no point in taking shelter under the rules framed by our colonial masters. Of course, a civil servant should try to function within the system without seeking undue publicity. But it happens often that he or she is trampled upon under foot by his or her own superiors, let alone the politicians, either for good initiatives as in the case of these three officers or for adopting a bold and objective stand against a corrupt system. Perhaps they cannot afford to resign from the service as some have done on the basis of conscience. So these bold officers have chosen to correct the system from within. They get the limelight because so many others in similar situations have chosen either to remain silent on account of sheer fright or whenever they have tried to defy the system from within, the system has only slapped them back and there is no way the outside world could know it. There is also no point in getting out of the system by resigning or hobnobbing with the same politicians who are the masters in a democratic system.

So, in my opinion, these three bold officers who have defied a corrupt system without any constitutional immunity for themselves should be encouraged so that many others would be encouraged to emulate their example, rather than stifling them by taking disciplinary action under archaic rules and regulations disregarding transparency and the people's right to know (There was no Right to Information Act when this was drafted). Of course, they should not try to combine roles, that is, a civil servant trying to be a politician or seeking undue publicity. (Alphons has since become a politician and Kiran Bedi dresses like a politician!)

It often happens in one's official career that one comes to know of one's transfer from newspapers or the TV. For instance, the creation of new departments and the postings were first announced on the TV and next morning in the newspapers and only hours later even the Establishment Officer came to know of it. I had also heard stories in my official career that some one suddenly appeared in an officer's room and told him that he had come there to take over from him. Whereas the officer concerned had no knowledge at all about it. Similarly, in some places the rooms of officers were locked up and they were told that they had already been transferred. I did not give much credence to these stories because it never happened to me.

But when I was placed in charge of the Department of Consumer Affairs and Public Distribution System, although I looked after it for more than a year as Secretary of the Ministry of Civil Supplies, Consumer Affairs and Public Distribution and also technically held charge of both Departments and I was shedding only the charge of the Department of Civil Supplies, my batch-mate who was put in charge of the Department of Civil Supplies wanted to occupy my room stating that it was his room. In fact, I was to attend an important meeting outside my office on that day at 11 a.m., Somehow I had a suspicion and also Providence told me that he might come at that time and occupy my chair. So I deliberately did not go to that meeting. As anticipated by me, he did not turn up at the scheduled time of 10.30 a.m., He rang me up on the RAX five minutes before 11 a.m., perhaps to find whether I was still in the room and if I was not there he could straightaway encroach on my room and occupy my chair. To his surprise, he found me still there and when he came in for signing the joining report, he demanded for my room. Of course, I refused to budge and told him that he was the new comer and there was no change in my situation as far as I was concerned. In fact, if he had occupied my room and sat in my chair, I would have physically thrown him out. But that would have created a scene and appeared the next day in the newspapers. Luckily the situation was averted. Later, for about a week till he was settled in some other room, I had to do the unpleasant thing of locking the room and taking the key with me lest he would occupy my room!

Some years back, the officers of the Central Secretariat Service remained in the same Ministry for ever. I had identified 'seven pillars of wisdom' in the Ministry of Commerce! This was not a healthy system and it was changed. But even now the private secretaries, personal assistants and drivers remain in the same ministry for ever. This is again not healthy although the PA network is useful. Some of them had drawn an 'iron curtain' around their ministers. For instance, P. Chidambaram was a rare person like Sripal to pick up the phone himself although he might disconnect abruptly. But, it is impossible to contact some ministers and officers because the PAs would not simply put you through. This is more true of the private sector. One could manage to speak to the PM on phone, but not to the chairman or MD of a company.

The liaison officers of big companies are another institution in Delhi. They carry news, right or wrong, all the time. Some of them manage to get suitable appointments for secretaries or for additional secretaries of their choice.

In the Indian context, the first six months are crucial for any government, secretary to the government or a head of the department to introduce policy or administrative changes. During this period of euphoria, the iron is hot and one should strike. After this period, some scandal or the other erupts and the people or the PAs get to know the weak points of the government or the boss and do not allow them to function. Press also become hostile. Governments also become shaky particularly the coalitions. So, once again, time is the essence.

Boards to select officers to certain positions (like the CVC) and to effect transfers do not work in fact in our 'sifarish' culture. So, in my opinion, there should be built-in mechanism, say, a unified civil service with compartments of specialization so that an officer cannot be transferred from finance to archives to environment to social welfare. A fixed tenure of two or three years, which is advocated often is only to favour their own persons. No cabinet secretary has put the Thames on fire, or even the Jamuna. He or she cannot bring about radical changes because the system is fairly well-set. So the fixed tenure is only an excuse and also the government cannot get rid of a bad fellow.

Lyngdoh very rightly stated that the collegiate mode of selection i.e., by the PM, HM and the Leader of the Opposition as for the CVC results only in 'lobbying' and the strongest lobbyist gets the post. So it would be honest to leave it to the PM, as in many other cases. Or we could even switch over to the American system of changing the top layers of the bureaucracy when there is a change of government.

Or, the IAS, the IPS and the Indian Forest Service officers including the promoted ones should be really all-India in character by transferring them anywhere in the country once in five years. This is also a built-in mechanism against the present prevailing corruption where many officers have developed deep roots in their states of allotment and nexus with corrupt businessmen and politicians. Transfer to other states and the centre will break this. Knowledge about a state, language, etc., are only arguments to perpetuate the present system. When specialised knowledge about departments like finance, power or the environment is not considered important and an officer could pick up, similarly an officer should be able to adjust to a new state like the officers in the Indian Foreign Service in different countries.

I have already written elsewhere that holders of Constitutional positions like High Court or Supreme Court judges, Election Commissioners, Comptroller and Auditor General and UPSC Chairman and Members and the CVC (although only statutory) should not be eligible for any other post including Constitutional positions like Governors except for President, Vice-President or for standing for elections only as an independents since this is a citizen's fundamental right. Nominations to the Rajya Sabha or positions like Human Rights Commission should also be excluded by a Constitutional Amendment. In the present system, there is favour-seeking at least by a few all the time and patronage, spoiling the sanctity of these august positions. There should not be even a shadow of suspicion against the holders of these offices.

These thoughts may appear a bit stray or disjointed. However, our system is not all that bad in spite of all the sham. But corruption is eating into the vitals of the system and it is necessary to plug it or cure it by requisite legislative means like Constitutional amendments. There should be new thinking and a felt need to perfect the present system instead of diluting it.

* * *

21

Astrology and all that

People believe in astrology throughout the world, rightly or wrongly. The Luxembourg TV used to finish the day or evening with forecasts for the next day as early as in 1971. Sir C.V. Raman, the Nobel Laureate, never believed in astrology. While scientists are trying to explore Mars, we feel that Mars has an influence over us. Even the famous Aerospace Museum of the Smithsonian Institute in Washington has a section on astrology from different parts of the world including India. Man has yet to fathom the mysteries of the universe or God.

I have not heard any Swamiji giving this example about God: ants and flies have life and they live in a world of their own. But we do not hesitate to kill an ant or swat a fly. Likewise, if there is a God managing the Universe, as somebody said that 'God is the best Manager', He would not hesitate or bother about a small human being on the earth unless he or she seeks Him.

Astrology did play a role in my life although I became skeptical on many occasions even about the existence of God. Looking back, the subject like God must have fascinated me. Though I had totally forgotten, I discovered the other day an article of mine in the Voorhees College journal way back in 1955 when I was sixteen and the other one published recently which may be of interest:

"About the Existence of God"- "The readers may think that I am venturing to repeat some common statements on the side of Theism by elaborating something here and there. But that is almost a symposium.

We can divide the modern world into two divisions, not by any colour prejudice but from a philosophical and common point of view. One is Theism and the other is the contrary. Many sparkling arguments and bitter disputes have been advanced on the same subject.

There are some common statements on one side: the blowing of wind, the feeling of pain and so on are some of them.

One fine morning, I was going through a collection of Tamil poems of modern literature. This anthology is the product of some modern poet of Tamil Nadu. In one of the poems, he is writing about the same subject in a dramatic form.

A discussion goes on between man and God. The individual says that he has no faith in the existence of the Almighty. God wants to lead him on the right path. So the Immortal tells him that God has created this universe and all other things and that the earth is a great house; God is the father; the men on earth are his sons. At once the atheist asks Him to show the man who created God himself. Unwilling to answer this question, God simply leaves the scene.

Being an atheist, the poet stops this here. We must recall here the words of C. Rajagopalchari who plays a vital role in the political as well as the religious fields of India. He says that man cannot know the Creator of God because the knowledge of man is limited to a certain extent. Man has discovered many things. Atom is the smallest thing. Atoms are the units of which matter is built. There are extremely small, even the heaviest ones, like uranium atoms, weighing only as much in comparison with a melon as the melon weighs in comparison with the earth. But the power of the atoms may be more readily imagined than described. Such is the power of God. But our astounding knowledge is not reached to the extent of knowing God thoroughly.

Suthananda Bharathi, the eminent scholar and poet of modern Tamil literature had toured Russia. In one of the Russian colleges, he had conversed with the Russian students on the same subject. They asked him the same thing as we find in the poetical section of the modern Tamil poet. But Bharathi cleared their doubts. He made them believe God. He erased the stain from their soul and made them once again wise because "the fear of the Lord is the beginning of knowledge; but fools despise wisdom and instruction".

Now we can see God through many a noble and supreme being of all beings. "Thou seest many stars at night in the sky" says Ramakrishna "but findest them not when sun rises. Canst thou say that there are no stars, then, in the heaven of day? So, O man, because thou beholdest not the Almighty in the days of thy ignorance, say not that there is no God. He is born to no purpose who having the rare privilege of being born a man is unable to realise God in this life." "If you want any good to come just throw your ceremonials over-board and worship the living God, Man. God created every being that wears a human form, God has universal as well as individual aspect." These words came from the lips of the indomitable frame, Swami Vivekananda.

Mahatma Gandhi had no belief in God during his early days. But after some time he realised the Lord and became a superman. He confessed that he has no "living faith in God". Who made the world?" he asked. "Who directed it?" He accordingly inclined "somewhat towards atheism". But after his realisation "the word Satya means truth, he writes, "and it derives from Sath which means to be. Sath also denotes God. Therefore, "Truth is God".

Over the years Gandhi tried to prove the existence of God. It is possible to reason out the existence of God to a limited extent. There is an orderliness in the Universe; there is an unalterable law governing everything and every being that exists or lives. It is not a blind law that can govern the conduct of human beings.... That law that which governs all life is God....... I do dimly perceive that whilst everything around me is ever-changing, ever dying, there is under-lying all that change a living Power that is changeless and holds all together, that creates, dissolves and re-creates. That informing Power or Spirit is God.... In the midst of death life persists, in the midst of untruth truth persists, in the midst of darkness light persists. Hence I gather that God is life, Truth and Love. He is

Love. He is the supreme God." "Faith transcends reason. If we could solve all the mysteries of the Universe, we would be co-equal with God. Every drop of ocean shares it glory but is not the ocean". "By analogy every human being partakes of the nature of God but is not God and cannot know what He is".

When Gandhi was shot by Godse, he at once uttered the words "Hey Ram" (Oh God).

Scientists like Einstein and Raman (Nobel Prize winner of South India) if they want, can destroy this world. They can make more powerful weapons than the thermo-nuclear weapons. Christians as well as Hindu missionaries are serving in the humanitarian fields of education and medicine. But they are working under the mission of God.

The ancient Tamil poet Tiruvalluvar was also a God-worshipping man. He writes in his immortal *Tirukkural,* "What profits have those derived from learning who worship not the good feet of Him who is possessed of pure knowledge?" "None can swim the great sea of birth, but those who are united to the feet of God".

The great biographer, Louis Fischer says in his biography of Mahatma,

"His legacy is courage, his lesson truth, his weapon Love,

His life is monument,

He now belongs to mankind. How? He achieved this and the limelight by the virtue of God".

Finally, the key "My brethren, be strong in the Lord and power of His might. He who believeth in Him should not perish but have ever-lasting life".

"God is formless and God is possessed of form too. And he is also that which transcends both visible and invisible. He alone knows what all He is".

I also wrote in *The Times of India* on June 28th, 1996: "God, Spirituality and All That": "Recently I had the opportunity of visiting the Swaminarayan Temple in London. The Swaminarayan sect, unlike the Sankaracharyas of Kanchi or any other Sankaracharya, has the munificence of the Gujaratis spread all over the world.

There is no dearth of men or material for free voluntary service. This is evident from the Akshardham complex and the headquarters of the sect appropriately located at Gandhinagar in Gujarat.

I took my customary visit to Tirupati in the beginning of last year. As I was standing there for darshan inside the sanctum with a little bit of lurking doubt as usual, I saw hundreds of men and women doing the 'angapradakshanam' i.e., going round the sanctum by rolling oneself on the floor. I believe President Shanker Dayal Sharma also does this whenever he goes to Tirupati. I felt convinced in my heart of hearts that all this depended upon one's faith and there was no rational explanation to it. As Aldous Huxley said that these were impervious to logic or arguments. This was followed by a series of visits to important temples purely by chance and not by any design or pre-plan.

A visit to Thiruvananthapuram enabled me to have darshan of the presiding deity, Shri Padmanabha Swami. I was told of an incident about the presiding deities in relation to Mrs Indira Gandhi. She was on a visit to Tirupati for some election or the other when she was Prime Minister. Since a visit to Tirumala was not on the schedule, she declined to visit Tirumala although she was told that, if a person came to that area, he or she should make it a point to have darshan of the presiding deity. On account of this lapse, I was told that she lost the elections! May be this was only a coincidence. When I went to Kathmandu once, I had decided not to have darshan of the famous Pasupathinath because I had already visited that temple on a previous visit. I was keen on taking the famous mountain-flight in Nepal by air to view the Everest at close quarters. When I went to the airport early in the morning, the flight was cancelled on account of inclement weather and I decided to use that time for visiting Pasupathinath. This was similar to Mrs Gandhi's experience, true or otherwise!

An official visit to Kashmir took me to the Shankaracharya Hill in Srinagar and also to the famous ice Lingam of Amarnath. I could also visit a Gurudwara in Baramulla in the Kashmir Valley in spite of the tight security restrictions. I had earlier visited the two Kanchi Acharyas at Kanyakumari. A visit to Madurai took me to the famous Meenakshi temple which included a darshan of Bhairava who was supposed to vanquish one's enemies. A visit to Kancheepuram to see the Sankaracharya provided an opportunity to have a darshan of Kanchi Kamakshi. The circuit of the three important deities was completed in the sense that a visit to U.P. by the end of the year enabled me to have a darshan of Visalakshi of Kashi.

A visit to Leh took me to some ancient Buddhist monasteries including the famous Hermes Monastery, which was visited by Pandit Nehru after days of trekking and pony-riding. An official visit to Istanbul enabled me to offer prayers at the world famous Blue Mosque and other mosques there. I was feeling sorry that I could not accompany my minister to Calcutta because his visit included a call on Mother Teresa. But Mother Teresa came to Delhi for a function to which I was also invited. Both my wife and I made it a point to go there and had the darshan of this noble soul.

So it was a year of visits to religious places and sages for spiritual satisfaction not by any design or pre-plan, but mostly by chance. However, it was not a year of any personal progress in the material sense. An ordinary human being always looks for material progress although the religious scriptures say that it should not be the goal. At the same time, one cannot be totally free from such mundane feelings and doubts about the efficacy of such visits to holy places, shrines and holy men. One should have abiding faith in the Almighty like the emperor Nala, Harishchandra, Mira and so on. If one has such unflinching devotion, one should not be driven to such extremes as in the case of Nala, Harishchandra or Mira, but remember that all of them and also Jesus, the Buddha, Mahatma Gandhi and Nelson Mandela had earned indelible places in history only by trials and tribulations without aspiring for benefits or results. However, thoughts as far as God, spirituality and all that are concerned, have made me an agnostic though not an atheist".

At the same time, I could not be totally rational however much I tried to rationalize. A debilitated Sun did make me struggle for recognition and my due was not given to me. Luckily, according to astrologers, this was rectified by the presence of other planets and turned out to be 'a neech-bang raj-yog'! A weak Sun is a minus factor, I believe, in any case. Whereas an exalted Sun brought due recognition in my wife's case! As I have already recorded, there were times when things happened automatically without much effort – in Pondicherry, in Ahmedabad as Additional Commissioner of Industries, postings to Brussels and the Commerce Ministry; and there were also times when things did not happen despite Herculean efforts and high-level interventions. Here, you believe in destiny or astrology.

Of course, if one has no horoscope, one should be happy. Astrology is also often negative. For example, 'Sadesathi' takes away twenty two years of life, let alone 'ashtama Sani', etc., Only five transits of Jupiter, 1,5,7,9 and 11 are good out of the twelve transits.

I came in contact with the Swaminarayans of Gujarat and the Shankaracharyas of Kanchi purely by chance. In fact, my wife and my parents do not believe in the Swamijis, but only in God. But I do not question any one including the Mother whom I used to visit often in Pondicherry in my official capacity escorting VIPs when I was there. At the same time, I believe in the saying, ' a man can also become God' – a means to or of God. Krishna, Jesus and Buddha were also human beings.

But the God, God-men or astrology should not totally guide one in one's life because all the three could go wrong as happened to me in post-retirement. Contrary to the rosy predictions of some big astrologers except M.O.H. Farook who told me not to worry at all at one time years ago, but not this time. I could get only a small assignment as tourism adviser to the government of Gujarat for a year, thanks to fomer PM Chandra Shekhar and the former Gujarat Chief Minister Shankersinh Waghela both of whom I did not even know. But when I told Chandra Shekhar that he was Prime Minister when I was Additional Secretary in Commerce and the need for a job for me, he appreciated my straightforward request to him because he was an old-timer who distinguished between good and bad, politicians and civil servants and their respective roles. He did not mix up the roles as the present day politician do. Although I was appointed by Waghela, a sworn enemy of the BJP, Keshubhai Patel who became Chief Minister later gave me an extension because Gujarat, unlike many other state governments today, believed in the intrinsic merit of civil servants and did not involve them in their politics.

L.K. Advani (because of my Gujarat connection) and Dr Manmohan Singh were well disposed towards me and the latter even promised me a position when Congress would come back to power—he himself became the PM. They were so courteous that they even spoke to me over phone or replied to my letters in spite of their busy schedules – some people may not even believe this. It is good fortune of India that we have an honest President (written during Kalam's time) and PM. This itself is more than ninety percent of the battle won. Dr. Manmohan Singh was always courteous to me and at times discussed or perhaps picked my brains about political matters. Before leaving Delhi, I called on him. He discussed even about the Congress. I told him that Mrs. Sonia Gandhi could continue as Congress President and place some one else as Prime Minister (though I did not tell him, I was keeping him in mind).

Similarly, on another occasion, I told him to his query that the Congress should go it alone in Tamil Nadu in the face of repeated defeats and improve the percentage of its vote-bank. This would make and help people that there is an alternative to the DMK or the AIADMK. To his query on alliance in Tamil Nadu, I gave my opinion, which I do not want to disclose here because I have to live in Tamil Nadu! (I do not know whether he remembers all this.)

But both Advani and Manmohan Singh could not do anything for me because of the former's conflict or supposed conflict with Vajpayee and more with the PMO. Since there was no Cabinet Secretary or Secretary to the PM from Gujarat, Keshubhai Patel wrote to Vajpayee to consider me for the post of Secretary to the PM, but as usual N.K. Singh knocked it off. I could not get anything later either from the BJP or the Congress. I had worked with a lot of people in the Congress including Dr Manmohan Singh et al. This is what is known as destiny. At a point of time, as described elsewhere, jobs were offered to me. The following letters would put it in the proper perspective:

(1)

15th April, 2003.

Respected Prime Minister,

I crave your indulgence for a few minutes to read this letter.

As soon as you took over as PM for the second time, I called on you with a letter from the Government of Gujarat suggesting that I could be considered for the PMO since no one from the Gujarat Cadre was ever a Secretary to PM or Cabinet Secretary. Further details were obtained as desired by your goodself, and I reasonably believe that I was considered. Of course, it was your personal choice and you had chosen another officer.

At that time, Ms Vasundhara Raje was the MOS (MEA) directly working with you and I believe that she had put up a note for your kind consideration for my posting as Ambassador to EU and Belgium. But the age of retirement was revised and the incumbent stayed on in Brussels.

Shri. Yashwant Sinha, the Minister for External Affairs, knows me for a long time.

*I now read in the newspapers that ******* Finance Secretary, is being considered for this post. I am afraid that he has no background to this post at all. I hasten to add that he might be eminently suitable for many other posts keeping in view his background and accomplishments. Similarly, I am not asking for a posting to the USA or the UK or Russia. Only in our country, a free-for-all seems to prevail. Merit and suitability should be first taken into consideration. Even from Iraq, I have read in the newspapers that the person who came as special envoy to Delhi before the war was their Ambassador to India earlier.*

Although a former Cabinet Secretary and some retiring officers tried for this position in 1993, the then Foreign Secretary was of the opinion that I was the most suitable candidate for the post. But my IFS batch-mates were chosen although this post was traditionally for the ICS/IAS.

I would request you to consider me for the post of Ambassador to the EU and Belgium. (I studied in Brussels; Ph.D.,; published books on the subject; Deputy Secretary and Additional Secretary in Commerce; was Counsellor in the same Mission (this was approved by your goodself when you were Minister for External Affairs in 1978 and it was noted that I was 'tailor-made' for the post); successfully negotiated our current Agreement with the EU.

I hope and trust you will do me justice. I thought that I would adopt this straightforward approach to you.

(G. Sundaram)

To

Shri A.B. Vajpayee,
Hon'ble Prime Minister,

Copy to
Shri L.K. Advani,
Hon'ble Deputy Prime Minister,

Shri Yashwant Sinha,
Hon'ble Minister for External Affairs.

---

(2)

19th July, 2003.

Respected Prime Minister,

Pranams

You have rightly appointed Dr Y.V. Reddy as Governor of the RBI – "right person for the right job" and "a man of tremendous integrity" as reported by some newspapers. Such appointments do enhance the stature of a government and governments should strive to do it. It was well known that Reddy was prevented from becoming Finance Secretary by some vested interests.

Pardon me for drawing a parallel of my case with that of Reddy's. As he specialised in economic affairs, I specialised in commerce. When I was due to become Commerce Secretary, Mr Tejendra Khanna was occupying the post not by any machination, but he was my senior in service and junior in age, which meant my retirement before him. Shri P.V. Narasimha Rao did consider me twice for the post of Ambassador to the European Union and Belgium because I had studied in Brussels, an M.Phil., and Ph.D., (from the Delhi School of Economics) in the subject of India-EU relations, Counsellor in the Embassy posted when you were Minister of External Affairs, negotiated and initialed as Additional Secretary, Commerce, the current India-EU Agreement, knowledge of French, etc., but my own batch-mates from the IFS – Shri A.N. Ram, Shri C. Dasgupta –knocked me out although the post was with the ICS and the IAS for a long time. I feel that we should not go by the service, but by expertise for such positions.

So, I hope and pray that you will also reward me with this post of Ambassador to the EU and Belgium as you have rightly done to Dr Y.V. Reddy, in case Shri P.K. Singh is moving out of Brussels.

(G. Sundaram)

To
Shri A.B. Vajpayee ji,
Hon'ble Prime Minister

Copy to
Shri Yashwant Sinha ji,
Minister for External Affairs
(3)

26th December, 2003.

Dear Shri Saikia,

Greetings of the Season.

I would request you to spare a few minutes of your precious time to read this letter. As I told you over phone, the Government of Gujarat wanted my name to be considered for the position of Secretary to the PM when the present PM took over. It was considered and, of course, it was the personal choice of the PM and also that no one could stand competition from Shri N.K. Singh. Even when Dr Manmohan Singh seriously recommended my name for the post of Secretary, Expenditure, Shri Singh came in the way. In all such circumstances, an equally important position was given to the losing candidate. It was not done in my case. But, later my name was considered for the BIFR and I was told by the then Cabinet Secretary that it would go through. But at your office level, it was turned down. You would recall that I never lobbied with you although I knew that you were looking after the appointments. Since I read recently in the newspapers that you were a fair-minded person, I spoke to you.

Be this as it may, my name was approved by no less a person than the then PM for the elective post of Secretary-General of the World Tourism Organisation when I was Secretary, Tourism. But the MEA did not oppose my candidacy on the basis of my suitability, but took the plea that they were busy lobbying for a permanent seat for India in the Security Council and so they were not in a position to lobby for me. Finally, India got only three votes – our own, Bhutan's and Libya's!

My name was also considered for the post of Ambassador in Brussels twice, but IFS officers got it. Whereas, when Dr. V. Kurien created a diplomatic post in the same Embassy, he selected me purely on the basis of my earlier education there, my Ph.D., in the subject, knowledge of French, etc. He wrote to the Government that I was "tailor-made" for the post. The then Ambassador also used to consult me on economic and commercial matters. Later too, I negotiated and initialed the current Agreement between the EU and India. But our 'sifarish' culture and the claim by the IFS (as the IAS too does for all posts under the sun) denied me the opportunity.

Many commerce and finance secretaries in the recent past had never worked in these ministries. No wonder it was a pathetic sight when Shri Ajit Kumar, Finance Secretary, confessed on TV camera that he could not fathom the undercurrents or understand the nuances whenever a paper or file came up to him. When I was to be appointed as Additional Secretary in Commerce, the then Minister Mr. Arun Nehru told the Secretary that he was not interested in any candidate, but the new incumbent should be able to start functioning from day one since a secretary or additional secretary cannot learn on the job, whereas a JS could do so because of the long tenure. I fitted in because I had worked as Deputy Secretary earlier.

Even for Nobel Prize, they cast the net wide and unheard of but suitable persons are chosen. But we do not see beyond our nose.

Many secretaries, though retiring at the age of 60, lined up positions for them and got them. But people like me who retired at the age of 58 were left high and dry.

I told you about my suitability for the position of L.G., Pondicherry, because I was the first Collector and DM. People there still remember me for my development work and knowledge of French. Incidentally, Shri N.N. Jha is a good friend of mine for a long time and he is suitable. But I could have done better there. Again and again, I feel that we do not seem to bother about anything these days. In the previous dispensations, even if they made three appointments on considerations other than merit, they did at least another two or three on merit and suitability.

You could call for my CRs and have a look provided it is still there. I had no difficulty in empanelment as secretary, nor was any adverse remark ever communicated to me. So I presume that I reasonably did well, to put it that way. Some Cabinet Secretary or Secretary (Personnel) with adverse remarks in his or her CRs must have given a ruling that these records should be destroyed after five years from retirement. I wrote to Shri Kamal Pande to reconsider this decision. But there is no reply, as usual.

Please do not think that I am either a mad-cap or naïve; Government is not obliged to give me any position at all. But there has to be an apparent norm and justice.

Sorry for this long letter. I felt that I should write to you because you advise on appointments. I shall be grateful, if you could kindly convey my feelings to the Hon. PM and the Hon. Deputy PM.

(G. Sundaram)

To:
Shri Ashok Saikia,
Additional Secretary to the PM,
Prime Minister's Office.

———

(4)

25th December 2004

Respected Sir,

Apropos administrative reforms, you are reported to have stated that officers' educational qualifications have often nothing to do with their experience. Very true—this is because of our system. I myself had occasions to tell your goodself that people who never worked in Finance or Commerce or even studied economics were appointed Finance Secretary, Commerce Secretary, Executive Director, World Bank and even Economic Adviser to PM!

Luckily, I had no such problem till I became secretary. I had no empanelment problem. But some seniors deliberately pushed me to civil supplies (although it is important), consumer affairs and tourism. This is the reason why, I repeatedly request you (mentioned to you even when you were out of office about my tenuous connection with the then government because of my Cadre, Gujarat, and they did nothing) to compensate for it.

Only Dr. V. Kurien selected me purely on the basis that I studied in Brussels (M.Phil.,), with the EEC, my Ph.D., from the Delhi School of Economics was on India-EEC Relations, I knew French well, etc., for aid co-ordination for Operation Flood-II as Counsellor in our Mission in Brussels. Ambassador Davé used me for my economic and commercial knowledge with the EEC too. When Shri Montek Singh was my secretary in commerce, he was good enough to assign me the EEC work and it fell to my lot to negotiate the third and current agreement between India and the EEC (It was initialed by me and later signed by Shri Pranab Mukherjee).

Mr. J.N. Dixit also felt in 1996 that should a non-IFS officer be appointed as Ambassador to Brussels as hitherto, I should be the one vis-à-vis M.S. Gill, Rajgopal and Sudarshan Agarwal who knew nothing about the EEC. But Shri A.N. Ram, IFS, my batch-mate was appointed. When he returned without completing his tenure, he was good enough to suggest my name. But again, an IFS officer, Shri. Chandrasekhar Dasgupta, my batch-mate was appointed. On both the occasions, Shri Narasimha Rao had cleared my name.

I had also met Mrs. Gandhi four or five months ago and presented my case. I told her that I was prepared to go to even Arunachal or Andamans (a small post: a BJP politician is now the Lt. Governor; Shri Shivraj-ji also knows me well; I worked with him in Defence). I requested her also to consider me for the Planning Commission or the Human Rights Commission where age is no problem – I am now 66. I briefed Shri Pulok Chatterjee also. Shri T.K.A. Nair and Shri B.K. Chaturvedi know me well.

I thought that I would renew my request by giving this background.

(G. Sundaram)

To:
Dr. Manmohan Singh,
Hon. Prime Minister.

(5)

1st March 2005

Respected Madam,

Greetings. I would request you to spare a few minutes of your valuable time for me in reading this letter.

You would recall that I had called on you a few months ago with my c.v., and my requests (only requests enclosed now). I have been keeping the Hon. PM also posted. He knows me for a long time. Although he is a fair-minded person, the coalition politics seems to be weighing him down and hence this letter to you.

*I understand that Mr. *****, the former Commerce Secretary, is likely to be posted as our Ambassador to Belgium and the EU. Although he never worked in the Commerce Ministry, he came straight as Commerce Secretary through the same coalition politics route during the BJP and NDA rule. He was even given extension beyond retirement. He was to go to the Competition Commission but for a court ruling against it. After a few months from retirement, he is brought in as Adviser in the Commerce Ministry en route to Brussels, I believe.*

Although it is extremely difficult to pick up in a Ministry, particularly in economic ministries like Commerce at the level of Additional Secretary or Secretary (many such appointments were made by the NDA), he might have done so and perhaps did well. I have no dispute with this. But as far as the Brussels post is concerned, I dare say that I have better credentials:

1. *Leather Export Promotion Council (field of the Commerce Ministry).*
2. *Deputy Secretary / Director – Commerce Ministry.*
3. *Additional Secretary, Commerce Ministry.*

4. Studied in the University of Brussels (M.Phil.,) on the same subject.

5. Was with the European Economic Commission for six months.

6. My Ph.D., on the subject from the Delhi School of Economics.

7. Worked as Counsellor in Brussels. (I was selected by Dr. V. Kurien purely on the basis of this background for his 'Operation Flood' co-ordination. But Ambassador used my economic and commercial knowledge.)

8. I know French well.

9. I would have become Commerce Secretary but for the fact that Mr. Tejendra Khanna was my senior in Service and junior in age and hence blocked me.

10. The third and current Agreement between India and EU was fully negotiated and initialed by me.

(Please see my web-site also)

The late J.N. Dixit also felt in 1996 that should a non-IFS officer be appointed as Ambassador to Brussels as hitherto, I should be the one vis-à-vis Messrs M.S. Gill, Rajgopal – the then Cabinet Secretary – and Sudarshan Agarwal because they knew nothing about the EEC. Though my name was cleared twice, it went to the IFS. It is my idea that the post should come back to the IAS and I am happy it is happening, but ironically not for me!

I understand political compulsions. This is also unfortunately a country of 'sifarish' and connections. I am not connected or related to any big-wig. But this should inevitably be only in a few cases as during Mrs. Gandhi's and Rajivji's times. Both of them went by merit for important positions – but for this, she would not have appointed Rao Sahib as Cabinet Secretary who was brought in by the Janata from the A.P. Cadre. When I was moved out of the Pollution Control Board in Gujarat, arbitrarily, I brought that to the notice of Rajivji through Mr. Mani Shankar Iyer and he rewarded me later. Incidentally, Mr. Mani Shankar Iyer knows my entire Brussels background; you could check with him and I have not briefed him.

Madam, sorry for having taken your time. I had made similar straightforward requests to the NDA too, but they never bothered.

I hate to make requests of this kind, but the wretched system makes me do so.

I am not trying to praise you - you must be having a logical mind. But for this, you would not have given up the Prime Ministership. No other person would have done it. I would only request you to apply the same logical mind to my case and appreciate my merit and my straightforward approach and do justice to me.

(G. SUNDARAM)

To:
Mrs. Sonia Gandhi ji,
10, Janpath,
New Delhi – 110 011

Only Mrs. Sonia Gandhi acknowledged my letter. I still feel that an occidental logical and analytical mind made her do this unlike the oriental example of Mrs. M.G. Ramachandran who was a Chief Minister only for eighteen days or so.

(1. For NDA in the letter, read Brajesh Mishra.

2. I wonder whether the reader will construe that I am sycophantic in my letter above. My favourite columnist, T.J.S. George also wrote recently that a Congressman was writing a sycophantic letter seeking a favour. My answer to such criticism:
   (a) How do I communicate with her? I have to state all the facts which is possible only in a letter;
   (b) the burden of this book is to abolish 'the sifarish' culture and encourage a straightforward approach based on merits. In this case, while the post was brought back to the IAS as argued by me, it was not given to me because of 'the sifarish' culture and also the coalition politics. But the candidate could have been given another post;
   (c) I have lived in Europe and know the West European mind. For instance, when the Embassy of India, Belgium, wanted me to go round to the households where Indian children were adopted, many Belgian parents told me that the Indian kids were more emotional, sentimental and strong in mathematics than their own kids who were more analytical in their approach. So I felt that way in respect of Mrs. Sonia

Gandhi too; (I have since been proved right by P.M. Nair's observations in his very recent book that President Abdul Kalam was indeed ready to swear her in as PM)

(d) Moreover, this is also the reality. She calls the shots in respect of important appointments!)

In this regard, I had read in the autobiography of that outstanding civil servant, Badr-ud-din Tyabji, ICS, when he did not get what he aspired for, he rationalised by stating that he thought well of himself for a particular post, but he did not know what others actually thought of him. So I wanted to see my CRs to know how I was assessed by others. I never had an adverse remark communicated to me. But they would not show it even after retirement. In fact, some one told me that the CRs were destroyed five years after one's retirement – this ruling or practice must have been introduced by a Cabinet Secretary or Secretary, Personnel, with some adverse remarks! I wrote to Kamal Pande, but there was no reply as usual. So I requested a close and objective officer who was also a Cabinet Secretary with whom I had worked and who had seen my CRs. He told me that there was not even a single adverse remark except for a tangential one by a non-IAS secretary to deflect me from Commerce. Some years, it was 'outstanding' as Director A.N. Jha in the Mussoorie training academy recorded in the first year itself. In my case, it would be 'Very Good +' to 'outstanding' on the whole, but not less than 'Very Good +', he told me.

* * *

22

Several Worlds

I have had the opportunity of visiting many parts of the world as the following article would show:

Indian Airlines Journal, *Swagat*, October 1996: "All the Capes": "There are several interesting spots in the world which are known as Capes – in Africa, in the Americas and in Europe. In India too, the edge of the subcontinent was once called Cape Comorin.

Some of these spots have been developed into towns while others remain only tourist spots with perhaps just a lighthouse. However, these places tell the visitor a lot about the country and its people.

Cape Comorin – 'The Land's End' and known now by a more attractive name, Kanyakumari, is a place where tourists flock to see the rising as well as the setting sun. Vivekananda Rock and a tall statue of Tiruvalluvar are also situated here. It used to be a small, beautiful township in the deep south of India, but has now fallen victim to haphazard constructions. This is a place where one can see the confluence of the three seas and one doesn't really know whether the sun rises from the Bay of Bengal or the Indian Ocean.

From Cape Comorin, Cape North in Norway is a long way off.

Norway itself is an interesting country apart from being 'The Land of the Midnight Sun'. Rugged mountains rise suddenly from the sea and there are innumerable fjords and lakes. There is practically no place without a mountain or a scenic lake. In this respect, one is reminded of Switzerland. But, in Norway, nature stands in naked beauty and it is not painted or manicured as in Switzerland.

There was a steady drizzle when we landed in Oslo almost near midnight. But it was twilight because of the midnight sun, and seemed as though there was no real darkness at all.

We took a flight in the morning from Oslo. Our first stop was a small town on the banks of a lake in the midst of mountains in north Norway. The next stop was Tromso, an important town in the north. From Tromso, we took a twenty-seater Twin-Otter plane to Hammerfest. The Twin-Otter bridges the islands of the far north with the rest of the world by connecting Tromso through regular flights. After crossing a number of wild mountain ranges and fjords, the plane landed in the northernmost town in the world, Hammerfest.

This region is now known as 'Land of the Lapps' with its vast open spaces and stretches of barren tundra. In area, it surpasses the whole of Denmark, but has a population of only 80 or 90 thousand and only three per cent of the land is arable. The interior consists of a mountain plateau 1,400 metres above sea level, dotted with lakes and sparse vegetation barely sufficient to provide winter pasture for reindeers.

We took off from Hammerfest within about 10 minutes. The plane flew over a range of mountains before landing in Honningsvag, which is situated on the island of Mageroya which houses Cape North.

Although Honningsvag is a small village cut off from the world, it has all the modern facilities including one or two very good hotels. TV and radio provide leisure time activities to the local population. The road to Cape North passes through mountains and lakes. There is practically nothing in this vast, vacant tundra. As you go along, you will see a few summer camps or grazing reindeer. You may meet one or two Lapplander families in their colourful costumes. Most of them have adapted to the modern way of life. But quite a few still follow their old style of living.

We started from Honningsvag around 11 pm, and found the place still bathed in sunlight. As we drove slowly through the mountains, we saw the sun behind the peaks and clouds—a breathtaking sight indeed! We reached Cape North which rises like a colossus from the Arctic Ocean to a height of 1000 feet. In spite of the sun around, we encountered a strong cold wind coming from the north. Unlike Cape Comorin, no construction has taken place on Cape North. There is only one small building with a restaurant, a curio shop and a post office, providing a view of the sun from the small building. You can post a letter from Cape North with a special postal stamp and cancellation. You also get a certificate saying you've crossed the Arctic Circle and visited Cape North.

On the day of the summer solstice on 21st June, the sun is well above the horizon at midnight. As the days pass, the sun begins its descent towards the horizon. At the end of July, it touches the horizon. At the end of July, it touches the horizon on the Arctic Ocean, but immediately starts moving up. This drama goes on till August in Cape North. There is no night for about three months in summer. But as the months pass by the sun goes down and is not seen at all for two or three months during the winter. During that period, there is no day in this part of the world. Winter darkness is pierced by "Pyrotechnics" – the Northern Lights or Aurora Borealis, enough to read a newspaper. There are long periods of snowfall in March and April and then finally it's time for spring.

Northern Norway should be perpetually covered with ice owing to its geographical position above the Arctic Circle. However, thanks to the warm Gulf Stream which creates favourable conditions for human beings, animals and plants, the place is habitable and provides a variety of attractions. In spite of nature's caprice, people enjoy a good life in these parts. Farming, forestry, fishing and mining provide the bulk of the population with a means of livelihood.

In many other respects too, northern Norway is a land of contrasts. The weather-beaten coast contrasts dramatically with the sheltered in-land districts; the desolate mountain moors with the bustling lives in the towns; the weathered rock of the rugged mountains with the sandy beaches, strewn with smooth stones. Vacationers come here for winter sports, for skiing and to enjoy the continuous sun during summer.

Compare this with Cape Horn on the other side of the world, near Antarctica. Before doing this, however, it would be advisable to take a look at another famous Cape – the Cape of Good Hope in South Africa. Very near the Cape of Good Hope, just a couple of miles away, is Cape Point in South Africa which juts into the sea trying to divide the Atlantic Ocean and the Indian Ocean. These Capes are about 100 kilometres away from Cape Town, the southernmost town in the African continent. Cape Town is beautiful with its beaches, Town Hall, ancient quarters where its original inhabitants settled and the Table Mountain as a backdrop to the town. The Table Mountain is like a 'table with a flat top, often covered with misty clouds which the local people liken to a 'table cloth'. The town very often faces strong winds so much so that it is difficult even to walk. But the wind keeps the town clean and free from pollution.

A drive on the well-paved mountain road through some beautiful towns takes one to the Cape Point and the Cape of Good Hope. On the way, one passes through Simons Town, which is the naval base in South Africa and also houses a memorial to Sir Cecil Rhodes, once Premier of Cape Province and who instituted the famous Rhodes Scholarship.

When one reaches Cape Point by car or bus, a van takes one to the highest point here. They are now constructing a cable car to that point. From the light house on this topmost point, one can see on the left Cape Bay and on the other side high majestic mountains. The landscape near Cape Point and the Cape of Good Hope is similar to the landscape near Cape North. Unlike Cape Comorin, which has become a bustling and haphazard town, these two Capes are without construction except for a restaurant and a shop as in Cape North.

Cape Horn, the southernmost point in South America, can be reached either from Buenos Aires in Argentina or Santiago in Chile. A flight to Ushuaia, the southernmost city in the world, from Buenos Aires takes three and a half hours – one could say the same time as a flight from Leh to Cape Comorin. From the flight, one can see vast stretches of vacant land with farm houses here and there. Tourists get off the plane in different cities for different attractions. For instance, in the southern Rio Grand, they get off to see not only the native people living here, but also the second largest glacier in the world. But as the plane approaches Ushuaia, the entire scenery changes and there are steep mountains particularly Mt Olivia, which dominates the scene. These peaks are snow-clad even in summer perhaps because of their closeness to Antarctica. One gets a birds-eye-view of Ushuaia and the mountainous surroundings, the sea and Beagle Bay on which Ushuaia is actually located.

Ushuaia's different panoramic views let you admire the town and its Andean maritime background. The present navy building was actually a prison long ago where murderers and other hardened criminals were sent. Today, however, it is a bustling tourist town with an increase in population of 400 per cent over the last 18 years. The Museum of the End of the World is also located in Ushuaia. Similarly, it also boasts of the End of the World train and station. The National Park of Tierra del Fuego can be reached by train via the End of the World station. Although Tierra del Fuego is above the Antarctic Circle, the weather is somewhat cold even in summer because of strong winds. You can also take a cruise in the Beagle Channel by catamaran. The cruise takes one very near Sea Lions Island on which one can see a large number of sea lions in their natural habitat. On Cormorants Island, one gets a glimpse of a lot of birds. There is also a light house in the middle of the channel which guides the boats. After about three hours, the catamaran takes you to Harberton where you can take a walking tour. The nearby Martillo Island is a rookery of penguins which is an excellent sight to see. Penguins migrate from these islands depending upon the weather.

The border between Argentina and Chile runs down the middle of Beagle Channel. The catamaran generally keeps itself to the Argentinian side. When I went there, the Government of Chile instructed their Consul General in Ushuaia to receive me and take me to Port Williams on their side. So the catamaran made a special stop. I was received by the local Naval Commander and Mayor and taken round the small town of 2,000 people. Port Williams, the southernmost town in the world, is located on Navarino Island. There is a museum here depicting the history of the island. The photographs in the museum indicated that the original inhabitants known as Yamanas, were progressively absorbed by invaders to these shores. When I went there, there were only two old Yamana women left speaking the Yamana language.

There is a comfortable hospice in Port Williams for visitors. The airport is small where small planes can land. As I have been repeatedly advocating, these small planes are used for the benefit of tourists. There is some sort of an informal schedule and there is no full-fledged airport. The tower ensures safety of landing and take-off. Otherwise, the arrangement is informal and the small planes take the tourist to different places of interest although remotely situated. They would have given me a flight over Cape Horn which is supposed to be the southernmost point in Latin America located in Chile, but for the bad weather that day. Unlike Cape North, Cape Comorin, Cape Point or the Cape of Good Hope, one cannot reach Cape Horn by road. It is still an unexplored rock where only naval planes land occasionally.

A cruise to Cape Horn takes about eight days and as in Cape Comorin, the Antarctic Ocean, the Pacific Ocean and the Atlantic Ocean meet here. It was also the passage of Sir Francis Drake.

There are also other Capes, which have yet to be reached easily. For instance, Cape San Pablo in Argentina, about 140 kilometres from Ushuaia, is reachable only by road. There is a hospice on the seafront for tourists. However, communication facilities could be better as in Norway or in South Africa.

There are also several boat excursions one can take including the one to the mysterious continent of Antarctica, which is about 1,000 kilometres.

It is also possible to reach Staten Island after some days of navigation on the east. This is an almost unexplored island which is also a cemetery of ships and is situated in the Atlantic Ocean on the east of Tierra del Fuego. Just above is the famous Falklands known in Argentina as the Malvinas.

After a seven-day journey by sea one can visit the fjords located in the western section of the Beagle Channel. Many glaciers belonging to the Darwin range can be seen here. In fact, some of the glaciers have no names yet!

In Tierra del Fuego, night lasts for about three hours during summer as it is above the Polar Antarctic Circle. In the Antarctic, however, since it is below the Polar Circle, there is no daylight around the winter solstice of June 21.

Contrast this to the summer solstice of North Cape and northern Norway where there is no night!

All the Capes have something distinctive to offer the traveller – a beauty that is awesome – making man feel 'tiny' in the face of nature."

(In the aforesaid article, the trip to North Cape was purely personal when I was posted in Brussels).

But not even a single trip of mine was a junket. When I was leading a delegation once, one of the members asked me whether I was an influential person or manipulating things to have trips abroad frequently. I replied to him that if that was so, I would have gone to the United States long ago. In fact, I had not gone to the United States at all till 1995 when I was in the Ministry of Civil Supplies, Consumer Affairs and Public Distribution – a year before my retirement. Our officer in charge of the Tea Board in New York had requested me to visit the USA when I was in the Ministry of Commerce. But there was no real opportunity in the public interest. Commerce Secretary A.V. Ganesan also felt that I was too senior for any training programme although the Additional Secretary and Financial Adviser – from the same cadre of Rajasthan as A.V. Ganesan – managed to go for a training programme. So when I had to study the Forward Markets and the Regulatory Commissions in the USA, I had that opportunity and visited the USA for the first time. Following that, for the first time a Cabinet note was prepared for creating Forward Commodity Market in India although it had not taken off because the elections were coming up and, as I had already indicated, many proposals took a long time to fructify in our country. In any case, I initiated an international commodity exchange for pepper in Cochin, which became a reality later.

Similarly, when I went to South Africa and came back, the South African Minister for Planning and Poverty Alleviation, Jay Naidoo, himself called on me here to collect some administrative details. I got one of the old Block Development Manuals of the government of Maharashtra from Bombay to pass on to them to set up an administrative set up at the village and district levels which was lacking in South Africa. Even after I left the Ministry of Civil Supplies, Consumer Affairs and Public Distribution, the Ministry of Agriculture invited me to a meeting to tie-up some arrangements for farms in Zambia on the basis of my tour report. In fact, a private company from Madras tried to make it a successful venture there. The tours, both within the country and abroad, should serve the pubic interest.

* * *

Epilogue

I have come a long way from Kilpattu. So I have no regrets.

I feel that I have served the public reasonably well. I would continue to do so in some form or the other. There would be no retirement for me.

Postscript

Several civic issues including water supply of the locality where I live have been tackled. As P.K. Davé, former adviser to the Governor of Tamil Nadu, told me that the Tamil Nadu administration had to be told and they would carry out the orders efficiently, even if they lacked the initiative themselves. But the people should also co-operate in civic matters; they should cultivate civic sense so that the environment could be preserved.

There was an ancient temple in my village not less than a hundred years old because I had seen my grandfather worshipping there. The Hindu Religious Endowment Department was prepared to help, but people of the village were not in a position to give a matching contribution. So the temple was renovated by me with the help of a philanthropist. The villagers, of course, gave physical help.

India is no doubt a vibrant democracy. But the politicians seem to be taking it in the reverse direction and democracy is facing silent danger. I am not stating that siblings of politicians should not take to politics at all; but it should not become a family occupation; politics should be a calling. It is good that many educated youngsters have taken to politics. But I do not know whether they would have the idealism or ethics of the old-world politicians like Gandhiji, Nehru, Rajaji, Kamaraj, Annadurai or even that of Indira, Rajiv, Chandra Shekhar, Vajpayee, Advani, EMS, AKG, Indrajit Gupta and so on. Money-making and corruption are justified in the name of politics and elections. Many of them have no ostensible means of livelihood except politics. Though politics is the art of the possible, it has become totally unprincipled; opportunistic alliances even by big parties have become the order of the day. They have taken the people for granted or for perfect fools. Since people have become helpless, they have also started making money during elections.

To get out of this vicious circle, I thought that I would form a political party myself and call it the **Honest People's Party** with these broad objectives:

1. Honesty and Clean Politics (possible!)
2. Self-discipline;
3. Credibility;
4. No religion, caste or pseudo-secularism;
5. No criminals (once a charge-sheet is filed, subject to scrutiny for false cases);
6. Transparency;
7. No business or big contributions (only small contributions of Re.1/- to Rs.10,000/- without multiplicity to circumvent);
8. Audited accounts and free inspection;
9. Payment of Tax;
10. Follow scrupulously even the unwritten rules of the Election Commission and the code.

In this regard, the USA is a bad example in many respects – even conduct of elections and campaign funds. Some of the Continental countries could be good examples. No high-power, costly campaigns; publicity about candidates only through advertisements in the media and in specific earmarked places (not posters or cut-outs everywhere disfiguring walls and digging roads or street politics). It will be 'E-Democracy'.

There is an interesting article on political parties by T.K. Arun in *The Economic Times* (March 17th, 2005): "Just being a collection of power-seekers or power-brokers is not sufficient to qualify as a political party ..... the political party is dead, whether it is the Congress, BJP or RJD ..... India's problems cannot be fixed without re-building the institution of the political party..... Constant engagement with civil society and mediation between the people and the state do not figure in the agenda of any party. India's problems cannot be fixed without putting these back on the agenda. And that calls for rebuilding the institution of the political party..... This kind of party building from the bottom is a lot of hard work, quite different from strategising in New Delhi". My party, I trust, will fulfill this with your cooperation.

You may feel that politics is the last refuge of only the scoundrels; it should not be so. I thought of an NGO, but there are many and they only advise. Politics should become a calling to serve the people and the public interest and not for personal aggrandisement.

You are most welcome to join this Party.

* * *

Index

INDIA'S
SPY
AGENCIES
Shaken not Stirred

AF519863

Lt Col Sunil S Parihar

MANAS PUBLICATIONS
(We Convert Fighters into Writers)
(Publishers, Library Suppliers, Importers & Exporters)
4402/5-A, Ansari Road (Opp HDFC Bank)
Darya Ganj, New Delhi-110 002 (India)
Off. (23260783, 23265523, Fax: 011-23272766
E-mail: manaspublications@vsnl.com
manaspublications@gmail.com

ISBN 978-81-7049-438-6
₹ 595/-

Designed at
Manas Publications

Printed in India at
HS Offsets, Delhi
and published by Suman Lata for
Manas Publications, 4402/5-A,
Ansari Road (Opp HDFC Bank),
Darya Ganj, New Delhi-110 002 (INDIA)

Contents

For

Anandita, Anaheeta and Ransher

INTRODUCTION

India's intelligence agencies, despite suffering many intelligence failures, are like James Bond's martinis – 'Shaken not Stirred'. Kargil shook them up a bit, but could not stir their mind-set and ethos, and they continued napping till 26/11, when they were shaken out of their deep slumber, but still remain largely unstirred as evidenced by Mumbai blasts on 13 July '11(13/7).

In India, everyone talks of an intelligence failure whenever a blast or an act of terror takes place. The central or the state intelligence agencies are held responsible by various politicians depending on their respective political affiliations. There are 'big fights' on TV where some arm-chair analysts talk big and end up stating the obvious about what went wrong and what needs to be done. The select audience expresses its concern even as most of them are there to grab their 15 seconds of fame. Then all is forgotten in a few days. Public memory is short after all. And life goes on.

Why our intelligence fails time and again? We all know that intelligence is a highly complex and critical aspect of a nation's security, which warrants expertise of specialists. But who are at the helm of India's spy machine? The generalist bureaucrats, of course. A recent report on Indian intelligence agencies by Institute of Defence Studies and Analysis (IDSA) blames the bureaucracy for standing in the way of comprehensive intelligence reforms. The report, apparently shelved for the time being, is unlikely to see the light of the day in its original form. The great Indian bureaucracy is always averse to any change that poses a challenge to their supremacy and as such, will ensure that suggested reforms remain on the backburner. The bureaucrats will also ensure that serving and retired officers and other professionals with ample expertise in the field of intelligence never get a controlling stake in the Indian intelligence set up. Bureaucrats virtually have a final say on intelligence issues, as their political masters seem to have neither the time nor inclination or expertise to oversee matters of such importance. Lack of political will to take the national security issues head on is quite clear from the fact that 64 years since her independence, India still doesn't have a National Security Doctrine.

But to be fair, one can't just blame only the usual suspects, the politicians and bureaucrats. There are so many other factors as well. The aim is not to witch-hunt or pin-point responsibility for India's various intelligence failures but to go beyond the obvious in answering the larger question: why our intelligence fails and why the Indian intelligence agencies are, the way they are? How do they compare with world's major intelligence agencies? What has been done since the 1999 Kargil war or post -26/11 and more important, what still needs to be done? What are the reasons behind India's continued vulnerability to terror attacks? Why history repeats itself with dreadful monotony?

This book is actually a reminder that unless the Indian intelligence agencies wake-up from their somnolence and work like a well-oiled spy machine, attacks such as Kargil and 26/11 may happen yet again.

PRELUDE

Sometime in the late sixties, as a school boy, I happened to lay my hands on a book titled - The Adventures of Sherlock Holmes. Having assumed that it would be something similar to the adventures of Hardy Boys, I was somewhat disappointed at first, to find that it wasn't anything like that. But as I kept turning the pages, the fictional detective from London's Baker Street, intrigued me so much that the Victorian English of the book notwithstanding, I was completely hooked. His astuteness, logical reasoning, ability to take almost any guise and forensic science skills that he used so effectively in solving highly complicated cases, deeply fascinated and intrigued me.

Well, that was school boy stuff. A couple of years later, when I saw the movie *Gold Finger*, I found James Bond even more spell-binding. Badly bitten by the spy bug, I often wondered if I could become a professional spy some day. I wanted to step into the shoes of James Bond. Who doesn't, actually? Guns, gals, gadgets and great destinations, all make for an exciting world every man would like to explore.

Or does it?

The real spy world, as one realised much later, isn't half as glamorous as depicted in the spy flicks. Espionage is actually not only a hi-risk and painstaking venture, but also a thankless one. Spy games are played by all countries to safeguard their national interests, and when a spy gets exposed or lost, s/he is quickly disowned and replaced by another one. All said and done, it's a fascinating world; strange and murky without doubt, but fascinating nonetheless. So after my initial brush with the fictitious spies and those that ruled the reel world, I graduated to following the adrenaline–pumping and spine chilling exploits of super spies of real world.

In the annals of espionage, one name towers above all others: that of India born 'Kim' Philby, the ring-leader of the legendary Cambridge spies. A member of the British establishment, Philby joined the Secret Intelligence Service in 1940, rose to the head of Soviet counter-intelligence, and, as MI6's liaison with the CIA and the FBI, betrayed every secret of Allied operations to the Russians, fatally compromising covert actions to roll back the Iron Curtain in the early years of cold war.

The most fascinating and legendary spy however, was Mata Hari. Her name has become synonymous with spying, espionage and intrigue, even though I personally feel that she wasn't really a spy but more of an adventurer; *a femme fatale*. The woman who adopted this name was born Margaretha Zelle on August 7, 1876 in Leeuwarden, the Netherlands. In the little Dutch town where she grew up, her shopkeeper father lavished extremes of affection on his 'little princess'. It made her vain, self-centred and spoilt, and with an insatiable longing for male attention. But, overall she had a deprived childhood, being forced to live with relatives after her mother's death.

Her marriage to a Dutch army captain wasn't a happy one either. There were problems almost right away. She couldn't keep her eyes off the other officers and, as she was the first to admit, she did not have it within her to be 'a good housewife'. 'I was not content at home,' she later confessed. "I wanted to live like a colourful butterfly in the sun". The marriage was short-lived as there were serious differences between the couple, and, after her divorce, she moved alone in Europe. She took up dancing to earn money and became a professional mistress.

The critics enthused, "feline, trembling in a thousand rhythms, exotic yet deeply austere, slender and supple like a sacred serpent". She added spice to her act with subterfuge and lies. First there was her name - *Mata Hari,* meaning 'sunrise' or, more literally, "the eye of the day", in the language of the Dutch East Indies. Then there were the stories to the press, that she was the daughter of an Indian temple dancer' who had died giving birth to her, and that she grew up in a jungle in Java.

Her life became an unending performance, both on stage and off. Her success seemed unstoppable and the money came rolling in. But she still managed to spend more than she earned as she travelled Europe, picking up lovers, dropping some, keeping others. And German spy? That is what - in the fevered atmosphere of France in World War I, with Kaiser's troops encamped within its borders - she was shot for. She was instrumental in causing the deaths of tens of thousands of French soldiers, it was said, a crime that would ever after make her synonymous with seduction and treachery, and the ultimate *femme fatale.*

Except that she may not have been guilty at all. In a fascinating biography, American academic Pat Shipman makes the case that, far from being the betrayer, she was the one betrayed, and that by the breed she loved all her life - men. She was executed after an allegedly dubious trial at the outskirts of Paris on the morning of October 15, 1917.

Cut to Circa 1981. After passing out from the Indian Military Academy, when I joined my unit as a Second Lieutenant, I thought my dream of entering the spy world had finally come true when the Adjutant told me that I'd been appointed as the unit's Intelligence Officer. The feeling of elation however didn't last long as I realised that one's primary task was to update and carry the Commanding Officer's maps and his lunch as well, during tactical exercises. This was heart breaking indeed for someone who'd been waiting to step into the shoes of James Bond. But then, they say, dreams never die. Do they?

Eight years later, I was posted as General Staff Officer (Intelligence) at a brigade headquarters. By now I'd matured enough to realise that my dream of being a James Bond will remain just that - a dream. The flights of Bondesque fantasies didn't take off anymore. No fast cars and fancy gizmos. No gals either, as I was engaged to marry, and fooling around was out of the question. Guns too had lost their charm as one had seen and handled them aplenty. The job was pretty exciting and satisfying though. I stayed in the brigade officers' mess and another officer who resided there happened to be the OC LU, an Intelligence Corps officer. He turned out to be a wonderful person, an excellent officer and a thorough professional. In fact, it is officers like him that make an otherwise lackadaisical Int Corps tick at times.

Anyway, I learnt a great deal about the intelligence organisations and their functioning from this officer and the knowledge I thus acquired came in handy during my tenure at the brigade headquarters. Not only that, I found the intelligence job so exciting that I decided to join the Int Corps. The opportunity presented itself sooner that I had reckoned. As part of their expansion drive, the Int Corps was looking for volunteer officers from various branches of the army. Before putting in my application as a matter of courtesy, I went to my immediate boss, the Deputy Brigade Commander for his verbal approval. The dyed in the wool infantry officer that he was, he gave me a solid dressing down for my decision, which he thought was tantamount to professional hara-kiri.

I tried to convince him that the Int Corps was after all a part of the same army as the Infantry, and, whether good or bad, could not be given the step-sisterly treatment. He was, of course, not convinced, but gave me the nod in a 'go-to-hell' kind of manner. My application for the switch, though accepted by the Int Corps, was not cleared by the Military Secretary's (MS) branch, the final authority in such matters at the Army Headquarters. On enquiring from the concerned officer at the MS branch why I was not being allowed to side step to the Int Corps, all I got was a rather curt response; "friend, I have gone through your dossier and you are doing pretty fine. And even though you are hell-bent, I won't let you dig your own grave. Period". And that was the end of the matter. I left his office humming, '*Que Sera Sera*' and have had no regrets ever after. In fact, a decade later, when I was posted at the Army Headquarters MI Directorate, I realised that a simple soldier like me wasn't really cut out for the Int Corps. I also realised that analysing stuff and joining the dots - whether pieces of information or aerial imagery - was my forte...and perhaps *karma*. That perhaps explains a rather long chapter in this book on analysing intelligence analysis.

Though I still love watching Bond movies, I now strongly feel, that in the world of spying and espionage, it is actually guys like Sherlock Holmes, who provide vital leads and complete the intelligence cycle. Get set for some interesting reading.

Abbreviations

AI	Artificial Intelligence
ARC	Aviation Research Centre
BSF	Border Security Force
CIA	Central Intelligence Agency
CBI	Central Bureau of Investigation
CCSA	Cabinet Committee for Security Affairs
COMINT	Communication Intelligence
DCI	Director Central Intelligence
DG	Director General
DGMI	Director General Military Intelligence
DIPAC	Defence Image Processing and Analysis Centre
DRDO	Defence Research and Development Organisation
ELINT	Electronic Intelligence
ECM	Electronic Counter Measures

ER	Enhanced Reality
ESM	Electronic Support Measures
FBI	Federal Bureau of Investigation
GOC	General Officer Commanding
GSO	General Staff Officer
HuM	Harkat-ul-Mujahideen
HUMINT	Human Intelligence
IAF	Indian Air Force
IB	Intelligence Bureau
IDSA	Institute of Defence Studies and Analysis
IFSU	Intelligence and Field Security Unit
IMINT	Imagery Intelligence
Int Corps	Intelligence Corps
ISI	Inter Services Intelligence
IPKF	Indian Peace Keeping Force
JIA	Joint Intelligence Administration
JCIB	Joint Counter-intelligence Bureau
JCO	Junior Commissioned Officer
JIB	Joint Intelligence Bureau
JIC	Joint Intelligence Committee
JIM	Joint Intelligence Miscellaneous
JIN	Joint Intelligence North
JIT	Joint Intelligence Technical
JSTARS	Joint Surveillance and Target Attack Radar System
LCA	Light Combat Aircraft
LIC	Low Intensity Conflict
LICO	Low Intensity Conflict Operation
LoC	Line of Control
LTTE	Liberation Tigers of Tamil Eelam

LU	Liaison Unit
MAC	Multi Agency Centre
MI	Military Intelligence
MS	Military Secretary
NCO	Non-Commissioned Officer
NCTC	National Counter Terrorism Centre
NTRO	National Technical Research Organisation
OSD	Officer on Special Duty
POK	Pakistan Occupied Kashmir
R&AW	Research and Analysis Wing
R&D	Research and Development
SAR	Synthetic Aperture Radar
SFF	Special Frontier Force
SIGINT	Signal Intelligence
SSB	Special Service Bureau
TECHINT	Technical Intelligence
UAV	Unarmed Aerial Vehicle
VR	Virtual Reality

Glossary of Spy Terms

The spy world is filled with terms and codes unique to the business of spying. From technical jargon to slang, acronyms to established codes, newcomers to the intelligence arena are likely to encounter speech that they'll find difficult to decipher. So, here's a glossary of common spy terms; some are not so common actually, having originated in cold war era and thus more relevant to CIA/erstwhile KGB, but interesting nevertheless.

Action officer – The case officer designated to perform an operational act during a clandestine operation, especially in hostile territory.

Agent – A person, usually a foreign national, who has been recruited by a staff case officer from an intelligence service to perform clandestine missions.

Agent-in-place – An agent serving as a penetration into an intelligence target who has been recruited or has volunteered to stay in place.

Ambush	–	The surprise capture and arrest of a case officer in an act of espionage by an opposing counter-intelligence or security service.
(the) Appendix	–	The tower in Lubyanka that houses the KGB's most sensitive departments. It is a nine-story tower that connects the old and new wings of the building and overlooks an inner courtyard.
Asset	–	A clandestine source or method, usually an agent.
Bailout point	–	The point, during a vehicular run under surveillance, at which the action officer riding as a passenger is planning to bail out of the car in order to elude surveillance.
Bang and burn	–	Demolition and sabotage operations.
BIGOT list	–	A list of the names of all persons, who are privy to the plans for a sensitive intelligence operation; it dates back to World War II when Allied orders for officers were stamped TO GIB for those being sent to Gibraltar for preparations for the invasion of North Africa; later their orders were stamped BIG OT (TO GIB backwards) when they were sent back to begin planning Operation Overlord, the invasion of Normandy.
Black bag job	–	A surreptitious entry operation usually conducted by the FBI against a domestically located foreign intelligence target.
Black operations	–	Clandestine or covert operations not attributable to the organisation carrying them out.
Bona fides	–	An operative's true identity, affiliation, or intentions.

Bridge agent – An agent who acts as a courier or go-between from a case officer to an agent in a denied area.

Brief encounter – Any brief physical contact between a case officer and an agent under threat of surveillance.

Brush pass – A brief encounter where something is passed between a case officer and an agent.

Bumper-lock – A harassing move in which vehicular surveillance follows the target officer so closely that the surveilling car's front bumper is almost locked to the rear bumper of the target car.

Bust-out – A leak of electronic communications from a secure enclosure before they are encrypted by the code machine.

Cam-car – A vehicle equipped with a concealed camera used for clandestine casing and surveillance operations.

Case officer – An operations officer serving as an official staffer of an intelligence service.

Casuals – Casual observers to a surveillance exercise; non-participants visible in the area.

(the) Centre – Russian intelligence headquarters in Moscow.

Cheka – Russian secret police founded in 1917 to serve the Bolshevik Party; one of the many forerunners of the KGB.

Chokepoint – A narrow passage, such as a bridge, tunnel, or Metro station, used as a surveillance or counter surveillance tool for channelling the opposing force or monitoring their passage.

CIA – The Central Intelligence Agency of the United States formed in 1947 to conduct foreign intelligence collection, covert action, and counter-intelligence operations abroad. Also responsible for providing finished intelligence to US policy-makers.

CID – The Clandestine Imaging Division of the Office of Technical Service of the CIA. Responsible for providing technical support to clandestine agent operations in the form of photography, secret writing, and video surveillance.

(the) Citadel – A super secret department in US intelligence responsible for collecting foreign signals and communications intelligence.

Clandestine operation – An intelligence operation designed to remain secret as long as possible.

Clandestine Service – The operational arm of the CIA responsible for classic espionage operations, usually with human assets. Also known as the Directorate of Operations (DO) and formerly the Directorate of Plans (DP).

CLOAK – A sensitive disguise and deception illusionary technique first deployed by the CIA in Moscow during the mid-1970s.

Code – A system used to obscure a message by use of a cipher, mark, symbol, sound, innocuous verse, or piece of music.

COMINT – Communications intelligence, usually gathered by technical interception and code breaking, but also by use of human agents and surreptitious entry.

Commo-communications	–	The various forms of secure electronic and nonelectronic communications used in clandestine operations.
Commo plan	–	The various secret communication methods employed with a particular agent.
Compartmenting: – vertical; lateral; double		Various ways to ensure that information is held by only those who have a 'need-to-know' in an organisation. Vertical denies information up or down the chain of command, and lateral denies information from peer groups. Double is spoofing the original group who held the information into believing the operation has ended when it has simply moved to a new compartment.
Compromised	–	When an operation, asset, or agent is uncovered and cannot remain secret.
Concealment device	–	Any one of a variety of innocuous devices used to secretly store and transport materials relating to an operation.
Control	–	In a surveillance exercise, the one directing the team remotely, usually by electronic communications.
Controller	–	Often used interchangeably with handler, but usually means a hostile force is involved, that is, the agent has come under control of the opposition.
Cover stop	–	A stop made while under-surveillance that provides an ostensibly innocent reason for a trip.
Covert action operation (CA)	–	An operation kept secret for only a finite period of time, or an operation whose real source remains secret

because the operation is attributed to another source.

Cryptonym – Code name; crypt or crypto for short, always capitalized. GT and CK prefixes to code names are used to identify the nature of the clandestine source. These two prefixes were both 'diagraph' identifiers for the Soviet and East European program during this period. The diagraph is used in front of the cryptonym of the source as a more formal way of referring to the subject, not unlike putting 'Mr' in front of 'Smallwood'.

Cutout – A mechanism or person that acts as a compartment between the members of an operation but which allows them to pass material or messages securely.

DAGGER – A sophisticated disguise first used in the Soviet Union in the 1970s.

Dangle operation – An operation in which an enticing intelligence target is dangled in front of an opposition service in hopes they will think him or her a bona fide recruit. The dangle is really a double agent.

Dead drop – A secret location where materials can be left in concealment for another party to retrieve. This eliminates the need for direct contact in hostile situations.

Dead telephone – A signal or code passed with the telephone without speaking.

Defector – A person who has intelligence value who volunteers to work for another intelligence service. He may be requesting asylum or can remain in place.

Double agent – An agent who has come under the control of another intelligence service and is being used against his original handlers.

Dzerzhinsky Square - Historic site in Moscow of Lubyanka Prison, longtime headquarters of the Soviet security organs, including Cheka, NKVD, and KGB. Now the headquarters of the FSB, the internal security service that replaced the Second Chief Directorate of the KGB.

EEI - Essential elements of information; an outline to be used for collecting intelligence on a particular topic.

ELINT - Electronic intelligence, usually collected by technical interception, such as telemetry from a rocket launch collected by receivers at a distance.

(the) Emerald City - The code name of the Special Surveillance Team used for the CIA Headquarters Building during their exercises.

Escort officer - The operations officer assigned to lead a defector along an exfiltration route.

Exfiltration operation - A clandestine rescue operation designed to get a defector, refugee, or operative and his or her family out of harm's way.

(the) Eye - The person on the surveillance team who has the target under visual observation at any given moment.

Film loop - A loop of film used to project or record a sequence of images on a continuous basis.

FINESSE - Sensitive disguises developed by the CIA using a Hollywood consultant and contractors.

First Chief Directorate (First CD) – The foreign intelligence arm of the KGB, now known as the SVR.

FLIR – Forward-looking infra-red device.

Foots (feet) – Members of a surveillance team who are working on foot and riding as passengers in a surveillance car.

(the) Forest – New location of KGB headquarters outside of the Moscow Ring Road.

FSB – Internal security service in Russia, successor to the KGB's Second Chief Directorate (internal counter-intelligence).

GAD – The Graphics and Authentication Division of the Office of Technical Service, responsible for operational disguise and false documentation capabilities for the CIA.

GAMBIT – A highly sensitive disguise developed for the CIA with the help of their Hollywood consultant. It was first used in Indo-China in 1971.

Ghost surveillance – Extremely discreet and seemingly omnipresent surveillance, working mostly out of the view of the target.

GRU – The Soviet military intelligence organisation.

Hostile service, surveillance, etc. – Terms used to describe the organisations and activities of the 'opposition services,' aka 'the enemy'.

HUMINT – Human intelligence, collected by human sources, such as agents.

HVA – East German foreign intelligence service.

Illegal – A KGB operative infiltrated into a target country and operating without the protection of diplomatic immunity.

IMINT – Image intelligence, usually collected by high-altitude planes or space vehicles.

Impersonal – Secret communication techniques used between a case officer and a human intelligence asset when no physical contact is possible or desired.

Infiltration operation communications – The covert moving of an operative into a target area with the idea that his presence or true affiliation will go undetected for the appropriate amount of time.

Internal Operations – CIA operations inside the Soviet Bloc during the Cold War.

In the black – Surveillance-free for a time span greater than a few seconds.

In the gap – Surveillance-free for a few seconds but not as long as a minute.

In the wind – When a target of surveillance has escaped and left for parts unknown.

KAPELLE device – A super secret communications security device used by the KGB.

KGB – The all-powerful intelligence and security service of the USSR during the Cold War. Ultimate successor to Cheka. Disbanded into the SVR and the FSB in 1991.

First CD – First Chief Directorate of the KGB; foreign intelligence.

Legend (cover) – The complete cover story developed for an operative.

Local agent – An agent recruited in a particular target area to do a local task.

Lockstep – When a surveillance team is following so close on foot they seem to be moving in lockstep with the target.

"L" pill – A lethal cyanide capsule issued to intelligence operatives, who would prefer to take their own life rather than be caught and tortured.

Lubyanka – The prison on Dzerzhinsky Square in Moscow that is the traditional headquarters of the Soviet intelligence services. Now occupied by the FSB.

METKA – A KGB umbrella program that encompassed research on all their various tagging and marking substances, like spy dust.

Microdot – A photographic reduction of a secret message so small it can be hidden in plain sight under the period at the end of this sentence.

MI5 – The British domestic and foreign counter-intelligence service responsible for national internal security.

MI6 – The British foreign intelligence service.

Mole – A human penetration into an intelligence service or other highly sensitive organisation. Quite often a mole is a defector who agrees to work in place.

Moscow rules – The ultimate tradecraft methods for use in the most hostile of the operational environments. During the Cold War, Moscow was considered the most difficult of operating environments.

Mossad – Israel's foreign intelligence service.

NIACT – The CIA cable slug that indicates that 'night action' is necessary.

NKVD – The Soviet security and intelligence service from 1934 to 1946.

NOC – A CIA case officer operating under non-official cover, similar to the KGB illegal.

OC, Operations Course	–	The eighteen-week course that all CIA case officers take at the beginning of their careers.
OGPU	–	The Soviet intelligence and security service from 1923 to 1934.
Okhrana	–	The secret police under the Russian czars, 1881-1917.
One-time pad (OTP)	–	Sheets of paper or silk printed with random five-number group ciphers to be used to encode and decode enciphered messages.
OP	–	An observation post manned by a static surveillant.
Operative	–	An intelligence officer or agent operating in the field.
Opposition	–	The enemy service; any hostile operational force.
Optical system	–	A tracking system that uses optical marks and sensors.
OSS	–	The Office of Strategic Services; forerunner of the CIA, 1942-1945.
OTS	–	The Office of Technical Service, formerly the Technical Services Division, the CIA's technical arm of the Clandestine Service. Develops and deploys technical tradecraft needed for clandestine and covert operations.
Overhead platform	–	A technical platform, aboard an airplane or satellite, used for technical surveillance and reconnaissance.
OWVL	–	One-way voice link; shortwave radio link used to transmit prerecorded enciphered messages to an operative, who is usually working in a hostile area.

Passive probe – Someone sent on an intelligence mission just to passively observe and record details about the target location or organisation.

Pattern – The overt behaviour and daily routine of an operative that makes his identity unique.

Personal meeting – A clandestine meeting between two operatives, always the most desirable but a more risky form of communication.

PHOTINT – Photographic intelligence; renamed IMINT, image intelligence. Usually, involves high-altitude reconnaissance using spy satellites or aircraft.

Pianist – A Kapelle operator. Also used to describe a clandestine radio operator.

PLASMA – A secret technique or device used to defeat a lock.

Point – The member of the surveillance team who is following the target from the closest position, the point position.

Prober – An operative assigned to test border controls before an exfiltration is mounted. Usually, a specialist in false documents.

Profile – All the aspects of an operative's or a target's overt physical or behavioural persona.

Provocateur – An operative sent to incite a target group to action for purposes of entrapping or embarrassing them.

Provocative – A harassing act or procedure designed to flush out surveillance.

Put up a signal – To clandestinely signal another operative or secret source, as in putting up a signal like a chalk mark on a light pole.

Q Branch	–	The fictional part of the British intelligence service (MI6) that provides spy gadgetry to James Bond. OTS is the real 'Q'.
Rabbit	–	The target in a surveillance operation
Remote viewing	–	The paranormal ability of a subject to have an out-of-body view of a facility or person from an extremely remote position.
Repro	–	Making a false document.
Rezident	–	A KGB chief of station in a foreign location, usually under diplomatic cover.
Rezidentura	–	A KGB station, usually located in their embassy in a foreign capital.
Roll-out	–	Surreptitious technique of rolling out the contents of a letter without opening it. It can be done with two knitting needles or a split chopstick.
Rolled up	–	When an operation goes bad and the agent is arrested.
Rolling car pickup	–	A clandestine car pickup executed so smoothly that the car hardly stops at all and seems to have kept moving forward.
RYBAT	–	A code word meaning that the subject matter is extremely sensitive.
Safe-house	–	An apartment, hotel room, or other similar site considered safe for use by operatives as a base of operations or for a personal meeting.
Sanctum	–	The secure location of a KAPELLE device in a Soviet stronghold abroad.
SDR	–	Surveillance detection run; a route designed to erode or flush out surveillance without alerting them to an operative's purpose.

Second Chief Directorate (Second CD) – The counter-intelligence arm of the KGB responsible for domestic counter-intelligence. Currently known as the FSB.

Secret writing – Any tradecraft technique employing invisible messages hidden in or on innocuous materials. This includes invisible inks and microdots, among many other variations.

Security service – Usually a country's internal counter-intelligence service.

SE Division – The Soviet and East European Division of the CIA's Directorate of Operations (DO) during the latter part of the Cold War.

Sensing device – A technical sensor designed to react to a concealed mark, chemical compound, or passive element.

Seventh Directorate – The internal surveillance arm of the KGB. These are the watchers that include the mobile surveillance teams and the technical eavesdroppers.

SIGINT – Signals intelligence; the amalgamation of COMINT and ELINT into one unit of intelligence gathering dealing with all electronic emanations and transmissions.

Signals – Any form of clandestine tradecraft using a system of marks, signs, or codes for signaling between operatives.

Silver bullet – The special disguise and deception tradecraft techniques developed under Moscow rules to help the CIA penetrate the KGB's security perimeter in Moscow.

Sixteenth Directorate – The science and technology directorate of the KGB.

Part One
Kargil Revisited

1

The Wake-Up Call

Kargil was not the first incident of a country having been surprised by an unexpected invasion. History is replete with many an episode where lack of intelligence led to some major military setbacks. The Americans were completely surprised by the Japanese attack on Pearl Harbour. Even an ever vigilant Israel was caught unaware by the Arab invasion on the Yom Kippur Day in 1967.

In Indian context, just when the nation started celebrating its independence, the Pakistanis carried out a series of raids in Kashmir beginning early September 1947. While in 1962, India was deceived by China, three years later it was Pakistan who surprised her again by launching Operation Gibraltar on August 5, '65. A newly-raised special task force nicknamed 'Gibraltar Force' comprising regular Pakistan Army soldiers, Militia, Frontier Force Scouts, Razakars and Mujahids with a combined strength of nearly thirty thousand, infiltrated across the ceasefire line in civil clothes in two's and three's along selected points between Kargil and Jammu. Some succeeded in penetrating deep into

Indian territory. Since no large-scale infiltration had been predicted by the Indian intelligence agencies, it came as a bolt from the blue for Indian Army.

Kargil, as such, was just a case of history repeating itself. But since it was a major intelligence failure, it shook the Indian government as also the intelligence agencies like never before. The Kargil Review Committee and the Group of Ministers made several recommendations and consequently, a number of new organisations were created and some effort was made to deal with the shortcomings highlighted by the reform committees. The Indian spy machine, however, continues to malfunction, as evidenced by 26/11 and several other intelligence failures post-Kargil.

It's pretty much obvious that to make the intelligence machine function efficiently, some trouble shooting is highly needed, which necessitates revisiting Kargil. The Kargil invasion after all was the first regular war fought by India since 1971, and is still considered the mother of all intelligence failures in India.

Warning Signals

For execution of any tactical plan, an adversary needs to carry out certain essential activities, which even under utmost secrecy cannot be concealed beyond a certain stage and time. Timely knowledge of these activities reveals the nature and method of conduct of the impending operations. These activities in military parlance are called battle indications. Did Pakistan give out any such indications prior to the Kargil intrusion?

There were, of course, some warning signals which were somehow overlooked by the intelligence agencies, or so it seems. There were major purchases of high altitude military equipment and certain Pakistan Army units on the Line of Control (LoC) in the Kargil Sector were reinforced through early spring. According to intelligence sources in Islamabad[1], the Mujahideen strength undergoing training in North East Pakistan was enhanced significantly towards the end of 1998 and as many as 40 new training camps were established in the Neelam Valley, Muzzaffarabad and

Baltistan. The Mujahideens were given intensive training in high altitude warfare by local mountain guides in the Skardu region by the end of winter.

As per the Intelligence Bureau (IB), a report regarding enhanced activity in the Kargil sector was forwarded to the Prime Minister, Home Minister, Cabinet Secretary, Defence Secretary and the Director General Military Operations (DGMO), as early as June 1998. The report explicitly warned of Pakistan army regulars building up at various posts and increased fighter aircraft activity in Skardu. The IB also forwarded a report to Home Ministry on 20 December, 1998 regarding intrusion of Pakistani remote-piloted vehicles into the Indian territory at least 20 times. [2]

In March 1999, the operatives of Military Intelligence Units - Intelligence and Field Security Units (IFSU) and Liaison Unit (LU) based in Leh sent reports about increased threat perception along the border, to the Army Headquarters. [3]

Bunkers or Sangars?

When Kargil happened, there was lot of hype created by the media about the kind of defence works that Pakistan army had constructed up there. Were these proper bunkers or makeshift sangars? To a lay person, the difference between a bunker and a sangar may not be of much consequence. But soldiers know the difference between the two, in terms of their defence potential and mode of construction. A sangar is essentially a stone-walled field fortification erected in a day or two by the defender while taking up a hasty defence. It provides limited protection against small arms and is highly vulnerable against artillery/mortar fire. A bunker on the other hand is a *pucca* defence work made of concrete that provides safety to the defender against small arms, artillery and mortar fire as also adequate cover against air attack. It can take a few weeks to construct a bunker and in a high altitude area like Kargil, may be even a couple of months.

As it turned out later, most of the defensive positions were actually sangars, but the fact that Pakistan army could keep them under wraps for so long, makes it pretty much evident that surveillance elements on the Indian side were either not there, or were perhaps napping.

The Overt Source

Contrary to the popular belief, about eighty per cent of the information that goes into finished intelligence reports is obtained from open sources such as professional journals, newspapers and other publications. As per an IB official[4] during the period just prior to the commencement of Operation Vijay in May 1999, "Language newspapers in Pakistan and in particular those in Pakistan occupied Kashmir were full of tales of so-called heroic exploits of the Pakistan army and the volunteers in Kargil, Drass and Muchkoh sectors". To assume that the Indian operatives failed to pick up this public information would be stretching things a bit too far. Right? Not really. The overt sources of information can be made use of only by open minds. More on this later.

Good Shepherds

It was reported by a section of the press that it was some local shepherd who informed the army about the presence of Pakistani intruders on Indian side of LoC. By a strange coincident, in 1965 also the first information about the infiltration came from the shepherds. One is not sure how far these reports are true, but yes, there is another interesting tale about the battle of Chushul. On 18 November, 1962, after fighting a pitched battle against Chinese human waves attacks, the Indian army formation defending the area, had to withdraw to the rear leaving behind many dead. In fact, an entire company of 13 Kumaon Regiment deployed at Rezang la – about 14 km East of Chushul – was wiped out as the gallant troops fought the attacking Chinese till last man, last round. Only nine survived out of a total strength of 123. Since the area was assumed to be under Chinese occupation, no one ventured up there. It was after a couple of months that a local shepherd – Rebo in Ladakhi language – happened to observe from afar, an Ibex (mountain goat) grazing on the Rezang la slopes. Ibex being a very shy animal, seldom strays into inhabited places; hence the shepherd ruled out the possibility of Chinese presence in that area and informed Indian troops accordingly. A patrol was tasked to ascertain the fact, and it was confirmed that the Chinese had vacated the area and had withdrawn across Rezang la. It was then that the dead bodies were recovered. This makes one wonder, why it's usually the shepherds who give Indian intelligencers the wake-up call.

2

Pakistan's Gameplan

The Terrain

To an uninstructed eye, the area of Pakistani intrusion in Kargil as also in the rest of Ladakh region, may appear as a formless muddle of mountains, but to those who are familiar with the maps, it will be evident that the main ranges follow the direction of the great Himalayas, that is from South East to North West. The height of the mountains varies from 15,000 to 18,000 feet. The higher reaches being glaciated and covered with about five feet of snow throughout the year, the area was likened to Siachen by the media. But having served in both the sectors, one must point out that Siachen is a different ball game but nevertheless, the going in Kargil is pretty tough. In fact, it is more hostile and desolate on the Indian side of LoC and relatively easy on the Pakistani side. It will, therefore, not be incorrect to state that the intruders were much better of than the attacking Indian troops, who had to negotiate the treacherous climb to almost vertical peaks where even eagles seldom dare.

Pakistan's Grand Design

Diplomatically, the Pakistan grand design was to bring the Kashmir issue back on the international agenda, notwithstanding the Lahore declaration. They endeavoured to alter the LoC, hoping to somehow legitimise the same through international intervention. Moreover, by controlling the heights, they could dominate the strategic Srinagar-Leh highway, thereby isolating Ladakh from the rest of India. This would have not only allowed them to push militants into the Kashmir valley at will, but also force India to back down in Siachen.

Also, as Ladakh had more or less remained untouched by militancy unlike elsewhere in Jammu and Kashmir, Pakistan wanted to unleash the demon of insurgency in this region as well. And since the local population in Kargil is mostly Shias, their harassment would not have harmed the cause of Sunni Muslim dominated Pakistan. The ultimate objective of Pakistan was actually as envisaged by Gen Zia-ul-Haq in Operation Topac, that is to wrest Kashmir.

However, the end result of the Pakistan's gamble was quite different from what had been hoped for. The Kashmir issue, of course was back in the media headlines, but for the wrong reasons. The international media in fact got after the Pakistan government as never before. The rogue nation stood exposed as a terrorist state, trying to fan the flames of Islamic militancy. India on the other hand was universally praised for its restraint against unprovoked Pakistani aggression.

By their own admission, certain ex-Pakistan Army Generals have described the Kargil operation as a disaster for Pakistan. Some of their senior defence officials including former chief of the ISI, Lt Gen Asad Durrani, criticised their government for embarking on the Kargil misadventure. Air Marshal (Retd) Noor Khan had gone on record saying[5], "We should have known that India will not be bogged down in Kargil and will expand the war to other fronts and the international community will not support us". Another senior ex-Pakistan Army officer described Kargil as a "complete fiasco and a failure".

The Pakistani adventure, nay misadventure, boomeranged on them indeed. But, all said and done, even though Pakistanis failed to achieve their military objectives as planned, they succeeded in opening up a Siachen like front for the Indian Army.

The Tapped Tapes

During the Kargil conflict, Gen Parvez Musharraf, then Chief of the Army Staff under Pakistan Prime Minister Nawaz Sharif, had gone on a visit to Beijing. Lt Gen Mohammad Aziz Khan, his trusted Chief of the General Staff, rang him up at his hotel in Beijing and reported to him about a meeting chaired by Nawaz Sharif at which the chiefs of the Pakistani Air Force and Navy complained that Musharraf had kept them in the dark about the invasion. This was wire-tapped by R&AW.

The public release of this tape turned out to be a grave mistake on India's part as the particular satellite link was promptly closed by the Pakistanis, drying up a valuable source of intelligence.

It is a sad reflection on the psyche of our media, that amidst continuing allegations of intelligence failure, they all but forgot to give a well-deserved pat to the Indian intelligencers for their stupendous scoop. The devils must be granted their due. Given that voice synthesising technology can reproduce voices with considerable accuracy, one can't be sure that the tapes were authentic. However, since the contents of the taped conversation between the two senior most Pakistan army officers was in consonance with their overall gameplan, it's a fair assumption that the tapes were real indeed. Besides, post Kargil, the Pakistan military authorities ordered a probe into the leakage of these tapes and thus added a new dimension to this episode. It was alleged that former ISI Chief, Lt Gen Ziauddin Butt got the conversation taped and later handed it over to the deposed Prime Minister Nawaz Sharif, who sent these to the Indian Prime Minister through Track-II diplomacy. A misnomer really as the tapes were actually the handiwork of R&AW. In any event, to get a clearer perspective about Pakistan's gameplan in Kargil, and more important, how effective and useful covert intelligence could be, a brief analysis of the following excerpts of conversation, sourced from the *Times of India* of August 7, 1999, is in order.

"On shooting down of the Mi-17 helicopter (29 May, 1999) :

Lt Gen Mohd Aziz (MA): This is Pakistan. Give me room number 83315. Hello.

Gen Parvez Musharraf (PM): Hello Aziz.

MA: The situation on ground is OK… one of their Mi-17 was brought down.

PM: Has this Mi-17 not fallen in our area?

MA: No sir. This has fallen in their area. We have not claimed it. We have got it claimed through the Mujahideen.

PM: Well done…Now are they facing any greater difficulty in flying them? Are they scared or not? This also you should note. Are they coming any less nearer?

MA: Yes. There is a lot of pressure on them. They were talking about greater air defence than they had anticipated. They can't afford to lose any more aircraft. There has been less intensity of air flying after that.

PM: Very good. First class…

On the line Sartaj Aziz must take and the stand on LoC (29 May) :

MA: There is a development. Have you listened to yesterday's news regarding Mian Saheb (Nawaz Sharif) speaking to his counterpart. He told him that the spirit of Lahore Declaration and escalation has been done by your people…. He told Indian PM they should have waited instead of upping the ante by using air force and other means… Sartaj Aziz could go to New Delhi to explore the possibility of defusing tension.

PM: OK.

MA: Aziz Saheb (Sartaj Aziz) has discussed with me and my recommendation is that dialogue option is always open. But in their first meeting, they must give no understanding or commitment on ground situation.

PM: Very correct. You or Mehmood (Commander X Corps, Rawalpindi) must go with Zafar because they don't know about ground situation.

MA: This week we are getting together. Zafar Saheb will deliberate it. We want to suggest to Zafar that they have to maintain that they will not be talking about ground situation.... .

PM: Idea on LoC?

MA: Hint is that, given that the LoC has many areas where the interpretation of either side is not what the other side believes. So, comprehensive deliberation is required. So that can be worked out by the DGMOs (Director General Military Operations).

PM: If they are assured that we are here for a long period. We have been sitting here for long. Like in the beginning, the matter is the same – no post was attacked and no post was captured. The situation is that we are along our defensive Line of Control (LoC). If it is not in his (Sartaj Aziz's) knowledge, then discuss it altogether. Emphasise that for years, we are here only. Yes, this point should be raised. We are sitting on the same LoC since a long period.

MA: This is their (India's) weakness. They are not agreed on the demarcation under UN's verification, whereas we are agreed. We want to exploit it.

PM: This is in Shimla Agreement that we cannot go for the UN intervention.

On Nawaz Sharif's ignorance and Pakistani army control over terrorists in Kashmir (26 May)

MA to PM:.... But he (unidentified top level person) was also saying that any escalation after that should be regulated as there may be danger of war. On this logic we give the suggestion that there was no such fear as the scruff of their (militants) neck is in our hands, whenever we want we could regulate it.... We told him (Nawaz Sharif) that there is no reason of alarm and panic. Then he said when I came to know seven days back, when corps commanders were told. The entire reason for the success of this operation was total secrecy. Our experience was that our earlier efforts failed because of secrecy. So,, the top priority is to be accorded to confidentiality, to ensure our success. We should respect this and the advantage we have from this would give us a handle.... ".

Even a casual study of the above conversation makes it quite obvious that:

- Pakistan regular army personnel had been fighting alongside Mujahideen from the very beginning
- One of their main objectives was to alter the LoC to their advantage.
- The Indian Air Force (IAF) MI-17 helicopter was fired at on the Indian side of LoC.
- They did not want the operation to escalate into a full-fledged war.
- Pakistan Army had full control over the militants'activities.

3

The Intruders

If you know the enemy and know yourself, you need not fear the result of a hundred battles. If you know yourself but not the enemy, for every victory gained you will suffer defeat. If you know neither the enemy nor yourself, you will succumb in every battle. – **Sun Tzu**.

How much did Indian intelligence know about the enemy, in the initial stages of the conflict?

Groping in the Dark

The first signs of intrusion were detected on 4/5 May, 1999. But it was only after about 10 days – around May 15 – that the extent of the intrusion became somewhat clear. It will not be fair to blame the Army for taking its own time to assess the ground reality. A proper review of the situation, especially in an unconventional scenario such as the Kargil invasion, takes time. The attacking force must get a fair estimate of the enemy strength, dispositions and capabilities before mounting the offensive. This is usually done by launching patrols or even probing attacks – and that's what was done by the army. Two patrols were dispatched on May 4/5, one to Khoberaro and another to Yaldor. The first patrol saw two men while the second observed seven intruders. Two officer-led patrols were launched the next day. However, both were ambushed and three soldiers were killed.

The Invading Force

As per the initial estimates the number of Pakistani intruders was put at around 300 Mujahideen which was enhanced to 700 Mujahideen reinforced by Pakistan Army regulars. Later the strength of the Pakistani invading force was estimated at over 1000 (mainly Pakistan regulars assisted by Mujahideen) consisting of the following:

- Units of Northern Light Infantry comprising troops of the Northern areas of Pakistan.
- Mercenaries of the Harkat-ul-Mujahideen (HuM). The group was known as Harkat-ul-Ansar before it was banned by the US after it abducted foreign tourists (including US citizens) in Kashmir. Its cadre comprising nearly 80 per cent foreign mercenaries apparently trained in Osama bin Laden's camps in Afghanistan.
- Lashkar-e-Taiba, a well-trained and heavily armed militant group formed in the early 1980s. Fighting the Ghazwa-e-Hind (holy war against India) the group with mostly militants from Afghanistan and Pakistan occupied Kashmir (POK) on its rolls, claimed to have had links with bin Laden.
- Al Badr, formed in 1998, comprising elements of the dreaded militant organisation Hizbul Mujahideen from both POK and J&K. Its training camps were located in POK.
- Osama bin Laden's Harkat-ul-Jihad-al-Islami, a.k.a Tehrik-e-Jihad popularly known as al Qaeda.

World's most wanted terrorist: Osama bin Laden, world's most wanted fugitive, who was killed in a US

Marines operation in Pakistan, was believed to have called for an all out jihad against India. In his threat that appeared in the September 16, 1999 issue of *Jang* - a popular Urdu daily published in Pakistan - bin Laden declared: ... all Mujahideen groups in Pakistan should come together now to target India... we are always ready to help the Kashmir Mujahideens.

During the Kargil conflict, there were rumours of the presence of bin Laden and his mercenaries in the battle zone. While the individual presence of the world's most wanted terrorist could not be established, there is little doubt about the presence of his followers in Kargil.

4

India's Response

The Kargil intrusion led to much mud-slinging between various political parties. But the fact is that after the initial setback the Indian Government played its cards rather well and was bold enough to take the Pakistani bull by its horns.

Diplomatic Initiative

Even though the government did not quite anticipate the massive intrusion in its own territory and was obviously unprepared for the same, it not only managed to defeat Pakistan's gameplan but also enhanced the country's prestige in the entire world. The government's overall approach on handling the issue was of low profile diplomacy coupled with stern action on ground.

As mentioned earlier, it is not the first time that India had been surprised by her adversary. But one must commend the government's overall response, who like Israel in the Yom Kippur war, turned the challenge inside out.

The Military Operations

Operation Vijay in Kargil was perhaps the most difficult, complicated and challenging operation undertaken anywhere in the world, wherein the Indian defence forces had to confront not only the heavily armed, fanatically trained mercenaries and regular Pakistan army soldiers but also the vagaries of the most inhospitable high-altitude battlefield. The army operations were launched with the following objectives:

- To prevent further ingress by the invading force
- To safeguard the strategic Srinagar-Leh Road
- Finally, to evict the infiltrators from own territory and thus restore the sanctity of the LoC.

The IAF was tasked to support the ground operations by softening the known enemy positions and to monitor the enemy activities through aerial surveillance.

The above objectives were successfully achieved after intense fighting at heights ranging from 15,000 to 18,000 feet across a frontage of over 60 kms. The army, mainly infantry, ably-supported by the air force, had to literally inch forward against all odds and heavy fire, to dislodge the well-entrenched enemy. The courage, grit and heroism displayed by the Indian soldier in accomplishing the daunting task, will no doubt remain unparalleled in the history of warfare, notwithstanding the fact that some wise men constituting the Fifth Pay Commission equated the same soldier to a police constable.

The army suffered over 2000 casualties during the two-month long operation; 523 soldiers including 25 officers killed and 1,363 soldiers including 35 officers wounded. The officer casualty rate as always was rather high, which speaks volumes about the quality of junior leaders of India's armed forces

Since the defences in Kargil sector now have to be manned even during winters, the army suffers casualties due to hostile weather. Well then that's the price Indian Army had to pay for intelligence failure in Kargil.

5

Kargil Review Committee

Soon after the culmination of Operation Vijay, the government ordered an inquiry into the events that led to Pakistan's intrusion in Kargil. But even as the inquiry committee was trying to find out the truth of the matter, the political parties went full lick to derive political mileage during election time out of this sorry affair. There were charges and counter-charges. Worse, even the armed forces were not spared in this blame game. The media too acted irresponsibly by unnecessarily raising controversial issues such as sacking of a brigadier by the army and his tendentious allegations against his own organisation. It's a sad reflection on the country's politics that even as the nation had just overcome a crisis of such an alarming magnitude, the political class got into their act of one-upmanship right away. But then, it was election time after all. While the Congress Party described Kargil as the 'mother of all strategic failures', the BJP retaliated by calling the IPKF mission in Sri Lanka the 'mother of all follies'. As their verbal duel continued unabated the army was unnecessarily dragged into the playing arena. Whether the Kargil conflict could have been averted and whether the senior military leaders were guilty of a monumental error of judgment was left to the Kargil Review Committee (KRC), headed by the renowned defence analyst, the late K Subrahmanyam.

The crux of the Committee's 250-page report is as follows:

- Kargil highlighted major inadequacies in the surveillance capability. The Review Committee pointed out that the intrusions could have been detected earlier if India had half-meter resolution satellite imagery capability, appropriate UAVs and better HUMINT. There was a complete intelligence failure. The intelligence agencies/army did not foresee the possibility of the kind of intrusions made by Pakistan and when actually their troops occupied the heights of Kargil.
- The Committee examined information based on documents captured by the Indian Army during Kargil operations and POW interrogation reports. This information when compared with information supplied by R&AW in June 1999 indicated that R&AW could not correctly identify as many as five infantry battalions deployed right across the LoC. A serious lapse indeed.
- Pakistan was able to achieve strategic surprise because this area had been free from LoC violations for long and was considered unsuitable for military operations, especially during winters.
- Certain structural changes in India's intelligence set-up were recommended by the Review Committee, some of which have not been implemented as yet.

Part Two
The Spy Machine - Bond and Beyond

6

Indian Intelligence - Inside Out

Why the Indian intelligence failed in Kargil? And why India's spy machine continues to malfunction even over two decades after Kargil? Some of the prominent defence analysts have tried to address this issue but have only scratched the crust of the matter, leaving the core untouched. While some have blamed lack of intelligence culture which is supposedly deep-rooted in India's history, others have outrightly criticised the intelligence agencies for being negligent and unprofessional. Lack of hi-tech surveillance equipment has also been cited as one of the reasons for the failure of Indian intelligence.

There is an element of truth in all these allegations, but the real malaise lies much deeper. For a comprehensive answer and to get a deeper insight into this burning issue, we must first critically analyse the existing intelligence set-up, changes brought in post-Kargil/terror attacks in Mumbai in 2008, and find out why India's intelligence agencies are, the way they are. It will also be prudent to compare the organisation and track record of the world's major intelligence agencies with the Indian intelligence outfits, not only for differentiation, but also to find out how they have evolved in recent times to counter terrorism. There are so many intelligence agencies across the globe, with each country having a few on board. The list, including arguably the world's top ten, is indexed at the end.

Historical

The aim is not to trace the history of Indian intelligence services in great detail, as the same has been adequately covered earlier by various contemporary publications on the subject, but to provide an element of continuity to the entire analysis, as also to point out how deep-rooted is the intelligence culture in India's history.

"As the wind moves everywhere and penetrates all created beings, so also should the king penetrate everywhere by means of his unidentified agents". Thus spake Manu, the mythological Hindu law-maker and progenitor of mankind.

Kautilya, considered as the master of espionage in ancient India, laid out an effective system of espionage in his '*Arthashastra*', the manual of statecraft. Espionage, both diplomatic and military, was highly organised. Kautilya described how spies were used to investigate enemy positions and numbers. He also mentioned sending messages in cipher through carrier pigeons, demoralising the enemy by circulating false information and attempting to seduce allegiance of important individuals in the army and the *harems*.

The Rig-Veda also makes a mention of '*dutas*' and '*prahitas*'. While the former was a diplomatic envoy of the king, the latter was supposed to be a regular spy. The great Indian epics, *Mahabharata* and *Ramayana* explicitly refer to the activity of secret agents. The art of spying was an important facet of good governance and spies were extensively employed by the kings, as is evident throughout India's recorded history up to the Mughal period.

Thus, espionage in India is as old as the origin of the state and can certainly be considered the second oldest profession.

Moving on through the time, it was during the British rule in India that India's present intelligence set-up was conceived and formalised. The first agency responsible for collecting intelligence on internal security was called the Anti-Thugee organisation which was established by the British in 1835[6]. However, one of the main intelligence agencies which exists today – the IB – was an offshoot of Police Department (CID) and came into existence much later in 1929, after undergoing a series of organisational and functional changes. Post independence, IB continued to be the sole agency responsible for both internal as well as external intelligence, till September 1968, when R&AW was created to look after the foreign affairs. Military intelligence service, the MI, based at Shimla was in existence throughout the British rule, however its main component, the Intelligence Corps was instituted in 1942 and was headquartered at Karachi.

7

The Intelligence Services

There are generally two types of intelligence services which gather and evaluate information for the country's political and military leaders to help them in decision-making during peace and in war. One gathers and analyses information about foreign countries and the other protects its own nation against espionage and other activities inimical to own interests. Processed and analysed information is called intelligence.

In India there are several agencies which carry out both the tasks. Mainly it's the IB, which is responsible for providing intelligence for the country's internal security and R&AW which looks after the external intelligence. The third component of the Indian intelligence machine is the Military Intelligence which is dedicated to all the three defence services.

Besides, some para-military forces like Border Security Force (BSF) have their own intelligence units called the 'G' Branch. There are others such as Directorate of Revenue

Intelligence (DRI), the Narcotics Control Bureau, and CBI who form an essential part of the entire intelligence set-up. Inputs from all the agencies are important to connect the dotted lines.

At the top of the intelligence hierarchy is the PMO (Prime Minister's Office) and the Cabinet Committee for Security Affairs (CCSA), followed by the Cabinet Secretariat. The highest intelligence assessment body, the Joint Intelligence Committee (JIC), comprising representatives of all the intelligence services, forms part of the National Security Council's secretariat. Its task is to coordinate all intelligence related activity *viz.*, political, economic, scientific and military and prepare weekly reviews and special reports, as required by the Prime Minister, the Cabinet, various ministries and government departments.

In the wake of 26/11, National Investigation Agency (NIA) was established by an act of Parliament in December 2008. NIA has concurrent jurisdiction which empowers the Centre to probe terror attacks in any part of the country, covering offences posing challenge to the country's sovereignty and integrity, bomb blasts, hijacking of aircraft and ships, and attacks on nuclear installations.

Other than offences of terrorism, it also deals with counterfeit currency, human-trafficking, narcotics or drugs and organised crime.

Another step taken by the government towards refurbishing the terror combat infrastructure was the establishment of a Multi-Agency Centre (MAC) and a Joint Task Force on Intelligence within IB as a hub of India's counter-terrorism effort. Patterned on the CIA's Counter-terrorism Center, the MAC is responsible for the joint analysis of intelligence flowing from different quarters and co-ordinating relevant follow-up actions

Yet another organisation that has come up to improve India's intelligence capability is the National Technical Research Organisation (NTRO), with a focus on collecting technical intelligence (TECHINT), cyber intelligence and cyber counter-intelligence. NTRO adds one more agency to the mix, as the IB, R&AW and the Army's Signals Directorate continue to maintain autonomous TECHINT units. The organisation unfortunately has been reeling under a series of scandals and allegations since its inception.

Intelligence Bureau

The Organisation

The IB is essentially a counter-intelligence organisation controlled by the Union Home Minister, which deals with all intelligence matters pertaining to India's internal security. It is divided into various headquarters and field units based on its specific functions such as security, insurgency and immigration etc, as also the regional or local situation. The Director IB is the country's highest ranking police officer and is a member of the JIC[7]. Right since its inception, IB has been a police oriented organisation and as such, not only its boss but also its main officer cadre is recruited from the Indian Police Service. Its technical manpower is inducted through Union Public Service Commission or directly from the universities.

The Track Record

Tribal Invasion of Kashmir - Soon after the partition, the newly-formed and belligerent Pakistan launched the tribal invasion of Kashmir in September 1947. The IB, despite its teething problems and limited resources, did provide some useful inputs regarding Pakistani intentions in Kashmir, based on which India could take the Pakistan challenge head on.

The China Aggression - Even though the IB had failed to report construction of the strategic road across Aksai Chin by China in the early 50s, it had apparently provided sufficient and timely information to the government regarding Chinese threat before the actual invasion in 1962[8]. However, the bits and pieces of information gathered by the IB remained more or less like a jig-saw puzzle, since the same were not processed into hard intelligence. Nehru's misguided policy on China did not help matters either. The Chinese attack was not unexpected as such, but they surprised India all the same.

Indo-Pak War 1965 – Three years after the 1962 debacle the Indian intelligencers had still not completely woken up, it seems. Not only were they surprised by Pakistan's 'Gibraltar Force', their assessment of Grand Slam, was also not up to the mark. The IB however claimed that it had provided adequate intelligence about Pakistan's grand design but the same was not properly interpreted by the end users[9].

If the IB's claim is correct and not a mere face-saving device, then the Indian Army must be blamed for its faulty assessment of the available intelligence. But then, was it intelligence or mere pieces of unprocessed information that were dished out by the IB?

Counter-insurgency Operations – India has been facing the menace of insurgency since the fifties. It started in the North East and has now spread almost throughout the country. IB painstakingly established its network in all the insurgency prone areas and had several successes to its credit in providing hard intelligence during counter-insurgency operations. However, it has failed miserably on some occasions resulting in serious setback to the end user, mainly the army. Operation Blue Star is one such instance. Being personally involved in the operation as a young officer, one regrets to point out that whatever limited intelligence was provided to us in the initial stages of the operation, was of little value and it was virtually like going blind-folded in a blind alley. My experience in counter-insurgency operations in Doda has been no different. When the elite Delta Force (Rashtriya Rifles) was inducted into Doda District in 1994 as part of the counter-insurgency grid in J&K, real time information from the existing IB sources was hard to come by.

Communal Riots – Ever since the time of partition

when India witnessed the worst riots between the Hindus and Muslims, communal disturbances have occurred on a number of occasions. Outbreak of communal violence of course is difficult to predict, but then isn't it the job of intelligence agencies to predict the unexpected? Acquisition of real time intelligence in such a scenario has to be an ongoing process, which the IB has not been able to follow. IB's inability to anticipate the aftermath of Bombay blasts in 1993 was a major failure on its part.

Research and Analysis Wing (R&AW)

The Organisation

R&AW was created in September 1968 as an offshoot of the IB – its foreign intelligence desk and the Directorate General of Security (DGS) are a legacy of the IB and was placed under the control of Cabinet Secretariat. It is responsible for collecting, analysing and disseminating intelligence, particularly external intelligence, which effects national security. It is headed by a Director, an officer of the rank of a secretary.

The organisation which is somewhat based on the CIA model, has three main functional components i.e. Office of Special Operations (OSO) under the Additional Director, the covert units *viz.* ARC, SSB, and SFF controlled by the Director-General Security (DGS) and various country/area specific research desks under the Joint Directors. At the time of its inception, the officer cadre was created by pooling in specialists from various civil services and other government organisations. Later, to streamline the outfit as also to rationalize the inter-se seniority and pay scales of its personnel, a regular cadre, the Research and Analysis Services was formed under Rajiv Gandhi led government. Since then R&AW has been recruiting its officer cadre by screening volunteers from the colleges on as required basis. Besides, officers from the armed forces are also deputed to the organisation to deal with intelligence pertaining to matters military [10].

The Covert Units – The Aviation Research Center (ARC),

Special Service Bureau (SSB) and Special Frontier Force (SFF) are primarily responsible for the conduct of covert operations. While ARC gathers intelligence from aerial surveillance and satellite communications, the SSB – a China specific outfit – is organised to conduct guerrilla and physiological warfare besides intelligence acquisition. The SFF came into existence in November 1962 and comprises mainly Tibetan refugees settled in India. Its battalions are trained in commando and counter-insurgency operations by officers of the army who are deputed for a three-year stint.

The Track Record

R&AW has been active both within and outside India for over four decades but its track record like the IB is a mixed bag. Within two years since its inception it performed stupendously alongside the Mukti Bahini for liberation of Bangladesh. However, its attempt to do a Bangladesh in Sri Lanka in the mid-1980s boomeranged on the IPKF (Indian Peace Keeping Force). But to be fair it's actually the political leadership that must be blamed for the Sri Lanka fiasco. On the insurgency front, especially in Punjab during Operation Blue Star and the J&K thereafter, R&AW has been off target more often than not. Inability to foresee Kargil and 26/11 has been one of its major failures.

Military Intelligence

The Organisation

Technically, Military Intelligence (MI) covers the intelligence set-up of all the three defence services, however its army component being the largest and most prominent, the term is commonly used with reference to the army intelligence. At the apex of the organisation is the Directorate General of Military Intelligence (DGMI) which is headed by a Lt Gen and functions under the Vice Chief of Army Staff. Similarly, there are directorates of air and naval intelligence functioning under their respective headquarters in New Delhi. The DGMI controls and coordinates the overall intelligence activities of the army and comprises of various country and function specific desks. Its main intelligence apparatus, the Intelligence Corps has two components, the LU and IFSU. While the former is responsible for counter-intelligence, the latter acquires external intelligence for the army. Both the units are manned by volunteer army officers and other ranks who are permanently seconded to the organisation after undergoing specialised training at the Military Intelligence School in Pune. Since the last few years officers are also being directly commissioned into Int Corps. Some specialised intelligence units *viz.* Regional Centres, Internal Security Groups and Counter-insurgency Intelligence Units have since been raised in insurgency infested areas.

Incidentally, the Directorate is always headed by a non-Int Corps Officer, since the highest rank in the Int Corps cadre is that of a Major General.

The Track Record

The MI too has not been very consistent in delivering the goods and its record of achievements is interlaced with failures like that of other two intelligence agencies. Whereas it performed admirably during the 1971 operations, its efficiency during the Chinese aggression in 1962 and Pakistan's offensives in 1948 and 1965 was far from satisfactory. However, it has played an important role in some of the major counter-insurgency operations undertaken by the army.

Operations in the North East – The Indian Army has been combating intelligence in the North East for several decades. But it was only in the 1990s that it intensified its operations to counter the growing menace of insurgency, especially in Assam. Operation Bajrang, Operation Cloud Burst and Operation Rhino were launched in quick succession, commencing towards the end of 1990. The MI had not much intelligence to offer to the army for planning and conduct of Operation Bajrang and same was the case with other intelligence agencies. However, by the time Operation Rhino was launched, the Int Corps was quite prepared and had acquired substantial information about the ULFA operatives which contributed to the success of the Operation.

Operation Pawan - The MI couldn't anticipate the government's rash and sudden decision to send IPKF to Sri Lanka and was caught off guard during the initial stage of Operation Pawan. But why R&AW, which had been training LTTE cadres all along, failed to provide any worthwhile information to the Indian Army, is something of a mystery that one has not been able to discern. Anyway, the army got down to business with locally acquired tourist maps and the MI, even though late off the starting blocks, got its act together and played a vital role in IPKF's operations by providing hard intelligence, mainly acquired through Signal Intelligence (SIGINT), to the army units.

Operation Rakshak - One of the major achievements of MI has been intelligence acquisition during 'Operation Rakshak', both in Punjab and J&K. Despite its perennial problem of co-ordinating the intelligence effort with other agencies, the Int Corps has been able to build its own network in both the States, especially the latter: a fact which is manifested in many a successful operation executed by the army units employed in Operation Rakshak.

On the flip side, the MI failed to detect Pakistani terrorists occupying about 100 square kilometers of Indian territory, 35 kilometres inside the LoC around Hilkaka in Jammu and Kashmir in May 2003; a failure that perhaps outdid the shame of the initially undetected Kargil incursions. The Kargil experience, wherein it was left to local shepherds to blow the whistle signaling presence of Pakistani infiltrators, should have taught the MI to be on guard. Nothing like that seemed to have happened, as the Indian Army intelligencers were shaken but not stirred and were caught napping again.

Defence Intelligence Agency (DIA) - This agency was established in March 2002, as part of post-Kargil reforms. The organisation is headed by Director General (DG), an officer of the rank of a Lieutenant General. It is supposed to be the nodal agency for all defence related intelligence, thus distinguishing it from the R&AW.

The DIA controls some of the army's coveted technical intelligence assets such as the Directorate of Signals Intelligence and the Defence Image Processing and Analysis Centre (DIPAC). The Signals Directorate is responsible for acquiring and decrypting enemy communications, whereas the DIPAC controls India's satellite-based image acquisition capabilities. The DIA also controls the Defence Information Warfare Agency (DIWA). DIWA handles all elements of the information warfare repertoire, including psychological operations, cyber-war, electronic intercepts and monitoring of sound waves.

Central Intelligence Agency (CIA)

CIA, arguably the world's most powerful intelligence service was established in 1947 with the signing of National Security Act by the then US President Truman. Developed from the Office of Strategic Services in World War II, the CIA gathers political, economic and military information about more than 150 countries around the world and evaluates it for the US government agencies.

The Organisation

The CIA is an independent agency, responsible to the US President through its director and accountable to the American people through the intelligence oversight committees of the US Congress. CIA's role is to support the US President, the National Security Council and all officials who make and execute US national security policy by[11] conducting counter-intelligence activities, special activities and other functions related to foreign intelligence and national security, as directed by the President. To accomplish its objectives, the CIA engages in research, development and deployment of high technology. The CIA serves as an independent source of analysis on topics of concern and works closely with other organisations in the intelligence community to ensure that the end-user, whether Washington policy-maker or battlefield commander, receives the best intelligence possible.

The changing global realities in the post cold war scenario reordered the US national security agenda and the CIA effectively took on the new challenge by:

- Creating special, multi-disciplinary centres to address high-priority issues such as non-proliferation, counter-terrorism, counter-intelligence, international organised crime, narcotics trafficking, environment, and arms control intelligence.
- Forging stronger partnerships between several intelligence collection disciplines and all – source analysis
- Taking an active part in intelligence community analytical efforts and producing all-source analysis on the full range of topics that affect the national security.
- Contributing to the effectiveness of the overall intelligence community by managing services of common concern in imagery analysis and open source collection and by participating in strategic partnership with other intelligence agencies in the areas of research and development and technical collection.

At the apex of the CIA organisational pyramid is the Director Central Intelligence (DCI) who acts as Adviser to the President on matters pertaining to intelligence and national security.

The number two man in the Agency is its Deputy Director who assists the Director in his duties as head of CIA and the intelligence community and exercises powers of the Director when the Director is not present. The Agency also has an Executive Director who manages the organisation on day-to-day basis. The main components of the organisation are:

- **The Directorate of Operations** – It is responsible for the clandestine collection of foreign intelligence, primarily through human intelligence and comprises 15 different components such as Foreign Intelligence (espionage) Staff, Operational Services Division, Technical Services Division,

Missions and Programmes Staff, Area Divisions including domestic operations and special operations sections, Field Stations and Bases. The CIA stations and bases around the world serve as principal headquarters of covert activities in the countries they are located. The stations are usually housed in the US Embassies in the capital cities whereas the bases are located in other major cities.

- **The Directorate of Science and Technology** – As the name suggests, the Directorate creates and applies innovative technology in support of the overall intelligence collection mission and collects information from the open sources as well as electronic and satellite photography. This Directorate is known to have indulged in certain improper and questionable activities such as testing the influence of dangerous drugs like LSD and tapping conversations of American people.
- **The Directorate of Intelligence** – This is the analytical branch of the CIA and is responsible for the production and dissemination of all source intelligence analysis on key foreign issues. This Directorate interprets and writes the finished product-based on information turned over by the first two Directorates. One of the most important tasks of this Directorate is the production of daily intelligence publications, designed to alert the foreign affairs community to significant developments abroad and to analyse specific problems of broad-based trends in the international arena. These publications comprise mainly of the President's daily brief, the National Intelligence Daily prepared for cabinet and sub-cabinet level consumers and the National Intelligence Bulletin distributed to the defence and foreign affairs department.
- **The Directorate of Administration** – It provides administrative backup to the CIA in areas such as communications, security, human resources and logistics and makes sure the whole operation runs smoothly. The organisation also has a centre for the study of Intelligence which maintains the agency's historical materials and promotes the study of intelligence as a legitimate and serious discipline. Besides, there is an Office of Public Affairs which serves as the communications focal point

for the media, the general public and the Agency employees.

The Track Record

Despite its rating as one of the world's best intelligence agencies, CIA's track record has not always been hunky dory. Vietnam, Korea, the Bay of Pigs fiasco, hostage crisis in Iran, to mention a few, do not make it a zero-error outfit. Its failure to anticipate, Pokharan II – not that it had predicted Pokharan I for that matter – was highly embarrassing for the elite organisation. And despite all its secrecy, the organisation was penetrated by several deep cover agents of KGB during the Cold War era.

In 1999, a year after the CIA's Director declared war on al Qaeda, the agency was still training its spy recruits in the art of working embassy cocktail parties and James Bond style evasive driving, according to a book by a lady who worked in CIA's clandestine service. Even after 9/11 attacks, CIA was slow to change espionage tactics, and was using the same training model that was used in Cold War years, says Lindsay Moran in her book, *Blowing My Cover: My Life as a CIA Spy*.

But the CIA was eventually shaken and stirred by the post-9/11 US intelligence reforms and its brilliant covert operation that resulted in the termination of world's most wanted terrorist Osama bin Laden just shows that the agency has evolved into an efficient intelligence machine. And that's the essential difference between a crack outfit and a mediocre one. No organisation can be expected to be always on target, but the pursuit for excellence is something that Indian intelligence agencies must pick up from the CIA.

Inter Services Intelligence (ISI)

An average Indian, who perhaps may not have ever heard of R&AW, is pretty much aware of Pakistan's Inter Services Intelligence, ISI. And, why not? After all, ISI's hand is seen in all the troubles from Kashmir to Kanyakumari and Kutch to Kohima, and has arguably been rated the world's best intelligence agency by a website. ISI has orchestrated many terrorist attacks against India, including the bombing of its Embassy in Kabul in 2008.

The ISI was founded in 1948 by a British army officer, Maj Gen R Cawthome, then Deputy Chief of Staff in Pakistan Army. In 1958, Field Marshal Ayub Khan, then President of Pakistan, enhanced the role of ISI in safeguarding Pakistan's interests, monitoring opposition politicians, and sustaining military rule. Comprising of hundreds of civilian and military officers, and thousands of other workers, the agency's headquarters is located in Islamabad.

The Organisation

The organisational structure of ISI is quite similar to most other intelligence agencies in the world but the absolute power it enjoys in Pakistan is something which even the omnipotent erstwhile KGB could never boast of.

The ISI is headed by a Director General (DG) of the rank of Lt Gen/Maj Gen, who is invariably a serving officer of the Pakistan Army. The ISI being an inter-services organisation, its DG can be from any one of the three services but ever since its inception this elite outfit has never been headed by an officer from Pakistan Air Force or Navy. The reason being that the DG is always the Army Chief's man, even though on paper he functions under the Ministry of Defence and is supposed to be the Adviser to the Prime Minister on intelligence matters.

The ISI is broadly structured as follows[12]:

- **The Joint Intelligence Bureau (JIB)** - Responsible for political intelligence, this is the largest Bureau of the ISI having three sub-sections including one dealing specifically with India. The JIB is not only responsible for posting and functioning of Pakistani defence attaches/advisers to foreign countries but also controls the movement of foreign defence attaches within Pakistan.

- **The Joint Counter-intelligence Bureau (JCIB)** - This Bureau is responsible for surveillance of foreign suspects as also the political leaders, civil servants, police and armed forces of Pakistan. Such misuse of intelligence services is quite common in other countries also. In fact, IB, is known to keep tabs on senior defence services officers among others, in India. However, while IB carries out such surveillance at the behest of the central government, the ISI does so on behalf of the Pakistan Army.

- **Joint Intelligence Miscellaneous (JIM)** – It is responsible for espionage activities in other countries and is perhaps the most destructive component of the ISI. The JIM carries out assigned tasks either through its own agents or through officers posted in cover appointments in Pakistani missions abroad. Trained spies are also sent to carry out offensive – read destructive – intelligence assignments in the target countries.

  While members of the JIM are known to have crossed international borders to keep in touch with their agents, most activities on and across the borders are controlled by the army's Field Intelligence Units.

- **Joint Intelligence North (JIN)** – This is a Kashmir specific Bureau which along with the JIM is presumably the hub of all ISI activities in J&K.
- **Joint Signals Intelligence Bureau (JSIB)** – As its name suggests, the bureau carries out SIGINT activities for the ISI.
- **Joint Intelligence Technical (JIT)** – This bureau functions alongside other bureaus especially JSIB – and advises ISI on technical aspects of counter-intelligence.
- **Joint Intelligence Administration (JIA)** – This bureau provides the administrative back-up to the ISI and its personnel posted abroad.
- **Joint Intelligence X (JIX)** – Serves as the secretariat which coordinates other ISI sections and provides administrative support.

The ISI, as such is a combination of the RAW, IB, CBI, various special agencies operating under the Indian Home Ministry, the intelligence directorates of our armed forces and para-military forces and the JIC, all rolled into one[13]. It is the sole and ultimate intelligence machine piloted through remote control or otherwise by the Pakistan Army Chief himself.

The Track Record

Considering its overall scheme of things, the ISI's track record needs to be judged essentially on three fronts i.e. on home turf inside Pakistan, in Afghanistan and most significantly inside India. On the home front, the ISI's role in toppling successive leaders from Zulfiqar Ali Bhutto to Nawaz Sharif – barring Gen Zia-ul-Haq – is too well-known to be repeated here. The ISI grew much stronger under the leadership of Lt Gen Hamid Gul in 1990, when the general elections in Pakistan were believed to have been rigged and a conglomerate of nine, mainly-rightist parties was formed by the ISI to ensure the defeat of Benazir Bhutto's Pakistan's People Party.

In Afghanistan, the ISI has always been active, especially since the time when the Russians invaded Afghanistan. It performed admirably alongside CIA and was largely credited for its efforts in evicting the Communist Regime and the Russians from Afghanistan. The ISI actively participated in Afghan Civil War, backing up the Taliban in their fight against the Rabbani government, and continues to maintain links with the Haqqani network and LeT in North Waziristan.

ISI's thrust on subversive activities and secessionist plans to destabilise the territorial integrity and sovereignty of India is an open secret. The increased infiltration from across the border and the frequent spurts in terrorist attacks across India unfold ISI's sinister gameplan.

The ISI taking advantage of India's soft approach in dealing with extremism and simmering discontent in sections of the Muslim youth, went about the task of creating a Jihadi network which is Jammu and Kashmir specific and India-centric. Their strategy is to keep Kashmir on the boil and to keep the Indian security forces preoccupied with internal security. It has trained and regularly sent militants to Kashmir since 1988. Even as Kashmir was returning to normalcy, at the behest of their ISI mentors, trouble makers reportedly infiltrated the stone-pelting agitation in the summer of 2010.

Kashmir apart, the ISI has slowly but surely shifted its focus of attention towards India's North Eastern border. Now that the entire North Western and North Eastern regions are under their concentration, they are looking towards the maritime borders of Gujarat and Maharashtra, as evidenced by the Mumbai attack on 26-28 November, 2008 (26/11).

That ISI is running a state within state, is by now common knowledge. Answerable neither to the army, nor political leadership, its ever-increasing power and influence, however, got a setback when the US Special Forces killed Osama bin Laden on 2 May, 2011 in Abbottabad, inside a compound located in close vicinity of Pakistan Military Academy. It was not only embarrassing for the ISI but humiliating for Pakistan military as well. The US, a contentious ally of Pakistan in its war against terror, did not take Pakistan into confidence because it feared the raid on Osama's hideout could be jeopardised by elements in the ISI, a fact that points out at growing distrust between the CIA and ISI, in recent times. Within one month after their successful operation, the then CIA Chief Leon Panetta visited Pakistan, with a view to solicit cooperation from Pakistan military and intelligence establishment. But surprised by rigidity shown by the military, which went to the extent of even declining an American offer of security assistance, he had to return without reaching a deal on resetting troubled relations with the ISI.

The death of bin Laden has put the ISI in a very uncomfortable position among the al Qaeda, Haqqani network and the LeT. Just when it was trying to bring about some sanity in its circles post bin Laden, the trial of both David Coleman Headley and Tahawwur Rana commenced in the US, causing more embarrassment for the ISI. And if that was not enough, a Taliban raid on a Pakistan Naval facility soon thereafter, added more insult to the injured pride of the ISI. It will be interesting to watch how the ISI gets out of this mess and tries to regain its past glory, in days to come.

8

What Ails India's Spy Machine?

After having had a look at the organisational structure and track record of some of the world's major intelligence services, one needs to delve into the next logical question: what exactly ails the Indian intelligence machine and why it malfunctions so often?

Even a cursory glance at the events as they unfolded in Kargil and beyond, will suggest that it's not one particular component of the intelligence machine that failed to function properly but it was a systemic failure in general. The whole machine as such, needs a thorough overhaul. It would therefore be in the fitness of things to look for the Achilles' heels in our intelligence system, and turn them into Samson's hair, rather than indulge in the futile blame game and witch hunting.

The Organisational Structure: From a mere study of organisation of Indian intelligence agencies, their basic structure appears to be more or less similar to other such organisations the world over. The problem seems to be at the top, that is the JIC, which like a toothless tiger lacks the regulatory authority and as such is not given due importance by the agencies functioning under it. The intelligence services often do not share the information among each other and if that is not bad enough, they also tend to directly access the powers that be, thus bypassing the JIC whose quintessential role is to coordinate and assess the entire intelligence effort. Their main rival, the ISI being the sole agency that collects, collates and converts information from all the available sources into intelligence, faces no such problem of coordination.

Another aspect connected with the organisation of our intelligence services that needs to be looked into is the autonomy enjoyed by them. While it is essential that such organisations must be given sufficient freedom to operate independently without undue government interference, for obvious reasons they cannot be allowed to build their independent empires free from any public scrutiny. The CIA even though being an independent agency is accountable to the American people through the US Congress Intelligence Oversight Committee. There's been talk of emulating the US model and bringing all intelligence agencies under the purview of a parliamentary overseeing committee.

Politicisation: Politicisation of any government organisation is bad for the system; Politicisation of intelligence services is even worse, especially in a democratic country like India. It not only curbs the initiative and independent functioning of an organisation but also leads to various other ills such as political vendetta and misuse of power for political gains. There have been a few occasions when services of covert units of R&AW have been utilised to destabilise certain state governments considered inimical to the political interests of the ruling party at the center.

At the time of its inception, R&AW would have been placed under the Ministry of Defence, but for Indira Gandhi who realised the value - read political benefit - of having such an organisation under the Cabinet Secretariat.

PN Haksar, her Principal Private Secretary at that time, backed her up and thus R&AW was instituted under the Cabinet Secretariat[14]. If it was Haskar who was instrumental in placing R&AW under direct control of the Cabinet Secretariat, then it was RN Kao who enjoyed maximum power as R&AW's Chief during Indira Gandhi's tenure as Prime Minister. And even as R&AW and Kao both became extremely pervasive and powerful when Indira Gandhi was at the helm, the IB was placed under the oversight control of the Policy Planning Cell, then headed by PN Dhar. Was it by design or default that Haskar, Kao and Dhar belonged to the Kashmiri pundit clan of Indira Gandhi. Needless to say, personal equations between political leaders and intelligence chiefs are not in organisational interest and in fact, prove counter-productive for both and should not be allowed.

Coordination - More often than not, intelligence failures could be largely attributed to lack of coordination between various agencies operating in the area. During my tenure in Ladakh, I had an opportunity to interact with intelligencers of as many five different organisations; the Int Corp, R&AW, IB, CID and Indo-Tibetan Border Police (ITBP). Even though they were all located in a small village within a radius of two kilometers or so, one could sense a feeling of mutual distrust amongst them and quite often they functioned at cross purposes instead of working in tandem. Ironically, the only common bond that existed amongst them was their source of information - a local guy who used to be hired by them all independently and perhaps unwittingly. Now imagine the end result. Information provided by this common source - for whatever its worth - when collated and processed at higher level would be treated as confirmed intelligence since it was supposedly acquired by different agencies and thus different sources.

While lack of coordination dissipates the overall intelligence effort, overlapping of functional roles of certain agencies results in duplication of their work. A case in point is the covert outfits functioning under the Cabinet Secretariat

- SSB and SFF - who seem to be duplicating the work of BSF and ITBP, the two border forces under the Ministry of Home Affairs. A three-member review committee under former Home Secretary K Padmanabhaiah, set up by the government in the 1990s to look into the functioning of these super secret services had recommended disbandment of SSB and absorption of its personnel in other intelligence agencies. However, the proposed disbandment did not take place, since the affected personnel apparently lobbied hard for maintenance of status quo to avoid loss of their seniority if they were side-stepped to other agencies.

Post 9/11, numerous US security agencies were directed to talk to each other and share as much information as they possibly could. This has held the Americans in good stead. A similar nudge needs to guide the Indian intelligence as well.

There is also a need for close coordination with international intelligence community. A lack of cooperation between the intelligence agencies of Russia and the US contributed to key mistakes in the past, but having learnt the lesson, Russia's FSB now routinely exchanges intelligence with its American counterparts as also with Israelis. Historically, R&AW has been close to its western allies and Israeli counterparts, though it doesn't have the kind of links that the CIA has with MI6 and Mossad. But that's okay because when it comes to intelligence issues, each country looks out for itself. Indian intelligence agencies, as such, must fend for themselves, yet on the basis of reciprocity and mutual benefit, cooperate with other intelligence agencies.

One-upmanship: One of the main reasons for lack of coordination in intelligence effort is the element of one-upmanship that exists among various agencies. Whereas healthy competition acts as a source of inspiration for any organisation, unhealthy professional rivalry wherein one tries to score a point over the other can be counter-productive. But unfortunately this happens quite often. As an intelligence staff officer of a brigade in Punjab in 1990, I accompanied an officer from the Int Corps to a police station, for interrogation of suspected militants who had been apprehended from a border village during a cordon-and-search operation the night before. My friend got down to business right away and took about three hours to interrogate 15 of them one by one. After concluding his preliminary interrogation, he asked me as to how many of them could actually be terrorists. "None. Because had there been even one, the BSF guys instead of handing him over to us, would have included him in their own score card", I told him. Later, after sustained interrogation, they were all released as none of them was graded 'Black' (confirmed militant) or even 'Grey' (suspect) – they were all 'Whites' (cleared) as I had predicted.

While this was the case of inter-organisation rivalry, one-upmanship persists within the same organisation also, as I experienced during Operation Rakshak in J&K. My rifle company (sub-unit of an infantry battalion) was deployed alongside the sector headquarters, close to international border. Another company of our neighbouring battalion was located about seven kilometers away along the border. It so happened one day that a local villager approached a Junior Commissioned Officer (JCO) of the other company and informed him about some weapons having been dumped in a well by the militants. The JCO hurried towards his Company Headquarters to inform his Company Commander about the tip off, but since the Company Commander was not available the JCO came to the sector headquarters to inform one of his battalion officers, who was attached there as a staff officer. As luck would have it, that officer along with the sector commander had gone out for reconnaissance. The JCO patiently waited for more than an hour for their return and by the time the two returned and rushed to the cache site, the civil police who were also tipped off by the villagers, had already captured a big haul of weapons and of course, the glory.

All this while I was present at my company location but the JCO did not want to share his information with me since I was not from his battalion. In any case, he could have rushed to the spot himself and taken over all the weapons which were there for the asking, but then initiative, or rather lack of it, amongst the JCO cadre of Indian Army is a different matter altogether.

Recently (June 2011), the IB wrote to the Union Home Ministry objecting to the role played by NTRO in internet interceptions, thus amplifying the turf battles amongst intelligence agencies. The IB reportedly pointed out that NTRO was not an authorised law enforcement agency and was therefore not authorised to carry out interception and certainly not on behalf of all the law enforcement agencies. This is when there is a dire need for a common intelligence database that allows all security agencies within India to speedily exchange and update information.

Professionalism: On January 19, 1953, like all young American men of the time were required to do at age 18, Elvis Presley, the famous American Pop icon, registered for the US Selective Service System. Under the draft system, young men of good health were expected to be available to serve in the military for two years of active duty and then four years in the reserves. (This system continued until after the Vietnam War when the US went to a voluntary military system).

In March 1958, Elvis, leaving behind his chauffeur driven Limousine, said his good-byes and Private Presley was bused with the others from Memphis to Fort Chaffee, Arkansas, for further processing.

The US Navy and the Air Force had offered bids for his services, the Navy offering to create a specially trained 'Elvis Presley Company'and the Air Force thinking it would be good for him to tour their recruiting centers. Elvis turned down their offers, not wanting any special treatment. He was going to serve like a regular GI. A thorough professional indeed.

Now compare his professional attitude with that of an Int Corps Officer who was entrusted with the challenging job of raising a special intelligence unit, the CIIU, as part of the elite Delta Force in the Doda Sector in J&K. Right from the word go, the gentleman started complaining to all who would care to listen about the meager resources available to him, poor standard of his officers and other ranks, paucity of vehicles and accommodation and just about everything. To be fair to him, there were some teething problems which are quite normal in an organisation under raising, but the problem with our man was that he had his priorities all mixed up. He tried endlessly to get a civil pattern vehicle - a car actually - released for himself rather than the essential equipment required for the smooth functioning of his unit. The unit did produce some commendable results but that was mainly because of certain dedicated officers who bashed on regardless of the lopsided sense of professionalism of their boss.

And then there was this Non-Commissioned Officer (NCO) of LU who happened to be operating in a border village in Ladakh. He used to often approach me for small administrative favours and I normally obliged. However, once he requested me to attach one of my Company boys with him as his helper who could cook for him and take care of his other personal chores. Now this wasn't only a case of asking for too much, but I thought this so-called intelligencer was not being professional. He was willing to compromise his undercover status for his personal comfort, and so I turned down his rather unreasonable and unprofessional demand. Later, his boss during one of his rare visits to our remote post also tried to convince - or rather pester - me to oblige the NCO, but I did not budge despite being threatened, albeit covertly, with dire consequences for not cooperating. Luckily, there were no skeletons hidden in my cupboard which these guys could expose and I was able to complete my tenure without any problem.

Anyway, it is not only the Int Corps which is lacking in professionalism. The other agencies are no different since this seems to be our national weakness. The recent goof-ups in the list of 50 most wanted fugitives handed over to Pakistan by the Indian government was not only embarrassing but our intelligence people should be responsible for such glaring gaffes, betrays a lack of professionalism. Of the 50 names in India's most wanted list, two were traced back to India, while three on the Red Corner Notices were dead and another two lodged in jail. With the recent economic liberalisation, our private sector has been forced to adopt virtues of professionalism of the multi-national companies. It's time our intelligence set up follows suit.

Foresight: To be successful in its missions, an intelligence organisation must be able to predict the unexpected. For this, besides the professional acumen, one needs to think ahead with foresight. Unfortunately, like professionalism, the sense of foresight also happens to be India's national weakness and is visible everywhere. Lack of adequate basic infrastructure, unplanned cities with heavily congested roads and choked drainage system, absence of effective disaster management plans, illiteracy with all its connected problems, lopsided health and education policies are all due to lack of foresight on the part of political leadership and bureaucracy.

Indian intelligence system obviously is no different. Some of the intelligence failures discussed earlier are attributable to lack of foresight, above all else. The fiascos of Operation Bluestar and Operation Pawan were actually quite predictable had the persons concerned bothered to look ahead. During Bluestar, why was it that the troops of only a few army units resorted to mutiny whereas other units having same class composition of troops, remained unaffected? The reason is simple. The Commanding Officers with foresight could anticipate the trouble and had motivated their men accordingly. Those who did not predict the unexpected were caught unaware by the pitfall.

Forget foresight, India's spy machine has quite often failed to use even hindsight; and that is inexcusable in the intelligence game.

Acceptance of Intelligence: As brought out earlier, some political parties had outrightly blamed the government for Kargil intrusion and in fact pronounced it guilty of deliberately ignoring vital information provided by the intelligence agencies about Pakistan gameplan well in time. Some opponents of the then Prime Minister Atal Behari Vajpayee had gone to the extent of blaming him for willfully ignoring the intelligence reports, as acceptance of same would have jeopardised his Lahore bus initiative. While these allegations were perhaps farfetched, there have been occasions in the past when hard intelligence was not accepted by the leaders, perhaps due to their political compulsions.

For instance in 1975, the then IB Chief, Jayaram had advised the Prime Minister against promulgation of emergency[15] but Indira Gandhi did not accept his advice as it was contrary to her political ambition and went on to impose emergency on the country and thus blemished the otherwise spotless image of India as the world's largest democracy.

Similarly, Rajiv Gandhi chose to ignore repeated warnings from the intelligence agencies regarding clear threats to his life but he probably did not want to lose his mass appeal and thus continued to mingle with the crowds at his own peril.

Acceptance of intelligence, or rather its non-acceptance, has been a perennial issue with all intelligence agencies around the world. The Arab-Israel war in 1973 happened, not because there were no prior inputs but because no intelligence analyst was prepared to stake his reputation on those inputs indicating that Egypt intended to launch an attack across the Suez against a militarily much stronger Israel.

Similarly, hard intelligence about Pakistan's moves prior to Indo-Pakistan war in 1965 was ignored by the CIA, because it was not in line with the known imbalance of power between the two countries. Interestingly, the information about Pakistan's plan for capture of Kashmir, was provided to a CIA agent, Duane R Clarridge, in Jeddah, Saudi Arabia, by guess who? Well, he was none other than the Lion of Kashmir, Sheikh Abdullah. Rating the information as 'Explosive', Clarridge thus recalls his meeting with Abdullah, in his book

A Spy For All Seasons – My Life in the CIA – "The Lion of Kashmir basically gave me the whole plan. Pakistanis were going to begin infiltrating small guerrilla units out of Azad Kashmir into Kashmir proper. Once the insurrection got under way in Kashmir, regular Pakistani military forces would come to Kashmir's aid". His report received little attention at the CIA Headquarters until just before the war, when the "Pakistani gameplan was unfolding according to the information Sheikh Abdullah had given me absolutely to the letter", rues Clarridge. Explosive intelligence indeed. One wonders why the Sheikh didn't share this with the Indian government. Or did he?

Needless to say, the best intelligence is of no value unless it is accepted by the decision makers, but unfortunately an unbiased objective analysis provided by the intelligence apparatus quite often finds no takers at the decisionmaking level. So, in order to please their political bosses, the intelligence heads sometimes modify their intelligence inputs instead of acquainting the decision maker with unvarnished bitter truth.

Consistency: No organisation can be expected to have a cent per cent success rate and capability to deliver goods unfailingly all the time, least of all the intelligence machine. Because more often than not, the intelligence analysts are required to grope in the dark, deal with intangibles and still make fairly accurate predictions. To add to their woes, many ambiguous situations and conflicting indicators are all part of the intelligence puzzle. And then the adversary obviously is not obliged to follow the pattern as may have been projected by the analysts after carefully and diligently processing all available inputs. Not surprisingly therefore, track record of all intelligence agencies including the highly rated CIA and ISI is a mixed bag. Even thoroughly professional outfits such as Mossad and the erstwhile KGB have sometimes gone completely off the target in their intelligence assignments.

In Kargil, the Indian intelligence machine did pick up bits and pieces of information but somehow failed to solve the complete jigsaw puzzle. The intelligence pundits could not provide an unambiguous, accurate and timely assessment of the Pakistan designs in Kargil to the government. They did anticipate some problem but could not perceive the magnitude of the Pakistan's efforts in the sector. Their threat perception at best was an underestimated one and therefore may have been underrated by the people at the helm.

But let's face the fact. Kargil wasn't really an exception. There have been quite a few intelligence failures before and since then owing to the dysfunctional intelligence machine. To be fair, the Indian intelligence agencies have had some remarkable successes as well. However, they need to be more consistent and if they improve upon their overall success rate, to say about 80 to 90 per cent hits on targets, things should be fine.

Killer Instinct: When Amritraj (Vijay), Borg (Bjorn) and Conners (Jimmy) hit the international tennis scene, the media called them ABC of tennis and talent wise they were rated in the same order. While Borg and Conners went on to become living legends by winning many grand slams, Vijay Amritraj lost his steam midway and was left far behind. The reason? Well, he lacked something that is a must to excel at the top – the killer instinct.

Same goes for the Indian intelligence agencies. They perhaps lack the killer instinct to take on the ISI. The question is why the Pakistanis, who were Indians before the partition, have it in them and the Indians don't. It is probably because of their upbringing. After all, it is Aurangzeb and not Akbar who figures in their children's history books, as an ideal hero worth emulating. The killer instinct is not something inborn as many of us would like to believe, but can be inculcated. Otherwise, why is it that despite all odds the Indian soldier was able to defeat his Pakistani counterpart in Kargil, or in all previous wars for that matter? The Indian soldier gets his killer instinct from training, motivation and *esprit-de-corps*. If that be so, why can't the Indian intelligencers adopt the same techniques to pep themselves up and beat the ISI at its own game?

Money Matters: 'Paucity of funds' is perhaps one of the most common excuses one makes to cover one's failures in India. Pakistanis are actually no different, as even the ISI blamed shortage of resources for their failure to detect and stop an American incursion into its sovereign space when they raided bin Laden's hideout in Abbotabad.

During Operation Vijay, some Indian Army officers blamed the decline in the country's defence budget over the years for their lack of preparedness in Kargil. While it's no secret that the Indian Army's operations in Kargil did get cramped due to some critical deficiencies of weapons, equipment and even clothing, but what about the deficiencies in intelligence acquisition? Were intelligence services suffering from resource crunch too? It does not seem very likely. Since their finances come mainly from secret funds, one cannot really quote any specific figures, but these organisations are known to be quite well off in terms of resources.

Whether their resources are optimally utilised is another issue. One has seen the MI funds of the Army of which very little trickles down at the unit level in any case, being frittered away on nonessentials by the commanders even as many useful sources of information went abegging for want of adequate compensation. The civil intelligence agencies are no different. They too believe in paying peanuts to their sources and not surprisingly often get monkeys to do their jobs, whereas their rivals like CIA and ISI are known to spend lavishly on their sources. But it is not as much a question of availability of funds as the power to spend the same.

While operating in the field, the CIA agents are given free hand to hire sources. In the late sixties, one of their agents operating in a banana republic was asked to provide an expensive sports car for one of the local politicians for return favours. He did not have to think twice to close the deal[16]. On the other hand, in 1978 one of R&AW's Pakistani agents had been offered the entire blue print and plans for the Kahuta nuclear plant for a mere $ 10,000 but the deal could not materialize. Why? Not because R&AW did not have sufficient funds but because of undue hierarchical control over the funds. The R&AW chief had to approach the then Prime Minister Morarji Desai for the approval of the deal, who believe it or not, refused. Worse, he apparently informed the Pakistani diplomats about it and the poor agent was left in the cold[17]. Ironically, Seymour Hersh , renowned American investigative journalist, in his 1983 book "*The Price of Power: Kissinger in the White House*" had accused Morarji Desai of selling secrets to the CIA during the Johnson and Nixon administrations, especially in 1971 when India and Pakistan went to war. Desai was allegedly paid $20,000 per month by the CIA for services rendered. But that's another story.

The point is, intelligence invariably fails not due to paucity of funds but probably due to unfocused expenditure.

Casual Attitude: Of the innumerable things which are peculiar to India, the '*Chalta Hai* attitude' - or casual approach towards everything - finds no parallel anywhere else in the world. Tsunami that hit Indian shores in December 2004, caused large scale destruction. No one could have done much to stop a cyclone of such severity but many human lives could have been saved had there been an effective disaster management plan in place. While the Met office had anticipated the storm four days in advance, warnings to various districts were issued by the State government two days later. Even then no warning ever reached a vast section of the local population. Worse, it took almost a week for the casual government machinery to get activated and provide rudimentary rescue and relief measures.

Seven years down the line, India still isn't really prepared for Tsunamis and other natural calamities. The so-called Disaster Management organisation is not adequately equipped to meet such challenges.

Indian intelligence community is no different and their psyche and basic attitude happens to be the same as the rest of the nation. Consider this: During one of my stints in a border area in the Jammu region, I was once woken up early in the morning by the local villagers who had nabbed a suspected Pakistani intruder who was moving around suspiciously in the village during the wee hours. The suspect however claimed that he was very much an Indian hailing from Gurdaspur in Punjab and was actually a source of the R&AW. He further stated that he had been launched the previous night but had got lost while crossing the IB and instead of reaching his destination across he had unwittingly strayed back into own village. I cross checked his alibi with an official of the R&AW in that area who confirmed it as true. While handing over the individual to the R&AW official I could not help asking him as to why their source was carrying tell tale stuff like Indian currency and a HMT (Indian make) watch on his person during his mission. The official had no valid answer to offer but tried to pass the buck by saying that since the source was launched through the BSF, they should have searched him before release. Anyway, the point is, this source - for whatever his worth - had been launched in a totally casual manner. *Chalta hai,* so what? Well, the intelligence game can never be won with such a lackadaisical and casual approach.

Tenacity: No other profession perhaps demands the kind of persistent, dogged and tenacious approach to work as spying. Behind every successful intelligence operation, there is painstaking intelligence work, which sometimes could stretch to years. Hunting down of Osama bin Laden by the CIA is a case in point. The violent final minutes when a team of US Navy SEALs shot bin Laden to death was the culmination of years of intelligence effort, including interrogation of CIA detainees, where sometimes what was not said was as useful as what was. Inside the CIA team hunting bin Laden, it always was clear that bin Laden's vulnerability was his couriers. He would never let al Qaida foot soldiers, or even his senior commanders, know the location of his hideout. But if he wanted to get his messages out, somebody had to carry them; someone he could trust with his life. If they could find that courier, he'd possibly lead them to bin Laden.

It was as far back as 2002, that in a secret CIA prison in Eastern Europe, al Qaida's No 3 leader, Khalid Sheikh Mohammed, gave authorities the nicknames of several of bin Laden's couriers. Those names were among thousands of leads the CIA was pursuing.

It took years of work for intelligence agencies to identify the courier's real name. When they did identify him, he was nowhere to be found. The CIA's sources didn't know where he was hiding. Bin Laden was famously insistent that no phones or computers be used near him, so the eavesdroppers at the National Security Agency kept coming up cold. Then in July 2010, the courier had a telephone conversation with someone who was being monitored by US intelligence. The courier was located in the bustling streets near Peshawar and after weeks of surveillance, he led the CIA agents to Osama's hideout, a sprawling compound in Abbottabad, close to Pakistan Military Academy. If bin Laden was hiding there, in a busy suburb, it challenged much of the agency's early assumptions. But there was this CIA analyst, John – his middle name – who had the ability to spot the importance of seemingly insignificant details and to weave disparate strands of information into a meaningful story. He could pretty much sense that bin Laden was probably hiding out there.

To confirm and be absolutely sure about Osama's presence inside the compound, the CIA ran a fake vaccination programme in Abbottabad with a view to obtain his DNA samples. A Pakistani doctor who ran the programme did manage to temporarily gain access to the compound, but he never saw bin Laden and wasn't successful in getting DNA samples from any of his family.

But owing to their dogged pursuit spread over many years, the CIA finally got their man anyway. Tenacity pays.

Mind matters: Indians are good losers. It shouldn't be so in a culture seemingly obsessed with winning and winners, where parents and teachers start early and put extra pressure on class I students to excel. Yet, we end up as losers. Is it because India didn't have a wild West, a Protestant work ethic, or a generation of baby boomers? Is it because the Independence Movement failed to create a surge of long lasting nationalism the same way little Boy and fat Man did for Japan? Or is it because the Indian state never veered far enough left off centre to instill in people an obsession to win. It could be any of these. Just as it could be the prevalent culture of mediocrity that makes us tolerate imperfection, the emphasis on quantity and not quality, even sheer lethargy. Then there's the fabled sense of fatalism. From the classroom to boardroom there's an almost universal belief in fate. To most Indians, victory and defeat are not mutually exclusive outcomes in a game of skill but preordained ends that no amount of human endeavour can alter. Expectedly, no one tries hard. Result: emotions, empty rhetoric, and sentimentalism invariably triumph over reason and logic.

There is, as anyone familiar with India must be aware, no such thing as singular Indian psyche. There are combinations of variables such as religion, region, caste, language, income and education. Still, there are common traits across this multitude of psyches. One such is negativity. The four major religions that have originated in India, Hinduism, Buddhism, Jainism and Sikhism preach tolerance and spirituality. Religious texts such as the *Bhagwad Gita* exhort believers to strive on selflessly without any expectation of a payback. And Gandhian thought espouses a moderate outlook towards life and material success. The little is much concept seems to be ingrained in Indian psyche. There's nothing wrong with austerity; only it gets in the way of single-minded pursuit of success, material or otherwise.

A couple of centuries of colonial rule have also left their mark on the Indian psyche, having bred a certain sense of inferiority and some diffidence. Also, there's a predilection for conventionalism. Individualism is frowned upon in India. None of these constraints matter out of the country. And so Indians have done very well for themselves out of India – in medicine, nuclear physics, finance, banking and technology. Indians have all that is required to succeed. If they are provided an environment to succeed, they are second to none. When the Americans couldn't crack an encrypted message they came across while investigating 9/11 attacks, they approached a 17-year-old Ankit Fardia in

Delhi about whom *The New York Times* had done a feature. Fardia, author of *Guide to Ethical Hacking,* came up with the key to crack the al Qaida message, within ten days. While this guy is an exceptional talent who has excelled on his own, you need support systems for ordinary talent to blossom into an extraordinary one. Management guru Peter Drucker once described an organisation as something that enabled ordinary people do extraordinary things. Creating winners then is the responsibility of the system.

The Human Factor: Any organisation is as good or bad as its men, or rather its personnel, to be politically correct. This may appear to be stating the obvious but its importance has not been fully understood by the Indian intelligence community, or so it seems. While the civilian agencies are officered by bureaucrats from IAS and IPS, supposedly brilliant people, their field operatives are not exactly the best in the business.

The human resource management of MI is apparently even worse as one comes across many odd balls in the organisation.

Sample this: An officer who was not found fit to be a Lt Col by the Army's Selection Board, was posted to MI-1, considered as one of the most important desks of the MI Directorate as it deals with Pakistan specific intelligence. An isolated case may be? Not really. Many officers in the MI Directorate are not high profile. Things are not much different with MI's cutting edge, the Int Corps. Though on paper only high/above average officers are seconded to Int Corps, on ground things seem to be quite different and I say that from my personal experience.

In Army, whatever the level of command, a Commander must have timely and accurate information about the adversary to plan a successful operation. That means intelligence is as important, if not more, as the operations and going by the same logic, intelligence appointments should be treated at par with the operational ones. But the army's MS Branch does not think that way. It's common knowledge that while only the best officers are posted as operations staff officers, the average officers - invariably superceded ones - are given the intelligence appointments, especially at the level of divisional headquarters and above. Ironically, the divisional headquarters is the first level in the chain of command which has various intelligence sources and agencies at its disposal. The senior most intelligence staff officer at the divisional headquarters - GSO1 (Int) - besides being the Adviser to the General Officer Commanding (GOC) of the division on all matters pertaining to intelligence and counter-intelligence is also responsible to coordinate the functioning of all intelligence elements of the formation and extract maximum output from them. But whereas his counterpart in the operations branch is always a Defence Services Staff College alumnus - read high flier - the intelligence staff officer despite the vital importance of his job is invariably a-no-longer-in-the-run kind of officer.

When Headquarters Delta Force, a divisional level headquarters of the Rashtriya Rifles, was raised in August 1994, it is said that the dossiers of all the officers (including the intelligence staff) were personally screened by the Deputy Military Secretary and only high profile officers were posted to this elite group. One is not really sure how far this is true, but since yours truly also happened to be part of this select group of officers, it is quite flattering for one's ego to accept it as a fact. I was posted as GSO2 (Intelligence) and rightly so as I had done the Intelligence Staff Officers Course at the Military Intelligence School at Pune, a year back, and moreover, hail from the Doda District of J&K, the area of operations of Delta Force. The MS Branch, for a change, had done its home work I thought. But it turned out to be by default rather than design, as by the time I reported on duty, the appointment of GSO2 (Intelligence) had been scrapped and I was absorbed in another non-intelligence position. The MS Branch may have had organisational constraints for doing so but the fact that I was the only officer in the entire Delta Force who happened to be a local was also ignored by the officers at the helm in the headquarters. Despite ample feelers from my side, no one thought it prudent to exploit my 'home ground advantage' in the intelligence field. They probably thought it's only in cricket that playing on home turf can be advantageous. Incidentally, in Kargil, best results were achieved by the sons of the soil from Ladakh Scouts. Isn't it time the MS Branch gets its priorities right and selects horses for the courses.

As far as the IB and R&AW are concerned, my interaction with these organisations has mainly been in the field and hence restricted to their junior cadre. But then, it is the field operatives who act as the anchor and can make or mar any organisation. I do not wish to generalise but I observed that most of their officials who I happened to interact with, were not really cut for the job at hand. They didn't have a flair and professional competence essential for intelligence work. Besides, some looked old, tired and jaded. One reason for this could probably be that both the organisations being top heavy tend to neglect their grassroots level cadre. Or perhaps the job on offer is not lucrative enough to attract the right material. The recruitment directly to R&AW of UPSC exam qualifiers hasn't thrown up the requisite material as just a few have opted for the organisation in the last ten years.

While surfing the CIA's web-site on the internet I was surprised to see their Kids Page to familiarise the young US citizens with the CIA's organisation and functioning in a very simple and forthright manner. It also has a games section, with games like Break the Code, Aerial Analysis Challenge, Photo Analysis Challenge and several other games for the kids to play the spy on line. Besides being educative, the site obviously aims at attracting their future agents to the organisation.

CIA, despite being the world's most hi-tech intelligence service, realises the importance of the human factor. The Indian intelligence agencies must do the same.

Part Three
Fixing the Spy Machine

9

Beyond the Obvious

There is this poster of Sir Isaac Newton that shows the legendary scientist sitting under a tree, having just been hit on the head by a falling apple. Its caption reads:

Experience is not what happens to you; it's what you do with what happens to you.

Had the Indian political and bureaucratic establishment followed Newton's advice and learnt lessons from Kargil, more than 200 people who made the mistake of being in Mumbai on 26/11 and 13/7, perhaps would have been alive today.

The Kargil war is now history. But Pakistan's proxy war against India is far from over. If anything, it seems to have been stepped up from time to time as indicated by militants attack on Indian Parliament and the carnage in Mumbai on 26/11. In fact, soon after the operations in Kargil were terminated, the Pakistani foreign minister was heard telling the BBC that there would be 'ten more Kargils' if the Kashmir problem was not resolved.

More recently, the Lashkar-e-Taiba's supreme religious and political head, Hafiz Mohammad Saeed, told his top functionaries: "The only language India understands is that of force, and that is the language it must be talked to in".

In any event, and sooner than later, fresh impetus to cross-border terrorism in India will be provided by Pashtun and Punjabi veterans of the US Af-Pak War. But despite being convinced about Pakistan's strategy to use terrorism to destabilise India, the Indian agencies have done precious little to develop a meaningful counter-terrorism strategy that can deter Pakistan.

Nineteenth century French diplomat Talleyrand's famous remark about the Bourbons could well apply to the rulers of India, who seem to have "learnt nothing and forgotten everything". Not learning a lesson from the attack on India's Parliament, Members of Legislative Assembly (MLAs) were up in arms over tightening of security set-up in Delhi Secretariat. When Delhi government introduced restricted access rules in the Secretariat, it fuelled a row with legislators describing it as a move to keep citizens away from government. Their protest was not only vocal but it had even turned physical. Some MLAs challenged security guards who tried to enforce the restrictions.

The attitude of the Members of Parliament (MPs) towards security is no different. Two years after the attack by terrorists, some of them were reportedly misusing car parking labels and carelessly handing out visitor passes. There were cases of MPs making colour photocopies of the parking labels issued to them which subsequently found their way to the windshields of other cars. Electronic car parking labels have since been introduced. With such an attitude, it's hardly surprising that India's top policy-makers haven't really bothered to put a cohesive counter-intelligence strategy in place. Worse, in each crisis the Indian leadership has emerged as a weak responder. From Kashmir to Kandahar and from 26 /11 the to 13/7, the leadership has repeatedly failed to take on the terror bull by its horns.

In the aftermath of 26/11, then Union Home Minister Shivraj Patil lost his job for his failure to anticipate the attack. The supposedly competent Chidambaram who replaced Patil, had this to say after 13/7 - "there's been no intelligence failure since there was no intelligence". Going by that logic, he might as well disband all intelligence agencies so that there is no intelligence and as such, no intelligence failure. Obviously, it doesn't seem to matter who happens to be at the helm of affairs; the system remains much the same. The Ram Pradhan Committee that was set up by the Maharashtra government post-26/11, had made a specific reference to the American experience after 9/11 while recommending ways to improve intelligence. The US carried out significant intelligence reforms and the results are there for all to see. There have been no terror attacks in the US since 9/11. Other countries have also fine tuned their intelligence agencies in the wake of ever growing menace of terrorism. While the Pradhan Committee report gathers dust, let's have a look at the US intelligence reforms post 9/11.

> *"Over the last two years, (since the enactment of the US Intelligence Reform and Terrorism Prevention Act –IRTPA – of 2004) the Intelligence Community has achieved good results through a concerted effort to integrate itself more tightly, share information more freely, coordinate its actions more efficiently, define its priorities more clearly, and align its resource expenditures against those priorities more strategically".*
>
> – Excerpt from Unclassified Statement of the Chairman, US Senate Select Committee on Intelligence, 23 January 2007

The US intelligence reforms were focused on structural change, analysis, collection, management, requirements, the information enterprise, and science and technology.

A great deal of structural change has occurred within the Intelligence Community in response both to past failures and pressing threats. The National Counter Terrorism Centre (NCTC) stands at the centre of the intelligence contribution to the War on Terror. NCTC is led by an official designated as the mission manager for counter-terrorism. It comprises officers representing all the relevant federal departments and draws on and shares information from thirty different intelligence networks, including foreign and domestic threat information. It guides the counter-terrorism analytic workload across the Intelligence community and when events mandate, it becomes a hub for critical intelligence support to the Nation's leaders.

The National Security Branch (NSB) and National Clandestine Service (NCS) were established within the FBI and CIA respectively. These two changes, the NCS and the NSB were major events, strengthening the human intelligence effort within US and abroad. In coordination with the National Clandestine Service, the FBI, the Defence Intelligence Agency, and the Military Services are improving the training, tradecraft, and integration of their case officers and operations.

Countries like UK and Israel which face terror threat have also carried out comprehensive intelligence reforms. France's international spy agency, the DGSE, has recently got a budget boost and recruited hundreds of people, to better fend off threats like terrorism and nuclear proliferation.

In India, nothing much has changed after Kargil and 26/11 and the nation's intelligence effort leaves a lot to be desired. That the India's Spy Machine needs fixing is pretty obvious but while overhauling it, people at the helm must look beyond the obvious. While it is obvious that India needs to equip itself with high-end security systems, the human factor is more important for future protection against intelligence failures.

For the ease of understanding of the lay reader, here's a brief introduction to sources of intelligence gathering. All intelligence acquisition systems are broadly classified into two main heads: Human Intelligence (HUMINT) and Technical Intelligence (TECHINT). The latter can be divided into two distinct categories. Imagery Intelligence (IMINT) and Signal Intelligence (SIGINT). These again can be further sub-divided into land based systems like Electronic Fighting Vehicles Systems capable of providing Electronic Support Measures (ESM), Electronic Counter Measures (ECM), Communication Intelligence (COMINT), Electronic Intelligence (ELINT) and the airborne systems such as the Unarmed Aerial Vehicles (UAV), Joint Surveillance and Target Attack Radar System (JSTARS), Advanced Tactical Air Reconnaissance Systems (ATAR) and the Satellites. Technical jargon be ignored; what all this simply means is that information can either by acquired by men - and, of course women - or by machines.

Let's first see what role the machines, or rather technology, can play in the intelligence wars of today and may be tomorrow.

10

Hi-Tech Intelligence

The Indian Army in Kargil lacked proper battlefield surveillance equipment. The Infantry man was dependent on second generation night vision goggles and obsolete devices such as BFSR Mark 1 (Battlefield Surveillance Radar) which could hardly discern enemy movement beyond half a kilometer or so. Now the army has medium range radars capable of detecting enemy movement upto 10 kilometers and the obsolete night vision goggles/binoculars have been replaced with the latest thermal imaging devices that can detect intruders several kilometers away.

Acquisition of UAVs and other state-of-the-art surveillance and communication equipment has enhanced India's intelligence acquisition capability post-Kargil. Better late than never? The cliché notwithstanding, the point is that it's not as if these technologies were futuristic when Kargil happened. In fact, the hi-tech equipment had been part of the army's shopping list for long. So, why the delay, one may ask. Some defence analysts and most bureaucrats put the blame squarely on India's limited defence budget. They say the cost of maintaining the massive manpower of the armed forces, leaves very little – not more than 10 per cent or so – for modernisation of weapons and equipment.

While the government did enhance the defence budget post-Kargil, things have not changed much because there hasn't been any change in bureaucratic attitude. Consider this: Gen VP Malik, the Indian Army Chief during Kargil, had proposed to downsize the army – the tail part – and thus save Rs 500 crore which could be utilised to enhance its combat efficiency. It was a laudable proposal and a step in the right direction but sadly, the response from the Defence Ministry if anything, was rather lukewarm. But then the bureaucrats are known to love the redtape and the great Indian bureaucracy continues to move at its own pace.

The Directorate of Perspective Planning under the Defence Ministry, while considering the requirement of men and material of the armed forces is supposed to look at least 15 years ahead. Ironically, the gestation period for India's major defence deals is about the same.

In any event, such quick fix solutions as enhancement of defence budget needs to be viewed from another angle. In view of the state of economy and limited means of the nation, how much can be really spent on defence, after all. Post Kargil, Siachenisation of the LoC has put an additional burden on the defence budget. Add on the cost of acquisitions underway as also planned and even an enhanced defence budget may not suffice. The long term perspective as such, should be viewed while considering defence expenditure *vis-a-vis* the GDP. Defence spending should not occur in spurts, driven by knee jerk responses to crisis but should be stepped up periodically in a planned manner.

And it's not just the defence budget that needs to be planned in phases but also defence R&D which must progress in stages to avoid overstrain and to ensure development of a sound technological base. Rather than stubbornly concentrate on the high end technology, the DRDO and other defence oriented labs shift their focus on more immediate concerns. The scientists at DRDO had themselves admitted that simple concepts like Infra Red or Synthetic Aperture Radar (SAR) fitted in a small aircraft – even a two-seater – could have been employed by the IAF on reconnaissance missions thereby substantially reducing the number of sorties that were actually flown by the fighters during Operation Vijay. "This does not involve technology which has to be imported. Our Remote Sensing Satellites employ such equipment to tell us about crop yield or flood damage. If we had flown an aircraft with SAR, the first bunkers built by the militants would have alerted us", observed the DRDO scientists[18].

Another facet of going all out in pursuit of high technology pertains to the dizzy advances made in the field of information technology (IT). This is one field where India is a force to reckon with. The army too seems to have latched on to the ubiquitous microchip and has started thinking in terms of cyber wars wherein surveillance is based on satellites, UAV and battlefield radar's capable of tracking the enemy beyond visual range thousands of kilometers across the battlefield.

The power of the microchip was abundantly displayed during the Gulf war two decades ago. According to Alan D Campen, a retired air force officer and formerly Director of Command and Control Policy in the US Defence Department, the Gulf was a war where an ounce of silicon in a computer may have had more effect than a ton of uranium".[19]

Cyber wars apart, one of the major concerns worldwide happens to be the fight against terrorism which besides all else requires extremely fine grained information and new computerised techniques for getting it. In the words of Count de Merenches, former Chief of French Intelligence "Precision personal intelligence can be more critical than precision guided munitions"[20]. While the use of IT in the ongoing war against terror is self-evident, one must not forget that the microchip can act as a double-edged sword. It can also be destructively used by terrorists having expertise in hacking. Today's terrorist can do more damage with a keyboard than with a bomb.

Hi-tech communication and intelligence gathering systems with automated data links, have their own inherent vulnerabilities not only against hackers and other external factors such as electronic warfare but can also breakdown at critical junctures due to mechanical failure. TECHINT as such can never replace, or even override HUMINT.

11

Importance of Human Intelligence

Many defence analysts are of the opinion that in the 21st century, Techint will surely replace Humint. IT, Artificial Intelligence (AI), Visual Reality (VR) and Enhanced Reality (ER) will give a new meaning to intelligence and will accord it the capability to analyse the intangibles such as feelings, mind-sets and intention. Maj Gen Yashwant Deva, (Retd), formerly Chief Signal Officer at Indian Army's Southern Command declared some 13 years back that "as technology leaps forward, it will replace human intellect in many ways with ER. Techint will acquire a new face and emerge as one of the most sought after intellectual pursuits. Agent provocateurs and 007s are out of fashion, and soon will be jobless."[21] Well, it hasn't happened so far and unlikely to happen in future either.

Technology has an edge over human brain as far as things like memory, storage and easy recall are concerned but to say that it will soon replace human intellect is stretching things a bit too far. General Deva being from the Corps of Signals is obviously an expert on matters technical but as an infantry man one does really wonder how technology can ever replace human intellect. Technology no doubt can provide the end user with a plethora of operational and intelligence related inputs at the press of a computer key, but can it provide the commander in the field, say an infantry battalion commander, with real time information during operations that his well trained reconnaissance parties can? Despite tremendous progress made in IT of late, is there any software presently available which can tell the commander anything about the state of morale of his troops or give him a feel of the pulse of his command? A computer can display the enemy's strength and general dispositions but what about his state of leadership, determination and drive? Only one computer is capable of analysing all this, the human brain. Technology can only augment the human effort by carrying out some mechanical functions but it cannot replace the human brain, not in the foreseeable future at least.

The point one is trying to make is best emphasised by the Tofflers in their extraordinary book *'War and Anti-War'*. They wrote "...the best satellites can't peer into a terrorist's mind. Nor can they reveal the intentions of Saddam Hussein. Satellites and other technical surveillance technologies told the United States that Saddam Hussein was massing troops near the Kuwait border. But the United States, short on spies in Baghdad's inner circle, brushed aside such warnings as alarmist and mistakenly concluded the troop movements were just a bluff. One human spy in or near Saddam's inner circle might have cast light on his intentions and changed history. The shift to Third Wave (the present era) intelligence system, paradoxically, means a stronger emphasis on human spies – the only kind available in the First Wave (10,000 years ago) world. Only now, First Wave spies come armed with sophisticated Third Wave technologies".

CIA's inability to predict Pokharan II is considered as one of its biggest intelligence failures. If there is any intelligence agency in the world that has all imaginable and unimaginable marvels of technology at its disposal, it's the CIA. As a matter of fact, the Pokharan test ranges were kept under constant surveillance for over four years by CIA's billion dollar spies in the sky that could possibly read out the time from a wrist watch of the Indian soldier far below on the ground.[22] And yet the world's most powerful and hi-tech secret service was so easily deceived by the Indian Army and other key players involved in the conduct of the most secret nuclear explosion. It was a victory of human intellect over technology indeed.

12

Dirty Tricks and Trump Cards

American intelligence operations have scored some successes in Afghanistan by helping tribal leaders score some as well. What do you give the tribal leader who has everything, including multiple wives? A bit of youth in a little blue pill apparently works wonders for friendship and cooperation. Factor this:

"The Afghan chieftain looked older than his 60-odd years, and his bearded face bore the creases of a man burdened with duties as tribal patriarch and husband to four younger women. His visitor, a CIA officer, saw an opportunity, and reached into his bag for a small gift.

Four blue pills. Viagra.

Take one of these. You'll love it, the officer said. Compliments of Uncle Sam.

The enticement worked. The officer, who described the encounter, returned four days later to an enthusiastic reception. The grinning chief offered up a bonanza of information about Taliban movements and supply routes – followed by a request for more pills".[23]

This is how US intelligence officials get their hard intelligence at times. While the CIA has a long history of buying information with cash, the growing Taliban insurgency prompted the use of novel incentives and creative bargaining to gain support in some of the country's toughest neighbourhoods.

The success of this strategy makes sense. Tossing cash at people can compromise sources. People who get large sums of money tend to flash it, and it becomes clear who they work with and terrorists obviously will avoid them like the plague.

Intelligence operatives ought to look for other less obvious enticements. In this case the CIA agents realised that few things would be more private in Muslim tribal life than bedroom performance. Many older tribal chiefs have multiple wives but may not have the physical ability to keep pace. And so few items would make the kind of impression that Viagra does for men in that position, and it's highly unlikely that they'd be chatting about it at the mosque.

In their efforts to win over notoriously fickle warlords and chieftains, the agency's operatives have used a variety of personal services. These include pocket-knives and tools, medicine or surgeries for ailing family members, toys and school equipment, tooth extractions, travel visas, and, occasionally, pharmaceutical enhancements for aging patriarchs with waning libidos. Whatever it takes to make friends and influence people – whether it's building a school or handing out Viagra.

The key is to find a way to meet the informant's personal needs in a way that keeps him firmly on your side but leaves little or no visible trace.

The Indian intelligencers need to do some out of the box thinking and reinvent their dirty tricks department, to obtain hard intelligence. Going by what one has experienced in the field, they are hardly innovative in handling their informers – the trump cards – and all they can think of is dishing out cash – which is peanuts mostly – or sexual favours.

Money and honey seems to be their all purpose remedy, which obviously doesn't work many a time.

Also, the way they treat their informants/agents makes the hard intelligence, harder to get. Sample this:

Surinder Kumar who served in the Indian Army from 1970 to 1978 was lured by an intelligence agency to join them as a spy. They promised him better pay and assured him that his family will be well looked after in case he was caught. He went to Pakistan five times and stayed there for about five years. However, in 1992 he was caught in Khiara village in Narowal district of Pakistan. Initially, he was kept in a military jail for about one year where he suffered third degree torture. Electric shocks deteriorated his health so he was shifted to the Kot Lakhpat jail and awarded twelve years of imprisonment. In jail he was operated upon seven times for reasons never explained to him. Feeling betrayed he told the media persons, "Now that I have returned home, I find my family shattered. Due to lack of support from the intelligence agencies my children have been deprived of education. My wife had to work as housemaid to make both ends meet".

As per Surinder, some of his Indian cell mates hailing from border villages/towns of Punjab and J&K had been in Pakistani jails for over 25 years. They were awarded sentence ranging from 10 to 15 years, however, due to lack of support from any quarter they had not been set free despite the completion of their sentence.

Another case in point is that of Mohanlal Bhaskar, who was circumcised in 1965 and sent across as a spy. After spending 14 years in Jail, Bhaskar penned his experience on spying in a book titled '*An Indian Spy in Pakistan*'. Khushwant Singh, the well-known author writes in the book's preface, "Not all the wealth of the world would persuade me to undergo what Mohanlal Bhaskar had to go through in the jails of Lahore, Kot Lakhpat, Mianwali and Multan. It is a miracle that after all that he lives to tell his tale, retain his sanity and teach in a school".

Bhaskar was on a mission to gather information about Pakistan's nuclear bombs. Betrayed by one of his colleagues, a double agent who was also subsequently arrested and had to face his own demons. He was condemned to prison and tortured in an alien country where he was to spend 14 years of his life. Perhaps he would not have been allowed to emerge alive but his salvation came when he was exchanged for Pakistani spies held by India.

Kashmir Singh, another Indian agent who languished in various jails in Pakistan for 35 years before being released, felt betrayed and has blamed successive governments of the country for not looking after his poor family.

So what needs to be done by India's intelligence community is something as simple as this: be really choosy in selecting the trump cards and not just recruit anybody; train them well and look after them like prized assets to ensure their unflinching loyalty, lest they get lured/trapped by the adversaries.

13

Love and Honey Pots

Madhuri Gupta, the plump, middle-aged, bespectacled plain Jane, anti-thesis of Mata Hari and an Indian Foreign Service official, shattered the belief that it's mostly men who fall for the honey trap. Madhuri apparently had an amorous affair with her Pakistani handler, with whom she shared information, while she was posted at the Indian High Commission in Islamabad. That makes her a lady who's been honey trapped, a rare case in the spy world, where exploiting sex to dig up secret information is usually a woman's domain.

The oldest case of honey trapping in India is an interesting one. When Nehru was the prime minister, an Indian diplomat was enticed by a Russian girl in Moscow. When the KGB exposed pictures of the diplomat with the girl, Nehru just laughed it off, warning the young diplomat to be more careful in future.

There are many examples of Indian men falling for the charms of foreign honey traps. In May 2008, Manmohan

Sharma, a senior R&AW officer, posted in Beijing was called back for falling to the charms of a Chinese honey trap. It was alleged that Sharma was having an affair with his Chinese language teacher, whom Indian authorities suspected to be an informant of the Chinese government. In October 2007, another R&AW officer Ravi Nair was called back from Hong Kong, for his close liaison with a girl believed to be working for a Chinese spy agency. One of the most prominent cases was that of K V Unnikrishnan, a R&AW officer, who fell in love with an air hostess suspected to be an agent.

In December 2011, a Lieutenant Colonel from the Indian Army was reportedly caught in a honey trap while attending a course at one of the military academies in Bangladesh by the ISI and forced to spy for Pakistan against Indian interests. The officer, from an infantry unit, is now facing a court of inquiry to ascertain if he passed on any sensitive information on the Indian Army's deployments and plans.

Unable to bear the pressure from ISI agents, who had videotaped him with a woman, the officer opened up about his unenviable position with the Indian High Commission authorities in Dhaka, following which he was immediately packed off to India.

This is the second incident of an Indian military officer falling prey to a honey trap in the recent years. In 2009, Indian Navy's Commodore Sukhjinder Singh was caught in a honey trap involving him and a Russian woman, after his photographs taken in a compromising position with her came out in the open. He was the Indian Navy's points man in Moscow between 2005 and 2008 to oversee the refit and repair of Admiral Gorshkov Aircraft Carrier that India had bought from Russia in 2004. Even as the Russians, beginning 2007, made demands for hiking the price of the warship, the Commodore was well entrenched in the honey trap. And this, perhaps, may have emboldened the Russians to jack up the cost of repair and refit of the warship progressing at the Sevmash shipyard in Russia. The naval officer was court-martialed for his indiscretion and discharged from service without pension benefits.

It needs no emphasis that India's spy machine must be guarded against such traps and those found guilty of compromising state secrets for sexual or other favours, should be given exemplary punishment.

14

Analysing Intelligence Analysis

Intelligence analysis happened to be my main task while serving with the MI at the Army Headquarters. And it's there that I got an opportunity to work on a project of national importance with a team of scientists from the Defence Institute of Psychological Research. One had always been interested in psychology and mind matters. Motivated by the scientists, I ended up doing a Masters in Psychology rather late in life and while doing so I realised that Intelligence Analysis and Psycho-Analysis are somewhat co-related. Intelligence Analysis is actually the KRA (Key Result Area) of the Intelligence Cycle and as such, is being dwelled upon in detail.

It has been observed that generally the reaction of the Intelligence Community to many problems is to collect more information, even though analysts in many cases already have more information than they can digest. What analysts need is more truly useful information, mostly reliable HUMINT from knowledgeable insiders, to help them make good decisions. Or they need a more accurate mental model and better analytical tools to help them sort through, make sense of, and get the most out of the available ambiguous and conflicting information.[24]

Of the diverse problems that impede accurate intelligence analysis, those inherent in human mental processes are surely among the most important and most difficult to deal with. Intelligence analysis is basically a mental process, but understanding this process is hindered by the lack of conscious awareness of the workings of our own minds.

A basic finding of cognitive psychology is that people have no conscious experience of most of what happens in the human mind. Many functions associated with perception, memory, and information processing are conducted prior to and independently of any conscious direction. What appears spontaneously in consciousness is the result of thinking, not the process of thinking.

Weaknesses and biases inherent in human thinking processes can be demonstrated through carefully designed experiments. They can be alleviated by conscious application of tools and techniques that should be in the analytical tradecraft tool-kit of all intelligence analysts.

When we talk of improving intelligence analysis, we are usually referring to the quality of writing, types of analytical products, relations between intelligence analysts and intelligence consumers, or organisation of the analytical process. Little attention is devoted to improving how analysts think.

Thinking analytically is a skill like carpentry or driving a car. It can be taught, it can be learned, and it can improve with practice. But like many other skills, such as riding a bike, it is not learnt by sitting in a classroom and being told how to do it. Analysts learn by doing. Most people achieve at least a minimally acceptable level of analytical performance with little conscious effort beyond completing their education. With much effort and hard work, however, analysts can achieve a level of excellence beyond what comes naturally.

Regular running enhances endurance but does not improve technique without expert guidance. Similarly, expert guidance may be required to modify long-established analytical habits to achieve an optimal level of analytical excellence. An analytical coaching staff to help young analysts hone their analytical tradecraft would be a valuable supplement to classroom instruction.

Much psychological research on perception, memory, attention span, and reasoning capacity documents the limitations in our mental machinery. Many scholars have applied these psychological insights to the study of international political behaviour. [25] A similar psychological perspective underlies some writings on intelligence failure and strategic surprise. [26]

Before obtaining a license to practice, psychoanalysts are required to undergo psycho-analysis themselves in order to become more aware of how their own personality interacts with and conditions their observations of others. The practice of psycho-analysis has not been so successful that its procedures should be emulated by the intelligence and foreign policy community. But the analogy highlights an interesting point: Intelligence analysts must understand themselves before they can understand others. Training is needed to increase self-awareness concerning generic problems in how people perceive and make analytical judgments concerning foreign events, as also to provide guidance and practice in overcoming these problems.

Not enough training is focused in this direction--that is, inward toward the analyst's own thought processes. Training of intelligence analysts generally means instruction in organisational procedures, methodological techniques, or substantive topics. More training time should be devoted to the mental act of thinking or analysing. It is simply assumed, incorrectly, that analysts know how to analyse. There is a need to support training that examines the thinking and reasoning processes involved in intelligence analysis.

A generation ago, few intelligence analysts were self-conscious and introspective about the process by which they did analysis. The accepted wisdom was the 'common sense' theory of knowledge that to perceive events accurately, it was necessary only to open one's eyes, look at the facts, and purge oneself of all preconceptions and prejudices in order to make an objective judgment.

Today, there is greatly increased understanding that intelligence analysts do not approach their tasks with empty minds. They start with a set of assumptions about how events normally transpire in the area for which they are responsible. Although this changed view is becoming conventional wisdom, the Intelligence Community has only begun to scratch the surface of its implications.

Implications for Intelligence Analysis

Comprehending the nature of perception has significant implications for understanding the nature and limitations of intelligence analysis. The circumstances under which accurate perception is most difficult are exactly the circumstances under which intelligence analysis is generally conducted; dealing with highly ambiguous situations on the basis of information that is processed incrementally under pressure for early judgment. This is a recipe for inaccurate perception.

Intelligence seeks to illuminate the unknown. Almost by definition, intelligence analysis deals with highly ambiguous situations. The greater the ambiguity of the stimuli, the greater the impact of expectations and pre-existing images on the perception of that stimuli. Thus, despite maximum striving for objectivity, the intelligence analyst's own preconceptions are likely to exert a greater impact on the analytical product than in other fields where an analyst is working with less ambiguous and less discordant information.

The receipt of information in small increments over time also facilitates assimilation of this information into the analyst's existing views. No one item of information may be sufficient to prompt the analyst to change a previous view. The cumulative message inherent in many pieces of information may be significant but is attenuated when this information is not examined as a whole. The US Intelligence Community's review of its performance before the 1973 Arab-Israeli War noted: The problem of incremental analysis – especially as it applies to the current intelligence process – was also at work in the period preceding hostilities. Analysts, according to their own accounts, were often proceeding on the basis of the day's take, hastily comparing it with material received the previous day. They then produced in 'assembly line fashion' items which may have reflected perceptive intuition but which (did not) accrue from a systematic consideration of an accumulated body of integrated evidence.

And finally, the intelligence analyst operates in an environment that exerts strong pressures for what psychologists call premature closure. Customer demand for interpretive analysis is greatest within two or three days after an event occurs. The system requires the intelligence analyst to come up with an almost instant diagnosis before sufficient hard information, and the broader background information that may be needed to gain perspective, become available to make possible a well-grounded judgment. This diagnosis can only be based upon the analyst's preconceptions concerning how and why events normally transpire in a given society.

As time passes and more information is received, a fresh look at all the evidence might suggest a different explanation. Yet, the perception experiments indicate that an early judgment adversely affects the formation of future perceptions. Once an observer thinks he or she knows what is happening, this perception tends to resist change. New data received incrementally can be fit easily into an analyst's previous image. This perceptual bias is reinforced by organisational pressures favouring consistent interpretation; once the analyst is committed in writing, both the analyst and the organisation have a vested interest in maintaining the original assessment.

That intelligence analysts perform as well as they do is testimony to their generally sound judgment, training, and dedication in performing a dauntingly difficult task.

The problems outlined here have implications for the management as well as the conduct of analysis. Given the difficulties inherent in the human processing of complex information, a prudent management system should:

- Encourage products that clearly delineate their assumptions and chains of inference and that specify the degree and source of uncertainty involved in the conclusions.
- Support analyses that periodically re-examine key problems from the ground up in order to avoid the pitfalls of the incremental approach.
- Emphasise procedures that expose and elaborate alternative points of view. Educate consumers about the limitations as well as the capabilities of intelligence analysis; define a set of realistic expectations as a standard against which to judge analytical performance.

Do We Really Need More Information?

The difficulties associated with intelligence analysis are often attributed to the inadequacy of available information. Thus the intelligence communities invest heavily in improved intelligence collection systems while managers of analysis lament the comparatively small sums devoted to enhancing analytical resources, improving analytical methods, or gaining better understanding of the cognitive processes involved in making analytical judgments. The often implicit assumption that lack of information is the main obstacle to accurate intelligence judgments needs to be questioned.

Using experts in a variety of fields as test subjects, experimental psychologists have examined the relationship between the amounts of information available to the experts, the accuracy of judgments they make based on this information and the experts'confidence in the accuracy of these judgments. The word 'information', as used in this context refers to the totality of material available with an analyst to work with in making a judgment.

Key findings from this research are:

- Once an experienced analyst has the minimum information necessary to make an informed judgment, obtaining additional information generally does not improve the accuracy of his or her estimates. Additional information does, however, lead the analyst to become more confident in the judgment, to the point of over-confidence
- Experienced analysts have an imperfect understanding of what information they actually use in making judgments. They are unaware of the extent to which their judgments are determined by a few dominant factors, rather than by the systematic integration of all available information. Analysts actually use much less of the available information than they think they do.

As will be noted below, these experimental findings should not necessarily be accepted at face value. For example, circumstances exist in which additional information does contribute to more accurate analysis. However, there also are circumstances in which additional information - particularly contradictory information - decreases rather than increases an analyst's confidence.

To interpret the disturbing but not surprising findings from these experiments, it is necessary to consider four different types of information and discuss their relative value in contributing to the accuracy of analytical judgments. It is also helpful to distinguish analysis in which results are driven by the data from analysis that is driven by the conceptual framework employed to interpret the data.

Understanding the complex relationship between amount of information and accuracy of judgment has implications for both the management and conduct of intelligence analysis. Such an understanding suggests analytical procedures and management initiatives that may indeed contribute to more accurate analytical judgments. It also suggests that resources needed to attain a better understanding of the entire analytical process might profitably be diverted from some of the more costly intelligence collection programs.

These findings have broad relevance beyond the Intelligence Community. Analysis of information to gain a better understanding of current developments and to estimate future outcomes is an essential component of decision-making in any field. In fact, the psychological experiments that are most relevant have been conducted with experts in such diverse fields as medical and psychological diagnosis, stock market analysis, weather forecasting, and horserace handicapping. The experiments reflect basic human processes that affect analysis of any subject.

One may conduct experiments to demonstrate these phenomena in any field in which experts analyse a finite number of identifiable and classifiable kinds of information to make judgments or estimates that can subsequently be checked for accuracy. The stock market analyst, for example, commonly works with information concerning price-earnings ratios, profit margins, earnings per share, market volume, and resistance and support levels, and it is relatively easy to measure quantitatively the accuracy of the resulting predictions. By controlling the information made available to a group of experts and then checking the accuracy of judgments based on this information, it is possible to investigate how people use information to arrive at analytical judgments.

Keeping an Open Mind

Minds are like parachutes. They only function when they are open. A new idea is the beginning, not the end, of the creative process. It must jump over many hurdles before being embraced as an organisational product or solution. The organisational climate plays a crucial role in determining whether new ideas bubble to the surface or are suppressed.

Major intelligence failures are usually caused by failures of analysis, not failures of collection. Relevant information is discounted, misinterpreted, ignored, rejected, or overlooked because it fails to fit a prevailing mental model or mind-set.[27] The 'signals' are lost in the 'noise'.[28] How can we ensure that analysts remain open to new experience and recognise when long-held views or conventional wisdom need to be revised in response to a changing world?

Beliefs, assumptions, concepts, and information retrieved from memory form a mind-set or mental model that guides perception and processing of new information. The nature of the intelligence business forces us to deal with issues at an early stage when hard information is incomplete. If there were no gaps in the information on an issue or situation, and no ambiguity, it would not be an interesting intelligence problem. When information is lacking, analysts often have no choice but to lean heavily on prior beliefs and assumptions about how and why events normally transpire in a given country.

A mind-set is neither good nor bad. It is unavoidable. It is, in essence, a distillation of all that analysts think they know about a subject. It forms a lens through which they perceive the world, and once formed, it resists change.

Stimulating Creative Thinking

Imagination and creativity play important roles in intelligence analysis as in most other human endeavours. Intelligence judgments require the ability to imagine possible causes and outcomes of a current situation. All possible outcomes are not given. The analyst must think of them by imagining scenarios that explicate how they might come about. Similarly, imagination as well as knowledge is required to reconstruct how a problem appears from the viewpoint of a foreign government. Creativity is required to question things that have long been taken for granted. The fact that apples fall from trees was well-known to everyone. Newton's creative genius was to ask "why?" Intelligence analysts, too, are expected to raise new questions that lead to the identification of previously unrecognised relationships or to possible outcomes that had not previously been foreseen.

A creative analytical product shows a flair for devising imaginative or innovative – but also accurate and effective –

ways to fulfill any of the major requirements of analysis: gathering information, analysing information, documenting evidence, and/or presenting conclusions. Tapping unusual sources of data, asking new questions, applying unusual analytic methods, and developing new types of products or new ways of fitting analysis to the needs of consumers are all examples of creative activity.

A person's intelligence, as measured by IQ tests, has little to do with creativity, but the organisational environment exercises a major influence. New but appropriate ideas are most likely to arise in an organisational climate that nurtures their development and communication.

The old view that creativity is something one is born with, and that it cannot be taught or developed, is largely untrue. While native talent, *per se*, is important and may be immutable, it is possible to learn to employ one's innate talents more productively. With understanding, practice, and conscious effort, analysts can learn to produce more imaginative, innovative, creative work.

Creativity, in the sense of new and useful ideas, is at least as important in intelligence analysis as in any other human endeavour. Procedures to enhance innovative thinking are not new. Creative thinkers have employed them successfully for centuries. The only new elements – and even they may not be new anymore – are the grounding of these procedures in psychological theory to explain how and why they work, and their formalisation in systematic creativity programs.

Learning creative problem-solving techniques does not change an analyst's native-born talents but helps an analyst achieve his or her full potential. Most people have the ability to be more innovative than they themselves realise. The effectiveness of these procedures depends, in large measure, upon the analyst's motivation, drive, and perseverance in taking the time required for thoughtful analysis despite the pressures of day-to-day duties, mail, and current intelligence reporting.

A questioning attitude is a prerequisite to a successful search for new ideas. Any analyst who is confident that he or she already knows the answer, and that this answer has not changed recently, is unlikely to produce innovative or imaginative work. Another prerequisite to creativity is sufficient strength of character to suggest new ideas to others, possibly at the expense of being rejected or even ridiculed on occasion. "The ideas of creative people often lead them into direct conflict with the trends of their time, and they need the courage to be able to stand alone".[29]

Biases in Evaluation of Evidence

Evaluation of evidence is a crucial step in analysis, but what evidence people rely on and how they interpret it are influenced by a variety of extraneous factors. Information presented in vivid and concrete detail often has unwarranted impact, and people tend to disregard abstract or statistical information that may have greater evidential value. We seldom take the absence of evidence into account. The human mind is also over-sensitive to the consistency of the evidence, and insufficiently sensitive to the reliability of the evidence. And, impressions often remain even after the evidence on which they are based has been totally discredited.

The intelligence analyst works in a somewhat unique informational environment. Evidence comes from an unusually diverse set of sources: newspapers and wire services, observations by embassy officers, reports from controlled agents and casual informants, information exchanges with foreign governments, photo reconnaissance, and communications intelligence. Each source has its own unique strengths, weaknesses, potential or actual biases, and vulnerability to manipulation and deception. The most salient characteristic of the information environment is its diversity - multiple sources, each with varying degrees of reliability, and each commonly reporting information which by itself is incomplete and sometimes inconsistent or even incompatible with reporting from other sources. Conflicting information of uncertain reliability is endemic to intelligence analysis, as is the need to make rapid judgments on current events even before all the evidence is in.

The analyst has only limited control over the stream of information. Tasking of sources to report on specific subjects is often a cumbersome and time-consuming process. Evidence on some important topics is sporadic or nonexistent. Most human-source information is second hand at best.

Recognising and avoiding biases under such circumstances is particularly difficult. Most of the biases discussed in this chapter are unrelated to each other and are grouped together here only because they all concern some aspect of the evaluation of evidence.

The Vividness Criterion

The impact of information on the human mind is only imperfectly related to its true value as evidence.[30] Specifically, information that is vivid, concrete, and personal has a greater impact on our thinking than pallid, abstract information that may actually have substantially greater value as evidence. For example:

- Information that people perceive directly, that they hear with their own ears or see with their own eyes, is likely to have greater impact than information received secondhand that may have greater evidential value.
- Case histories and anecdotes will have greater impact than more informative but abstract aggregate or statistical data.

Events that people experience personally are more memorable than those they only read about. Concrete words are easier to remember than abstract words,[31] and words of all types are easier to recall than numbers. In short, information having the qualities cited in the preceding paragraph is more likely to attract and hold our attention. It is more likely to be stored and remembered than abstract reasoning or statistical summaries, and therefore can be expected to have a greater immediate effect as well as a continuing impact on our thinking in the future.

Intelligence analysts generally work with secondhand information. The information that analysts receive is mediated by the written words of others rather than perceived directly with their own eyes and ears. That concrete, sensory data do and should enjoy a certain priority when weighing evidence is well established. When an abstract theory or secondhand report is contradicted by personal observation, the latter properly prevails under most circumstances. There are a number of popular adages that advise mistrust of secondhand data: "Don't believe everything you read", "You can prove anything with statistics", "Seeing is believing"...

It is curious that there are no comparable maxims to warn against being misled by our own observations. Seeing should not always be believing.

Personal observations by intelligence analysts and agents can be as deceptive as secondhand accounts. Most individuals visiting foreign countries become familiar with only a small sample of people representing a narrow segment of the total society. Incomplete and distorted perceptions are a common result. Analysts should give little weight to anecdotes and personal case histories unless they are known to be typical, and perhaps no weight at all if aggregate data based on a more valid sample can be obtained.

Absence of Evidence

A principal characteristic of intelligence analysis is that key information is often lacking. Analytical problems are selected on the basis of their importance and the perceived needs of the consumers, without much regard for availability of information. Analysts have to do the best they can with what they have, somehow taking into account the fact that much relevant information is known to be missing.

Ideally, intelligence analysts should be able to recognise what relevant evidence is lacking and factor this into their calculations. They should also be able to estimate the potential impact of the missing data and to adjust confidence in their judgment accordingly. Unfortunately, this ideal does not appear to be the norm. Experiments suggest that "out of sight, out of mind" is a better description of the impact of gaps in the evidence. As an antidote for this problem, analysts should identify explicitly those relevant variables on which information is lacking, consider alternative hypotheses concerning the status of these variables, and then modify their judgment and especially confidence in their judgment accordingly. They should also consider whether the absence of information is normal or is itself an indicator of unusual activity or inactivity.

Oversensitivity to Consistency

The internal consistency in a pattern of evidence helps determine our confidence in judgments based on that evidence.[32] In one sense, consistency is clearly an appropriate guideline for evaluating evidence. People formulate alternative explanations or estimates and select the one that encompasses the greatest amount of evidence within a logically consistent scenario. Under some circumstances, however, consistency can be deceptive. Information may be consistent only because it is highly correlated or redundant, in which case many related reports may be no more informative than a single report. Or it may be consistent only because information is drawn from a very small sample or a biased sample.

The tendency to place too much reliance on small samples has been dubbed the "law of small numbers".[33] This is a parody on the law of large numbers, the basic statistical principle that says very large samples will be highly representative of the population from which they are drawn. This is the principle that underlies opinion polling, but most people are not good intuitive statisticians. People do not have much intuitive feel for how large a sample has to be before they can draw valid conclusions from it. The so-called law of small numbers means that, intuitively, we make the mistake of treating small samples as though they were large ones.

Are intelligence analysts also overly confident of conclusions drawn from very little data – especially if the data seem to be consistent? When working with a small but consistent body of evidence, analysts need to consider how representative that evidence is of the total body of potentially available information. If more reporting were available, how likely is it that this information, too, would be consistent with the already available evidence? If an analyst is stuck with only a small amount of evidence and cannot determine how representative this evidence is, confidence in judgments based on this evidence should be low regardless of the consistency of the information.

Improving Intelligence Analysis

How can intelligence analysis be improved? That is the challenge. A variety of traditional approaches are used in pursuing this goal: collecting more and better information for analysts to work with, changing the management of the analytical process, increasing the number of analysts, providing language and area studies to improve analysts' substantive expertise, revising employee selection and retention criteria, improving report-writing skills, fine-tuning the relationship between intelligence analysts and intelligence consumers, and modifying the types of analytical products.

Any of these measures may play an important role, but analysis is, above all, a mental process. Traditionally, analysts at all levels devote little attention to improving how they think. To penetrate the heart and soul of the problem of improving analysis, it is necessary to better understand, influence, and guide the mental processes of analysts themselves.

Checklist for Analysts

This checklist for analysts summarises guidelines for manoeuvring through the minefields encountered while proceeding through the analytical process. Following the guidelines will help analysts protect themselves from avoidable error and improve their chances of making the right calls. The discussion is organised around six key steps in the analytical process: defining the problem, generating hypotheses, collecting information, evaluating hypotheses, selecting the most likely hypothesis, and the ongoing monitoring of new information.

Defining the Problem

Start out by making certain one is asking - or being asked- the right questions. Do not hesitate to go back up the chain of command with a suggestion for doing something a little different from what was asked for. The policy-maker, who originated the requirement may not have thought through his or her needs, or the requirement may be somewhat garbled as it passes down through several echelons of management. You may have a better understanding than the policy-maker of what he or she needs, or should have, or what is possible to do. At the outset, also be sure your supervisor is aware of any tradeoff between quality of analysis and what you can accomplish within a specified time deadline.

Generating Hypotheses

Identify all the plausible hypotheses that need to be considered. Make a list of as many ideas as possible by consulting colleagues and outside experts. Do this in a brainstorming mode, suspending judgment for as long as possible until all the ideas are out on the table. Then whittle the list down to a workable number of hypotheses for more detailed analysis. At this stage, do not screen out reasonable hypotheses only because there is no evidence to support them. This applies in particular to the deception hypothesis. If another country is concealing its intent through denial and deception, you should probably not expect to see evidence of it without completing a very careful analysis of this possibility. The deception hypothesis and other plausible hypotheses for which there may be no immediate evidence should be carried forward to the next stage of analysis until they can be carefully considered and, if appropriate, rejected with good cause.

Collecting Information

Relying only on information that is automatically delivered to you will probably not solve all your analytical problems. To do the job right, it will probably be necessary to look elsewhere and dig for more information. Contact with the collectors, or first-cut analysts often yields additional information. Also check academic specialists, foreign newspapers, and specialised journals.

Collect information to evaluate all the reasonable hypotheses, not just the one that seems most likely. Exploring alternative hypotheses that have not been seriously considered before often leads an analyst into unexpected and unfamiliar territory. It is important to suspend judgment while information is being assembled on each of the hypotheses. It is easy to form impressions about a hypothesis on the basis of very little information, but hard to change an impression once it has taken root. If you find yourself thinking you already know the answer, ask yourself what would cause you to change your mind; then look for that information.

Try to develop alternative hypotheses in order to determine if some alternative – when given a fair chance – might not be as compelling as your own preconceived view. Systematic development of an alternative hypothesis usually increases the perceived likelihood of that hypothesis".A willingness to play with material from different angles and in the context of unpopular as well as popular hypotheses is an essential ingredient of a good detective, whether the end is the solution of a crime or an intelligence estimate".[34]

Evaluating Hypotheses

Do not be misled by the fact that so much evidence supports your preconceived idea of which is the most likely hypothesis. That same evidence may be consistent with several different hypotheses. Focus on developing arguments against each hypothesis rather than trying to confirm hypotheses. In other words, pay particular attention to evidence or assumptions that suggest one or more hypotheses are less likely than the others.

Selecting the Most Likely Hypothesis

Proceed by trying to reject hypotheses rather than confirm them. The most likely hypothesis is usually the one with the least evidence against it, not the one with the most evidence for it.

In presenting your conclusions, note all the reasonable hypotheses that were considered. Cite the arguments and evidence supporting your judgment, but also justify briefly why other alternatives were rejected or considered less likely. To avoid ambiguity, insert an odds ratio or probability range in parentheses after expressions of uncertainty in key judgments.

Ongoing Monitoring

In a rapidly changing, probabilistic world, analytical conclusions are always tentative. The situation may change, or it may remain unchanged while you receive new information that alters your understanding of it. Specify things to look for that, if observed, would suggest a significant change in the probabilities.

Pay particular attention to any feeling of surprise when new information does not fit your prior understanding. Consider whether this surprising information is consistent with an alternative hypothesis. A surprise or two, however small, may be the first clue that your understanding of what is happening requires some adjustment, is at best incomplete, or may be quite wrong Management of Analysis.

The cognitive problems described in this book have implications for the management as well as the conduct of intelligence analysis. This concluding section looks at what managers of intelligence analysis can do to help create an organisational environment in which analytical excellence flourishes. These measures fall into four general categories: research, training, exposure to alternative mind-sets, and guiding analytical products.

Support for Research

Management should support research to gain a better understanding of the cognitive processes involved in making intelligence judgments. There is a need for better understanding of the thinking skills involved in intelligence analysis, how to test job applicants for these skills, and how to train analysts to improve these skills. Analysts also need a fuller understanding of how cognitive limitations affect intelligence analysis and how to minimise their impact. They need simple tools and techniques to help protect themselves from avoidable error. There is so much research to be done that it is difficult to know where to start.

Training

Most training of intelligence analysts is focused on organisational procedures, writing style, and methodological techniques. Analysts who write clearly are assumed to be thinking clearly. Yet it is quite possible to follow a faulty analytical process and write a clear and persuasive argument in support of an erroneous judgment.

More training time should be devoted to the thinking and reasoning processes involved in making intelligence judgments, and to the tools of the trade that are available to alleviate or compensate for the known cognitive problems encountered in analysis. This book is intended to support such training. Training will be more effective if supplemented with ongoing advice and assistance. An experienced coach who can monitor and guide ongoing performance is a valuable supplement to classroom instruction in many fields, probably including intelligence analysis. This is supposed to be the job of the branch chief or senior analyst, but these officers are often too busy responding to other pressing demands on their time.

It would be worthwhile to consider how an analytical coaching staff might be formed to mentor new analysts or consult with analysts working particularly difficult issues. One possible model is the SCORE organisation that exists in many communities. SCORE stands for Senior Corps of Retired Executives. It is a US organisation of retired executives, who volunteer their time to counsel young entrepreneurs starting their own businesses. It should be possible to form a small group of retired analysts, who possess the skills and values that should be imparted to new analysts, and who would be willing to volunteer or be hired, to come in several days a week to counsel junior analysts.

Exposure to Alternative Mind-Sets

The realities of bureaucratic life produce strong pressures for conformity. Management needs to make conscious efforts to ensure that well-reasoned competing views have the opportunity to surface within the Intelligence Community. Analysts need to enjoy a sense of security, so that partially developed new ideas may be expressed and bounced off others as sounding boards with minimal fear of criticism for deviating from established conformity.

The Bottom Line

Analysis can be improved. None of the measures discussed in this book will guarantee that accurate conclusions will be drawn from the incomplete and ambiguous information that intelligence analysts typically work with. Occasional intelligence failures must be expected. Collectively, however, the measures discussed here can certainly improve the odds in the analysts' favour.

Joining the Dots: Open Source Intelligence Acquisition

The proliferation of social networking software and communications technology has provided incredible opportunity for open source collaboration on knowledge projects. Wikipedia is the best example of a public refereed system for collaborative knowledge. What if we were to match this collaborative knowledge-building approach with open source intelligence acquisition?

The intelligence agencies could provide a site where whistle-blowers could collaborate with experts, journalists, and authorities to build a picture of what's happening across India and elsewhere. The Delhi Police has recently started a public campaign – Be Our Eyes and Ears – urging people to inform the police about any suspicious activity or person/s, which is a step in the right direction. However, using some sort of technology that allows anonymous posting, a whistle-blower could post inputs on a website, using an open source version of software like 'Analyst's Notebook', which provides a visual representation of intelligence data (essentially a detailed mind map which can be extensively manipulated). An interested individual could add to the data by asking specific questions or drawing connections of their own. Some members of the public might have a particular expertise and could add their insight to the analysis.

As mentioned earlier, most of the intelligence is acquired through open sources and if the dots are joined properly, the picture that emerges is generally clear. Even a cursory perusal of the India Timeline – 2011[35] given at the end, makes it pretty clear that the Maoist insurgency threat in several states in India is now more serious than militancy in Kashmir. Besides, it also points out that, ISI is making efforts to revive militant groups in Punjab as also trying to destabilise India's economy by induction of huge amounts of fake currency. In India, terror related incidents/activities occur on daily basis. Well, almost. India's intelligence community is certainly aware of all this but sadly, not enough is being done by the government to take the terror bull by its horns. As things stand today, India Timeline -2012, and subsequent years, will be no different.

15

Integration is the key

In the corporate world it's called M&A - Mergers and Acquisitions - where two or more companies join hands and integrate their resources and efforts to deal with the challenge posed by their competitors. Indian intelligence services also need to integrate their activities if they are to succeed in facing the challenges posed by their adversaries. The strength of ISI lies in its being the sole agency that runs the intelligence machine of Pakistan and as such does not face the problems of lack of coordination and one-upmanship that Indian intelligence agencies do. While it is neither feasible nor desirable - omnipotent organisations such as ISI pose dangerous pitfalls - to roll all intelligence agencies into one, it is essential to integrate their overall effort in a more competent and homogeneous manner than being done at present.

One way of doing this is to have a separate central ministry whose writ prevails over the entire intelligence community. While this would have obvious advantage in that it will be a regulatory authority unlike the toothless

JIC, it may disturb the present hierarchy and is likely to face opposition from various quarters. Besides, it will be yet another addition to the long list of existing ministries and its creation will entail substantial expenditure. For effective command and control as also for driving intelligence policies and implementation, an additional Department of Intelligence Coordination (DICA) under the Union Home Minister should be established. The home minister can directly interact with the Director DICA and Officers on Special Duty (OSD) of various agencies thus overcoming the bureaucratic red tape. A broad organisational structure of this additional complement of Ministry of Home Affairs is annexed at the end.

There is also a need to set up a joint Civil-Military intelligence organisation tailor-made for LICO. Also, cross attachment of Int Corps officers to civil agencies and vice versa on fixed tenure basis will also go a long way in inculcating better understanding of each other's constraints, problems and prospects.

While NATGRID, the National Intelligence Grid, an integrated facility which aims to link databases of 21 departments and ministries to improve counter-terror country's capability has finally been given the go-ahead by the government, there is need to appoint a Director of National Intelligence, as in US, to integrate efforts of all the intelligence agencies.

The shortage of police personnel across the country is well-known. The home ministry had itself admitted after 26/11 that 5,40,00 policemen were required to make up the shortage in police forces, however, less than a third have actually been recruited since then. Even if recruitment target is fully achieved, India's projections for policing will still be much lower than the UN recommended ratio of 222 policemen per 1,00,000 citizens. There is, therefore, a need to integrate security and intelligence effort of police and private security agencies and even the citizens of the country. This will essentially involve close coordination between beat constables and police station/chowkis on one hand and the private security agencies and the citizens on the other. Some routine chores such as verification of antecedents of people applying for passports and arms licence etc could be passed on to reputed private agencies. This, of course, will entail strict enforcement of the Private Security Agencies Regulation Act (PSARA 2005), which even after seven years of its enactment in the Parliament, is still not being followed in letter and spirit.

The two main systems of intelligence acquisition, Humint and Techint need integration as well, since both are important and are in fact complementary to each other.

Besides, with the growing complexity of Techint, there is a need to work towards systems integration of various communication links such as computers, data bases and satellites. There is also a strong case for integrating the country's defence R&D with civil R&D to encourage competitiveness, free control and intellectual simulation in the technical field. As a matter of fact, for best results, integration of the entire process of research, development, production and procurement of defence requirements, must be ensured.

The craft of intelligence is a multi-disciplinary and cerebral one. It's not merely about knowing what the enemy is up to, but being a step ahead by going deep into the enemy's psyche to find out what he is likely to do in the future. This calls for integrating expertise of intelligence community and universities. The university departments can be utilised to study and analyse future trends while intelligencers focus more on gathering intelligence.

Though there had been much talk of integrating all three service headquarters (CDS) with the defence ministry, the idea is yet to be executed on ground. And it is not only the bureaucrats who for obvious reasons have shown reluctance to implement this long standing proposal; difference of opinion exists even among the services in this regard. Needless to say, unless the three Chiefs of Staff follow an integrated approach in advising the government on matters military, nothing worthwhile will be achieved in integrating their headquarters with the Ministry of Defence. It will also be prudent for all political parties not to indulge in politicking but to adopt an integrated stance while deciding issues pertaining to the country's defence. In short, integration is the name of the game.

Can India prevent the next terror attack?

As mentioned at the outset, history is replete with instances of intelligence failure not only in India, but worldwide. The opaque and uncertain nature of intelligence makes intelligence failure inevitable at times. Terrorists with determination and ingenuity will sneak in and hit their target anyway. Like they did recently (13/7) in Mumbai. A day after serial blasts ripped through India's financial capital, the Congress General Secretary Rahul Gandhi said "It's very difficult to stop every single terror attack. Terrorism is impossible to stop all the time. But ninety nine per cent terror attacks have been stopped due to strong vigilance and intelligence efforts". While one wonders from where and how the ruling party's heir apparent derived a success rate of 99 per cent, fact remains that attacks like this one, manifest a much larger failure on the part of successive governments to create an effective intelligence machinery that could counter the complex terrorist threat India faces today.

There were lessons to be learned from Kargil and 26/11 that never got learnt. Every time there's an intelligence or security failure, a spate of promises are made to make India better prepared to meet the terror challenge but then all is forgotten and nothing gets done. As one writes this, 13/7 that happened just a month back, seems to have vanished from everyone's memory.

Finally the quintessential poser: Can India prevent the next terror attack? As things stand today, the answer unfortunately is no. But if intelligence gets top priority which is long overdue, terrorists can be kept at bay for long, if not for ever. Let Bond relish his martinis the way he likes. India's spy machine needs to be thoroughly overhauled and not just shaken and stirred.

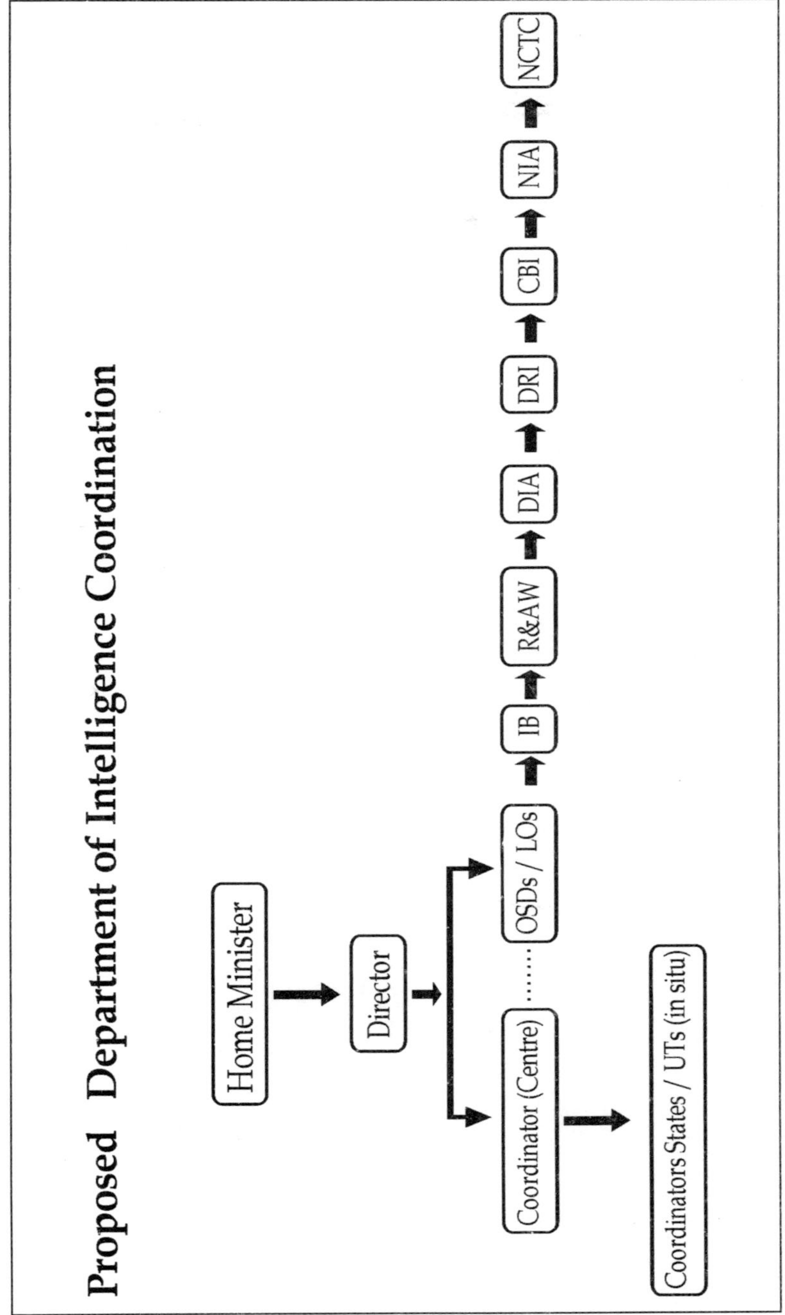
Proposed Department of Intelligence Coordination
Home Minister
Director
Coordinator (Centre)
OSDs / LOs
IB
R&AW
DIA
DRI
CBI
NIA
NCTC
Coordinators States / UTs (in situ)

16

The Top Ten Spy Agencies

Source: www.smashinglists.com and Wikipedia

People generally know very little as to what the intelligence agencies actually do, so figuring out which is the best intelligence service can be rather difficult. The very opaque nature of intelligence often means that the successes will not be public knowledge for years, whereas failures or controversial operations will be taken to the press. It's a thankless situation. Still, from what little has emerged, one can have an idea of some of the better intelligence services out there, with the understanding that this is based on incomplete data.

10. ASIS - Australia

Australian Secret Intelligence Service (ASIS) was formed on 13 May, 1952 and is headquartered in Canberra. The agency is responsible for collecting foreign intelligence, undertaking counter-intelligence activities and cooperation with other intelligence agencies overseas. For more than twenty years, the existence of the agency was a secret even from its own government. Its primary responsibility is gathering intelligence from mainly Asian and Pacific interests using agents stationed across the globe. Its main purpose, as with most agencies, is to protect the country's political and economic interests while ensuring safety for the people of Australia against national threats.

9. R&AW - India

The Research and Analysis Wing (R&AW or RAW) is India's external intelligence agency. It was formed in September 1968 after the poor performance of the Intelligence Bureau (which handled both internal and external intelligence) in the Sino-Indian war of 1962 and the India-Pakistan war of 1965 convinced the then government of India that a specialised, independent agency was required for competent external intelligence gathering.

The primary function of the R&AW is collection of external intelligence, counter-terrorism and covert operations. In addition, it is responsible for obtaining and analysing information about foreign governments, corporations, and persons, in order to advise Indian policy makers. The agency has its headquarters in New Delhi.

8. DGSE - France

Directorate General for External Security (French: *Direction Générale de la Sécurité Extérieure,* or DGSE) is France's external intelligence agency having its headquarters in Paris. Operating under the direction of the French ministry of defence, the agency works alongside the DCRI (the Central Directorate of Interior Intelligence) in providing intelligence and national security, notably by performing paramilitary and counter-intelligence operations abroad. The DGSE has a rather short history compared to other intelligence agencies in the region. It was officially founded on April 2, 1982 from a multitude of pre-existing intelligence agencies in the country. Its primary focus is to gather intelligence from foreign sources to assist in military and strategic decisions for the country. The agency employs more than five thousand people.

7. FSB - Russia

The Federal Security Service of Russian Federation (FSB) is the main domestic security agency of the Russian Federation and the main successor agency of the Soviet-era Cheka, NKVD and KGB. Formed on April 3, 1995 with its headquarters at Lubyanka Square, the FSB is involved in counter-intelligence, internal and border security, counter-terrorism, and surveillance. All law enforcement and intelligence agencies in Russia work under the guidance of FSB. For example, the GRU, spetsnaz and Internal Troops detachments of Russian Ministry of Internal Affairs work together with the FSB in Chechnya. The FSB is responsible for internal security of the Russian state, counter-espionage, and the fight against organised crime, terrorism, and drug smuggling. The number of FSB personnel and its budget remain state secrets, although the budget was reported to jump nearly 40 per cent in 2006.

6. BND - Germany

The Bundesnachrichtendienst (Federal Intelligence Service, BND) is Germany's foreign intelligence agency functioning under the Chancellor's Office. The BND which was raised on April 1, 1956 and having its headquarters at Pullach (near Munich), the agency acts as an early warning system to alert the German government regarding threats to German interests from abroad. It depends heavily on wire-tapping and electronic surveillance of international communications. It collects and evaluates information areas such as international terrorism, WMD proliferation and illegal transfer of technology, organised crime, weapons and drug-trafficking, money-laundering, illegal migration and information warfare. As Germany's only overseas intelligence service, the BND gathers both military and civil intelligence.

5. MSS - China

Formed in 1949 , Ministry of State Security (MSS) is the security agency of the People's Republic of China. It is also probably the Chinese government's largest and most active foreign intelligence agency, though it is also involved in domestic security matters. Article 4 of the Criminal Procedure Law gives the MSS the same authority to arrest or detain people as regular police for crimes involving state security with identical supervision by the procuratorates and the courts. It is headquartered near the Ministry of Public Security of the People's Republic of China in Beijing. According to Liu Fuzhi, Secretary-General of the Commission for Politics and Law under the Central Committee of the Communist Party of China and Minister of Public Security, the mission of the MSS is to ensure "the security of the state through effective measures against enemy agents, spies, and counter-revolutionary activities designed to sabotage or overthrow China's socialist system". One of the primary missions of the MSS is undoubtedly to gather foreign intelligence from targets in various countries overseas. Many MSS agents are said to have operated in the Greater China region (Hong Kong, Macau, and Taiwan) and to have integrated themselves into the world's numerous overseas Chinese communities. At one point, nearly 120 agents who had been operating under non-official cover in the US, Canada, Western and Northern Europe, and Japan as businessmen, bankers, scholars, and journalists were recalled to China, a fact that demonstrates the broad geographical scope of MSS agent coverage.

4. CIA - America

Headquartered at Langley, Virginia and established on September 18, 1947, the Central Intelligence Agency (CIA) is a civilian intelligence agency of the United States government. It is an executive agency and reports directly to the Director of National Intelligence, with responsibility for providing national security intelligence assessment to senior United States policy-makers. Intelligence gathering is performed by non-military commissioned civilian intelligence agents, many of whom are trained to avoid tactical situations. The CIA also oversees and sometimes engages in tactical and covert activities at the request of the President of the United States. Often, when such field operations are organised, the US military or other warfare tacticians carry these tactical operations out on behalf of the agency while the CIA oversees them. Although intelligence gathering is the agency's main agenda, tactical divisions were established in the agency to carry out emergency field operations that require immediate suppression or dismantling of a threat or weapon. The CIA is often used for intelligence gathering instead of the US military to avoid a declaration of war.

3. MI6 - United Kingdom

The British have had a long public perception of an effective intelligence agency, due to the success of the unrealistic, yet entertaining, James Bond (fictional super agent of MI6) movies. This perception matches reality. SIS–the Special Intelligence Services - or MI6, as it's commonly known, the British equivalent to the CIA, has had two big advantages in staying effective: The British Official Secrets Act and D notices can often prevent leaks which have been the bane of the CIA's existence.

The agency , originally formed as Secret Service Bureau in 1909 with its headquarters at Vauxhall Cross, London, is tasked by the British Government to collect intelligence world-wide in support of its security, defence, foreign and economic policies. SIS does not itself decide on the intelligence requirements placed on the Service. These requirements are regularly reviewed by Government and are classified.

2. Mossad - Israel

Established on December 13, 1949, it has its headquarters in Tel Aviv. Mossad is responsible for intelligence collection and covert operations including paramilitary activities. It is one of the main entities in the Israeli Intelligence

Community, along with Aman (military intelligence) and Shin Bet (internal security), but its director reports directly to the Prime Minister. The list of its successes is long. Israel's intelligence agency is most famous for having taken out a number of PLO operatives in retaliation for the attack that killed eleven Israeli athletes at the 1972 Olympic Games in Munich. However, this agency has other successes to its name, including the acquisition of a MiG-21 prior to the Yom Kippur war of 1967 and the theft of the plans for the Mirage-5 after the deal with France went sour. Mossad also assisted the United States in supporting Solidarity in Poland during the 1980s.

1. ISI – Pakistan

The Directorate for Inter Services Intelligence more commonly known as Inter Services Intelligence or simply by its initials ISI, is Pakistan's premier intelligence agency, responsible for providing critical national security intelligence assessment to the Government of Pakistan. ISI is the largest of the three intelligence service agencies of Pakistan, the others being the Intelligence Bureau (IB) and Military Intelligence (MI). Its work has included supporting the Mujahideen in Afghanistan against the Soviets in the 1980s (in conjunction with CIA and its Allies) and supporting Taliban against the India and Iran backed Northern Alliance in the Afghanistan Civil War in the 1990s.

The ISI was established as an independent intelligence agency in 1948 with its headquarters at Islamabad, in order to strengthen sharing of military intelligence between the three branches of Pakistan's armed forces in the aftermath of the Indo-Pakistan War, which had exposed weaknesses in intelligence gathering, sharing and coordination between the Army, Air Force and Navy. From its inception, the agency is headed by an appointed 3-Star General Officer of the Pakistan Army, despite officers from all three branches of the Pakistan Armed Forces serving with the agency.

17

World's Major Intelligence Agencies

Australia

- Australian Secret Intelligence Service (ASIS)
- Australian Security Intelligence organisation (ASIO)
- Australian Army Intelligence Corps (AUSTINT)
- Australian Federal Police (AFP) Intelligence
- Defence Imagery and Geo-spatial organisation (DIGO)
- Defence Intelligence organisation (DIO)
- Defence Signals Directorate (DSD)
- Office of National Assessments (ONA)

Bangladesh

- Directorate General of Forces Intelligence (DGFI)
- National Security Intelligence (NSI)

Belgium

- Staatsveiligheid/Sûreté de l'État (SV/SE) - State Security Service

Brazil

- Agência Brasileira de Inteligência (ABIN) - Brazilian Intelligence Agency

Canada

- Canadian Security Intelligence Service/Service Canadien du renseignement de sécurité (CSIS/SCRS)
- Communications Security Establishment (CSE)
- Canadian Forces Intelligence Branch

Chile

- Agencia Nacional de Inteligencia (ANI) National Intelligence Agency
- People's Republic of China
- Ministry of State Security (MSS)

Colombia

- Departamento Administrativo de Seguridad (DAS) Administrative Department of Security (of Colombia)

Cuba

- Dirección General de Intelligence (DGI) General Directorate of Intelligence

Czech Republic

- Bezpečnostní informační služba (BIS) - Security Information Service
- Úřad pro zahraniční styky a informace (ÚZSI) - Office for Foreign Relations and Information
- Vojenské zpravodajství (VZ) - Military Intelligence

Denmark

- Politiets Efterretningstjeneste (PET) - Danish Security and Intelligence Service
- Forsvarets Efterretningstjeneste (FE) - Danish Defence Intelligence Service

Egypt

- Al-Mukhabarat al-'Ammah - Egyptian General Intelligence Directorate
- Mabahith Amn al-Dawla al-'Ulya - State Security Investigation Bureau
- Al-Mukhabarat al-Harbeya (Military Intelligence)

Finland

- Suojelupoliisi (SUPO) -- Security Intelligence Service

France

- Direction Générale de la Sécurité Extérieure (DGSE) - General Directorate of External Security
- Direction Centrale du Renseignement Intérieur (DCRI) - Central Directorate of Interior Intelligence

Germany

- Bundesnachrichtendienst (BND) - Federal Intelligence Service
- Bundesamt für Verfassungsschutz (BfV) - Federal Office for the Protection of the Constitution
- Militärischer Abschirmdienst (MAD) - Military Counter-intelligence Service

Greece

- Ethniki Ypiresia Pliroforion (NIS) - Hellenic National Intelligence Service

India

- Central Bureau of Investigation (CBI)
- Defence Intelligence Agency (DIA)
- Intelligence Bureau (IB)
- National Investigation Agency (NIA)
- Research and Analysis Wing (R&AW)

Indonesia

- Badan Intelijen Negara (BIN)

Iran

- Ministry of Intelligence and National Security (VEVAK)
- NAJA
- Intelligence and Security Organisation of Islamic Revolutionary Guards Corps (SASA)
- SAVAK Defunct secret police, replaced by VEVAK

Ireland

- G2 Army Intelligence (G2)
- Garda National Surveillance Unit (NSU)
- Irish Secret Service (ISS)

Israel

- ha-Mossad le-Modiin u-le-Tafkidim Myukhadim (Mossad) – Institute for Intelligence and Special Operations
- Shirut Bitahon Klali (ISA) – Israel Security Agency
- Aman – Military Intelligence Directorate

Italy

- Agenzia Informazioni e Sicurezza Interna (AISI) – Agency for Internal Information and Security
- Agenzia Informazioni e Sicurezza Esterna (AISE) – Agency for External Information and Security

Jordan

- Dairat al-Mukhabarat al-Ammah

Lithuania

- Valstybės Saugumo Departamentas (VSD) – State Security Department
- Antrasis operatyvinių tarnybų departamentas prie Krašto apsaugos ministerijos (AOTD) – II-nd Investigation Department

Malaysia

- Kor Risik DiRaja – Royal Intelligence Corps
- Malaysian Special Branch of the Royal Malaysian Police
- National Security Council (Malaysia)
- National Security Division (BKN)
- Defence Staff Intelligence Division
- Public Safety and Security Division

Mexico

- Centro de Investigación y Seguridad Nacional (CISEN) – National Security and Investigation Center
- Agencia Federal de Investigacion (AFI) – Federal Investigation Agency
- Morocco
- Direction de la Surveillance du Territoire (DST) – Directorate of Territorial Surveillance
- Direction Generale des Etudes et la Documentation (DGED) –

Netherlands

- Algemene Inlichtingen- en Veiligheidsdienst (AIVD) – General Intelligence and Security Service
- Militaire Inlichtingen- en Veiligheidsdienst (MIVD) – Military Intelligence and Security Service
- Nationaal Coördinator Terrorismebestrijding (NCTb) – Domestic Counter-Terrorist Unit
- 'Fiscale inlichtingen- en opsporingsdienst (FOID-ECD) – Fiscal Information and Investigation Service

New Zealand

- New Zealand Security Intelligence Service (NZSIS)
- Government Communications Security Bureau (GCSB)

Norway

- National Security Authority (NSM)
- Norwegian Police Security Service (PST)
- Norwegian Intelligence Service (E-tjenesten)

Pakistan

- Inter-Services Intelligence (ISI)
- Military Intelligence (MI)
- Intelligence Bureau (IB)
- Federal Investigation Agency (FIA)
- Criminal Investigation Department (CID)

Philippines

- Office of the President
- National Intelligence Co-ordinating Agency (NICA)
- Philippine Drug Enforcement Agency (PDEA)
- PresidentialSecurityGroup-PresidentialIntelligence Company (PSG-PIC)
- Department of National Defense
- Intelligence Service of the Armed Forces of the Philippines (ISAFP)
- Philippine Air force''' - 300th Air Intelligence and Security Squadron (300TH AISG)
- Philippine Army - Intelligence Security Group (PA-ISG)
- Philippine Navy - Naval Intelligence and Security Force (PN-NISF)
- Department of Justice
- National Bureau of Investigation (NBI)
- Department of Interior and Local Government
- Philippine National Police - Intelligence Group (PNP-IG)

- Department of Finance
- Bureau of Customs - Intelligence Group (BOC-IG)
- Bureau of Internal Revenue - National Investigation Division (BIR-NID)
- Department of Transportation and Communications
- Civil Aviation Authority of the Philippines - Security and Intelligence Service (CAAP-SIS)
- Land Transportation Office - Intelligence and Investigation Division (LTO-IID)
- Philippine Coast Guard - Intelligence, Security and Law Enforcement (PCG-ISLE)

Poland

- Agencja Wywiadu (AW) – Foreign Intelligence Agency
- Agencja Bezpieczeństwa Wewnętrznego (ABW) – Internal Security Agency
- Służba Wywiadu Wojskowego (SWW) – Military Intelligence Service
- Służba Kontrwywiadu Wojskowego (SKW) – Military Counter-intelligence Service

Portugal

- Serviço de Informações de Segurança (SIS) – Security Intelligence Service
- Serviço de Informações Estratégicas de Defesa (SIED) – Strategic Defense Intelligence Service
- Sistema de Informações da República Portuguesa (SIRP) – Intelligence System of the Portuguese Republic

Romania

- Serviciul Roman de Informatii (SRI) – Romanian Information Service

Russian Federation

- Federalnaya Sluzhba Bezopasnosti (FSB) - Federal Security Service
- Glavnoye Razvedyvatelnoye Upravlenie Genshtaba (GRU) - Main Intelligence Directorate of General Staff
- Sluzhba Vneshney Razvedki (SVR) - Foreign Intelligence Service

Saudi Arabia

- Al Mukhabarat Al A'amah - General Intelligence Directorate

Serbia

- Bezbednosno Informativna Agencija (BIA) Security Informative Agency
- Vojnoobavestajna agencija (VOA) Military Intelligence Agency

Singapore

- Security and Intelligence Division (SID)
- Internal Security Department (ISD)

Slovakia

- Slovenská informačná služba (SIS) - Slovak Information Service
- Vojenské spravodajská služba (VSS) - Military Intelligence Service

South Africa

- National Intelligence Agency (NIA)
- South African Secret Service (SASS)

South Korea

- National Intelligence Service (NIS)

Spain

- Centro Nacional de Inteligencia (CNI) - National Intelligence Centre

Sweden

- Kontoret för särskild inhämtning (KSI) - Office for Special Acquisition
- Underrättelsekontoret (UNDK) - Intelligence Office

Taiwan

- National Security Bureau (NSB)
- Ministry of Justice Investigation Bureau (MJIB)
- Bureau of Military Intelligence

Turkey

- Milli İstihbarat Teşkilatı (MİT) - National Intelligence Organisation

Ukraine

- Holovne Upravlinnya Rozvidky (HUR) - Central Intelligence Directorate
- Sluzhba Bezpeky Ukrayiny (SBU) - Security Service of Ukraine
- Sluzhba Zovnishnioyi Rozvidky Ukrayiny (SZR or SZRU) - Foreign Intelligence Service of Ukraine

United Kingdom

- Defence Intelligence
- Secret Intelligence Service (SIS or MI6)
- Special Branch
- Security Service (colloquially MI5)
- Government Communications Headquarters (GCHQ)

United States

- Independent agencies
- Central Intelligence Agency (CIA)
- United States Department of Defense
- Air Force Intelligence, Surveillance and Reconnaissance Agency (AFISRA)
- United States Army Intelligence and Security Command (MI)
- Defense Intelligence Agency (DIA)
- Marine Corps Intelligence Activity (MCIA)
- National Geo-spatial-Intelligence Agency (NGA)
- National Reconnaissance Office (NRO)
- National Security Agency (NSA)
- Office of Naval Intelligence (ONI)
- United States Department of Energy
- Office of Intelligence and Counter-intelligence (OICI)
- United States Department of Homeland Security
- Office of Intelligence and Analysis (I and A)
- Coast Guard Investigative Service (CGIS)
- United States Department of Justice
- Federal Bureau of Investigation (FBI)
- Drug Enforcement Administration (DEA)
- United States Department of State
- Bureau of Intelligence and Research (INR)
- United States Department of the Treasury
- Office of Terrorism and Financial Intelligence

Vietnam

- Tong cuc2 (TC2)

18

Joining the Dots

India Time Line - 2011

Date	Internal Security Related Information
January 2	A Delhi court convicted five JeM militants, for waging war against the country and being involved in spreading terror.
January 3	Foreign Minister SM Krishna, warned Pakistan that 'compulsive hostility' is not going to help the process of dialogue. India is most likely to be given a key responsibility by the UN Security Council in its fight against terrorism in acknowledgement of New Delhi's prominent role in the global war against terror
January 4	The Union Ministry of Home Affairs (MHA) called a meeting of the Police Chiefs of Naxal [Left Wing Extremism (LWE)]-affected States in New Delhi on January 10-11 to discuss the overall situation in the CPI-Maoist zone. India to deploy naval spy drones on the Gujarat coast to detect terror and conventional threats emanating from sea from across the border in real time.

January 6	Five JeM militants sentenced to life imprisonment by a Delhi trial court in connection with Millennium Park encounter case (August 30, 2003). Hardeep Puri, India's permanent representative in the United Nations elected to chair the key counter-terrorism committee and international security committee in the United Nations Security Council (UNSC). India will also chair two other committees on Somalia and Eritrea. India to deploy naval spy drones on the Gujarat coast to detect terror and conventional threats emanating from sea from across the border in real-time. As part of its effort to crackdown on terrorism, the Maharashtra Government makes it harder for people convicted of terrorist and extremist activities to get out of jail early.
January 7	The intelligence agencies issue a fresh terror alert stating that Pakistani terrorists are procuring fake continuous discharge certificates (CDC), which have to be carried by sailors, from the Republic of Liberia and trying to sneak in through sea routes. Prime Minister Manmohan Singh said that India was not satisfied with the pace of progress in the Mumbai terror attack (November 26, 2008, also known as 26/11) trial in Pakistan and would like the cases against the suspects expedited.
January 8	Swami Aseemanand, the hard-line Hindutva leader, confessed of his involvement in the terror attack on Hyderabad's Mecca Masjid.
January 10	In the course of his confessions Swami Aseemanand, the hard-line religious leader, revealed that he had paid INR 25,000 to his co-conspirator Sunil Joshi (who was later murdered) before the bomb explosions in Malegaon (September 8, 2008) in Maharashtra.

January 11	Union Home Minister P Chidambaram took stock of anti- CPI-Maoist operations and coordination amongst State Police and Paramilitary officers of Naxal -affected States of the country as he met the top brass of these forces in New Delhi on January 10.
January 11	The Union government ruled out the prospect of sharing information with Pakistan on the probe into the Samjhauta Express bomb blast case at present, saying it was too premature. External Affairs Minister SM Krishna, during an interaction with visiting journalists from eastern European countries in New Delhi said that India was looking forward to Pakistan addressing its core concern regarding terrorism and tackling the militant outfits effectively.
January 13	A special court in Mumbai granted permission to the CBI for reinvestigating the Malegaon blast case in Maharashtra in the wake of Swami Aseemanand's (the hardliner religious leader accused of involvement in terrorist activities and currently in Police custody) statement linking Hindu groups to the case.
January 14	The Special Investigation Team (SIT) of the CBI to question nine persons arrested in connection with the Malegaon mosque blast case. The state-of-the-art control rooms with giant TV screens that will help track the movement of Security Forces in thick forests and hilly terrain of Naxal-affected areas with satellite-based navigation (SATNAV) imaging and Global Positioning System (GPS) have been activated at the Central Reserve Police Force (CRPF), headquarters in New Delhi.
January 15	The Army asked the Government to finalize "Rules of Engagement" as it gets ready to open a new training facility in Chhattisgarh, but denied the move is linked to combating Naxalites in the State. A Delhi court awarded rigorous life imprisonment to six HUJI militants, including three Pakistani nationals, for plotting to abduct cricketers Sachin Tendulkar and Saurav Ganguly in 2002

January 16	The Home Secretary GK Pillai said that India would share information with Pakistan on the investigation into the Samjhauta Express blast case (February 17, 2007) once the probe was completed.
January 18	Pakistan has reportedly pumped in Fake Indian Currency Notes (FICN) worth several crores in Jammu and Kashmir, New Delhi and Bangalore through Bangladesh-West Bengal border using a number of fresh recruit of Jammu and Kashmir (J&K), Bihar, West Bengal and other parts of the country. The Special Investigation Team probing the Ishrat Jahan encounter case (June 15, 2004) claimed to have found that both the alleged Pakistani militants who were shot dead along with Ishrat and Pranesh Pillai alias Javed Sheikh had faked their identities as Kashmiris.
January 19	The Indore Bench of the Madhya Pradesh High Court directed the Central Bureau of Investigation (CBI) to complete, within two months, the probe in the case of missing witness, Dilip Patidar, in the Malegaon blast incident.
January 26	Indian Foreign Secretary Nirupama Rao, said that India is looking forward to receiving the Pakistani Foreign Minister Shah Mahmood Qureshi for talks in the next couple of months and is serious about dialogues but wants Pakistan to take action against perpetrators of the Mumbai terrorist attacks (November 26, 2008 also known as 26/11).
January 27	National Investigation Agency (NIA) failed to produce Swami Aseemanand before the Panchkula District court in connection with Samjhauta blast case (February 17, 2007). India accused Pakistan of not doing enough to check terrorism. Foreign secretary Nirupama Rao said there were elements in Pakistan who believed in violence and were allowing terror to grow further
January 29	Former Deputy Speaker of Punjab, Bir Devinder Singh, reportedly received a threatening email from militant outfit Babbar Khalsa International (BKI)

February 1	Indian security and intelligence agencies are probing into possible links between Pakistan-based militant outfits and Somali pirates, who are now operating much closer to Indian waters off the Lakshadweep Islands. The Maharashtra ATS arrested Praveen Mutalik, an accused in the Malegaon blast case, from Gokak in Belgaum District of Karnataka. Union Home Minister P Chidambaram said that new groups from neighbouring countries were suspected to be behind some terror attacks that took place in recent years. Chief Ministers of different States discussed various facets of internal security scenario in the conference convened by the Centre in New Delhi.
February 2	Militant outfits of the North East have to express desire for peace and show willingness to abjure violence for the Centre to respond positively in considering their demands, said Prime Minister Manmohan Singh. Ahead of the Foreign Secretary-level talks, Union External Affairs Minister SM Krishna said that India felt let down by Pakistan on the issue of bringing the perpetrators of Mumbai terror attacks (26/11) to justice.
February 3	A Chicago court in the US, on an unspecified date in 2010, sent a Letter Rogatory (communication sent by a court to a foreign court for judicial assistance) to a Mumbai court, requesting assistance for the FBI in the Mumbai terror attacks investigations.
February 4	According to secret diplomatic cables released by WikiLeaks, terror training camps, though not directly run by the Pakistan Government, continue to operate along India-Pakistan border creating potential for conflict with India and instability in the region. The Supreme Court ruled that members of banned organisations cannot be treated as criminals by the Police till they indulge in or incite violence. The Staff Selection Commission (SSC) to recruit 53,200 constables for Central para-military forces through a common recruitment examination.

February 5	The ULFA general council endorsed the resolution of the central executive council (CEC) to sit for talks with the Centre without any precondition.
February 8	The Union Government will approach a larger Bench of the Supreme Court seeking a review of a recent ruling, which held that mere membership of a banned outfit would not attract criminal action. Brijesh Kumar Singh, the Indian Army trooper arrested on February 5 for his links with the ISI, was in constant touch with Pakistani authorities. Singh was charged under the Official Secrets Act after he was found providing vital information to Vishambhar Tarachand Agarwal, who was arrested by the Crime Branch on February 2 for collecting information from Singh and passing it on to the ISI. Foreign Secretary Nirupama Rao said that the India-Pakistan dialogue process could be back on track. She added that the two sides intend to resume activities that had been put in abeyance.
February 9	A change of guard in the Central Committee leadership is being considered during CPI-Maoist plenary that is on in Bihar. The Indian Air Force will deploy more low-level aerial surveillance systems in the peninsular region to guard the country's 4,000-km-long coastline against hostile low-flying aircraft, gliders, and unmanned surveillance drones. Defence Minister AK Antony said that the Union Government was aiming at rapid modernisation of the Armed Forces and that the defence expenditure was bound to go up in the coming decades.
February 10	The Supreme Court reiterated that mere membership of a banned outfit without indulging in or inciting violence is not a crime.
February 12	The CPI-Maoist threatened to launch an indefinite bandh (general shut down) in Jharkhand and Odisha from February 14, if one of its members and two others of an Assam-based outfit, arrested by joint forces on Odisha-Jharkhand border, were not produced in court by February 13.

February 13	Central intelligence agencies communicated specific inputs to the Tamil Nadu Police that suspected LTTE cadres are conspiring to carry out attacks on VVIPs during forthcoming Assembly elections in the State.
February 14	India is considering sending a commission to the US to get evidence against Pakistani-American militant David Coleman Headley and questioning his Chicago-based wife, Shazia, who has so far been kept away from Indian investigators.
February 15	Union Home Secretary Gopal K Pillai said that the emergence of right-wing terror elements in the country was a cause of worry for the Government.
February 17	Restrictions on movement of passenger trains during night in CPI-Maoist affected areas of West Bengal, Odisha and Jharkhand will continue till February 24, a Railway statement said

Cont...

February 21	The CPI-Maoist are garnering international support. A solidarity initiative is being launched by Maoist parties and groups across the world. The Bombay High Court upheld the death sentence awarded by the trial court to the lone surviving Pakistani gunman, Mohammad Ajmal Amir Kasab who is accused of involvement in the Mumbai terror attacks. It also upheld the acquittal of co-accused Fahim Ansari and Sabahuddin Ahmed for want of corroborative evidence. Among the several charges against Kasab, the most serious was his waging a war against the Indian government, the Bombay High Court said. Upholding his death sentence, Justice Ranjan Desai said, "Perhaps the weightiest aggravating circumstance is that Kasab waged a war against the Government of India pursuant to a conspiracy which was hatched in Pakistan, the object of which was to *inter alia* destabilise the Government of India and to weaken India's economic might. " India proposed two sets of dates, March 21-22 and March 28-29 to Pakistan for Home Secretary-level talks which will have counter-terrorism high on its agenda. The special cell of Delhi Police has confirmed that it has asked All Parties Hurriyat Conference (APHC-G) Chairman Syed Ali Shah Geelani not to leave the city after one of his close associates was found involved in a hawala (illegal money transfer) racket. Ministry of Home Affairs (MHA) is worried over the growing nexus of CPI-Maoist leaders with North East militant groups as a huge cache of sophisticated weapons in possession of North East insurgent groups, particularly the ULFA, PLA and NSCN-IM, is feared to have been finding route to Maoists in West Bengal, Jharkhand and Bihar.

February 22	Huge vacancies in the administrative set-up and large-scale absenteeism have been reported from the Naxal-affected areas. There are over 94,800 vacancies to be filled up as on December 31, 2010, by these states. These are indicative of poor presence of government machinery in the affected areas. Such trends would further alienate the people and render the entire exercise of countering Naxalism futile. Of the 94,800 vacancies, as many as 33,000 alone are from Andhra Pradesh, 18,000 in Jharkhand, 14,000 in Maharashtra, 12,300 in West Bengal, 5,000 in Odisha, 4,500 in Bihar and 3,500 in Chhattisgarh. States have communicated to the Home Ministry that most of these posts would be filled up during 2011. 10 battalions of specialised force trained and equipped for counter-insurgency and jungle warfare operations named Commando Battalion for Resolute Action are being raised as a part of the Central Reserve Police Force during the period 2008 -2011. In 2008-09, two battalions were raised, one each at Jagadlpur (Chhattisgarh) and Koraput (Odisha). The next year, four battalions were raised comprising one each at Hazaribagh (Jharkhand), Jagdalpur (Chhattisgarh), Gaya (Bihar) and Bhandara (Maharashtra). Alerting ex-servicemen to the plan of ISI to spread its network, senior Police officers from six northern states discussed issues like terrorism, security of national installations and crime when they met in Shimla to work out a more coordinated intelligence sharing system. .

February 23	The links of the militant groups of North East with China came to the fore yet again as Indian security agencies came to know about a meeting that the leaders of the militant groups had with Chinese Government officials in April, 2010. So,urces in the MHA told *Assam Tribune* that leaders of the militant groups like United National Liberation Front (UNLF) and People's Liberation Army (PLA) of Manipur, 'chairman'of the National Socialist Council of Nagaland-Khaplang (NSCN-K), S S Khaplang and the 'commander in chief'of the ULFA, Paresh Baruah among others attended the meeting held in Ruili in Yunan Province of China. The Home Secretaries of both India and Pakistan will hold talks in New Delhi on March 28 and 29 on a host of issues including the progress in the 26/11 attacks trial in a Rawalpindi court.
February 25-26	A local court in Mumbai granted four days'transit remand to Mohammed Asad Siddiqui, a SIMI cadre and an accused in the August 14, 2000 Kanpur blast case, arrested in a joint operation by the Maharashtra Anti-Terrorism Squad (ATS) and Uttar Pradesh ATS in Mumbai on February 25.
February 27	The Cricket World Cup is facing threat as 29 trained militants of LeT have entered the country as per Intelligence agencies. According to sources, among the militants there are cadres of IM as well. The militants have been asked to target cricket teams and venues of matches. Mumbai – where World Cup final will be played on April 2 – is reportedly a prime target.
March 1	India is awaiting a reply from Pakistan on its request to send a team there to question some suspects in 26/11 case before it takes a decision on allowing a commission from Islamabad to visit India.
March 3	The Director General of BSF Raman Srivastava said that BSF gave Bangladesh Rifles (BDR) a list of camps of Indian militant outfits operating in North East and will discuss the issue of presence of the militant leaders of those groups there.

March 6	A joint operation by the Coast Guard and Gujarat Police neutralised a live grenade lodged in a sea-tanker and averted a major maritime disaster. The tanker was registered in Greece. European countries are being used as hot destinations by terror group al Qaeda to route money to India, as per a Peruvian Financial Intelligence Unit (FIU) report.
March 7	Three militants, including one who worked as a communication expert with HM, were arrested near Khan Market area of New Delhi for allegedly running a fake currency racket. The Amritsar police on arrested Sohan Singh alias Sohanjit Singh, a close associate of a Pakistan-based terrorist Paramjit Singh Panjwar, 'chief'of KCF. The MHA warned that the SIM cards becoming the new national security risk. The information came out that many of the SIM cards being used by nearly 700 million mobile users in the country may have malevolent embedded software, which has put India's security agencies on tenterhooks.
March 8	Over 2,600 civilians and SF personnel were killed between 2008 and 2010 in several incidents of LWE violence across the country, said Minister of State (Home Affairs) Gurudas Kamat. Taking note of reports of Pune-based real estate agent and stud farm owner Hasan Ali Khan's alleged links with arms dealers and people associated with terror activities, the Supreme Court asked the Centre to indicate whether he could be booked under the anti-terror law.
March 9	Somali pirates freed all crew members of a hijacked ship MV Rak Afrikana including 11 Indians, who have since been shifted to a Spanish naval ship. A foreign intelligence agency conveyed to India that Islamist militant outfits al Qaeda and LeT may target ongoing World Cup cricket matches in India and vital oil installations along the coastline.

March 10	The Director General of Police of Tamil Nadu, Letika Saran dismissed as baseless the Sri Lankan Prime Minister DM Jayaratne's allegation that the LTTE had three secret training camps in the State close to its border with Kerala.
March 11	The Supreme Court penalised the Maharashtra Government for not responding to its notice for more than a year on a petition by the kin of the Mumbai terror attack victims (November 26, 2008, also known as 26/11), who demanded compensation from Taj and Oberoi hotels and a security regime for the hospitality industry.
March 12	In its anti-piracy operations, the Indian Navy intercepted a mother vessel of Somali pirates in the Arabian Sea about 700 nautical miles off Kochi and rescued 13 crew members apart from arresting 61 pirates.
March 13	Khalistani militant Jagtar Singh Tara, who was involved in the assassination of former Punjab chief minister Beant Singh, is reportedly planning to launch his own outfit, Khalistan Tiger Force (KTF) breaking away from the parent outfit BKI.
March 15	A special MCOCA court rejected the bail application of all the nine persons accused in the Malegaon blast case.
March 16	SFs arrested of four ISI agents from a Agartala Hospital.
March 21	The Centre warned Maharashtra Police about a possible terror plot to target the cricket World Cup final in Mumbai on April 2.
March 22	NIA to launch a thorough probe relating to cases involving Hindutva militant groups.
March 23	An ISI agent was arrested from a hotel in Agartala.
March 28	In a recent interview in Dhaka, Bangladesh, Robert Blake, the US Assistant Secretary of State for South and Central Asia observed that his government was worried about prospect of a terror attack in India from outfits like the LeT.

March 29	During the India-Pakistan Home Secretary level talks which ended in New Delhi, Pakistan conveyed its readiness, in principle, to entertain a commission from India with respect to the Mumbai terror attack probe, on the principle of comity and reciprocity.
March 30	The Union Government claimed that a 'breakthrough' in the Samjhauta Express blast case was achieved in December 2010 when a 'key conspirator' had not only confessed of his involvement but had also divulged the names of co-conspirators who carried out the blasts. This was the first statement on the subject issued by the Home Ministry.
March 31	Shivshankar Menon-, who was Foreign Secretary at the time of the 2008 Mumbai attacks, believed that the crisis presented India with an opportunity to build closer ties with the United States. In a WikiLeaks cable dated November 30, 2008 (180629: confidential), US Ambassador David Mulford wrote that Mr. Menon saw this as the 'only silver lining' of the gruesome attacks.
April 1	According to Intelligence shared by high ranking Delhi intelligence officials at a meeting with the State and City Police Officers, the Railway Minister and Trinamool Congress Chief, Mamata Banerjee is on the CPI-Maoist hit list.
April 2	Prime Minister Manmohan Singh said that the Union Government was open to talks with all militant outfits and the discussions with the ULFA are a good beginning.
April 3	A special NIA court in Panchkula in Haryana issued fresh production warrants against the arrested extremist leader Swami Aseemanand.
April 6	Foreign Secretary Nirupama Rao said that despite India's re-engagement with Pakistan on a wide range of issues that need to be addressed, India had made it clear that the wounds of Mumbai terror attack had not healed as yet and stressed on Islamabad taking with 'utmost seriousness' its request for voice samples of the 26/11 accused.

April 7	A local court in Ajmer rejected the application of extremist leader Swami Aseemanand, an accused in several terror cases, to turn an approver in the Ajmer Dargah blast
April 8	Separatists and terrorists in the North East states of India committed serious human rights abuses, as per an official US report.
April 9	Many industries located in CPI-Maoist dominated areas are forced to buy peace with the Left Wing Extremists due to insecure environment, stated the Union Home Secretary Gopal K Pillai.
April 12	Pakistani-American militant David Coleman Headley alias Daood Gilani and Pakistani-Canadian Tahawwur Hussain Rana, who allegedly planned and conducted recce before terror attacks in Mumbai, implicated the Pakistani Government and its intelligence agency, ISI, in the attack,
April 13	India is sending a two-member team to Chile to probe claims that the authorities in the Capital city of Santiago had detained a person wanted in the hijacking of the Indian Airlines aircraft, IC-814 on December 24, 1999 in Kandahar (Afghanistan). The detainee, identified as Abdul Rauf has been charged of possessing fake travel documents.
April 14	The Union Government said that there was no dilution in its position that all those responsible for the Mumbai terror attacks should be brought to justice expeditiously and the on-going dialogue with Pakistan will seek to address the country's terrorism-related concerns.
April 15	Pakistan's Interior Minister Rehman Malik, said that India had provided a report on the probe into the Samjhauta Express blast case to Pakistan, but declined to give details.
April 17	A scrap dealer was arrested in New Delhi, along with counterfeit currency with a face value of INR 1,10,000. The accused, identified as Zubair Alam, was arrested from East Delhi after the police received an input about a gang supplying fake notes in the Capital.

April 20	The crew of the Denmark-flagged ship MV Danica Sunrise, which was intercepted and detained by the Coast Guard in Mumbai port on April 17, admitted of having dumped two AK-47 rifles in the Arabian Sea. The Home Ministry asked intelligence agencies to verify records and see whether the suspected money-launderer Hasan Ali Khan or his alleged hawala network had links with any terror outfit or was ever used to transfer money to any of them or their fronts.
April 24	Police arrested five persons and seized fake Indian currency INR 9,54,000 from their possession in Mianwali, Punjab. Also, customs officials recovered fake currency worth two lakh Rupees from a goods train, which runs between India and Pakistan for trade activities. The recovery was made at Attari railway station located close to Pakistan.
April 21	Six Pakistani nationals, including two militants, lodged in Jammu and Kashmir and Tihar jails were released by India.
April 22	Extremist leader Swami Aseemanand, who is accused of masterminding bomb explosions in Ajmer Dargah, Mecca mosque, Malegaon and Samjhauta Express, told a trial court in Ajmer that he was innocent and that probe agencies had extracted a confession from him under duress.
April 25	Three crude bombs were recovered on Sealdah-Rajdhani Express (Train no-12313) between Asansol and Dhanbad stations. During Army and Air force commanders'conference in New Delhi, it was assessed that India was faced with unconventional threats emanating from jihadi outfits getting hold of 'dirty' nuclear bombs, crippling cyber-attacks and "hybrid forms of warfare" which were actually more worrying than full-blown conventional wars with Pakistan or China,
April 27	PLGA, the military wing of the CPI-Maoist, is training its cadres to counter aerial attacks in the event of air strikes by the Indian Air Force.

April 29	The Karnataka Government strongly opposed granting of bail to Abdul Nasir Maudany, an accused in the Bangalore serial bomb blast cases (July 25, 2008). Former British foreign secretary David Miliband stated that Pakistan was not doing enough to bring the perpetrators of the Mumbai terrorist attack to justice.
April 30	India has to play an important role in supporting the Afghan people, said Marc Grossman, the US special envoy for Afghanistan and Pakistan.
May 2	Indian Government demanded custody of the perpetrators of the Mumbai terror attacks from Pakistan, following US President Barack Obama's announcement about the killing of the al Qaeda leader Osama bin Laden by American forces.
May 3	Union Home Minister P Chidambaram said that the death of Osama bin Laden would not mean the end of terror and India would have to be 'very vigilant' until Pakistan dismantled terror infrastructure within its territory. The Union Government has decided to recruit more than 2000 retired Army personnel to help the CRPF troopers to gain expertise in crippling IED and hidden landmines while undertaking anti-Naxal operations.
May 4	US ambassador to India Timothy Roemer said that Pakistan must do more in terms of progress and results in the trial of Mumbai terror attack case. Army Chief General VK Singh said the Indian Armed Forces were capable of carrying out surgical operations against terrorists similar to the one conducted by the US in Pakistan to kill al Qaeda chief Osama bin Laden.
May 6	A District Court in Delhi framed charges against 13 suspected IM militants for their alleged role in the September 2008 Delhi serial blasts (September 13, 2008), which killed 26 people and injured 135.
May 9	Delhi-based religious organisation Tablighi Jamaat (TJ) is under increasing suspicion for having links with the al Qaeda. Indian authorities released detailed dossiers of five Pakistani nationals, including a serving Major of Pakistan's ISI who have been charge-sheeted by US authorities in connection with the Mumbai terror attacks.

May 10	One Indian national was arrested along with six other suspected Islamist militants in a counter-terrorism operation conducted by the French Police raids in Paris and its suburbs. The arrested Indian had 'links with Pakistan'. Indian authorities rejected Pakistani Interior Minister Rehman Malik's claim that the designated international terrorist Dawood Ibrahim was not in his country, insisting that Pakistan needed to disclose the whereabouts of the don, who has houses in Karachi, Lahore and Islamabad. US Ambassador in India, Timothy Roemer denied that his country viewed differently the terror attacks in New York (9/11) and in Mumbai (26/11).
May 11	The Union Government came out with a list of 50 "most wanted fugitives" hiding in Pakistan. Indian intelligence agencies claimed having credible evidence that several hundred Chinese nationals working in PoK are People's Liberation Army (PLA) engineers. Foreign Secretary Nirupama Rao said there was no 'use by date' on India's demand for prosecution of all those involved in the Mumbai terror attacks. Prime Minister Manmohan Singh called for a "thorough investigation" into the presence of Osama bin Laden in Pakistan. Union Home Minister P Chidambaram scotched the perception of rift in Government over engaging Pakistan.
May 12	The Union Government deleted 142 names of Sikh Non-Resident Indians (NRIs) from the dreaded 'black list', which had 169 names in all.
May 13	Afghanistan National Intelligence Agency spokesperson Lutfullah Mashal said that ISI hired two persons, identified as Sher Zamin and Khan Zamin, to kill the Indian Consul General of Jalalabad province. The Government decided to recruit 20,000 more armed women personnel in Paramilitary Forces (PMFs) in the next three to five years.

May 14	The Indian Army warned that Pakistan may sneak - in more militants into Jammu and Kashmir to divert attention from its 'internal problems' after the killing of Osama bin Laden.
May 15	India has started working on a network of air-defence systems which would be able to shoot down any enemy missile even at a distance of 5,000 kilometers, before it can enter the Indian air space.
May 16	The NIA filed a charge-sheet against the arrested extremist leader Swami Aseemanand for his alleged role in the conspiracy behind the Mecca Masjid blast (May 18, 2007) case.
May 20	While denying that ISI had a hand in the bombing of the Indian Embassy in Kabul (July 7, 2008), Mahmud Ali Durrani, Pakistan's National Security Adviser to the Prime Minister admitted to his Indian counterpart MK Narayanan that Pakistan had contacts with 'bad guys' and 'one of them' could have carried out the attack, according to WikiLeaks. Following a statement made by Shuja Ahmad Pasha, the Chief of Pakistan's ISI,, that they had 'identified targets' and carried out 'rehearsal' for an attack on India, Prime Minister Manmohan Singh met the three Service Chiefs to make a fresh assessment of the security situation. India and Pakistan resumed talks on the Sir Creek boundary dispute after a gap of four years. Defence Minister AK Antony on May 20 termed the killing of Osama bin Laden by the US Forces in Pakistan a 'watershed' event which would have a 'ripple effect' in the India's 'strategic neighbourhood' and asked the Armed Forces to be prepared for any eventuality.
May 22	Admitting there is a development deficit in areas affected by LWE, Prime Minister Manmohan Singh said his Government is determined to address the deficit, while maintaining that the menace remains a 'major problem'.

May 23	Two letters received by the police in Punjab threatened that LeT will blow up key temples in Punjab and Himachal Pradesh on June 5 to avenge the killing of Osama bin Laden. Union Home Minister P Chidambaram said that Mohammad Niaz Abdul Rashid, the Indian engineer, who was arrested by French Police for alleged links with al Qaeda, had been involved with the affiliates of the outlawed SIMI in Tamil Nadu. As per a police official, who had interrogated Varanasi Subramanian, one of the three Central Committee members of the CPI-Maoist, the Maoist leader confessed that the outfit's annual income by way of collecting levy from big companies and loot is to the tune of INR 400 billion. David Coleman Headley confessed in a Chicago court that the LeT and Pakistan's ISI had coordinated the 26/11 attacks.
May 24	Fresh evidence in the form of *e*-mails emerged during the trial of David Coleman Headley which showed that Pakistan's ISI played a key role in funding and organising the Mumbai terror attacks. Headley said that there was a plot involving his handlers in ISI and LeT to assassinate Shiv Sena party Chief Bal Thackeray.
May 25	A low intensity explosion was reported outside the Delhi High Court. CPI-Maoist cadres are using innocent children and women as shields to escape during encounters with Security Forces, as per a senior CRPF official.

May 26	One person from Ghaziabad in Uttar Pradesh was arrested by the Delhi Police in connection with the low-intensity explosion outside the Delhi High Court. During the trial of Tahawwur Hussein Rana, his accomplice and co-accused, David Coleman Headley testified that Pakistani Navy, at the behest of ISI had trained the 26/11 terrorists. Referring to the threat posed by the Pakistan-based militant outfit LeT, visiting Secretary of the Department of Homeland Security, Janet Napolitano, said, "I think, in my judgment, the LeT ranks right up there in the al Qaeda and related groups as terrorist organisations, one that seeks to harm people and takes innocent lives. Our perspective, the US perspective, is LeT is very, very, I do not want to say, important as that gives it too much credibility, but an organisation that is of the same ranking as al Qaeda-related groups". France has assured India it has for now put on hold supply of 'heavy' military hardware to Pakistan, in the back of concerns over the huge amounts of arms Pakistan is getting from the West in the name of the so-called global war on terrorism.
May 27	Admitting his involvement in the killing of VHP leader, Swami Laxmanananda Saraswati, surrendered CPI-Maoist leader, Dunna Keshav Rao alias Azad said that the decision to eliminate him was taken by the top leadership of the CPI-Maoist. Union Home minister P Chidambaram said that Pakistan, was "global epicentre of terrorism", which was promoting terror infrastructure as 'state policy' against India.
May 30	US authorities did not intend to press Pakistan for the extradition of suspects sought by federal prosecutors for their role in the terrorist attacks on Mumbai, lest it should lead to a further breakdown of its increasingly fraught relationship with Pakistan.

May 31	A diplomatic cable dated December 30, 2009 (242073: secret), sent under the name of US Secretary of State Hillary Clinton stated that despite public disavowals, some officials of Pakistan's ISI Directorate continued to maintain ties with a wide array of extremist organisations, in particular the Taliban and the LeT. The Maharashtra Anti-Terrorism Squad,, arrested a person in Mumbai, who allegedly sent an *e*-mail to the CBI giving information about future terror strikes in ten large cities of India, including Mumbai and Delhi. Prime Minister Manmohan Singh said that terrorism had to be fought on all fronts and not selectively.
June 1	Union Home Minister P Chidambaram said that beginning of dialogue with insurgent groups in the North Eastern region helped to bring down the level of violence in that part of the country. . Union Home Minister P Chidambaram said that most of the aspects of LeT operative David Coleman Headley's on-going deposition before a Chicago court were known to the Government. A newly-released WikiLeaks cable revealed that Libyan leader Muammar Gaddafi could be financing a Pakistan-based anti-India militant outfit, Sipah-e-Sahaba Pakistan (SSP). A suspected agent of the Pakistani intelligence agency ISI was arrested near Haridwar in Uttarakhand.
June 3	An unidentified Pakistani intruder was shot dead by Border Security Force (BSF) troops at Mullankot post in Amritsar. .
June 4	Minister of State for Defence MM Pallam Raju warned that India would retaliate, if another terror attack on its soil is linked to members of Pakistan's security apparatus.
June 5	The Madhya Pradesh ATS arrested eight suspected militants belonging to the Indian Mujahideen (IM) and the banned outfit SIMI in Bhopal.

June 6	Union Government approved of the use of MI 17 Russian helicopters for CPI-Maoist-hit areas in Chhattisgarh, Maharashtra, Andhra Pradesh, Odisha, West Bengal, Jharkhand, Bihar, Madhya Pradesh and Uttar Pradesh. From a confidential cable, dated August 21, 2009 sent by the American Embassy in Beijing to Washington, it has come to light that Chinese authorities had placed a technical hold on an Indian request to impose sanctions on three high-ranking Pakistan-based operatives of the LeT and JeM.
June 7	In order to tackle terrorist threats from the seas, India is going in for 'a major upgrade' of its harbour protection systems (HPSs) at the naval bases in Mumbai, Visakhapatnam, Karwar, Kochi and Port Blair along with the ongoing security audit of ports, airfields, naval facilities, offshore installations and the like.
June 8	According to highly placed sources in the Indian intelligence agencies, the SIMI and the CPI-Maoist have recently conducted a secret meeting in Kottayam District of Kerala. Eight militants who were arrested on June 5 by the Madhya Pradesh Anti-Terrorist Squad (ATS) had planned to attack judges involved in the Ayodhya verdict. Union Home Minister P Chidambaram said that confidence could not be restored between India and Pakistan till Islamabad took action against the 'real culprits' responsible for the Mumbai terror attack.
June 9	Pakistani-Canadian operative of the militant outfit LeT, Tahawwur Hussain Rana was acquitted by a US court on charges of abetting Mumbai terror attacks but was convicted for providing material support to LeT and helping a terror plot in Denmark.
June 11	Union Home Minister P Chidambaram said that the National Intelligence Grid (NATGRID), which had been given an 'in principle' clearance by the Cabinet, would be in place in 18 months, and would be able to prevent 26/11-type terror attacks.

June 12	Punjab Police arrested a person in Jalandhar for facilitating the family of the militant Paramjit Singh Panjwar (who is on India's most wanted list) procure passports on fake credentials.
June 13	Police arrested 10 cadres of the banned SIMI from a house in Khandwa in Madhya Pradesh. An Anti – Talk Faction of NDFB-ATF militant, identified as Subhrugsha Brahma alias Jagrith was arrested by Security Forces (SFs) at the Rajiv Gandhi International Airport in Hyderabad.
June 14	The Union Government will try to sort out border coordination issues between Chhattisgarh and Odisha, which blocks seamless anti-Naxal operations in Naxal-infested Mahasamund-Nuapada inter-state junction.
June 15	Having met barely 10 per cent of its road-construction target in the eight Naxalites-hit states, the Government plans to enlist locals as workers and settle for 'semi-kuchcha' or simple motorable surfaces in place of the metalled ones that are standard for national highways. Militants of LeT used videos of the 2002 Gujarat riots to motivate David Coleman Headley, a co-accused in the Mumbai terror attacks case to carry out 'jihad' against India.
June 16	Following the appointment of the new 'chief'of al Qaeda, Ayman al-Zawahiri, intelligence sources fear that India may figure as a potential target of the international terrorist outfit. India and Nepal decided to monitor the activities of Pakistan's intelligence agency ISI on the porous India-Nepal border.
June 20	India will seek a 'satisfactory closure' to the Mumbai terror attacks case when it will hold extensive bilateral talks with Pakistan during which they will also review the Nuclear Confidence Building Measures (CBMs). Pakistani-American operative of the militant outfit LeT had testified before a 12-member jury of a Chicago court that some Indian nationals living in Karachi were willing to work with LeT to carry out terror attacks in India.

June 20	Indian Foreign Minister SM Krishna said that terror would remain on India's agenda during the forthcoming Foreign Secretary talks with Pakistan.
June 22	A new front of the banned outfit SIMI was uncovered by the Police in Karnataka following the arrest of six youths from Mysore after a two-week long investigation into the kidnapping for ransom and murder of two young business management students.
June 23	The Planning Commission proposed setting up telecom towers in Police compounds in 60 Naxalite -hit districts, to help tackle extremist violence.
June 24	An Indian national was abducted in the Philippines by suspected gunmen belonging to banned militant Islamist outfit, Abu Sayyaf, which is linked to al Qaeda. Asserting that nothing could be achieved through violence, President Pratibha Patil exhorted the CPI-Maoist to shun violence, think practically and come forward for talks.
June 25	Madhya Pradesh Police arrested a former cadre of the SIMI at the Cochin International Airport.
June 26	Pakistan-based LeT outfit runs a series of well-oiled courses for budding terrorists, ranging from religious indoctrination to military and intelligence training, which are aimed at boosting militancy in Jammu and Kashmir revealed David Coleman Headley, in his testimony during the recently-concluded trial of co-accused Tahawwur Rana in Chicago. The Centre plans to set up an elite unit within the Home Ministry to deal effectively with cases of terror financing and money laundering, which have a direct bearing on the country's internal Security.
June 28	Pakistani Interior Minister Rehman Malik said that his country would act against JuD (a front of the militant outfit LeT) chief Hafiz Mohammad Saeed if India provided actionable evidence against him.

June 29	Indian Foreign Secretary Nirupama Rao said that better relations with Pakistan could be achieved only in "an atmosphere free of terror and violence". New Zealand Prime Minister John Key said that his country had put in all efforts to tackle terrorism and was partnering with India on many fronts. SFs arrested Chirom Premkumar alias Prem alias Tiken alias Sunil Meitei, the 'commander-in-chief'of Mobile Task Force faction of the KCP-MTF, from Ejipura in Bangalore.
June 30	Intelligence reports indicated possibility of CPI-Maoist cadres establishing Orissa-Chhattisgarh corridor. Maoists have formed a Bargarh-Mahasamund Divisional Committee that reports to the larger Dandakaranya Special Zonal Committee (DKSZC). A White House report said that the Pakistan-based militant outfit LeT posed serious threat to both India and the US and a global effort was required to eliminate its menace.
July 1	A special NIA court in Panchkula in Haryana declared two persons, Sandeep Dange and Ram Chandra Kalasangra, as proclaimed offenders in the Samjhauta Express blast case.
July 3	Indian Foreign Secretary Nirupama Rao said that Pakistan's attitude towards tackling terror had altered and India should take note of this 'concrete' development.
July 4	In order to control cross-border crimes and check illegal infiltration, the BSF has installed alarm system at its North Bengal Frontier with Bangladesh. Union Home Minister P Chidambaram asked LWE-hit States to adopt a unified approach to deal with the CPI-Maoist, underlining that while some states had performed well, there were some who had fared poorly in anti-Naxal operations.

July 5	NIA is exploring the possibility of taking over investigations into the murder of two college students in Karnataka following alleged involvement of members of an organisation known as the Karnataka Forum for Dignity (KFD), considered to be a new front of SIMI. Centre will shortly deploy Unmanned Aerial Vehicles (UAVs) in select Naxal strongholds to track Maoist movements and camps.
July 6	Huge cache of arms and ammunition was recovered by the police from a village in Tarn Taran District of Punjab.
July 7	Restrictions on the movement of passenger trains at night in the CP I-Maoist-affected areas of West Bengal, Odisha and Jharkhand will continue till July 14.
July 8	The CBI has recently uploaded an updated version of most wanted men on its website.
July 9	The Army is firming up plans for anti-Naxal operations and has sounded out the Government to define Rules of Engagement (RoE) and guidelines for combat role. The Police busted a gang involved in manufacture of fake currency and arrested one person in Bahraich in Uttar Pradesh.
July 10	Ahead of the crucial Indo-US strategic dialogue, the Obama administration has said that counter-terrorism cooperation with India is a "very high priority" as it would help prevent Mumbai-type attacks in future. Prime Minister Manmohan Singh on July 9, highlighted the dangers posed by terrorism in the region and called for greater efforts to fight it.
July 12	Defence Minister AK Antony ruled out Army's involvement in Naxal operations and said the Army would react only in self-defence if it was attacked.
July 13	Three serial bomb blasts in the span of 10 minutes ripped through three of the busiest hubs in Mumbai city-Zaveri Bazar, Opera House and Dadar, killing 17 people and injuring 131 others. Police, arrested three illegal migrants from Bangladesh in Nagpur.

July 14	ATS of Maharashtra confirmed that timer devices were used in the three blasts which hit Mumbai yesterday. The explosive used was ammonium nitrate. Police sources reported discovery of an unidentified body with an embedded electric circuit from the blast site at Zaveri Bazar.
July 15	A dozen suspected IM operatives were arrested as investigators searched a number of locations. Security agencies identified the owner of the two-wheeler in which explosive material was planted at Zaveri Bazar. IB has intercepted a terror threat to the Bhakra Nangal dam in Himachal Pradesh. Investigating agencies believe the IM, suspected behind July 13 serial blasts of Mumbai may have procured ammonium nitrate used in the bombs from Maoists in Maharashtra. Maharashtra Chief Minister Prithviraj Chavan said that Mumbai was ill-equipped to tackle terror. US media pointed out that the attacks in Mumbai on July 13 had all the markings of LeT.
July 16	On being alerted by the Intelligence Bureau, the Bihar Police conducted raids at Barchaundhi village in Kisanganj District and arrested a suspected cadre of the militant outfit HuJI. Crime branch officers of Gujarat Police, who had arrested a key operative of the IM, Danish Riyaz, from Vadodara railway station on June 23, claimed to have unearthed details of a joint venture between IM and Taliban to orchestrate terrorist attacks in India.

July 18	The Gujarat ATS arrested one more person in Ahmedabad following the arrest of Shahzad Rangrez, who was arrested a day earlier with eight crude bombs. Uttar Pradesh Police is probing two mysterious calls that asked a meat-trader in Meerut and a farmer in Baghpat to plant bombs. Both the calls have been traced to Iran but routed through the US. Investigations into the Mumbai serial blasts were focusing heavily on suspects in Gujarat, with the Maharashtra ATS reportedly getting major leads pointing towards involvement of the IM. Intelligence Agencies suspect that militant outfits targeting India have moved their communications significantly to Internet and other innovative means.
July 19	The death toll of the Mumbai serial blasts rose to 20 as one more person succumbed to his injuries.
July 21	Maharashtra rural development minister Jayant Patil today said that he had cleared a proposal to install 5,000 CCTVs across Mumbai, but did not know "what happened to it" subsequently. A NIA-team quizzed terror convict Dr Jalees Shakil Ansari at Ajmer Central jail on early Sunday morning for his possible role in the recent terror attacks in Mumbai. Scotland Yard initiated a probe into the activities and financing of London-based Kashmir lobby group, Justice Foundation, suspected to be a front of Pakistan's Inter Services Intelligence ISI. Union Government, in the aftermath of the Mumbai serial blasts case (13/7), has taken a long overdue initiative to set up the National Counter-Terrorism Centre (NCTC) – an umbrella body to deal with terror threats in the country.

July 22	Indian security agencies believe that the mastermind of the recent Mumbai blasts, Abdullah Khan of the IM is hiding in Bangladesh. Ghulam Nabi Fai's Kashmiri American Centre in various countries, not just in US but also in the UK was being used to spread Pakistan's ISI's anti-India agenda. India and UK will hold a joint combat exercise to hone the counter-terrorism skills of their soldiers at the high-tech Land Warfare Centre in Warminster, near Salisbury in England in August, 2011 Death toll in Mumbai serial blasts rose to 21.
July 23	One person with alleged terror links was arrested by the Police in Maldah in West Bengal and fake currency worth INR 15,000 was recovered from him. Death toll in Mumbai serial blasts rose to 22.
July 24	Death toll in Mumbai serial blasts rose to 24.
July 25	In response to India's request for the voice samples of the seven militants accused in the Mumbai terror attack case (26/11), Pakistan's Interior Minister Rehman Malik stated that as per the Pakistan Penal Code, the only identification of an accused acceptable was the thumb impression and officially no photograph or voice sample of any accused could be taken.
July 26	There is increasing evidence of very active and growing collaboration between the CPI-Maoist and militant groups of northeast India, according to intelligence agencies. CPI-Maoist is planning to spread its tentacles in urban areas after consolidating their position in rural pockets. Union Home Minister P Chidambaram described home-grown terror groups as experts in destruction, and said the threat from such outfits was pretty high.

July 27	The Police of Uttar Pradesh, Bihar, Jharkhand and Chhattisgarh will now focus on identifying and cracking down on persons and organisations providing financial and other support to the CPI-Maoist. Authorities of the Lord Krishna Temple at Guruvayur in Kerala received a letter which warned of bomb attacks from al Qaeda on the temple.
July 28	Union Home Minister P Chidambaram stated that the lack of a stable elected Government in Nepal has increased the security vulnerability of India. Death toll in Mumbai serial blasts rose to 25.
July 29	In response to a request made by the FBI to share with it all the samples of evidence collected in the Mumbai terror attack case, the Mumbai Police expressed its inability to do so since several items on the FBI's long wish list have already been disposed of by local authorities. Central Security agencies have identified 20-odd organisations - based in Delhi, Kolkata, Mumbai, Nagpur and Gurgaon - suspected to be working as fronts of the CPI-Maoist with an aim to expand their bases in urban areas.
July 30	India plans to approach a global inter-governmental body – Financial Action Task Force (FATF) – asking it to treat the issue of 'fake currency notes'as an instrument of 'terror funding'. Death toll in Mumbai serial blasts rose to 26.
July 31	An alert has been sounded and security cover increased in Kheda District (Gujarat), on receipt of an anonymous letter threatening a terror attack at a temple on Independence Day.
August 1	India has requested Bangladesh to hand over 'as early as possible' banned ULFA's 'general secretary'Anup Chetia.

August 2	As many as 35 Army personnel have been killed in different operations in various parts of the country so far this year. Jitendra Singh, Minister of State in the MHA in a written reply informed the Lok Sabha (lower house of Parliament) that the current year (up to 26th July, 2011) witnessed 999 incidents of Naxal violence leading to 333 deaths (241 civilians and 92 Security Forces).
August 3	LeT has threatened to blow up railway stations in Haridwar, Dehradun and Rishikesh on the Independence Day.
August 4	Union Home Minister P Chidambaram stated the Security Forces should deal with right-wing terror groups "sternly and fearlessly" as they were enemies of the country as much as IM and SIMI. Gujarat Police arrested a man, identified as Bhavesh Patel, and seized as many as 31 detonators at Nadiad in Kheda District, ahead of Independence Day function which would be attended by Gujarat Chief Minister Narendra Modi. Union Home Minister P Chidambaram said that the July 13 blasts in Mumbai could be the handiwork of a homegrown terror module, possibly the one which also carried out the German Bakery blast in Pune (February 14, 2010).
August 5	Two persons, identified as Mohammad Farookh Sheikh (21) and Farida Begam alias Rashida were arrested by the police for circulating fake currency of INR 1,000 denomination in Nagpur City. Further, the Police investigations have revealed that the currency seized in Pune last week came from Malda District (bordering Bangladesh) in West Bengal.

August 9	Search is on for a ship that had a suspicious communication with contacts in Karachi, Pakistan. NIA is expected to file a charge-sheet against Mumbai terror attacks mastermind David Headley and co-accused Tahawwur Hussain Rana in a court on the basis of documents provided by the US. The Parliament was informed that CPI-Maoist affected States have witnessed more incidents of terrorist violence in the last six months than Jammu and Kashmir and northeastern states.
August 10	Arrest of a 'bike thief' by the Maharashtra ATS is a significant development that could potentially lead investigators to crack the 13/7 Mumbai terror blasts case. The suspect had allegedly stolen a two-wheeler used by terrorists to plant a bomb in Mumbai's Zaveri Bazar on July 13.
August 10	Indian President Pratibha Patil has been advised by the Centre to reject the mercy plea filed by Parliament Attack (December 13, 2001) convict Mohammad Afzal Guru. The Supreme Court upheld the death sentence awarded to LeT militant Mohammad Arif alias Ashfaq for the December 22, 2000 attack at the Red Fort in which three army men were killed. Nearly 1,300 Pakistanis on visit to India are traceless after their visa expired, even as the Government has created an online data sharing system to track every person traveling from Pakistan. Defence Minister AK Anthony asked Navy Chief Admiral Nirmal Verma and Coast Guard Chief Vice-Admiral Anil Chopra to 'take all steps' to ensure that the recent episode of MT Pavit, which drifted to Mumbai (Maharashtra) shore without being detected, did not occur in the future.

August 11	A Pakistani national, identified as Niyamatullah alias Aftab staying in Delhi for the past two years while posing as an Afghan national, was arrested from Tilak Nagar in New Delhi. Hemant Chodankar alias Chintamani, an accused in a FICN racket that was busted on August 2, was a regular visitor at a Goa's State Civil Supplies Minister, Jose Phillip D'Souza's house, as per the police.
August 12	The NIA Special Court in Kochi (Kerala) sentenced the self-styled South Indian 'commander' of LeT, Thadiynatavide Nazeer, and his accomplice M Shafaz to life imprisonment for twin blasts in Kozhikode in 2006. A secret report prepared by R&AW, IB, Department of Revenue Intelligence (DRI) and the CBI revealed that the infusion of FICN into India to destabilise the economy and fund terror activities were being actively supported by Pakistan's High Commissions in Dhaka (Bangladesh) and Kathmandu (Nepal) through ISI. It has also been reported that China was emerging as a major staging post for FICN flooding into India.
August 13	The Centre filed a petition in the Supreme Court, seeking recall and review of two crucial paras in its July 5 ruling, through which a bench banned the use of SPOs in the fight against Naxalites.
August 15	The Indian Navy captured a 'hijacked' Iran flagged cargo vessel, Nafis-1 with nine persons on board off the Mumbai coast following intelligence inputs that it may be carrying arms, ammunition and contraband. In a major bid to overhaul governance in areas vulnerable to Naxalism, the Central Government is all set to launch a Centrally-sponsored scheme for nearly 300 blocks across the seven affected States. .
August 16	Minister of State for Home Jitendra Singh informed Lok Sabha that a total of 100 people have been killed in 202 incidents of terrorist violence in Jammu and Kashmir till July 2011. He also stated that during 2001-2011 a total of 174 Pakistan-based espionage modules were neutralised by Central and State intelligence and security agencies.

August 18	The Government fears that nuclear establishments in the country continue to be vulnerable to terrorist attacks.
August 19	A report published from the US observed that India experienced a lesser number of deaths due to terrorist attacks in 2010, but still remained one of the most terrorism-afflicted nations in the world.
August 22	CRPF has trained and deployed an elite squad of snipers for the first time.
August 23	The Union Government said that terror threats to coastal cities still existed and it was reviewing security arrangements to face emerging challenges.
August 24	NIA probing the Samjhauta Express blast case informed the Punjab and Haryana High Court (HC) that it needed to re-examine the samples gathered after bomb blast in the train to find any link with the explosions that took place in Malegaon, Hyderabad and Ajmer. The Department of Telecommunications asked the External Affairs Ministry to discuss with Islamabad and Dhaka the issue of mobile signals being available in Indian territory even though telecom operators are not allowed to provide cellular service within 500 metres of the international border.
August 26	MHA organised a day-long workshop for SPs of CPI-Maoist-hit Districts to acquaint them about the Centre's policy on tackling Maoist menace and urged them to 'catch the big fish' who have been leading the cadres. Director General of Assam Rifles (DGAR) Lieutenant General Rameshwar Roy said that insurgency in North Eastern India is on decline due to domination of Security Forces (SFs), split amongst militant groups, disenchantment of the people and growing economic activities but extortion remains a point of concern.

August 27	Three persons, Murugan alias Sriharan, Chinna Santhan and Perarivalan convicted in the assassination case of former Indian Prime Minister Rajiv Gandhi were sentenced to death will be hanged at the Vellore Central Prison in Tamil Nadu on September 9. Material evidence hinting at a Pakistani link to Somali pirates has been recently recovered with the arrest of nine foreign nationals from a hijacked Iranian vessel – MV Nafis-1, by the Indian Navy 170 nautical miles off Mumbai.
August 29	A sessions court in Mumbai convicted two persons, allegedly linked to the Hindutva outfit Sanatan Sanstha, of conspiring and carrying out blasts at theatres around Mumbai in 2008. Four other accused charged with the same offences were acquitted of all charges against them.
August 30	The Parliament was informed that India has signed legal assistance pacts that deal with combating terrorism with 35 countries including the neighbouring Myanmar, Sri Lanka and Bangladesh.
August 31	MHA has formed a new cell which will focus on effectively dealing with funding of terrorist activities in the country. Reserve Bank of India warned that FICNs are steadily making their presence felt in the Indian monetary system. Concerned at the recent surfacing of an abandoned merchant vessel in Mumbai, Union Defence Minister AK Antony told all stakeholders in maritime security that there was no room for delay or slackness on the issue.

September 2	NATO has sought a deeper engagement with India in fields ranging from counter-terrorism and anti-piracy to cyber-security and Ballistic Missile Defence (BMD). In view of threat to security along the shores, the BSF will deploy its newly-formed marine battalion in the Arabian Sea. Turning down the appeal made by the arrested extremist leader Swami Aseemanand, who had sought directions to restrain NIA from re-examining samples gathered after bomb blasts in Samjhauta Express on February 18, 2007, the Punjab and Haryana High Court ruled that NIA's move cannot be termed as re-investigation, but is further investigation in the case, which is permissible under law.
September 3	In order to thwart any intrusion bid through the river waters, the BSF has enforced its water wing to conduct round-the-clock patrolling in the river running along the border in Fazilka sector in Punjab. Maharashtra state ATS believes that the Mumbai serial blasts strike was funded by the Pakistani intelligence agency ISI through the Saudi Arabian route and executed with the help of local city youth.
September 4	A leaked American cable revealed that India's former national security advisor MK Narayanan, during his conversation with the then US ambassador had hinted at the possibility of involvement of Indian nationals in international Islamist outfits like, al Qaeda. NIA concluded that the Mumbai serial blasts was the handiwork of the homegrown militant outfit IM.
September 6	According to US cables leaked by WikiLeaks, Indian Muslims were upset over the muted reaction of their leaders to the phenomenon of 'Islamist terrorism'. Minister of State in the MHA, Jitendra Singh, in a written reply to a question in the Lok Sabha informed that a total of 816 Naxalites have surrendered from 2008 to 2010.

September 7	At least 11 people were killed and about 91 others injured in a powerful blast outside Delhi High Court this morning. Latest US cables released by WikiLeaks reveal that in the run up to the hijacking of the Indian Airlines Flight 814 (December 24, 1999) by Pakistan-based militant outfits, the ISI had made Nepal a hub of anti-India terror activities from where it pushed huge quantities of RDX into the country.
September 8	Union Home Minister P Chidambaram said that Delhi was a target for terrorist groups, admitting that the incident had taken place even though the national Capital was on high alert. NIA detained three persons in Kishtwar, Jammu and Kashmir in connection with the case. The detained persons include the owner of a cyber cafe from where an *e*-mail from the Pakistan-based militant outfit HuJI claiming responsibility of the blast had been sent. Death toll in the blast outside the Delhi High Court rose to 12.
September 8	Following the trail of the first e-mail which was sent three hours after the blast claiming that the outfit HuJI was behind the attacks, the NIA detained five persons from down town Kishtwar. The Union Government is about to finalise a National Telecom Security Policy to beef up national security. Death toll in the Delhi High Court blast case rose to 13.

September 9	Two suspects from Jammu and Kashmir were detained in Alwar, Rajasthan on the basis of their resemblance to the sketches of suspects released in connection with the Delhi High Court blast. Tripura Chief Minister Manik Sarkar said that Bangladesh Prime Minister Sheikh Hasina has assured to take steps against anti-India militants operating out of Bangladesh. Four *e*-mails claiming responsibility for the Delhi High Court attack have been received so far. Agencies investigating the Delhi High Court blast are probing two calls made on the evening of the blast from two different places in Uttar Pradesh to Bangladesh. Union Home Minister P Chidambaram said there were 'promising' but not 'very conclusive leads' in the Delhi High Court blast case and that foreign agencies had been roped in. Forensic scientists of the National Security Guard (NSG) said that that the lethal high explosive PETN (Penta Erythritol Tetra Nitrate) was used in the Delhi High Court blast. Union Home minister P Chidambaram expressed the hope that there might be a breakthrough in the July 13, 2011 Mumbai blasts.
September 10	ULFA and NSCN-K are planning to shift their camps in Myanmar amid reports of a crackdown by the Myanmar's army.
September 11	CRPF has earmarked 70 exclusive battalions for counter-insurgency and Naxal operations which will be insulated from regular law and order duties performed by the force.
September 12	Union Government is going to install static coastal radar chain and national AIS (Automatic Identification System) network to dynamically detect and track suspicious vessels entering Indian waters. Two persons were detained in Kishtwar District in Jammu and Kashmir in connection with the Delhi High Court blast.

September 13	Calling Naxalism a bigger challenge than terrorism or insurgency, Union Home Minister P Chidambaram said that the burden of governance in the Maoist-affected Districts must rest with the States as the Central Government" does not have that much human resource" and can only provide help. Observing that the Maoists had not targeted works done under the Integrated Action Plan (IAP), the Government said efforts are on to extend the ambitious programme to 20 more Naxal – hit Districts.
September 14	The death toll in Delhi High Court blast rose to 14 as a 34-year-old victim succumbed to his injuries. NIA arrested two persons from Jammu and Kashmir for sending an *e*-mail claiming responsibility for the attacks on behalf of the militant terror outfit HuJI.
September 15	Union Home Minister P Chidambaram said that Pakistan and Afghanistan are the epicenters of terror activities. A conference of top police officials will begin today in New Delhi where issues concerning continuing terror attacks (including the recent blasts in Mumbai and Delhi), Naxalism (LEFT-wing Extremism), cyber security and circulation/printing of fake Indian currency notes will be the top agenda.
September 16	Maharashtra Police received inputs from central intelligence agencies about possible terror attacks on luxury buses plying between Mumbai and Ahmedabad and steps have been taken to foil any such bid. Union Home Minister P Chidambaram pushed for continued deployment of SFs to tackle threat of violence and extortions in the North Eastern region of India. Prime Minister Manmohan Singh stated that the "cross-border camps for terrorists" were being "reactivated" and there were attempts to induct fresh batches of militants into the country.

September 17	The Death toll in Delhi High Court blast rose to 15 as one more person succumbed to his injuries. At least 15 persons were injured in an IED explosion at Jai Hospital in Agra (Uttar Pradesh).
September 18	Police arrested a suspected agent of Pakistan's ISI, near Kanpur Central Railway station in Uttar Pradesh. NIA, probing the Delhi High Court blast case, suspects that sleeper cells of the Islamist outfits HuJI and the IM in Kerala could have had a hand in the terror strike.
September 19	CBI has added the name of Iqbal Bhatkal, the co-founder of IM, to the recently updated list of fugitives most wanted by Indian enforcement agencies.
September 21	Government sources claimed that the Investigating agencies are on the verge of solving the Varanasi blast case (December 7, 2010). Conspiracy to carry out bomb blast at the Delhi High Court was hatched in Nepal by HuJI, according to an intelligence input generated in Kolkata.
September 22	NIA court in Delhi sent Aamir Abbas Dev, one of the teenagers arrested for allegedly sending e-mail which claimed responsibility for the Delhi High Court blast, to judicial custody.
September 23	Supreme Court refused to grant bail to Sadhvi Pragya Singh Thakur, who is facing charges under Maharashtra Control of Organised Crime Act (MCOCA) for her alleged involvement in the Malegaon bomb blast case.
September 25	India expressed satisfaction over the fact that US recognized the link between the Haqqani network and ISI, both of which have been blamed for the assassination of former Afghan President Burhanudin Rabbani. Mumbai Police Chief claimed that the group which carried out the triple blasts in Mumbai on July 13, 2011 has been identified.
September 26	India conveyed to the US that the fight against terrorism required a united and non-selective approach.

September 27	India asked Pakistan to destroy 42 terror camps which are operational in its territory and warned that a resurgent Taliban could be a security threat to the country after US forces pull out from Afghanistan. "There are 42 terror camps which are still operational. We want all of them to be destroyed", said Defence Minister AK Antony. Indian External Affairs Minister SM Krishna during a meeting with his Pakistan counterpart Hina Rabbani Khar in New York in US, expressed the hope that Pakistan would be 'serious' in dismantling terror camps in its soil and live up to its pronouncements. Frequent use of illegally procured satellite phones in the North East region, calls of which can be traced by China, poses a grave threat to the National Security, according to sources.
September 28	Nine persons who were arrested in Kerala on September 26 on the charge of cheating 34 Sri Lankans at refugee camps in Tamil Nadu are suspected by the police to have links with the LTTE.
September 30	Union Home Minister P Chidambaram said that India knew the whereabouts of underworld don Dawood Ibrahim in Pakistan. During the biannual conference of BSF and Border Guard Bangladesh (BGB) held in Dhaka from September 25 to 30, the BSF handed over a fresh list of Indian insurgents hiding in Bangladesh to the BGB and demanded action against them even as the latter ruled out presence of rebels in Bangladesh.
October 3	Illegal firearms being channelled into the North East are going to emerge as a major concern in maintaining law and order in a region already infested by dozens of insurgents and subversive groups, according to reports.
October 4	India urged the UN to adopt Comprehensive Convention against International Terrorism insisting that UN's global counter-terrorism strategy would be incomplete without such a convention.

October 6	NIA has detained one more suspect from Kishtwar for the September 7 blast outside Delhi High Court. According to NIA officials, the suspect, identified as Wasim, is one of the key conspirators and had been studying in Bangladesh.
October 7	Results of the polygraph test performed on at least one of the accused picked up from Kishtwar has indicated HuJI hand in the blast.
October 8	NIA has sensitized all the states, border forces and immigration authorities as intelligence inputs suggest that Junaid, who has been missing since November last year, is in India and may try to sneak out of the country following Wasim's arrest.
October 9	A team of NIA officials arrived in Bangladesh to probe into the Delhi High Court blast case. The team, headed by a SP, left for Dhaka recently and quizzed some of the Kashmiri students studying in Jalalabad Ragib Rabeya Medical College and Hospital at Sylhet, near Dhaka.
October 10	Supreme Court stayed the execution of the death sentence awarded to Ajmal Kasab.
October 11	Memon Iqbal Mohammed alias Iqbal Mirchi, a close aide of underworld don Dawood Ibrahim and an accused in the serial bomb attacks on Mumbai (March 12, 1993) was arrested by London Police for a local offence in the UK.
October 12	A suspected terror plot was foiled in Ambala in Haryana with the recovery of over five kilograms explosives and detonators from a car-parked outside Cantonment Railway Station of the city. Following the arrest of underworld don Iqbal Mirchi in UK, the Indian Government said that it had initiated the process for his extradition to India.
October 13	As per Delhi Police sources, the explosives-laden car found in Ambala was headed towards the national Capital for a terror strike.

October 17	Recent intelligence reports cautioned the Punjab Government about renewed efforts by the ISI and Pakistan-based militant outfits, including BKI, to send consignment of arms, explosives, fake currency and drugs in the state. Indian authorities sought the help of Bangladesh in tracking two cadres of the banned militant outfit ICS for their alleged involvement in the Delhi High Court blast.
October 18	While probing the seizure of fake currency worth INR 10 million, the CBI has discovered the involvement of an international racket with roots in Pakistan. Four hand grenades, two of them live, were recovered from an irrigation canal in the Naroda area on the outskirts of Ahmedabad in Gujarat.
October 19	US issued a travel alert for its citizens travelling to India reminding them of the continued possibility of terrorist attacks throughout the country ahead of the festival season. Security at the Karkardooma court complex in New Delhi was strengthened following Intelligence inputs about senior Congress leader Sajjan Kumar, who was to appear in court in connection with the anti-Sikh riots case, being target of Khalistani militants.
October 20	Union Home Ministry issued a confidential note to security agencies in the country warning them about the use of satellite phones of service providers like Thuraya, Iridium and Inmarsat by militants.
October 21	Joint exercise of Indian and French armies, aimed at improving their counter-terrorism and counter-insurgency skills, culminated in Almora district in Uttarakhand.
October 22	Wasim Akram Malik, who masterminded the Delhi High Court blast has revealed that the attack was carried out by two Pakistanis from Lahore. A Bangladeshi ship, suspected to be carrying arms and ammunition, was intercepted by authorities of the Indian Coast Guard at Sagar Island in the State's South 24 Parganas District.
October 24	DRI recovered a cache of arms and ammunitions and arrested one person in Firozpur District in Punjab.

October 27	CRPF is seeking the help of the ISRO in the fight against the Maoists. In an endeavour to start a major developmental initiative in the 60 Maoist-affected Districts, the Centre has drawn up a blue-print to provide jobs to three-hundred thousand youth.
October 28	Senior Indian politician and the leader of the BJP, LK Advani escaped an alleged attempt on his life in Madurai in Chennai following the discovery of explosives in his scheduled route of travel.
October 29	Union Minister for Rural Development, Jairam Ramesh remarked that the trustworthiness of the administration among tribal population is 'very low' due to unresolved land issues that have led to escalation in Naxal menace.
October 31	Banned terror outfit KTF claimed responsibility for the huge haul of explosives recovered from an abandoned car in Ambala and stated that their motive was to eliminate senior Congress leader Sajjan Kumar to avenge the 1984 anti-Sikh riots.
November 1	Pentagon has expressed willingness to enhance its co-operation with India in the fields of maritime security and counter-terrorism, especially through special operations engagement.
November 2	Faced with growing Chinese military presence along the border and other complex security challenges in the region, the Government is planning to increase the strength of the Indian Army by almost one lakh soldiers over the next five years.
November 3	NIA is said to have found that Hindu extremists, who are suspected of orchestrating the Malegaon bomb blasts had allegedly used two Muslim men to plant the bombs in and around a mosque in the textile town. Two HM militants were arrested from Jammu and Kashmir's Udhampur District in connection with the Delhi High Court blast case.

November 4	Pakistani authorities finally informed their Indian counterparts that a judicial commission on the Mumbai terror attack case (26/11) would soon visit India. ISI was behind the Mumbai terror attacks as also bombing of the Indian embassy in Kabul (July 7, 2008), the British Broadcasting Corporation (BBC) said in a report.
November 5	A special MCOCA court granted bail to all nine persons accused in the Malegaon blasts case after the NIA told the court it had no objection to any of their bail pleas.
November 6	NIA is all set to expand its wings by opening three new offices and increasing the organisation strength from existing 400 to nearly 900. The Government has decided to create nearly 500 more posts raising the strength of the counter-terror agency to 900 besides opening offices in Lucknow, Kochi and Mumbai.
November 9	Ministry of Defence officials said that plans were afoot to ensure Coast Guard to increase its force levels to around 200 ships and 100 aircraft by 2018 to effectively tackle its operational tasks, which includes piracy and the terror threat emanating from sea. In the short-term, three more Coast Guard stations will come up at Dahanu, Androth and Krishnapatnam to add to the existing 31, apart from a new regional HQ (North East) and a station at Kolkata.
November 10	Meeting on the sidelines of the 17th SAARC summit in Addu City of Maldives, India and Pakistan talked about writing 'a new chapter' in their tense ties, with Islamabad assuring New Delhi that the terrorists behind the Mumbai terror attacks would be brought to justice soon.
November 11	An Indian warship intercepted three boats with 26 Somali pirates in the Gulf of Aden and foiled an attack on merchant vessels. The declaration adopted by member nations during the 17th SAARC summit in Addu City of Maldives adopted a joint commitment to fight all terror threats, transnational organised crime and illegal drugs.

November 14	The Union Government has given approval to a plan for creating an exclusive intelligence wing in the CRPF for aiding the forces'operations in the Naxal affected states of the country. Union Rural Development Minister, Jairam Ramesh admitted that introducing MGNREGA in Maoist affected districts was not practical.
November 15	Union Home Minister P Chidambaram who was on a tour of Chhattisgarh to review the situation there called the Maoists "biggest violators of human rights".
November 17	The Centre has sanctioned seven battalions of a 'specialised' force, who will execute basic infrastructure projects, including construction of roads, under their protection in Naxalism-affected parts of the country.
November 18	India is expected to raise concerns about militant outfit HuJI in the forthcoming 12th round of home secretary-level talks with Bangladesh.
November 19	The Centre informed Assam, Manipur and Arunachal Pradesh that there was no move to grant a 'supra state body'status to Nagas settled across the North East and the negotiators, who have been talking to the National Socialist Council of NSCN-IM, had never promised the outfit any such arrangement that may have severe inter-state ramifications.
November 21	Addressing a joint press conference at the end of the 12th India-Bangladesh Home Secretary-level talks, Union Home Secretary R K Singh and his Bangladesh counterpart Monzur Hossain reaffirmed their commitment not to allow the territory of either country to be used for any activity inimical to each other's interests.

November 22	An accused in the Ghatkopar blast (a bomb explosion in a bus at Ghatkopar in Mumbai in Maharashtra on December 2, 2002 which killed two persons and injured over 50 others) was arrested from Morna in Noida by a team of UP ATS, Tamil Nadu SIT and Noida Police when he was about to leave for Dubai. As per a media report, 26/11 could have been averted if the then Bush administration had taken seriously the warning and threat perception of Lashkar-e-Taiba's global operations by a renowned French judge. The Central Government has formally confirmed that several militant outfits of North East, including ULFA, NDFB, and both factions of NSCN have camps in Sagaing Region, and States of Chin and Kachin in Myanmar. Union Home Ministry statistics put out in the Lok Sabha reveal that CPI-Maoist have been forced to back out from 41 districts over the last three years and have a presence in about 182 districts.
November 23	A new investigative report published by ProPublica, a Washington-based investigative journalism website claimed that David Coleman Headley was in fact a double agent under the employment of the US and the Pakistani spy agency ISI. The Union Government said Mumbai airport in Maharashtra faced a potential threat of air borne attack and the intelligence was shared with concerned authorities to prevent it. Rajya Sabha (upper house of Parliament) was informed that Maoist violence has left over 500 people dead this year and their front organisations are 'very active' in urban and semi-urban areas. Union Minister of State for Home Affairs, Jitendra Singh told the Rajya Sabha that incidents of CPI-Maoist violence have declined in all affected states in 2011 (till November 14), except in Bihar and Maharashtra, as compared to corresponding period of 2010.

November 25	The Union Government is all set to formally launch hunt for over 75 heavy-duty 'stealth' naval helicopters with potent anti-submarine and anti-warship warfare capabilities, customised for amphibious assaults and commando operations against conventional, terror, piracy and other threats.
November 26	On the third anniversary of 26/11, India reminded Pakistan it was still awaiting 'decisive' action against the perpetrators of the crime, and said evidence provided by it was sufficient to prosecute those behind the 'inhuman act'.
November 28	Central Committee of the CPI-Maoist issued a statement regarding a protest week from November 29 and also-called for a 48-hour All India bandh (shut down strike) on 4-5 December.
November 29	In an estimate made by the Union Government, Maharashtra reported nearly 85 per cent of the total seizure of fake Indian currency in India during the year 2011.
November 30	Delhi Police investigators announced the neutralisation of a pan-India module of militant outfit IM which they claimed was responsible for a string of nationwide attacks in the year 2010. Delhi Police's Special Cell announced that it had arrested six persons, including a Pakistani operative of the militant Islamist outfit JeM. Union Home Minister P Chidambaram said that Pakistani Prime Minister Yousuf Raza Gilani may be a 'man of peace' but he had not delivered on the 26/11 probe, whether it was arresting the real culprits or giving India voice samples of those who are in jails there.
December 1	A project, codenamed 'Karachi Project', undertaken by ISI to spread terror in India using local recruits through LeT network will soon find its place in the charge-sheet to be filed by the NIA against American-Pakistani terrorist David Coleman Headley and his accomplices, including serving and retired Army officials of Pakistan.
December 3	Sources in the IB and State security agencies suspect that the militant Islamist outfit IM has established more than seven sleeper cells in North Bihar.

December 4	Union Rural Development Minister Jairam Ramesh said there were 'liberated' zones in the country dominated by the CPI-Maoist, thus corroborating the Maoists' claims that the State's writ doesn't run in West Jharkhand and South Chhattisgarh,
December 5	According to Delhi Police, interrogation of the six IM operatives arrested from various locations across the country has revealed that the IM has sleeper cells in Chennai, Bangalore, Pune apart from New Delhi.
December 6	Over 500 people including 124 SF personnel were killed in 1,476 attacks carried out by Naxals in various affected states till November this year, reports '*Outlook India*'. Law enforcement agencies have arrested 1,728 Naxals, recovered 546 arms and 344 Maoists surrendered during last eleven months. There were 219 incidents in which LWE targeted industries, railways, telephone exchange towers, power plants, mines, panchayat bhawans (buildings of village level local self-government institutions), and school buildings among others. Of these, basic transport infrastructure like roads in Naxal areas bore the brunt with 119 strikes, followed by 31 attacks on telephone towers, 23 on railways properties, 21 school buildings and 12 on economic installations including uranium mines and pipe lines.
December 10	Union Minister for Rural Development Jairam Ramesh was forced to cancel his visit to Madhya Pradesh in the wake of inputs of CPI-Maoist's threat.
December 12	Delhi Police revealed that they had arrested two Pakistani spies, identified as Soofia Kanwal and Imran, trained in Nepal, on December 5, from New Delhi Railway Station.
December 13	After facing some reverses in their strongholds, the CPI-Maoist has formed a 'Golden Corridor Committee' to build its base in hitherto untouched industrial areas of Gujarat and Maharashtra, stretching from Pune to Ahmedabad, including commercial hubs like Mumbai, Nashik, Surat and Vadodara.

December 14	Pakistani spies Soofia Kanwal and her accomplice Imran, arrested on December 12, were pushed into India from ISI's launch pad in Nepal, to attack Gujarat Chief Minister Narendra Modi and other terror targets in the state.
December 16	MHA will chalk out strategies to deal with the CPI-Maoist problem in a meeting of the heads of the Police Forces of the North East, convened by the IB in Guwahati on December 19 and 20. Interpol General Secretary Robert K Noble along with CBI Director AP Singh announced, the setting up of a CBI-Interpol 'Research and Innovation Centre' for prevention of telecommunications crime, keeping in mind the growing popularity of mobile phones and devices as carriers of sensitive information. They also agreed that the present procedure to get information and evidence with regard to IP addresses and details of alleged cyber criminals from different countries was 'cumbersome', resulting in loss of evidence.
December 18	Indian Government has recently notified R&AW as one of the eight agencies to intercept phone calls, *e*-mails and voice and data communication's within the country.

December 19	CRPF Director General K Vijay Kumar said mosquitoes have claimed more CRPF personnel in the forests than the Maoists. According to CRPF sources, 17 troopers posted in the Maoist-infested areas have lost their lives to dengue and malaria in the last 10 months. According to recent official reports there is a shortage of over 100,000 personnel: BSF, which is deployed on the sensitive Indo-Pak border, tops the list with 25,000 vacancies. In addition, ITBP, which mans the disputed border with China, CRPF, which is engaged in anti-militancy operations, and the CISF, in charge of the security of vital installations and industrial units, are all short of around 17,000 personnel each. Other forces are also reeling under a shortage of personnel. Even the elite NSG is not fully staffed. The fact that most of the vacancies are at the lower levels makes the situation worse because the operational efficiency of the forces is critically dependent on the strength of the manpower at these levels. Even by the Union Home Ministry's admission the existing vacancies will be filled only in the next two years. Defence services also suffer from an estimated shortage of about 15,000 officers.
December 21	Proposal to create a NCTC is set for a final nod with the three-member committee headed by the national security adviser reconciling differences and drawing up a note for the Cabinet Committee on Security.
December 22	Two suspected BKI militants were arrested by Delhi Police. The arrests were made based on leads that they planned to assassinate some religious and political leaders.
December 24	The NIA, filed charge-sheet against nine persons including two serving Pakistan ISI officers - Major Iqbal and Major Samir Ali as well as David Headley and Hafiz Saeed, founder of LeT, for the 26/11 attacks in India.

December 25	The 60-page NIA charge-sheet (filed on December 24), highlighted roles of LeT founder Hafiz Saeed, LeT commander Zakir-ur-Rehman Lakhvi, al Qaeda operative Ilyas Kashmiri and two serving Pakistani ISI officers - Major Iqbal and Major Sameer Ali in "larger conspiracy to organise spectacular terrorist attacks on places of iconic importance in India".
December 26	According to the Police, the BKI is on an overdrive to recruit cadre.
December 27	Union Rural Development Minister Jairam Ramesh has pointed out 'operational' shortcomings in the Government's efforts to tackle CPI-Maoist insurgency through developmental work and urged greater political involvement to deal with it more effectively.
December 28	Uttar Pradesh ATS in coordination with a crime branch team from Ahmedabad arrested an alleged SIMI operative wanted in 2008 Ahmedabad blast case.
December 29	India will consider the Pakistani proposal to withdraw heavy artillery from the LoC in Jammu and Kashmir, only if Pakistan stops cross-border infiltration bids.
December 30	MHA in its year-end review for 2011 termed it as one of the most successful years in terms of bringing rebel groups to the negotiation table in Assam as well as in other North Eastern states.

Endnotes

1. In the Land of the Enemy, *India Today,* July 12, '99
2. The Men Who Knew, *Outlook,* September 6, '98
3. *Ibid*
4. *The Times of India,* August 31, '99
5. *The Times of India,* July 19, '99
6. *India Police Journal,* 1998. IB Centenary Issue. Page 16
7. Anjali Nirmal, *Role and Functioning of Central Police Organisation* (Delhi 1992) page 284
8. Dr Bhashyam Kasturi, Lancer Papers 6, 1995, page 36
9. *India Today,* July 15, '89
10. Dr Bhashyam Kasturi. *Op cit.* page 70
11. The role and organisational structure described herein is primarily based on inputs gathered from CIA's home-page on the internet.
12. Lt Gen Vijay Madan, PVSM, VSM (Retd). The Face behind the Mask behind the Veil - Pakistan's Inter Services Intelligence, *USI Journal,* April-June '94
13. *Ibid*
14. Dr Bhashyam Kasturi, *Op cit.* page 42
15. Shah Commission of Inquiry, Interim report, Vol-1, page 26
16. Philip Agee. Inside The Company - CIA Diary (Penguin Books)
17. *Sunday,* 18-24 September, '98
18. *Outlook,* August 2, '99
19. Alvin and Heidi Toffler. *War and Anti-War,* Warner Books, 1994, page 86
20. *Ibid,* page 205
21. Maj Gen Yashwant Deva, AVSM (Retd) Open Source, Virtual and Public Domain Intelligence, *USI Journal,* October-December, '95
22. How the CIA Was Fooled, *India Today,* May 17, '99

23. Joby Warrick's article in the *Washington Post,* December 26, '08
24. CIA's website.
25. Among the early scholars, who wrote on this subject were Joseph De Rivera, *The Psychological Dimension of Foreign Policy* (Columbus, OH: Merrill, 1968), and *Perception and Misperception in International Politics* (Princeton, NJ: Princeton University Press, 1976).
26. Christopher Brady, Intelligence and National Security, Vol 8, No 4 (October 1993). "The Intelligence Community Post-mortem Program, 1973-1975", *Studies in Intelligence,* Vol 21, No 1 (Fall 1977).
27. JJ Wirtz, *The Tet Offensive: Intelligence Failure in War* (New York, 1991).
28. Roberta Wohlstetter, *Pearl Harbor: Warning and Decision* (Stanford University Press, 1962). Roberta Wohlstetter, "Cuba and Pearl Harbor: Hindsight and Foresight", *Foreign Affairs,* Vol 43, No 4 (July 1965).
29. Robin Hogarth, *Judgment and Choice* (New York: Wiley, 1980), p 117.
30. Most of the ideas expressed here are from Richard Nisbett and Lee Ross, *Human Inference: Strategies and Shortcomings of Social Judgment* (Englewood Cliffs, NJ: Prentice-Hall, 1980), Chapter 3.
31. A Paivio, *Imagery and Verbal Processes* (New York: Holt, Rinehart and Winston, 1971).
32. Amos Tversky and Daniel Kahneman, "Judgment under Uncertainty: Heuristics and Biases", *Science,* Vol 185 (27 September 1974), 1126.
33. *Ibid* p. 1125-1126.
34. Roberta Wohlstetter, *Pearl Harbor: Warning and Decision* (Stanford: Stanford University Press, 1962), p 302.
35. South Asia Terrorism Portal.

Index

Inside IB and RAW: The Rolling Stone that Gathered Moss by K Sankaran Nair, IPS (Former Head: Research and Analysis Wing (RAW)

Intelligence: Corporate Success and Vigilance by D C Pathak, IPS (Ex Chief – IB)

The Undisclosed Punjab: India Besieged by Terror by Birbal Nath, IPS (Former DGP, Punjab)

The Folds of Insurgency by AP Maheshwari, IPS

Who Owns CBI: The Naked Truth by BR Lall, IPS (Former: Joint Director, CBI)

Saga of Civil Services by Dr Yogendra Narain, IAS (Former Defence Secretary)

Open Secrets: India's Intelligence Unveiled by M K Dhar, IPS

Security Manual by P Benjamin

SPYMASTER: My Life in the CIA by Ted Shackley

VIP Security: What You Need to know by Kanchan Sinha

Armed Forces Tribunal by Dr UC Jha

Ultimate Handbook of Jungle Warfare by Dr NC Asthana, IPS

Ultimate Handbook of Urban Warfare by Dr NC Asthana, IPS

Beyond North East: Insurgency-History-Development by HN Das (Former Chief Secretary, Assam)

Why Bureaucracy Fails by Kalyan Ray, IAS

WMD Terrorism: Strategy for Consequences Management by Brig MS Patial

Intelligence Manual by Department of Defence, USA

The ISI Game Plan by Brig Yash Mohan, VSM

Terror, Insurgency and the State: Ending Protracted Conflicts by Marianne Heiberg etc.

Operation Triple X: An Indian Spy-Run in Pakistan A Novel by MK Dhar, IPS

Legal Safeguards for Defence Personnel by Air Cmde. Ranvir Kumar (Former Judge Advocate General)

Reforming Intelligence Agencies: Pakistan's Transitional Democracy by Frederic Grare

Combating Terrorism: Strategies of Ten Countries by Yonah Alexander

Strategies in Defence and Intelligence by Lt Gen S Pattabhiraman & MK Dhar, IPS

Sports, Games and Adventure Sports by Air Cmde (Dr) CN Ghosh

The Craft of Intelligence by Allen W Dulles

Fulcrum of Evil: ISI-CIA-Al Qaeda Nexus by MK Dhar (Former Joint Chief of IB)

The Conspirators: Fiction of Facts (A Book on Pakistan's Intelligence) by Brig Yash Mohan, VSM

Silent Warfare: Understanding the World of Intelligence by Abram N Shulsky & Gary J Schmitt

Wages of Crime: Black Markets, Illegal Finance and the Underworld Economy by R T Naylor

The Peace Keepers: Indian Police Service (IPS) by SR Arun, IPS

Para-Military Forces: Central Reserve and Foreign Policy by Dr AK Pasha

Human Rights Training by Dr S Subramanian, IPS

Industrial Espionage: Causes and Cure by Dr S Subramaniam, IPS

Executive Protection by Dr S Subramaniam, IPS

CIA's Eye on South Asia by Anuj Dhar, Journalist

Threat to Security: How Secured is India from within by PC Dogra, IPS (Former DGP, Punjab)